The
Illustrated
Encyclopedia of
THE WORLD'S GREAT
MOVIE STARS
AND THEIR FILMS

The
Illustrated
Encyclopedia of
THE WORLD'S GREAT
MOVIE STARS
AND THEIR FILMS

Ken Wlaschin

BONANZA BOOKS
New York

First English edition published by
Salamander Books Ltd

Copyright©1979 by Salamander Books Ltd
27 Old Gloucester Street
London WC1N 3AF
United Kingdom

This edition is published by Bonanza Books
a division of Crown Publishers, Inc
by arrangement with Salamander Books Ltd
a b c d e f g h
BONANZA 1980 EDITION

Wlaschin, Ken.
The illustrated encyclopedia of the world's great
movie stars and their films.
1. Moving-picture actors and actresses – Biography.
2. Moving-pictures – Dictionaries. 3. Moving-pictures –
Catalogs. I. Title.
PN1998.A2W64 1980   791.43'028'0922 [B]   80-15161
ISBN 0-517-32123-8

All correspondence concerning the
content of this volume should be addressed to
Salamander Books Ltd

Credits

Editor: Trisha Palmer
Designer: Roger Hyde
Picture research: Maureen Kennedy Martin
Filmsetting: Modern Text Typesetting, England
Colour reproduction: Process Colour Centre Ltd,
                Tenreck Ltd, England
Printed in Belgium by
                Henri Proost & Cie, Turnhout

The Author

Ken Wlaschin, born in Nebraska in 1934, has been Programme Director of the London Film Festival and National Film Theatre since 1969, and is editor of the monthly National Film Theatre magazine. He was educated at Dartmouth College in the USA, University College, Dublin, and the University of Poitiers, graduating with a Master's Degree in English. He subsequently worked as diarist and film/theatre/art critic on the Daily American newspaper in Rome, as diarist and critic on the Daily Sketch in London, and as drama series story editor for London Weekend Television.

He writes on a freelance basis for many magazines and is also a poet, TV writer and novelist; books published include The Bluffer's Guide to the Cinema, The Italian Job, Rome: A Portrait, and To Kill The Pope. Film articles have appeared in various newspapers and periodicals including Films and Filming, The Sunday Times and The Observer, and he makes regular BBC radio reports on the cinema. He visits most major international film festivals and film theatres, and is involved with screening films from all countries of the world.

Contents

Introduction

This is a book of opinions. The opinions are backed by research, experience, analysis and "facts" but they are still subjective. It is an attempt to select the 400 most important movie stars of all times and countries, show the reasons for their importance when they made their reputations, discuss their value for us as movie enthusiasts today and list their ten best films. There are sections devoted to the stars of the silent, classic and modern eras, but it was neither possible nor desirable to include all of the known actors and actresses of all periods.

There are many books about movie stars. Most of them are love letters from fans; some are purely factual; very few help you to understand what a star is and why some actors become stars and others don't. Fans often consider stars as magical beings, studios think of them as investments (or "properties") and directors have been known to describe them as workhorses and cattle. For the purposes of this book stars are considered as myths. Their effectiveness can be described in relationship to three factors: image, personality and persona.

Personality is the easiest to apprehend. "Show me an actress who isn't a personality and I'll show you an actress who isn't a star", said Katharine Hepburn. A movie star either creates a screen personality or he/she/it remains simply an actor/actress/screen character/animal/cartoon figure. The greatest stars have created such powerful personalities that they have become a part of popular culture: everyone "knows" Charlie Chaplin, Mickey Mouse and John Wayne. A screen personality is not the same as an actor's off-screen personality, but the great ones are close reflections of their creator's inner selves. This "personality" is composed of almost every aspect of the star, from timbre of voice and way of speaking to bodily movement and unconscious mannerisms. Some of these are part of what an actor considers his image.

Image is a combination of screen roles, screen personality and screen presentation with off-screen behaviour and public relations. Stars don't often worry about their personalities, but they are very concerned about their image. In the old days a marriage or a divorce might be kept secret because it would affect a star's image; a star will

refuse a role or a new hairstyle because it might be bad for his/her image. In fact, image is not a combination of a star's assets but simply the public's opinion and assessment of that star.

Persona is the most intriguing aspect of a star and is usually developed over a period of time in conjunction with the personality. It is the most mythical part because it is the basis of what a star means. Although it derives from the roles that stars play in films, it soon becomes a separate entity which links the different roles. Personas tend to be more complex than simply "tough guy" or "sexy slut", and are always reflections of the needs, desires and interests of audiences (otherwise they're not accepted and disappear). Charles Chaplin's tramp and Woody Allen's worrier are both "little guy" personas but they are very different, each suitable for its own time and audience. Close examinations of personas is stressed in much of this book.

This is not, however, intended to be a "serious" study of stars. Seriousness is too often the refuge of the shallow, as Wilde noted. Serious critics tend to dismiss many of the stars in this book as mere entertainers and therefore unimportant; they rarely discuss Abbott and Costello, Gracie Fields or Fernandel. This is, therefore, a non-serious book which believes that movies can be, have been and will continue to be great fun as well as great art.

Another contentious matter is screen acting. Critics and occasionally audiences admire those who "act" on the screen. Real screen acting is so natural that it is never thought of as acting, and the greatest screen actors rarely win prizes (Astaire, Grant, etc). Theatre actors have traditionally looked down on movie stars because they don't "act" like stage actors. The reverse should be true. Very few stage actors are natural enough to act properly on screen, and even fewer have created screen personalities and personas. Many critics overrate theatre actors in their film appearances because of their stage prestige. This is not true of this book.

Most stage actors have been omitted from this selection of stars. They are not stars, they are simply actors who appear in films. Most leading men and women (ie escorts and decoration) have also been omitted unless they became stars in their own right (created a personality/persona). Other notable omissions include stars whose reputations are no longer valid and those whose personas are of little interest today even in buff circles (ie George Arliss). Obviously this kind of selection/omission will not meet with everyone's approval, but all of the superstars have been included and most of the important secondary stars.

Audience popularity has been considered as important as critical prestige in making the selection. Every year American exhibitors are polled on the stars they consider the biggest box-office attractions, and nearly all the top box-office stars are here. Tabulated numerically the most popular star of the sound cinema (by a long way) is John Wayne. Bing Crosby comes in second with Gary Cooper and Clark Gable close behind. In the silent era the most popular stars were Charles Chaplin, Mary Pickford and Douglas Fairbanks. Breaking box-office appeal down by decades shows Gable as the top star of the '30s, Crosby No 1 in the '40s, Wayne No 1 in both the '50s and '60s and Clint Eastwood heading the ratings in the '70s.

The Ten Best Films listed after every star (a few more than ten for the greatest stars) can be treated as subjective opinions (which they are) or carefully considered selections (by those who agree with me), but hopefully will prove generally to be of interest and help. Rather than list all of a star's films, it was felt to be more useful to list only those in which he/she gave his/her best performances. These are the films on which a star's reputation really rests. The arbitrary number of ten films was not too few for most stars; surprisingly few have made even that many outstanding movies. The listed films invariably include the ones in which the star's persona first developed and those that made him famous. Titles are original release titles in country of origin.

The arrows » used throughout the book denote that the artist has his or her own main biographical entry.

This is not an academic book, so I will not attempt to list the thousands of books, magazines, brochures, press releases and other material consulted in writing it. I would, however, like to thank those critics whose ideas about stars and films have been particularly stimulating, including Edgar Morin, Richard Griffith, Giulio Cesare Castello, Robin Wood, David Thomson, James Agee, William K. Everson, Arthur Myer, David Shipman, James Robert Parrish, Andrew Sarris, Manny Farber, Pauline Kael, Parker Tyler, Kevin Brownlow and Ian and Elisabeth Cameron. I am also particularly indebted to my wife Maureen Kennedy Martin whose creative picture research brought together what may be the finest collection of movie star photographs ever assembled, and to Adrian Turner and John Gillett for their help in checking and captioning.

KEN WLASCHIN

1 THE SILENT MOVIE STARS

The stars of the silent cinema were popular and influential to a degree that is almost impossible to imagine today. In the days before rock and pop stars and TV and radio celebrities, all the dreams and fantasy projections of the mass public were focused on the movie star. In many ways they were the first and the greatest of the popular stars that have been a feature of the twentieth century. Stardom, as we know it, was a new concept at the beginning of the century; there had been stage stars and music hall stars, of course, but the kind of adulation that the modern star gets needs the mass media to promote it, and the movie was the first of these to emerge after the popular newspaper.

The earliest films were simple documentaries made by the Lumière brothers in France and Edison in America, and the first actors with a memorable scene were May Irwin and John C. Rice in their scandalous The Kiss in 1896. They were middle-aged, but the kiss was too titillating for some and the first moves to censor the cinema were made. These early films featured nameless actors; they did not have stars. When the five major American companies producing film in the earliest years of the cinema (Edison, Vitagraph, Biograph, Essanay and Selig) got together to form the exclusive trust known as the Motion Picture Patents Company in 1909, there were already contract performers but they were kept anonymous. The studios feared (rightly as it turned out) that if they identified these performers to the public, then they might have to pay them more money. But the public insisted on creating stars anyway, using sudio names like "The Vitagraph Girl" or "The Biograph Girl" or visual characteristics like "The little girl with the golden curls" or screen names like "Broncho Billy", "Max" or "Little Mary", and in 1910 Carl Laemmle of the Independent Motion Picture Company (it later grew into Universal Pictures) gave the world its first named motion picture star—Florence Lawrence. Other actors quickly began to perceive their worth, and after Mary Pickford's big success stars multiplied enormously and every film soon had to have a star to sell it. The growth of studio power in the twenties meant that most stars were quickly typecast into vehicles that made money for a short period but used up the star's charisma in an average of five years. Only the greatest stars were able to extend their popularity, and even the greatest were generally defeated by sound. About a dozen made the transition without trouble, achieving even greater stardom in the sound period—notably Greta Garbo—but most were forced to retire or become supporting character actors—mainly because of identification with an earlier era rather than poor voice technique. Luminaries like Mary Pickford and Gloria Swanson may have been temporarily humbled by sound, but they did not lose their stardom permanently; they are still stars today and likely to remain so. A really great star can lose his or her popularity (or bankability) but star quality will endure. This selection of the 50 greatest silent stars is obviously subjective and arbitrary. Many important actors and actresses of the silent era have had to be left out, but the selection has been made as carefully as possible from the whole of world cinema. Stars have been chosen for their memorability, mythical qualities and great performances in great films. Some major '20s stars are not included here because they were also sound stars and will be found in Part II (ie Garbo, Crawford, Colman); others are not listed simply because their enormous popularity in the '20s does not seem to have made them into myth figures (ie Thomas Meighan, Richard Dix, Florence Vidor). One of the difficulties in assessing these stars is that so many films have been lost. The "best" films listed after these 50 stars include some major movies that appear to have vanished forever; however, most of the key films, like the stars, have survived the ravages of time and seem likely to become a permanent part of our culture.

GILBERT M. 'BRONCHO BILLY' ANDERSON

The first movie star character, the first motion picture cowboy hero and the first genuinely tinselled phoney in Hollywood. Anderson, known on screen and to his international public as "Broncho Billy", was actually born with the name Max Aaronson in Little Rock, Arkansas, in 1882. He had no connection with the West and couldn't even get on a horse, let alone ride one. Yet he virtually created the Western film out of his pulp magazine imagination and became the symbol to the world of the heroic cowboy. Anderson was genial and hard-working as well as phoney, so he eventually learned not only to ride a horse but also to write and direct exciting cowboy films.

His movie career began appropriately in 1903 with Edwin S. Porter's **The Great Train Robbery**, the first memorable American narrative film and a Western. It inspired Anderson to devote himself to cowboy movies; "Broncho Billy", a good badman, was his screen *alter ego* and the star of over 500 films. The first was **Broncho Billy and the Baby**, a sentimental story based on a tale by Peter B. Kyne. It was a huge hit and Anderson soon succeeded in making action-filled authentic-looking Westerns that were popular all over the world; the series lasted until 1915, when the features of William S. Hart began to win over audiences.

Essanay, founded by Anderson, was one of the most important early studios, with films featuring Chaplin », Bushman » and Swanson ». He more or less retired in 1920 but made a cameo appearance with other old-time cowboy stars in the 1965 **The Bounty Killers,** and was given a Special Academy Award in 1957 for his "contributions to the development of motion pictures as entertainment". He died in 1971.

BEST FILMS:
1903 The Great Train Robbery
Edwin S. Porter (Edison)
1908 Broncho Billy and the Baby
Reginald Barker (Essanay)
1909 Broncho Billy's Redemption
Reginald Barker (Essanay)
1911 Broncho Billy's Adventure
Reginald Barker (Essanay)
1912 Broncho Billy and the Bandits
G. M. Anderson (Essanay)
1913 Broncho Billy's Oath
G. M. Anderson (Essanay)
1914 Broncho Billy and the Sisters
G. M. Anderson (Essanay)
1915 The Indians' Narrow Escape
G. M. Anderson (Essanay)
1916 The Champion
Charles Chaplin (Essanay)
1965 The Bounty Killers
Spencer Bennett (Premiere Productions)

Below: Broncho Billy Anderson was the American cinema's first cowboy star, the predecessor of John Wayne et al. He made more than 500 films before he was shot out of the saddle of stardom by William S. Hart.

ROSCOE 'FATTY' ARBUCKLE

Arbuckle was the King of Custard Pies in the heyday of the slapstick comedy era. Newspaperman Gene Fowler once rhapsodised about him as so far surpassing others as to be the "Hercules of the winged dessert". He could heave pies in two directions at once with great accuracy and his huge, bouncy innocence made him one of the most popular comedians of the time, vying with Chaplin » and Keaton », with whom he worked. He was probably most popular of all with children. In his seven-year career he rose from Keystone Kop with Mack Sennett through stardom with Chaplin and Mabel Normand » to directing himself and Keaton in some of the best short comedies of the period.

In 1921 he was given a three-year contract for $3 million. Then the sky fell in. He was involved in the most notorious of all Hollywood scandals, acquitted by a jury but convicted by the public of having caused the death of a girl through rape or worse at a Labour Day party. His films were withdrawn, he was barred from film-making and he died almost a forgotten man in 1933 after trying to direct under pseudonyms. His work with the top silent comedians ensures that his films will live on, though the shadow of his tragedy has affected his cinematic reputation. Ironically, however, the scandal ensures that his work and name will never be ignored.

Above: Fatty Arbuckle became a comedy star with a huge following among children in the late 1910s before a tragic scandal involving model Virginia Rappe ended in his complete rejection by the public and the industry.

BEST FILMS:
1913 In the Clutches of the Gang
Mack Sennett (Keystone)
1914 The Masquerader
Charles Chaplin (Keystone)
1914 The Rounders
Charles Chaplin (Keystone)

1916 **Fatty and Mabel Adrift**
Roscoe Arbuckle (Paramount)
1917 **The Butcher Boy**
Roscoe Arbuckle (Paramount)
1917 **A Country Hero**
Roscoe Arbuckle (Paramount)
1918 **Out West**
Roscoe Arbuckle (Paramount)
1919 **The Garage**
Roscoe Arbuckle (Paramount)
1921 **Brewster's Millions**
Joe Henaberry (Famous Players)
1921 **The Dollar-a-Year Man**
James Cruze (Famous Players)

BETTY BALFOUR

One of the few bright spots in the British cinema of the 1920s was the pert and pretty Betty Balfour. Like her movies, she was jolly and unpretentious; she appeared in more films in the 1920s than any other British actress, and was voted top British star by a *Daily News* poll in 1924 and top world star by a *Daily Mirror* poll in 1928.

Miss Balfour, born in 1903, made her reputation in a minor part in the best British film of 1920, **Nothing Else Matters,** and became a major star the following year with the first of the **Squibs** series. These films featured her as a Piccadilly flower girl engaged to a policeman but somewhat troubled over her father being a bookmaker. Scenes from the four **Squibs** films were adventurously shot on location (rather illegally) in Piccadilly Circus. The bright and cheerful heroine made a number of successful films for director George Pearson, who launched her through his company Welsh-Pearson—including one based loosely on the life of Marie Lloyd, **Love, Life and Laughter**— but by the end of the decade she was working for British International in films like Alfred Hitchcock's frothy **Champagne.** Her career continued spasmodically through the '30s and '40s with films like **Evergreen** and a remake of **Squibs,** but her star never shone as brightly again after the coming of sound. The genial lack of pretension of her films makes them enjoyable even today.

BEST FILMS:
1920 **Nothing Else Matters**
George Pearson (Welsh-Pearson)
1921 **Squibs**
George Pearson (Welsh-Pearson)
1922 **Mord Em'ly**
George Pearson (Welsh-Pearson)
1922 **Wee MacGregor's Sweetheart**
George Pearson (Welsh-Pearson)
1922 **Squibs Wins the Calcutta Sweep**
George Pearson (Welsh-Pearson)
1923 **Squibs M.P.**
George Pearson (Welsh-Pearson)
1923 **Squibs' Honeymoon**
George Pearson (Welsh-Pearson)
1924 **Reveille**
George Pearson (Welsh-Pearson)
1925 **Love, Life and Laughter**
George Pearson (Welsh-Pearson)
1928 **Champagne**
Alfred Hitchcock (British International)

SILENT MOVIE STARS

Left: George Pearson directed most of Betty Balfour's charming comedies, including **Love, Life and Laughter,** *loosely based on the career of Marie Lloyd.*
Below: Bright-eyed Betty Balfour was the most popular British star of the 1920s.

THEDA BARA

Theda Bara was the first sex star of the movies: they called them "vamps" in those days—the word (from "vampire") had been coined to describe her. She was also the first totally manufactured star. Theda, whose name was said by studio publicity to be an anagram of Arab Death, was introduced to the gullible public as the frightfully evil daughter of an Egyptian seeress, and photographed with skulls, Nubian slaves and white limousines. She was actually a bit-part player named Theodosia Goodman, born in Cincinnati, Ohio, in 1890, but the hokum worked. Her initial film, **A Fool There Was,** loosely based on Kipling, was the box-office sensation of 1915, the word "vamp" passed into popular usage as a euphemism for "sexy" and her phrase "Kiss me, my fool" was quoted for years afterwards.

Her screen persona was manufactured by director Frank J. Powell and studio boss William Fox. It was such a success that she made 39 films in four years, became the biggest ever box office star, and provided the revenue for the development of the Fox Company (later 20th Century Fox). Her reputation today suffers because only her first, crudest Fox film survives. Most of the lavish spectaculars in which she played the great sex stars of history (**Cleopatra, Salome,**

Left: Theda Bara, the first cinematic vamp. Tastes have changed.
Inset: Like Elizabeth Taylor in recent years, Theda Bara just had to star in **Cleopatra.**

11

Madame Dubarry) were huge hits, 23 of them directed by J. Gordon Edwards and others by Raoul Walsh and Herbert Brenon. Her career ended abruptly in 1919 when she asked for more money, public taste began to change and she went on stage. Her comebacks, even burlesqueing her film persona, were not successful, but she kept her name in the casting directories until her death in 1955.

BEST FILMS:
1915 A Fool There Was
Frank J. Powell (Box Office Attractions)
1915 Kreutzer Sonata
Herbert Brenon (Fox)
1915 Carmen
Raoul Walsh (Fox)
1916 The Serpent
Raoul Walsh (Fox)
1916 Romeo and Juliet
J. Gordon Edwards (Fox)
1917 Camille
J. Gordon Edwards (Fox)
1917 Cleopatra
J. Gordon Edwards (Fox)
1918 Madame Dubarry
J. Gordon Edwards (Fox)
1918 Salome
J. Gordon Edwards (Fox)
1919 Kathleen Mavourneen
Charles Brabin (Fox)

JOHN BARRYMORE

Barrymore was billed as "The World's Greatest Actor" in his heyday in the 1920s. He was Warner Brothers' biggest prestige star, a member of the Royal Family of Broadway along with brother and sister Lionel and Ethel. He was considered so highbrow that his films were not big box-office outside the major cities. He was also one of the great tragi-comedians of the cinema, an incredible ham in many of his films, a lady chaser who tried to live up to his publicity slogan as "The Greatest Lover of the Screen", and an alcoholic who became so famous for being drunk that audiences went to see him in bad plays to watch him fall down. He was the Great Profile and Great Boozer rolled into one, and one of his best performances was playing exactly that role in Howard Hawks' satirical sound film **Twentieth Century**. Barrymore's greatest stardom, however, was in silents.

Born into a famous acting family in Philadelphia in 1882, he became a top stage actor and entered films in 1913 with **An American Citizen**. He made dozens of two-reelers during the next four years, first became widely known through starring in the 1917 **Raffles the Amateur Cracksman**, and his 1920 **Dr Jekyll and Mr Hyde** made him world famous. His Broadway career was at its height and he toured in **Hamlet** before making the hugely successful **Beau Brummel** for Warner Brothers, who paid him vast sums, followed

Above: John Barrymore relished villainous character roles like **Svengali** *(Archie Mayo, 1931) with Marian Marsh as Trilby. Inset: John Barrymore, great actor and matinée idol, in the elegant 1924* **Beau Brummel**.

by eye-rolling versions of **Moby Dick** and **The Sea Beast** and a rather delightful **Don Juan** with one of the best duelling scenes ever. This was actually the first sound film with music synchronised on discs.

Barrymore then moved to United Artists and made the famous **Beloved Rogue** (portraying François Villon) and Lubitsch's **Eternal Love**. His voice was eminently suitable for sound and he had no trouble getting work, but his drinking had become a major problem and he often needed cue cards to remember his lines. He starred opposite Garbo ➤ in **Grand Hotel** but almost did not complete **Romeo and Juliet** because of his drinking; immediately after it finished he entered an alcoholics' clinic. He was then demoted to feature roles and sometimes even portrayed parodies of himself as a broken-down old ham.

He died in Hollywood in 1942 and has been portrayed in several Hollywood films by Errol Flynn ➤ in **Too Much Too Soon**, about Barrymore's daughter and by Jack Cassidy in **W. C. Fields and Me**). Probably the greatest

role of his career, and the one for which he will be longest remembered, was as his flamboyant self, the leading man, the great John Barrymore.

BEST FILMS:
1920 Dr Jekyll and Mr Hyde
John S. Robertson (Famous Players-Lasky)
1922 Sherlock Holmes
Albert Parker (in England)
1924 Beau Brummel
Harry Beaumont (Warner Brothers)
1926 The Sea Beast
Millard Webb (Warner Brothers)
1926 Don Juan
Alan Crosland (United Artists)
1927 Beloved Rogue
Alan Crosland (United Artists)
1929 Eternal Love
Ernst Lubitsch (United Artists)
1932 Grand Hotel
Edmund Goulding (MGM)
1934 Twentieth Century
Howard Hawks (Columbia)
1936 Romeo and Juliet
George Cukor (MGM)
1939 Midnight
Mitchell Leisen (Paramount)

RICHARD BARTHELMESS
see **Classic Stars**

WALLACE BEERY
see **Classic Stars**

FRANCESCA BERTINI

La Bertini was the first great screen *diva* She became world famous in the 1910s, not only for being a good actress (which she was) but for being temperamental, capricious, wilful, egocentric, elegant and beautiful. Italian cinema at that time was leading the world by producing the first feature films and Bertini became the major Italian film star, a kind of combination of Maria Callas and Sophia Loren ≫. She was born Elena Vitiello in Florence in 1888, started in films in 1904, and became an Italian star in 1912 in **The Rose of Thebes.** Her international reputation began with the world hit **The Story of a Pierrot**.

She was given great glamour roles in lavish productions of **Tosca, Fedora** and **The Lady of the Camellias** and set fashion

Above: Italian diva *Francesca Bertini in the early 1930s.*

styles around the world. Parisian dressmakers and perfume manufacturers named their products after her and in 1919 she signed the largest contract ever up to that time, two million lire for eight films; but by then her career was virtually over. She made a few films in the '20s but she was no longer the grand *diva.*

Her finest film, **Assunta Spina**, is one of the classics of Italian cinema, and in the galaxy of Italian film stars she is the most brilliant. As befits the Gloria Swanson ≫ of Italy, she made a small come-back recently, portraying a nun in Bernardo Bertolucci's epic, **1900.**

BEST FILMS:
1912 The Rose of Thebes
Amleto Novelli (Cines)
1913 The Story of a Pierrot
Baldassare Negroni (Caesar)
1915 Assunta Spina
Gustavo Serena (Caesar)
1915 The Lady of the Camellias
Gustavo Serena (Caesar)
1916 Don Pietro Caruso
Emilio Ghione (Caesar)

1916 Odette
Giuseppe de'Liguoro (Caesar)
1916 Fedora
Giuseppe de'Liguoro (Caesar)
1918 Tosca
Alfredo de Antoni (Caesar)
1920 Maddalena Ferat
Roberto Roberti (Caesar)
1976 1900
Bernardo Bertolucci (PEA)

CLARA BOW

Clara Bow was one of the great "sex goddesses" of the American cinema, and her reputation as the "It Girl" has continued down through the years, even with those who have never seen any of her 56 films. Most sex symbols of yesteryear look merely quaint; Clara still looks vivacious and appealing. The red-headed No 1 jazz baby of the Roaring Twenties, she was the embodiment of the independent-minded flapper with bobbed hair and cupid bow lips, but the coming of sound and the new morality of the Depression years, coupled with a scandalous trial and ill-health, kept her from fluttering to stardom in the '30s.

Born in Brooklyn in 1905, she made her film début in 1922 under the wing of B. P. Schulberg, who brought her with him to Paramount after a series of lesser films. Under the direction of Herbert Brenon **(Dancing**

Mothers), Victor Fleming **(Mantrap)** and Clarence Badger **(It)**, she became Paramount's biggest star during 1927 and 1928. Elinor Glyn's "It" (a euphemism for sex appeal) may have been poorly defined, but Clara Bow had it and a lot of men (and women) admired her for it. Her most famous films followed rapidly **(Wings, Three Weekends** and **Red Hair,** with a colour sequence to show her russet tresses), and then her first sound film **The Wild Party.** Her voice disappointed her fans and her career lasted only a few years more as her health deteriorated; she married cowboy star Rex Bell and then retired from movies at the age of 26. She died in 1965, but her most famous films are still revived.

BEST FILMS:
1925 Kiss Me Again
Ernst Lubitsch (Warner Brothers)
1925 The Plastic Age
Wesley Ruggles (Preferred)
1925 Mantrap
Victor Fleming (Paramount)
1926 Dancing Mothers
Herbert Brenon (Paramount)
1927 It
Clarence Badger (Paramount)
1927 Wings
William Wellman (Paramount)
1928 Red Hair
Clarence Badger (Paramount)
1928 Three Weekends
Clarence Badger (Paramount)
1929 The Wild Party
Dorothy Arzner (Paramount)
1932 Call Her Savage
John Dillon (Fox)

Left: Clara Bow in her most famous role as the "It Girl".
Below: Clara Bow first gained critical acclaim in a film called **Down to the Sea in Ships.**

BETTY BRONSON

Betty Bronson had, for a while, the kind of fairy tale success in the silent era that Judy Garland ≫ had in the sound period with **The Wizard of Oz.** She was the pert pixie star of **Peter Pan** in 1924 and its delightful sequel, **A Kiss for Cinderella,** both directed by Herbert Brenon. The adulation that she received as the result of these charming bits of whimsey made her the only real challenge that Mary Pickford ≫ ever had as America's Sweetheart. Her delightful personification of the Pickfordish roles of Cinderella and Peter Pan made her more popular with children than anyone else, and the adults and critics also adored her; unfortunately her studio, Paramount, regretted that such a screen persona had been created for their five-foot star, fearing that audiences were changing and that fantasy had lost its appeal. She appeared in many different kinds of roles and even some fine films, but her period as a major star was limited to two short, glorious years.

Betty was born in Newark, New Jersey, in 1907, and became a teenage movie star with virtually no experience. James Barrie considered her perfect as Peter Pan and she more or less stole the show from everyone, including director Herbert Brenon. Her best film, **A Kiss for Cinderella,** was less successful commercially and she began to appear in Westerns and comedies, like the delightful **Are Parents People?** She was the Madonna in **Ben-Hur** and starred opposite Al Jolson ≫ as a wistful cigarette girl in **The Singing Fool,**

but her talkies career was not successful and she retired in 1932, returning to make the Gene Autry ≫ film **The Yodellin' Kid from Pine Ridge** in 1937 and the Samuel Fuller film **The Naked Kiss** in 1963. She died in 1971.

BEST FILMS:
1924 Peter Pan
Herbert Brenon (Paramount)
1925 Are Parents People?
Malcolm St Clair (Paramount)
1925 A Kiss for Cinderella
Herbert Brenon (Paramount)
1926 The Cat's Pajamas
William Wellman (Paramount)
1926 Ben-Hur
Fred Niblo (MGM)
1926 Everybody's Acting
Marshall Neilan (Paramount)
1927 Paradise for Two
Gregory La Cava (Paramount)
1928 The Singing Fool
Lloyd Bacon (Warner Brothers)
1929 Sonny Boy
Archie Mayo (Warner Brothers)
1963 The Naked Kiss
Samuel Fuller (Allied Artists)

Below: Betty Bronson in her greatest film, the 1925 **A Kiss for Cinderella.**
Below left: **Are Parents People?** *starred Betty Bronson in a delightful "modern" comedy.*

her cult began to grow in the '50s and she came out of seclusion to adulation. French director Jean-Luc Godard paid homage to her in **Vivre sa Vie** and film archives around the world mounted tributes to her. Her star seems likely to glow for a long time yet.

BEST FILMS:
1926 It's the Old Army Game
Edward Sutherland (Paramount)
1926 Love 'em and Leave 'em
Frank Tuttle (Paramount)
1927 Evening Clothes
Luther Reed (Paramount)
1927 The City Gone Wild
James Cruze (Paramount)
1927 Rolled Stockings
Richard Rossen (Paramount)
1928 A Girl in Every Port
Howard Hawks (Fox)
1928 Beggars of Life
William Wellman (Paramount)
1929 Pandora's Box
G. W. Pabst (Nero Films)—Germany
1929 Diary of a Lost Girl
G. W. Pabst (G. W. Pabst Films)—
Germany
1930 Prix de Beauté
Augusto Genina (Sofar)—France

FRANCIS X. BUSHMAN

Francis Xavier Bushman, born in Norfolk, Virginia in 1885, was considered the handsomest man in the world in the early 1910s. He was the first screen matinée idol, the most popular leading man in the American cinema from 1914 to 1917 and probably the first film pin-up boy (posing beefily in Tarzan-type tights). This prototype Clark Gable » entered films in 1911 after winning a Most Handsome Man competition. He was half of the first screen love team with wife Beverly Bayne, and just their initials inter-twined were enough to attract audiences; their films with Essanay and Metro were so popular that the studios contrived to keep their marriage secret in order not to destroy Bushman's "attainability". Their most popular film was the 1915 **Graustark,** but their greatest moment together was probably the lavish 1916 Metro version of **Romeo and Juliet.** Bushman had star adulation from 1911 on, even causing riots in Chicago, but the peak of his career and his best-remembered role was as Messala, the chariot-driving villain of the 1926 **Ben-Hur.** His career faded away after that, although he continued to work in B-pictures and serials, but he had starred in more than 400 films before he died in 1966. His most notable recent films were Henry King's **David and Bathsheba** (he played King Saul) and Billy Wilder's **Sabrina,** and his last film, in the year of his death, was **The Ghost in the Invisible Bikini.** His name is still magically synonymous with the dashing romantic hero of a bygone era.

LOUISE BROOKS

Louise Brooks is the Mona Lisa of the movies, the most paradoxical of all the silent cinema stars. She is certainly the only star whose fame has grown with the years to the point where she is probably more admired now than at the height of her career. This remarkably intelligent, dazzlingly beautiful and utterly enigmatic actress, after a series of films in America, became a top star in Germany at the age of 23 in G. W. Pabst's 1929 classic **Pandora's Box,** but was unable afterwards to find work in America despite an already flourishing career. Her "intense isolation", in the words of film historian Lotte Eisner, has since helped to make her a major cult figure with cinema enthusiasts all over the world. Miss Brooks, a wily as well as a witty sphinx, has

cleverly nurtured her own legend, writing more brilliantly than most critics about the cinema.

Born in Cherryvale, Kansas, in 1906, she became a dancer at the age of 15 and eventually appeared in the Ziegfeld Follies. She made her screen début in 1925 at Paramount in Herbert Brenon's **The Street of Forgotten Men.** She quickly became a star as a classic, lovely, bob-haired modern vamp in a series of flapper-age comedies, but gave up her contract to go to Germany when Pabst decided she could be the most memorable nymphomaniac in film history; as Lulu in **Pandora's Box** the intense sexuality of her face in close-up astonished even Pabst and he quickly starred her in **Diary of a Lost Girl.** Despite his warnings, she returned to America but her career there was ruined and effectively over—except for B-Westerns and shorts. She retired forgotten by all until

Top: Louise Brooks as the night-club entertainer murder victim of the 1929 Philo Vance mystery **The Canary Murder Case.**
Above: Louise Brooks in her greatest role as Lulu, the heroine of G. W. Pabst's master-piece **Pandora's Box.**

BEST FILMS:
1912 The Fall of Montezuma
Harry McRae Webster (Essanay)
1914 A Million a Minute
John Noble (Essanay)
1915 Graustark
Fred Wright (Essanay)
1916 Romeo and Juliet
John Noble (Metro)
1917 Red, White and Blue Blood
Charles Brabin (Metro)
1923 Modern Marriage
Lawrence Windom (FXB Pictures)
1925 The Masked Bride
Josef von Sternberg & Christy
Cabanne (MGM)
1926 Ben Hur
Fred Niblo (MGM)
1951 David and Bathsheba
Henry King (20th Century Fox)
1954 Sabrina
Billy Wilder (Paramount)

Below: Bushman as the villainous Messala in Ben-Hur, enjoying himself with Iras (Carmel Myers) before the fatal chariot race.
Bottom: Bushman and Novarro in the most famous chariot race of the cinema.

LON CHANEY

The first great horror film star and, indeed, the creator of the horror film as we know it today. Known as "The Man of a Thousand Faces", Chaney was an internationally recognised expert on make-up (he wrote the entry on that subject for the *Encyclopedia Britannica*) and had an obsessive fascination with disguising himself as grotesque, maimed and crippled monstrosities. His greatest make-up achievements came in his most famous film. In **The Hunchback of Notre Dame** he originated the role of the hunchback Quasimodo with a 70-pound rubber hump, misshapen face, bulging eye and animal-like teeth. In **The Phantom of the Opera,** he is the ghoul-like Erik the Phantom whose misshapen, skull-like face has seared itself onto the collective memory of the cinema public. Although most of his major films were made for MGM, these two classics were done for Universal

and started them on the way to becoming the king of the horror studios.

Chaney's own life was as distressing as one of his film roles. Both of his parents were deaf mutes—he learned pantomime to communicate with them—and his mother became an invalid when he was nine. Born in Colorado Springs, Colorado, in 1883, he first went into stage work but then took his make-up box to Universal in 1912 and started a film career, his first credit coming on **Poor Jake's Demise** (1913). He worked for Allan Dwan and others in over 70 shorts between 1913 and 1917 and appeared in his first feature in 1917, **Hell Morgan's Girl,** as a gangster. He was well liked as the villain in William S. Hart's **Riddle Gawne** (1918) and made his first film with his favourite and greatest director, Tod Browning, in 1919, **The Wicked Darling.** His first major horror film was **The Miracle Man** (1919) at Paramount (he portrayed a sham cripple, and it made him a star. His films improved rapidly after that and he was outstanding as Fagin opposite Jackie Coogan » in **Oliver Twist,** fearful as the blind pirate Pew in **Treasure Island,** and extraordinary in double roles like the gangster and Chinese in Browning's **Outside the Law** and as blind scientist and ape-man in **A Blind Bargain. The Hunchback of Notre Dame** raised him to major star status and won him a lucrative contract with MGM, where his films were consistently outstandingly directed by major creative figures, especially Victor Sjöström (**He Who Gets Slapped, The Tower of Lies**) and Tod Browning (seven films including **The Unholy Three, The Unknown** and **London After**

Above: Lon Chaney portraying
The Hunchback of Notre Dame.

Midnight). He was not just a horror star, as his excellent straight performances in Sjöström's pictures showed, and he was very popular without make-up as the tough sergeant in **Tell It to the Marines,** but it is for his gallery of grotesques that he is most remembered. He laid down the physical and psychological basics of the horror film. The incredible make-up jobs he did on himself created a tradition carried on by Universal in the 1930s with Frankenstein and Dracula; equally important was the tradition he established that the monster should be a romantic at heart, frustrated by social and sexual barriers and turned brutal and revengeful because of them. The monster is a creation of society, not an aberration, and his inner nature is usually revealed through the symbolic girl he captures.

Chaney would have made a great talkie star but he died of cancer just as he was finishing the sound re-make of his film **The Unholy Three.** He was the subject of a reasonable film biography in 1957, **Man of a Thousand Faces,** with James Cagney » portraying Chaney.

BEST FILMS:
1919 The Miracle Man
George L. Tucker (Paramount)
1923 The Hunchback of Notre Dame
Wallace Worsley (Universal)
1924 He Who Gets Slapped
Victor Sjöström (MGM)
1925 The Tower of Lies
Victor Sjöström (MGM)
1925 The Unholy Three
Tod Browning (MGM)
1925 The Phantom of the Opera
Rupert Julien (Universal)
1927 The Unknown
Tod Browning (MGM)
1927 Tell It to the Marines
George W. Hill (MGM)
1927 London After Midnight
Tod Browning (MGM)
1929 Where East is East
Tod Browning (MGM)

CHARLES CHAPLIN

Chaplin must be considered the most famous movie star of all time; the kind of enduring fame and myth creation that was his is unlikely ever to be surpassed. To many present-day audiences this is difficult to understand because, although his films are fairly widely shown now, his reputation is not what it once was and his kind of humour is less popular than that of Buster Keaton » or Laurel and Hardy ». The real problem, however, as with most things affecting the reputation of movie stars, is mythical, not cinematic. The persona created by Chaplin, the Tramp (or the Little Fella as Chaplin called him), the best-known of all screen personas with roots going back in the tradition of comedy for hundreds of years, is no longer one with which many audiences today can or wish to identify. The sassy, ornery, obstreperous down-and-out pitted against authority and the system (usually represented by the cop, but sometimes by impersonal forces like the machine) represents an out-of-fashion kind of individualism which audiences nowadays find less sympathetic than they did a few decades ago. The Tramp is not a "nice guy" and sometimes he seems downright mean-spirited and cruel. It is this aspect of his personality that annoys or repels some modern audiences, and not his humour (which is still as fine as anything done in the silent cinema) nor his supposed lack of directorial ability, as some critics claim (his direction, though traditional, is exactly suitable for his style of comedy). The very concept of pathos, which underlies so much of Chaplin's work, is not a fashionable emotion either. And yet his fame endures, his films are still shown and a future generation may consider his work entirely differently.

Chaplin was born in Lambeth in South London in 1889, made his first music hall appearance at the age of five and became a professional music hall comic in 1898. He came to America on tour with Fred Karno's company and was persuaded to work for Mack Sennett and Keystone for $150 a week. His first film was **Making A Living,** released in February 1914. In his second film, **Kid Auto Races in Venice,** he wore his famous tramp costume for the first time and the persona that was to make him world famous grew gradually in stature. He starred opposite Mabel Normand » in many of these films but it was the feature **Tillie's Punctured Romance** with Marie Dressler » that really made him famous. He moved to the Essanay Studios at $1250 a week in 1915 and was already being called "the world's greatest comedian". Here he starred opposite Ben Turpin » and his star-to-be, Edna Purviance, and made what some critics think was his first masterpiece, **The Tramp.**

In 1916 he moved to Mutual for $10,000 a week and was now being copied and caricatured around the world. Pathos began to creep into the figure of the Tramp and these Mutual shorts are as good in many ways as anything he was ever to do; for many people **The Cure** is the funniest of all Chaplin pictures, but there is also brilliance in **The Pawnshop, The Rink, Easy Street** (trying to rob the mission poorbox) and the poignant **The Immigrant.**

In 1918 he went to First National to make films at $150,000 each, the magical **A Dog's Life, Shoulder Arms** and **Sunnyside,** and then his first feature, **The Kid.** In it Jackie Coogan » portrays a small-fry version of the Tramp and this combination of sentiment and comedy made it the biggest grossing film of Chaplin's career. After making **The Pilgrim,** Chaplin joined United Artists, which he had co-founded with Mary Pickford », Douglas Fairbanks » and D. W. Griffith. He directed but did not act in his delightful comedy of manners **A Woman of Paris** in 1923, and then sent the Tramp to the Yukon for the imaginative **The Gold Rush** (1925). This was again a huge public and critical success, though it seems episodic now and best in its amazing hunger sequences in the cabin. **The Circus** (1928) was not so popular, but he received a Best Actor nomination and a special Academy Award for his "versatility and genius" in connection with making the film.

Sound didn't bother him; he simply stayed silent, adding music only. The sentimental **City Lights** (the tramp in love with a blind girl, played by Virginia Cherrill) was again a big hit. He was still silent in 1935 in his satire against the machine age **Modern Times,** except for a few words of gibberish. His sweetheart was Paulette Goddard » and the public loved her and the film. His outrage at what was happening in Europe was channelled into **The Great Dictator,** a memorable lampoon of Hitler opposite Jack Oakie's clownish Mussolini.

After the war his popularity suffered a decline. Although his **Monsieur Verdoux** was brilliant (some critics today consider it his best), it was ahead of its time, a black comedy about a mass murderer. The Tramp figure had seemingly disappeared, transmuted into a fastidious fop. **Limelight** in 1952 was better received but was more popular in Europe than in America. Chaplin was perfect as an ageing clown, especially opposite Buster Keaton » in the film's highlight.

At this time he left the USA for good (his popularity and image had suffered through paternity suits, his seeming non-Americanism and his support of the Soviet Union during the war). He settled in Vevey in Switzerland with his fourth wife Oona, the daughter of playwright Eugene O'Neill, and his last two films were disappointments but not failures.

He died in Switzerland on Christmas Day 1977, having finally been honoured by his English homeland with a knighthood. Some of his children have also gone into acting, and daughter Geraldine has become a star in her own right.

BEST FILMS:
1915 The Tramp
Charles Chaplin (Essanay)
1916 The Pawnshop
Charles Chaplin (Mutual)
1916 The Rink
Charles Chaplin (Mutual)
1917 Easy Street
Charles Chaplin (Mutual)
1917 The Cure
Charles Chaplin (Mutual)
1917 The Immigrant
Charles Chaplin (Mutual)
1918 A Dog's Life
Charles Chaplin (First National)

*Above: One of Chaplin's most popular films, **City Lights**, with Virginia Cherrill as the blind flower-girl whose sight he is finally able to restore.*
Right: Charlie Chaplin kept his hat and cane even on skates.

1919 Shoulder Arms
Charles Chaplin (First National)
1921 The Kid
Charles Chaplin (First National)
1925 The Gold Rush
Charles Chaplin (United Artists)
1931 City Lights
Charles Chaplin (United Artists)
1936 Modern Times
Charles Chaplin (United Artists)
1940 The Great Dictator
Charles Chaplin (United Artists)
1947 Monsieur Verdoux
Charles Chaplin (United Artists)
1952 Limelight
Charles Chaplin (United Artists)

RONALD COLMAN
see **Classic Stars**

JACKIE COOGAN

Billed as "The Greatest Boy Actor in the World", Jackie Coogan was the most phenomenal child star of the silent era, the counterpart of Shirley Temple » in the sound film. He became a star in the greatest child role in the cinema, Charlie Chaplin's » **The Kid** in 1921. An orphan junior tramp, his enormous eyes and cherubic five-year-old face set off by an oversized cap, he was irresistible to the sentimental '20s. Chaplin's brilliant mixture of comedy and pathos brought two and a half million dollars' worth of laughter and tears to the coffers of the First National Company.

John Leslie Coogan Jr was born in Los Angeles in 1915 and made his stage début at the age of two. He acted in Chaplin's 1919 short **A Day's Pleasure** before helping to create Chaplin's greatest box-office success ever as **The Kid**; he starred in a dozen films during the next six years including **Oliver Twist** (with Lon Chaney » as Fagin), **Old Clothes** (with Joan Crawford » as his co-star), and **Daddy**. They made over one million dollars, and he became one of the major box-office attractions of the time. All of his films were unashamedly sentimental and remained smash hits until he began to grow up; then his star gradually dimmed. He made two reasonable sound films based on Mark Twain novels (**Tom Sawyer, Huckleberry Finn**) and then was old enough to marry Betty Grable », the first of his four wives. He sued his parents for the money he had made (he lost the case) and continued to work in films and TV in a minor way. Today Mr Coogan is a bald and beefy character actor in his 60s, but the child he once was remains an eternally young movie star.

*Above right: Jackie Coogan became the greatest child star of the silent cinema as the five-year-old co-star of Chaplin in the 1921 **The Kid**. He stayed at the top for ten years.*

BEST FILMS:
1921 The Kid
Charles Chaplin (First National)
1921 Peck's Bad Boy
Sam Wood (First National)
1922 Oliver Twist
Frank Lloyd (First National)
1923 Daddy
E. Mason Hopper (First National)
1924 Little Robinson Crusoe
Edward Cline (Metro-Goldwyn)
1924 The Rag Man
Edward Cline (Metro-Goldwyn)
1925 Old Clothes
Edward Cline (MGM)
1926 Johnny Get Your Hair Cut
Archie Mayo & B. Reeves Eason (MGM)
1927 Buttons
George Hill (MGM)
1930 Tom Sawyer
John Cromwell (Paramount)

*Above: Jackie Coogan as the orphan junior tramp in **The Kid**.*

JOAN CRAWFORD
see **Classic Stars**

BEBE DANIELS
see **Classic Stars**

17

BEST FILMS:
1922 When Knighthood was in Flower
Robert G. Vignola (Paramount)
1923 Little Old New York
Sidney Olcott (Goldwyn)
1927 The Fair Coed
Sam Wood (MGM)
1927 Quality Street
Sidney Franklin (MGM)
1928 The Patsy
King Vidor (MGM)
1928 Show People
King Vidor (MGM)
1930 Not So Dumb
King Vidor (MGM)
1932 Blondie of the Follies
Edmund Goulding (MGM)
1933 Peg O' My Heart
Robert Z. Leonard (MGM)
1933 Going Hollywood
Raoul Walsh (MGM)

*Left: One of Marion Davies'
biggest successes was
Show People, loosely based on
the career of Gloria Swanson. It
featured most of the MGM
stars of the time in a famous
studio lunch scene. Here she
is shown at the casting office.*

*Below left: Marion Davies was
witty and talented as well as
lovely, so the caricature of her
in **Citizen Kane** is deceptive.*

DOUGLAS FAIRBANKS

Doug Fairbanks' films are probably the only non-comedy silent pictures which are enjoyed as much by general audiences today as they were in their era. His reign as the King of Hollywood (with Mary Pickford » as his Queen and Pickfair as their Buckingham Palace) is long over, but he is still the King of Swashbucklers—Errol Flynn » was the heir to this crown but Flynn was unable to match the athletic stunting fantasies of Fairbanks at his best. He set the standard for Flynn, Power » and others to follow with such wondrous escapism as **The Mark of Zorro, The Three Musketeers, Robin Hood** and **The Thief of Bagdad.** These films may be dismissed by the serious-minded as "mere entertainment", but there is nothing mere about great entertainment and these cinematic achievements have never been surpassed. Mary Pickford put her finger on the secret of his appeal when she said he was "a little boy who never grew up". For that part

MARION DAVIES

Marion Davies is famous for three things. First, she was a brilliant comedienne whose career as a movie star began in 1917 and included three excellent comedies directed by King Vidor. Second, she was the acknowledged mistress of newspaper magnate William Randolph Hearst, who founded a production company (Cosmopolitan) just to make her films and who ordered his papers to mention her name daily in his determination to make her a major star. Third, their relationship inspired Orson Welles » who cruelly satirised her as Susan Alexander in his masterpiece **Citizen Kane,** based on the life of Hearst and featuring a talentless mistress "opera singer" pushed to stardom. Unfortunately the last two items are far better known than the movies, which actually prove two other things: that Marion would have been a bigger star without Hearst, as she would have been able to concentrate on the comedy that suited her best rather than star vehicles, and that Welles' caricature was not the reality: King Vidor praised her talent highly in his autobiography.

She was born Marion Douras in Brooklyn in 1897, was a Ziegfeld Follies girl by 1917 and started in movies the same year, making **Runaway Romany** for Pathé. The witty and talented blonde beauty was then discovered by Hearst and he founded the film company that continued making her films until 1937. Her early films were released through Paramount, the most successful being the lavish

one and a half million dollar production **When Knighthood was in Flower,** an historical romp with Marion as Mary Tudor. Hearst moved his company to the MGM Studios in 1923 (MGM wanted more publicity in his papers) and there she made her best and most popular films with King Vidor: **Show People, The Patsy** and **Not So Dumb.** She was a brilliant mimic and did some wonderful send-ups in these films, notably of Mae Murray », Pola Negri » and Lillian Gish ». In **Blondie of the Follies** she and Jimmy Durante took off Garbo » and Barrymore ».

Sound was not the problem it could have been to a star without Hearst's backing (she stammered), but it worried her. She made some reasonable films in the '30s and co-starred with Clark Gable », Dick Powell » and Bing Crosby » but her career went downhill after Hearst broke away from MGM. She made her last film in 1937 but stayed with Hearst until his death in 1951; then she finally married someone else. She died in 1961.

of us that never grows up, the daredevil superman that was Doug will continue to be idolised.

He was born as Douglas Elton Ulman in Denver, Colorado, in 1883 and studied briefly at Harvard before travelling around and becoming an actor. He had become fairly well known by 1915 when he was enticed to Triangle to make films at $2000 a week; his first picture was **The Lamb** and he immediately attracted the attention of scriptwriter Anita Loos (the author of **Gentlemen Prefer Blondes**) who helped him forge his screen character. Although some critics consider these early films as his best and liveliest, they do not really appeal to audiences today. Doug's persona then, as an all-American all-round super extrovert with a grin on his face at all times and a propensity for being a do-gooder, seems like a caricature of the American back-slapping stereotype. Nevertheless his stunting is magnificent, a kind of poetry of motion that bears comparison to certain areas of modern ballet. Fairbanks had become an enormous star by this time and he joined forces with D. W. Griffith, Charles Chaplin » and Mary Pickford to form the United Artists company to produce and distribute their films. He also joined forces with Mary Pickford on a personal basis; they shed their respective spouses somewhat nervously (but there was no adverse reaction from the public) and became the reigning monarchs of Hollywood, including receiving official visitors in their mansion.

Fairbanks now began his greatest creative period, not only as an actor but as a producer of lavish, spectacular, swashbuckling epics. Working with first-class directors including Allan Dwan, Fred Niblo and Raoul Walsh, he made one masterpiece after another. **The Mark of Zorro** was the paciest, **The Three Musketeers** was the most romantic, **Robin Hood** had the biggest set and cast ever put together in Hollywood and **The Thief of Bagdad** set new standards for fantasy film-making. Chaplin may have been the spirit of comedy and Valentino » the spirit of romance, but Fairbanks became the most glorious of them all—the spirit of adventure. His later films were still good fun (the two-colour Technicolor **The Black Pirate** is a technical marvel) but these four films were the zenith of his career. Although his speaking voice was fine, he did not survive the coming of sound and retired in 1934 after making his last film in Britain, **The Private Life of Don Juan**. He divorced Mary, married Sylvia, Lady Ashley, after a bit of a scandal and died in Hollywood in 1939.

Left: Douglas Fairbanks, shown in a scene from the 1921 **The Three Musketeers,** *was the King of the silent swashbucklers.*

BEST FILMS:
1917 A Modern Musketeer
Allan Dwan (Famous Players-Lasky)
1919 His Majesty the American
Joseph Henaberry (United Artists)
1920 The Mark of Zorro
Fred Niblo (United Artists)
1921 The Three Musketeers
Fred Niblo (United Artists)
1922 Robin Hood
Allan Dwan (United Artists)
1924 The Thief of Bagdad
Raoul Walsh (United Artists)
1925 Don Q, Son of Zorro
Donald Crisp (United Artists)
1926 The Black Pirate
Albert Parker (United Artists)
1927 The Gaucho
F. Richard Jones (United Artists)
1929 The Iron Mask
Allan Dwan (United Artists)

FALCONETTI

The greatest single performance in the history of the cinema was achieved by French actress Renée (Marie) Falconetti in the greatest work of the silent era, **The Passion of Joan of Arc**, directed by Carl Dreyer. The film is almost wholly close-ups, and most of the

close-ups are of Falconetti's tortured face. This is not acting in the normal sense of the word, but rather opening up the soul and allowing a director to make a concentrated exploration of the inner self. It is almost painful to watch (Dreyer is said to have made her kneel on stone floors until she reached the right degree of suffering) and it drained so much out of Falconetti that she never made another film. Such a performance is unlikely ever to be repeated, but it was enough to make her a major star. It was not glamorous; she wore no make-up and Rudolph Maté's harsh penetrating camera allows no evasions. Her head was shaved for the part

and she was allowed only one change of clothes, a light-coloured sackcloth dress in which to be burned at the stake. She was probably lucky to survive that fire as Dreyer continued to demand real suffering.

Born in Sermano, Corsica, in 1893, Falconetti became a stage actress in 1918 and one of her theatre directors was film pioneer Alberto Cavalcanti. Dreyer selected her as Joan after seeing her perform in a light comedy and she then worked on the film for 18 months; afterwards she turned stage producer, as well as appearing with the Comédie Française. She spent World War II in Switzerland and afterwards left for South America to act in the classics, and died in Buenos Aires in 1946.

Only Film:
1928 La Passion de Jeanne d'Arc
Carl Dreyer (Société Générale de Films)—France

Below: Falconetti was apparently made to kneel on stone floors to make Joan's suffering more convincing in Carl Dreyer's masterpiece **The Passion of Joan of Arc.**

FELIX THE CAT

Felix the Cat may have been "alive" only as long as his cartoons were being projected, but he was still one of the major movie stars of the silent cinema, rivalled only by Chaplin » and Keaton ». It has been estimated that at one time three-quarters of the world population had either seen him or knew his name, and the song *Felix kept on walking* was sung internationally. Felix was no ordinary cat: Marcel Brion of the Académie Française noted in 1928 that "He has escaped the reality of being a cat; he has

Above: Felix the Cat was the top animated cartoon star in the '20s.

become an extraordinary personality". Felix, in the pre-Disney era, could do anything on screen: he turned himself into a bag in order to stow away on a plane, he fenced with a mosquito and he skated on the question marks that appeared over his baffled head. He was the brilliant creation of two people: animator-director Otto Messmer and producer Pat Sullivan. Messmer first drew him in 1919, he was named by Paramount producer John King shortly afterwards and he was copyrighted by Sullivan in 1922. His personality was in some ways a reflection of Chaplin: he was a loner in a hostile world who had to use resourcefulness to survive.

Felix was one of the first cartoon characters whose appeal was based on continuing adventures as well as on gags. Like most other silent stars, he did not survive the coming of the talkies and was replaced in international affection by Mickey Mouse ». The character was twice revived for new film series but never successfully; even cartoon movie stars can't make comebacks.

BEST FILMS:
1923 Felix Revolts
Otto Messmer/Pat Sullivan
(W. J. Winkler)
1923 Felix Minds the Baby
Messmer/Sullivan (W. J. Winkler)
1924 Felix Makes a Movie
Messmer/Sullivan (Flim-Flam Films)
1925 Felix the Cat on the Farm
Messmer/Sullivan (Educational Pictures)
1926 Felix Wins and Loses
Messmer/Sullivan (Pathé Animated)
1926 Felix the Cat Hunts the Hunter
Messmer/Sullivan (Educational Pictures)
1927 Felix the Cat in Hollywood
Messmer/Sullivan (Educational Pictures)
1928 Felix the Cat in The Oily Bird
Messmer/Sullivan (Educational Pictures)
1928 Felix the Cat in Ohm Sweet Ohm
Messmer/Sullivan (Educational Pictures)
1930 Felix the Cat in Oceantics
Messmer/Sullivan (Educational Pictures)

GRETA GARBO
see **Classic Stars**

JOHN GILBERT

John Gilbert is most often remembered as the great silent film star destroyed by the coming of sound. He was at the height of his career when the talkies arrived, the top male star of the time billed over Greta Garbo » in three films and considered the Greatest Screen Lover after the death of Valentino ». His masterpiece, King Vidor's **The Big Parade,** was the most popular film of 1925 and grossed $15 million. MGM gave him a fantastic, four-year, million-dollar contract. Then he spoke his first words on the screen: he attempted the balcony scene from **Romeo and Juliet** opposite Norma Shearer » in **The Hollywood Review of 1929.** Audiences sniggered and even laughed, and his next film, **His Glorious Night,** was no better. It wasn't that his voice was bad, it was simply that it didn't suit his image, his style of acting or his face: the dashing, swashbuckling personality of the silent cinema lost credibility. Gilbert kept on making films; he was even acceptable opposite Garbo in **Queen Christina** (the best of his 15 sound pictures), but he was washed up and he knew it. He literally drank himself to death, in 1936, at the age of 38.

Gilbert (born John Pringle in Logan, Utah, in 1897) had started in the cinema in 1916 as an extra in William S. Hart's **Hell's Hinges** and his career progressed slowly through the Triangle, Paramount, Metro and Fox Studios. He first attracted real attention as a Mississippi riverboat gambler in John Ford's 1923 **Cameo Kirby,** after which MGM signed him up,

and made him their major male star of the late '20s in a series of fine films directed by King Vidor, Victor Sjöström, Erich von Stroheim and Clarence Brown. Despite his sudden fall from grace, these films will keep his name remembered for many years to come.

BEST FILMS:
1923 Cameo Kirby
John Ford (Fox)
1924 He Who Gets Slapped
Victor Sjöström (MGM)
1925 The Merry Widow
Erich von Stroheim (MGM)
1925 The Big Parade
King Vidor (MGM)
1926 La Bohème
King Vidor (MGM)
1926 Flesh and the Devil
Clarence Brown (MGM)
1927 Love
Edmund Goulding (MGM)
1928 A Woman of Affairs
Clarence Brown (MGM)
1932 Downstairs
Monta Bell (MGM)
1933 Queen Christina
Rouben Mamoulian (MGM)

Right: John Gilbert's most famous sound role was in **Queen Christina** *with Greta Garbo, but his greatest period of stardom was in the '20s.*

Above: Lillian Gish, top silent star and still active today.
Left: Gish in one of her finest roles, as heroine of **The Wind.**

LILLIAN GISH

One of the cinema's most enduring and endearing stars, Lillian Gish has literally become a legend in her own lifetime. To many people she is the personification of the silent cinema heroine. She would hardly seem the stuff of which legends are made, being frail, almost ethereal, a wispy wraith with little overt sex appeal, and unquestionably pure and virginal. Yet she was constantly under attack from virile men in her films, to the point where her helpless "heroine in distress" became almost a cliché and contributed to

her downfall at the coming of sound. However, behind that façade of frail helplessness is a tremendous strength and a perceptive intelligence. To many critics she is not only the greatest actress of the silent cinema but one of the greatest actresses of all time, comparable to Duse and Bernhardt. She starred in more acknowledged masterpieces and in more of D. W. Griffith's features than any other silent star. She was, first and last, a creation of D. W. Griffith and she continues to

acknowledge his mastery to the present day, but she was also a fine enough actress to continue as a star without him.

Born Lillian de Guiche in Springfield, Ohio, in 1896, she was put on the stage by her mother at the age of five with younger sister Dorothy. Both girls joined their friend Mary Pickford », who was working for D. W. Griffith at Biograph, and made their cinema début together in **An Unseen Enemy;** Lillian rose to stardom when she was given the lead role as Elsie Stoneman in Griffith's 1915 **The Birth of a Nation,** one of the biggest box-office hits of all time as well as a great work of art. In 1916 she was the link character in the epic **Intolerance,** rocking the cradle of humanity. She then starred in some of Griffith's greatest tear-jerkers (no denigration intended), almost always as the pure and self-sacrificing heroine. She was heart-rending as the bride-to-be who loses her groom to the horrors of war in **Hearts of the World,** tragically pitiful as the Limehouse waif beaten to death in **Broken Blossoms,** full of incredible self-sacrifice paying anonymously for her secret love's training as a minister in **True Heart Susie,** driven out into the snow when her "past" is revealed in the melodramatic **Way Down East** and an ill-fated French Revolutionary orphan with her sister Dorothy in **Orphans of the Storm.** The plots and sentiments of these films often seem ludicrous today, but Gish's sensitive playing is enough to make us believe in them.

After **Orphans** she left Griffith

and made two good films with Henry King in Italy before being enticed to MGM. There she made two of her greatest films with the Swedish director Victor Sjöström, **The Scarlet Letter** and **The Wind,** as well as a fine **La Bohème** with King Vidor. When sound arrived, her voice seemed perfectly suitable for the new medium, but new faces were wanted and she had become too identified with the silent era.

She returned to stage work and later came back to the cinema in character roles, receiving an Oscar nomination for her performance as Lionel Barrymore's. wife in **Duel in the Sun** (1946), thereafter working regularly in cinema, TV and stage. She was superb in Charles Laughton's » **The Night of the Hunter** as a seemingly helpless old lady protecting two children from mad preacher Robert Mitchum » with a shotgun hidden under her shawl. Her disclaimer that nowadays she only plays "old ladies" is true but over-modest: she plays them to perfection. She was given a special Academy Award in 1970 for her "superlative artistry" and has continued promoting her master Griffith in books and personal tours. In 1975, at the age of 80, she appeared on Broadway, singing and dancing in a musical, and in 1978 she starred in Robert Altman's **A Wedding.**

BEST FILMS:
1915 The Birth of a Nation
D. W. Griffith (Epoch)
1916 Intolerance
D. W. Griffith (Wark)
1918 Hearts of the World
D. W. Griffith (Griffith)
1919 Broken Blossoms
D. W. Griffith (United Artists)
1919 True Heart Susie
D. W. Griffith (United Artists)
1920 Way Down East
D. W. Griffith (United Artists)
1921 Orphans of the Storm
D. W. Griffith (United Artists)
1923 The White Sister
Henry King (Inspiration)
1926 La Bohème
King Vidor (MGM)
1926 The Scarlet Letter
Victor Sjöström (MGM)
1927 The Wind
Victor Sjöström (MGM)

WILLIAM S. HART

Hart was a prototype of the cowboy film star. If we think of the Western hero as being a tall, dark, silent loner, it is because this is the image that Hart created and which he brought to perfection in some of the most authentic and "adult" Westerns ever made. Hart's stardom lasted from 1914 to 1925, but in that time he took the fledgling Western genre and injected it with documentary realism, harsh poetry and psychological weight, profoundly influencing its development.

Hart was able to bring authenticity to the cowboy movie because he had grown up in the West. Born in 1870 in Newburgh, New York, he travelled to the Dakotas with his family, learned Sioux at an early age and even worked as a trail herd cowboy. He spent 20 years on Broadway as a stage actor before joining his old friend Thomas Ince in California with a burning desire to make realistic Westerns; his first feature film, **The Bargain,** which he wrote, made him a star and Ince signed him as both actor and director. His memorable stone face and almost evangelical bearing seemed to

Above: William S. Hart, the first outstanding cowboy star.

hide a terrible past, and this creation of the Good Bad Man had a lasting influence on other Western stars. He was austere when confronting his enemies, chivalrous to women and sometimes sentimental. His best Westerns, like **Hell's Hinges, The Toll Gate** and **The Aryan,** are major cinematic achievements. The coming of fancy cowboy showmanship in the form of Tom Mix » and Hoot Gibson signalled the end of his career, but he refused to alter his authenticity. He produced his swan song **Tumbleweeds** in 1925, and then retired except for occasional guest appearances.

Hart was the predecessor and trail blazer for the great cowboy stars like Gary Cooper , Randolph Scott » and John Wayne », but was in no way their inferior. His contribution to the Western film came from his writing and directing as well as his acting, especially through his infusion of the genuine West into the genre. He hired real Indians and real Westerners for the lesser roles in his films, and his characters and sets were as authentic as the West itself, down to the dirt, grime and sweat. His pinto pony Fritz was the first well-known horse star. Even off-screen Hart maintained his loner image. Except for a brief marriage, his closest friends were Old West heroes like Bat Masterson and Wyatt Earp. His last screen appearance was in 1939, a kind of rugged Last Will and Testament in the form of an eight-minute prologue to the re-release

of his film **Tumbleweeds.** He died in Los Angeles in 1946 and his Horseshoe Ranch is now a public park.

BEST FILMS:
1914 The Bargain
Reginald Barker (New York Motion Picture Co)
1915 The Darkening Trail
William S. Hart (New York Motion Picture Co)
1916 The Return of Draw Egan
William S. Hart (Triangle)
1916 Hell's Hinges
William S. Hart (Triangle)
1917 The Aryan
William S. Hart (Triangle)
1917 The Narrow Trail
Lambert Hillyer (Artcraft)
1918 Branding Broadway
Lambert Hillyer (Artcraft)
1920 The Toll Gate
Lambert Hillyer (Artcraft)
1920 The Testing Block
Lambert Hillyer (Artcraft)
1925 Tumbleweeds
William S. Hart & King Baggot (United Artists)

BRIGITTE HELM

One of the most memorable images in the cinema is the birth of Brigitte Helm as a sinister robot in Fritz Lang's 1926 **Metropolis.** It was also the birth of an international star, for her double role as a beautiful, innocent girl with an erotic robot duplicate charged her with a double magnetism (sexy and nice) that few actresses have been given. She was only 18 years old at the time and totally inexperienced, but she instantly became one of the leading stars of the German cinema.

Born Gisele Eve Schittenhelm in Berlin in 1908, she was discovered by Lang in a student play and worked constantly for the following ten years with leading directors from Germany,

France, England and Italy. The dichotomous bad-good element of her nature as revealed by Lang was seized upon by other directors with relish. Pabst starred her in three films, most notably as the French bourgeois girl in love with a Russian communist in **The Love of Jeanne Ney,** and she appeared in the starring role in two German versions of **Alraune** in 1928 and 1930. Her career seemed to be set to continue successfully in sound films with such pleasant cinematic fairy tales as **The Countess of Monte Cristo** and even an English film with Herbert Wilcox, but Nazi Germany did not allow it. She was judged guilty of "race defilement" for having married a Jew in 1933 and ended up living in exile in Paris, making no more movies after 1936. She lives today in West Berlin with her industrialist husband, Hugh Kunheim, and her magnificent films are still constantly shown in cinémathèques and film societies.

BEST FILMS:
1926 Metropolis
Fritz Lang (Ufa)
1927 The Love of Jeanne Ney
G. W. Pabst (Ufa)
1928 Crisis
G. W. Pabst (Erda Film)
1928 L'Argent
Marcel l'Herbier (in France)
1929 The Wonderful Life of Nina Petrovna
Hans Schwarz (Ufa)
1932 The Countess of Monte Cristo
Karl Hartl (Ufa)
1932 The Blue Danube
Herbert Wilcox (in England)
1932 The Mistress of Atlantis
G. W. Pabst (Nero-film)
1933 The Marathon Runner
E. A. Dupont (Ufa)
1934 Gold
Karl Hartl (Ufa)

*Below Brigitte Helm became a major star in the German cinema, but made **The Blue Danube** in England with Joseph Schildkraut as her romantic co-star.*

EMIL JANNINGS

Jannings used to be considered "the greatest screen actor of all time", a contentious ranking held by international critics for at least two decades. He was the magnificent star of some of the greatest German films of the 1920s (major works by Murnau, Pabst, Dupont and Lubitsch) and also a star of the American silent cinema, winning the first Academy Award for Best Actor for two films (**The Way of All Flesh** and **The Last Command**). Today, although his films and performances still astonish, the limitations of his "whisper-scream" technique have become noticeable and have lessened his stature. We are also able to see how his usual self-abasement role as a figure of power brought low reflected the German nation's personality crisis; Jannings later became the favourite male star of the Third Reich. His enthusiastic work for the Hitler regime, including starring in the anti-British film **Ohm Kruger,** has also affected his international reputation.

Jannings was born Theodor Friedrich Emil Janenz in Rorschach, Switzerland, in 1884, worked on stage with Max Reinhardt in Berlin and made his film début in 1914 in Robert Wiene's **Arme Eva.** His triumphant film career includes some of the finest silent cinema acting performances, including the proud hotel doorman reduced to toilet attendant in F. W. Murnau's **The Last Laugh,** Louis XV in Ernst Lubitsch's **Madame Dubarry,** the jealous trapeze artist in E. A.

Above: Jannings, one of the great character stars, usually portrayed figures of power brought low. He won the first Best Actor Oscar for his role in **The Last Command,** *portraying a former Czarist general in Hollywood who ends up playing himself in a movie.*

Dupont's **Variety** and Haroun al Raschid in Paul Leni's **Waxworks;** the climax was his role as the professor destroyed by Marlene Dietrich » in Josef von Sternberg's **The Blue Angel.** His American career with Paramount was triumphant, but the coming of sound ended his chances of continuing US stardom, as audiences disliked his accent. In the Germany of the 1930s he was by far the most prestigious actor and he went on making films till the end of the war, when he was forced to retire. He died in Austria in 1950.

MAIN FILMS:
1919 Madame Dubarry
Ernst Lubitsch (Union Film-Ufa)
1924 Waxworks
Paul Leni (Neptun-film)
1924 The Last Laugh
F. W. Murnau (Ufa)
1925 Variety
E. A. Dupont (Ufa)
1925 Tartuffe
F. W. Murnau (Ufa)
1926 Faust
F. W. Murnau (Ufa)
1927 The Way of All Flesh
Victor Fleming (Ufa)
1928 The Last Command
Josef von Sternberg (Paramount)
1928 The Patriot
Ernst Lubitsch (Paramount)
1930 The Blue Angel
Josef von Sternberg (Ufa)

BUSTER KEATON

Keaton, for most critics today, is the greatest of the silent film comedians—not only because of his appealing sense of humour and screen persona, but also because he was an outstanding director, an inventive genius the equal of any other great film-maker of the time. The only comparable figure in cinema history is Jacques Tati », also a brilliant director as well as a comic genius, and there are certainly parallels between the unemotional, basically pessimistic personae they created. Keaton is often described as the "Great Stone Face" because of his deadpan, never-smiling face (usually topped by a thin, flat hat), but his devotees know that this impassivity simply allows him to impart feeling with the subtlest of movements. Like Garbo's face at the end of **Queen Christina**, this blank quality allows audiences to read into it whatever they themselves feel.

Buster was born Joseph Francis Keaton in Piqua, Kansas, in 1895, the child of vaudeville performers, and began his stage career at the age of three. The nickname Buster was reportedly given to him by escapologist Harry Houdini after watching the child fall down a flight of stairs. He began his film career with Fatty Arbuckle » in 1917 in **The Butcher Boy** and quickly surpassed his employer; his last film for Arbuckle was the 1919 **The Garage.**

In 1920 he made his first feature, the relatively unsuccessful **The Saphead,** directed by Winchell Smith and based on a Broadway melodrama. After that he produced and directed or co-directed most of his major silent films, beginning the nine most creative years of his life by making 20 brilliant shorts. Keaton never made a bad film but some of these two- and three-reelers are among his masterpieces. The finest is probably the 1922 **Cops,** in which Buster is conned into buying furniture that actually belongs to a policeman.

Keaton always got into trouble in his films but he never felt sorry for himself, nor asked for audience sympathy. Unlike Chaplin », whose Tramp figure is linked unfashionably to pathos, there was no sentiment in a Keaton film and the Stone Face was sad but never pathetic. His deadpan expression seemed to assume that things would go wrong and in this he was the opposite of Harold Lloyd ». Both were brilliant acrobats and stuntmen but Keaton could surpass even the daring Lloyd; in **Steamboat Bill Jr** he allows a whole house to collapse on him, having calculated to the inch where to stand so that a window space would fall around him.

Keaton turned completely to

Above: Buster Keaton always seemed to be scanning the horizon in his films. Here he is seen in **The Navigator,** *in which he and a girl are the only passengers on a deserted ship in the middle of the ocean. Right: Buster Keaton was known as the Great Stone Face, but his impassivity was only a façade.*

feature production in 1923, making **The Three Ages** and **Our Hospitality**. In the next three years he made his greatest films and the ones by which he is best remembered: **The General,** his most famous, is the story of a Northern soldier in the Civil War who steals a locomotive (called the General) from the South and gets involved in one of the greatest chases in film history. **Sherlock Jr** is a technical marvel in which Keaton plays a movie projectionist who imagines himself acting in the pictures he shows, especially as a great detective. **Seven Chances** allows Keaton half a day to find a bride and he soon has more than he can cope with. In **The Navigator** he finds himself alone at sea with a girl, trying to operate a mammoth ocean liner designed to be run by a vast crew. In these films Keaton's co-star is often a machine (a locomotive, a ship, a cinema projector); he loved mechanical devices and this is often reflected in the gags that run through these films, from the gigantic pot in which he tries to boil two eggs in **The Navigator** to his attempts to use a cannon in **The General.**

Keaton tried to continue his career in the talkie era, but either sound slowed his inventiveness or (more likely) MGM was unable to accept his improvisational method of working. At any rate

KEYSTONE KOPS

The Keystone Kops were the first group to become a collective movie star, and are still the most famous: many people's idea of a silent comedy is simply the Keystone Kops falling over or out of a fast-moving vehicle. They were the brainchild of comedy king Mack Sennett, who founded the Keystone Film Company in 1912, borrowing the name from a Pennsylvania railroad. One of the three actors who set up the studio was Ford Sterling (1893-1939), the funny-bearded chief of the Keystone Kops. The original seven Kops (according to Sennett) were Edgar Kennedy (1890-1948), the bald master of the slow burn, well known for later RKO shorts; Hank Mann (1897-1971), the great walrus-moustached comedian with a hound-dog look who lent support to stars from Chaplin » through to Jerry Lewis » for over 40 years; George (Slim) Summerville (1892-1946), a long, lanky, mournful comic who later became an ace Sennett director and then actor, most notably in **All Quiet on the Western Front**; Bobby Dunn (1891-1939), who starred in the Mirthquake series of the 1920s; George Jesks (1891-1951), who became a scriptwriter; Charles Avery and Mack Riley. The Kops were the crown princes of zany incompetence and their chase scenes are among the most memorable achievements of popular art.

The Kops first appeared in December 1912 in the film **Hoffmeyer's Legacy,** but their first starring role was in the April 1913 **The Bangville Police.** Thereafter they were featured in a very large number of the Keystone comedies—many critics consider the 1914 **In the Clutches of a Gang** to be their best—and most new actors joining the studio were tried out as Kops; among the more famous graduates of the Kop Korps were Roscoe (Fatty) Arbuckle », Chester Conklin (1888-1971) and Charlie Chase (1893-1940), all of whom became stars in their own right; James Finlayson (1887-1953), well known for his Laurel and Hardy » comedies; Henry ("Pathé") Lehrman, who became a director for Sennett, Hal Roach and other studios; and Eddie Sutherland and Eddie Cline, who also became comedy directors.

The Keystone Kops' slapstick brand of comedy did not survive the coming of sound, and an attempt to bring them to life again in 1955 in **Abbott and Costello Meet the Keystone Cops** was not successful.

BEST FILMS:
1913 The Bangville Police
Henry Lehrman (Keystone)
1914 In the Clutches of a Gang
George Nichols (Keystone)
1914 The Alarm
Roscoe Arbuckle (Keystone)
1914 The Knockout
Mack Sennett (Keystone)
1914 Barney Oldfield's Race for Life
Mack Sennett (Keystone)
1914 Those Country Kids
Roscoe Arbuckle (Keystone)
1914 Tillie's Punctured Romance
Mack Sennett (Keystone)
1915 Our Daredevil Chief
Mack Sennett (Keystone)
1916 Because He Loved Her
Dell Henderson (Triangle-Keystone)
1924 Hollywood Kid
Mack Sennett & Billy Bevan (Keystone)

his films deteriorated, he began to drink heavily and he ended up doing bit parts and gag writing. He still appeared in some notable films, including Chaplin's **Limelight** and shorts like **The Railrodder** and Samuel Beckett's **Film.** His reputation began to revive in the 1950s and Donald O'Connor » portrayed him in a not very good biopic, **The Buster Keaton Story.** Promoted by Raymond Rohauer, Keaton's films were re-released to universal acclaim in the 1960s. Before his death in 1966, he had the satisfaction of knowing that he had finally surpassed Chaplin in both critical and popular acclaim. The comedian whose most typical pose was that of a man scanning the horizon could finally see that his greatness would continue to be recognised.

BEST FILMS:
1922 Cops
Buster Keaton & Eddie Cline (Keaton)
1923 The Balloonatic
Keaton & Cline (Keaton)
1923 Our Hospitality
Keaton & Jack Blystone (Metro)
1924 Sherlock Jr
Keaton (Metro)
1924 The Navigator
Keaton & Donald Crisp (Metro-Goldwyn)
1925 Seven Chances
Keaton (Metro-Goldwyn)

1926 The General
Keaton & Clyde Bruckman (United Artists)
1927 Steamboat Bill Jr
Charles Reisner (United Artists)
1928 The Cameraman
Edward Sedgwick, Jr (MGM)
1929 Spite Marriage
Edward Sedgwick, Jr (MGM)

Below: Many critics consider **In the Clutches of a Gang** *to be the best of all Keystone Kop films. At the desk is Kop chief Ford Sterling while the Kops include (starting right) Fatty Arbuckle, Rube Miller, Hank Mann, Al St John and George Jesky. They were the first group star.*

Rudolf Klein-Rogge

One of the all-time great villains of the cinema, the prototype master criminal and mad scientist, Rudolf Klein-Rogge was the favourite actor of director Fritz Lang in the '20s. His greatest creations were the mad superman-master criminal Dr Mabuse, the crazy scientist Rotwang in **Metropolis**, the master spy Haghi in **Spies**, and Attila the Hun in **Kriemhild's Revenge**. His criminal tendencies go back to the very beginnings of his cinema career; he portrayed one in an early film, Wiene's 1919 **The Cabinet of Dr Caligari**.

Klein-Rogge was born in Cologne in 1888, began a stage career in Vienna and came to Berlin in 1918. He started filming the following year; his wife at this time was Thea von Harbou, who worked as a writer on all of Lang's films in the '20s (she married Lang in 1924 after divorcing Klein-Rogge). He was featured in their first collaboration, **The Wandering Picture,** in 1920 and then in most of Lang's films until the 1933 **The Testament of Dr Mabuse.** This was so clearly an indictment of Hitler (Klein-Rogge is a master criminal ruling his empire from a madhouse) that Goebbels immediately banned it.

Although Klein-Rogge worked with other directors in the '20s and his sound career continued into the 1940s, his greatest films were all made with Lang. The great screen villain died in Graz in 1955, but he will always be remembered as the predecessor (and superior) of such contemporary master criminals as James Bond's opponent Goldfinger.

BEST FILMS:
1919 The Cabinet of Dr Caligari
Robert Wiene (Decla-Bioscop)
1920 The Wandering Picture
Fritz Lang (May Film)
1920 Fighting Hearts
Fritz Lang (Decla-Bioscop)
1921 Destiny
Fritz Lang (Decla-Bioscop)
1922 Dr Mabuse the Gambler
Fritz Lang (Uco/Decla-Bioscop)
1923 The Stone Rider
Fritz Wendhausen (Decla-Bioscop)
1924 Kriemhild's Revenge
Fritz Lang (Ufa)
1926 Metropolis
Fritz Lang (Ufa)
1928 Spies
Fritz Lang (Lang/Ufa)
1933 The Testament of Dr Mabuse
Fritz Lang (Nero)

Werner Krauss

Krauss is one of the most fear-inspiring and evil-invoking stars in the history of the movies, and not just for cinematic reasons; he

Above: Rudolf Klein-Rogge was the first and perhaps greatest mad scientist/master criminal, especially as Dr Mabuse.

was the sinister, crippled personification of evil in the most famous of all German silent pictures, as the doctor in Wiene's **The Cabinet of Dr Caligari.** This strange foreshadowing of Hitler reached its awful conclusion in 1940, when Goebbels chose Krauss to be one of the stars of one of the vilest of all Nazi anti-semitic films, Viet Harlan's **Jud Süss;** Krauss claimed he was forced to make the film against his will, but he was blacklisted after the war and was forced to live and work in Austria until his death in 1959. This sad conclusion to the career of one of the greatest actors of the great German silent cinema does not erase his enormous contribution to the art of film; he starred in many of the most important films of Pabst and Murnau in addition to **Caligari.**

Born in Gestungshausen, Germany, in 1884, he became one of the leading German stage actors at the height of "expressionism" and entered the cinema in 1916. His geometric movements in **Caligari** reflected the tortured Cubist style of the film and contributed greatly to its success. He was the gross butcher in **Joyless Street**, a peasant in **Burning Acre,** a tortured mind in **Secrets of the Soul** and the devil in **The Student of Prague.** He was one of the "big four" of the German acting profession who stayed in Germany under the Nazis (along with Jannings ≫, George and Gründgens) and claimed he could not emigrate because Goebbels discovered his son had a Jewish wife. Whatever the reason, that decision eventually destroyed him.

BEST FILMS:
1919 The Cabinet of Dr Caligari
Robert Wiene (Decla-Bioscop)
1922 The Burning Earth
F. W. Murnau (Goron-Deulig Exklusiv Film)
1923 The Treasure
G. W. Pabst (Froelich Film)
1924 Waxworks
Paul Leni (Neptun Film)
1925 Tartuffe
F. W. Murnau (Ufa)
1925 The Joyless Street
G. W. Pabst (Sofar Film)
1926 The Student of Prague
Henrik Galeen (Soldat Film)
1926 Secrets of a Soul
G. W. Pabst (Neumann Film)
1926 Nana
Jean Renoir (in France)
1927 Royal Scandal
Hans Behrendt

*Below: Werner Krauss (standing right) in his most famous role as Caligari in **The Cabinet of Dr Caligari,** with Conrad Veidt as Cesare in the cabinet.*

HARRY LANGDON

Langdon is one of the Big Four of silent film comedy, the Baby who for a time rivalled the Tramp, the Stone Face and the College Kid. Langdon's screen persona, however, was the strangest of the four, a psychologically weird combination of innocence and age, a mélange of whimsy and depravity. Langdon was actually 40 years old when he became a baby-faced star; it would have been impossible to predict that this middle-aged former vaudevillean would become the screen's greatest child adult.

He was born in Council Bluffs, Iowa, in 1884 and spent nearly 20 years in show business (medicine shows, circuses, vaudeville) before turning to the cinema. He began working for comedy king Mack Sennett in 1924 and his bizarre baby characterisation was probably developed for him by gag writer Frank Capra, who later became a major director. Langdon made 30 comedies for Sennett in two years and became so popular that Warner Brothers offered him $6000 a week to work for them; he cleverly took Capra and his best director, Harry Edwards, along with him, and they helped him produce his three greatest films: in **Tramp, Tramp, Tramp** he attempts to win a cross-country race and Joan Crawford », hindered by cyclones and prison: in **The Strong Man** he is an ex-soldier who poses as a muscle man and wins the love of a blind girl: in **Long Pants** he is a country boy with his first pair of long trousers, bewitched by a vamp. After these three masterpieces, Langdon apparently convinced himself that he knew best how to make his own films and sacked Capra. His error was soon apparent—the three films he directed himself were total failures and his career nosedived, never to rise again. He continued working in sound films but mostly in supporting roles, most notably opposite Al Jolson » in Lewis Milestone's 1933 **Hallelujah I'm a Bum** and paired with Oliver Hardy » in Gordon Douglas's 1939 **Zenobia**. He died bankrupt in 1944, still trying to make a comeback.

BEST FILMS:
1924 Picking Peaches
Erle C. Kenton (Sennett)
1924 Luck of the Foolish
Harry Edwards (Sennett)
1925 There He Goes
Harry Edwards (Sennett)
1925 Lucky Stars
Harry Edwards (Sennett)
1926 Soldier Man
Harry Edwards (Sennett)
1926 His First Flame
Harry Edwards (Sennett)
1926 Ella Cinders
Alfred E. Green (Sennett)

Above: **Long Pants** *is considered by many critics as Harry Langdon's finest film, his child-man character baffled by the big city and bewitched by a vamp.*
Inset: Langdon created one of the oddest personas in film history, the 40-year-old Baby.

1926 Tramp, Tramp, Tramp
Harry Edwards (Warner Brothers)
1926 The Strong Man
Frank Capra (Warner Brothers)
1927 Long Pants
Frank Capra (Warner Brothers)

LAUREL AND HARDY
see **Classic Stars**

FLORENCE LAWRENCE

The movie star system as we know it today began in 1910 with Florence Lawrence, the first actor/actress to become famous by name; she is usually considered to be the first movie star, even though "Broncho Billy" Anderson » had become known a little earlier as a screen character.

Miss Lawrence, the most famous star from 1910 to 1912 and a major figure until 1915, was the first object of Hollywood ballyhoo and the focus of the first publicity stunt—prior to 1910 she had worked anonymously for Biograph and was known to her fans simply as "the Biograph girl"; Carl Laemmle, the founder of Universal Pictures, lured her to his new IMP Company with the offer of more money and then circulated a rumour that she had been killed in St Louis in a streetcar accident. He then "nailed" the lie by taking out big ads in the newspapers saying she was still alive and now working for the IMP Company, and when he produced her in person in St Louis, the crowds were bigger than those that had greeted the President a week earlier.

Miss Lawrence, born in 1888, was on the vaudeville circuit from the age of four as Baby Flo, the Child Wonder Whistler; she made her cinema début in 1907 at Vitagraph in **Daniel Boone** and then became the leading performer at Biograph. After achieving stardom she switched companies almost yearly. Her comedies with Arthur Johnson and the Jones series with John Compson were extremely popular, but the artistic highpoint of her career was being directed by D. W. Griffith in **Resurrection.**

Her career ended tragically. She was badly burned in a studio fire in 1915 trying to save someone else, and a comeback attempt in the 1920 **The Enfoldment** was unsuccessful. She ended up playing bit parts for MGM and killed herself with poison in 1938.

BEST FILMS:
1908 Romeo and Juliet
Paul Panzer (Vitagraph)
1909 Miss Jones Entertains
(Biograph)
1909 Resurrection
D. W. Griffith (Biograph)
1910 The Forest Ranger's Daughter
(IMP)
1910 The Angel of the Studio
(IMP)
1911 The Two Fathers
(Lubin)
1911 Her Two Sons
(Lubin)
1912 Swift Waters
(Victor)
1914 A Singular Cynic
(Universal)
1920 The Enfoldment
(Independent)

Left: Florence Lawrence was the first American movie star to become famous by name, and the star system began with her in 1910. Today she is virtually unknown, except to film historians, despite her importance.

MAX LINDER

Linder was the first great screen comedian, the predecessor of Charles Chaplin »; he is generally regarded as also the first truly international movie star.

He began acting in comedy shorts in 1905 and made some 400 films for the Pathé Studio in Paris over the next ten years. His screen persona as the sleek and elegant dandy "Max" did not really emerge until 1910 (the great first year of movie stars),but he had already acquired enormous popularity in Europe. Although he is not as well known today as he should be, because most of his films are no longer available, Max was one of the superstars of the 1910s and a major influence on Chaplin and other comedians.

Linder was born with the name Gabriel Levielle in Saint-Loubes, France, on December 16, 1883, and began his acting career in the theatre, turning to the cinema simply to earn money. By 1907 he had become Pathé's leading comedian, and from 1913 he wrote and directed his own films. His screen character was unlike any of the other early comics; he dressed in the finest quality top hat, tails and cloak, wore a svelte moustache, was precise in his gestures if dreamy in his manner and seemed only slightly perturbed by the frantic difficulties he experienced. His popularity in 1916 was so international that he was brought to Hollywood by the Essanay Studio to replace the departing Chaplin; he made three good films there, but his American career did not jell and he returned to Europe for two features. In 1921 he again tried to succeed in America and produced his three finest films, but sadly they were coolly received by the public, and after two more films in Europe he and his wife committed suicide in 1925. The great American comedies were re-released in 1963 as the compilation **Laugh with Max Linder.**

BEST FILMS:
1913 Max's Duel
Max Linder (Pathé)
1917 Max Comes Across
Max Linder (Essanay)
1917 Max Wants a Divorce
Max Linder (Essanay)
1917 Max in a Taxi
Max Linder (Essanay)
1919 Le Petit Café
Raymond Bernard (Pathé)
1921 Seven Years Bad Luck
Max Linder (United Artists)
1921 Be My Wife
Max Linder (Goldwyn)
1922 The Three Must-Get-Theres
Max Linder (United Artists)
1923 Au Secours!
Abel Gance (in France)
1925 The King of the Circus
Édouard-Émile Violet & Linder
(in Austria)

Below: Max Linder created a screen comedy persona that influenced most other silent comics, an elegant dreamer in top hat and tails. He was the first major funny man of the cinema, and has claims to be the first international star.

Above: Harold Lloyd scaled the heights of stardom with thrill comedies like the famous **Safety Last.** *Here he is seen on his way up a 20-storey building trying to make his way past a clock that falls apart as he clings to its face.*

HAROLD LLOYD

Harold Lloyd was the king of suspense comedy, memorable as much for his acrobatic laugh-provoking thrills as for his persona, the brash and breezy College Kid with horn-rimmed glasses and straw hat. Lloyd, the All-American boy go-getter with an Horatio Alger confidence in the world, called these films "thrill pictures", and began perfecting them as early as 1918 in **Look Out Below.** They depended on mixing laughs with danger by performing humorous stunts in a perilously lofty place. The high point of Lloyd's career was **Safety Last** (1923) in which he desperately tries to scale a 20-storey building continually hampered by windows, mice, people and a large clock that falls apart as he tries to climb it. Lloyd did his own stunts and they look just as spectacular today.

He actually started out on the flat plains of Nebraska, where he was born in Burchard in 1894, entering films from stage work in 1905. His first film was **Just Nuts** for Hal Roach; in the same year he developed a character called Lonesome Luke and made it reasonably popular in hundreds of films for Roach. His brash, optimistic, bespectacled College Kid persona emerged in the late 1910s and was first seen fully developed in **A Sailor Made Man** in 1921.

Although Lloyd did not direct his own films he controlled every detail of them, and his enormous success in the '20s with **Safety Last, The Freshman** and **The Kid Brother** was due to his own genius. His popularity diminished when sound arrived, and he retired a very wealthy man, emerging only to make a Preston Sturges film in 1946, **The Sin of Harold Diddlebock.** He re-issued the best of his work in two compilations in the early '60s (**Harold Lloyd's World of Comedy** and **The Funny Side of Life**), and they again proved a success with world audiences. He died in Hollywood in 1971.

BEST FILMS:
1921 A Sailor Made Man
Fred Newmeyer (Associated Exhibitors)
1922 Grandma's Boy
Fred Newmeyer (Pathé)
1923 Safety Last
Fred Newmeyer & Sam Taylor (Pathé)
1923 Why Worry?
Newmeyer & Taylor (Pathé)
1924 Girl Shy
Newmeyer & Taylor (Pathé)
1924 Hot Water
Newmeyer & Taylor (Pathé)
1925 The Freshman
Newmeyer & Taylor (Pathé)
1927 The Kid Brother
Ted Wilde (Paramount)
1930 Feet First
Clyde Bruckman (Paramount)
1932 Movie Crazy
Clyde Bruckman (Paramount)

BESSIE LOVE

One of the most popular of the American silent film stars in England, where she moved to in 1935, this 80-year-old is still making movies and recently published her autobiography, *From Hollywood With Love.* Her amazing career stretches from 1916 (when she starred in D. W. Griffith's masterpiece **Intolerance** and William S. Hart's superb **The Aryan**), through the first Hollywood musicals at MGM (**Broadway Melody**, which won the second Academy Award for Best Picture in 1929 and an Oscar nomination for Bessie as Best Actress, plus **The Hollywood Revue** in which she introduced the world to the hit song *Singin' in the Rain*), until today and brilliant cameo roles in British films (including the busy-body telephone operator in John Schlesinger's 1971 **Sunday, Bloody Sunday**).

Above: Bessie Love remains one of the best-loved stars of the silent cinema, though her films are rarely seen. Here she is pictured in the 1927 Donald Crisp movie **Dress Parade** *with co-star Hugh Allen. She was the first MGM musical star.*

Splendid as she is now, she was still more splendid in the heyday of the silent cinema, appearing opposite such stars as Douglas Fairbanks Sr » in **Reggie Moves In** at Triangle and Richard Barthelmess » in **Soul Fire** at First National. She was born Juanita Horton in Midland, Texas, in 1898 (Griffith told her to change her name) and combined all the qualities of the great silent actresses. She had the round, ethereal face of Lillian Gish », the tomboy humour of Mary Pickford » and the big-eyed sweet demureness of all the Griffith heroines. Her genuine acting skill was never really properly used, and her biggest commercial hit was playing opposite Willis O'Brien's dinosaurs in **The Lost World**; she introduced the Charleston to the screen in **The King on Main Street**, and

ended her silent stardom gloriously by becoming the first MGM musical star.

BEST FILMS:
1916 Intolerance
D. W. Griffith (Wark)
1916 The Aryan
Reginald Barker and William S. Hart (Triangle)
1916 Reggie Moves In
Christy Cabanne (Triangle)
1922 Forget-Me-Not
W. S. Van Dyke (Metro)
1925 Soul Fire
John Robertson (First National)
1925 The Lost World
Harry Hoyt (First National)
1926 Lovely Mary
King Baggot (MGM)
1927 Dress Parade
Donald Crisp (Pathé)
1928 Broadway Melody
Edmund Goulding (MGM)
1929 The Hollywood Revue
Charles Reisner (MGM)

MACISTE

Maciste was the first film character to become a major movie star; his popularity was similar to Tarzan's » in the '30s and James Bond's » today.

Maciste was originally the creation of Italian writer Gabriele D'Annunzio, who scripted the 1914 Italian epic **Cabiria**; Maciste was a Roman slave strong-man, a gentle giant who protected his master as well as the humble and oppressed. He was portrayed by an uneducated giant docker from Genoa named Bartolomeo Pagano (born in San Ilario in 1878, who was personally selected by **Cabiria's** director Giovanni Pastrone. This super-spectacular epic turned out to be the **Gone With the Wind** of its time, an astonishing international success; the illiterate Genoese became such a hot movie property that he was accepted as a mythical figure (he changed his name legally to Maciste) and was the star of Maciste films for 14 years. These

films (some of them directed by Pastrone) were extremely popular, amd "Maciste" retired a rich man in 1928.

The character survived Pagano's death in 1947 and was revived with great success by the Italian cinema in 1960. The new Maciste was even more like Hercules than his predecessor, and was portrayed by a number of American beefcake actors including Mark Forrest, Gordon Scott, Kirk Morris and Ed Fury. In 1962 five Maciste films were made in what was described as a mythological-historical movie boom, some of them remakes of silent originals like **Maciste in Hell**. At the moment the Maciste character is resting, but it seems probable that he will return to the limelight yet again.

BEST FILMS:
1914 Cabiria
Giovanni Pastrone (Itala)
1915 Maciste
Giovanni Pastrone (Itala)
1916 Maciste the Alphinist
Giovanni Pastrone (Itala)
1919 Maciste the Athlete
Giovanni Pastrone (Itala)
1923 Maciste and the Chinese Cabinet
Carl Boese (in Germany)
1925 Maciste Against the Sheik
Mario Camerini (Pittaluga)
1926 Maciste in Hell
Guido Brignone (Pittaluga)
1960 Maciste in the Valley of the Kings
Carlo Campogalliani (Donati-Carpentieri)
1961 Maciste at the Court of the Great Khan
Riccardo Freda (Panda)
1962 Maciste in Hell
Riccardo Freda (Panda)

Left: Maciste was the strong-man superstar of his era, an international success overnight because of stunts like this in the epic spectacular **Cabiria**.

Above: Mae Marsh, as The Dear One in the modern section of **Intolerance**, *trying to protect her baby from women reformers. Left: Mae Marsh as Little Sister in* **The Birth of a Nation**, *found dead by Henry B. Walthall.*

MAE MARSH

Some critics consider Mae Marsh the greatest actress of the silent cinema, comparable to Duse and Bernhardt in the theatre. It is unquestionably true that she turned in magnificent performances in two of the major cinema classics, D. W. Griffith's **The Birth of a Nation** and **Intolerance**; the scene in **Birth** in which Mae, as Little Sister, is discovered by returning Confederate soldier Henry B. Walthall to have faked the ermine on her supposedly new dress by using cotton is one of the most memorable funny-sad scenes in the cinema. Equally unforgettable is her scene of terror-inspired laughter as she hides during a renewed outbreak of fighting, and her sensitive underplaying of Dear One, the wife of the unjustly condemned man in the modern section of **Intolerance**, is rightly ranked as one of the supreme acting performances of the silent cinema.

Mary "Mae" Marsh was born in Madrid, New Mexico, in 1895 and began working with Griffith at Biograph in 1912; he said she was "born a film star" and she certainly had all the innocence and girlish looks that Griffith liked —a slight, freckled red-head, she could betray a fearful agitation when confronted with adult realities in her films. She stayed with Griffith until 1917 and then left to become one of Samuel Goldwyn's first stars for $2500 a week, but her pictures away from Griffith never really brought out her best and she returned to make one film with him in 1923, **The White Rose**, co-starring with Ivor Novello. She also joined forces with Novello for the British film **The Rat**, but the coming of sound ended her stardom, though she continued working in small roles and appeared in virtually every film made by her close friend John Ford (her last film was his 1961 picture **Two Rode Together**). Poet Vachel Lindsay wrote two poems about her in the 1920s, calling her the "madonna" of the new art of cinema, but it was Griffith who paid her the ultimate compliment; after attending a revival of **Birth of a Nation**, he sent her a cable: "Just saw the greatest performance ever seen on any screen—that of the Little Sister played by Mae Marsh." She died in California in 1968.

BEST FILMS:
1913 Judith of Bethulia
D. W. Griffith (Biograph)
1914 Home Sweet Home
D. W. Griffith (Reliance-Majestic)
1915 The Birth of a Nation
D. W. Griffith (Epoch)
1916 Intolerance
D. W. Griffith (Wark)
1916 Hoodoo Ann
Lloyd Ingraham (Triangle)
1916 The Wharf Rat
Chester Withy (Triangle)
1916 The Wild Girl of the Sierras
Paul Powell (Triangle)
1923 The White Rose
D. W. Griffith (United Artists)
1924 Daddies
William A. Seiter (Warner Brothers)
1925 The Rat
Graham Cutts (Gainsborough)—in England

Tom Mix

Tom Mix was King of the Cowboys in the 1920s, the highest-paid cowboy film star of all time and the direct inspiration of Gene Autry » and the other fancy-dressed Western stars of the '30s and '40s. Mix was the complete opposite of the authentic William S. Hart », whom he replaced as the leading Western star, believing in showmanship and brilliant stunting instead of gritty reality. In fact his Western background was just as genuine as Hart's (he had been a rodeo performer, cowboy and marshal, but he chose to emphasise the other facet of the cowboy personality— showing off. His elaborate costumes, mostly solid white with black boots and peaked sombrero (which is why we think heroes wear white hats), and his screen code (no drinking, smoking, swearing, or killing unless absolutely necessary) set a style for Westerns that continued into the '50s.

Mix was born in Mix Run, Pennsylvania, in 1881 and made his first Western in 1910, for Selig, before joining Fox in 1917 and becoming their major star and the financial backbone of the studio during the 1920s. His 60 films for Fox were distinguished by superb stunt work, outstanding outdoor photography (mostly by

*Above: Colleen Moore aroused the ire (and envy) of parents by setting free-thinking flapper standards for their daughters in films like this one, **Why Be Good?** with Neil Hamilton. She inspired many imitations at other Hollywood studios.*
Right: Colleen Moore set fashions around the world with her flapper-style bobbed hair.

Daniel Clark) and excellent production values; Mix did not normally direct himself but his films were very much his own creations, even when the directors were of the calibre of John Ford. His handsome black horse Tony was also the most famous equine star of the time, and by 1925 Mix was earning $17,000 a week, with a basic film plot he described as "getting into trouble when doing the right thing for somebody else". He moved from Fox to FBO at the end of the decade and then on to Universal, but his voice was apparently not right for the talkies (although it seems fine in **Destry Rides Again**). He died in a car crash in Arizona in 1940, daredevilling to the end.

BEST FILMS:
1919 The Daredevil
Tom Mix (Fox)
1922 Just Tony
Lynn Reynolds (Fox)
1922 Sky High
Lynn Reynolds (Fox)
1923 The Lone Star Ranger
Lambert Hillyer (Fox)
1923 Three Jumps Ahead
John Ford (Fox)
1924 North of Hudson Bay
John Ford (Fox)
1925 The Rainbow Trail
Lynn Reynolds (Fox)
1925 Riders of the Purple Sage
Lynn Reynolds (Fox)
1926 The Great K & A Train Robbery
Lewis Seiler (Fox)
1932 Destry Rides Again
Ben Stoloff (Universal)

Left: Tom Mix took over from William S. Hart as the top cowboy star at the beginning of the 1920s. He brought a new kind of showmanship to the Western—plus his horse Tony.

PHOTOPLAY

Colleen Moore

The delightful prototype flapper, Colleen Moore became a top star in 1923 in **Flaming Youth** and set fashions around the world with her flat-chested boyish look and short skirts. Her standards of dance and drinking inspired daughters and distressed their mothers; the titles of many of her films reflected this image, including **The Perfect Flapper, Naughty But Nice, Synthetic Sin** and **Why Be Good?** She was more than just a tantalising flapper: an intelligent, hard-working actress, she made a number of films outside the flapper persona, including **So Big** and **Lilac Time;** she was an excellent comedienne in **Irene** and **Orchids and Ermine** and her co-stars included Gary Cooper », John Barrymore », Mickey Rooney » and Harry Langdon ».

Born Kathleen Morrison in Port Huron, Michigan, in 1900, she started her film career under D. W. Griffith at Triangle in 1916. She worked with Selig, Christie and Goldwyn and became Tom Mix's » leading lady at Fox in 1919. Most of her major films were made for First National; sadly, she did not survive after the silent era, despite brains and beauty as well as fame, probably because the vogue of the flapper had waned.

Her best sound film was **The Power and the Glory** opposite Spencer Tracy ».

Enormously rich when she retired, she invested money wisely and became even more wealthy. She has written three books including her autobiography (*Silent Star*) and a guide to making money on the stock market, and lives today in southern California.

BEST FILMS:
1921 The Sky Pilot
King Vidor (First National)
1923 Flaming Youth
John Francis Dillon (First National)
1924 The Perfect Flapper
John Francis Dillon (First National)
1925 Sally
Alfred E. Green (First National)
1925 So Big
Charles Brabin (First National)
1926 Ella Cinders
Alfred E. Green (First National)
1926 Irene
Alfred E. Green (First National)
1928 Synthetic Sin
William A. Seiter (First National)
1928 Oh Kay
Mervyn Le Roy (First National)
1933 The Power and the Glory
William K. Howard (Fox)

Mae Murray

Mae Murray, born Marie Adrienne Koenig in Portsmouth, Virginia in 1889, was the deliciously outrageous caricature of a silent cinema sex star. She was the girl with the "bee-stung lips" and the frizzy blonde hair whose flashy roles in films like **Circe the Enchantress** and **The Delicious Little Devil** were meant to show off her sexual attraction rather than her acting ability; her greatest talent was her sense of movement (she began as a dancer) and her walk was sensual poetry in motion rather than just a way of getting across a room—she may well have been the model for Mae West's » satire of sexuality. Her director-husband Robert Z. Leonard (they divorced in 1924) guided her career at Universal and Paramount from 1916 and practically invented the soft-focus close-up through gauze for her films. She was one of the great glamour figures of the '20s; her parties were the rage, her gowns were the envy of the fans and she married a prince (one of the dubious Mdivanis of Georgia) in 1926. In short, she lived and behaved like a superstar; to top it all she even made a great film, Erich von Stroheim's **The Merry Widow**. The making of the film was an amazing conflict of personalities, with director and star constantly hurling insults at each other, but in the end von Stroheim succeeded in revealing Mae's qualities on screen as no other director ever had. It was the zenith of her career. With the coming of sound her popularity waned, but not her extravagant sense of stardom, which she retained until

her death in 1965, still planning a comeback. She will long be remembered for her classic remark after seeing **Sunset Boulevard**: "None of us floozies was ever *that* nuts."

BEST FILMS:
1917 A Mormon Maid
Robert Z. Leonard (Universal)
1919 The Delicious Little Devil
Robert Z. Leonard (Universal)
1922 Peacock Alley
Robert Z. Leonard (Metro)
1923 Jazz Mania
Robert Z. Leonard (Metro)
1924 Mademoiselle Midnight
Robert Z. Leonard (Metro-Goldwyn)
1924 Circe the Enchantress
Robert Z. Leonard (MGM)
1925 The Merry Widow
Erich von Stroheim (MGM)
1925 The Masked Bride
Josef von Sternberg & Christy Cabanne (MGM)
1926 Valencia
Dimitre Buchowezki (MGM)
1926 Altars of Desire
Christy Cabanne (MGM)

Above: Mae Murray was the most sensual of stars, with bee-stung lips and a walk like poetry.

Musidora

The French cinema produced only one genuinely mythical movie star in the silent era, the bizarre black-clad villainess of Louis Feuillade's surrealistic adventure serials, **Les Vampires** and **Judex**. Her poetic personification of evil beauty in moulded black silk tights led writer Louis Aragon to call her the "Tenth Muse" and she was admired by many members of the French avant-garde, including Apollinaire. Musidora, born Jeanne Roques in Paris in 1889, became the image of larger-than-life amorality, the woman with eyes of velvet, a far more powerfully sex-charged and ambiguous heroine than the vamp figure created by the American cinema at this time. Ostensibly the villainess Irma Vep in **Les Vampires**, she became, in the eyes of the audience, the heroine of this film about a gang of arch-criminals tracked down by a

crusading journalist. In **Judex** she is the gang leader Diana Monti whom the avenging Judex has to combat as part of his righteous campaign.

Musidora made many other films in the 1910s and 1920s and was one of the first women directors, but she never again reached the pinnacle of success she achieved in her Feuillade pictures. She became a journalist when sound films arrived, after filming both in Italy and Spain, and also worked at the French Cinémathèque. She died in Paris in 1957, but her black-garbed figure will continue to personify the best of the French silent cinema.

BEST FILMS:
1914 Severo Torrelli
Louis Feuillade (Gaumont)
1915 Les Vampires (10 episodes)
Louis Feuillade (Gaumont)
1916 Judex (12 episodes)
Louis Feuillade (Gaumont)
1918 La Vagabonda
Eugenio Perego (in Italy)
1919 Les Chacals
André Hugon
1919 Johannès fils de Johannès
André Hugon
1921 Pour Don Carlos
Jacques Lasseyre & Musidora
1921 La Geôle
Gaston Ravel
1924 La Tierra de Los Toros
Antonio Anero & Musidora (in Spain)
1926 Le Berceau de Dieu
Fred Leroy (Granville)

Alla Nazimova

Nazimova is best remembered for one film, the extraordinary 1923 **Salome**, but she was a major star of a most unusual kind. She was one of the leading stage actresses of her time, especially in the plays

*Above: Musidora was perhaps the only truly mythical star in European silent films, and won praise from the French avant-garde for her amoral villainess roles in Feuillade serials. Here she is seen as gang leader Diana Monti in the 1916 **Judex**.*

*Above: Alla Nazimova in her greatest and most extravagant performance as **Salome**. The costumes were sumptuous, the acting was stylised and the public was not interested.*

of Ibsen and Chekhov, and a great tragic pantomime artist, but her mass appeal to the cinema public was as a kind of super-vamp. She slowly transformed herself into a

29

goddess-like prototype Garbo », but became so remote from her audiences that she eventually lost her popularity.

She was born Alla Nazimoff in Yalta, Russia, in 1879 and came to the US as a successful stage actress after studying under Stanislavsky, and Lewis J. Selznick brought her into the cinema in 1916 with the film **War Brides.**

In 1918 she was signed by Metro and became the studio's most popular star the following year; at this time she began her campaign to bring culture to the masses and produced adaptations of Dumas (**Camille** in which she starred with Valentino »), Ibsen (**A Doll's House**) and Wilde (**Salome**), the last two directed by her co-star (and probable husband) Charles Bryant. **Salome** was heavily influenced by the German Expressionistic cinema, combining sumptuous costumes with bizarre, ballet-like, stylised acting. Playwright Robert E. Sherwood called it "the most extraordinarily beautiful picture ever produced", but it cost Nazimova her life's savings and was a financial failure. She went back to money-making movies but was soon shadowed by Garbo. She quit the cinema in the late '20s for the theatre, although she returned as an excellent character actress in the 1940s, notably as Tyrone Power's » mother in **Blood and Sand**. She died in 1945.

One of her most memorable legacies was the famous hotel of the stars called the Garden of Allah, which she built for herself and later converted into what became Hollywood's most notable and exclusive residence.

BEST FILMS:
1916 War Brides
Herbert Brenon (Selznick)
1918 The Revelation
George Baker (Metro)
1919 The Brat
Herbert Blanche (Metro)
1920 The Heart of a Child
Ray C. Smallwood (Metro)
1921 Camille
Ray C. Smallwood (Metro)
1922 A Doll's House
Charles Bryant (United Artists)
1923 Salome
Charles Bryant (United Artists)
1924 Madonna of the Streets
Edwin Carewe (First National)
1925 The Redeeming Sin
J. Stewart Blackton (Vitagraph)
1941 Blood and Sand
Rouben Mamoulian (20th Century Fox)

POLA NEGRI

Pola Negri (born Barbara Appolonia Chalupec in Janowa, Poland, in 1894) was the first European actress to be wooed, won and misunderstood by Hollywood. She was the hottest property in Europe at the beginning of the 1920s on the strength of her sexually irresistible performances in the first films of Ernst Lubitsch in Germany; he was almost the only director to use her looks and personality to advantage. The costume dramas she made for him personifying Dubarry, Carmen, Medea and others were among the first foreign films to be major hits in the US; her American films, however, except for one by Lubitsch and one by Stiller, were fairly ordinary—"all slink and mink", as one contemporary critic described them.

She had the kind of down-to-earth animal magnetism that more recent audiences associate with a Bardot » or a Loren ». She was a descendant of Polish gypsies and her ancestry was reflected in the demeanour and tatty clothes of her screen image—it added to her desirability. As one critic engagingly noted at the time, trying to explain her attraction, "You had the feeling that the back of her neck was dirty". Hollywood imported her and immediately sanitised her, washing off the dirt and replacing her tatters with elegant clothes and elaborate coiffures—it didn't work, but she made a hell of a name for herself during her tempestuous decade in the movie capital. After three marriages—to a baron, a count and a prince, she went back to Europe and made an excellent

*Below: Pola Negri became a star in the films of Ernst Lubitsch in Germany. Here she is seen in the 1921 **Die Bergkatze** as a wild mountain girl, the high-spirited daughter of a brigand chief, with five Balkan bandits. Right: Pola Negri was featured on a '30s German cigarette card.*

German drama with Willi Forst, attracting Goebbels' hatred and Hitler's favour. She made a few more films but faded away except for a cameo role in the Disney film **The Moonspinners** in 1964, and now lives in retirement in Texas, still fiercely loved by her fans and misunderstood by others. Her Lubitsch films continue to amaze new admirers.

BEST FILMS:
1918 The Eyes of the Mummy
Ernst Lubitsch (Union)—Germany
1918 Carmen/Gypsy Blood
Ernst Lubitsch (Union-Ufa)—Germany
1919 Madame Dubarry/Passion
Ernst Lubitsch (Union-Ufa)—Germany
1921 Die Bergkatze/The Wildcat
Ernst Lubitsch (Union-Ufa)—Germany
1923 Die Flamme/Montmartre
Ernst Lubitsch (Efa-Ufa)—Germany
1924 Forbidden Paradise
Ernst Lubitsch (Paramount)
1925 East of Suez
Raoul Walsh (Paramount)
1926 Hotel Imperial
Mauritz Stiller (Paramount)
1927 Barbed Wire
Rowland V. Lee (Paramount)
1935 Mazurka
Willi Forst (Ciné-Allianz)

ASTA NIELSEN

Danish actress Asta Nielsen was the first international female star, achieving fame in the same year that Florence Lawrence » set the pattern for stars in America (1910) and two years before Italy's Francesca Bertini ». She was also probably one of the greatest actresses ever in the cinema: Apollinaire called her "the drunkard's vision and the

Above: Asta Nielsen, the first international female star.

hermit's dream"; Bela Balazs bade the world "Dip the flags before her, for she is unique"; Lotte Eisner eulogised her "subtle intellectuality" and authentic passion. Because she never went to Hollywood and did not continue working after the arrival of the talkies, she is not well known today except for her female **Hamlet** and her remarkable performance in Pabst's **The Joyless Street** (overshadowing even Greta Garbo »).

Nielsen was born in Copenhagen in 1881 and first worked in the theatre. She made her first Danish film, **Afgrunden,** in 1910 and it created a sensation; she was then lured to Germany where she became the top star and made over 70 films, becoming the predecessor of Garbo and Dietrich » with a similar kind of reputation in the 1910s and early 1920s—her pale face and immense blazing eyes were immediately recognisable by admirers throughout the world. Her style was controlled and very modern, and she was as well known for comedy (**The Little Angel**) as for tragedy (**The Joyless Street**). Her **Hamlet** is brilliant, but she was perhaps at her finest as an ageing prostitute in **Street Tragedy**. She died in 1972, aged 91, and her films are still being revived and admired.

BEST FILMS:
1913 The Little Angel
Urban Gad (Union-Bioscop)
1916 The Lover's ABC
Magnus Shifter (in Germany)
1919 Intoxication
Ernst Lubitsch (Argus-Film)
1920 Hamlet
Sven Gade and Heinz Schall (in Germany)
1920 Der Reigen
Richard Oswald (Oswald Films)
1922 Vanina
Arthur von Gerlach (in Germany)
1923 The House by the Side of the Sea
Fritz Kaufman (Metro)
1924 Hedda Gabler
Fritz Eckstein (in Germany)
1925 The Joyless Street
G. W. Pabst (Sofar)
1927 Street Tragedy
Bruno Rahn (Pantomin)

Above: Mabel Normand, greatest comedienne of the silent screen and friend of Fatty Arbuckle. Scandals wrecked both their careers.

MABEL NORMAND

The first great screen comedienne and probably unsurpassed to this day, Mabel Normand was one of the progenitors of the American screen comedy: it was Mabel who introduced the custard pie to the screen; it was Mabel who helped Mack Sennett found the Keystone Film Company in 1912; and it was Mabel who starred in many of his best films, including those with Charlie Chaplin » and Arbuckle ». A mere five-foot-three, she was irresistible in her good humour and irrepressible vitality. She was utterly natural before the camera, superbly inventive and funny without recourse to gimmicks or make-up—and she was also beautiful. Her love affair with Sennett was one of the most enduring (and fascinating) in Hollywood and became the basis of a Broadway musical, *Mack and Mabel*, in 1974 (Bernadette Peters

was Mabel to Robert Preston's Sennett).

Born in Boston in 1894, she began as an artists' and fashion model (and a Gibson Girl) and started her film career in 1911. She was featured in Vitagraph and Biograph films (under D. W. Griffith) for two years and then left Biograph with Sennett to set up Keystone. She made hundreds of comedies for Sennett, many in a "Mabel" series, often directed by Sennett himself; the most famous film of this early period is **Tillie's Punctured Romance** with Chaplin and Marie Dressler ». Her first solo starring feature film, **Mickey**, came in 1917, and it eventually became her biggest-ever hit. By then she had already been enticed away by Samuel Goldwyn who offered her $3500 a week (the biggest salary up to that time), but the Goldwyn films were unsuccessful and she returned to Sennett.

Mabel was almost as famous for her off-camera antics as for her films, including highly publicised pranks, a fabulous wardrobe, wild living and (possibly) drugs. She was involved in two scandals that completely destroyed her career. She was the last person to see director William Desmond Taylor alive before his murder on February 1, 1922, and the popular

press had a field day with her in the wake of the scandal about her old friend Fatty Arbuckle. She almost weathered the Taylor storm, but was ruined when her name was associated with a second scandal: her chauffeur shot a millionaire friend, reportedly because of a quarrel over her. She made a couple more good films with Sennett, but the public did not want to know. She died in 1930, a great and unique talent lost to the sound cinema.

BEST FILMS:
1912 Mabel's Lovers
Mack Sennett (Keystone)
1913 Foiling Fickle Father
Mabel Normand (Keystone)
1914 Tillie's Strange Predicament
Henry Lehrman and Mack Sennett (Keystone)
1914 Tillie's Punctured Romance
Mack Sennett (Keystone)
1916 Fatty and Mabel Adrift
Roscoe Arbuckle (Triangle-Keystone)
1918 Mickey
F. Richard Jones (Keystone)
1919 Sis Hopkins
Clarence Badger (Goldwyn)
1921 Molly O
F. Richard Jones (Sennett)
1923 The Extra Girl
F. Richard Jones (Sennett)
1926 The Nickel Hopper
Hal Roach (Roach)

Left: Ramon Navarro, heroic as Ben-Hur, comforting his beloved Esther (May McAvoy).

RAMON NOVARRO

One of the great swashbuckling heroes of the cinema, Novarro is too often thought of simply as a second-string Latin Lover brought to prominence in the wake of Valentino ». He deserves to be remembered for his own insouciant qualities; he never really took himself seriously, especially as a Great Lover. He is most famous for his starring role in the 1926 **Ben-Hur,** the Charlton Heston » of his time, with biceps glistening as he lashed his horse to victory over villain Francis X. Bushman ». He was at his best in his first two swashbucklers, twirling swords with the best of them as Rupert in **The Prisoner of Zenda** and as the eponymous hero of **Scaramouche**. Both were directed by Rex Ingram, who made him a star but also tried to push him into the unsuitable mould of the Latin Lover.

Born Ramon Sumaniegos in Durango, Mexico, in 1899, the son of a dentist, he came to the US in flight from a revolution in 1914 and became a film extra in 1917. His first important role was as a turbaned and loin-clothed dancer in Mack Sennett's 1921 **A Small Town Idol.** Ingram starred him in four more films after the success of **The Prisoner of Zenda**; he then became an MGM contract star at $10,000 a week. **Ben-Hur** was his biggest hit at MGM, but his finest film was **The Student Prince**: Ernst Lubitsch took the hoary old musical comedy and with his incomparable touch made it a cinematic delight. The coming of sound effectively ended Novarro's career, although he continued in starring roles until 1935 and played opposite Garbo » in **Mata Hari**. He ended up drinking quite a lot and playing character roles. He died in 1968, the victim of a brutal murder.

BEST FILMS:
1922 The Prisoner of Zenda
Rex Ingram (MGM)
1922 Trifling Women
Rex Ingram (MGM)
1923 Scaramouche
Rex Ingram (MGM)
1923 Where the Pavement Ends
Rex Ingram (MGM)
1924 The Arab
Rex Ingram (MGM)
1924 The Red Lily
Fred Niblo (MGM)
1925 The Midshipman
Christy Cabanne (MGM)
1926 Ben-Hur
Fred Niblo (MGM)
1927 The Student Prince in Old Heidelberg
Ernst Lubitsch (MGM)
1932 Mata Hari
George Fitzmaurice (MGM)

IVOR NOVELLO

Novello was the most popular male British film star of the 1920s and made notable films in America, France and Hungary as well as England. His romantic, black-haired, Welsh, matinée idol appearance made him the European counterpart of John Barrymore » and Ramon Novarro ». Born Ivor Davies in Cardiff in 1893, Novello's later reputation as a stage musical comedy star, composer and writer has tended to eclipse the importance of his silent film career. He starred in some of the most important British films of the '20s, including the first major Alfred Hitchcock film **The Lodger** (Novello portrayed the Jack the Ripper suspect protagonist) and Graham Cutts' **The Rat,** based on Novello's own play. He also found time to go to America to star opposite Mae Marsh » in D. W. Griffith's **The White Rose.**

Three of his films opened within one month in 1923 and a Novello boom soon made him the hottest property in British pictures. The success of his film career persuaded him to abandon the stage in 1927 to devote himself to becoming the leading star for Gainsborough under Michael Balcon, but the coming of sound lessened his success. His last silent film was **The South Sea Bubble** and, following a writing but non-acting stint in Hollywood, his last movie was the 1935 **Autumn Crocus.** His stage career continued to prosper until his death in 1951.

BEST FILMS:
1919 The Call of the Blood
Louis Mercanton (in France)
1921 Carnival
Harley Knowles (London Films)
1923 The Man Without Desire
Adrian Brunel (Novello-Atlas)
1923 The White Rose
D. W. Griffith (Griffith Films)
1925 The Rat
Graham Cutts (Gainsborough)

Above: Ivor Novello was the most popular British actor in the '20s, a true matinée idol.

1926 The Lodger
Alfred Hitchcock (Gainsborough)
1927 Downhill
Alfred Hitchcock (Gainsborough)
1927 The Vortex
Adrian Brunel (Gainsborough)
1928 The Constant Nymph
Adrian Brunel (Gainsborough)
1928 The South Sea Bubble
T. H. Hunter

MARY PICKFORD

Mary Pickford could be considered the most popular star in the history of the cinema; she was for some years even ranked as the most popular woman in the world. This may seem incredible to those unacquainted with film history, especially as her films are no longer widely admired and her myth as the child-woman Little Mary, America's (and the World's) Sweetheart, has not endured. Revivals of her films in London and New York create interest but little excitement, despite the ardent love and promotion of her admirers. The sad truth is that Mary, the Girl with the Golden Curls, embodied an ideal of plucky rural innocence that harmonised perfectly with the coming-of-age of society in America and elsewhere in the 1910s and early 1920s—but that age and sentiment has vanished forever.

Little Mary was a good actress and a highly photogenic film star; she had charisma before the word was in vogue, but she also became typecast very early in her career as a mixture of Victoriana and modernity that inhibited her full development. God knows she tried, even to the extent of importing sophisticated European director Ernst Lubitsch to Hollywood to direct her in **Rosita,** but even his touch could not shift the inertia imposed by public expectation. Pickford was the first and greatest victim of typecasting, not by some insensitive film mogul but by herself in her aim to retain her popularity at the box office. Perhaps her star will shine brightly again—fashions change, even among film historians—but for the moment she is definitely in eclipse.

Mary was born Gladys Smith in Toronto, Canada, in 1893 and went on the stage to help support her family at the age of five. She

*Left: Mary Pickford was possibly the most popular star in the history of the cinema, even as late as the 1926 **Sparrows.**
Below left: Mary Pickford's Pollyanna golden-curled persona was permanently fixed in her 1917 **The Poor Little Rich Girl.***

began working with D. W. Griffith at the Biograph Company in 1909 and by 1910 was the star of the company, known around the world as Little Mary from the dialogue titles on **The Little Teacher,** her 27th film. She was exceedingly ambitious and intelligent and moved to the IMP Company after 77 films to get more salary. In 1912 she became the first film star to win acclaim on stage; this reflected favourably on her cinema career. Her salary began to escalate sensationally, from $10 a day in 1909 to $10,000 a week in 1916; she became the unquestioned number one star of the cinema and the biggest box office attraction bar none, not even Chaplin ».

In her early films she played all kinds of different roles and played them well, but her huge success in **Tess of the Storm Country** in 1914 under Edwin S. Porter's direction set the mould for years to come. The Little Mary characterisation was fixed in **Poor Little Rich Girl** and **Rebecca of Sunnybrook Farm** and all her greatest hits were variations of it. This does not mean that the screen persona she evolved was sickly sweet, naive or helpless; her audiences loved her for her humour as well as for her willingness to struggle against the odds while being self-sacrificing and lovable. They were, however, unwilling to let her grow up, insisting that a 30-year-old woman wear long golden girls and portray Heidi and Cinderella.

The shrewd brain concealed behind those curls (Mary was a first-class business woman) decided to go along with the public and retain popularity. With Chaplin, Griffith and Fairbanks », she founded United Artists to make films (and money) the way she wanted. Her business acumen kept her a top star for 20 years, but there was no way to carry Little Mary into the sound era. She won the Best Actress Oscar in 1929 as a trendy, shingle-haired flirt in **Coquette,** but the film made her just another flapper; her uniqueness was gone and her follow-up films, including a creaky version of **The Taming of the Shrew** opposite husband Douglas Fairbanks, were not successes. She retired, split with Doug, married Buddy Rogers and retired to her "Pickfair" home. She lived there until her death on 28 May 1979. With the help of her great cameraman Charles Rosher, she succeeded in prolonging childhood longer than anyone else. Little Mary never had a chance to grow up.

BEST FILMS:
1917 Poor Little Rich Girl
Maurice Tourneur (Famous Players)
1917 Rebecca of Sunnybrook Farm
Marshall Neilan (Famous Players)
1918 Stella Maris
Marshall Neilan (Famous Players)
1919 Daddy Long Legs
Marshall Neilan (First National)
1920 Pollyanna
Paul Powell (United Artists)
1921 Little Lord Fauntleroy
Alfred Green & Jack Pickford (United Artists)
1923 Rosita
Ernst Lubitsch (United Artists)
1926 Sparrows
William Beaudine (United Artists)
1927 My Best Girl
Sam Taylor (United Artist)
1929 Coquette
Sam Taylor (United Artists)

RIN TIN TIN

The most popular film star in the United States in 1925 was a German Shepherd dog named Rin Tin Tin. He was the biggest animal movie star of all time and the biggest box office attraction at Warner Brothers throughout the 1920s. He was a true superstar with 12,000 fan letters a week. He earned $6000 a month, starred in more than 40 films, and was even cited by his trainer's wife as cause for divorce. Rinty, as he was popularly called, was known as

A WARNER BROS. PRODUCTION

Above: Rin Tin Tin became the Warner Brothers superstar of the '20s in adventures like this.

the "mortgage lifter" because of his unfailing commercial success. He was also, surprisingly, rather a good actor. He developed his acting range from film to film until he could go through long and complicated routines without looking to his trainer for direction. He even played a long scene in close-up in the 1925 **The Night Cry,** his eyes moist with emotion and his ears drooping.

Rin Tin Tin was discovered as a puppy by his master, Captain Lee Duncan, in a German dugout near Metz in World War I. Duncan

brought the dog back to Los Angeles and turned him into a film actor. He was not docile (he sometimes attacked other actors and directors), but he was handsome and very clever and his rise to stardom was fast. He made the fortune of a young writer named Darryl Zanuck, who helped direct the dog's meteoric rise and went on to become the head of 20th Century Fox.

Rin Tin Tin had good scriptwriters and directors and was the only Hollywood star not worried by the coming of sound. Unfortunately, he died in 1932, but his offspring continue to use his name.

BEST FILMS:
1923 When the North Begins
Chester Franklin (Warner Brothers)
1923 Tiger Rose
Sidney Franklin (Warner Brothers)
1924 The Lighthouse by the Sea
Malcolm St Clair (Warner Brothers)
1924 Find Your Man
Malcolm St Clair (Warner Brothers)
1925 The Night Cry
Herman Raymaker (Warner Brothers)
1925 Clash of the Wolves
Noel Mason Smith (Warner Brothers)
1926 A Hero of the Big Snows
Herman Raymaker (Warner Brothers)
1927 Jaws of Steel
Ray Enright (Warner Brothers)
1927 Tracked by the Police
Ray Enright (Warner Brothers)
1927 A Dog of the Regiment
Ross Lederman (Warner Brothers)

NORMA SHEARER

see **Classic Stars**

GLORIA SWANSON

"I'm still big, it's the pictures that got smaller." Gloria Swanson's famous comment in **Sunset Boulevard** reflected her character in the same way that the film reflected her career. Erich von Stroheim », who portrays her ex-director, now her butler, was actually the director of Swanson's greatest film—and greatest folly—**Queen Kelly.** She was the grandest of the great silent glamour stars—in her own words "every inch and every moment a star". By 1926 she was Paramount's highest-paid star, and she turned down an incredible offer of $1 million a year to renew her contract. She worked as hard at being glamorous as she did at being an actress and lived up to her legend on every occasion: she wore only the most fashionable clothes and was said never to wear the same dress twice. When her popularity seemed to be diminishing, she dashed off to Europe and came back with a genuine Marquis for a husband (and thereby caused a

Left: Gloria Swanson was the grandest glamour star of all. Below: Great comebacks are rare in the cinema, but Gloria Swanson's return as a silent movie glamour queen in Billy Wilder's **Sunset Boulevard** *was magnificently successful.*

veritable flood of Hollywood marriages to European aristocrats). When she returned to America, she was greeted by crowds and bands like a queen coming home. She had come a long way from being a shop assistant in Chicago only ten years before.

Gloria May Swanson was born in the Windy City in 1898, the daughter of a US Army civilian employee, and entered films via the Essanay studios in Chicago, mostly playing small parts in Wallace Beery » films. He married her and took her to Hollywood, where she appeared in a dozen Sennett comedies. She soon progressed to being a misunderstood wife or girl friend in eight Triangle domestic dramas and then went to work for Cecil B. de Mille, who starred her in six films between 1919 and 1921; they made her famous and helped shape the manners and morals of America in the '20s. These were erotic films disguised as morality plays, in which the de Mille bathroom first became notorious and in which sex was seen as the most interesting aspect of marriage. They had come-on titles like **Don't Change Your Husband** and **Why Change Your Wife?,** and de Mille spent lavishly on clothes for his star to make her that extra bit attractive.

Paramount took over her contract from de Mille (they released his films) and built her up even more, capitalising on an imaginary rivalry with their other sex star, Pola Negri ». Swanson was featured in a series of star vehicles with Sam Wood as director, and co-starred with Valentino » in

Beyond the Rocks, but then she began fighting to get more control of her films. Allan Dwan directed eight of her best films, including **Manhandled** and **Stage Struck,** before she broke away from Paramount, at the height of her fame, to form her own production company and release films through United Artists. The first effort, **The Loves of Sunya,** was unimportant, but the second was a magnificent calamity, half failure and half masterpiece. Erich von Stroheim was at his most extravagant and baroque in creating the sexually-charged **Queen Kelly,** with Swanson as a schoolgirl losing her knickers to a prince and winning the hatred of his queen. Joseph Kennedy (father of the future president) was one of the backers, but Swanson finally had to sack von Stroheim and take charge herself. The film was never released in the US, but even in its mutilated, salvaged form it is a great work of art.

After this financial disaster, Swanson began to recoup her losses in a sultry **Sadie Thompson** (Best Actress Oscar nomination), with Raoul Walsh directing and co-starring, and her first talkie, **The Trespasser** (another Academy Award nomination). Her voice was fine and she seemed all set to go on with a major career in talkies in the '30s when suddenly her star lost its brightness. She was too closely identified with the past; audiences seemed to want new faces. She kept on trying to make comebacks and almost succeeded back at Paramount in 1950 with **Sunset Boulevard,** under Billy Wilder's direction. But no studio was really interested and she played only minor roles afterwards, including herself in **Airport '75**. In 1976, glamorous as ever at the age of 77, she married her sixth husband and began work on her auto-biography. The legendary Gloria Swanson is just as full of surprises as ever.

BEST FILMS:
1919 Male and Female
Cecil B. de Mille (FPL-Paramount)
1920 Why Change Your Wife?
Cecil B. de Mille (FPL-Paramount)
1922 Beyond the Rocks
Sam Wood (Paramount)
1924 Manhandled
Allan Dwan (Paramount)
1925 Madame Sans-Gêne
Léonie Perret (Paramount)-France
1925 Stage Struck
Allan Dwan (Paramount)
1928 Queen Kelly
Erich von Stroheim (United Artists)
1928 Sadie Thompson
Raoul Walsh (United Artists)
1929 The Trespasser
Edmund Goulding (United Artists)
1950 Sunset Boulevard
Billy Wilder (Paramount)

NORMA TALMADGE

Norma Talmadge was Noble Womanhood personified in the silent cinema era and this charac-terisation made her one of the most popular stars of this period. She was the first protagonist of the "woman's film", a genre repopularised in the sound era by Crawford ≫, Davis ≫ and Garson ≫ Norma almost patented the clichés of the genre: she smiled through her tears, defiantly pitted herself against a cruel world, and was long-suffering for the sake of love—but she was also and always elegant, beautifully coif-fured and fashionably gowned, for the sake of the millions of fans who wanted to emulate her. Norma could afford the clothes: she was paid $250,000 a film and was promoted by husband Joseph Schenck, who became president of United Artists in 1924.

Norma's reputation today has faded because few of her films survive; most audiences and critics have never had the chance to see her on the screen. She was born in Niagara Falls, New York, in 1897, and was the most famous of the Talmadge dynasty that included sisters Constance (a fine comedi-enne) and Natalie (who married Buster Keaton ≫ and mother Peggy (who pushed them all to stardom). She started in films with Vitagraph in Brooklyn in 1910 with **The Household Pest** and her first notable film was the 1911 **A Tale of Two Cities**. Schenck married her in 1917 and gave her stardom on a silver platter as his wedding present (he was 19 years older; she always called him Daddy). Clarence Brown, who directed her most

famous film, **Kiki**, praised her as "the greatest pantomimist that ever drew breath", applauding especially her comic abilities. In most of her films, however, she was required to suffer to love. Perhaps **The Lady**, in which she portrayed a tough 70-year-old reminiscing about her pathetic career, was the best film of this kind, but she suffered well in many other films, including **Camille, The Branded Woman** and **Graustark**. Her Brooklyn accent destroyed her career as soon as sound arrived. The disas-trous **Dubarry, Woman of Paris**, was released in 1930 to utter dismay from her fans; she immediately retired. She also divorced Mr Schenck, married George Jessel and went on the radio, where her voice was no handicap. She died, a nearly for-gotten first-magnitude star, in Las Vegas in 1957.

BEST FILMS:
1911 A Tale of Two Cities
James Stuart Blackton (Vitagraph)
1920 The Branded Woman
Albert Parker (First National)
1921 The Passion Flower
Herbert Brenon (First National)
1924 Secrets
Frank Borzage (First National)
1925 Graustark
Dmitri Buchowetzki (First National)
1925 The Lady
Frank Borzage (First National)
1926 Kiki
Clarence Brown (First National)
1927 Camille
Fred Niblo (First National)
1928 The Woman Disputed
Henry King & Sam Taylor (United Artists)
1928 The Dove
Roland West (United Artists)

Above: Norma Talmadge, one of the major stars of the silent cinema in nobly suffering roles, was ruined by the coming of sound and especially by this film, **Dubarry, Woman of Passion.**

BEN TURPIN

The only cross-eyed star in the history of the cinema. Comedians are rarely taken seriously by critics, so Turpin has not generally been ranked as one of the great stars, even though his face is one of the few from the silent cinema remembered by the general public today. Turpin was more than just an immortal cross-eyed comic, he was one of the great iconoclasts of Hollywood in the '20s. He poked

fun at the cinema's pretensions and became the most notable lampoonist of the movie hero. He could rib Valentino ≫ in **The Shreik of Araby**, Fairbanks ≫ in **The Daredevil** or von Stroheim ≫ in **Three Foolish Weeks** and delight the Hollywood community as much as the wider public. He was a prototype Goon or Monty Python, just as eccentric in his private life as on screen (he was said to act as the janitor of his apartment block and advise bus passengers how much he earned).

Turpin started out in movies by sweeping floors at the Essanay studio in 1907, then made his début in **Ben Gets a Duck and is Ducked**. Born in New Orleans in 1874, he worked in vaudeville for many years before turning to films. It was Chaplin ≫ who really put him on the road to stardom, selecting Turpin as his foil at Essanay in 1915 for **The Cham-pion** and **A Night Out**. He became a leading star for Sennett in 1917 with **A Clever Dummy** and remained big throughout the '20s. His crossed eyes (actually just one eye) quickly became identifiable to the public as his trademark and eventually were even insured at Lloyd's. Despite his outlandish face (deadpan like Keaton's ≫) his roles were often as heroes highly attracted by and attractive to women—husbands were always chasing him—but somewhat bumbling and con-fused in sexual action. This persona made him eminently suitable for parodying Holly-wood's leading men. Many of his films were scripted by Frank Capra and he was often co-starred with Louise Fazenda. His persona was not really suitable for sound, although he did appear in some important films, including **The Love Parade** in 1929 and **Million Dollar Legs** in 1932. His last film appearance was opposite Laurel and Hardy ≫ in the 1940 **Saps at Sea** shortly before his death that same year.

BEST FILMS:
1915 The Champion
Charles Chaplin (Essanay)
1915 A Night Out
Charles Chaplin (Essanay)
1919 Uncle Tom Without the Cabin
Ray Hunt (Sennett Pathé)
1921 A Small Town Idol
Erle C. Kenton (Sennett)
1923 The Shreik of Araby
F. Richard Jones (Sennett)
1923 The Daredevil
Del Lord (Sennett)
1924 Three Foolish Weeks
Reggie Morris & Edgar Kennedy (Sennett)
1924 The Hollywood Kid
Mack Sennett & Billy Bevan (Sennett)
1925 The Wild Goose Chaser
Lloyd Bacon (Sennett)
1927 A Hollywood Hero
Harry Edwards (Sennett)

Left: Ben Turpin made a fortune from his crossed eyes and had them insured for $500,000.

RUDOLPH VALENTINO

The Valentino legend refuses to diminish, even 50 years after his death. People who have never seen a silent film are well aware of his reputation and associate the tango with his sexual prowess. Books and films about him are still popular: Rudolf Nureyev recently portrayed the Great Lover as visualised by Ken Russell in one film and Gene Wilder parodied the legend in another.

There has been no other movie star with Valentino's kind of fame and lasting reputation, although these were based on very little: he was a star for only six years, from 1921 to 1926, and he made no great films. His reputation as a great lover has been exposed many times, revealing him as both a hen-pecked husband and a distinctly unsatisfactory sexual partner. His admirers were mostly women; men considered him weak and effeminate, a "Pink Powder Puff" who wore make-up and jewellery like a whore. Yet he is one of the great stars and is likely to remain so for many years to come. His appeal is a strange combination of smouldering sex appeal for many women (the exotic stuff of fantasy as evidenced in the still massive sales of romantic novels) and androgynous interest for a unisex modern age, in which Valentino's possible homosexuality makes him more interesting than he might otherwise have been. He embodies a Great Romantic Fantasy which may at times seem downright silly but appears to be a part of many people's nature. The films themselves may no longer have much attraction, but the legend does. The Sheik lives on and his real life story seems an improbable fiction.

He was born in Castellaneta in southern Italy as Rodolfo Alfonzo Raffaelo Pierre Filibert Guglielmi di Valentino d'Antonguolla, the son of an army veterinarian. He came to New York in 1913, as a poor immigrant aged 18, and became a professional dancer. He went to California and began working in films in 1918—as a dancer—and had only minor success until 1921, when a scriptwriter named June Mathis persuaded director Rex Ingram to cast him in **The Four Horsemen of the Apocalypse**, based on a best-selling novel by Blasco Ibañez. Valentino portrayed a South American who becomes a World War I hero—and touched a responsive chord in the world public.

The film grossed nearly $5 million, and is one of the biggest successes of all time. Metro immediately starred him opposite the goddess-like Alla Nazimova ❯ in a new version of **Camille**, but did not yet seem to realise just what magnitude their new star had

Above: Rudolph Valentino, like the bullfighter he portrayed in the 1922 **Blood and Sand,** *lived too close to the horns of myth to survive very long. In fact, he died after six years of stardom.*

attained: they refused a small salary rise, so Paramount snapped him up along with his mentor June Mathis. His first Paramount film, **The Sheik,** based on a wonderful piece of trash written by E. M. Hull, was another box office smash and seared the Valentino legend permanently onto the public consciousness. The film wasn't very good, but the women of the world adored it. The myth of the Latin Lover was born. It established the image that most people visualise—an exotic, dusky, half-naked man about to rape a nice middle-class girl.

In a sense, Valentino's career after **The Sheik** was an anti-climax. His popularity could get no higher and his films did not improve much either, especially because of the interference of his dominating second wife, Natacha Rambova. His best pictures were made with Clarence Brown and George Fitzmaurice. In 1926, just as it seemed his popularity was starting to wane and with the impassable barrier of sound just around the corner, he died. In such circumstances, death was the capstone of the romantic hero legend and rounded off his career perfectly. The romantic lover with the flashing eyes, flaring nostrils and sleek black hair had acquired immortality at the cost of his life.

BEST FILMS:
1921 The Four Horsemen of the Apocalypse
Rex Ingram (Metro)

1921 **Camille**
Ray Smallwood (Metro)
1921 **The Sheik**
George Melford (Paramount)
1922 **Beyond the Rocks**
Sam Wood (Paramount)
1922 **Blood and Sand**
Fred Niblo (Paramount)
1924 **Monsieur Beaucaire**
Sidney Olcott (Paramount)
1924 **A Sainted Devil**
Joseph Henaberry (Paramount)
1925 **Cobra**
Joseph Henaberry (Paramount)
1925 **The Eagle**
Clarence Brown (United Artists)
1925 **The Son of the Sheik**
George Fitzmaurice (United Artists)

CONRAD VEIDT

see **Classic Stars.**

ERICH VON STROHEIM

see **Classic Stars.**

PEARL WHITE

"The Fearless Peerless Pearl White," as they used to call her, was the Queen of the Silent Serials and the all-time champion cliff-hanger. She was the reckless female equivalent of Doug Fairbanks ❯, full of derring-do, good humour, a bouncing personality and healthy good looks. She didn't really need a man to look after her, but her tomboyishness was all the more attractive for that. Whether being threatened by a buzz saw, a rolling mill or one of a dozen diabolically clever master villains, she always came out triumphant.

She was born Victoria Evans White in Springfield, Missouri, in 1889, ran away from home to join a circus as a teenager, worked in various theatrical companies, and began her film career in 1910. Her early slapstick comedies and dramas made little impression, but the April 1914 release of the first episode of **The Perils of Pauline** made her an instant star. She made a dozen more breakneck, thrill-filled serials for Pathé, whose top star she became, apparently performing most of her daredevil stunts herself. The serials, from 10 to 15 episodes, were shot around Ithaca, New York, and Fort Lee, New Jersey. She eventually grew tired of them and tried to make straight features for Fox; all ten were lacklustre pictures, so she made two more serials before retiring in 1925. She died in France in 1938. Her legend was reincarnated in 1947 by Betty Hutton ❯ in the biographical film **The Perils of Pauline.**

BEST SERIALS:
1914 The Perils of Pauline
Donald McKenzie & Louis Gasnier (Pathé)
1915 The Exploits of Elaine
Donald McKenzie & Louis Gasnier (Pathé)
1915 The New Exploits of Elaine
McKenzie, Gasnier & George Seitz (Pathé)
1916 The Iron Claw
Edward Jose (Pathé)
1917 Pearl of the Army
George B. Seitz (Pathé)
1918 The Fatal Ring
George B. Seitz (Pathé)
1918 The House of Hate
George B. Seitz (Pathé)
1919 The Black Secret
George B. Seitz (Pathé)
1919 The Lightning Raider
George B. Seitz (Pathé)
1923 Plunder
George B. Seitz (Pathé)

Left: Pearl White, the queen of the silent serial, in her famous **The Perils of Pauline.**

2 THE CLASSIC MOVIE STARS

The classic, golden era of the cinema was the period from the coming of sound to the coming of television. Movies were the unrivalled world entertainment medium, barely challenged by stage or radio, and Hollywood was the international centre of cinema art and commerce. It was the age of the studio and absolute studio control.

The public images of the studios depended upon their stars, so each studio groomed its stars to reflect the kind of corporate image it tried to maintain. MGM was glossy glamour; it had the biggest box office stars, including Greta Garbo, Clark Gable, Greer Garson, Spencer Tracy and Mickey Rooney. Warner Brothers aimed for a more restrained emotional sophistication, with stars like Bette Davis, Errol Flynn, Joan Crawford, Paul Muni, Humphrey Bogart, James Cagney, Lauren Bacall and Barbara Stanwyck. Paramount was suave, elegant and charming, with Cary Grant, Marlene Dietrich, Paulette Goddard, Claudette Colbert, Mae West, Alan Ladd, Veronica Lake, Ray Milland, Bing Crosby, Kirk Douglas and Burt Lancaster. Columbia borrowed a lot of actors but had only one major star of its own, Rita Hayworth, and its image was as closely identified with her as Republic's was with Vera Hruba Ralston. Twentieth Century Fox was bright, brassy and scintillating with a wide range of musical stars, from Betty Grable, Alice Faye and Tyrone Power to Shirley Temple, Carmen Miranda and Sonja Henie. Universal was an odd mixture of horror and tuneful kitsch, with Deanna Durbin and Maria Montez rubbing shoulders with Boris Karloff, Bela Lugosi and Lionel Atwill. RKO was the snappy patter home of Katharine Hepburn, Fred Astaire, Ginger Rogers, Irene Dunne, Jane Russell and Lucille Ball. The major films they starred in at this time were the glamour films, the escapist pictures, the prestige movies. Gone With the Wind broke box office records; Casablanca and It Happened One Night won multiple Academy Awards; Garbo's pictures set the standard. Outside the Hollywood studios, only France and England were producing stars of international calibre. German films were hardly seen abroad after Hitler came to power, and the Italian cinema was relatively unknown.

During the '30s and early '40s, Hollywood studios averaged nearly 500 films a year. Admissions reached an all-time high in 1946, at $1692 million, and then began to decline; the end of the classic era was marked by the rise of television, from 11,000 sets in 1946 to 14 million in 1952. Out of this slough the new Hollywood and the international new wave would emerge, but in the '50s the industry desperately sought gimmicks like Cinemascope to bring back the audiences and the year 1957 is generally considered the nadir of movies as business.

The stars included here are only a selection of the great actors and actresses of the period. Like all selections, it is subjective and idiosyncratic, but it includes all the superstars from Garbo to Gable and most of the major names. The criterion was that they became major stars in the period from the coming of sound to the mid-'50s. The approximate cut-off date is 1957, but some actors who came to prominence before this time are considered modern (ie James Dean) while others are placed in this classic section (Kirk Douglas, Burt Lancaster). A few character actors have been included as stars in their own way, even though they never got their names above the title.

The classic stars lived in a glamorous world of sleek limousines, luxurious restaurants and elegant clothes — a dream vision that appealed to Depression-humbled audiences. The glamour remained, for Europe, until well after 1945, but when rationing ended and Europe's economic miracle began, it signalled the end of classic Hollywood.

ABBOTT AND COSTELLO

Bud Abbott was the tall, thin, wise-guy with the manner of a confidence trickster. Lou Costello was the short, fat, gullible innocent who was always being conned. Together they were one of the greatest comedy teams ever in the cinema, the No 1 box office attraction in 1942 and in the top ten for eight years. Although they have never been properly appreciated by "serious" critics, they were as outstanding in their own way as Laurel and Hardy ». They were also very funny, bringing to the movies the highly-polished, fast-talking routines that they had perfected while filling the bill between strip acts in burlesque houses in the '30s. Some of their classic patter acts, like the "Who's on first?" routine, have become a part of American folklore, as has Lou's quivering-jelly cowardice. They made what is possibly the finest of all comedy-horror films, **Abbott and Costello Meet Frankenstein,** which featured Universal's three greatest horror creations: Glenn Strange as the Monster, Bela Lugosi » as Dracula and Lon Chaney, Jr, as the Wolfman.

William "Bud" Abbott, born in Asbury Park, New Jersey, in 1895, and Louis Francis Costello (real name Cristillo), born in Paterson, New Jersey, in 1906, had separate showbiz careers until 1930, when they met in a burlesque house and teamed up. They made a reputation on stage and on radio in the late '30s and were given supporting comic roles in Universal's 1940 film **One**

Below: The comedy team of **Abbott and Costello in Hollywood** *with a mogul-sized telephone for making important calls.*

Night in the Tropics. They made an immediate appeal to the average American's sense of humour and became instant stars. Abbott and Costello appeared in 37 films together, remaining popular until 1951, when their joint career declined as public tastes became more sophisticated. They made their last film together, **Dance With Me, Henry,** in 1956 and broke up in 1957. Costello died in 1959; Abbott in 1974.

BEST FILMS:
1941 Buck Privates
Arthur Lubin (Universal)
1941 Hold That Ghost
Arthur Lubin (Universal)
1942 Pardon My Sarong
Erle C. Kenton (Universal)
1942 Who Done It?
Erle C. Kenton (Universal)
1944 In Society
Jean Yarborough (Universal)
1944 Lost in a Harem
Charles Reisner (MGM)
1946 The Time of Their Lives
Charles Barton (Universal)
1947 Buck Privates Come Home
Charles Barton (Universal)
1948 Abbott and Costello Meet Frankenstein
Charles Barton (Universal)
1949 Abbott and Costello Meet the Killer, Boris Karloff
Charles Barton (Universal)

GRACIE ALLEN
see **George Burns**

JUNE ALLYSON

The girl-next-door of '40s movies, whose teaming with boy-next-door Van Johnson » led one critic to describe her as the "improbable distillation of the non-existent thing we call average", June was the *summa non ultra* of cheerful wholesomeness; the image created by her (and by her studio,

MGM) was exactly right for the period. Her long, blonde hair and instantly recognisable voice, soft and a little husky, exactly fitted her for the part of the gentle, affectionate, virtuous wife or girl-friend of a soldier or man under stress. She was often starred opposite Van Johnson after their initial success together in **Two Girls and a Sailor,** but was also teamed with Robert Walker in **Her Highness and the Bellboy** (as an invalid in love with bellboy Walker) and Peter Lawford in **Good News** (a '20s college musical). Her greatest partnership, however, and the fullest realisation of her sentimental persona, was with James Stewart ». In **The Stratton Story** she is the plucky, loving wife standing by her man, with Stewart as the baseball player Monty Stratton, who loses a leg but gamely carries on. Stewart asked her to star opposite him again in the hugely successful (and only slightly less sentimental) biopic **The Glenn Miller Story.**

June Allyson was born Ella Geisman on October 7, 1917, in the Bronx, New York City, and became a dancer to recover from a back injury. She graduated to the chorus lines of Broadway musicals and, in true Hollywood fashion, was discovered by a director (George Abbott) when she had to take over the lead from a sick Betty Hutton. Her film career took off immediately and flourished until the late '50s, when her wholesome persona became less fashionable. Although she wisely altered course with such shrewish roles as **The Shrike,** her career still faltered. Her last film was as a murderess in **They Only Kill Their Masters** in 1972. She was married to Dick Powell » from 1945 to 1963 and today lives with her third husband in southern California.

BEST FILMS:
1944 Two Girls and a Sailor
Richard Thorpe (MGM)
1945 Music for Millions
Henry Koster (MGM)
1945 Her Highness and the Bell Boy
Richard Thorpe (MGM)
1946 Till the Clouds Roll By
Richard Whorf (MGM)
1947 Good News
Charles Walters (MGM)
1948 The Bride Goes Wild
Norman Taurog (MGM)
1949 Little Women
Mervyn Le Roy (MGM)
1949 The Stratton Story
Sam Wood (MGM)
1954 The Glenn Miller Story
Anthony Mann (Universal)
1955 The Shrike
José Ferrer (Universal)

DANA ANDREWS

Born as Carver Dan Andrews in Collins, Mississippi, on January 1, 1909, Dana Andrews made his film début in 1940 in The

Westerner. He represents a fascinating inversion of the square-jawed, honest screen hero; the characters he portrays usually turn out to be losers. This nice-guy-transmuted-into-victim persona runs through his entire career. In his first important role, in **The Ox-Bow Incident** in 1943, he tries to convince a lynch mob of his innocence, fails and is hung (and he *is* innocent). In one of his most recent films, **Airport 75,** he is the harassed pilot of a small plane trying to fly home in a storm and crashing into a Boeing 747. His

*Left: June Allyson looked sad even when she was happy. Below: She usually played the patient, loving wife/girlfriend in her movies. Here she is the patient, loving wife of jet fighter ace Alan Ladd in **The McConnell Story** in 1955.*

is a writer framed for murder when he tries to find out how just the law really is.

What is especially interesting about Andrews' screen persona is that he looks like a decent all-American boy who is no longer quite certain what is right. He was a favourite actor of Otto Preminger and Lewis Milestone in the '40s; they seemed to relish the ambiguity of a flawed hero. His best performances were given in Preminger's **Laura** (as a cynical private-eye trying to find out the truth about lovely Gene Tierney ➤) and in Milestone's **A Walk in the Sun** (as a tough sergeant who takes over his platoon after the other officers are killed). He had the knack of working with the right directors in good films (some critics consider **Walk** as the best film made about World War II), even when he had only a small part. Howard Hawks used him as Barbara Stanwyck's ➤ gangster boyfriend in **Ball of Fire** (naturally he loses her in the end) at the beginning of his career, and Fritz Lang starred him in two outstanding crime thrillers (**While the City Sleeps** and **Beyond a Reasonable Doubt**) in the mid-'50s, when his star was beginning to wane. Since his major star period ended in the '50s, he has worked largely in supporting roles—but has done them well.

BEST FILMS:
1943 The Ox-Bow Incident
William Wellman (20th Century Fox)
1944 Laura
Otto Preminger (20th Century Fox)
1945 State Fair
Walter Lang (20th Century Fox)
1946 A Walk in the Sun
Lewis Milestone (20th Century Fox)
1946 The Best Years of Our Lives
William Wyler (RKO)
1947 Boomerang
Elia Kazan (20th Century Fox)
1950 Where the Sidewalk Ends
Otto Preminger (20th Century Fox)
1956 While the City Sleeps
Fritz Lang (20th Century Fox)
1956 Beyond a Reasonable Doubt
Fritz Lang (RKO)
1957 Night of the Demon
Jacques Tourneur (Columbia) in England

*Above: Dana Andrews (right) with Danny Kaye in **Up in Arms**, as new Army recruits. Andrews usually turned out to be a loser in the end.*

biggest prestige picture, the multiple Oscar-winner **The Best Years of Our Lives,** showed him as the returning heroic veteran whose wife proves to be such a no-good tramp that he turns to drink. In **Where the Sidewalk Ends** he is the honest but tough cop who accidentally kills a suspect. In **Beyond a Reasonable Doubt** he

*Above: French star Annabella came to England in 1937 to star in the first British Technicolor film, **Wings of the Morning.***

ANNABELLA

The first big star of the French sound cinema and the first French actress to achieve international stardom, working in America and England as well as France. Annabella was the imported star of Britain's first Technicolor film, the 1936 **Wings of the Morning,** and won the Best Actress Award at the 1936 Venice Film Festival for Marcel L'Herbier's **Veille d'Armes.** She is best remembered as the charming star of major films by such leading French directors as Gance, Clair and Carné.

Annabella was born in La Varenne - Saint - Hilaire, outside Paris, in 1909, as Suzanne Georgette Charpentier. Her first important film role was in Abel Gance's epic **Napoléon** but it was René Clair's films **Le Million** and **Quatorze Juillet** that made her famous as the typical French working-class girl. Critics admired her enormously for her portrayal of a poor servant girl in **Marie, Légende Hongroise,** while others praised especially her depiction of Denise in Litvak's **L'Équipage,** but she is probably best known for her role in Carné's **Hotel du Nord,** a film that was built around her. She made one film in Hollywood **Caravan,** with Charles Boyer ➤, in 1934, but did not become an American star until the late '30s, at Fox. When she starred opposite Tyrone Power ➤ in the 1938 **Suez,** sparks flew: her French marriage to Jean Murat went up in flames and she married Power in 1939. Annabella continued working on stage and in American films until 1946, when she made Henry Hathaway's **13 Rue Madeleine.** Afterwards she returned to France and eventually retired after divorcing Power in 1948. Annabella divides her time now between her home in Paris and her farm in the Pyrenees.

BEST FILMS:
1926 Napoléon
Abel Gance (WESTI/SGF)
1927 Maldone
Jean Grémillon (Dullin)
1931 Le Million
René Clair (Tobis)
1932 Marie, Légende Hongroise
Paul Fejös (Osso)
1933 Quatorze Juillet
René Clair (Tobis)
1936 La Bandéra
Julien Duvivier (SNC)
1936 L'Équipage
Anatole Litvak (Pathé Nathan)
1936 Wings of the Morning
Harold Schuster (20th Century Fox)
1938 Hôtel Du Nord
Marcel Carné (Sedif)

EVE ARDEN

Eve Arden is one of the great pleasures of movie-going: if she's in a film, you know you will enjoy at least part of it. Her usual role was as the tall, cool, wisecracking friend of the heroine, with an inexhaustible stock of witty ripostes, caustic quips and snappy replies; it was exactly this kind of part that won her her only Oscar acting nomination in **Mildred Pierce** (1945). She portrays Joan Crawford's ➤ knowledgeable best friend and has the best lines in the movie, including her classic comment about Crawford's horrible daughter: "Veda's convinced me that alligators have the right idea. They eat their young."

Eve Arden rarely had starring roles in the usual sense, but she was actually a star in every movie

Above: Eve Arden, Hollywood's wise-cracking friend of heroines.

she appeared in, from the brassy, wisecracking show girls of her earliest films (**Stage Door, Ziegfeld Girl**) to her recent show-stopping appearance as the high school principal in the 1978 musical **Grease.** She often stole the picture from the nominal stars, most notably in **Cover Girl** as fashion editor Otto Kruger's assistant and in **The Doughgirls** as the Russian girl who likes to shoot pigeons from the hotel terrace. She was always good humoured and loyal even when being caustic, as in **Anatomy of a Murder,** where she goes on working for lawyer James Stewart ❯ although her salary is long overdue. For many Americans she is most closely identified with Connie Brooks, the sharp-tongued teacher of the long-running radio and TV series **Our Miss Brooks;** a film version was made in 1956.

Eve Arden was born as (unfortunately, she would probably say) Eunice Quedens, in Mill Valley, California, on April 30, 1912, and took her stage name from a cold-cream jar. As Eunice, she made her film début in 1929 in **Song of Love,** but her career dragged until she changed her name, became a Ziegfeld girl, and came back to movies in the 1937 **Oh Doctor!** She was soon one of the busiest actresses in Hollywood (she made ten films in 1941 and was delightful in all of them). She has had occasional dramatic roles (as the bossy sister in **The Dark at the Top of the Stairs**) and bitchy ones (as the sister-in-law in **The Unfaithful**) but it is for her portrayals of barbed-tongued but warm-hearted friends that she will always be remembered.

BEST FILMS:
1937 Stage Door
Gregory La Cava (RKO)
1941 That Uncertain Feeling
Ernst Lubitsch (United Artists)
1944 Cover Girl
Charles Vidor (Columbia)
1944 The Doughgirls
James V. Kern (Warner Brothers)
1945 Mildred Pierce
Michael Curtiz (Warner Brothers)
1947 The Voice of the Turtle
Irving Rapper (Warner Brothers)
1956 Our Miss Brooks
Al Lewis (Warner Brothers)
1959 Anatomy of a Murder
Otto Preminger (Columbia)
1960 The Dark at the Top of the Stairs
Delbert Mann (Warner Brothers)
1978 Grease
Randal Kleiser (Paramount)

Arletty

The unforgettable star of the best films of Marcel Carné and one of the most memorable actresses in French cinema. Arletty was at her best as Garance, the woman loved by mime Jean-Louis Barrault in **Les Enfants du Paradis,** but was also splendid as the Devil's emissary in **Les Visiteurs du Soir,**

Above: Arletty, a French star with truly international appeal.

the mistress of Jean Gabin ❯ in **Le Jour se Lève,** and as the street-walker paired with Louis Jouvet ❯ in **Hôtel du Nord.** She was very beautiful in a peculiarly dry French way with a sharpish wit, a touch of erotic vulgarity and a virtually inimitable voice. Many of her lines in these films are extremely famous in France (the scriptwriters were Jacques Prévert and Henri Jeanson) and there has never been another screen persona quite like hers.

Born as Arlette-Léonie Bathiat in Courbevoie, France, in 1898, she worked as a factory girl, secretary and model before coming into the cinema as a singer and dancer after a success in operetta. Arletty's first film was the 1930 **La Douceur d'Aimer** but her first memorable appearance was as the streetwalker Parasol in Jacques Feyder's 1935 **Pension Mimosas.** Sacha Guitry developed her screen personality in his films **Désiré** and **Les Perles de la Couronne,** and her career

really took off in 1938 with **Hôtel du Nord.** The good-hearted, rather dashing and very amusing "bad girl" image was used nicely in **Fric-Frac,** which she first did on stage and then in the cinema with Michel Simon ❯ and Fernandel ❯. The marked slang dialogue of this film and its sequels, **Circonstances atténuantes** and **Tempête,** has probably kept them from being well known abroad, but they made Arletty the *grande dame* of the French cinema of this period.

After World War II Arletty worked in fewer films but continued her stage career. Her last film was the 1962 **Le Voyage à Biarritz** (she appeared in Daryl Zanuck's **The Longest Day** in 1961) and her last stage appearance was in 1966 in Jean Cocteau's **Monstres Sacrés.** She is now over 80 and almost blind, retaining partial vision in only one eye, but to cinema enthusiasts everywhere she will always remain the young and beautiful Arletty of her Carné masterpieces.

BEST FILMS:
1935 Pension Mimosas
Jacques Feyder (Tobis)
1938 Hôtel du Nord
Marcel Carné (Sedif)
1939 Fric-Frac
Maurice Lehmann (CCFC)
1939 Le Jour se Lève
Marcel Carné (Vog/Sigma)
1939 Circonstances atténuantes
Jean Boyer (Berchulz)
1941 Madame Sans-Gêne
Roger Richebé (Ciné-Alliance)
1942 Les Visiteurs du Soir
Marcel Carné (Paulvé)
1944 Les Enfants du Paradis
Marcel Carné (Pathé)
1954 Le Grand Jeu
Robert Siodmak (Speva/Rizzoli)
1954 Huis Clos
Jacqueline Audry (Films Marceau)

Jean Arthur

The quirkily humorous star of outstanding films by Capra, Ford, Hawks, Stevens and Wilder, Jean Arthur apparently remains convinced even now that she can't really act. Capra, who decribed her as his favourite actress, noted that she was chronically nervous about facing the camera, and to this day continues to back out of stage, TV and film commitments when possible. The persona she created at the Columbia Studios, where she was one of the major stars in the 1930s, was that of a liberated woman in the Hawks style: durable, resilient, honest in emotions and with a no-nonsense air. She always had a slight look of astonishment on her face and her slightly cracked, throaty voice added to her pert charm.

Her lack of confidence in her acting ability went back a long way. Born as Gladys Georgianna Greene, in New York, on October 17, 1905, Jean Arthur had her first film role in John Ford's **Cameo Kirby.** She failed to impress in more than 20 silent films and ended up in slapstick as a target for custard pies. The initial sound period was no better, and her break was a long time coming. But perhaps her very shyness and lack of confidence made her so attractive when Ford once again directed her in 1935 in **The Whole Town's Talking,** opposite Edward G. Robinson ❯. Her

*Below: Jean Arthur between husband Van Heflin and former gunfighter Alan Ladd in **Shane.** As usual she had mixed feelings about the men in her life, but kept a no-nonsense façade.*

image as a self-reliant woman who first takes pity on a man and then falls for him was established in this film and repeated with Gary Cooper » in **Mr Deeds Goes to Town**, Cary Grant » in **Only Angels Have Wings** and James Stewart » in **Mr Smith Goes to Washington**. She was paired with Charles Boyer » in the shipboard romance **History is Made at Night**, with Edward Arnold in the delectable **Easy Living**, with Joel McCrea » in **Adventure in Manhattan** and with William Powell » in **The Ex-Mrs Bradford**. She did not really like being a star and having to live up to her screen image, and she reportedly whooped with joy when her Columbia contract expired in 1944. Thereafter she alternated academic studies with only a few plays and films and drama teaching at Vassar. Today she is a slender, silver-haired 70-year-old and still shy. If you see her, tell her what a good actress she is.

BEST FILMS:
1935 The Whole Town's Talking
John Ford (Columbia)
1936 Mr Deeds Goes to Town
Frank Capra (Columbia)
1937 History is Made at Night
Frank Borzage (United Artists)
1938 You Can't Take It With You
Frank Capra (Columbia)
1939 Only Angels Have Wings
Howard Hawks (Columbia)
1939 Mr Smith Goes to Washington
Frank Capra (Columbia)
1942 The Talk of the Town
George Stevens (Columbia)
1943 The More the Merrier
George Stevens (Columbia)
1948 A Foreign Affair
Billy Wilder (Paramount)
1953 Shane
George Stevens (Paramount)

FRED ASTAIRE

Fred Astaire is the real tinsel beneath the false tinsel of Hollywood, the ultimate confectioner of style-as-art, the apotheosis of acting as movement. He is much more than just the greatest dancer in the history of the cinema. American critic James Agee (who compared him to Mozart and Chaplin ») suggested in 1943 that a new cinematic form would have to be developed to adequately realise his qualities. One might say that that form has already been created and is called the Astaire movie. These are not like other films. One searches vainly through Astaire's 1959 autobiography, **Steps in Time,** in hope of finding the basis for his screen charisma; the book, like his screen characterisations, his seemingly ordinary voice, his suave good humour—and his films—is insubstantial. His insubstantiality, however, is that of illusion and magic. Astaire bewitches audiences as soon as he appears on the screen, and not

only when dancing. His sophisticated finesse, his devil-may-care, optimistic attitudes and his elegant and precise grace of movement charm even the stone deaf. When he begins to dance, he wins over all the rest—pity poor Dolores del Rio and Gene Raymond in the 1933 **Flying Down to Rio,** in which they were the ostensible stars: low-billed Astaire and new girl Ginger Rogers » walked off with the picture, the screen's greatest dancing partnership was born, and doleful Dolores lost her RKO contract.

Right: Fred Astaire teamed with Cyd Charisse in **Silk Stockings,** *a musical version of* **Ninotchka.**

Below: Fred Astaire and Ginger Rogers back together again in 1948: **The Barkleys of Broadway.**

Astaire, of course, had been dancing for a long time before this. He was born in Omaha, Nebraska, on May 10, 1899, as Frederick Austerlitz. His mother set him dancing with sister Adele from the age of five and they were soon in vaudeville and then Broadway musicals. By 1922 people were writing shows just for them — and soon those writers had names like George Gershwin, who gave them **Funny Face** and **Lady Be Good.** When Adele retired and got married, Fred decided to go into the movies. His first was at MGM with Joan Crawford » in **Dancing Lady,** in 1933. Then RKO teamed him with Ginger Rogers. The chemistry was perfect; she gave him substantiality and he gave her style. Her dancing could not match his, but she worked very hard. He was a perfectionist and he was like the wind, the ultimate in movement; she gave colour and shape to his flow. He pursued her through nine films as the most debonair of playboys, and there have rarely been more enjoyable musicals. Critics described Astaire as one of the greatest joys of the cinema

and audiences flocked to **The Gay Divorcée, Top Hat, Roberta** and the rest. Astaire in top hat and tails became a symbol of the American cinema at its best and most enjoyable — it may not have been great art to the serious critics (who mistakenly never seem to list his pictures among the enduring masterpieces) but it was great fun, the joyous victory of style over content. Some critics consider **Swing Time** as the best Astaire and Rogers film (because it has a famous director, George Stevens), but really there is great enjoyment in all of them.

At the end of the '30s, Ginger decided to give up dancing for dramatics and Astaire set out to find a new partner; surprisingly, he never found a permanent one nor even a better one, though many of them were far better dancers than Ginger. One of the great teamings was with Eleanor Powell », a dancing star in her own right, in **Broadway Melody of 1940;** she was the only partner ever able to match him in dancing dexterity. He was good with a series of ladies after that, including Rita Hayworth » and Paulette Goddard

», and then was matched against his greatest rival, Gene Kelly », in **Ziegfeld Follies** (Astaire won). This was the beginning of the great second half of his career, working with Vincente Minnelli and other outstanding musical directors. Minnelli pushed Astaire into a brilliant but less popular style in **Yolanda and the Thief** (with Lucille Bremer) and the truly magnificent **The Band Wagon** (with Cyd Charisse »). Charles Walters used him in a much more open and pleasant style in **Easter Parade** with Judy Garland » and **The Belle of New York** with Vera-Ellen, and reunited him with Ginger in the relatively weak **The Barkleys of Broadway.** Stanley Donen brought a nice briskness to the Astaire musical, directing **Royal Wedding** with Jane Powell and the delightful **Funny Face** with Audrey Hepburn ».

Astaire's last real musical was one of his best and most visually opulent, Rouben Mamoulian's 1957 **Silk Stockings,** with Cyd Charisse dancing the role that Garbo » had once played in **Ninotchka.** It was a great film but not a popular success, and Astaire turned to straight acting in films like **On the Beach** and **The Notorious Landlady.**

In 1968 he made not so much a comeback as a homage to his career in musicals with Francis Ford Coppola's enjoyably schmaltzy **Finian's Rainbow.** He has continued to work in films, including an excellent performance in debonair if elderly form in **The Towering Inferno** (1975), and in TV. He was given a special Academy Award in 1949 for his "unique artistry" and received a nomination for Best Supporting Actor for **Towering Inferno.** His greatest films and his greatest performances won no awards and need none; they will be remembered and enjoyed long after most of the prizewinners have been forgotten.

BEST FILMS:
1934 The Gay Divorcee
Mark Sandrich (RKO)
1935 Top Hat
Mark Sandrich (RKO)
1936 Swing Time
George Stevens (RKO)
1937 Shall We Dance?
Mark Sandrich (RKO)
1940 Broadway Melody of 1940
Norman Taurog (MGM)
1945 Yolanda and the Thief
Vincente Minnelli (MGM)
1948 Easter Parade
Charles Walters (MGM)
1953 The Band Wagon
Vincente Minnelli (MGM)
1957 Funny Face
Stanley Donen (Paramount)
1957 Silk Stockings
Rouben Mamoulian (MGM)

MARY ASTOR

Mary Astor will be remembered for at least three things. First, she was the only person ever able to steal a film from Bette Davis » (she got an Academy Award for **The Great Lie** of 1941 because of it). Second, she was the focus of the biggest Hollywood scandal of the '30s when newspapers published lurid extracts from an alleged diary describing her torrid love affair with writer George S. Kaufman (it actually helped her career rather than hindered it). Finally, she was a highly intelligent and charismatic actress who starred in movies for 40 years, with especial brilliance at playing a twofaced bitch and a softhearted mother. The pinnacle of her long career was opposite Humphrey Bogart » in **The Maltese Falcon** (1941) as the deceptively helpless Brigid O'Shaughnessy.

Mary Astor began life as Lucille Vasconcells Langehanke in Quincy, Illinois, where she was born on May 3, 1906. Her ambitious father pushed her into movies at the first possible opportunity; she made her début in 1921 in **Sentimental Tommy,** but it was the 1924 **Beau Brummel** that sparked her career. Co-star John Barrymore » became her first lover (as she later admitted in her autobiography *My Story*) and also starred her in the first sound film **Don Juan.** She appeared opposite Douglas Fairbanks Sr » in **Don Q, Son of Zorro,** but her career faltered with the arrival of sound. She had reasonable parts in the early '30s but it was the scandalous publication of her diary that brought her national fame, heralding the period of her finest films; audiences burst into applause when she appeared in **Dodsworth**

(as Walter Huston's tender friend) and she was outstanding in **The Prisoner of Zenda** and **The Hurricane.** She was a memorable society bitch with a sharp tongue in **Midnight,** and Bette Davis handed her an Oscar on a platter as the rival wife in **The Great Lie.** After **Maltese Falcon** and **Across the Pacific** with Bogart, she was mostly stuck in motherly roles **(Meet Me in St Louis, Little Women)** which she hated — but in which she excelled. In 1961 she again won critical kudos for stealing the show in **Return to Peyton Place.** Her last film was the 1965 **Hush, Hush . . . Sweet Charlotte.** She lives today at the Motion Picture and TV Country Home in California, where a chronic heart condition limits her activity to writing novels.

BEST FILMS:
1926 Don Juan
Alan Crosland (Warner Brothers)
1936 Dodsworth
William Wyler (United Artists)
1937 The Prisoner of Zenda
John Cromwell (United Artists)
1937 Hurricane
John Ford (United Artists)
1939 Midnight
Mitchell Leisen (Paramount)
1941 The Great Lie
Edmund Goulding (Warner Brothers)
1941 The Maltese Falcon
John Huston (Warner Brothers)
1942 Palm Beach Story
Preston Sturges (Paramount)
1944 Meet Me in St Louis
Vincente Minnelli (MGM)
1949 Little Women
Mervyn Le Roy (MGM)

Left: Mary Astor as the double-dealing and deadly Brigid O'Shaughnessy in the 1941 **The Maltese Falcon** *with Humphrey Bogart as Sam Spade, Sydney Greenstreet as Kaspar Gutman and Peter Lorre as Joel Cairo. From early typecasting as a bitch she graduated to motherly roles.*

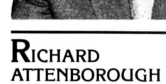

RICHARD ATTENBOROUGH

The cowardliness popularly associated with Richard Attenborough's screen persona in the early part of his career was a misconception; what he really reflects in his films is an instinct for survival which often emerges in panic-striken or even psychopathic behaviour. In his first film, the 1942 **In Which We Serve,** in the role that made his teenage reputation, he is a stoker who loses his nerve but survives the torpedoing of a destroyer. In **Brighton Rock** he is a teenage psychopath willing to marry and kill a waitress to protect himself from a murder charge. Whether trying to escape from a POW camp **(The Great Escape),** or wishing not to be involved in a kidnap plot **(Seance on a Wet Afternoon),** or cracking up after a plane crash **(The Flight of the Phoenix),** his basic concern is survival. It is a limited persona and Attenborough is not the most talented of actors, but his long movie career (34 years) shows his strength. Despite more than the usual number of weak movies, his position as one of the doyens of the British cinema is stronger than ever today, and he received a knighthood in 1976.

Left: Richard Attenborough (right) was the nervous navigator to James Stewart's pilot in the 1965 Robert Aldrich film **The Flight of the Phoenix.** *Below left: Attenborough, actor and director, knighted in 1976 after 34 years in movies.*

Attenborough was born in Cambridge, England, in 1923 and began working on stage in the early '40s, making his film début in **In Which We Serve.** He has not been very lucky in getting first-class directors for his films but when he does he can be very good indeed, especially under the guidance of Satyajit Ray in the Indian epic **The Chess Players,** John Sturges in **The Great Escape** and Robert Aldrich in **The Flight of the Phoenix.** He has received British film industry recognition for his performances in **Seance on a Wet Afternoon** and **Guns at Batasi** and has been highly popular with audiences in films like **Private's Progress.** He has consolidated his position in the British cinema by directing some notable films, especially **Oh What a Lovely War!** (1969), **Young Winston** (1972), **A Bridge Too Far** (1978) and, most recently, **Magic** (1979).

BEST FILMS:
1942 In Which We Serve
Noel Coward & David Lean (Rank)
1947 Brighton Rock
John Boulting (Associated British)
1956 Private's Progress
John Boulting (British Lion)
1960 The League of Gentlemen
Basil Dearden (Rank)
1963 The Great Escape
John Sturges (United Artists)
1964 Seance on a Wet Afternoon
Bryan Forbes (Rank)
1964 Guns at Batasi
John Guillermin (20th Century Fox)
1965 The Flight of the Phoenix
Robert Aldrich (20th Century Fox)
1970 Ten Rillington Place
Richard Fleischer (Columbia)
1977 The Chess Players
Satyajit Ray (Devki Chitra Productions)

Jean-Pierre Aumont

The screen persona of Jean-Pierre Aumont as the suavest and most enduring "Continental lover" reached its brilliant apogee in François Truffaut's tribute to the movies, **Day for Night.** Aumont is the star of a film-with-in-the-film whose co-star "wife" is astonished that her old lover is still playing romantic leads (he is scripted to run off with their son's bride). It was all superbly done and was doubly enjoyable for audiences who knew that Aumont had been making films for more than 40 years and was the great "jeune premier" of the French cinema in the '30s. It was Aumont who was chosen as Annabella's ❯ romantic

Above: Jean-Pierre Aumont was almost playing himself as the suavest of Continental lovers in François Truffaut's **Day For Night** *but the director kept a surprise up his sleeve. Here Aumont talks to his co-star Valentina Cortese.*

co-star for Marcel Carnés 1938 **Hôtel du Nord** (although Arletty ❯ and Louis Jouvet ❯ stole the film from them), and it was Aumont who was the romantic Resistance hero of the 1943 **Assignment in Brittany** (by taking advantage of the fact that he looked like a Nazi leader). Aumont has made his share of pretty awful movies; in **Song of Scheherezade** he is naval cadet composer Rimsky-Korsakov, enchanted in lurid colour by dancer Yvonne de Carlo, but he has also made some charming ones — he was superb as the sophisticated magician with an eye for the ladies in **Lili** (bewitching Leslie Caron ❯; he was pleasant opposite Ginger Rogers ❯ in **Heartbeat;** and he did his best to help Lynn Redgrave make a go of **The Happy Hooker.** He was very effective as the French count who owns the castle in **Castle Keep,** encouraging Burt Lancaster ❯ to have an affair with his wife so that he can have an heir.

Aumont, born in Paris in 1913 as Jean-Pierre Salomons, is married to another film star, Marisa Pavan, the Italian-born (1913) sister of Pier Angeli. They have been married since 1956, have two teenage sons, own homes in Paris and Ibiza, and worked together in a supper-club act in the '60s. Aumont's first wife was the late Maria Montez; the daughter of that marriage is Italian movie star Tina Aumont. His most recent films include **Mahoganny,** with Diana Ross ❯ and the Canadian picture **Two Solitudes,** in which he stars opposite Stacy Keach as the ageing headman of a small Quebec town.

BEST FILMS:
1934 Lac aux Dames
Marc Allégret (Filmor)
1934 Maria Chapdelaine
Julien Duvivier (France Film)
1936 Drôle de Drame
Marcel Carné (Corniglion-Molinier)
1938 Hôtel du Nord
Marcel Carné (Sedif)
1943 Assignment in Brittany
Jack Conway (MGM)
1946 Heartbeat
Sam Wood (RKO)
1952 Lili
Charles Walters (MGM)
1969 Castle Keep
Sydney Pollack (Columbia)
1973 La Nuit Américaine (Day for Night)
François Truffaut (Films du Carosse)
1978 Two Solitudes
Lionel Chetwynd (Compass)

Below: Gene Autry was never admired by critics, but the public kept him a top star for 16 years.

Gene Autry

The first singing cowboy star has been returning to popularity lately with re-releases of his records and a cinematic homage in the Burt Reynolds ❯ Kris Kristofferson ❯ film **Semi-Tough,** whose sound track is all Autry music. He was the biggest thing in cowboy movies for much of the period from 1935 to 1951 (mostly with Republic) and was the first Western star to become a Top Ten box-office favourite. He created a cleancut, amiable, honest fellow called "Gene Autry" and portrayed him with great success in most of his 93 films. Serious critics have never responded to him — a pity, because he reflected audience needs which would reward study. His Boy Scout-style code of conduct (he never shot or hit a man first, he didn't smoke or drink and he always kept his word) was what US audiences at the time (especially boys) thought was right and "American." He was also, of course, one of the most popular singing stars of all time, as his record sales show, and will always be identified with such songs as *Back in the Saddle Again* (his theme) and *Tumbling Tumbleweeds*

Born Orvon Gene Autry on September 29, 1907, in Tioga, Texas, he was a radio star on the National Barn Dance before making his first film in 1934 (**In Old Santa Fé,** starring Ken Maynard). He wasn't the first singing cowboy (Maynard and even John Wayne ❯ had sung before) but he was the first successful one and he was an instant hit — even in that bizarre science-fiction serial, **The Phantom Empire.** His films were never particularly outstanding but they had action and good songs, along with a memorable humorous

sidekick named Frog (Smiley Burnette), a wonder horse (Champion), and a highly talented musical support group (the Sons of the Pioneers). Autry's films remained popular until 1953 when he made his last starring vehicle, **Last of the Pony Riders.** He has since used his accumulated wealth to go into TV and other business ventures and has become a financial tycoon worth well over one hundred million dollars. He lives today on his "Melody Ranch" in California.

BEST FILMS:
1935 The Phantom Empire
B. Reeves Eason & Otto Brewer (Mascot)
1935 Tumbling Tumbleweeds
Joseph Kane (Republic)
1936 Red River Valley
B. Reeves Eason (Republic)
1936 The Old Corral
Joseph Kane (Republic)
1939 Mexicali Rose
George Sherman (Republic)
1939 In Old Monterey
Joseph Kane (Republic)
1939 South of the Border
George Sherman (Republic)
1940 Melody Ranch
Joseph Santley (Republic)
1949 Riders in the Sky
John English (Columbia)
1950 Mule Train
John English (Columbia)

LAUREN BACALL

Lauren Bacall was the closest there has ever been to a female Humphrey Bogart ❯—and a wonderful achievement it was. She was a major star from her first film opposite Bogart in 1944, **To Have and Have Not.** Critic James Agee fell in love with both her voice ("like a chorus by Kid Ory") and her persona ("It has been years since I have seen such amusing pseudo-toughness on the

Top: Lauren Bacall made her screen debut in 1944 opposite Humphrey Bogart in To Have and Have Not with such lines as "Was you ever bit by a dead bee?".
Inset: Bacall's image was inspired by director Howard Hawks.

screen"), and her studio, Warner Brothers, immediately dubbed her "The Look." Bogart himself was so impressed that he married his slim, sultry co-star the following year, and in 1946 they starred together in one of the greatest American films of all time, **The Big Sleep.** These two pictures, with Howard Hawks directing and Bogart as the co-star, remain Bacall's finest achievements, although she has made other good films.

She was born as Betty Jane Perske in New York City on September 16, 1924, and was a not very successful stage actress and model when Hawks' wife saw her photo on the cover of the magazine *Harper's Bazaar.* Only 19 years old, she dominated **To Have and Have Not** as a girl named Slim who insouciantly taught Bogart to whistle ("just put your lips together and blow"). She was just as cynical, cool and independent as Bogart—and rather more beautiful, especially when she walked (it was suggested that there must have been a panther in her family tree) and

her voice was incredibly husky; it made everything she said sound insinuating and sexy. In **The Big Sleep** she was the rich, insolent, antagonistic daughter of Bogart's employer in an inspired adaptation of Raymond Chandler's novel; she made two more films with Bogart, **Dark Passage** and **Key Largo,** but Warner's did not really seem to know how to develop her screen personality and most of her parts were simply

straightforward heroines. She later showed a nice flair for comedy in films like **How to Marry a Millionaire** and **A Woman's World** under Jean Negulesco's direction, and was excellent opposite Richard Widmark ❯ in **The Cobweb.** ❯ Following Bogart's death in 1957, she married Jason Robards ❯ in 1961 (they divorced in 1969). She starred in **Harper,** a loving homage to Bogart with Paul Newman ❯, in 1966, but since then has worked mostly on stage in New York except for occasional films like **Murder on the Orient Express** (1974) and **The Shootist** (1976), a superb performance being nicely antagonistic towards John Wayne ❯.

BEST FILMS:
1944 To Have and Have Not
Howard Hawks (Warner Brothers)
1946 The Big Sleep
Howard Hawks (Warner Brothers)
1947 Dark Passage
Delmer Daves (Warner Brothers)
1948 Key Largo
John Huston (Warner Brothers)
1953 How to Marry a Millionaire
Jean Negulesco (20th-Century Fox)
1956 The Cobweb
Vincente Minnelli (MGM)
1957 Written on the Wind
Douglas Sirk (Universal)
1957 Designing Woman
Vincente Minnelli (MGM)
1966 Harper
Jack Smight (Warner Brothers)
1976 The Shootist
Don Siegel (CIC)

STANLEY BAKER

Stanley Baker brought a new kind of virile, aggressive, working-class Welsh power to the British cinema in the early '50s that was very much in line with the changing patterns of British culture at that time, but he reached his peak as an actor in the '60s in a series of films with expatriate American director Joseph Losey. There was a strength and vigour

in his screen personality rare in British films, making him ideally suited to the roles of tough policeman **(Blind Date)**, criminal gang leader **(The Criminal, Robbery, Perfect Friday)**, or fighter against the odds in heroic war pictures **(Zulu, The Guns of Navarone)**.

Baker was born in Wales on February 27, 1927, and made his cinema début as a teenager in the 1943 **Undercover**. He was generally given unsympathetic and boorish roles during his cinema apprenticeship and first made a real impact as a bullying officer on a corvette in **The Cruel Sea** (1952). His almost American-style toughness was exploited in '50s films like **Hell Below Zero, Hell Drivers** and **Sea Fury**, although he was also good as the Welshman Henry Tudor in Laurence Olivier's ≫ film version of **Richard III**. His first film with Losey was the 1959 **Blind Date** (as a police inspector investigating a murder), followed in 1960 by the even better **The Criminal** (portraying an imprisoned gang leader who is hunted down and killed by other criminals when he comes out to get the loot he had hidden years before). Losey's Italian-made **Eva** starred Baker as a British writer in Venice who becomes involved with mysterious *femme fatale* Jeanne Moreau ≫, while **Accident** featured him in a supporting role to Dirk Bogarde ≫ as an Oxford professor.

Peter Hall used him well as a bank manager who arranges to rob his own bank in **Perfect Friday**, but his biggest commercial successes were the large-budget epics **The Guns of Navarone** and **Zulu**. He died of cancer in 1976, having received a knighthood shortly before his death.

BEST FILMS:
1952 The Cruel Sea
Charles Frend (Ealing)
1956 Richard III
Laurence Olivier (London Films)
1959 Blind Date
Joseph Losey (Rank)
1960 The Criminal
Joseph Losey (Merton Park)
1961 The Guns of Navarone
J. Lee Thompson (Columbia)
1962 Eva
Joseph Losey (Interopa Film)
1963 Zulu
Cy Endfield (Paramount)
1967 Accident
Joseph Losey (London Independent Producers)
1967 Robbery
Peter Yates (Joseph E. Levine)
1970 Perfect Friday
Peter Hall (London Screenplays)

Left: Stanley Baker surrounded by bodies in one of his most successful films, the 1964 epic **Zulu**. *Baker usually portrayed strong-minded tough guys able to battle against the odds and keep audiences in doubt as to whether he could win out in the end. Often he didn't.*

LUCILLE BALL

Lucille Ball is one of the great female clowns of cinema and television, but she will also go down in history as the only star ever able to get the ultimate revenge on her studio—by buying it up. RKO never realised Ball's full potential as a comedienne in her long years with them, but she certainly realised the potential of the RKO studios, and bought them for her television production company, Desilu, in 1957. Her film career was quite extraordinary: she became one of the best known screen personalities of the '40s without ever making a really good film. She was instantly recognisable, very likeable and extremely funny, and she could steal scenes from any of the stars she was billed with, but she seemed to have terrible luck in getting the right script or the right director. Bright, brassy and breezy, she enlivened almost everything she was in and was an excellent partner to Red Skelton **(Dubarry Was a Lady)** and Bob Hope ≫ **(Sorrowful Jones, Fancy Pants)**. She was delightful with other bright ladies as well, notably in her first really successful film, the 1937 **Stage Door** (with Katharine Hepburn ≫ and Ginger Rogers ≫, and in **Dance, Girl, Dance** (with Maureen O'Hara ≫). But it took television to give her the opportunities she deserved—three series, beginning with **I Love Lucy** in 1951, proved that she was a brilliant businesswoman as well as comedienne, and made her a multi-millionairess.

"Lucy" was born as Lucille Desirée Ball in Jamestown, New York, on August 6, 1910. She worked as a model and on stage until she came to Hollywood in 1933 as a Goldwyn Girl to appear in **Roman Scandals** and played

Left: Lucille Ball teamed up with Bob Hope in 1963 for the comedy **Critic's Choice**. *He's a New York drama critic, she's his wife and a playwright.*

bit parts for years before making a breakthrough with **Stage Door**, tossing off smart remarks with fellow low-billed Eve Arden ≫. The RKO company was going downhill, but she made it as a star of their films—even if most were unexceptional. She was a fireball stripper in **Dance, Girl, Dance** and had her finest dramatic role in the Damon Runyon adaptation **The Big Street** (as a crippled ex-gold-digger worshipped by Henry Fonda ≫. She was funny with Hope and Skelton, but her most popular films came later; Minnelli's **The Long, Long Trailer** with husband Desi Arnaz was probably her best comedy, and she had a resounding commercial success when she re-teamed with Henry Fonda in the family comedy **Yours, Mine and Ours**. Her last film was a big one, the lavish, energetic musical **Mame**. Her 20-year marriage to Desi Arnaz ended in 1960 and she married comedian Gary Morton in 1961. She currently lives in Beverly Hills.

BEST FILMS:
1937 Stage Door
Gregory La Cava (RKO)
1939 Five Came Back
John Farrow (RKO)
1940 Dance, Girl, Dance
Dorothy Arzner (RKO)
1942 The Big Street
Irving Reis (RKO)
1943 Dubarry Was A Lady
Roy Del Ruth (MGM)
1949 Sorrowful Jones
Sidney Lanfield (Paramount)
1954 The Long, Long Trailer
Vincente Minnelli (MGM)
1960 The Facts of Life
Melvin Frank (United Artists)
1968 Yours, Mine and Ours
Melville Shavelson (United Artists)
1974 Mame
Gene Saks (Warner Brothers)

RICHARD BARTHELMESS

Barthelmess was a major star of both the silent and sound cinema. He was D. W. Griffith's favourite male actor and was the epitome of the romantic hero in Griffith's **Way Down East** and **Broken Blossoms** and Henry King's **Tol'able David**. The screen persona he created under Griffith's tutelage was that of a modest, gentle, handsome young man with hidden reserves of toughness and strength; this characterisation is seen at its best in **Tol'able David**, in which he wins through against terrific obstacles. The persona was flavoured with a touch of bitters when sound arrived, and he often portrayed disillusioned heroes, war veterans who no longer fit in. He was brilliant as a "lost generation" ex-pilot in Dieterle's **The Last Flight**, as a war veteran turned drug addict in Wellman's **Heroes for Sale**, and as a circus performer in Pabst's **A Modern Hero**. His greatest sound films were, however, made for Howard Hawks. He was superb as the heroic pilot who learns the

Bottom: Barthelmess rescues Lillian Gish from the ice in D.W. Griffith's **Way Down East**. *Below: Richard Barthelmess as the officer sending friends to their death in* **Dawn Patrol**.

bitterness of command in **The Dawn Patrol** and unforgettable as Rita Hayworth's supposedly cowardly pilot husband in **Only Angels Have Wings.**

Barthelmess was born in New York City in 1895 and started in films as an extra in 1913. His official début was in George King's 1916 **Gloria's Romance** with Billie Burke, and he worked with Herbert Brenon and others before Griffith put him under personal contract in 1919. He often starred opposite Lillian Gish ≫, most notably as her Chinese admirer in **Broken Blossoms** and as the farm boy who rescues her from the snow in **Way Down East.** He formed his own company, Inspiration, in 1921, and produced his great **Tol'able David**, one of the classics of Americana; he made films all through the '20s and won Best Actor nominations for two films at the first Academy Awards in 1927. He remained one of the ten most popular stars for many years in the early sound period, but his career gradually lost impetus and he retired after making **The Spoilers** in 1942. He died in 1963.

BEST FILMS:
1919 Broken Blossoms
D. W. Griffith (FPL)
1920 Way Down East
D. W. Griffith (United Artists)
1921 Tol'able David
Henry King (Inspiration)
1927 The Patent Leather Kid
Alfred Santell (First National)
1930 The Dawn Patrol
Howard Hawks (First National)
1931 The Last Flight
William Dieterle (First National)
1932 Cabin in the Cotton
Michael Curtiz (First National)
1933 Central Airport
William Wellman (Warner Brothers)
1933 Heroes for Sale
William Wellman (Warner Brothers)
1934 A Modern Hero
G. W. Pabst (Warner Brothers)
1939 Only Angels Have Wings
Howard Hawks (Columbia)

ANNE BAXTER

Anne Baxter was the smiling schemer in **All About Eve**, climbing to stardom over Bette Davis's ≫ still-warm body, and the tragic Sophie in **The Razor's Edge** (wallowing in grief-stricken debauchery). She should have become a major star after winning a Supporting Actress Oscar for **Razor's Edge** and a Best Actress nomination for **All About Eve**, but didn't—primarily because she never developed that smiling schemer into the screen persona that would have fitted her so well. She was well aware of this: "I'm an actress, not a personality," she told an interviewer. "It's more successful to be a personality." She still did pretty well for herself, working with top directors, appearing in excellent films and achieving a noteworthy, if limited, stardom.

Above: Anne Baxter at her best as the sweet schemer in **All Above Eve,** *using Bette Davis and George Sanders as stepping stones to success (and an Oscar nomination).*

Born in Michigan City, Indiana, on May 7, 1923, she made her cinema début in the 1940 **Twenty Mule Team** after a short stage career. Her first good role was as a poor swamp girl opposite Dana Andrews ≫ in Jean Renoir's **Swamp Water**; she had a bigger and meatier part as Joseph Cotten's ≫ daughter in Orson Welles' ≫ **The Magnificent Ambersons.** She played nice, innocent girls until the 1944 **Guest in the House** provided her with a trial run of the sweet schemer role (as a seemingly nice house guest wreaking havoc among a family). She was popular in the sentimental **Sunday Dinner for a Soldier** (inviting John Hodiak over to share meagre rations and falling in love with him). Her breakthrough came with her sensitive and very effective portrayal in **The Razor's Edge**—but her career didn't really take off. She made a good Western **(Yellow Sky)** and an enjoyable musical satirising jazz babies **(You're My Everything),** but it was not until the 1950 **All About Eve** that she really had another role to get her teeth into. She plays Eve Harrington, an apparently innocent would-be actress who uses every dirty trick possible in her climb to success; it is a brilliant, satirical film and was the high point of Anne's career. She was notable in later films (for Hitchcock and Fritz Lang) and was a sexy Nefertiti in de Mille's **The Ten Commandments**, but her screen characterisation did not develop and most of her later roles were only so-so. Much of her work in recent years has been for television.

Above: Anne Baxter portrayed a saloon girl in Oklahoma Territory in the epic Western **Cimarron** *(1961).*

BEST FILMS:
1942 The Magnificent Ambersons
Orson Welles (RKO)
1944 Guest in the House
John Brahm (United Artists)
1946 The Razor's Edge
Edmund Goulding (20th Century Fox)
1949 Yellow Sky
William Wellman (20th Century Fox)
1949 You're My Everything
Walter Lang (20th Century Fox)
1950 All About Eve
Joseph Mankiewicz (20th Century Fox)
1953 I Confess
Alfred Hitchcock (Warner Brothers)
1953 The Blue Gardenia
Fritz Lang (Warner Brothers)
1956 The Ten Commandments
Cecil B. De Mille (Paramount)
1961 Cimarron
Anthony Mann (MGM)

WARNER BAXTER

Warner Baxter created two of Hollywood's most enjoyable series, the **Cisco Kid** and the **Crime Doctor**; he won the Best Actor Academy Award in 1929 for **In Old Arizona**; starred in some outstanding films, including John Ford's **The Prisoner of Shark Island** and Howard Hawks' **The Road to Glory**; and for a while in the '30s was one of the most popular and highest-paid male actors in Hollywood. It was Baxter who told Ruby Keeler ≫ that she was going out there a nobody and coming back a star in **42nd Street**, and he was Ginger Rogers' ≫ mature admirer in **Lady in the Dark.** He was a handsome, pencil-moustached leading man— but he was best as the reckless, romantic Cisco Kid.

Baxter was born on March 29, 1892, in Columbus, Ohio, and entered movies after a theatrical career. His first screen role was in the 1918 **All Woman** with Mae Marsh ≫. He gradually became a minor star in the '20s, playing the lead in Herbert Brenon's version of **The Great Gatsby** in 1926 and opposite Lon Chaney, Snr ≫ in Tod Browning's 1929 **West of Zanzibar.** He was chosen to be the Cisco Kid for **In Old Arizona** after director/star-designate Raoul Walsh had an accident and lost an eye. Baxter was perfect for the character; a romantic, dashing Mexican hero with a penchant for the ladies, originally created by O. Henry in his short story "The Caballero's Way" and he played the role twice more (in **The Cisco Kid** in 1931 and **The Return of the Cisco Kid** in 1939); the character stayed alive for 20 more films (played by Cesar Romero, Duncan Renaldo and Gilbert Roland). Baxter's film career in the '30s had

Above: Warner Baxter looks after Elisabeth Allen in the 1937 **Slave Ship** *prior to mutiny on the high seas. Baxter was enjoyable in every kind of film, from the* **Cisco Kid** *series to musicals.*

its ups and downs, but he stayed a top star until 1941, making some quality films, like Capra's **Broadway Bill** and Cromwell's **To Mary With Love,** along with many programmers. He was reduced to B-pictures in the '40s, but cinema buffs remember with pleasure his 10-picture Columbia **Crime Doctor** series, as an amnesiac criminologist who discovers that he was formerly a criminal mastermind; he made two a year from 1943 on. He died in 1951, relatively ignored by critics but warmly remembered by audiences.

BEST FILMS:
1929 West of Zanzibar
Tod Browning (MGM)
1929 In Old Arizona
Irving Cummings (Fox)
1931 Daddy Long Legs
Alfred Santell (Fox)
1933 42nd Street
Lloyd Bacon (Warner Brothers)
1933 Penthouse
W. S. Van Dyke (MGM)
1934 Broadway Bill
Frank Capra (Columbia)
1935 King of Burlesque
Sidney Lanfield (Fox)
1936 The Prisoner of Shark Island
John Ford (20th Century Fox)
1936 The Road to Glory
Howard Hawks (20th Century Fox)
1936 To Mary With Love
John Cromwell (20th Century Fox)

WALLACE BEERY

Wallace Beery was the lovable rogue of '30s cinema, with an ugly face but a beautiful heart. Whether

Above: Wallace Beery in an earlier non-starring role in Tod Browning's 1923 **The White Tiger.**

portraying a washed-up boxer, a pot-bellied lush or a roughneck revolutionary, he was always himself; his endearing naiveté and gravelly voice made him a major MGM star for nearly 20 years. This persona was seen at its most characteristic in King Vidor's 1931 **The Champ,** the film that won him an Academy Award for his portrayal of a boozy, broken-down boxer worshipped by a young boy (Jackie Cooper). His biggest box-office role was as sparring partner to Marie Dressler ≫ in the sentimental but charming films **Min and Bill** (which won Dressler an Oscar) and **Tugboat Annie** (in which heavy-drinking Beery tries to down hair oil), and his greatest performance was as a Mexican revolutionary bandit in the Hawks-Conway **Viva Villa!** in

1934. Beery's greatest period was in the early '30s, but he remained a favourite of rural America until his death in 1949. His beat-up almost boorish face was his greatest asset in 37 years in movies (as he put it, "My mug is my fortune"), but his gruff voice was also memorable (with such trademark lines as "Aw, shucks!"

Beery was born in Kansas City, Missouri, on April 1, 1886 (his brother Noah (1884-1946) was a notable villain in the silent era). After a stage career, he entered films in 1912, with the Essanay company in Chicago, and made his first reputation as a drag artist playing a Swedish housemaid in the "Sweedie" comedy series. The surprising attraction of his "mug" persuaded glamour girl Gloria Swanson ≫ to marry him in 1916, although they divorced a couple of years later, and by the '20s he was getting important roles. He was Richard the Lionheart in Fairbanks' ≫ **Robin Hood,** the villain in Keaton's ≫ **The Three Ages** and a heavy in many major films. He teamed with Raymond Hatton in a series of popular comedies for Paramount and then joined MGM in 1930 for the big part of a rebellious prison thug in **The Big House.** It made his reputation and he was a major star from then on (and a gangster again in **The Secret Six**). After his biggest period in the '30s, he was often teamed with Marjorie Main in very popular low-budget '40s films; his last picture was **Big Jack** in 1949.

BEST FILMS:
1930 The Big House
George Hill (MGM)
1930 Billy the Kid
King Vidor (MGM)
1930 Min and Bill
George Hill (MGM)
1931 The Secret Six
George Hill (MGM)
1931 The Champ
King Vidor (MGM)
1932 Grand Hotel
Edmund Goulding (MGM)
1933 Dinner at Eight
George Cukor (MGM)
1933 Tugboat Annie
Mervyn Le Roy (MGM)
1934 Viva Villa!
Howard Hawks and Jack Conway (MGM)
1935 Ah, Wilderness!
Clarence Brown (MGM)

ROBERT BENCHLEY

In 1935 an amiable, middle-aged and rather portly New York writer won an Academy Award for a "scientific lecture" on **How To Sleep** (one of the MGM **How To** shorts). In it he portrayed an amiable, middle-aged and rather portly bumbler who has become one of the most memorable comic creations of the American cinema;

Above: Robert Benchley shows how easy it is to tie a tie in one of his brilliant **How To** *shorts that enlivened cinema-going in the 1930s. The Benchley screen persona is still effective.*

Benchley's character, a distorted version of himself, starred in 48 shorts and 40 feature films, sometimes as incompetent lecturer (in the MGM series), sometimes as a wonderfully engaging drunk (opposite Clark Gable ≫ and Jean Harlow ≫ in **China Seas**), and sometimes as screen star Robert Benchley (narrating the Hope ≫-Crosby ≫ **Road to Utopia,** with "explanations"). His first short, **The Treasurer's Report,** of 1928, was so popular that exhibitors billed it above the feature, and the persona he perfected in his 17-year film career is likely to endure for many years.

Benchley was an unlikely movie star. Born in 1889, and a graduate of Harvard where he edited the humour magazine, he became a top drama critic in the '20s, a famous *New Yorker* humourist and one of the wittiest stalwarts of the Algonquin group (he cabled them from Venice: "STREETS FLOODED. PLEASE ADVISE."). His "Treasurer's Report" monologue became so famous that he was asked to make a film of it for Fox in 1928; its success led to further films with RKO, MGM and Paramount. Sometimes the lecturer was seen in ordinary life as the "Normal Bumbler; (who later became "Joe Doakes"), but he always seemed self-confident, even when the situation was out of control. He died in 1945.

BEST FILMS:
1928 The Treasurer's Report
Thomas Chalmers (Fox)
1928 The Sex Life of the Polyp
Thomas Chalmers (Fox)

CONSTANCE BENNETT

Constance Bennett is best remembered today as the blonde, beautiful and very funny ghost who starred with Cary Grant ≫ in **Topper** and its sequel, **Topper Takes a Trip**. She was a brilliant sophisticated comedienne, as she showed by stealing the film from Greta Garbo ≫ in **Two-Faced Woman**—and from everyone else in her delightful family in **Merrily We Live**. She was a major star in Hollywood for a very long time and in the early '30s was said to be the highest-paid actress in the world. She was extremely popular and her sleek page-boy haircut was a much imitated trademark. In most of her romantic comedies she played a kind of worldly-wise flapper, with an attractive, husky voice and a wonderful air of slight disdain and amusement. Sadly, her early pictures are rarely shown, but she is especially notable in Cukor's **What Price Hollywood?** (a predecessor of **A Star is Born**), portraying a waitress who becomes a star.

Constance Campbell Bennett was born in New York City on October 22, 1905, the eldest of stage actor Richard Bennett's three daughters (Joan Bennett ≫ also became a star and Barbara had a short film career). She began acting in films in the early '20s and had her first major role in George Fitzmaurice's 1924 **Cyntherea**. She was exceptional in 1925 in Brown's **The Goose Woman** and Goulding's **Sally, Irene and Mary** (as a flapper with Joan Crawford ≫) but she then dropped out of movies and eloped with a millionaire (just like sister Joan) in 1929. She came back to films in 1929, at an enormous salary, and stayed a top star until the '40s, when her career began to lose momentum. She was as good as ever, but audiences seemed to want comediennes in other styles. She made films of many different kinds and ended her career in excellent form portraying Lana Turner's ≫ mother in Donald Lowell Rich's 1965 **Madame X**. She died the same year, the last of her five husbands by her side.

BEST FILMS:
1925 The Goose Woman
Clarence Brown (Universal)
1925 Sally, Irene and Mary
Edmund Goulding (MGM)
1930 Three Faces East
Roy Del Ruth (Warner Brothers)
1932 What Price Hollywood?
George Cukor (RKO)
1933 Bed of Roses
Gregory La Cava (RKO)
1934 The Affairs of Cellini
Gregory La Cava (United Artists)
1937 Topper
Norman Z. McLeod (MGM)
1938 Merrily We Live
Norman Z. McLeod (MGM)
1939 Topper Takes a Trip
Norman Z. McLeod (MGM)
1941 Two-Faced Woman
George Cukor (MGM)

Below: Constance Bennett as Lana Turner's mother in the 1965 **Madame X.** *Her more usual role was as a sophisticated wordly-wise comedienne.*

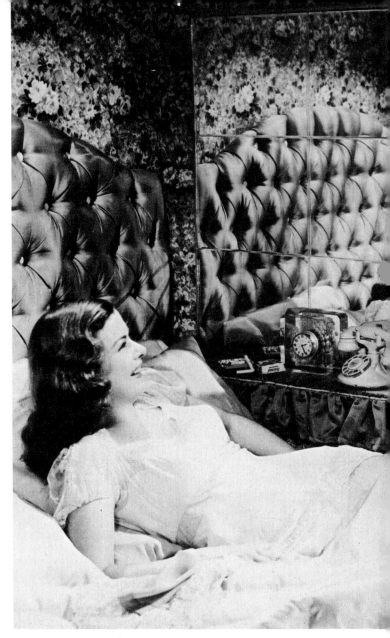

JOAN BENNETT

Joan Bennett has the unique distinction of being the only Hollywood glamour star to be featured in continental-type roles by such major European directors as Fritz Lang, Max Ophuls and Jean Renoir. It is also worthy of note that she was a star both as a blonde (in the '30s) and a brunette (in the '40s), as she changed from a lovely lightweight leading lady to an alluring, corrupt and even vulgar *film noir* heroine. Her screen persona as a glamorous, man-hungry and usually evil (but never unattractive) *femme fatale* in the '40s was destroyed, rather brilliantly, when she played the mother to Spencer Tracy's ≫ **Father of the Bride** in 1950. An era had ended, but she will always be remembered for her four Lang films: the sensual Lazy Legs in **Scarlet Street** (murdered by Edward G. Robinson ≫ after she has ruined him); the cockney tart in **Man Hunt** (involved with Walter Pidgeon ≫ on the run); the mysterious woman-in-the-painting in **The Woman in the Window** (again with Edward G. Robinson); and the suspicious wife in **Secret Beyond the Door**. She was also excellent as a murderess pursued by James Mason ≫ in Ophuls' **The Reckless Moment** and as Renoir's **The Woman on the Beach,** enticing Robert Ryan ≫ in spite of her blind husband (Charles Bickford).

Joan Bennett was born in Palisades, New Jersey, on February 27, 1910. She eloped with a millionaire at the age of 16, married him, had a baby, divorced him and started her film career in 1928; sister Constance was already a star by this time, but Joan quickly caught up. Most of her 40-odd '30s movies (as a blonde) are relatively unimportant (the best was Cukor's 1933 **Little Women,** as Amy). It was producer and husband-to-be Walter Wanger who changed her to a brunette in **Trade Winds,** in 1938, to cash in on the Hedy Lamarr ≫ vogue. Her career took off like a shot in the *noir,* notably in **The House Across the Bay** and **The Man I Married,** followed by her Lang pictures. Her film career was fatally damaged when husband Wanger shot agent Jennings Lang in 1953 and went to jail, but she has continued to make a few movies, the last being the TV film **The Eyes of Charles Sand.** She starred

*Above: Joan Bennett made her greatest impact as a star in four Fritz Lang films in the '40s. Here she is seen with Edward G. Robinson as the corrupt and sensual Lazy Legs in the 1946 **Scarlet Street**. He is driven to murder when he finds she has another lover (Dan Duryea).*

in a TV soap opera (**Dark Shadows**), wrote the family history (**The Bennett Playbill**), and now lives in Scarsdale, New York.

BEST FILMS:
1933 Little Women
George Cukor (RKO)
1940 The House Across the Bay
Archie Mayo (United Artists)
1941 Man Hunt
Fritz Lang (20th Century Fox)
1944 The Woman in the Window
Fritz Lang (RKO)
1946 Scarlet Street
Fritz Lang (Universal)
1947 The Macomber Affair
Zoltan Korda (United Artists)
1947 The Woman on the Beach
Jean Renoir (RKO)
1948 Secret Beyond the Door
Fritz Lang (Universal)
1949 The Reckless Moment
Max Ophuls (Columbia)
1950 Father of the Bride
Vincente Minnelli (MGM)

JACK BENNY

Jack Benny was one of the major Hollywood comedy stars of the late '30s and early '40s, though he is now known less for his films than for his radio and TV shows. This is a pity: not only was he a highly enjoyable movie comic, often opposite radio colleagues, like Fred Allen, George Burns ≫ and Gracie Allen ≫, he also starred in the greatest of all American black comedies, **To Be or Not To Be.**

*Below: Jack Benny's greatest film role was the actor-manager of Ernst Lubitsch's acid-edged comedy **To Be Or Not To Be**. Here he is in his Hamlet costume.*

This acid-etched satire on Nazi domination featured Benny as the head of an acting troupe in Poland at the time of the German invasion; Carole Lombard ≫, in her last film, is the wife who continually causes him to dry up during his "To be or not to be" speech.

Benny's persona as "the meanest man in the world" was developed as much on the radio as in movies, but films actually came first. Born Benjamin Kubelsky in Waukegan, Illinois, on February 14, 1894, he began in vaudeville (already kidding his own violin playing) and was signed by MGM in 1929. His first film was **The Hollywood Revue of 1929** (in a sketch only), followed up by the part of stage manager in **Chasing Rainbows** (1930), with Bessie Love ≫. His real reputation developed in radio, however, from 1932 on, with wife Mary Livingstone (whom he married in 1927), Eddie "Rochester" Anderson and a host of others who became a part of American folklore. He was cowardly, miserly, boastful, a never-aging 39, driving an old Maxwell and playing a mean violin. He expected to be attacked about all these faults and was continually hurt and reproach-

ful. Paramount took this image and used it astutely (often utilising Benny's radio colleagues) from 1936 to 1940, with good directors like Mitchell Leisen and Raoul Walsh. Benny's best films, however, came in the '40s beginning with an excellent version of **Charley's Aunt** (as a slightly over-aged undergraduate), the masterpiece **To Be or Not To Be,** and the very funny stage-derived **George Washington Slept Here,** with Ann Sheridan ≫. **The Meanest Man in the World** (1943) guyed his own image, and he ended his movie star career in the fantasy **The Horn Blows at Midnight** (not at all bad, despite his own jokes about it). He later appeared in small parts in films, but concentrated on his hugely successful television series **The Jack Benny Show.** His last film was the 1967 **A Guide for the Married Man.** He died in 1974.

BEST FILMS:
1936 The Big Broadcast of 1937
Mitchell Leisen (Paramount)
1937 College Holiday
Frank Tuttle (Paramount)
1937 Artists and Models
Raoul Walsh (Paramount)
1938 Artists and Models Abroad
Mitchell Leisen (Paramount)
1940 Buck Benny Rides Again
Mark Sandrich (Paramount)
1940 Love Thy Neighbour
Mark Sandrich (Paramount)
1941 Charley's Aunt
Archie Mayor (20th Century Fox)
1942 To Be or Not To Be
Ernst Lubitsch (United Artists)
1942 George Washington Slept Here
William Keighley (Warner Brothers)
1945 The Horn Blows at Midnight
Raoul Walsh (Warner Brothers)

INGRID BERGMAN

Ingrid Bergman has been a movie star for more than 40 years and her popularity remains amazingly strong. Born in Stockholm on August 29, 1915, she made her first film in 1934 (**Munkbrogreven**), became a major Swedish star in 1936 (in Gustav Molander's **Intermezzo**), and a major American star in 1939 (in Gregory Ratoff's re-make, **Intermezzo: A Love Story**). She won her first Academy Award for her acting ability in 1944 (for **Gaslight**), became the top woman box-office star in America in 1946, won a second Oscar in 1956 (for **Anastasia**) and a third in 1974 (as Supporting Actress in **Murder on the Orient Express**). She has starred in some of the most popular films made in Hollywood (**Casablanca, The Bells of St Mary's**) and worked with four of the greatest masters of the cinema, Alfred Hitchcock (three films), Roberto Rossellini (six films), Jean Renoir and Ingmar Bergman. She took over from Greta Garbo ≫ as the world's leading Swedish film actress, and has shown herself intelligent and candid off screen.

Yet despite her undoubted greatness, one is a little disappointed by Bergman's persona.

*Above: Ingrid Bergman as she looked in her Academy Award-winning performance in the 1974 **Murder On the Orient Express**. Left: Ingrid Bergman as Joan in the $5 million 1948 **Joan of Arc**. She exactly suited the role of Joan as a beautiful victim.*

Unlike other major female stars (Garbo, Dietrich ❯, Davis ❯, Crawford ❯ and Hepburn ❯, with whom she can be compared as a dramatic actress, she has created a screen personality of remarkable colourlessness. Her early image was that of a natural, forthright, healthy and sexy girl, without make-up or sophistication; she quickly became a suffering child of nature, a beautiful victim doomed to various kinds of unhappiness, as was evident in **Casablanca** (twice forced to part from Bogart ❯ for duty's sake), **Gaslight** (husband Charles Boyer ❯ tried to drive her crazy), and **For Whom the Bell Tolls** (doomed love with Gary Cooper ❯)—she has appeared on screen primarily in a woman-in-distress role. This was her forte, as she knew (she played Joan of Arc three times, in movies and on stage) and as Rossellini realised when he used her magnificently in his '50s movies; these films, although never widely popular, have been among the most influential in the development of the modern cinema—**Viaggio in Italia,** for example, in which Bergman portrays an overwrought woman whose marriage with George Sanders ❯ is on the point of breaking up, is considered the beginning of a new genre by the younger Italian and French filmmakers and was a decisive influence on the French New Wave. Her martyr-woman was evident in all these films, from the first, **Stromboli** (a war refugee trying to escape from her marriage-prison on a volcanic island), to the last, **Joan of Arc at the Stake.**

Bergman's liaison with Rossellini made her a real-life victim, in an ironic twist that shows that not only is life like the movies, but that the screen characterisations of the stars are accurate reflections of their personalities. She had gone to Italy after seeing **Rome, Open City** and became Rossellini's lover (and later wife) while shooting **Stromboli;** when she candidly admitted to the world that she was to have Rossellini's baby while still married to another man, a ridiculous and vituperous scandal blew up that killed her American career. But Bergman weathered the storm well, made the brilliant, light and lyrical **Éléna et les Hommes** with Jean Renoir in 1956 after her marriage to Rossellini began to go wrong, and made a triumphal return to American movies in **Anastasia** in the same year. Her Oscar for portraying the pretender to the Russian royal family was as much a gesture of forgiveness as an acting award, but Bergman did not return to America in person until 1967.

Her later films have been mostly enjoyable, although not always exceptional; she made a good team with Cary Grant ❯ in Stanley Donen's **Indiscreet** and a likeable missionary in China in **The Inn of the Sixth Happiness.** Her finest Hollywood films, how-

Right: One of the greatest romantic partnerships in the history of the cinema, Humphrey Bogart and Ingrid Bergman in the 1942 **Casablanca.** *He portrays tough café owner Rick Blaine, she is his old love Ilsa Lund.*

ever, remain her pictures with Hitchcock in her early period: as a worried psychiatrist in **Spellbound** trying to cure Gregory Peck ❯, as a despairing secret agent helping Cary Grant in **Notorious,** and as the suffering wife of an ex-convict in Australia in **Under Capricorn.** She was remarkably good in her Oscar-winning performance as a dowdy Swedish missionary in **Murder on the Orient Express,** but one of her greatest-ever performances was in the 1978 Ingmar Bergman film **Autumn Sonata,** portraying a concert pianist reunited with daughter Liv Ullmann ❯ in scenes of terrible intensity.

BEST FILMS:
1942 Casablanca
Michael Curtiz (Warner Brothers)
1944 Gaslight
George Cukor (MGM)
1945 Spellbound
Alfred Hitchcock (Selznick)
1946 Notorious
Alfred Hitchcock (Selznick)
1949 Under Capricorn
Alfred Hitchcock (Warner Brothers)
1950 Stromboli
Roberto Rossellini (RKO)
1952 Europa 51
Roberto Rossellini (Ponti and De Laurentiis)
1953 Viaggio in Italia
Robert Rossellini (Sveva-Junior-Italia-film)
1956 Éléna et les Hommes
Jean Renoir (Franco-London Films)
1957 Anastasia
Anatole Litvak (20th Century Fox)
1974 Murder on the Orient Express
Sidney Lumet (EMI)
1978 Autumn Sonata
Ingmar Bergman (ITC)

JOAN BLONDELL

The apotheosis of the wise-cracking broad, the breezy blonde, the predatory gold-digger, Joan Blondell never gave a bad performance and her gum-chewing roles put snap into many of the most enjoyable Warner Brothers films of the '30s. She may never have been a major star (she once said; "My can got me into pictures."), although she eventually got star billing, but she remains one of the most memorable actresses of the period. Whether she was dancing with a pair of long-johns in **Dames,** singing about her *Forgotten Man* in **Gold Diggers of 1933,** or exchanging wisecracks with James Cagney ❯ in many films, she was never less than wonderful. She was probably the only Warner's actress who could really stand up to Cagney, with whom she played

her first lead in 1931 in **Blonde Crazy;** they had actually come to Hollywood together when Warner's bought the play in which they were starring and invited them West.

Joan was born with the poetic name of Rosebud Blondell in New York City on August 13, 1909. Her parents were in vaudeville and she was in showbiz from childhood, as is instantly apparent in the worldly-wise screen persona she developed at Warner's. She made a record 32 films in 27 months for the studio in her first years and actually shot 54 pictures in the '30s, mostly for Warner's. Delightful as her image was (even Leslie

Below: Joan Blondell was such a likeable, wise-cracking, happy dame that she gave gold-diggers a good reputation in her many films, and even brought James Cagney to a standstill.

Howard ❯ asked to borrow her for a film), it was not the kind of characterisation around which a studio could build a major star; she was superb in everything she did, but she won no awards and not much prestige—except from millions of admirers and from three husbands (George Barnes, Dick Powell ❯ and Mike Todd). She became a fine character actress in the '40s (notably as Aunt Cissy in **A Tree Grows in Brooklyn**), and has continued giving memorable performances up to the present day. She was outstanding as the card dealer to big-time gamblers Steve McQueen ❯ and Edward G. Robinson ❯ in the 1965 **Cincinnati Kid,** and devastating as the playwright and former actress in Cassavetes' 1978 **Opening Night** (she has never been in a film where she was more herself). As always, she stole the notices.

Above: A Belgian poster of the 1951 **The African Queen,** in which Humphrey Bogart was abrasively paired with Katharine Hepburn and won his first and only acting Academy Award.
Right: Humphrey Bogart in typical sardonic pose. He is possibly the greatest hero figure of the American cinema, still a cult figure today.

BEST FILMS:
1931 Blonde Crazy
Roy Del Ruth (Warner Brothers)
1932 The Crowd Roars
Howard Hawks (Warner Brothers)
1933 Gold Diggers of 1933
Mervyn Le Roy (Warner Brothers)
1933 Footlight Parade
Lloyd Bacon (Warner Brothers)
1934 Dames
Ray Enright (Warner Brothers)
1936 Stage Struck
Busby Berkeley (Warner Brothers)
1937 Stand-In
Tay Garnett (United Artists)
1945 A Tree Grows in Brooklyn
Elia Kazan (20th Century Fox)
1951 The Blue Veil
Curtis Bernhardt (RKO)
1978 Opening Night
John Cassavetes (Faces Pictures)

HUMPHREY BOGART

Humphrey DeForest Bogart became a star after 11 years of making movies, playing in everything from cowboy pictures to hillbilly comedies but mostly as the fourth-ranked gangster on the Warner Brothers lot (behind Robinson ❯, Cagney ❯ and Raft ❯. He was good in most of these '30s films, although not really memorable; then, suddenly, in the '40s, he became not merely a great film star but one of the legends of the cinema. This happened within the space of five years, under the guidance of four of America's greatest directors, Raoul Walsh, John Huston, Michael Curtiz and Howard Hawks. The transformation seems so simple that one wonders why it hadn't been tried before; basically all these directors did was to invert Bogart's cynical, tough gangster persona and make him the good guy, the hero. He became the epitome of the disillusioned anti-hero opposed to any form of authority, the embodiment of the modern hero envisioned in the novels of Dashiell Hammett, Ernest Hemingway and Raymond Chandler. He was the black knight, himself honest in a dishonest world, perfectly fitting Chandler's famous dictum: "Down these mean streets a man must go who is not himself mean, who is neither tarnished nor afraid."

The revamping of Bogart's screen image was begun by Walsh, who gave his gangster character some hard-boiled wisecracks in **The Roaring Twenties,** humanised him as a tough long-distance truck driver with a cynical sense of humour in **They Drive By Night,** and brought the new persona to life as the gangster with integrity who dominates **High Sierra.** Huston developed this new Bogart anti-hero as the disenchanted but perceptive private eye Sam Spade in his adaptation of Hammett's great novel **The Maltese Falcon,** and again as the cashiered army officer on the trail of a spy ring in **Across the Pacific** (working brilliantly with Sydney Greenstreet ❯ and Mary Astor ❯ in both pictures). Michael Curtiz, the cleverest of Hollywood craftsmen, took all the new and old Bogart characteristics and crystallised them brilliantly in the figure of Rick Blaine, the tough existential hero of **Casablanca.** The proprietor of Rick's Café is still part of the underworld (able, for example, to deal with crooked colleague Sydney Greenstreet on an equal basis) but underneath his cynical façade he is a man of romantic ideals and integrity who can give up the woman he loves (Ingrid Bergman ❯) because it is the right thing to do. The apotheosis of this new, incredibly effective Bogart image came under Howard Hawks, first as the Hemingway hero of **To Have and Have Not** and finally, in his greatest role, as Philip Marlowe in Chandler's **The Big Sleep.**

This has many claims to being the best American film—certainly it has never been surpassed—and Bogart is the centre of its greatness. His cynical but uncorrupted private-eye Marlowe has more humanity than Spade, less sentimentality than Rick, greater understanding of the imperfections of the world that surrounds him than earlier Bogart screen manifestations, and full awareness of the limitations on his power to change the situation. Bogart had become the greatest hero figure of the '40s American cinema, a sardonic man of honour who could take on the system as an individual and not be cowed by it, a legend in his own lifetime.

His physical characteristics were hardly those of the conventional hero. He was ugly-handsome with a permanent squint, a peculiar lisping voice and rather ill-fitting clothes. His usual facial expression on screen was one of cynical disbelief and he rarely smiled except in contempt. He treated women with distant courtesy but did not trust them, and he rarely let his real feelings show. We are surprised at the end of **The Maltese Falcon** when he turns the woman he loves over to the police (because she's a murderer), and we are surprised at the end of **Casablanca** when he sends the woman he loves off with another man (because he cannot accept her self-sacrifice).

Bogart was born in New York City on December 25, 1899, into a wealthy family. He began acting on stage in 1920. He made his first film, **Broadway's Like That** (a short), in 1930, and his feature début the same year for Fox in **A Devil with Women.** He appeared in pictures with Bette Davis ➤ (**Bad Sister**), Spencer Tracy ➤ (**Up the River**) and Joan Blondell ➤ (**Big City Blues**), but his career did not develop until after he returned to the stage to portray the gangster, Duke Mantee, in Robert E. Sherwood's play **The Petrified Forest.** Leslie Howard ➤, the star of the play, persuaded Warner Brothers to feature Bogart and himself in the film version in the same roles, in 1936, and Bogart's tough gangster personality stuck with him for his next 30 pictures. The best of his performances in these early films came in William Wyler's **Dead End,** Michael Curtiz's **Angels with Dirty Faces** and Lloyd Bacon's **Invisible Stripes.** His great '40s films led to a wider variation in the kind of role he was asked to play—but he was always Bogart and never lost that identity in his later characterisations. Huston used him brilliantly in four films after **The Maltese Falcon.** The chemistry with Lauren Bacall ➤ (who had become his fourth wife after appearing with him in her début film, **To Have and Have Not**) was again apparent in **Key Largo,** a slightly dated adaptation of Maxwell Anderson's play with Edward G. Robinson as a gangster holding them both prisoner, a neat reversal of Bogart's position in **The Petrified Forest.** In **The African Queen,** a different kind of chemical reaction emerged when he was abrasively paired with missionary Katharine Hepburn ➤; his performance won him an Academy Award. Finally, Huston delightfully parodied the Bogart-type murder mystery-adventure in **Beat the Devil.** Bogart was the good guy in these three pictures but Huston also used him superbly in a villainous role—the gold-hungry prospector of **The Treasure**

of the Sierra Madre.

Other directors used Bogart rather differently. Nicholas Ray cast him as a defence attorney in **Knock on Any Door,** and then showed some of the bitterness beneath the toughness when Bogart portrayed a Hollywood screenwriter in **In a Lonely Place.** Billy Wilder slightly miscast him as an older man fighting William Holden ➤ for Audrey Hepburn ➤ in **Sabrina** (a part originally meant for Cary Grant ➤), but he was still superb. He made a terrific impact in 1954 as the neurotic Captain Queeg in **The Caine Mutiny,** especially in his crack-up in the court-martial sequence, unforgettably rolling steel ball-bearings in his hand. He was also excellent as the film director in Joseph Mankiewicz's **The Barefoot Contessa,** cynically promoting Ava Gardner's ➤ movie career. His last film was the fairly good **The Harder They Fall** in 1956. He died on January 14, 1957.

BEST FILMS:
1941 High Sierra
Raoul Walsh (Warner Brothers)
1941 The Maltese Falcon
John Huston (Warner Brothers)
1942 Casablanca
Michael Curtiz (Warner Brothers)
1944 To Have and Have Not
Howard Hawks (Warner Brothers)
1946 The Big Sleep
Howard Hawks (Warner Brothers)
1948 The Treasure of the Sierra Madre
John Huston (Warner Brothers)
1950 In a Lonely Place
Nicholas Ray (Columbia)
1951 The African Queen
John Huston (United Artists)
1954 Beat the Devil
John Huston (United Artists)
1954 The Caine Mutiny
Edward Dmytryk (Columbia)
1954 Sabrina
Billy Wilder (Paramount)
1954 The Barefoot Contessa
Joseph Mankiewicz (United Artists)

Above: Ernest Borgnine (right) won an Academy Award in **Marty** for expressive inarticulateness.

ERNEST BORGNINE

Ernest Borgnine tried to convince movie audiences that he was a nice guy in **Marty,** even to the extent of marrying fellow dog Betsy Blair, but those who have seen his films before and after that Oscar-winning performance can't be deceived; they know how basically nasty he really is. It is Borgnine who beats Frank Sinatra ➤ to death in **From Here to Eternity,** stabs Royal Dano in the back in **Johnny Guitar,** and throws hoboes off trains as the vicious guard of **Emperor of the North Pole.** Admittedly he did a fine job in **Marty** and deserved his Oscar, but that toad-like face and bulging eyes are really more suitable for the villains he usually portrays. He has worked regularly with violent action directors Robert Aldrich (**The Dirty Dozen, The Legend of Lylah Clare, The Flight of the Phoenix, Emperor of the North Pole, Hustle**) and Sam Peckinpah (**Convoy**), and this is probably an indication of where his real interest lies. He was pretty nasty as the belligerent policeman disagreeing with Gene Hackman ➤ in **The Poseidon Adventure,** and in **The Dirty Dozen** he's the mean general who sends the convicts off on their mission. In **Bad Day at Black Rock** he pours ketchup all over one-armed Spencer Tracy's ➤ dinner, and he was even meaner in **The Vikings** and **The Badlanders.**

Born in Hamden, Connecticut, on January 24, 1917, as Ermes Effron Borgnine, he worked as a truck driver and then was a fitter's mate during World War II

before beginning to act on stage and in television. He made his film début in the 1951 **China Corsair,** but didn't really establish himself as a screen heavy until his sweating, hateful performance as the sadistic sergeant Fatso Judson of **From Here to Eternity.** After **Marty,** he had more sympathetic roles for a time, notably in **Jubal, The Catered Affair** and **The Best Things in Life Are Free,** but soon slipped back into the villainy that was his screen destiny. His career has continued successfully into the '70s, as good villains are always in demand, and he was memorably nasty as a cop in **Convoy.** He also had a big success on TV in the '60s with his series *McHale's Navy.*

Above: Charles Boyer was loved by most of the movie glamour ladies during his long career. Here it is Margaret Sullavan willing to give up everything and sacrifice her whole life for Boyer in the 1941 version of Fannie Hurst's novel Back Street.

Left: Charles Boyer as he looked towards the end of his career portraying Charles Monod in the all-star Is Paris Burning? made in France in 1965.

BEST FILMS:
1953 From Here to Eternity
Fred Zinnemann (Columbia)
1954 Bad Day at Black Rock
John Sturges (MGM)
1955 Marty
Delbert Mann (United Artists)
1958 The Badlanders
Delmer Daves (MGM)
1966 The Dirty Dozen
Robert Aldrich (MGM)
1968 The Legend of Lylah Clare
Robert Aldrich (MGM)
1969 The Wild Bunch
Sam Peckinpah (Warner Brothers)
1972 The Poseidon Adventure
Ronald Neame (20th Century Fox)
1973 Emperor of the North Pole
Robert Aldrich (20th Century Fox)
1978 Convoy
Sam Peckinpah (EMI-United Artists)

CHARLES BOYER

Charles Boyer was easily the greatest lover in the history of the cinema, as well as being one of the most imitated. He didn't actually say "Come wiz me to the Casbah" to Hedy Lamarr ❯ in **Algiers,** but he did star opposite more glamour stars than any one man has the right to do. What is more incredible is that he was still doing it more than 50 years after his cinema début. Among the more memorable screen partners of the man who created the cliché of the "French lover" were Greta Garbo ❯ (who loved him as Napoleon in **Conquest**), Danielle Darrieux ❯ (who adored him as Prince Rudolph in **Mayerling**), Irene Dunne ❯ (who got run over by a car because she was so eager to see him in **Love Affair**), Ingrid Bergman ❯ (whom he tried to get rid of in **Gaslight**), Marlene Dietrich ❯ (who loved him in the middle of the desert in **The Garden of Allah**), Lauren Bacall ❯ (who was fascinated by his shabby intellect in **The Confidential Agent**), and Jennifer Jones ❯ (who loved him as a Czech refugee in **Cluny Brown**). The list is almost endless, down to such recent films as **Fanny** (with Leslie Caron ❯, 1960) and **Stavisky** (with a bevy of young French ladies 1974). He was a fine actor as well, with five Academy Award nominations, including one for **Stavisky.**

Boyer was born in Figeac, France, on August 28, 1899, and made his first film, Marcel L'Herbier's **L'Homme du Large,** in 1920. He was soon a star of both theatre and cinema, notably in Alberto Cavalcanti's 1927 **Le Capitaine Fracasse.** His first English-language film in America was the 1931 **The Magnificent Lie** (with Ruth Chatterton), and he starred opposite Claudette Colbert ❯ in **The Man from Yesterday** in the following year. He was with Annabella ❯ in **The Battle,** Loretta Young ❯ in **Caravan** and Katharine Hepburn ❯ in **Break of Hearts,** but it was his teaming with Darrieux in **Mayerling** that made him internationally famous as *the* great lover. He was more than just that, of course, as he proved in such delightful comedies as **Tovarich** (with Colbert) and **History is Made at Night** (with Jean Arthur ❯).

Boyer's longevity was truly astonishing; he remained a convincing lover (though sometimes in character parts) all through the '50s and '60s. He was at his best in **Madame de . . .** (with Darrieux once again), and still persuasive opposite Brigitte Bardot ❯ in **Une Parisienne,** Sophia Loren ❯ in **La Fortuna di essere Donna,** Martine Carol ❯ in **Nana,** Michèle Morgan ❯ in **Maxime** and a host of others. Off-screen Boyer was happily married to the same woman,

English actress Patricia Paterson, for 44 years, despite the most awe-inspiring competition any wife ever had to face. She died of cancer in August 1978, and the grief-stricken Boyer killed himself two days later.

BEST FILMS:
1936 Mayerling
Anatole Litvak (in France)
1937 Conquest (Marie Walewska)
Clarence Brown (MGM)
1937 History is Made at Night
Frank Borzage (United Artists)
1938 Algiers
John Cromwell (United Artists)
1939 Love Affair
Leo McCarey (RKO)
1944 Gaslight
George Cukor (MGM)
1945 The Confidential Agent
Herman Shumlin (Warner Brothers)
1946 Cluny Brown
Ernst Lubitsch (20th Century Fox)
1953 Madame de . . .
Max Ophuls (in France)
1960 Fanny
Joshua Logan (Warner Brothers)
1974 Stavisky
Alain Resnais (Cerito-Ariane)

MARLON BRANDO

see **Modern Stars**

WALTER BRENNAN

Walter Brennan played cantankerous old men in so many classic Westerns that he has become as identified with the genre as major stars like John Wayne ❯. Brennan was the king of character actors, the star of supporting stars. He was the only man to win the Best Supporting Actor Oscar three times (and in fact the only three-time winner until Katharine Hepburn ❯ caught up with him in 1968). He worked in an amazing number of good films, but will be best remembered for his outstanding contributions to Hawks and Ford Westerns. He was born on July 25, 1894, in Swampscott, Massachusetts, served in World War I as a private, and went into movies in 1923 as a stuntman. He had his first important character role as "Old Atrocity" in Hawks' **Barbary Coast.** His greatest role was probably that of Stumpy, the cranky old man with a shotgun guarding the jail for John Wayne in **Rio Bravo,** but he was also outstanding as Old Man Clanton opposing Wyatt Earp (Henry Fonda ❯) in **My Darling Clementine.** Hawks used him again as the pastor in **Sergeant York** in 1941, and as Eddie the rummy, Bogart's ❯ friend in **To Have and Have Not.** His petulant old-timer role began as Groot in Hawks' **Red River** and was followed by marvellous performances in

many great Westerns, including Sturges' **Bad Day at Black Rock,** Mann's **The Far Country** and Walsh's **Along the Great Divide.** And these are only some of the films he didn't win Academy Awards for. The prizes came for the 1936 **Come and Get It** (in the lumberjack trade), the 1938 **Kentucky** (he was now into horse-racing) and the 1940 **The Westerner** (getting closer to his great cranky persona in portraying Judge Roy Bean). Brennan played toothless old men for most of his career, following an accident in 1932 when he lost his teeth.

He stayed a top character star until his death in 1974, working in TV as well as in the cinema.

BEST FILMS:
1935 Barbary Coast
Howard Hawks (United Artists)
1936 Come and Get It
William Wyler and Howard Hawks (United Artists)
1938 Kentucky
David Butler (20th Century Fox)
1940 The Westerner
William Wyler (United Artists)
1941 Sergeant York
Howard Hawks (Warner Brothers)
1944 To Have and Have Not
Howard Hawks (Warner Brothers)
1946 My Darling Clementine
John Ford (20th Century Fox)
1948 Red River
Howard Hawks (United Artists)
1955 The Far Country
Anthony Mann (Universal)
1959 Rio Bravo
Howard Hawks (Warner Brothers)

*Below: Three-times-Oscar winning Walter Brennan usually portrayed old-timers. In the 1969 **Support Your Local Sheriff** he co-starred with James Garner.*

CLIVE BROOK

The suave, handsome leading man of both British and American cinema who is best remembered as the first gentleman gangster (Rolls Royce, the melancholic intellectual in Josef von Sternberg's 1928 **Underworld**) and as Marlene Dietrich's ❯ most gentlemanly screen partner (Captain Harvey in von Sternberg's 1932 **Shanghai Express**). He was usually the perfect upper-class gentleman in his films, but he could use that screen image superbly in various ways, most notably as an Edwardian duke involved with an American heiress (Beatrice Lillie) in the sparkling 1945 comedy **On Approval**. He was the very symbol of British upper-class values in the film of Noël Coward's ❯ play **Cavalcade**, fitted perfectly into the first version of **The Four Feathers** in 1929, and played Sherlock Holmes on two occasions (**The Return of Sherlock Holmes** in 1929 and **Sherlock Holmes** in 1932). He began and ended his acting career in the theatre, but from 1920 to 1945 he devoted himself almost wholly to films.

Born Clifford Brook on June 1, 1891, in London he made his first stage appearance in 1918 after service in World War I. His first film was the 1920 version of **Trent's Last Case**, directed by Richard Garrick, and he then starred in a number of films directed by Maurice Elvey and Graham Cutts. His 1923 weepie **Woman to Woman** (British officer returns as amnesiac, child by French dancer, etc) was a formidable hit in both England and America (only to be expected, with Cutts directing, Alfred Hitchcock as writer and assistant director, and Michael Balcon and Victor Saville as producer). His American career began in 1924 with George Archainbaud's **Christine of the Hungry Heart**; he quickly became a major US star, playing opposite Clara Bow ❯ in **Hula** (as a gentlemanly engineer

in Hawaii) and winning the heart of Feathers (Evelyn Brent) from Bull Weed (George Bancroft) in the first gangster film, **Underworld.** Brook was at his suavest portraying Tallulah Bankhead's husband in George Cukor's **Tarnished Lady**, and then gave his great performance as the former lover of Shanghai Lily (Marlene Dietrich) in **Shanghai Express**, projecting great depth into his portrait of the most polished of army officers. Brook returned to England in the mid-'30s and made notable films for Victor Saville and Robert Stevenson, but his best work came at the beginning of the war in Penrose Tennyson's forgotten gem **Convoy** and Anthony Asquith's **Freedom Radio**. His film career virtually ended in 1945, when he returned to the theatre after directing himself and Bea Lillie in the matchless **On Approval**. He made one enjoyable comeback, joining many other stars in John Huston's entertaining **The List of Adrian Messenger** in 1963. He died in 1974.

BEST FILMS:
1927 Hula
Victor Fleming (Paramount)
1928 Underworld
Josef von Sternberg (Paramount)
1929 The Four Feathers
Ernest Schoedsack, Merian Cooper and Lothar Mendes (Paramount)
1931 Tarnished Lady
George Cukor (Paramount)
1932 Shanghai Express
Josef von Sternberg (Paramount)
1932 Sherlock Holmes
William K. Howard (Fox)
1933 Cavalcade
Frank Lloyd (Fox)
1941 Convoy
Penrose Tennyson (Ealing)
1945 On Approval
Clive Brook (GFD)
1963 The List of Adrian Messenger
John Huston (Universal-International)

*Below: London-born Clive Brook in his outstanding film role as Marlene Dietrich's army-officer ex-lover in **Shanghai Express** (1932), directed by Josef von Sternberg.*

JACK BUCHANAN

Jack Buchanan was the debonair king of the British musical in the 1930s (when Jessie Matthews ❯ was the queen), but he was also the star of two of the greatest American musicals, Ernst Lubitsch's 1930 **Monte Carlo** and Vincente Minnelli's 1953 **The Band Wagon**. He was the personification of the Mayfair man-about-town, always immaculately dressed (usually in white tie and tails), delightfully teasing his leading ladies, and bringing bright and brittle good humour to Britain during the Depression. He wasn't as good a dancer as his American counterpart Fred Astaire ❯, but he was highly entertaining, with long, dangling legs and a pleasantly catarrhal voice.

"Johnny B," as he was often called, was born near Glasgow on April 12, 1891, and made his stage début in 1912. He starred in a number of silent films, beginning with **Auld Lang Syne** in 1917, but it wasn't until the coming of sound that his screen personality made an impact. After success on Broadway as a song-and-dance man, he went to Hollywood in 1929 to film **Paris** and **The Show of Shows**. Lubitsch then teamed him with Jeanette MacDonald ❯ in the captivating **Monte Carlo**, one of the most innovatory of musicals with its famous *Beyond the Blue Horizon* train sequence and delightful dialogue. He returned to Britain to make **Man of**

*Above: Jack Buchanan was bright, brittle and debonair in his delightful 1930s British musicals, the public's favourite Man-about-Mayfair. Here he is seen in the 1935 **Brewster's Millions** with Lili Damita.*

Mayfair and other popular musicals, many directed by Herbert Wilcox. His favourite partner in these light-hearted films was Elsie Randolph (**Yes Mr Brown, That's A Good Girl, This'll Make You Whistle**), but he also joined forces with American star Fay Wray ❯ in **When Knights Were Bold**. He co-starred with Maurice Chevalier in René Clair's **Break the News** (they both play song-and-dance men) and was enjoyable in non-musicals like **Smash and Grab** and **The Gang's All Here**. The war put an end to his supposedly frivolous kind of film but he made an outstanding comeback in 1953 as the hilarious producer in Minnelli's **The Band Wagon,** with Fred Astaire and Nanette Fabray. He proved an able dancing partner for Astaire in their white-tie-and-tails soft-shoe duet *I Guess I'll Have to Change My Plan* and the wonderful *Triplets* number. He made only two more films, however, before his death in 1957, the last being Preston Sturges's **Les Carnets de Major Thompson**, made in France.

BEST FILMS:
1930 Monte Carlo
Ernst Lubitsch (Paramount)
1933 Yes Mr Brown
Herbert Wilcox (British & Dominion)

BUGS BUNNY

Bugs Bunny is possibly the greatest cartoon star of them all, and is certainly unmatched in continuing inventiveness and characterisation over his 25-year career. He won an Academy Award in 1958 for **Knighty Knight**

Above: Bugs Bunny, most popular cartoon star from 1945 to 1960, plus his favourite food.

Bugs (directed by Friz Freleng), but every one of his films was a joy and the best are among the masterpieces of world animation. He was a sassy, wisecracking Brooklyn tough-guy, the perfect cartoon counterpart at his studio, Warner Brothers, for their live-action toughies Bogart ❯ and Cagney ❯. His catchphrase "What's up, Doc?" has become a part of movie mythology and was used by Peter Bogdanovich as the title of his 1972 feature homage to the good old days.

Bugs is primarily associated with animation genius Chuck Jones, who made many of his best films, but he was actually a

studio product; his superb voice was the creation of Mel Blanc, and many great animation masters contributed to his career. He was initially the brainchild of Bob Clampett, who did the original design for the character. His first film was the 1938 **Porky's Hare Hunt**, made by Cal Dalton and Ben "Bugs" Hardaway, who gave him his gangster monicker. Chuck Jones directed his first Bugs film in 1940 (**Elmer's Candid Camera**), but it was that other animation genius, Tex Avery, who first gave Bugs his lasting lunatic characterisation in the 1940 **A Wild Hare** (the first film in which he says "What's Up, Doc?"). Avery did three more splendid Bugs films (**Tortoise Beats Hare, The Heckling Hare** and **All This and Rabbit Stew**) before leaving the studio. Robert Clampett, Friz Freleng and Robert McKimson created superb films with the character, but it was Jones who did more for him than anyone else, with assistance from writer Michael Maltese and designer Maurice Noble. The greatest Bugs film, and one of the masterworks of animation, was the 1957 **What's Opera, Doc?** Jones thought of Bugs as a combination of Groucho and Harpo Marx ❯, zany, unpredictable but always a winner in every situation. His usual opponent was Elmer Fudd, who even became the giant in **Beanstalk Bunny**, but he was also brilliantly teamed with Daffy Duck in three films, **Rabbit Fire, Rabbit Seasoning** and **Duck! Rabbit! Duck!**. Bugs retired from the screen in 1963 after starring in 159 films.

BEST FILMS:
1940 A Wild Hare
Tex Avery (Warner Brothers)
1941 The Heckling Hare
Tex Avery (Warner Brothers)
1943 Corny Concerto
Robert Clampett (Warner Brothers)
1944 Gorilla My Dreams
Robert McKimson (Warner Brothers)
1945 Stage Door Cartoon
Friz Freleng (Warner Brothers)
1949 Rabbit of Seville
Chuck Jones (Warner Brothers)

1951 Rabbit Fire
Chuck Jones (Warner Brothers)
1955 Beanstalk Bunny
Chuck Jones (Warner Brothers)
1957 What's Opera, Doc?
Chuck Jones (Warner Brothers)
1958 Knighty Knight Bugs
Friz Freleng (Warner Brothers)

GEORGE BURNS AND GRACIE ALLEN

George Burns and Gracie Allen were among the funniest people on the screen in the 1930s and their performances stand up uproariously well today. It is a great shame that Hollywood did not use them after the '30s (they are better know now as radio and TV stars than as movie comedians), for what they did was outstanding and will last. It was ironic that official recognition did not come until 1975, when Burns won the Best Supporting Actor Academy Award for his marvellous performance as an aged vaudeville star in **The Sunshine Boys.** He was outstanding, but no more so than he had been back in his heyday. Light, "frivolous" entertainment rarely gets its due from the serious critics, but Burns' and Allen's contribution to the cinema will be re-assessed in the years to come. Their screen personalities (as on radio and TV) were of a cigar-smoking, quiet man with the patience of Job, putting up with and actually loving a scatter-brained, feather-headed and foolish woman with a wonderful gift for malapropism. Off-screen, Burns was considered one of the wittiest people in show business, while Gracie was the quiet one.

Burns was born as Nathan Birnbaum on January 20, 1896, in New York; Allen was christened Grace Ethel Cecile Rosalie Allen on July 26, 1902, in San Francisco. They got together somewhere between the coasts in 1926, married, and became vaudeville and radio stars. Their first film was

Above left: The 1933 **College Humor** *helped to make Burns & Allen popular with American film audiences. They played eccentric caterers. Above: George Burns and Gracie Allen began their movie careers in* **The Big Broadcast** *(1932).*

The Big Broadcast (1932), also starring Bing Crosby ❯, with Burns as the owner of a radio station, and it was such a success that two sequels were made. They appeared in a series of delightful films (mostly at Paramount) with major stars including W. C. Fields ❯ (in the early TV-orientated **International House** and the zany **Six of a Kind**), Crosby again with Carole Lombard ❯ (**We're Not Dressing**), Jack Benny ❯ (**College Holiday**), Eleanor Powell ❯ and Red Skelton (**Honolulu**) and did some singing and dancing with Fred Astaire ❯ and Joan Fontaine ❯ in **A Damsel in Distress**. Gracie was in two films alone, playing herself (**The Gracie Allen Murder Case** and **Mr and Mrs North**), both murder mysteries, but their movie career ended in the early '40s. Gracie died in 1964 and Burns returned to the cinema ten years later, proving more than a match for the accomplished Walter Matthau ❯ in **The Sunshine Boys**. It was an extraordinary comeback for an 80-year-old star, who suddenly became a hot Hollywood property again; he was a box-office smash playing God to John Denver in **Oh, God!**, and a delight as the mayor in **Sergeant Pepper's Lonely Hearts Club Band.**

RICHARD BURTON

see **Modern Stars**

JAMES CAGNEY

The greatest gangster of the cinema and one of its most original stars, James Cagney's staccato delivery of dialogue sounded like a machine gun even in musical comedy. His cardinal rule for acting was "Never relax!" The persona he created at Warner Brothers in the 1930s is well-known and often mimicked, but it was actually a highly complex characterisation. He was always the tough guy, even in light-hearted efforts like **Footlight Parade**, but his was a believable toughness with layers of nervousness under the dapper, bouncing and often smug exterior. He always seemed to be on the balls of his feet, ready for something to happen, warily observant but eager for action. He never did relax—and nor could the audience.

Although he claimed to act only for money, he was actually a consummate professional whose grace of movement and delivery is equal to any "serious" actor.

Cagney was born in the lower East Side of New York City on July 17, 1904, and began his show business career as a dancer—in drag. He married in 1922 (they're still together) and toured with his wife before starring with Joan Blondell ❯ in Broadway productions that brought him to Hollywood. His first film was the 1930 **Sinner's Holiday**, based on his Broadway play **Penny Arcade**, but it was the 1931 **Public Enemy** that made him a star. He was a fast-talking gangster who ends up dead on his mother's doorstep—but not before a famous breakfast scene in which he shoves half a grapefruit in Mae Clarke's face. It was this film that formed the Cagney tough guy image; he later grew to resent it but was unable to

change it, no matter how good he was in other roles. To the general public, nobody was better at being bad, ill-treating women, machine-gunning speakeasies or breaking out of jail, but he played all kinds of roles, from a fast-talking theatre producer in **Footlight Parade** (in which he danced and sang *Shanghai Lil*), to Bottom

*Above: The contemporary poster for **Public Enemy** in 1931 with both James Cagney and Jean Harlow billed below the title, as they weren't yet major stars. Below: James Cagney became a major star for his tough, fast-talking performance as a gangster in **Public Enemy**; here he is "persuading" a victim.*

in Max Reinhardt's elaborate production of **A Midsummer Night's Dream**, to a prison governor in **Mayor of Hell**. One of his most popular roles was that of a gangster in **Angels With Dirty Faces** opposite Pat O'Brien; he teamed with fellow gangsters George Raft ❯ (in **Each Dawn I Die**), Humphrey Bogart ❯ (**Angels with Dirty Faces**), and Edward G. Robinson ❯ (**Smart Money**), and made the last important gangster film of the '30s with Bogart (**The Roaring Twenties**).Two of his best '30 films were with Howard Hawks, as a cocky racing driver in **The Crowd Roars** (1932) and as a commercial airline pilot and ladies' man in **Ceiling Zero** (1936). He co-starred in this with Pat O'Brien, his partner in many Warner films. By this time he had become one of the top ten American box-office attractions and more or less had his choice of roles. In 1941 he received the second highest salary in the USA, only slightly less than that of MGM mogul Louis B. Mayer.

Cagney's acting ability finally received its due when he made **Yankee Doodle Dandy** in 1942 and won the Best Actor Oscar and the New York critics' acting award. This jingoistic biopic about patriotic songwriter George M. Cohan allowed full range to Cagney's dynamic tap-dancing energy; his personality kept the sentiment from becoming too cloying. His next great film was a return to gangsterism in the 1949 **White Heat,** when Raoul Walsh gave him one of his most famous scenes—screaming "Top of the world, Ma!" as he blows himself up by emptying his gun into the huge gas container on which he is standing. His '50s films were still pretty good, especially **Love me or Leave Me,** in which he plays the

racketeer boyfriend of Doris Day ➤, the Gimp to her songstress Ruth Etting. He was very good as the eccentric captain of a World War II cargo ship in **Mr Roberts**, and absolutely brilliant in a brief tap-dancing-on-the-table appearance as George M. Cohan in **The Seven Little Foys**. He did a good job impersonating Lon Chaney, Snr ➤, in **The Man of a Thousand Faces**, directed a re-make of **This Gun for Hire** titled **Short Cut to Hell**, and ended his film career in a blaze of glory in 1961 in Billy Wilder's **One, Two, Three**, as a fast-talking Coca Cola executive in West Berlin. Now a little more stocky but still not relaxed, he breeds horses and cattle on a 500-acre farm near Stanfordville, New York, and tap-dances every morning to keep in shape.

BEST FILMS:
1931 Public Enemy
William Wellman (Warner Brothers)
1932 The Crowd Roars
Howard Hawks (Warner Brothers)
1933 Footlight Parade
Lloyd Bacon (Warner Brothers)
1935 G-Men
William Keighley (Warner Brothers)
1936 Ceiling Zero
Howard Hawks (Warner Brothers)
1938 Angels With Dirty Faces
Michael Curtiz (Warner Brothers)
1939 The Roaring Twenties
Raoul Walsh (Warner Brothers)
1942 Yankee Doodle Dandy
Michael Curtiz (Warner Brothers)
1949 White Heat
Raoul Walsh (Warner Brothers)
1955 Love Me or Leave Me
Charles Vidor (MGM)
1961, One, Two, Three
Billy Wilder (United Artists)

Eddie Cantor

Eddie Cantor's popping "banjo eyes" were almost as well known to cinema audiences in the '30s as Crosby's ➤ voice and Astaire's ➤ feet. He was one of the few radio stars to become known in movies first; in fact, his career had begun in the silent cinema, starring opposite Clara Bow ➤ in the 1926 **Kid Boots**, adapted from his Ziegfeld stage success. But Cantor was best known for his songs (like *Ida, Sweet as Apple Cider,* written for Ida Tobias whom he married in 1915, and *If You Knew Susie*) and his enthusiastic, fast-talking way of telling old vaudeville jokes (often about Ida and their five daughters) — so it was not until sound cinema that he became a major star. His lavish musicals were mostly made for Sam Goldwyn and featured bevies of beautiful Goldwyn girls, not to mention such talents as cameraman Gregg Toland, who worked on four of his pictures, and choreographer Busby Berkeley. He also had top stars with him in these frothy but enjoyable romps, including Ethel Merman in **Strike Me Pink** (songs by Harold Arlen), Charlotte Greenwood and George

Above: Eddie Cantor was usually surrounded by beautiful girls in his films, even as late as the 1944 comedy **Show Business**.

Raft ➤ in **Palmy Days,** and Merman and Ann Sothern in **Kid Millions.**

Cantor, who was born Edward Israel Iskowitz in New York on January 31, 1893, was in show business from an early age and a top Ziegfeld star by 1917. His biggest movie stardom was in the early '30s, most notably for the elaborate **Roman Scandals** and **The Kid from Spain** (which Leo McCarey directed), but he continued to make films until 1948. He was the centrepiece of the all-star Warner Brothers extravaganza **Thank Your Lucky Stars** in 1943 and made his last two films with the brilliant comedienne Joan Davis, **Show Business** and **If You Knew Susie.** A poor biopic starring Keefe Brasselle as Cantor (**The Eddie Cantor Story**) was made in 1953, and Hollywood honoured him with a special Oscar in 1956. He died in 1964.

BEST FILMS:
1926 Kid Boots
Frank Tuttle (Paramount)
1930 Whoopee
Thornton Freeland (Goldwyn/United Artists)
1931 Palmy Days
Edward Sutherland (Goldwyn/United Artists)
1933 The Kid from Spain
Leo McCarey (Goldwyn/United Artists)

1934 Roman Scandals
Frank Tuttle (Goldwyn/United Artists)
1934 Kid Millions
Roy Del Ruth (Goldwyn/United Artists)
1936 Strike Me Pink
Norman Taurog (Goldwyn/United Artists)
1937 Ali Baba Goes to Town
David Butler (20th Century Fox)
1943 Thank Your Lucky Stars
David Butler (Warner Brothers)
1944 Show Business
Edwin L. Marin (RKO)

Martine Carol

Martine Carol was the first erotic star of the postwar cinema, the unclad heroine of early '50s French films, continually slipping in and out of baths and elaborate costumes. She seemed remarkably daring and sexy at the time, the Gallic rival of the emerging Marilyn Monroe, but it was clean, antiseptic sex, fit for the whole family and especially for export. As it turned out, she was merely the predecessor to Brigitte Bardot, but in her time — beginning with the 1950 **Caroline Chérie** — she was the queen of the cinema boudoir. She also starred in one of the greatest films of all time (American critic Andrew Sarris

Right: Martine Carol was the first famous sex star of the postwar cinema, taking off her clothes in a series of French films noted for "daringness."

considers it the greatest, although it was a financial failure), Max Ophuls' **Lola Montès.** It was a big-budget film, meant to show off her glory at the peak of her popularity, portraying the most famous courtesan of the nineteenth century, but instead Ophuls treated her very much as Orson Welles ➤ had treated sex goddess Rita Hayworth ➤ in **The Lady From Shanghai,** stripping her screen persona down to its essentials and destroying her myth.

She was born as Marie-Louise Mourer in Biarritz, France, in 1922, began appearing on stage in 1942, and made her film début in the 1943 **La Ferme aux loups. Caroline Chérie,** a kind of French Revolution **Gone With the Wind** with Carol sacrificing her virtue for the best of causes, was an international hit, and her stardom was then developed through the astuteness of her husband, director Christian-Jaque. He featured her as the unclad centrepiece of a series of costume dramas like **Lucrezia Borgia, Madame Dubarry** and **Nana.** Carol continued to make films after Ophuls had exposed her emptiness but was down-graded to third billing in Robert Aldrich's **Ten Seconds to Hell** (after Jack Palance ➤ and Jeff Chandler) and in Roberto Rossellini's **Vanina Vanini** (after Sandra Milo and Laurent Terzieff). Her last film was the 1966 **Hell Is Empty.** She died in 1967.

BEST FILMS:
1950 Caroline Chérie
Richard Pottier (Cinéphonie/SNEG)
1952 Beauties of the Night
(Belles de Nuit)
René Clair (Franco-London/Rizzoli)
1952 Adorable Creatures
Christian-Jaque (Ariane/Rizzoli)
1952 Lucrezia Borgia
Christian-Jaque (Filmsonar/Ariane)

LESLIE CARON
see Modern Stars

MADELEINE CARROLL

The first British actress to become a major star in both England and America, Madeleine Carroll is fondly remembered today as Alfred Hitchcock's prototype icy blonde heroine—she was sexily handcuffed to Robert Donat ❯ in **The Thirty-Nine Steps** (he politely asks if he can help while she struggles to remove her stockings) and then portrayed John Gielgud's bogus wife in the spy story **The Secret Agent.** She was extremely beautiful, and rather good at cinematic espionage, both in England (Saville's **I Was a Spy** with Conrad Veidt ❯) and America (**My Favourite Blonde** with Bob Hope ❯ and a penguin). She was the most popular female star in Britain in the early '30s (with the possible exception of comedienne Gracie Fields ❯) and she had no trouble at all in maintaining star status in the US when Hollywood called. She was peaches-and-cream perfection as the Ruritanian romantic heroine of **The Prisoner of Zenda** (adored by Ronald Colman ❯) and equally lovely as the object of everybody's affection in **Lloyds of London** (with Tyrone Power ❯ competing with George Sanders ❯ for her favours).

Born in West Bromwich, Staffordshire, England, on February 26, 1906, as Marie-Madeleine Bernadette O'Carroll, she was initially a stage actress and made her first film, **The Guns of Loos,** in 1928. She had climbed rapidly to stardom with films like **The W Plan** (co-starring Brian Aherne) and **Sleeping Car** (with Ivor Novello ❯) when Fox brought her to Hollywood in 1934 to make the John Ford film **The World Moves On** (a lesser effort he wished to forget). She returned to Britain for her great Hitchcock films and then began her major American period with pictures like **The General Died at Dawn** (as a spy once again, loved by Gary Cooper ❯ and the musical **On The Avenue** (as a socialite romanced by Dick Powell ❯; she didn't have to sing). Her finest dramatic role was in the sudsby but effective **My Son, My Son!,** once more with

Right: Madeleine Carroll looking peaches-and-cream at Gary Cooper in Cecil B. de Mille's 1940 epic **Northwest Mounted Police.**

Brian Aherne, but two years later her very funny Bob Hope picture signalled the effective end of her Hollywood career, although she came back in the late '40s to star in **Don't Trust Your Husband** and the Otto Preminger picture **The Fan.** She has done no performing of any kind since 1964 and now lives on a farm near Paris, where she grows apples.

BEST FILMS:
1933 I Was A Spy
Victor Saville (Fox)
1935 The Thirty-Nine Steps
Alfred Hitchcock (Gaumont-British)
1936 Secret Agent
Alfred Hitchcock (Gaumont-British)
1936 The General Died at Dawn
Lewis Milestone (Paramount)
1936 Lloyds of London
Henry King (20th Century Fox)
1937 On the Avenue
Roy Del Ruth (20th Century Fox)
1937 The Prisoner of Zenda
John Cromwell (United Artists)
1938 Blockade
William Dieterle (United Artists)
1940 My Son, My Son!
Charles Vidor (United Artists)
1942 My Favourite Blonde
Sidney Lanfield (Paramount)

MARIA CASARÈS

A major star of French cinema and theatre, Maria Casarès was actually Spanish in origin, born Maria Casarès Quiroga in Corunna, Spain, in 1922, the daughter of a diplomat. She was a hospital nurse during the Spanish Civil War, came to France afterwards as a refugee and took up acting in Paris, studying at the Conservatoire, then worked in many theatres, including the Théâtre des Mathurins and the TNP.

She made very few films, but she made some great ones; she was excellent in her first, as Jean-Louis Barrault's unloved wife Nathalie in Marcel Carné's **Les Enfants du Paradis** and was a worthy partner to Gérard Philipe ❯ in Christian-Jaque's adaptation of Stendhal's **La Chartreuse de Parme.** Her unsurpassed portrait of a jealous woman in Robert Bresson's **Les Dames du Bois de Boulogne** (as the vengeful, slighted Hélène, a symbolic fury in a long black dress, implacably pursuing her prey) must have impressed dialogue writer Jean Cocteau, who later used her to stunning effect in **Orphée** and its sequel **Le Testament d'Orphée** as the cinema's greatest and most effective image of Death. Between these two films she gave a magnificent example of her theatrical art as Lady Macbeth in Georges Franju's **Le Théâtre National Populaire** but subsequently appeared in very few pictures, the last being the

Above: Maria Casarès, the unforgettable personification of Death in Cocteau's **Orphée.**

lamentable 1974 **Flavia la Monaca Musulmana,** as the lunatic nun Sister Agatha.

BEST FILMS:
1943 Les Enfants du Paradis
Marcel Carné (Pathé-Cinéma)
1944 Les Dames du Bois de Boulogne
Robert Bresson (UGC)
1946 Le Septième Porte
Andre Zwobada (Ciné Reportage)
1947 La Chartreuse de Parme
Christian-Jaque (Scalera)
1949 Orphée
Jean Cocteau (Paulvé/Palais Royal)
1956 Le Théâtre National Populaire
Georges Franju (Procinex/Antinex)
1959 Le Testament d'Orphée
Jean Cocteau (Editions Cinématographiques)

CYD CHARISSE

Cyd Charisse has two great claims to cinema immortality: she was the finest female dancer on film and she had the greatest legs ever to grace a movie. It is unfortunate that she arrived near the end of the musical (and studio) era, but while she had the chance she

burned up the screen with her dancing—she was not a particularly interesting actress, but when she danced she was what Fred Astaire described as "beautiful dynamite."

She was born with the unlikely name of Tula Ellice Finklea in Amarillo, Texas, on March 8, 1921. Her nickname was Sid; the Charisse came from her ballet teacher, whom she married. Through him she got into pictures after a tour with the Ballet Russe, and made her début in the 1943 **Mission to Moscow.** MGM then put her under contract and she had small dancing roles in **Ziegfeld Follies, The Harvey Girls** and **Three Wise Fools.** She began to attract wider notice in **Till The Clouds Roll By, Fiesta** and **Words and Music,** but a broken leg kept her out of **Easter Parade** and pregnancy out of **An American in Paris.** She wowed the world as the provocative gangster's moll in **Singin' in the Rain,** however, and was thereafter featured in **Sombrero** and **The Band Wagon;** this was probably her greatest film— the *Girl Hunt* ballet was a delightful satire on Mickey Spillane and *Dancing in the Dark* showed off her sensuality to perfection. She was with Kelly in **It's Always Fair Weather,** teamed with Dan Dailey for **Meet Me in Las Vegas,** joined Kelly for his fine ballet film **Invitation to the Dance,** and was back with Astaire in **Silk Stockings.** She was notable in **Party Girl** and **Two Weeks in Another Town,** but her acting ability wasn't enough to carry her through the post-musical era; she retired from movies after the 1967 **Marco 7,** except for **Warlords of Atlantis** in 1978.

BEST FILMS:
1952 Singin' in the Rain
Stanley Donen and Gene Kelly MGM)
1953 Sombrero
Norman Foster (MGM)
1953 The Band Wagon
Vincente Minnelli (MGM)
1954 Brigadoon
Vincente Minnelli (MGM)
1955 It's Always Fair Weather
Stanley Donen and Gene Kelly (MGM)

greatest epic film ever made. Eisenstein forced his actor to strain his muscles and remain in awkward positions so that the right pictorial compositions could be obtained; Cherkassov complained bitterly about it afterwards, but it is a truly majestic achievement.

After the war, Cherkassov starred in Kozintsev's **Pirogov** (about a nineteenth-century surgeon) and two big biographies directed by Roshal, **Mussorgsky** and **Rimsky-Korsakov.** His last great role was as the gentle, other-world knight **Don Quixote** in the best of all film versions of Cervantes' novel. He died in 1966.

BEST FILMS:
1937 Baltic Deputy
Zarkhi and Heifëtz (Lenfilm)
1937 Peter the First (Parts I & II)
Vladimir Petrov (Lenfilm)

Above: Nicolai Cherkassov, at his best as Ivan the Terrible.

1938 Alexander Nevsky
Sergei Eisenstein (Mosfilm)
1939 Lenin in 1918
Mikhail Romm (Mosfilm)
1942 His Name is Sukhe-Bator
Zarkhi and Heifitz (Lenfilm)
1942-46 Ivan the Terrible (Parts I & II)
Sergei Eisenstein (Mosfilm)
1947 Pirogov
Grigori Kozintsev (Lenfilm)
1951 Mussorgsky
Grigori Roshal (Lenfilm)
1953 Rimsky-Korsakov
Grigori Roshal (Lenfilm)
1957 Don Quixote
Grigori Kozintsev (Lenfilm)

MAURICE CHEVALIER

Chevalier became the cinematic cliché of a Frenchman almost against his will, but he will be forever identified with the carefree, debonair Parisian boulevardier he portrayed in his Hollywood movies. He was more than that, of course, but his other attractions were less publicised.

Behind the trademark French accent, straw hat and jaunty, jutting lower lip was a vivacious

Above: Cyd Charisse and Gene Kelly in **Singin' In The Rain.**

1956 Meet Me in Las Vegas
Douglas Sirk (MGM)
1957 Invitation to the Dance
Gene Kelly (MGM)
1957 Silk Stockings
Rouben Mamoulian (MGM)
1958 Party Girl
Nicholas Ray (MGM)
1962 Two Weeks in Another Town
Vincente Minnelli (MGM)

NICOLAI CHERKASSOV

The greatest "star" of the Soviet cinema and probably the greatest epic hero of the movies, Cherkassov is best known for his superhuman portrayal of Tsar Ivan in Eisenstein's **Ivan the Terrible.** He was equally memorable as the legendary hero of Eisenstein's first epic, **Alexander Nevsky,** and as the tall, gaunt and chivalrous hero of Kozintsev's **Don Quixote.** There has never been another movie star quite like him, able to portray the "utmost grandiloquence of manner," in James Agee's telling phrase. He did what John Barrymore », George Arliss and Paul Muni » could

never do, for all their fame—portray great historical figures in a cinematic manner. He was helped enormously by working with one of the world's finest directors, but his success was also due to his own acting genius; at the age of 32, relatively unknown, he persuaded Josef Heifitz and Alexander Zarkhi to star him in **Baltic Deputy**—as 75-year-old Professor Polezhayev. The portrayal made him world famous.

Cherkassov was born in St Petersburg (Leningrad) in 1903 and was a musician and dancer before turning to acting. He made his film début in 1927, but was a theatre student until 1933, when he joined the Pushkin Theatre in Leningrad. After his success in **Baltic Deputy** in 1937, he was seen as the Tsarevich Alexei, the weakling villain of Petrov's **Peter the First** (a big-budget, two-part epic) and then as the remarkable **Alexander Nevsky,** defeating the Teutonic Knights in the thirteenth century (and winning Cherkassov the Order of Lenin from Stalin). In Romm's **Lenin in 1918** he played Maxim Gorky and was again featured by Heifitz and Zarkhi in **His Name is Sukhe-Bator. Ivan the Terrible** was begun in 1942 and finished in 1946; a grandiose two-part life-story of Tsar Ivan (a reflection of Stalin) and surely the

Above: **Love Me Tonight** *starred Maurice Chevalier in the famous* I'm An Apache *number that stressed his Gallic image.*

sexuality that came out in both halves of his long film career. In the early '30s, when he had his greatest period of fame and made his best movies, he was able to suggest erotic ideas that a more "serious" actor could never have got away with, and as an old man, in the second half of his career in the '50s and '60s, he was able to be absolutely outrageous because he was so charming (how else could a 70-year-old roué be allowed to sing *Thank Heaven for Little Girls).* He was a major movie star as well as being an inimitable singer and his films with Lubitsch, Cukor and Mamoulian have never been bettered (critic John Baxter, for example, thinks his **Love Me Tonight** the greatest of all '30s musicals).

Maurice Auguste Chevalier was born in Paris on September 12, 1888, and, after an unfortunate childhood, began to sing in the cafés. He danced with Mistinguett before World War I and became an operetta star in the '20s. Although he had earlier made short films with Max Linder, his featured début but was in Hollywood in 1929, in Richard Wallace's

Innocents of Paris; he sang *Every Little Breeze Seems to Whisper Louise* and became world-famous overnight. He was then teamed with Jeanette MacDonald ➤ in Lubitsch's **The Love Parade**, setting new standards for the musical—and for sexual roguishness. He was with Claudette Colbert ➤ in two films (including Lubitsch's delightful **The Smiling Lieutenant**) and then at his most risqué with MacDonald again in their **One Hour With You** and Mamoulian's **Love Me Tonight** (which includes Chevalier's famous *I'm an Apache* number). The vogue for musicals was passing, however, and after the sparkling **The Merry Widow** (Lubitsch again) and **Folies Bergères** (which won a dance direction Oscar for Dave Gould), Chevalier returned to Paris.

He made films in France and England (including René Clair's **Break the News** with Jack Buchanan ➤ as co-star), but with only moderate success; he had a good character role as an old film director in Clair's 1947 **Le Silence est d'Or**, but it was not until 1957 that he came back to Hollywood. Billy Wilder cast him brilliantly as Audrey Hepburn's ➤ private-eye father in **Love in the Afternoon** (set in Paris), and he then made his great comeback in Vincente Minnelli's **Gigi**. The film got the 1958 Best Picture Oscar (among others) and Chevalier was given a special award for his 50 years of entertaining. As an old roué he stole the film, with such delights as a duet with Hermione Gingold — *I Remember It Well*. He was a big movie star once more, starring opposite Frank Sinatra ➤ and Shirley MacLaine ➤ in **Can-Can**, Leslie Caron ➤ in **Fanny**, and even playing himself with Paul Newman ➤ and Joanne Woodward ➤ in **A New Kind of Love**. He was nearly 80 when he made his last film in 1967, **Monkeys Go Home**, directed by Andrew V. McLaglen. He died in Paris in 1972.

BEST FILMS:
1929 The Love Parade
Ernst Lubitsch (MGM)
1931 The Smiling Lieutenant
Ernst Lubitsch (Paramount)
1932 One Hour With You
George Cukor (Paramount)
1932 Love Me Tonight
Rouben Mamoulian (Paramount)
1934 The Merry Widow
Ernst Lubitsch (MGM)
1935 Folies Bergères
Roy Del Ruth (United Artists)
1947 Le Silence est d'Or
René Clair (in France)
1957 Love in the Afternoon
Billy Wilder (Allied Artists)
1958 Gigi
Vincente Minnelli (MGM)
1961 Fanny
Joshua Logan (Warner Brothers)

MONTGOMERY CLIFT
see **Modern Stars**

LEE J. COBB

Lee J. Cobb was one of the great heavies of the cinema, a snarling, sweating, loud-mouthed, boorish gangster, at his best in such films as **On The Waterfront** and **Party Girl**. An excellent actor, he created the role of Willy Loman in the Broadway production of *Death of a Salesman* and was able to move from the villain roles of his earlier career to more sympathetic but still tough patriarchal figures in his later years. One of his most memorable non-gangster performances was as the jury man who holds out for conviction until the very end in **Twelve Angry Men**, although he himself found more satisfaction in portraying the Karamazov father in **The Brothers Karamazov**. He was also very strong in police lieutenant roles, trying to control Clint Eastwood in **Coogan's Bluff** or investigating the strange goings-

*Above: Lee J. Cobb as he was seen in the violent 1970 **Lawman**, directed by Michael Winner.*

on of **The Exorcist**. His voice was as much a part of his personality as his sneer, seeming to convey a snarl even when he was speaking softly, and excellent for intemperate ranting.

Born in New York City on December 8, 1911, as Leo Jacob, he worked in the theatre during the '30s and made his film début in the 1937 **North of the Rio Grande**. He was a leading character actor in the '40s, coming into his own in the postwar period in some of the best thrillers of time, including **Johnny O'Clock, The Dark Past, Call Northside 777** and **Boomerang**. His Academy Award nomination for **On The Waterfront**, as Johnny Friendly, the crooked boss of the longshoremen, boosted his career considerably and helped make him a major star. His finest performances thereafter came in

*Above right: One of Claudette Colbert's finest performances was in **The Gilded Lily** (1935). Right: Claudette Colbert and Ray Milland in the 1940 Mitchell Leisen film **Arise My Love**.*

two 1958 films, as the mobster boss demonstrating the effects of acid on Cyd Charisse ➤ in Nicholas Ray's **Party Girl**, and as the chief outlaw in Anthony Mann's **Man of the West**.

He died in 1976.

BEST FILMS:
1947 Boomerang
Elia Kazan (20th Century Fox)
1947 Johnny O'Clock
Robert Rossen (Columbia)
1949 The Dark Past
Rudolph Maté (Columbia)
1954 On The Waterfront
Elia Kazan (Columbia)
1957 Twelve Angry Men
Sidney Lumet (United Artists)
1958 Party Girl
Nicholas Ray (MGM)
1958 Man of the West
Anthony Mann (United Artists)
1963 Come Blow Your Horn
Bud Yorkin (Paramount)
1968 Coogan's Bluff
Don Siegel (Universal)
1973 The Exorcist
William Friedkin (Warner Brothers)

CLAUDETTE COLBERT

She was never quite believable when taking baths in asses' milk (the "wickedest woman in the world") in **The Sign of the Cross**, nor when disporting herself in scanty clothing in **Cleopatra**. Claudette Colbert was too amusing, too "normal," too frothy; her tongue was usually in the cheek of that unique heart-shaped face. It's not that she wasn't sexy, but she had too much light comedy in her to be a vamp or a glamorous goddess; as a comedienne she was second to none, wiping up the opposition in such delectable confections as the multiple Oscar-winning **It Happened One Night** (with Clark Gable ➤ on the other side of that famous Wall of Jericho), **The Gilded Lily** (with Fred MacMurray ➤), **She Married Her Boss** with Melvyn Douglas ➤

(gaining a wife but losing his office efficiency), **Midnight** (as a showgirl in Paris pretending to be a Hungarian aristocrat) and **The Palm Beach Story**. In 1936 she was the highest paid star in Hollywood, and she received another Academy Award nomination for her dramatic role as a psychiatrist opposite Charles Boyer ❯ in **Private Worlds**.

Colbert began life as Lily Claudette Chaunchoin, in Paris, on September 13, 1905. Her family came to the US when she was six; she was a secretary and then a stage star before appearing in her first film in 1927, Frank Capra's **For the Love of Mike**. Paramount gave her a contract but did not really develop her potential until Cecil B. DeMille unveiled the sexiness hidden behind her demure exterior and Capra proved how brilliant she was at comedy in **It Happened One Night**. She was a top star for 20 years, winning another Oscar nomination for **Since You Went Away** (1944) and working with many top directors, including Lubitsch, DeMille, Ford, Capra, La Cava, Stahl, Cukor, Sirk and Leisen. Her last big box-office success was the enjoyable **The Egg and I** in 1947, but she continued making occasional films until 1961 (**Parrish**). Her husband of 33 years, Dr Joel Pressman, died in 1968, and she now lives most of the year in Barbados. In 1974 she toured the US in a stage play, and, hopefully, she may yet make another film.

BEST FILMS:
1931 The Smiling Lieutenant
Ernst Lubitsch (Paramount)
1934 It Happened One Night
Frank Capra (Columbia)
1934 Cleopatra
Cecil B. De Mille (Paramount)
1935 The Gilded Lily
Wesley Ruggles (Paramount)
1935 Private Worlds
Gregory La Cava (Paramount)
1935 She Married Her Boss
Gregory La Cava (Paramount)
1939 Midnight
Mitchell Leisen (Paramount)
1942 The Palm Beach Story
Preston Sturges (Paramount)
1944 Since You Went Away
John Cromwell (United Artists)
1947 The Egg and I
Chester Erskine (Universal)

RONALD COLMAN

The greatest "gentleman hero" in the history of the cinema and a major star for nearly 30 years, Colman was one of the few top silent actors to become an even bigger talkie star. He was the distinguished, romantic figure *par excellence,* combining in his screen persona almost all the qualities a woman could wish for in a man. He was handsome and charming, with a glorious speaking voice and the finest moustache on the screen. There was a slightly sad cast to his face which helped project his image of absolute integrity, inner strength, reliability and gentleness; he was also urbane and witty, with the remarkable ability to be romantic through understatement and amusing through restraint. He stamped his personality on every film, achieving perfection as Sidney Carton making the ultimate sacrifice in **The Tale of Two Cities** and as the look-alike commoner nobly giving up Madeleine Carroll ❯ and the Ruritanian throne in **The Prisoner of Zenda**. He was the perfect hero for Frank Capra's original **Lost Horizon** in 1937: Shangri-La would not have been the perfect place it was without him. He was the prototype self-sacrificing doctor in John Ford's remarkable **Arrowsmith** and even more noble in the original, silent version of **Beau Geste**. Colman's nobility was so understated that it was convincing, but he was also excellent as a dashing, romantic adventure hero in films like **Under Two Flags** and **Clive of India**. His gentleman-hero persona was seen at its debonair best in **Bulldog Drummond** (on the right side of the law) and **Raffles** (on the wrong side). He had, after all, polished it for a good many years.

Colman was born on February 9, 1891, in Richmond, Surrey, and went to America to make his fortune in 1920 after making a few minor films in Britain. He worked in both theatre and cinema and then had his break playing opposite Lillian Gish ❯ in Henry King's excellent **The White Sister** in 1923; Samuel Goldwyn put him under contract and he soon became one of the leading romantic heroes of the silent era. He was co-starred with lovely Vilma Banky in the weepie **The Dark Angel,** and they became one of the great love teams of the period in films like **The Winning of Barbara Worth** and **Two Lovers.** His finest silent films were probably **Stella Dallas** (remade in 1937) and **Beau Geste** (first and best of the three versions).

Sound was not only not a problem for Colman, it actually increased his star magnitude; nobody else in the movies had such a rich, distinctive voice, and one that matched so well with his screen persona. His first talkie, **Bulldog Drummond,** was a box-office and critical hit and won him an Oscar nomination. He was nominated twice more (for **Condemned** and **Random Harvest**) but did not actually win that acting award until 1947, in **A Double Life** (as a Shakespearian actor who thinks he's Othello in real life). He was then 57 years old and silver-haired, but just as charming and attractive to women as ever. His greatest popular success in the '40s was in **Random Harvest,** a finely acted if implausible James Hilton story about an amnesiac who marries Greer Garson ❯ twice. His last starring film was a light-hearted romp called **Champagne for Caesar**, in which he portrayed a quiz programme genius. He then gracefully retired with his wife, English actress Benita Hume, except for guest appearances in **Around the World in 80 Days** and **The Story of Mankind.** He died on May 19, 1958. His daughter, Juliet Benita Colman, published his biography, *A Very Private Person,* in 1975.

BEST FILMS:
1925 Stella Dallas
Henry King (Goldwyn/United Artists)
1926 Beau Geste
Herbert Brenon (Paramount)
1929 Bulldog Drummond
F. Richard Jones (Goldwyn/United Artists)

1931 Arrowsmith
John Ford (Goldwyn/United Artists)
1933 Cynara
King Vidor (Goldwyn/United Artists)
1935 A Tale of Two Cities
Jack Conway (20th Century Fox)
1937 Lost Horizon
Frank Capra (Columbia)
1937 The Prisoner of Zenda
John Cromwell (Selznick/United Artists)
1942 Talk of the Town
George Stevens (Columbia)
1943 Random Harvest
Mervyn Le Roy (MGM)
1947 A Double Life
George Cukor (Universal)

Below: Ronald Colman was 57 when he won an Oscar in the 1947 film **A Double Life,** *portraying an actor obsessed by Othello.*

Above: Ronald Colman and co-star Joan Bennett in the 1929 **Bulldog Drummond,** *directed by F. Richard Jones. Colman was the greatest of all the screen Drummonds.*

GARY COOPER

One of the half-dozen greatest stars of the cinema and one of the finest of all movie actors, Gary Cooper was a towering screen personality for 35 years. He acted in outstanding films by an impressive number of major American directors (including Hawks, von Sternberg, Mamoulian, Lubitsch, Capra, Wyler, Aldrich and Mann), won two Academy Awards for memorable performances (as the pacifist war hero of **Sergeant York** and the sheriff standing alone in **High Noon**), and must be considered as the almost perfect American screen hero. The very concept of the tall, taciturn hero who "has to do what he has to do" is based on Cooper's screen

Above: Gary Cooper as an admiral about to retire in Delmer Daves' **Task Force.**

LOU COSTELLO
see **Abbott and Costello**

JOSEPH COTTEN

Above: Gary Cooper in one of his finest early roles, opposite Marlene Dietrich in Josef von Sternberg's 1930 **Morocco.**
Right: Gary Cooper and his fellow encyclopedia writers in the 1941 comedy **Ball of Fire,** learning from Barbara Stanwyck.

persona as the slow-speaking, deep-thinking, utterly-determined man of integrity. He never portrayed a villain on the screen, nor even a dishonest man: it was too contrary to his character. His mannerisms were under control, he was believable in films ranging from sophisticated comedy to Hemingway tragedy — and yet he was never lost in his roles; he always remained Gary Cooper.

He was probably best, and is certainly best remembered, as the star of cowboy films, the ultimate personification of the heroic American West, beginning with his first sound film in 1929, **The Virginian** (laconically giving the world his first "yup"), and including such superb movies as **The Plainsman, The Westerner, High Noon, Vera Cruz** and **Man of the West.** These aloof cowboy roles are possibly the reason for critical underestimation of his acting ability (one critic claimed he had only two looks — a stern one and a not-so-stern one), but even stage actors like Charles Laughton ➤ were stunned by his screen performances. His persona did not noticeably change in his comedies, but nobody is more skilled nor funnier on screen than Cooper in **Ball of Fire** (as a professor hiding stripper Barbara Stanwyck ➤), **Mr Deeds Goes To Town** (as the apparently naive heir to a fortune), or **Design for Living** (matched against Fredric

March ➤ and Miriam Hopkins ➤ in a Noël Coward ➤ love triangle. He was just as good in romantic films, believably attractive to a wide array of glamorous ladies, including Marlene Dietrich ➤ (**Morocco, Desire**), Helen Hayes ➤ (**A Farewell to Arms**), Tallulah Bankhead (**Devil and the Deep**), Ingrid Bergman ➤ (**For Whom the Bell Tolls**), Audrey Hepburn ➤ (**Love in the Afternoon**) and Suzy Parker (**Ten North Frederick**). He was an all-round film actor whose style of performance is unlikely to date, even if his type of hero becomes unfashionable.

Cooper was born in Helena, Montana, on May 7, 1901, of English parents, and spent his early years on a ranch (although his father was a lawyer). He began working in Hollywood in 1925 as a stuntman and had his first featured role in Henry King's 1926 **The Winning of Barbara Worth.** He quickly became an important star for Paramount in films with Clara Bow ➤ and Fay Wray ➤, and then a really major one in 1929 with **The Virgininan,** an outstanding screen adaptation of the first great Western novel.

Virtually every film he made in the '30s was good, and he became a perennial top ten box office attraction and one of the highest paid actors in Hollywood. He was magnificently heroic in two of the greatest adventure films of the decade, **Lives of a Bengal Lancer** and **Beau Geste,** and then, with the arrival of the '40s, became the most magnificent of war heroes, **Sergeant York.** His other film roles in that decade were pretty good, including the nuclear scientist in **Cloak and Dagger** and the architect in **The Fountainhead.** He had nowhere to go but up in the '50s; he totally dominated **High Noon,** becoming forever the image of a lawman involved in a showdown with bad men, and then made two more major Westerns, **Vera Cruz** and **Man of the West,** and a brilliant romantic comedy, **Love in the Afternoon.** His last picture was **The Naked Edge** in 1961 with Deborah Kerr ➤. He was given a special Academy Award on April 17, 1961, when James Stewart ➤ revealed that Cooper had less than a month to live. He died on May 13 of that year.

Joseph Cotten is a superb screen actor whose talents have been virtually wasted since his great string of classic films in the '40s. He was a protégé of Orson Welles ➤ on stage in the late '30s, and it was Welles who really began his film career as the drama critic in **Citizen Kane.** He was featured in two other Welles films, **The Magnificent Ambersons** and **Journey into Fear,** had a brief role in **Touch of Evil,** and was completely overshadowed by Welles in **The Third Man** (of which Cotten is actually the hero). He was at his very best in two films for Alfred Hitchcock, **Shadow of a Doubt** (the pleasant, murdering uncle of Teresa Wright) and **Under Capricorn** (the hardened ex-convict husband of Ingrid Bergman ➤). He was good, although dominated by the performances of Jennifer Jones ➤ and Gregory Peck ➤ in **Duel in the Sun,** but in prize-winning form with Jennifer Jones again in **Portrait of Jennie** (as an artist inspired by her). This last was directed by William Dieterle, who elicited some of Cotten's most memorable performances in **I'll Be Seeing You, Love Letters** and especially **September Affair,** a marvellously romantic fling with Joan Fontaine ➤. Unfortunately, that 1950 film was one of his last outstanding movies.

Cotten was born in Peterburg, Virginia, on May 15, 1905, and was an important theatre star in the '30s (he appeared with Katharine Hepburn ➤ in the stage production of **The Philadelphia Story**). After his outstanding '40s

Above: Joseph Cotten looking suspiciously like a murderer in Hitchcock's **Shadow of a Doubt.**

film career, he continued to turn in good but lesser performances. He was Marilyn Monroe's ❯ husband in **Niagara,** and fine opposite Teresa Wright again in the dramatic **The Steel Trap,** but was soon reduced to being featured in Westerns and Italian films. Among his more impressive later performances were the Army major in **The Great Sioux Massacre** and Richard Chamberlain's father in **Petulia.**

He has continued working regularly in the '70s. One of his last strong roles was in the 1973 **A Delicate Balance,** but he also made notable contributions to **Airport '77** and **Twilight's Last Gleaming.**

BEST FILMS:
1941 Citizen Kane
Orson Welles (RKO)
1942 The Magnificent Ambersons
Orson Welles (RKO)
1942 Journey into Fear
Norman Foster (RKO)
1944 I'll Be Seeing You
William Dieterle (Selznick/United Artists)
1945 Love Letters
William Dieterle (Paramount)
1946 Duel in the Sun
King Vidor (Selznick/United Artists)
1948 Portrait of Jennie
William Dieterle (Selznick/United Artists)
1949 Under Capricorn
Alfred Hitchcock (Warner Brothers)
1949 The Third Man
Carol Reed (British Lion)
1950 September Affair
William Dieterle (Paramount)

CICELY COURTNEIDGE AND JACK HULBERT

The leading comedy team of the British cinema in the 1930s, the stars of unpretentious but highly popular entertainments which are still enjoyable today. Their successful stage career has kept their names in the limelight, but their

Right: Cicely Courtneidge and Jack Hulbert in **Under Your Hat.**

fine work in films is unjustly neglected. Cicely was the bubbly, uninhibited clown of the duo, while Jack was the long-chinned fellow with a wide grin and dancing feet. They made their first film together in 1930, the all-star revue **Elstree Calling,** and then made two of their best pictures with director Walter Forde, **The Ghost Train** and **Jack's the Boy.** The plots of their films were silly but amiable, almost always involving them in pretending to be somebody else. In **Falling for You** they were rival reporters in disguise, in **Take My Tip** aristocrats disguised as hotel servants, and in **Under Your Hat** film stars in disguise out to foil spies.

Cicely Courtneidge was born in Sydney, Australia, in 1893; Jack Hulbert was born in Ely, Cambridgeshire, in 1892. They met in a London play called *The Pearl Girl* and married in 1919. Although most of their good films were made together, they were also featured separately; Cicely starred opposite Edward Everett Horton in a double role in the comedy **Soldiers of the King,** and pretended to be someone else, as usual, in **Aunt Sally, Things Are Looking Up** and **Me and Marlborough** (with Victor Saville directing). She went to Hollywood in 1935 to star opposite Frank Morgan in **The Perfect Gentleman,** but the film was unsuccessful and she returned to England. Jack was seen at his best in films directed by Walter Forde, especially opposite Fay Wray ❯ in **Bulldog Jack** (playboy posing as detective) and **Jack Ahoy.** World War II ended their kind of frivolous comedy, but they did small roles separately and appeared together in **Spider's Web** in 1960 and **Not Now Darling** in 1972. Cicely gave an especially notable performance as an ageing lesbian in Bryan Forbes' **The L-Shaped Room.** She published her autobiography, *Cicely* in 1953. Jack brought out his, *The Little Woman's Always Right,* in 1976, two years before his death.

BEST FILMS:
1931 The Ghost Train
Walter Forde (Gainsborough)
1932 Jack's The Boy
Walter Forde (Gainsborough)
1933 Soldiers of the King
Maurice Elvey (Gainsborough)
1933 Falling For You
Jack Hulbert & Robert Stevenson (Gainsborough)
1934 Jack Ahoy
Walter Forde (Gainsborough)
1934 Bulldog Jack
Walter Forde (Gainsborough)
1935 Things Are Looking Up
Albert de Courville (Gaumont)
1935 Me and Marlborough
Victor Saville (Gaumont)
1937 Take My Tip
Herbert Mason (Gaumont)
1940 Under Your Hat
Maurice Elvey (Grand National)

Above: Noël Coward as a warlock of inimitable sophistication in Joseph Losey's bizarre **Boom!**

NOEL COWARD

Noël Coward's persona as the ultimate sophisticate has helped make him one of the best known personalities of the entertainment world this century. Although his contribution to the cinema was a limited one, he was certainly one of its most charismatic stars. He appeared in only 11 films, but he also had considerable impact on the cinema as a writer, producer and director. He is best remembered by the modern public as the sophisticated master criminal planning jobs from the security of prison in **The Italian Job;** as the exceedingly strange character who keeps a rack full of whips in **Bunny Lake is Missing,** and as the unflappable, highly sophisticated and very funny Foreign Office gentleman who hires Alec Guinness to be a spy in **Our Man in Havana.** His finest screen acting performances, however, were probably in his first two sound films in **The Scoundrel** in 1935, and **In Which We Serve** in 1942. He had made his cinema début in

the early silent days with a tiny part in D. W. Griffith's **Hearts of the World,** which was shot in France in 1918 with Lillian Gish ❯.

Noël Peirce Coward was born in Teddington, Middlesex, on December 16, 1899, and made his stage début at the age of 12. His playwriting career was so successful by 1931 that three of his plays were made into silent films, notably **Easy Virtue,** directed by Alfred Hitchcock, and **The Vortex,** starring Ivor Novello ❯. Coward went before the cameras himself in 1935 as a cynical, witty publisher in the Ben Hecht and Charles MacArthur film **The Scoundrel.** The script glittered with epigrams, the film became a New York cult, and Coward won warm praise. He did not, however, appear in another film until 1942, when he was the producer, director and writer of the patriotic **In Which We Serve,** also starring as the gallant naval commander, in what was considered one of the most important films of the war.

He did not normally act in the film versions of his plays but can be seen in the 1949 **The Astonished Heart** (as a highly sophisticated psychiatrist involved in a love triangle). He was one of the celebrities Mike Todd persuaded to appear in **Around the World in 80 Days** (as the head of the employment exchange who sends Cantinflas to work for David Niven ❯), and he did his only singing and dancing on film in Stanley Donen's not very successful gangster comedy, **Surprise Package** (he plays the poverty-stricken ex-King of Anatolia). In 1963 he was a guest star again in **Paris When It Sizzles**, with Audrey Hepburn ❯ and William Holden ❯, and in 1966 he was a male witch opposite Elizabeth Taylor ❯ and Richard Burton ❯ in Joseph Losey's **Boom**. His last film was **The Italian Job** in 1969. In 1970 the National Film theatre in London mounted a tribute to his 50-year film career. He was given a knighthood and died in 1973.

COMPLETE FILMS:
1918 Hearts of the World
D. W. Griffith (Griffith)
1935 The Scoundrel
Ben Hecht and Charles MacArthur (Paramount)
1942 In Which We Serve
Noël Coward & David Lean (Rank/Two Cities)
1949 The Astonished Heart
Terence-Fisher & Antony Darnborough (Gainsborough)
1955 Around the World in 80 Days
Michael Anderson (Mike Todd/United Artists)
1959 Our Man in Havana
Carol Reed (Columbia)
1960 Surprise Package
Stanley Donen (Columbia)
1963 Paris When It Sizzles
Richard Quine (Paramount)
1965 Bunny Lake is Missing
Otto Preminger (Columbia)
1968 Boom
Joseph Losey (Universal)
1969 The Italian Job
Peter Collinson (Paramount)

Above: Jeanne Crain could be glamorous as well as girlish. Right: Hattie McDaniel helps Jeanne Crain get dressed in her romantic 1946 hit **Margie,** *but neglects those vital bloomers.*

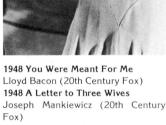

Cary Grant ❯ in **People Will Talk.** After she left Fox in 1953 her career lost momentum, though she was nicely stiff opposite Kirk Douglas ❯ in the Western **Man Without a Star.**

She was born in Barstow, California, on May 25, 1925, and made her film début in a bathing suit in **The Gang's All Here** in 1943. She became a star in Henry Hathaway's 1944 **Home in Indiana** opposite June Haver and a lot of horses, and from then on had major parts. She was a soldier's wife in George Cukor's **Winged Victor**, bandleader Dan Dailey's wife in **You Were Meant for Me**, and a pretty model in the comedy **The Model and the Marriage Broker**. She has made occasional films in the '60s and '70s, one of the last being the 1972 **Skyjacked.**

BEST FILMS:
1945 State Fair
Walter Lang (20th Century Fox)
1946 Centennial Summer
Otto Preminger (20th Century Fox)
1946 Margie
Henry King (20th Century Fox)

JEANNE CRAIN

Jeanne Crain was pretty, sweet, sometimes a little over-cute—and usually the girl-next-door type—in 20th Century Fox films of the late '40s and early '50s. Her best and most representative performance was as the schoolgirl who loses her knickers but marries her French teacher in the charming 1946 **Margie,** but she got her only Oscar nomination as a black girl trying to pass for white in **Pinky,** a well-intentioned but now dated picture. She was really better in period family comedies like **State Fair, Centennial Summer** and **Cheaper by the Dozen** and its sequel **Belles on Their Toes.** She was good but still sweet as one of the wives in **A Letter to Three Wives** and excellent opposite

1948 You Were Meant For Me
Lloyd Bacon (20th Century Fox)
1948 A Letter to Three Wives
Joseph Mankiewicz (20th Century Fox)
1949 Pinky
Elia Kazan (20th Century Fox)
1950 Cheaper By The Dozen
Walter Lang (20th Century Fox)
1951 People Will Talk
Joseph Mankiewicz (20th Century Fox)
1951 The Model and the Marriage Broker
George Cukor (20th Century Fox)
1955 Man Without a Star
King Vidor (Universal)

BRODERICK CRAWFORD

Broderick Crawford is the best Hollywood personification of the Damon Runyon gangster—big, fast-talking, blustering, often crude, sometimes nasty but always a strong, positive personality. Crawford actually starred in two

Damon Runyon films early in his career, **Tight Shoes** (as a big-shot gangster with equally big feet) and **Butch Minds The Baby** (helping a mother down on her luck), but the epitome of this characterisation was in a non-Runyon film, **Born Yesterday.** As junk merchant Harry Brock brawling with dumb broad Judy Holliday ❯, who turns out to be a little brighter than he bargained for, Crawford was at the peak of his screen career. The year before, 1949, he had won the Academy Award for a nastier version of the same persona in **All The King's Men,** portraying a southern political boss based on Huey Long. Unfortunately, these two roles were the best he ever had in Hollywood; in the majority of his films he was a more ordinary tough detective, villain or cowboy. He made one more great film, but that was in Italy under Federico Fellini's direction; in **Il Bidone** he is a con-man down on his luck, trying one last swindle and killed by his fellows when he begins to feel remorse.

Crawford was born in Philadelphia, Pennsylvania, on December 11, 1911, the son of stage and film actress Helen Broderick and actor Lester Crawford. After radio and stage work, he made his film début in a leading role in the 1937 comedy **Woman Chases Man.** He played Lennie in the stage production of **Of Mice and Men** and then spent the '40s in gangster and detective parts. He had a popular TV success in the '50s with the series **Highway Patrol** and went to Italy again in 1960 to star for director Vittorio Cottafavi in **Goliath and the Dragon.** He has continued to work through the '60s and '70s, but has never again

Left: Broderick Crawford as junk merchant wheeler-dealer Harry Brock—a typical role— about to be beaten at gin rummy by not-so-dumb broad Judy Holliday in **Born Yesterday.**

had the impact he had in the '50s. One of his better recent roles was in the 1972 **Embassy**, but he was at his very best as J. Edgar Hoover in the controversial **The Private Files of J. Edgar Hoover.**

BEST FILMS:
1941 Tight Shoes
Albert S. Rogell (Universal)
1942 Butch Minds the Baby
Albert S. Rogell (Universal)
1949 All the King's Men
Robert Rossen (Columbia)
1950 Born Yesterday
George Cukor (Columbia)
1951 The Mob
Robert Parrish (Columbia)
1954 Human Desire
Fritz Lang (Columbia)
1955 New York Confidential
Russell Rouse (Warner Brothers)
1955 Big House USA
Howard W. Koch (United Artists)
1955 Il Bidone (The Swindlers)
Federico Fellini (in Italy)
1978 The Private Files of J. Edgar Hoover
Larry Cohen (AIP)

JOAN CRAWFORD

Hollywood's most representative "Great Movie Star" and the screen's finest personification of no-holds-barred ambition, Joan Crawford created her screen persona early, doubtless basing it on her own desperate climb from the bottom of society, and pushed this screen image to the very peak of stardom. The outward manifestations changed (she was a flapper in the '20s, ambitious working girl or social climber in the '30s, and crafty business woman in the '40s), but the core of the image never altered: she was a tough, shrewd, determined woman who wanted the best things in life and would do anything to get them—even murder. "I love to play bitches," she once said, and in the end she came to symbolise the bitch-goddess success, the dark side of the American dream. She looked like a star, she behaved like a star, she was a star. Her broad mouth and even broader shoulders (especially in the '40s with shoulder pads), her arched eyebrows and fixed determined look, and her expensively groomed but somehow trying-too-hard-to-impress clothes have become a part of movie folklore. She was one of the most durable of American actresses (the only silent cinema star still at the top in the '70s), both because of her image and because of the ambition behind it. Critics who criticise her limited acting ability do not fully understand what screen acting is all about because she is a formidable "screen actress". F. Scott Fitzgerald, who considered her the "best example of the flapper" during the '20s, was amusing but mistaken in his oft-quoted denigration of her acting ability—he said that you couldn't give her a direction to tell

Left: Joan Crawford in an early "hard-boiled" role, using her glamour and beauty on Spencer Tracy in Frank Borzage's 1937 **Mannequin** *as she climbs from factory to fashionable success.*

a lie "because if you did she would practically give a representation of Benedict Arnold selling West Point to the British." It's true she went in for big, broad and overwhelming emotions, but she showcased them magnificently.

After 20 years of movie stardom, she put all her expertise together in one package and won the acting Oscar for **Mildred Pierce.** It was the apotheosis of the ambitious Crawford screen persona, a tough-minded woman who had fought her way to the top without losing her femininity and feminine weaknesses. She portrayed a waitress who has struggled to success only to find that her spoiled daughter is uncontrollable. Glossy and glamorous as well as grubby, Crawford seemed to be playing out a movie version of her own life.

She was born Billie Cassin in San Antonio, Texas, on March 28, 1906, to a difficult life: her parents separated before she was born, her step-father left while she was still a child, and she spent her early years living in cheap hotels with her mother. She worked as a laundry helper, a shop assistant and a waitress before advancing to the heights of being a chorus girl. When she was taken out of the chorus line and screen-tested in 1925, she channelled her burning ambition into becoming a movie star. Her first film was nothing, simply the double in long shots for Norma Shearer ≫ in **Lady of the Night,** but she had a real part in the next, **Pretty Ladies** (type-cast as a chorine). After that she never slowed down. She had good films, playing the love interest to Harry Langdon in **Tramp, Tramp, Tramp** and to Lon Chaney, Snr ≫ in **The Unknown,** but it was **Our Dancing Daughters** in 1928 that made her a big star, the wildest flapper of them all. She jumped feet first into the new sound films (her tap-dance in **Hollywood Revue of 1929** was the first one heard in the movies) and became one of MGM's major ladies. She wasn't quite as big a star as Greta Garbo ≫ or Norma Shearer—but she was pretty big, and she outlasted them both.

Her '30s films are not bad, but are rarely exceptional; she had not yet fully developed her screen image. One of the best was Frank Borzage's **Mannequin,** a prototype Crawford vehicle, the rags-to-riches story of a factory girl climbing to fashionable success with the help of Spencer Tracy ≫

Left: Joan Crawford in her element as a tough publishing executive in Jean Negulesco's 1959 **The Best of Everything,** *from the novel by Rona Jaffe.*

and MGM gloss. She was a formidable hard-boiled bitch in George Cukor's **The Women** and even better as a scarred and bitter woman in his 1941 **A Woman's Face.** Cukor directed her with greater sensitivity than anyone before or since, but **A Woman's Face** also contained some of the most inane lines ever spoken in the cinema (He: "Do you like music? Symphonies? Concertos?" She: "Some symphonies, most concertos".); the scriptwriter was Donald Ogden Stewart, so maybe it was on purpose.

Crawford then left MGM after a long association and moved to Warner Brothers, where she had her finest moment in Michael Curtiz's **Mildred Pierce** and her career went into high gear. She followed **Mildred Pierce** with another classic of the women's picture genre, Jean Negulesco's **Humoresque;** she was in love with violinist John Garfield », but couldn't compete with his music; she listened to him play one last time and then walked into the ocean wearing a stylish evening dress. It was almost as awe-inspiring as Marlene Dietrich's » walk into the desert in **Morocco.** Crawford was equally powerful in **Possessed** (in love with, and murdering for, not-nice Van Heflin) and in Otto Preminger's **Daisy Kenyon** (torn between Henry Fonda » and Dana Andrews »). She was even tougher in the 1949 **Flamingo Road**, with Curtiz directing her again as a carny girl who finds love with Sydney Greenstreet », and varied the formula with a thriller called **Sudden Fear,** in which she discovered that new husband Jack Palance » was out to kill her. She was a singer and a dancer in **Torch Song** (her legs looked great for a lady past 40), and she was outstanding under Nicholas Ray's direction in the 1954 **Johnny Guitar** (one of the few really interesting Westerns with a female star). In **Female on the Beach** she was worried that new lover Jeff Chandler was trying to kill her, and in **Queen Bee** she tries to dominate everyone within her claustrophobic circle—but her star had begun to shine a little less brightly. She came back strongly in 1962 in **Whatever Happened to Baby Jane?,** with Bette Davis » co-starring in a Grand Guignol mixture of horror and Hollywood. That was her last good film, but she kept on working. Her last starring role was in the 1970 British film **Trog.** She died on 10 May 1977.

BEST FILMS:
1928 Our Dancing Daughters
Harry Beaumont (MGM)
1938 Mannequin
Frank Borzage (MGM)
1939 The Women
George Cukor (MGM)
1941 A Woman's Face
George Cukor (MGM)
1945 Mildred Pierce
Michael Curtiz (Warner Brothers)
1945 Humoresque
Jean Negulesco (Warner Brothers)
1947 Possessed
Curtis Bernhardt (Warner Brothers)
1949 Flamingo Road
Michael Curtiz (Warner Brothers)
1952 Sudden Fear
David Miller (RKO)
1954 Johnny Guitar
Nicholas Ray (Republic)
1962 Whatever Happened to Baby Jane?
Robert Aldrich (Warner Brothers)

BING CROSBY

The most popular American entertainer of the twentieth century, with equally big careers in radio, music and cinema, Crosby is one of the major movie stars—even if film historians have rarely accorded him his rightful place. His screen persona seems so relaxed and easy and his movies such pure entertainment that serious critics have largely ignored his outstanding contribution to the development of the cinema comedy and musical genres. As one admirer noted, there is nothing as relaxing as watching and listening to Bing Crosby. His voice, his manner, his attitude and his songs were "laid back" before

the concept originated, and the sheer pleasure of seeing and hearing Crosby has made him as popular internationally as in America. He is the second most popular star of the sound cinema, a top star for over 40 years and, for a period in the '40s, the number one box-office draw. He won an Academy Award for Best Actor for his 1944 portrayal of a priest in **Going My Way** (which also won the Best Picture Oscar) and more critical kudos for his fine performance as an alcoholic ex-star trying for a comeback in **The Country Girl** (although Grace Kelly » got the Oscar as his patient wife). His '30s, radio-orientated, films are among the most enjoyable musicals of that period, and his '40s **Road** films with Bob Hope » and Dorothy Lamour » are so much a part of their era that the period wouldn't be the same without them. In the '50s, he starred in some of the most enjoyable musicals to come out of Hollywood, especially the Frank Capra-directed **Riding High** and **Here Comes the Groom,** and a delightful musical re-make of **The Philadelphia Story, High Society.**

Crosby's greatest contribution to the movies, apart from his singing, was his attitude to light comedy acting. His influential,

Above: Bing Crosby, in his golden era of stardom, won an Oscar for his role as an ultra-relaxed priest opposite crotchety Barry Fitzgerald in **Going My Way.**

unforced style helped other actors realise that they could be film stars without forcing themselves to be anyone other than themselves. It wasn't the only way (James Cagney » was the complete antithesis, with his idea that the actor must never relax), but it was a good one, and its effects can be seen in the work of many modern stars, most notably Dean Martin » and James Garner ». In addition to his film success, Crosby is also the greatest selling recording artist of all time, with sales close to 400 million. His hit song White Christmas, from the 1942 musical **Holiday Inn,** is the biggest selling single at about 100 million copies. His death in 1977, while playing a relaxed game of golf (the game most associated with him), seemed an entirely appropriate end to a legend.

He was born as Harry Lillis Crosby on May 2, 1901, in Tacoma, Washington, and acquired his nickname "Bing" from the comic strip **The Bingsville Bugle** because both he and the strip's main character had big ears. His lackadaisical approach to his career kept him from major stardom until 1932, although he began singing as early as 1921. His movie career began in Mack Sennett shorts, and with Paul Whiteman's Orchestra as one of the Rhythm Boys in the 1930 **King of Jazz.** He got his own radio show in 1931 and achieved immediate fame. Paramount starred him in the delightful 1932 **The Big Broadcast** as a crooner (he always played variations of himself in his films) and his movie career took off in a big way. His '30s films are very pleasant, with such excellent co-stars as W.C. Fields ≫, Carole Lombard ≫, Marion Davies ≫, Ethel Merman and Burns and Allen ≫. Two of the best were the Cole Porter musical **Anything Goes** (with Merman)

Above: Bing Crosby, the most popular movie star of the sound era after John Wayne.

and **Pennies From Heaven** (with Louis Armstrong), both in 1936. His star climbed even higher in 1940 with the first of the **Road** films, **The Road to Singapore;** the combination of Crosby, Hope and Lamour was irresistible. The film was the most popular of the year and Crosby entered his golden era of movie stardom. He made the classic musicals **Birth of the Blues** (with Mary Martin) and **Holiday Inn** (with Fred Astaire ≫), and then became the top star in America and Britain with his multiple-Oscar-winning **Going My Way,** as a relaxed, singing priest solving the problems of a slum parish with song and winning over cantankerous older priest Barry Fitzgerald ≫ (who also got an acting Oscar). The film was highly approved of by mid-west and Catholic America, as was its sequel the following year, **The Bells of St Mary's** (with Ingrid Bergman ≫ as a nun).

Crosby was then at the peak of his movie career and could do no wrong. He made a series of hits including **Road to Utopia, Blue Skies, The Emperor Waltz** (with Billy Wilder directing), and **Wel-**

come **Stranger.** His success continued into the '50s in his charming musicals with Frank Capra, the box-office smash **White Christmas,** the dramatic **Country Girl** and the memorable **High Society.** He continued to make pleasant films but his movie stardom was fading and the films were no longer as popular as the earlier ones. His last role was a good one in an unsuccessful film: the drunken doctor in the 1966 remake of **Stagecoach.** Thereafter he devoted most of his time to TV and personal appearances and to his second family—his first wife, Dixie Lee (they married in 1930), had died in 1952, and he had married Kathryn Grant in 1957.

One of the few critics properly to appreciate Crosby's work was the great James Agee, who described his acting style as "the unaffected exploitation of an amiable personality, which at its best could not possibly be beat."

BEST FILMS:
1932 The Big Broadcast
Frank Tuttle (Paramount)
1936 Anything Goes
Lewis Milestone (Paramount)
1940 The Road to Morocco
David Butler (Paramount)
1942 Holiday Inn
Mark Sandrich (Paramount)
1944 Going My Way
Leo McCarey (Paramount)
1945 The Bells of St Mary's
Leo McCarey (Paramount)
1951 Here Comes the Groom
Frank Capra (Paramount)
1954 White Christmas
Michael Curtiz (Paramount)
1954 The Country Girl
George Seaton (Paramount)
1956 High Society
Charles Walters (MGM)

BEBE DANIELS

Bebe Daniels was a major star in the silent era but is more likely to be remembered for her excellent, though fewer, sound films and her popular British radio and TV shows with husband Ben Lyon (**Hi Gang!** and **Life with the Lyons**). Despite her extraordinarily long career (she appeared in her first film in 1908) and her great versatility, she never really created an identifiable screen personality. In the 1910s she was the little innocent paired with Harold Lloyd ≫ in most of his "Lonesome Luke" comedies; in the early '20s she was a mildly risqué playgirl in the films of Cecil B. De Mille and later in the decade she was a delightful light comedienne in a series of entertainments, mostly directed by Clarence Badger. She was a top star at Paramount, but always behind Swanson ≫ and Negri ≫. When Paramount dropped her with the arrival of sound, she switched to RKO and became one of the first big musical stars in the hit **Rio Rita** (re-made with Abbott and Costello ≫ in 1942) and its sequel **Dixiana.** She had some of

Above: Bebe Daniels as she appeared to a movie magazine artist in the early 1920s.

Above: Bebe Daniels with Thomas Meighan in **Why Change Your Wife?,** the epitome of 1920 sexual sophistication. She later became a top musical star.

her most rewarding parts during this period, creating the role of Miss Wonderly in the excellent first version of **The Maltese Falcon** (the part played in the 1941 version by Mary Astor ≫). She starred opposite Douglas Fairbanks, Snr ≫ in **Reaching for the Moon,** saved John Barrymore ≫ from himself in **Counsellor at Law,** and sang You're Getting to be a Habit with Me in the Busby Berkeley musical **42nd Street** (she then gets temperamental and lets Ruby Keeler ≫ be shoved forward to become a star).

Bebe Daniels married Ben Lyon in 1930 and played opposite him in films like **Alias French Gertie** and **My Past.** Her career started to falter; she was even cast as a has-been movie star in **Music is Music** with Alice Faye ≫. Although both were as American as could be (she was born in Dallas, Texas, on January 14, 1901, as Virginia Daniels, and he was born in Atlanta, Georgia, the same year), she went to England with her husband and they became bigger

stars than ever in live shows and their two BBC radio series. Both series inspired British films. They remained in Britain (except for a short American stay after World War II) until Bebe's death in 1971. Ben remarried in 1972, and lived in Beverly Hills until his death in 1979. A biography, Bebe and Ben, was published in 1975.

BEST FILMS:
1924 Monsieur Beaucaire
Sidney Olcott (Paramount)
1926 Miss Brewster's Millions
Clarence Badger (Paramount)
1927 A Kiss in a Taxi
Clarence Badger (Paramount)
1928 Feel My Pulse
Gregory La Cava (Paramount)
1929 Rio Rita
Luther Reed (RKO)
1931 The Maltese Falcon
Roy Del Ruth (Warner Brothers)
1933 42nd Street
Lloyd Bacon (Warner Brothers)
1933 Counsellor at Law
William Wyler (Universal)
1941 Hi Gang!
Marcel Varnel (in England)
1953 Life with the Lyons
Val Guest (in England)

DANIELLE DARRIEUX

Danielle Darrieux has become the world's idea of the ideal French woman, probably because that image has been based on her for the past 40 years. She became an international star in 1936 at the age of 19, portraying the pathetic Marie to Charles Boyer's ≫ Prince Rudolph in Anatole Litvak's romantic tragedy **Mayerling;** in 1975 she was singled out for praise as the best thing in a new movie opening in Paris. In between, she made an enormous number of good, bad and indifferent films, but only three great ones, all directed by Max Ophuls: **La Ronde** (as the sympathetic married woman who goes to bed with student Daniel Gélin), **Le Plaisir** (as a prostitute in love with Jean Gabin ≫), and **Madame de..**

(her greatest film and greatest performance, as a woman who loses the love of her life because of a pair of earrings). Darrieux was a good actress, exceptionally beautiful and unfailingly elegant, and Ophuls' baroque style fitted her perfectly: a woman who is romantic but also knowing, her charm almost an armour, her defence a deft and light sarcasm. One critic described her as "a flutter of steel".

Born in Bordeaux in 1917, she made her first movie at the age of 14, the 1931 **Le Bal** directed by Wilhelm Thiele. She appeared in several films in the next few years, including the early Billy Wilder picture **Mauvaise Graine** (1933). After the success of **Mayerling** in the US, Hollywood wanted to make her into an American star, but she preferred Europe (although she made one good American picture in 1938, **The Rage to Live** with Douglas Fairbanks, Jr ❯, and appeared in many popular French comedies with her director husband Henri Decoin (she later married playboy Porfirio Rubirosa, and then her present husband George Mitsinkides). The post-war period brought even greater popular success; apart from her Ophuls films, she upstaged Jane Powell in the MGM musical **Rich, Young and Pretty** (1951), singing a duet with Fernando Lamas, and was a double-crossing match for James Mason ❯ in **Five Fingers** (1952). Her career peaked in the '50s, after she appeared in her own favourite role as Madame de Renal opposite Gérard Philipe in **Le Rouge et le Noir.** She has continued making films in the '60s and '70s, and even appeared on Broadway in 1970 in **Coco.** As the ads for her first American film aptly said, "Fifty Million Frenchmen Can't Be Wrong."

*Above: Danielle Darrieux in her greatest role as the wife (of Charles Boyer) in Max Ophuls' **Madame De . . .***

BEST FILMS:
1936 Mayerling
Anatole Litvak (Nero)
1938 The Rage of Paris
Henry Koster (Universal)
1939 Battement de Coeur
Henri Decoin (Ciné-Alliance-Gerder)
1949 Occupe-toi d'Amélie
Claude Autant-Lara (Lux)
1950 La Ronde
Max Ophuls (Sacha Gordine)
1951 Le Plaisir
Max Ophuls (Stera/CCFC)
1952 Five Fingers
Joseph Mankiewicz (20th Century Fox)
1953 Madame de . . .
Max Ophuls (Franco-London)
1954 Le Rouge et le Noir
Claude Autant-Lara (Franco-London)
1968 24 Heures de la Vie d'une Femme
Dominique Delouche (Progefi/Roxy)

BETTE DAVIS

Bette Davis's greatest creation was Bette Davis. She was—indeed —a fine actress, but she made sure that the world knew it, knew how hard she had worked and what opposition she had to overcome to get great acting roles. She wanted to be known as an "actress" and she gritted her teeth, bulged her eyes and succeeded, winning two Oscars (for **Dangerous** and **Jezebel**), eight nominations and numerous other awards. She became the Queen of Hollywood as surely as Clark Gable ❯ became its King, and she was a big box-office star to boot. She also became one of the greatest show-offs in the history of the movies, a manneristic *grande dame* whom one critic aptly described as "breathtakingly" absurd." She fought, loudly and publicly, for the freedom to make better films—and when she got it, she mostly chose trashy (though highly enjoyable) women's pictures. The majority of her films are magnificent hokum: there is nothing in her career remotely comparable to Falconetti's ❯ performance in **The Passion of Joan of Arc.**

Davis's greatest performance was not in her early soap operas and over-heated, four-handkerchief melodramas, but in the sparkling satiric comedy **All About Eve.** Joseph Mankiewicz directed her into a delightful reflection of her own show business personality and she was never more truly a great screen actress. The mannerisms, the bitchiness, the unique vocal inflections and the gutsy intensity that she had built up over the years in her screen persona were finally given their proper setting. Sadly, it came virtually at the end of her great Hollywood years and she was only able to use this approach to her style twice more, as an Oscar-winning actress trying to make a comeback in **The Star** (1953), and as the demented, bizarre former movie star in **Whatever Happened to Baby Jane?** in 1962.

She was born as Ruth Elizabeth Davis in Lowell, Massachusetts, on April 15, 1908, and borrowed the "Bette" for her stage name from Balzac. She started in theatre in 1928 and made her first film in 1931 at Universal, **Bad Sister.** But it was at Warner Brothers that she became a star, and it was probably that studio's reputation for tough guys and brassy dames that helped form her screen personality. Her first important movie was the 1932 **Cabin in the Cotton** with Michael Curtiz directing her for the first time in the type of conniving Southern vixen role that she was to make famous. Her career went nowhere until 1934, when she gave one of her most memorable performances as the sluttish, grasping waitress who hooks Leslie Howard ❯ in **Of Human Bondage,** thus beginning the greatest period of her cinema career. She was impressive with Paul Muni ❯ in the love-triangle **Bordertown,** and then won her first Academy Award in **Dangerous,** portraying a film star on the skids saved by Franchot Tone. She was exceptional (as she always was when playing actresses) in her next film as well, teamed with Humphrey Bogart ❯ and Leslie Howard in the screen version of **The Petrified Forest.** Her fight with the studio to get more meaty roles ended in a court case in London when she went abroad to film; she lost, but came back to enhanced prestige.

Davis's next great vehicle was the 1938 **Jezebel,** which won her a second Oscar (as a prototype Scarlett O'Hara in a scandalous red dress). She had become a

bravura actress. The flouncing walk and staccato style of delivery were never better, but she was no longer simply an actress playing a role—she was Bette Davis giving a mesmeric performance. It is impossible to take your eyes off her when she is on screen in her memorable films, although many of them are pure schmaltz. She was a rich socialite dying of a tumour in the great weepie **Dark Victory,** an unwed mother whose daughter prefers nasty Miriam Hopkins ❯ in the tear-jerker **The Old Maid,** and an incomparable Queen Elizabeth in the historical pageant **The Private Lives of Elizabeth and Essex** (co-starring with Errol Flynn ❯ in her first colour film). At the beginning of

shall »). She proved herself equally adept at witty comedy in **The Man Who Came to Dinner** (portraying Monty Woolley's secretary), but was probably more popular as the ultimate bitch destroying Olivia de Havilland's life (and everybody else's) in **In This Our Life**. She was back in sudsy hokum with Miriam Hopkins in **Old Acquaintance**, teamed up with Claude Rains again for more soap-opera in **Mr Skeffington**, and even tried her hand at singing in **Thank Your Lucky Stars**.

Her post-war films fell off sharply, and it was not until **All About Eve** in 1950 that she was back in form. She was memorable in **The Star** in 1952 and **The Virgin Queen** in 1955, but her career slackened—she even had to advertise for work in 1961, before making a smashing comeback with Joan Crawford » in Robert Aldrich's macabre **Whatever Happened to Baby Jane?** Its combination of horror, Hollywood and manneristic acting put her back in the star class again—but few good films followed, with the exception of Aldrich's sequel **Hush, Hush . . . Sweet Charlotte**. She made films in England and Italy as well as in America, but none was particularly successful, although she still had charisma on the screen. She has also done TV work. Among her more succesful recent films were the 1976 **Burnt Offerings**, and the 1978 **Return from Witch Mountain**. She remains a truly wondrous star but, as Brian Aherne once remarked, nobody but a mother could have loved her at the height of her career.

BEST FILMS:

1934 Of Human Bondage
John Cromwell (RKO)
1935 Dangerous
Alfred E. Green (Warner Brothers)
1938 Jezebel
William Wyler (Warner Brothers)
1939 Dark Victory
Edmund Goulding (Warner Brothers)
1940 The Letter
William Wyler (Warner Brothers)
1941 The Little Foxes
William Wyler (RKO/Goldwyn)
1942 In This Our Life
John Huston (Warner Brothers)
1942 Now Voyager
Irving Rapper (Warner Brothers)
1950 All About Eve
Joseph Mankiewicz (20th Century Fox)
1962 Whatever Happened to Baby Jane?
Robert Aldrich (Warner Brothers)

DORIS DAY

It is fashionable to sneer at Doris Day's screen image as a freckle-faced, wholesome, professional virgin with a clean-scrubbed voice and reticent sexuality, but the wheels of fashion continue to revolve and that facile assessment is likely to alter considerably in the years to come. She was

Above: Doris Day and "husband" Rock Hudson in the 1964 **Send Me No Flowers**, *in which he wanted to marry her off.*

indeed professional, one of the best comediennes and most enjoyable singers of the modern cinema, but her much-touted and joked-about persona as a "virgin" needs re-examination. If she wasn't sexy, then why were Rock Hudson », Cary Grant » and her other leading men always trying to get her into bed? Perhaps the key lies in Oscar Levant's famous quip: "I knew Doris Day before she was a virgin." In fact, she had been married twice before she became a movie star, and her life as a band singer with Bob Crosby and Les Brown was hardly conducive to an image of pristine purity.

One of the most appealing aspects of her screen persona was her independence—and the hints of previous experiences that made her wary of falling for masculine (and often chauvinist) wiles. In her best films she was just as tough-minded as the men she was involved with; this was noticeable even in her '50s films like **Calamity Jane** and **Love Me or Leave Me**. In her delightful later comedies (beginning with the 1959 **Pillow Talk**), the "virgin" aspect was stressed (by the men), but what she actually portrayed was a woman who was not against the idea, but unwilling to succumb on the terms offered. The central subject of these comedies was sex and, considering the restrictions of Hollywood films of the time, they were fairly open about it.

Day's immense popularity as a movie star should not be overlooked. She was probably the top woman box office star of all time, if the annual top ten list is anything to go by; she was number one for four years in the

early '60s (a record unequalled by any other woman), and was highly ranked through most of the '50s and '60s.

She was born as Doris Kappelhoff in Cincinnati on April 3, 1924, planned to be a dancer before a bad automobile accident, and instead became a band singer (her million-selling *Sentimental Journey* with the Les Brown Orchestra remains a classic). Two early marriages to musicians didn't work out, and her career was not going well when Michael Curtiz cast her in the 1948 **Romance on the High Seas**, replacing pregnant Betty Hutton ». Her pleasant rendition of *It's Magic* made her an instant hit, and she became a big star as both a recording artist and a movie actress—one of the first to have cross-over success between the two industries; she had six million-selling records, starting with *Confess* and including *It's Magic, Secret Love* (from **Calamity Jane**) and *Que Sera Sera* (from **The Man Who Knew Too Much**). She made a series of frothy but enjoyable musicals in the early '50s, as well as demonstrating her abilities as an actress in films like **Storm Warning** (getting shot by the Ku Klux Klan) and Alfred Hitchcock's **The Man Who Knew Too Much** (as an ex-actress whose son is kidnapped). She proved that she was just as good at being "immoral" as at being "virginal" in **Love Me or Leave Me,** portraying singer Ruth Etting. She was bouncy and tomboyish in **Calamity Jane** and even better as the high-spirited union leader in **The Pajama Game**.

Day began her brilliant series of comedies at Universal in 1959 with **Pillow Talk**. They were glossily mounted by producer Ross Hunter, and all extremely popular under the direction of

Above: Bette Davis gave one of her finest performances in **The Little Foxes**. *Inset: Davis in* **Whatever Happened to Baby Jane?**

the '40s she was at the peak of her career, the most popular female star in America.

Her films during the war years were among her most popular; they were mainly women's pictures and sob-stories, but there have never been more tearfully enjoyable romps than **All This and Heaven Too, The Great Lie,** and, greatest of them all, **Now Voyager**, with Claude Rains ». She had the moon—but she also had the stars, in some high quality films by her greatest director, William Wyler: **The Letter** (magnificently deceptive as a murderess in Malaya), and **The Little Foxes** (again as a murderess, viciously withholding pills from husband Herbert Mar-

Michael Gordon, Delbert Mann and Norman Jewison. By the time of **The Thrill of It All** in 1964, there were even Freudian showers of fireworks when she headed for the bedroom with James Garner ❯. Her third husband and manager, Martin Melcher, died in 1968, and she made no more films after the 1969 **With Six You Get Eggroll,** although that was a big commercial success. She hosted the TV series *The Doris Day Show* from 1968 to 1972, and in 1976 published her revealing autobiography, *Doris Day: Her Story.*

BEST FILMS:
1948 Romance on the High Seas
Michael Curtiz (Warner Brothers)
1951 On Moonlight Bay
Roy Del Ruth (Warner Brothers)
1953 Calamity Jane
David Butler (Warner Brothers)
1955 Love Me or Leave Me
Charles Vidor (MGM)
1956 The Man Who Knew Too Much
Alfred Hitchcock (Paramount)
1957 The Pajama Game
Stanley Donen and George Abbott (Warner Brothers)
1959 Pillow Talk
Michael Gordon (Universal)
1962 Lover Come Back
Delbert Mann (Universal)
1963 The Thrill of It All
Norman Jewison (Universal)
1966 The Glass Bottom Boat
Frank Tashlin (MGM)

OLIVIA DE HAVILLAND

One of the major Hollywood glamour stars, with a long list of notable films, Olivia de Havilland's screen career divides into two sections. In the '30s she was the lightweight but delectable heroine of Errol Flynn's ❯ best swashbucklers, including the sweet heroine of **Captain Blood,** the demure Maid Marian of **The Adventures of Robin Hood,** and the refined maid-in-waiting of **The Private Lives of Elizabeth and Essex,** all under the direction of Michael Curtiz. She was even able to make wishy-washy Melanie an enjoyable characterisation in **Gone With the Wind.** Her second career, in the '40s, came after a struggle with Warners for the right to choose better parts without the threat of an extended contract, and two years of litigation —which she won. She then became the leading "dramatic actress" of the American cinema of the period, winning Academy Awards for Leisen's **To Each His Own** (as an unwed mother making a brave sacrifice) and Wyler's **The Heiress** as a spinster wooed by and rejecting Montgomery Clift ❯, and great critical acclaim for Litvak's **The Snake Pit** (a patient in a mental home) and **The Dark Mirror** (playing good and bad twins). She rounded off this period nicely with the highly dramatic **My Cousin Rachel.** De

Above: Olivia de Havilland looked exceptionally good in period costume frills.

Below: Olivia de Havilland as Maid Marian with Errol Flynn in **The Adventures of Robin Hood.**

Havilland was outstanding in both periods, but although she won the most prestige for her heavyweight dramatic films, it is her earlier lightweight entertainments that are most enjoyed today—and most often revived.

She was born of British parents in Tokyo on July 1, 1916, and discovered in a stage production of **A Midsummer's Night's Dream** by Max Reinhardt, who put her in his film version as Hermia. Warners put her under contract, and she became Errol Flynn's love interest in most of his great pictures for Michael Curtiz. She was a natural for the vapid Melanie in **Gone With the Wind,** and this helped her get meatier roles. She won an Academy Award acting nomination for **Hold Back the Dawn** (as a schoolteacher wooed by Charles Boyer ❯, but did not get her great dramatic roles until after she left Warners in 1946. Her career has continued into the '70s, but she lost interest in film-making for a while after her marriage in 1955 to the editor of *Paris Match* (they later separated). She made two notable thrillers in 1964, **Lady in a Cage** and **Hush, Hush . . . Sweet Charlotte** (with old friend Bette Davis ❯), and was in **The Adventurers** in 1969. Her '70s films include **Airport '77** and **The Swarm.**

BEST FILMS:
1935 Captain Blood
Michael Curtiz (Warner Brothers)
1938 The Adventures of Robin Hood
Michael Curtiz (Warner Brothers)
1939 Gone With the Wind
Victor Fleming (MGM)
1941 Hold Back the Dawn
Mitchell Leisen (Paramount)
1946 The Dark Mirror
Robert Siodmak (Universal)
1946 To Each His Own
Mitchell Leisen (Paramount)
1948 The Snake Pit
Anatole Litvak (20th Century Fox)
1949 The Heiress
William Wyler (Paramount)
1952 My Cousin Rachel
Henry Koster (20th Century Fox)
1964 Hush, Hush . . . Sweet Charlotte
Robert Aldrich (20th Century Fox)

MARLENE DIETRICH

One of the greatest glamour figures of the twentieth century, Marlene Dietrich had a rather extraordinary film career that is now only part of her chic image as an all-round entertainer. However, the public image of Dietrich was created by the movies and everything that she became is based on her films of the '30s. Her Svengali was director Josef von Sternberg, who starred her in **The Blue Angel** in Germany in 1930 and then made her into Greta Garbo's ❯ only real rival in Hollywood. That

Above: Marlene Dietrich—the movie star as a living legend.

stardom lasted an amazingly short time. By 1936, she was not even among the 100 most popular stars and had to begin making the first of many comebacks—highly successfully, in the 1939 **Destry Rides Again**. That film brought her exotic, untouchable, man-destroying *femme fatale* image down to earth with a bump (including a fist fight with Una Merkel), but it kept her in movies for two more decades, even if she was no longer the main attraction of the films in which she appeared.

Marlene was born as Maria Magdalena Dietrich in Berlin in December 27, 1901 (she later acquired the surname von Lösch when her widowed mother remarried). She began with stage work and had her first film part as a maid in the 1923 film **Der kleine Napoleon**, directed by Georg Jacoby. She recorded her first song in 1927 (*Peter*) and was signed by von Sternberg to star opposite Emil Jannings ≯ in **The Blue Angel**. Her performance as a new kind of cruel vamp in top hat and silk stockings, enticing school-teacher Jannings to destruction, was a resounding international hit, especially when she sang *Falling in Love Again*. Von Sternberg may have created the characterisation of the screen Dietrich and put it in its proper setting, and certainly cameraman Lee Garmes was responsible for her Paramount look, but it was Dietrich herself who provided the beauty, the voice, and the enigmatic personality at its core. The screen "Marlene" was the creation of all three, but she took the combined creation and has literally lived it up to the present day. Her six Paramount films for von Sternberg were her (and his) masterpieces. In **Morocco** she is cabaret singer Amy Jolly, so in love with Foreign Legionnaire Gary Cooper ≯ that she follows him into the desert in her evening dress. In **Dishonored** she is a streetwalker-turned-spy in World-War-I Vienna, tracking down Russian Victor McLaglen ≯.

In **Shanghai Express**, probably her finest film, she is a woman of easy virtue willing to sacrifice all for Clive Brook ≯ in China (and has the immortal line, "It took more than one man to change my name to Shanghai Lily"). In the relatively less successful **Blonde Venus** she is a café singer involved with Herbert Marshall ≯ and Cary Grant ≯, doing one number in a gorilla suit and another in her famous white tie, tails and top hat. In the opulent and magnificent **The Scarlet Empress** she is a jewel-hard Catherine the Great of Russia in what is probably her most visually stunning film. Her last von Sternberg picture was **The Devil is a Woman**, with Marlene in the

Left: Marlene Dietrich as Lola-Lola in von Sternberg's 1930 **The Blue Angel**, *the role that made her into an international movie and singing star.*

Spain of the 1890s involved with César Romero and Lionel Atwill (a financial flop but one of her favourite films). In all of these films, von Sternberg stressed the visual element and lighting almost to the exclusion of the Dietrich personality, smothering her in ever more elaborate costumes and sets.

Paramount took Dietrich away from von Sternberg (she was too big an investment to hide behind even the most stunning costumes) and tried to restore her falling popularity with rather good films by Frank Borzage (**Desire**) and Ernst Lubitsch (**Angel**). It didn't work, and nor did anything else (including a British film, **Knight Without Armour**) until (at von Sternberg's suggestion) she returned to demolish her untouchable image in **Destry Rides Again** opposite James Stewart ≯. She has made many films since then and has often been brilliant—but nothing has matched her early period. She was especially notable as a nightclub tramp in Wilder's **A Foreign Affair** (1948) and as a saloon singer hiding outlaws in Lang's **Rancho Notorious**; in the '50s she more or less gave up films for singing, and her persona has worked just as well in night clubs and on records as in the cinema. The 1964 **Paris When It Sizzles** was her last film until 1978, when she made **Just A Gigolo** with rock star David Bowie.

As Ernest Hemingway once observed: "If she had nothing more than her voice, she could break your heart." She had a lot more—and she is destined to be one of the cinema's immortals.

BEST FILMS:
1930 The Blue Angel (Der blaue Engel)
Josef von Sternberg (Ufa), in Germany
1930 Morocco
Josef von Sternberg (Paramount)
1931 Dishonored
Josef von Sternberg (Paramount)
1932 Shanghai Express
Josef von Sternberg (Paramount)
1932 Blonde Venus
Josef von Sternberg (Paramount)
1934 The Scarlet Empress
Josef von Sternberg (Paramount)
1935 The Devil is a Woman
Josef von Sternberg (Paramount)
1939 Destry Rides Again
George Marshall (Universal)
1948 A Foreign Affair
Billy Wilder (Paramount)
1952 Rancho Notorious
Fritz Lang (RKO)

DONALD DUCK

see **Mickey Mouse**

ROBERT DONAT

For America in the 1930s, Donat was the personification of the British gentleman film star, with unequalled performances in such classics as **The Thirty-Nine Steps** and **Goodbye Mr Chips**. For England, he was something else again—the unfulfilled greatest actor of his generation, with a career blighted by ill-health. He may not have reached the heights that might have been possible (only 19 films in 26 years), but his cinema achievement was consider-

Left: Robert Donat in one of his greatest roles, as Richard Hannay in Alfred Hitchcock's classic 1935 version of John Buchan's thriller about a man on the run, **The Thirty-Nine Steps.**

able all the same. As Richard Hannay in Alfred Hitchcock's **The Thirty Nine Steps**, he gave one of the all-time best portrayals of the man on the run. In **Goodbye Mr Chips**, his frail, melodious voice was heard at its finest in a sentimental but still moving portrait of the life of a schoolmaster (for which he won the 1939 Academy Award). In **The Citadel**, he brought genuine believability to the role of A. J. Cronin's doctor who gives up idealism for wealth until tragedy gives him understanding. He was even a good swashbuckler in the excellent 1934 version of **The Count of Monte Cristo**. He should have become a star of the stature of Olivier ≯, but he was dogged by chronic asthma; he was too ill to make many films in the '40s and '50s and he died at the age of 53.

Donat was born in Withington, Manchester, in 1905, and made his stage début in 1921. Alexander Korda discovered him for films and he made his first movie, **Men of Tomorrow**, in 1932. His supporting role as Culpepper to Laughton's ≯ **Henry VIII** made him famous and he quickly became *the* British prestige actor, starring in René Clair's **The Ghost Goes West** (as both a ghost and his modern descendant in a haunted castle) and Jacques Feyder's **Knight Without Armour** (the very expensive production Korda set up for Marlene Dietrich ≯). After the '30s, Donat's film career was spasmodic. He was a brilliant, fiery politician in Reed's patriotic **The Young Mr Pitt** and was at the peak of his eloquence as the barrister in Asquith's **The Winslow Boy** in 1948. He was desperately ill during much of the '50s, but did manage a superb supporting role as the Chinese mandarin in **The Inn of the Sixth Happiness** in 1958. His last words in the film were: "We shall not see each other again, I think." He died shortly afterwards.

BEST FILMS:
1933 The Private Life of Henry VIII
Alexander Korda (London Films)
1934 The Count of Monte Cristo
Rowland V. Lee (Reliance)
1935 The Thirty-Nine Steps
Alfred Hitchcock (Gaumont-British)
1936 The Ghost Goes West
René Clair (London Films)
1937 Knight Without Armour
Jacques Feyder (London Films)
1938 The Citadel
King Vidor (MGM)
1939 Goodbye Mr Chips
Sam Wood (MGM)
1942 The Young Mr Pitt
Carol Reed (20th Century Fox)
1943 The Adventures of Tartu
Harold Bucquet (MGM)
1948 The Winslow Boy
Anthony Asquith (British Lion)

KIRK DOUGLAS

Kirk Douglas fought his way to stardom in the 1949 **Champion** as an unscrupulous boxer who wouldn't let anything or anyone prevent him from reaching the top. The film was a good metaphor for Douglas's screen personality and doubtless reflected the personal drives of a man who worked at menial jobs to pay his way through drama school and retained a relentless drive once he became a star. His clenched-teeth determination is a part of the iconography of the cinema (along with that cleft in his chin), and he used it to brilliant effect in a series of outstanding movies in the '50s, culminating in his performance in one of the greatest films ever made in Hollywood, **Paths of Glory.**

Douglas was born as Issur Danielovitch Demsky in Amsterdam, New York, on December 9, 1916, and made his initial reputation acting on stage in the '40s. He had a good, big role in his first film, **The Strange Love of Martha Ivers,** in 1946, opposite Barbara Stanwyck ≯, and the 1949 **Champion** made him the hottest new star in Hollywood. He didn't let up for a moment, and made one exceptional film after another, including **Along the Great Divide, Ace in the Hole, Detective Story, The Big Sky** and **The Bad and the Beautiful,** all classics of their kind. He was as powerful in Westerns (**Man Without A Star, Gunfight at the OK Corral, Last Train to Gun Hill**) as he was playing the ambitious reporter in **Ace in the Hole** and as the vicious movie producer of **The Bad and The Beautiful.** He had to extend himself considerably to portray Vincent Van Gogh in **Lust For**

Above left: Kirk Douglas as a film director trying for a comeback in **Two Weeks in Another Town.**
Above: Douglas having a smirky chat with Claire Trevor in the 1955 **Man Without a Star.**

Life — a brilliant performance despite critical carping. Then came Stanley Kubrick's **Paths of Glory,** the greatest role of Douglas's remarkable career. His relentless, driving idealism as a World War I French officer who tries to save his men from the juggernaut of corrupt Army bureaucracy set in motion by unscrupulous superiors, was the fulcrum of this astounding pacifist film. He loses, but it is only because of his forceful attempt to secure justice that we realize how powerful corruption can be. The situation was repeated under Kubrick's direction in **Spartacus** three years later. Douglas again portrays a tough-minded and ruthlessly determined idealist trying to protect his followers from the oppression of the mighty (in this case they are slaves from Imperial Rome), and again he loses bitterly.

After these two towering achievements, Douglas continued to portray the idea of the man fighting against impossible odds for what he thinks is right — but the scale came down considerably. In **Lonely Are The Brave** he is a lone cowboy on the run, beaten and killed by the mechanical juggernauts of modern life. In **Two Weeks in Another Town** he is a shattered movie director trying to make a comeback in Rome. In **Seven Days in May** he once again opposes the Army establishment, which is attempting an American *coup d'etat,* but this time he succeeds.

In 1969, he and director Elia Kazan combined their talents on what seemed oddly like a doubly-autobiographical movie, **The Arrangement.** His films in the '70s have been less notable, though his Western political allegory **Posse** (which he directed) was a considerable achievement.

BEST FILMS:
1949 Champion
Mark Robson (United Artists)
1951 Ace in the Hole
Billy Wilder (Paramount)

1951 Detective Story
William Wyler (Paramount)
1951 Along the Great Divide
Raoul Walsh (Warner Brothers)
1952 The Big Sky
Howard Hawks (RKO)
1952 The Bad and the Beautiful
Vincente Minnelli (MGM)
1955 Man Without a Star
King Vidor (Universal)
1956 Lust For Life
Vincente Minnelli (MGM)
1957 Gunfight at the OK Corral
John Sturges (Paramount)
1957 Paths of Glory
Stanley Kubrick (United Artists)
1960 Spartacus
Stanley Kubrick (Universal)
1962 Lonely Are The Brave
David Miller (Universal)
1962 Two Weeks In Another Town
Vincente Minnelli (MGM)
1964 Seven Days in May
John Frankenheimer (Paramount)
1969 The Arrangement
Elia Kazan (Warner Brothers)

MELVYN DOUGLAS

In the '30s Melvyn Douglas would have been unrecognisable without an elegant glamorous star on his arm, the perfect escort to such ladies as Greta Garbo ≯, Joan Crawford ≯, Claudette Colbert ≯, Marlene Dietrich ≯. In the '60s he was the epitome of opinionated old fathers in conflict with their sons, notably Paul Newman ≯ in **Hud** and Gene Hackman ≯ in **I Never Sang for My Father.** But he also starred in some of the most delightful light comedies of the '30s and early '40s. He was frivolous, frothy and funny, almost always wearing a memorably quizzical look as partners like Irene Dunne, Joan Blondell ≯ and Myrna Loy ≯ behaved in odd ways. He was Garbo's partner in her delicious Ernst Lubitsch comedy **Ninotchka,** and he was equally amusing trading quips with Colbert in **She Married Her Boss,** Dunne in **Theodora Grows Wild,** Blondell in **There's Always a Woman,** and Loy in **Third Finger Left Hand.** Lubitsch used his stylish playing to excellent effect opposite Dietrich in **Angel** and Merle Oberon in **That Uncertain Feeling.** He was brilliant — but nobody thought of it as "acting" at the time; he didn't get an Academy Award until 1962 (for his "serious" role in **Hud**), and then was nominated again for **I Never Sang for My Father.** Acting, as the Academy stresses, is a serious business.

Douglas was born as Melvyn C. Hesselberg in Macon, Georgia, on April 5, 1901. He had a successful stage career and was transferred to Hollywood with a hit play, **Tonight or Never,** to star opposite Gloria Swanson ≯ in 1931. He "starred opposite" a lot of glamour ladies after that, including Garbo in **As You Desire Me** and Ann Harding in **Prestige,** but the focus

Above: Melvyn Douglas turned out to be one of the most suitable partners ever for Greta Garbo in the witty 1939 Ernst Lubitsch comedy Ninotchka. She plays a hard-line Soviet woman who is softened by Douglas's charms.

was never on him. His first great comedy role was in the wonderful horror spoof **The Old Dark House**, but he wasn't really recognised for his stylish playing until the 1935 **She Married Her Boss**. After that he had a fine run of comedies until he joined the Army. After the war, he concentrated more on theatre work than cinema, but still made some good films, including the 1948 **Mr Blandings Builds His Dream House.** He began appearing regularly again in the '60s, in films like **Billy Budd** and **Hud**, and showed his comic genius once more in the under-rated **The Americanization of Emily.** His recent films include **The Candidate, The Tenant** and **Twilight's Last Gleaming.**

BEST FILMS:
1932 The Old Dark House
James Whale (Universal)
1935 She Married Her Boss
Gregory La Cava (Columbia)
1936 Theodora Goes Wild
Richard Boleslavsky (Columbia)
1937 Angel
Ernst Lubitsch (Paramount)
1939 Ninotchka
Ernst Lubitsch (MGM)
1941 That Uncertain Feeling
Ernst Lubitsch (Columbia)
1941 A Woman's Face
George Cukor (MGM)
1942 Two-Faced Woman
George Cukor (MGM)
1962 Hud
Martin Ritt (Paramount)
1969 I Never Sang for My Father
Gilbert Cates (Columbia)

MARIE DRESSLER

MGM called her "The World's Greatest Actress" in the early '30s when she was that studio's highest paid performer and the most popular star in movies. She was also one of the unlikeliest movie stars of all time being a 60-year-old fat and flabby harridan with a broken-down face that looked like the back of a barge. She stole the attention from Greta Garbo ❯ in her first sound film **Anna Christie** (as the gritty-humoured Marthy) and suddenly became everybody's favourite star after years in the wilderness.

She was born as Leila von Koerber in Coburg, Ontario, on November 9, 1869, and became a popular vaudeville star and comedienne. She was persuaded to make her first film in 1914 by Mack Sennett, based on her stage work, and it became the comedy classic **Tillie's Punctured Romance.** It was the first comedy feature and her co-stars were Charles Chaplin ❯ and Mabel Normand ❯. Later films did not go well and her part in the 1917 chorus girl strike affected her career badly. She was very much down-and-out in the '20s and had almost abandoned acting when screenwriter Frances Marion found her and persuaded MGM to hire her. Her career revived but did not really take off until Marion talked MGM boss Irving Thalberg into using her in **Anna Christie**: that was the turning point in the most extraordinary comeback ever.

Her performance as a tough, boozy waterfront hotel operator (with a heart of gold) with Wallace Beery in **Min and Bill** won her the Best Actress Oscar in 1931 and the film was a smash at the box office. She was teamed again with Beery in the equally-successful **Tugboat Annie** (she was the tough-talking captain and Beery was the heavy-drinking husband "who never struck me except in self defense.") She got another Oscar nomination for **Emma** (as the maidservant and finally bride of Jean Hersholt) and made a series of highly popular comedies with Polly Moran as her fighting friend (**Caught Short, Reducing, Politics**). She was wonderfully funny as a cynical old actress in **Dinner at Eight** and gave one of her greatest performances as the housekeeper in **The Late Christopher Bean**, who prefers large families she can feel a part of. She died in July, 1934, after a truly amazing career.

BEST FILMS:
1914 Tillie's Punctured Romance
Mack Sennett (Keystone)
1928 The Patsy
King Vidor (MGM)
1930 Anna Christie
Clarence Brown (MGM)
1930 Caught Short
Charles Reisner (MGM)
1932 Min and Bill
George Hill (MGM)
1931 Reducing
Charles Reisner (MGM)
1932 Emma
Clarence Brown (MGM)
1933 Tugboat Annie
Mervyn LeRoy (MGM)
1933 Dinner at Eight
George Cukor (MGM)
1933 The Late Christopher Bean
Sam Wood (MGM)

IRENE DUNNE

The chic, elegant and noble Queen of the Weepies in the '30s and early '40s, who also excelled in musical and screwball comedies. Her title as the First Lady of Soap

Opera came after superbly suffering performances in classics like **Back Street** and **Magnificent Obsession.** She told interviewers that her success was based on tears in multiple-handkerchief movies, but she was loved by audiences for other things as well. She became a star in her second film, the epic 1931 Western **Cimarron** (as a pioneer housewife). It won the Best Picture Oscar and Dunne was nominated for Best Actress (as she was four later films, but she never won). She starred coolly opposite Fred Astaire ❯ and Ginger Rogers ❯ in **Roberta** in 1935 (singing *Smoke Gets in Your Eyes*), was at her singing-and-dancing best in the 1936 **Showboat** as Magnolia (singing *Make Believe*), and was relatively less successful in **High, Wide and Handsome** with Randolph Scott ❯ (singing *The Folk Who Live on the Hill*). Her funniest performances were in the screwball comedies **Theodora Goes Wild** (as a small-town girl who is the secret author of a naughty novel) and the even more delightful **The Awful Truth** (with Leo McCarey directing and Cary Grant ❯ as co-star). Having proved she was versatile, Dunne then went back to soap opera never-never land (rather splendidly) opposite Charles Boyer ❯ in the 1939 **Love Affair** (another Oscar nomination, and her favourite film).

Born Irene Marie Dunn in Louisville, Kentucky, on December 20, 1901, she came to the cinema after a very successful stage career in the '20s. Her first film was **Leathernecking** in 1930, and then **Cimarron** made her a star. Her graceful, sophisticated style kept her a major star in the '40s with such hits as the fantasy **A Guy Named Joe** and the weepie **The White Cliffs of Dover.** After World War II she made three outstanding films: **Anna and the King of Siam** (the first and best version, with Rex Harrison ❯ as

Below: Irene Dunne was both elegant and convincing in Anna and the King of Siam.

Below: Marie Dressler as a decaying grande dame in the all-star comedy Dinner at Eight.

the King), **Life With Father** (as the matronly but lively wife of William Powell ») and **I Remember Mama** (as the kindest and cleverest of all screen mamas in 1910 San Francisco). It looked as if her career would go on indefinitely, until she suddenly flopped in 1950 in **The Mudlark** (as a static and dowdy Queen Victoria). She made only one more film, the unsuccessful 1952 comedy **It Grows on Trees.** Her place in film history is secure but has probably not been properly recognised because so many of her best films have been re-made (and her earlier version withdrawn from circulation). There is a subtle kind of flattery in the fact that there were new versions of her greatest hits (**Cimarron, Back Street, Magnificent Obsession, Roberta, Show Boat, Anna and the King of Siam,** etc). They certainly did not improve on the originals.

Above: Deanna Durbin described herself as a "fairy tale character" in her 21 movies.

BEST FILMS:
1931 Cimarron
Wesley Ruggles (RKO)
1932 Back Street
John Stahl (Universal)
1935 Roberta
William A. Seiter (RKO)
1935 Magnificent Obsession
John Stahl (Universal)
1936 Show Boat
James Whale (Universal)
1936 Theodora Goes Wild
Richard Boleslawski (Columbia)
1937 The Awful Truth
Leo McCarey (Columbia)
1939 Love Affair
Leo McCarey (RKO)
1946 Anna and the King of Siam
John Cromwell (20th Century Fox)
1947 Life With Father
Michael Curtiz (Warner Brothers)
1948 I Remember Mama
George Stevens (RKO)

DEANNA DURBIN

One of the most popular teenage movie stars of all time, Deanna Durbin was the high-spirited Little Miss Fixit of 21 contemporary fairy tales for Universal in the late '30s and early '40s. Her clear, natural singing voice made her a star, but it was her warmth and agreeable spontaneity that made her screen image. She was just as popular in Britain as in America, but was unable to break out of her teenage persona and retired at the age of 27.

She was born as Edna Mae Dubrin in Winnipeg, Canada, on December 4, 1921, and made her first film, a short called **Every Sunday,** for MGM in 1936. It co-starred Judy Garland (an extract is included in **That's Entertainment**). Durbin was then whisked away to Universal by producer Joseph Pasternak, who made her that studio's biggest star (thereby saving it from bankruptcy).

Durbin's first feature was **Three Smart Girls,** directed by Henry Koster, who made six of her best films. As in many of her movies, she was matchmaking (her parents this time), a little bit cleverer than the adults and a superb singer (including *Someone to Care for Me*). The film was such a hit that she was culturally upgraded for her next picture, **100 Men and a Girl,** co-starring with Leopold Stokowski and a symphony orchestra, with Adolphe Menjou » as her violinist father. In it, like most of her films, she was a "fairy tale character" (as she herself has recently described her image), but her self-assurance, likeable personality and amazing voice gave it appeal to all ages. She made two hit films a year after that, most of them cut to the same pattern but still enjoyable, and was given a special miniature Academy Award in 1938 (in tandem with Mickey Rooney ») for "bringing to the screen the spirit and personification of youth." Her career faltered badly in the mid-40's, probably because Pasternak left Universal and no-one developed her screen personality in a new way, as was done with Judy Garland at MGM. She retired in 1949 after making her last film, **For the Love of Mary.** She married French director Charles-Henri David (who made her 1945 **Lady on a Train**) and moved to the French village of Neauphle-le-Château near Paris, where she still lives.

BEST FILMS:
1936 Three Smart Girls
Henry Koster (Universal)
1937 100 Men and a Girl
Henry Koster (Universal)
1938 Mad About Music
Norman Taurog (Universal)
1938 That Certain Age
Edward Ludwig (Universal)
1939 Three Smart Girls Grow Up
Henry Koster (Universal)
1939 First Love
Henry Koster (Universal)
1940 It's a Date
William A. Seiter (Universal)
1940 Spring Parade
Henry Koster (Universal)
1941 It Started with Eve
Henry Koster (Universal)
1943 His Butler's Sister
Frank Borzage (Universal)

NELSON EDDY
see **Jeanette MacDonald**

DOUGLAS FAIRBANKS JR

Douglas Fairbanks, Jr, almost took over his father's swashbuckling persona in the early '40s, starring in a highly entertaining series of fun films (**The Corsican Brothers, Sinbad the Sailor** and **The Exile**). Unfortunately they came too late in his career for him to become truly immersed in that delectable genre and he retired very shortly afterwards. Throughout his 28 years in the cinema he had had trouble establishing a screen image in the shadow of his father's fame; if Jesse Lasky of Paramount, who put him in his first film in 1923 (a flop called **Stephen Steps Out**), had not been so intent on exploiting the Fairbanks name, an entirely different persona might have been built up. Fairbanks, Jr, was at his most memorable in the kind of British roles played by Colman » and Flynn » notably in **The Dawn Patrol** and **Gunga Din,** but his finest creation was the caddish Rupert of Hentzau in **The Prisoner of Zenda.**

Fairbanks was actually not British at all. He was born in New York City on December 9, 1909, as Douglas Elton Ulman, Jr, and his mother was a Rhode Island girl named Beth Sully. He went to Hollywood to earn money against his father's wishes, but had little luck in the silent era; sound advanced his career and he made notable appearances in Hawks' **The Dawn Patrol** (the man who will follow Richard Barthelmess » into the death seat), **Outward Bound** (Leslie Howard's » first talkie) and **Little Caesar** (as the gigolo). He was well teamed with Joan Blondell » in **Union Depot,** Bette Davis » in **Parachute Jumper** and Katharine Hepburn » in **Morning Glory,** but his screen image failed to grow. He was a convincing Czar to Elisabeth Bergner's **Catherine the Great** in England, but other films in Britain were expensive failures. He returned to Hollywood for his finest period, starting with **The**

Left: Douglas Fairbanks Jr inherited a good deal of his father's swashbuckling zest, as he showed in the 1948 **The Exile.**

Prisoner of Zenda, followed by **Joy of Living** (with Irene Dunne ≫), **Having A Wonderful Time** (with Ginger Rogers ≫) and **The Rage of Paris** (with Danielle Darrieux ≫). He was a wacky con-man in **The Young in Heart** and a strange swindler with Rita Hayworth ≫ in Ben Hecht's odd **Angels Over Broadway;** then he made his delightful series of swashbucklers. He rounded off his career with a frothy Lubitsch film, **That Lady in Ermine,** opposite Betty Grable ≫ and a dandy British suspense thriller **State Secret.** His last film was the improbable **Mr Drake's Duck** in 1951. He retired from the cinema and devoted his energy to TV films shown under the title *Douglas Fairbanks Presents.* He was a prominent British socialite but finally sold his London home and moved to Palm Beach with his second wife Mary Lee (his first was Joan Crawford ≫), from 1928 to 1933).

BEST FILMS:
1930 The Dawn Patrol
Howard Hawks (Warner Brothers)
1937 The Prisoner of Zenda
John Cromwell (Selznick/United Artists)
1938 The Rage of Paris
Henry Koster (Universal)
1938 Young in Heart
Richard Wallace (Selznick/United Artists)
1939 Gunga Din
George Stevens (RKO)
1942 The Corsican Brothers
Gregory Ratoff (United Artists)
1947 Sinbad the Sailor
Richard Wallace (RKO)
1948 The Exile
Max Ophuls (Universal)
1948 That Lady in Ermine
Otto Preminger & Ernst Lubitsch (20th Century Fox)
1950 State Secret
Sidney Gilliat (in England)

CHARLES FARRELL
see **Janet Gaynor**

ALICE FAYE

The gentle, soft-eyed queen of the Fox musical in the late '30s and early '40s, Alice Faye is sometimes under-rated simply because of her lack of forcefulness. She was admired not only by audiences but also by song-writers like Cole Porter and Irving Berlin, who praised her ability to project their songs. Alice was unlike other '30s blondes in her lack of brassiness; she was amiable, tearful, a little plump and a little cow-like in her attitudes, but she projected a unique kind of cuddly fragility which makes her seem at times

Above: Alice Faye as a cover girl in 1939, when she was ranked as a top box office star.

like a prototype Marilyn Monroe ≫. Faye was born as Alice Jeanne Leppert in New York City on May 5, 1912, and came into films after being a chorus girl. She made her début in 1934 in **George White's Scandals,** replacing Lilian Harvey ≫. She made 32 films between 1934 and 1945, of which a good few are still revived; she was at her best in period films, especially in the three directed by Henry King, for her figure seemed just right in costume. She was the flashy (well, not too flashy) singer Belle Fawcett, involved with Tyrone Power ≫ and the great fire in **In Old Chicago.** She was a musical comedy star through three decades, again entangled with Power in **Alexander's Ragtime Band** and singing some of Irving Berlin's best songs, and was a bar-maid in love with the inventor of the steamboat in **Little Old New York.**

It is for her musicals that Faye is best known: singing *I've Got My Love to Keep Me Warm* in **On the Avenue,** portraying a thinly-disguised Fanny Brice in **Rose of Washington Square,** and re-creating the past of Hollywood in **Hollywood Cavalcade.** She was highly enjoyable as a famous nineteenth-century singer in **Lillian Russell** and she made a wonderful contrast to Carmen Miranda ≫ in **That Night in Rio** and **Weekend in Havana.** She sang the Academy Award-winning song *You'll Never Know* in the big 1943 costume musical **Hello, Frisco, Hello** and Busby Berkeley arranged two elaborate productions for her in **The Gang's All Here.** And then, suddenly, her career was over. After two more small roles she retired, turning her attention to radio and TV with husband Phil Harris. She has since been featured in two films, playing the mother in the 1962 version of **State Fair** and a small singing role in **The Magic of Lassie** in 1978.

BEST FILMS:
1937 On the Avenue
Roy Del Ruth (20th Century Fox)
1938 In Old Chicago
Henry King (20th Century Fox)
1938 Alexander's Ragtime Band
Henry King (20th Century Fox)
1939 Rose of Washington Square
Gregory Ratoff (20th Century Fox)
1939 Hollywood Cavalcade
Irving Cummings (20th Century Fox)
1940 Little Old New York
Henry King (20th Century Fox)
1940 Lillian Russell
Irving Cummings (20th Century Fox)
1940 Tin Pan Alley
Walter Lang (20th Century Fox)
1943 Hello, Frisco, Hello
Bruce Humberstone (20th Century Fox)
1943 The Gang's All Here
Busby Berkeley (20th Century Fox)

FERNANDEL

The French comedian with the toothy horseface and the rubber features is best known inter-nationally as the Italian village priest on a first-name relationship with God in the **Don Camillo** series of the '50s. In France, he was the top popular comedian for nearly 40 years and a number one box-office attraction as early as 1937. His critical reputation has never been very high because he made so many mediocre vehicle films, but his exceptional talents can be seen at their best in films directed by Marcel Pagnol, Jean Renoir, Julien Duvivier, Claude Autant-Lara and Sacha Guitry. He made few films in English and those were not his most successful: he was David Niven's ≫ coachman in **Around the World in 80 Days** in 1956 (Mike Todd wanted him to play the Cantinflas role) and he was Bob Hope's ≫ rival for Anita Ekberg ≫ in the uneasy 1958 comedy **Paris Holiday.**

He was born Fernand Joseph Désiré Contandin in Marseilles on May 8, 1903, and entered show business as a comic singer (his first hit was *Mad'moiselle Rose*). His horse face quickly became his fortune and he made his first film in 1930, Robert Florey's **Le Blanc et le Noir.** He was featured in Renoir's first film, **On Purge Bébé,** a Feydeau farce with Michel Simon ≫, but it was Bernard Deschamps' 1932 **Le Rosier de Madame Husson** with Françoise Rosay that really made him famous in France and abroad (as a stupid but touching village boy given an award for virtue). His long association with Pagnol began in 1934 with **Angèle,** again as a good-hearted and comical imbecile. (This was to be his basic screen persona for most of his career, but it was elastic enough to take in a wide range of characterisations.) He made two of his best films in 1937: in Duvivier's **Un Carnet de Bal** he was the old flame of Marie Bell's who has become a hairdresser with a large family; in Pagnol's **Harvest** he was a knife-grinder who loses his girl to his best friend. Both films were inter-national successes and **Harvest** was named the best foreign film of the year by New York critics. Fernandel starred for Pagnol agin the following year in **Le Schpountz** and then was a great hit playing opposite Arletty ≫ and Michel Simon ≫ in **Fric-Frac.** He was Raimu's ≫ buddy in another Pagnol success, **La Fille du Puisatier,** and continued to make films throughout the Occupation.

Most of Fernandel's '40s films are forgettable, but he came back strongly at the end of the decade

Left: French comedian Fernandel had his greatest success as the priest in **The Little World of Don Camillo.**

in Carlo Rim's black comedy **L'Armoir Volante** (as a man looking for his aunt's corpse), then in Sacha Guitry's farce **Tu m'as sauvé la vie** (as a bum befriended by a baron), Pagnol's **Topaze** (the oft-filmed play about a maths teacher who becomes the brains of a gang), and Autant-Lara's black comedy **The Red Inn** (as a slightly odd monk). In 1952 he made the first of the Don Camillo pictures, **The Little World of Don Camillo,** and established himself once again internationally. In this film and its many sequels he portrays a kind-hearted if slightly nutty priest who has a running war with the Communist mayor of his village (Italian actor Gino Cervi). He had another international success playing quintuplets (and their father) in the bizarre **The Sheep Has Five Legs.** He continued film making until his death in 1971, but this later work was weaker, although still entertaining.

BEST FILMS:
1931 On Purge Bébé
Jean Renoir (Braunberger/Richebé)
1934 Angèle
Marcel Pagnol (Pagnol)
1937 Un Carnet de Bal
Julien Duvivier (Lévy-Strauss Sigma)
1937 Regain (Harvest)
Marcel Pagnol (Pagnol)
1939 Fric-Frac
Maurice Lehmann (CCFC)
1940 La Fille du Puisatier
Marcel Pagnol (Pagnol)
1951 L'Auberge Rouge (The Red Inn)
Claude Autant-Lara (Memnon)
1952 Le Petit Monde de Don Camillo (The Little World of Don Camillo)
Julien Duvivier (Amato)
1953 Le Retour de Don Camillo (The Return of Don Camillo)
Julien Duvivier (Francinex-Rizzoli)
1954 Le Mouton à Cinq Pattes (The Sheep Has Five Legs)
Henry Verneuil (Ploquin)

JOSÉ FERRER

José Ferrer has been making films for 30 years but remains essentially a one-picture star. The

movie, of course, was **Cyrano de Bergerac:** Ferrer's dazzling theatrical acting style was perfectly suited to this screen adaptation of the Rostand play. He is flamboyant, eloquent, and moving as the long-nosed swordsman with the soul of a poet, whose love for the beautiful Roxanne is expressed through another man. Ferrer won the 1950 Best Actor Oscar for his performance; he was never again to achieve such success in a film, through he has continued to work in movies up to the present time. He is said to have one of the finest speaking voices on the stage and it is his voice more than his presence which has been the mainstay of his cinema career. His other relatively famous film role was as Toulouse-Lautrec in John Huston's **Moulin Rouge,** courageously playing the entire film with his legs strapped up to emulate the dwarfish painter, and again using his fine voice to good effect.

Ferrer was born as José Vincente Ferrer Otero y Cintron in Santurce, Puerto Rico, on January 8, 1909, studied at Princeton, and began to work on stage from 1935. He made his film début as the Dauphin opposite Ingrid Bergman ❯ in the stodgy 1948 **Joan of Arc.** He had roles in two other films, **Whirlpool** (as a murdering hypnotist) and **Crisis** (as a South American dictator), before winning his Oscar for **Cyrano.** He continued to work on stage as well as in the cinema, and was impressive as the defending lawyer in **The Caine Mutiny,** Sigmund Romberg in **Deep in My Heart,** and the husband of domineering June Allyson ❯ in the film version of his stage success **The Shrike.** He directed this and other films, notably **The Great Man,** an exposé of a TV personality. In the '60s he turned to character acting, playing a Turkish Bey in **Lawrence of Arabia,** an Indian policeman in **Nine Hours to Rama,** a Nazi type in **Ship of Fools** and a drunken actor in **Enter Laughing.** He has continued to work in both TV and cinema films in the '70s, including **The Sentinel, The Swarm, The Amazing Captain Nemo** (duelling

Left: José Ferrer strapped up his legs to play the dwarfish painter Toulouse-Lautrec in **Moulin Rouge** *(1953), one of his most famous roles. The other was* **Cyrano de Bergerac,** *floridly scripted by Carl Foreman, for which Ferrer won that year's Best Actor Award.*

with Mel Ferrer) and Billy Wilder's **Fedora.**

BEST FILMS:
1949 Whirlpool
Otto Preminger (20th Century Fox)
1950 Crisis
Richard Brooks (MGM)
1950 Cyrano de Bergerac
Michael Gordon (United Artists)
1952 Moulin Rouge
John Huston (United Artists)
1954 The Caine Mutiny
Edward Dmytryk (Columbia)
1955 The Shrike
José Ferrer (Universal)
1956 The Great Man
José Ferrer (Universal)
1961 Enter Laughing
Carl Reiner (Columbia)
1962 Lawrence of Arabia
David Lean (Columbia)
1978 Fedora
Billy Wilder (Bavaria)

GRACIE FIELDS

"The Pride of Lancashire" was the most popular and the highest-paid film star in Britain in the '30s, and was considered (by Hollywood) to be the British equivalent of Will Rogers ❯. "Our Gracie" was liked both as a singing star (her *Sing as We Go* was practically the national anthem of the working class in the depression era) and as a down-to-earth no-nonsense film comedienne who genuinely reflected aspects of working life in England in the '30s. It has been argued that her supposedly escapist entertainment was actually a far truer reflection of the times than the poetic, artistic documentary movement. She never became quite as big a myth figure as the biggest American stars of

Above: Gracie Fields. Her early success led to a Hollywood contract, but she continued to film mostly in England and never really made it in the States.

the period, probably because she was too northern-working-class in her screen image (the mill girl who made good)—but that was also her magical attraction (she felt so uncomfortable keeping chauffeur-driven cars waiting for her that she would send the drivers off and go home by bus).

Her best films are part of the British national heritage, especially **Sally in Our Alley** (her first), **Sing as We Go** (with an excellent script by J. B. Priestley), **Queen of Hearts** (glamourised a bit, in the first film directed by husband-to-be Monty Banks) and **Keep Smiling.** Her success brought a contract from 20th Century Fox for four films for £200,000, but she made most of those films in England and never really became an American movie star. Her best American picture was the delightful comedy **Holy Matrimony,** teamed with Monty Woolley, but she did not get a chance to sing in it. Good as it was, she will really be remembered for her British musicals as an ordinary girl with a voice and a penchant for slapstick humour (a singer in a workmen's café, a manicurist, a factory girl—and even a factory girl who becomes a singing movie star in the strangely autobiographical **The Show Goes On**). Gracie, who was born as Grace Stansfield in Rochdale, Lancashire, in 1898, started singing at the age of seven, made her name in music hall and theatre, and made her first film in 1931. Her cinema career ended in 1946, starring opposite Constance Bennett ❯ in the Resistance drama **Madam Pimpernel,** but she continued to make occasional singing appearances on TV and radio. She published her autobiography (*Sing as We Go*) in 1960 and presently lives in semi-retirement in Capri (of which she is the uncrowned queen).

BEST FILMS:
1931 Sally in Our Alley
Maurice Elvey (Associated Talking Pictures)
1932 Looking on the Bright Side
Basil Dean (Associated Talking Pictures)
1934 Love, Life and Laughter
Maurice Elvey (Associated Talking Pictures)
1934 Sing as We Go
Basil Dean (Associated Talking Pictures)
1936 Queen of Hearts
Monty Banks (Associated Talking Pictures)
1937 The Show Goes On
Basil Dean (Associated Talking Pictures)
1937 We're Going to be Rich
Monty Banks (20th Century Productions)
1938 Keep Smiling
Monty Banks (20th Century Productions)
1939 Shipyard Sally
Monty Banks (20th Century Productions)
1943 Holy Matrimony
John Stahl (20th Century Fox)

W.C. FIELDS

W.C. Fields created one of the best-known, best-loved and most-imitated screen personalities in the history of the cinema. Despite his fame as a pool shark and a juggler (stretching back to 1900), his impeccable comic timing, and his hilarious scripts for most of his films, it is essentially his screen persona that makes him one of the immortals of the movies; all his best films are simply vehicles to allow an incredible eccentric with a bulbous nose, beat-up top hat and bottles of booze to put across his attitudes and ideas. More than anything else, it is his voice which embodies that image, a unique wheezing, croaking growl which conveys utter disdain for and absolute superiority to the malevolent nincompoops who people the world. There are still misguided critics who like to single out for praise his Mr Micawber in **David Copperfield** or his Humpty Dumpty in **Alice in Wonderland** because these roles gave him the chance for "real acting", thereby apparently writing off his great performances as himself on screen as some kind of non-acting. Admittedly, Fields is superb in these roles, but they are simply prestige sidelights in his film career. In his greatest films he was simply W.C. Fields; the movies run together as the continuing saga of a true comic genius. He disguised himself under fantastic names like Egbert Souse, A. Pismo Clam and Larson E. Whipsnade, but no one was deceived by such *alter egos*. He was always the sane clown at the centre of a whirlwind of disasters, opposing the malevolence of people and things with caustic, half-whispered asides and disgruntled resignation. No matter how bad things are, he seemed to imply, they're going to get worse. There were a few things he liked in the absurd world in which he was forced to exist—booze, storytelling and suckers were high on the list—but mainly he despised the things that most respectable people care for, especially children, animals and respectability. No one who hates dogs and children can be all bad, he noted. He had a particular aversion for water ("Fish fuck in it," he complained off screen), but was not averse to any form of skullduggery, fakery or cheating scheme that might deprive a sucker of a few bucks. The titles of his films convey his philosophy—**You Can't Cheat an Honest Man** and **Never Give a Sucker an Even Break**—and one of the most joyous things about him is that he was apparently exactly the same in real life.

Fields' real name was William Claude Dukenfield (hence his love for pretentious character names) and he was born in Philadelphia, Pennsylvania, in February 10, 1879. He ran away from home

at 11, had become a skilled juggler by the age of 14, and a top vaudeville star by the year 1900. He made his film début in 1915 in the short **Pool Sharks,** but his film career didn't really start until the 1924 **Janice Meredith** and the film version of his stage success *Poppy* in 1925 (retitled **Sally of the Sawdust** and directed by D.W. Griffith). His conniving conman character was established in this and two Gregory La Cava movies.

He was a star of silent films, but it was not until the advent of sound that he really came into his own. He made four superb shorts for Mack Sennett (**The Dentist, The Fatal Glass of Beer, The Pharmacist** and **The Barber Shop**) and then began his great feature career at Paramount with **Million Dollar Legs** in 1932. Not all of his films were good in themselves, but Fields himself was always magnificent. He rarely had top directors, although Leo McCarey made a splendid comedy with him (**Six of a Kind**) and he responded well to George Cukor in **David Copperfield.** His most representative films, however, are probably those made with Edward Cline (**The Bank Dick, Million Dollar Legs,** etc) for they allowed Fields to dominate the action. He was obviously a difficult person to deal with and left Paramount for Universal in the mid-'30s, but his films at both studios were equally good. His most famous film is the 1939 **My Little Chickadee** which teamed him with Mae West ➤ (very funny, but not as funny as hoped for) but his most hilarious are **It's A Gift** and **The Bank Dick.** His last starring film was the 1941 **Never Give a Sucker an Even Break**; afterwards, he only did small roles as a guest artist. He died on Christmas Day, 1946, obviously relishing to the end his dislike of that holiday. He was the subject of a film biography in 1976, **W.C. Fields and Me,** with Rod Steiger ➤ trying hard to emulate the master.

BEST FILMS:
1932 Million Dollar Legs
Edward Cline (Paramount)
1933 Tillie and Gus
Francis Martin (Paramount)
1934 Six of a Kind
Leo McCarey (Paramount)
1934 The Old Fashioned Way
William Beaudine (Paramount)
1934 It's A Gift
Norman Taurog (Paramount)

Above: W.C. Fields was so fond of his comedy stage success Poppy *that he made two films of it, in 1925 and 1936.*
Right: Fields was full of tales about his athletic skills and was able to demonstrate them in the 1932 **Million Dollar Legs.**

1935 The Man on the Flying Trapeze
Clyde Bruckman (Paramount)
1939 You Can't Cheat an Honest Man
George Marshall (Universal)
1939 My Little Chickadee
Edward Cline (Universal)
1940 The Bank Dick
Edward Cline (Universal)
1941 Never Give a Sucker an Even Break
Edward Cline (Universal)

PETER FINCH
see **Modern Stars**

BARRY FITZGERALD

Hollywood's ideal Irishman, full of blarney and tears, sharp of tongue and sentimental to the core, sometimes whimsical, usually irascible, and always leaning on his "brogue" for all it was worth. He was also a splendid actor: playwright Sean O'Casey eulogised him as "the greatest comic actor in the world". His immensely enjoyable performance as a crotchety, stubborn, old-fashioned priest in **Going My Way** very deservedly won him the Best Supporting Actor Academy Award for 1944. As critic James Agee noted at the time, Fitzgerald lifted the part into "the quintessence of the pathos, dignity and ludicrousness which old age can display". He was also notable in two film adaptations of O'Casey plays, as the orator in Alfred Hitchcock's **Juno and the Paycock** and as Fluther in John Ford's **The Plough and the Stars.** He was one of Ford's favourite actors and appeared in a number of his films, most memorably in that brawling, blustering hymn to Ireland **The Quiet Man.**

Fitzgerald was born on March 10, 1888, in Dublin, with the name William Shields (his younger brother, Arthur Shields, also became a well-known Hollywood Irishman and was featured in Ford films). He spent 20 years as a civil servant before becoming an actor at the renowned Abbey Theatre in Dublin. His first film was Hitchcock's 1930 **Juno,** but his real film career did not begin until 1936, when Ford persuaded him to star in **The Plough and the Stars.** He worked regularly in Hollywood after that in big and small parts, including a brilliantly funny performance opposite Cary Grant ➤ and Katharine Hepburn ➤ in Howard Hawks' **Bringing Up Baby** (as a drunken Irish gardener who can't quite believe that he is sitting beside a leopard), and as Lieutenant Muldoon in Dassin's police thriller **The Naked City.** His last American film was **The Catered Affair** in 1956, with Bette Davis ➤ , and his last two films were British productions directed by George Pollock— **Rooney** (1957) and **Broth of a Boy** (1958). He died in Dublin in 1961.

BEST FILMS:
1930 Juno and the Paycock
Alfred Hitchcock (BIP)
1936 The Plough and the Stars
John Ford (RKO)
1938 Bringing Up Baby
Howard Hawks (RKO)
1938 Four Men and a Prayer
John Ford (20th Century Fox)
1940 The Long Voyage Home
John Ford (United Artists)
1941 How Green Was My Valley
John Ford (20th Century Fox)
1944 Going My Way
Leo McCarey (Paramount)
1945 And Then There Were None
René Clair (20th Century Fox)
1948 The Naked City
Jules Dassin (Universal)
1952 The Quiet Man
John Ford (Republic)

Below: Barry Fitzgerald lecturing as Lieutenant Muldoon in Jules Dassin's superb 1948 police thriller **The Naked City.**

ERROL FLYNN

Errol Flynn was the best swashbuckler of the sound cinema, the sprightly tongue-in-cheek, devil-may-care hero of such classics as **The Adventures of Robin Hood, Captain Blood** and **The Sea Hawk.** Later on he became one of the screen's great drunks as well, in films like **The Sun Also Rises, Too Much Too Soon** and **The Roots of Heaven.** In between, he practically won the war for America in such films as **Desperate Journey, Northern Pursuit** and **Objective, Burma!** And yet there are still critics who insist that Flynn was not a good screen actor. In fact, he was a very good one and will remain a screen immortal as long as there are people who like sword fights, war adventures and booze. Off screen he was almost as fascinating as he was on, involved in a series of amatory escapades that at one

point led to a famous statutory rape trial (he was acquitted). He was a Sabatini hero brought to life and his screen persona is one of the delights of movie-going. He made most of his good films at Warner Brothers in their heyday in the late '30s and early '40's, directed by two of the masters of action cinema, Michael Curtiz and Raoul Walsh, backed by the splendour of Erich Wolfgang Korngold's music, partnered with the delectable Olivia de Havilland ➤ and duelling to the death with the villainous Basil Rathbone ➤ . He had dash, flair, grace and a sense of humour; he made these films believable on their own level because he treated them with the mock-heroic, light-hearted seriousness that they required. A good swashbuckler is as difficult to make as a good musical; Flynn dominates the genre as much as Fred Astaire ➤ dominates the song-and-dance film.

Erroll Leslie Flynn was born in Hobart, Tasmania, on June 20, 1909, and made his screen début in an Australian semi-documentary in 1933, **In the Wake of the Bounty.** He made one film in Britain (**Murder at Monte Carlo**) before going to America, and immediately began making Warner Brothers films for Michael Curtiz, the director who did more than anyone else to create Flynn's screen image. He became a star in 1935 with **Captain Blood,** then making a wondrous series of films with Curtiz until 1941, when they quarrelled and regrettably stopped working together. These included **The Charge of the Light Brigade** (gallant in India), **The Perfect Specimen** (a good comedy with Joan Blondell ➤), **The Adventures of Robin Hood** (probably the best of all swashbuckling films), **The Private Lives of Elizabeth and Essex** (where he proved to be a match even for the

Above: Errol Flynn duelling with Basil Rathbone in the dashing **The Adventures of Robin Hood.**
Left: Flynn, with Olivia de Havilland, playing Custer in **They Died With Their Boots On.**

Malone ≫, and more philosophically in John Huston's adaptation of Romain Gary's **The Roots of Heaven** with Juliette Greco. His last film was the 1959 **Cuban Rebel Girls,** which suitably featured his last teenage girl friend. He died the same year and his autobiography, *My Wicked, Wicked Ways* was published posthumously in 1960.

BEST FILMS:
1935 Captain Blood
Michael Curtiz (Warner Brothers)
1936 The Charge of the Light Brigade
Michael Curtiz (Warner Brothers)
1938 The Adventures of Robin Hood
Michael Curtiz (Warner Brothers)
1938 The Dawn Patrol
Edmund Goulding (Warner Brothers)
1939 The Private Lives of Elizabeth and Essex
Michael Curtiz (Warner Brothers)
1939 Dodge City
Michael Curtiz (Warner Brothers)
1940 The Sea Hawk
Michael Curtiz (Warner Brothers)
1941 They Died With Their Boots On
Raoul Walsh (Warner Brothers)
1943 Northern Pursuit
Raoul Walsh (Warner Brothers)
1945 Objective Burma
Raoul Walsh (Warner Brothers)
1957 The Sun Also Rises
Harry King (20th Century Fox)

imperious Bette Davis ≫), **Dodge City** (taming the West just like Wyatt Earp), **Four's A Crowd** (a light comedy with Olivia de Havilland), **Virginia City** (a Civil War Western with the added attractions of Humphrey Bogart ≫ and Randolph Scott ≫), **The Sea Hawk** (swashbuckling again for Queen Elizabeth, this time played by Flora Robson, **Santa Fe Trail** (in fighting form as Jeb Stuart), and the final one, **Dive Bomber** (experimenting with blacking out). Raoul Walsh then took over and made some good pictures, including **They Died With Their Boots On** (Flynn as General Custer), **Gentleman Jim** (as heavyweight champion Jim Corbett) and those exciting war pictures that culminated in **Objective, Burma!** The British objected to Flynn winning the war single-handed in the last and actually banned the picture.

Flynn was reportedly drinking quite heavily by this time but he was back in good swashbuckling form in the 1948 **The Adventures of Don Juan** and was quite a reasonable Soames in **That Forsyte Woman** in 1949. After that, his films seemed to lose his new panache until he took up his new image as a rather personable drinker in 1957, in Henry King's version of Hemingway's **The Sun Also Rises.** He hit the bottle theatrically as John Barrymore in **Too Much Too Soon** with Dorothy

HENRY FONDA

The Henry Fonda screen image as the noble, honest man of conscience, the idealistic hero of **Young Mr Lincoln** and **The Grapes of Wrath,** was rudely shattered in 1968, when he suddenly turned into the most callous of villains, gunning down children, in Sergio Leone's **Once Upon a Time in the West.** It was as if one of the bedrocks of American liberalism had been turned over to reveal a hitherto hidden and loathsome side. The end of the '60s was the end of innocence for America—and it was ironically appropriate that the very symbol of American goodheartedness had turned evil.

Fonda is one of the great screen actors and, despite his recent transfiguration, one of the great Western heroes as well. He was

the very personification of American frontier justice as Wyatt Earp in John Ford's **My Darling Clementine,** possibly the best film in the genre. A large percentage of his movies have been in the cowboy/pioneer mould; there is something particularly suitable about him for outdoor pictures, and it was just such a film, **The Trail of the Lonesome Pine,** in 1936, that first made him famous and shaped his image for the next 30 years.

Like many of the great Western stars, Fonda grew up on the prairie and never lost his Nebraska twang nor his rolling plains walk. He was born in Grand Island, Nebraska, on May 16, 1905, and began his career as a stage actor. He made his professional début in 1928 and his first Hollywood film, **The Farmer Takes a Wife** (1935), was an adaptation of a play he had done on Broadway. He was an immediate success as a film actor under contract to Walter Wanger and starred in the first outdoor Technicolor picture (**The Trail of the Lonesome Pine**) and the first British Technicolor picture (**Wings of the Morning**). He was outstanding in Lang's **You Only Live Once** with Sylvia Sidney, starred opposite Bette Davis ≫ in **Jezebel**

and **That Certain Woman,** and then made the first of his major Westerns in 1939, Henry King's **Jesse James** (he was brother Frank). In the same year he began his long association with his greatest director, John Ford, as the gauche but strong-minded idealist **Young Mr Lincoln.** Two fine Ford films followed in quick succession, the spectacular **Drums Along the Mohawk** and the powerful film version of John Steinbeck's **The Grapes of Wrath.** He worked for Lang again in **The Return of Frank James** and then made his best-ever comedy opposite Barbara Stanwyck ≫ , Preston Sturges' **The Lady Eve.** Most of his films at this time were pretty good, but the biggest critical success was William Wellman's **The Ox-Bow Incident,** acting once more as the liberal conscience of the American people. In 1946 he made his greatest film, **My Darling Clementine,** a remarkably beautiful evocation of pioneer life as well as the finest cinema enactment of the gunfight at the OK Corral. Despite critical reservations, he was also excellent as the whisky-sodden priest in Ford's **The Fugitive,** an adaptation of Graham Greene's **The Power and the Glory** which was superbly

Left: Henry Fonda had to face many "problems" during his long career, but none of them were more formidable than Bette Davis in **Jezebel.**
Below: Henry Fonda has a face that seems absolutely right for cowboy/pioneer roles. Here he is seen as a gangleader in the 1968 western **Firecreek.**

photographed but rather too studied. Ford featured him again in **Fort Apache,** their last Western together, but this time he was less sympathetic as an authoritarian cavalry officer.

Fonda then returned to stage work, but after his success in the play *Mister Roberts* was brought back to Hollywood to star in the 1955 film version. Ford and he quarrelled over the interpretation and never worked together again, but his film career continued strong. He was only adequate as Pierre in the epic **War and Peace,** but terrifyingly credible in Alfred Hitchcock's **The Wrong Man** as a musician falsely accused of murder. He was back as the best of liberals with a brilliant performance in **Twelve Angry Men,** convincing 11 other jurors that they were wrong about the defendant. Next came two of his best-ever Westerns, a bounty-hunter in Anthony Mann's **The Tin Star** and a psychologically strange gunfighter in Edward Dmytryk's **Warlock.** He then moved into screen politics, causing the President problems because of his liberalism in **Advise and Consent** (brilliant casting by Otto Preminger), going after the Presidency himself in **The Best Man,** and becoming President in **Fail-Safe.** He was mainly in weaker Westerns and epic war films after that, but came back very strongly indeed in Leone's brutal Italian Western **Once Upon a Time in the West** (in which the more-or-less hero who shoots him down in the end is Charles Bronson ❯ , a former villain). He has continued to work sporadically in the '70s, including another war epic, the 1976 **Midway.**

BEST FILMS:
1937 You Only Live Once
Fritz Lang (United Artists)
1939 Young Mr Lincoln
John Ford (20th Century Fox)
1940 The Grapes of Wrath
John Ford (20th Century Fox)
1941 The Lady Eve
Preston Sturges (Paramount)
1943 The Ox-Bow Incident
William Wellman (20th Century Fox)
1946 My Darling Clementine
John Ford (20th Century Fox)
1955 Mister Roberts
John Ford and Mervyn LeRoy (Warner Brothers)
1957 The Wrong Man
Alfred Hitchcock (Warner Brothers)
1957 Twelve Angry Men
Sidney Lumet (United Artists)
1957 The Tin Star
Anthony Mann (Paramount)
1968 Once Upon a Time in the West
Sergio Leone (Paramount)

JOAN FONTAINE

Joan Fontaine is best remembered for being a very frightened lady in two of Alfred Hitchcock's most disturbing thrillers. In the 1940

Above: Joan Fontaine as a swank society woman who discovers singer Mario Lanza in the 1956 Anthony Mann movie **Serenade.**

Rebecca, based on Daphne du Maurier's novel, she was the insecure bride of Laurence Olivier ❯, brought back to a house-full of the memories of Olivier's first wife and presided over by the terrifying Judith Anderson. In the 1941 **Suspicion** she was the insecure bride of Cary Grant ❯, whom she thinks is trying to kill her. Presumably her real husband at that time, Brian Aherne, must have been quite concerned about her film roles: they had just got married, in 1939. In any event, **Suspicion** won her an Academy Award for acting and (or so it was said at the time) a great deal of animosity from her more famous

sister, Olivia de Havilland ❯, who had been nominated for the same Oscar. Although Fontaine never went on to create a really identifiable screen persona, presumably preferring glamour to insecurity, she made other excellent films. She had a nice penchant for falling in love with musicians in her better pictures, including Charles Boyer ❯ in **The Constant Nymph** (another Oscar nomination) and Louis Jourdan ❯ in **Letter from an Unknown Woman** (an outstanding performance). She usually had a lot of trouble with her love affairs, whether she was nicely bitchy, as in **Born to Be Bad** with two men on her string, or sweetly romantic, as in **September Affair** with the already married Joseph Cotten ❯, but she had a good film career all the same.

Joan de Beauvoir de Havilland (her real name; she borrowed Fontaine from her stepfather) was born in Tokyo on October 22, 1917. She soon followed her sister's movie success—but it took her longer. In 1935 she had a small part in **No More Ladies,** then she starred opposite Fred Astaire ❯ in the 1937 **A Damsel in Distress** (a tentative replacement for Ginger Rogers ❯, and had a nice part in **Gunga Din** and a better one in **The Women.** David Selznick made her into a star with **Rebecca** and she quickly became very glamorous indeed in films like **Frenchman's Creek** and **The Affairs of Susan.** She portrayed an actress with drinking problems for director George Stevens in **Something to Live For** in 1952, and starred in Fritz Lang's 1956 **Beyond a Reasonable Doubt,** but her career ran out of steam in the late '50s. Her last film was the Hammer horror picture **The Witches** in 1966.

BEST FILMS:
1937 A Damsel in Distress
George Stevens (RKO)
1939 The Women
George Cukor (MGM)
1940 Rebecca
Alfred Hitchcock (Selznick/United Artists)
1941 Suspicion
Alfred Hitchcock (RKO)
1943 The Constant Nymph
Edmund Goulding (Warner Brothers)
1944 Jane Eyre
Robert Stevenson (20th Century Fox)
1948 Letter from an Unknown Woman
Max Ophuls (Universal)
1950 Born to be Bad
Nicholas Ray (RKO)
1950 September Affair
William Dieterle (Paramount)
1956 Beyond a Reasonable Doubt
Fritz Lang (RKO)

GLENN FORD

Glenn Ford is a solid, dependable, genial actor, with a screen personality that combines relaxed amiability with determination. He does not generate much charisma on film but is always watchable and, given a good script and a good director, he can be a very fine actor indeed. He is as adept in romantic melodrama (**Gilda,** with Rita Hayworth ❯ ; **A Stolen Life,** with Bette Davis ❯) as in comedies (**The Teahouse of the August Moon, A Pocketful of Miracles**), but his strongest movies have been action ones. He was, perhaps, at his very best as the dogged detective whose wife is blown up by a bomb meant for him in **The Big Heat,** winning through with the help of Gloria Grahame ❯ . He has been very impressive in a number of Wes-

Above left: Glenn Ford created a persona of relaxed geniality.
Left: **The Teahouse of the August Moon** *(1956) featured Glenn Ford as an Army officer in Okinawa having trouble with interpreter Marlon Brando.*

terns, especially **The Violent Men, Jubal, The Sheepman** and **3:10 to Yuma** (in which he was the villain).

Born in Quebec, Canada, on May 1, 1916, as Gwyllyn Ford, he worked on stage in the late '30s and made his film début in the 1940 **Heaven with a Barbed Wire Fence**. He worked mainly in B-pictures and supporting roles until after his war service, when his studio, Columbia, starred him opposite Rita Hayworth in the hit **Gilda**; he starred with her in later movies, but none had the ambiguous chemistry of this key '40s film. Ford got more and more popular as the years went by, probably reaching the peak of his popularity in 1958, when he was rated as the number one box office star. He was helped by the notoriety of **The Blackboard Jungle**, which introduced rock 'n' roll to the screen through its Bill Haley theme song *Rock Around the Clock* (Ford was a determined teacher in a tough school), and the great success of **The Teahouse of the August Moon**. His star dimmed slightly in the '60s, although he gave fine comedy performances in **A Pocketful of Miracles** and **The Courtship of Eddie's Father** (he was father), and in some reasonable Westerns. In the '70s he mainly worked in TV movies and the series *Cade's County*.

BEST FILMS:
1946 Gilda
Charles Vidor (Columbia)
1953 The Big Heat
Fritz Lang (Columbia)
1954 Human Desire
Fritz Lang (Columbia)
1955 The Blackboard Jungle
Richard Brooks (MGM)
1956 Jubal
Delmer Daves (Columbia)
1956 The Teahouse of the August Moon
Daniel Mann (MGM)
1957 3:10 to Yuma
Delmer Daves (Columbia)
1958 The Sheepman
George Marshall (MGM)
1961 A Pocketful of Miracles
Frank Capra (United Artists)
1963 The Courtship of Eddie's Father
Vincente Minnelli (MGM)

GEORGE FORMBY

There are still George Formby fan clubs in Blackpool, and young people who weren't alive at the height of his fame play his songs and enjoy his movies. Formby is often unjustly overlooked by serious film critics as being "merely popular" when, in fact, he created a rather splendid screen persona. He was the most popular British star for five years (1938-1942) and a major box office attraction for ten (1935 to 1945). He was the "little man" personified, gormless certainly, semi-imbecilic perhaps, but always genuinely winning with his toothy smile, his

Above: George Formby retains an amazing popularity today in England, both for his lively film comedies and for his infectious "ukelele" songs.

naïve innocence, his infectious good-humour and, of course, his lilting ukelele songs. He was never popular in America (the equivalent would be a singing Joe E. Brown), but he was absolutely right for Britain during the Depression and the early war years.

He was born in Wigan, Lancashire, in 1904, the son of a popular comedian, George Formby Sr, and was a music hall star before turning to films in 1934, in the cheaply-made **Boots Boots**. His career was built up at ATP (Ealing Studios) by producer Basil Dean, beginning in 1935 with **No Limit,** in which he plays a motorcyclist winning the Tourist

Trophy in the Isle of Man TT races. Most of his '30s films were written and directed by Anthony Kimmins and they were usually cut to a pattern; he is the innocent to whom every possible disaster occurs, but he always win through in the end with dogged optimism, usually getting a pretty girl as well. **Keep Your Seats Please** was based on the famous Soviet novel *The Twelve Chairs* by Ilf and Petrov (later remade by Mel Brooks), but his Kimmins films were more typical. In **Keep Fit** he was a barber, in **I See Ice** he gets mixed up with an ice ballet, in **It's in the Air** he was once again a motor cycle enthusiast, and in **Trouble Brewing** he was a printer. All of his films had a good chase sequence and memorable songs like *The Window Cleaner* (in **Keep Your Seats, Please**) and *Auntie Maggie's Remedy* (in **Turned Out Nice Again**). Two of his best films were directed by Marcel Varnel (who made many Will Hay ≫ comedies); their 1940 **Let George Do It** is often considered Formby's outstanding film. When the war ended, his kind of comedy became less popular and he made his last film in 1947, **George in Civvy Street**. He returned to music hall entertaining and died in 1961.

BEST FILMS:
1936 No Limit
Monty Banks (ATP)
1936 Keep Your Seats, Please
Monty Banks (ATP)
1937 Feather Your Nest
William Beaudine (ATP)
1937 Keep Fit
Anthony Kimmins (ATP)
1938 I See Ice
Anthony Kimmins (ATP)
1938 It's in the Air
Anthony Kimmins (ATP)
1939 Come On, George
Anthony Kimmins (ATP)
1940 Let George Do It
Marcel Varnel (ATP)
1940 Spare a Copper
John Paddy Carstairs (ATP)
1941 Turned Out Nice Again
Marcel Varnel (ATP)

JEAN GABIN

The greatest star in the history of the French cinema, Jean Gabin was a top box-office attraction (often No 1) and a fine screen actor for more than 40 years. He was the Gallic equivalent of Bogart ≫ and Tracy ≫ combined, and he also became the embodiment of changing French values. In the '30s he was a romantic anti-hero, doomed but resigned to his fate, usually involved with a beautiful woman who almost always represented death. After a confused period in the '40s, his persona re-developed into a more materialistic representation of conservative values; Gabin was solid and reliable, whether portraying a police inspector or a gangster. In the earlier films he was usually working class, often on the run, and more often than not a petty criminal. In the later ones he was usually bourgeois, tended to be gruffly lovable, and was a cop as often as he was a criminal. The attitudes he embodied in the 1939 **Le Jour se Lève** (as a murderer-on-the-run holed up in a hotel, waiting for the police to arrive and dreaming about the past) exactly reflected the mood of France on the eve of the German Occupation. His modern persona, with its white-haired solidity and old-fashioned values presumably reflected the more hopeful mood of post-war France. The quality of his films is also reflected in this change; his '30s films are among the great masterpieces of the cinema, but his modern films are simply well-crafted and well-acted movies. It is doubtful if many of his later pictures will be revived in a hundred years' time, but it is inconceivable that those of the '30s will ever be forgotten—films like Renoir's **La Grande Illusion, Les Bas-Fonds** and **La Bête Humaine** and Carnés **Quai des Brumes and Le Jour se Lève** have become milestones in cinema history.

Gabin was born as Jean-Alexis Moncourge in Meriel, Oise, France, on May 17, 1904. His parents were in music hall and he followed them onto the stage, turning full-time to the cinema. His first film was the 1930 **Chacun sa Chance,** and over the next few years he became a star as the Gabin screen persona took shape. He was a

Left: Jean Gabin with Simone Simon, the woman who pushes him to murder in his 1938 Renoir masterpiece La Bête Humaine.

Above: Jean Gabin stayed a major star until the end of his career, in gangster films like the 1968 **Le Clan des Siciliens.**

petty crook in **Coeur de Lilas,** a new cavalry recruit in **Les Gaités de l'Escadron,** and then, for the first time, a man on the run from the police, involved in a tragic romance, in Duvivier's **Maria Chapdelaine.** The Gabin screen image had become a huge success and the actor soon began the greatest period of his life (1936-1939). In 1936 he was the anti-romantic Legionnaire, on the run from the police and dying heroically, in Duvivier's influential **La Bandéra.** Next, Duvivier starred him in **La Belle Équipe** as the leader of five unemployed men who win the lottery and end up quarrelling over a woman, with Gabin killing Charles Vanel. In his first film with Renoir, **Les Bas-Fonds** (an adaptation of Gorki's play **The Lower Depths**), he was again the doomed hero on the bottom stratum of society with other down-and-outs, but still involved with women. In 1937 he created one of his most famous parts in Duvivier's **Pépé Le Moko,** portraying the king of crime in the Algiers Casbah, gunned down by the police when he comes out for love of a woman (the film was remade in Hollywood with Charles Boyer ≫ inviting Hedy Lamarr ≫ into the Casbah). Next, he starred in his greatest film, Renoir's pacifist but patriotic **La Grande Illusion.** Gabin is a working-class officer, contrasted with aristocratic officer Pierre Fresnay but united with him and their fellow Frenchmen against ultra-aristocratic Erich von Stroheim ≫, commandant of their World-War-I prison camp — Fresnay is killed by von Stroheim while helping Gabin to escape (it was said at the time that Gabin insisted on a death scene clause in his contracts). In 1938, Gabin was again the doomed anti-hero in Carné's **Quai des Brumes,** an Army deserter waiting for a ship in Le Havre and becoming entangled with Michèle Morgan ≫. He kills her protector (Michel Simon ≫) and is in turned killed by a gangster (Pierre Brasseur) while trying to escape. In Renoir's **La**

Bête Humaine he gave one of his finest acting performances as a railway worker pushed to murder by Simone Simon, whom he strangles. In 1939 he was the ultimate in doomed heros in Carné's **Le Jour se Lève,** the justified killer calmly and fatalistically waiting in his hotel room for the police to come and kill him. His last '30s film was the flawed but fascinating **Remorques,** directed by Jean Gremillon, a tragic love triangle story with Gabin as a tugboat captain involved once again with mysterious Michèle Morgan.

Gabin was never again to make films of such consistent quality. In 1940 he left for America, via Lisbon, and made two Hollywood films, **Moontide** and **The Imposter.** They were not successful and he returned to North Africa to join the French armed forces. When he resumed his career in 1946, he was at first unsuccessful, but he found his way back with the tried-and-tested doomed romance formula. This time he was a murderer on the run from the law in Genoa, in love with waitress Isa Miranda as the police closed in. The film was called **Au-delà des Grilles,** was directed by René Clement, and won the American Academy Award as the Best Foreign Film of the year. After that the movies came thick and fast and Gabin was soon back as the top male star in France. He was good once again under Carné's direction in **La Marie du Port** (an older man falling for a young waitress) and had a big popular hit with the gangster picture **Touchez Pas au Grisbi.** His popularity never waned after this, no matter the film — and there were still some good roles. He was superb as Danielle Darrieux ≫ admirer in a small role in Max Ophuls' **Le Plaisir,** and he was outstanding as the impresario and club-owner in Renoir's **French Can-Can.** Every film he made was worth seeing for his reliable performances, but perhaps the most impressive were his personifications of Georges Simenon's detective, Inspector Maigret. He played the role for the first time in 1958 in **Maigret Tend un Piège,** and it was among his finest later work. He returned to the role in later films and played other police inspectors as well, alternating with roles as gangsters and Mafia men. In the 1970s, despite everything that had happened to the French cinema, including the arrival of the *nouvelle vague* (which ignored him completely) and the rise of younger stars like Jean-Paul Belmondo ≫ (who admired him enormously), he was still by far the most popular actor in France. He died in 1976, his last film being Jean Girault's **L'Année Sainte.**

BEST FILMS:
1936 La Belle Équipe
Julien Duvivier (Ciné Arys)
1936 Les Bas-Fonds (The Lower Depths)
Jean Renoir (Albatros)

1937 Pépé Le Moko
Julien Duvivier (Paris Films)
1937 Le Grande Illusion
Jean Renoir (RAC)
1938 Quai des Brumes
Marcel Carné (Rabinovich)
1938 La Bête Humaine
Jean Renoir (Paris Films)
1939 Le Jour se Lève
Marcel Carné (Vog/Sigma)
1939 Remorques (Stormy Waters)
Jean Gremillon (Sedif)
1954 Touchez Pas au Grisbi
Jacques Becker (Del Duca/ Silver/Antares)
1955 French Can Can
Jean Renoir (Franco-London/Jolly)

CLARK GABLE

"Clark Gable was the King of an empire called Hollywood", noted Joan Crawford ≫ in a famous eulogy. "The empire is not what it once was — but the King has not been dethroned, even after death." The amazing charisma of Gable still survives nearly 20 years after his passing and 40 years after his major film, **Gone With the Wind.** This extraordinary longevity as a top star has been achieved despite the fact that he made few really good films and was never a notable "actor" in the narrow sense of the word. "I can't act

Above: Clark Gable romancing a somewhat unwilling Jeanette MacDonald in the 1936 epic **San Francisco.** *The earthquake finally shakes up her ideas. Above right: Clark Gable as Rhett Butler in* **Gone With the Wind.** *Here he is seen confronting Olivia de Havilland with Leslie Howard. Right: Clark Gable's last film was the ill-fated 1960 picture* **The Misfits.** *It was also the last for co-star Marilyn Monroe, seen here with Eli Wallach.*

worth a damn", he once stated, and this (untrue, but typical) assessment of his talent was generally accepted. He was liked, it was said, because he was natural, because he was manly and sexually attractive to women and a regular outdoor he-man to other men — because he was a new type of tough hero. While all this is true, and certainly helped boost his career, it is only necessary to look at his best films to see what a good "screen actor" he really was when he had a worthwhile script and director. The character he played was, of course, Clark Gable, but he was truly magnificent at it, grinning impudently and knowingly at his co-stars and timing his gestures and movements so well that he was irresistible in comedy. He

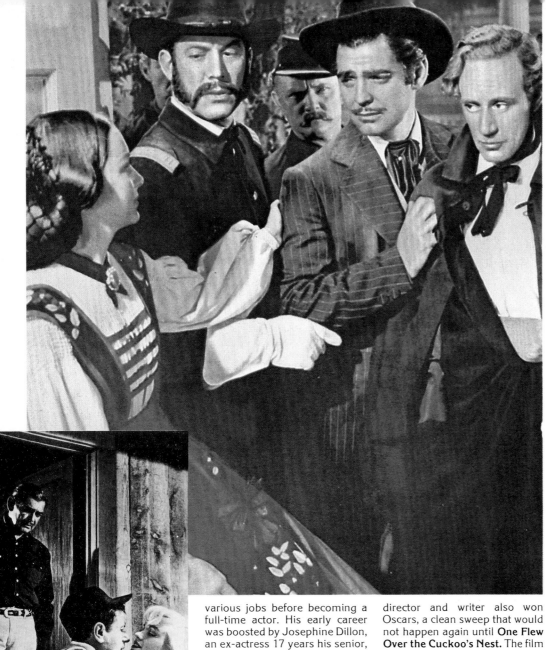

King of Hollywood, but his next really good film was not until 1938, an action-comedy called **Too Hot To Handle,** with Gable and Walter Pidgeon ❯ as rival newsreel men vying for the favours of Myrna Loy. He was back in another delightful comedy in 1939, a screen version of Robert Sherwood's play **Idiot's Delight,** playing a stranded song-and-dance man opposite Norma Shearer ❯. Then came **Gone With the Wind,** the pinnacle of Gable's career; he was never better or more enjoyable to watch on the screen. It is possible that author Margaret Mitchell had Gable in mind when she created the character of Rhett Butler in the book; certainly his screen persona and the role were exactly matched. Producer David Selznick delayed shooting the film for two years in order to secure Gable's services from MGM on very unfavourable terms. Vivien Leigh ❯ was a perfect Scarlett as counter-weight to his Rhett, each playing against the other with impeccable awareness of the other's deceptions. The film deserved its overwhelming success at the time, and remains effective today.

Gable's career was never the same after this peak. He made a lot more films but after his bride of 22 months, Carole Lombard ❯, was killed in a plane crash he joined the Army. He came back to Greer Garson's ❯ arms in the 1945 film **Adventure**—but it failed. He was back in form in **The Hucksters** in 1947, battling for integrity in the advertising industry; after that, his films were rather ordinary until John Ford directed him in a good remake of **Red Dust** called **Mogambo,** with Ava Gardner ❯ and Grace Kelly ❯. He parted from MGM in 1954 after 23 years, and immediately had a hit with a superb Raoul Walsh Western **The Tall Men.** Nothing was up to that standard again until his last film, John Huston's **The Misfits,** with Marilyn Monroe ❯ and Montgomery Clift ❯. It was his valedictory to Hollywood. He died a few weeks after he finished it, on November 16, 1960. The King was dead—and no-one could replace him.

"acted" with his whole body and his whole personality, as all the greatest movie stars have done, and no-one else could have performed as well in **Gone With the Wind, It Happened One Night, Mutiny on the Bounty** or **The Misfits.** He will continue to be watchable on the screen, even magnetic, a hundred years from now, when great prestige "actors" like George Arliss are forgotten—popular taste, especially in the cinema, is often a more reliable yardstick than critical acclaim. Gable was one of the top box-office stars for most of his 30 years of stardom—and usually in the top ten.

He was born in Cadiz, Ohio, on February 1, 1901, and worked at various jobs before becoming a full-time actor. His early career was boosted by Josephine Dillon, an ex-actress 17 years his senior, who taught him the craft of acting and married him in 1924. He did some work as an extra in films in 1925 and 1926, but did not really break into movies until 1931—as a villain in **The Painted Desert.** He had charisma even at this point and was rushed into film after film by MGM, who desperately needed a new romantic leading man to replace their fading silent stars John Gilbert ❯ and Ramon Novarro ❯. Gable took over the lead from Gilbert opposite Greta Garbo ❯ in **Susan Lenox—Her Fall and Rise,** and starred opposite Norma Shearer ❯, Joan Crawford ❯ and Constance Bennett ❯ in his first year in pictures. He became a major star the following year, when he was featured in smouldering love scenes with Jean Harlow ❯ and Mary Astor ❯ in **Red Dust,** and given some classic wise-cracking dialogue as well. He then became the major MGM star, but it was on a loan to the minor studio (as it was then) Columbia that he collected the ultimate accolade of his peers, an Academy Award. It came from his role in Frank Capra's **It Happened One Night,** which was also named Best Picture; co-star Claudette Colbert ❯ was named Best Actress and the

director and writer also won Oscars, a clean sweep that would not happen again until **One Flew Over the Cuckoo's Nest.** The film should have established Gable's reputation as a great comedy actor—but it did not, partly because he seemed to do it so easily and partly because he was so modest about his achievement. He was "just playing himself" it was said, even through his thumb-jerking hitch-hiking scene became as famous as his tumbling down of the "Walls of Jericho" (a blanket decorously dividing a room he shared with Colbert) at the climax of the film.

Gable was good opposite Harlow again in the 1935 **China Seas,** but his major film of that year was **Mutiny on the Bounty.** He was Mr Christian to Charles Laughton's ❯ powerful Captain Bligh, proving that he was able to hold his own in the acting department against even the greatest competition. His principal female co-stars at this time were Harlow, Crawford and Myrna Loy ❯, but he was teamed with Jeanette MacDonald ❯ for his biggest film of 1936, **San Francisco.** Despite the heavyweight acting competition from another great screen actor, Spencer Tracy ❯, Gable was as good as ever and gave one of his most effective performances. In 1937 a public opinion poll named him the

BEST FILMS:
1932 Red Dust
Victor Fleming (MGM)
1934 It Happened One Night
Frank Capra (Columbia)
1935 Mutiny on the Bounty
Frank Lloyd (MGM)
1936 San Francisco
W.S. Van Dyke (MGM)
1939 Idiot's Delight
Clarence Brown (MGM)
1939 Gone With the Wind
Victor Fleming (Selznick/MGM)
1947 The Hucksters
Jack Conway (MGM)
1953 Mogambo
John Ford (MGM)
1955 The Tall Men
Raoul Walsh (20th Century Fox)
1960 The Misfits
John Huston (United Artists)

GRETA GARBO

Greta Garbo is the major myth figure of the cinema and probably the most adulated star. Whether she is actually the greatest screen actress, as many critics claim, is open to question, but she certainly had the greatest charisma, although she did not star in very many good pictures. Her career consists of three silent films in Europe, ten silent films in Hollywood, and 14 American sound pictures. She was the centre of MGM's reputation as the great star studio, but she was also the most elusive and enigmatic of all the major movie personalities. If one peels off the false myth of her stardom, one finds only a real myth underneath. The most revealing aspect of her screen image is the way in which she was photographed in her Hollywood films: always in close-ups or long shot, almost never in medium or full-length shot, and usually with high-key lighting; her cameraman for 12 of her sound films was the great William Daniels, who found that she did not come out well as a medium person—like all myths, she needed to be seen at a great distance or with utter intimacy. Her personality was a major part of her image, her shyness making her withdrawn and thus apparently aloof, her probable sensuality masked by wary reserve. Her famous catch-phrase, "I want to be alone", conveys this timorous inhibition. Most of her films were tragic love stories in which she died or sacrificed herself in some way for love of a man—this is especially true of her greatest film, Rouben Mamoulian's **Queen Christina**, in which she gives up the throne of Sweden for a man who then dies. It is in this film, if anywhere, that the key to her greatness lies. In the famous final shot on a ship taking the body of her dead lover back to Spain, Garbo is seen in enormous close-up for almost a full minute. Critics have read in her face as many conflicting meanings as in the Mona Lisa. What she was told by Mamoulian to convey was "absolutely nothing", to make her mind and heart a complete blank.

Garbo was born as Greta Gustafsson in Stockholm, Sweden, on September 18, 1905, of a poor family, and was working in a barber shop by the age of 14. She was featured in short films in 1921 and made her feature début in 1924 in Mauritz Stiller's **The Atonement of Gösta Berling**. Stiller was her formative influence, and after making G. W. Pabst's **Joyless Street** in Germany she went with him to Hollywood, having been signed by MGM at his insistence. Strangely, they only completed one film together, for in Hollywood she was immediately turned over to other directors. Her first American film was **The**

Torrent in 1925, opposite Ricardo Cortez, and she immediately became a major star. Stiller's US career fizzled out and he returned to Sweden in 1928, dying the same year, but his protégé quickly became the major Hollywood star in her ten silent films and was especially popular in films co-starring John Gilbert ❯, including **Flesh and the Devil, Love** (a version of **Anna Karenina**) and **A Woman of Affairs.** The best was probably Victor Sjöström's **The Divine Woman**, but the most representative were those directed by Clarence Brown (**Flesh and the Devil, A Woman of Affairs**), who made six films with her.

MGM cleverly waited until almost two years after the coming of sound to star Garbo in a talkie (most European stars in Hollywood were destroyed by sound), and then astutely featured her in a version of Eugene O'Neill's **Anna Christie**, where her heavy accent seemed completely appropriate. By now she had become a living legend and her very remoteness was capitalized upon in the studio's publicity. She was extremely popular opposite Clark Gable ❯ in **Susan Lenox—Her Fall and Rise** and was truly marvellous as a famous ballerina in **Grand Hotel**, a role that seemed to mirror her own position as a star. Her career progressed with great critical acclaim through **As Your Desire Me, Queen Christina, The Painted Veil, Anna Karenina, Camille** and **Marie Walewska**, but her box-office appeal was beginning to diminish, so she was put in a comedy. This was Ernst Lubitsch's

*Above: Garbo posed as her twin sister in her last film, the 1941 **Two-Faced Woman.***
Below: Greta Garbo, the major myth figure of world cinema.

brilliant **Ninotchka**, one of her very best films, which was promoted with the slogan "Garbo Laughs". She was now more popular in Europe than in America, but the coming of the war closed that market, and her last film was the relatively unsuccessful **Two-Faced Woman.** She went into what was supposed to be temporary retirement, but never returned to the screen, and soon she became an absolute recluse, known only through photographs taken at various international airports. She never married (in **Queen Christina** she says, "I shall die a bachelor") and lives as privately as possible in a New York apartment.

BEST FILMS:
1925 Die Freudlose Gasse (Joyless Street)
G. W. Pabst (Sofar)
1926 Flesh and the Devil
Clarence Brown (MGM)
1928 The Divine Woman
Victor Sjöström (MGM)
1930 Anna Christie
Clarence Brown (MGM)
1931 Susan Lenox—Her Fall and Rise
Robert Z. Leonard (MGM)
1932 Grand Hotel
Edmund Goulding (MGM)
1933 Queen Christina
Rouben Mamoulian (MGM)
1935 Anna Karenina
Clarence Brown (MGM)
1936 Camille
George Cukor (MGM)
1939 Ninotchka
Ernst Lubitsch (MGM)

AVA GARDNER

Ava Gardner used to be known as the most beautiful woman in the world (and was once fancifully publicised as the World's Most Beautiful Animal), but it was not wholly her looks that made her one of the great movie stars. Her image, which she quickly developed, was that of the independent-minded, wordly-wise and sexually knowledgeable good bad woman who fascinates men and worries wives. She was eminently suitable to be a Hemingway heroine, as she proved in **The Sun Also Rises** and **The Snows of Kilimanjaro**, and her highly publicised off-screen life was built into her screen personality. Joseph Mankiewicz's **The Barefoot Contessa** appears almost biographical (sensual, temperamental beauty built to stardom) and certainly he never considered anybody else for the part. Her marriages to Mickey Rooney ≫, Artie Shaw and Frank Sinatra ≫, like her friendships with Howard Hughes and others, are all a part of her cinema legend; she is the epitome of the girl from the other side of the tracks who has made it big without kow-towing to anybody.

Gardner's own life has not been that different. She was born as poor as can be on a tenant farm in Grabtown, North Carolina, on December 24, 1922, and her father died when she was 12. Glamorous photographs taken in New York won her an MGM contract in 1941, and she made her feature début in a bit part in the 1942 **We Were Dancing**, but her career didn't really develop until she was cast as gangsters' molls in **Whistle Stop** and **The Killers** in 1946, and opposite Clark Gable ≫ in a small role in **The Hucksters**. She was deftly cast as a statue of Venus come to life in **One Touch of Venus** in 1948, and was alluring as the Dostoevsky-inspired countess in Robert Siodmak's **The Great Sinner**. She was at her most beautiful in another almost biographical role, as a restless playgirl involved with James Mason ≫, in **Pandora and the Flying Dutchman**, and very good indeed as the half-caste Julie in **Show Boat**. She seemed particularly right in Africa, first with Clark Gable and Grace Kelly ≫ in **Mogambo** (a re-make of **Red Dust** with Gardner in the Jean Harlow ≫ part) and then with Stewart Granger ≫ in **Bhowani Junction** (once again playing a half-caste). In the '60s she was notable in featured roles in **55 Days at Peking**, **Seven Days in May** and **The Night of the Iguana**. She has continued working steadily in the 70's, with relatively small roles in films like **The Life and Times of Judge Roy Bean** (as Lillie Langtry), **Earthquake, The Sentinel** and **The Cassandra Crossing**.

*Above: Ava Gardner as she looked in **The Naked Maja**, the story of the romance between the painter Goya and the beautiful Duchess of Alba.*

BEST FILMS:
1946 The Killers
Robert Siodmak (Universal)
1947 The Hucksters
Jack Conway (MGM)
1951 Pandora and the Flying Dutchman
Albert Lewin (MGM)
1951 Show Boat
George Sidney (MGM)
1952 The Snows of Kilimanjaro
Henry King (20th Century Fox)
1953 Mogambo
John Ford (MGM)
1954 The Barefoot Contessa
Joseph Mankiewicz (United Artists)
1956 Bhowani Junction
George Cukor (MGM)
1957 The Sun Also Rises
Henry King (20th Century Fox)
1964 The Night of the Iguana
John Huston (MGM)

JOHN GARFIELD

Garfield was the equivalent of James Dean ≫ and Marlon Brando ≫ in the late '30s and '40s; he was the aggressive boy from the other side of the tracks, with a chip on his shoulder and a tough, embittered cynicism; he was often the ugly outsider, forced to become a criminal because of society's attitude. His real life paralleled his screen persona: he rose to stardom from the street gangs of the Bronx

*Above: John Garfield as the hustler in the 1946 **Nobody Lives Forever**, who falls in love with the girl he tries to swindle.*

and was eventually hounded to death by society in the form of the righteous anti-Communist crusaders of the House Un-American Activities Committee.

Garfield was born as Julius Garfinkle on March 4, 1913, in New York City. He won a scholarship to drama school and became associated with the left-wing Group Theatre, where he attracted attention in Clifford Odets' **Golden Boy**. Warner Brothers put him under contract and starred him in the highly successful **Four Daughters** (one of whom falls in love with a poor boy, played by Garfield) and its sequels. He was excellent in an adaptation of Jack London's novel **The Sea Wolf**, and very impressive in such war films as Hawks' **Air Force** (as an air force hero in the Pacific) and Daves' **The Pride of the Marines** (as a blinded veteran). He rang bells with audiences in his virile performance opposite Lana Turner ≫ in an adaptation of James M. Cain's thriller **The Postman Always Rings Twice** (this version kept Visconti's unauthorised Italian adaptation, **Ossessione,** from being seen abroad). Garfield was defiantly himself as the violinist lover of Joan Crawford in **Humoresque** in 1947, and then left Warner Brothers to make more committed films. The first was Rossen's brilliant **Body and Soul**, perhaps the best boxing movie ever made. Next came **Gentleman's Agreement**, with Kazan casting him as a Jew in that exposé of anti-Semitism. Finally, he made what many critics consider his finest film, Polonsky's **Force of Evil**, in which he is utterly convincing as a numbers racket organiser. He also starred in an excellent remake of **To Have and Have Not** (**The Breaking Point**), but his supposed leftist sympathies made it difficult for him to get work after that; he was blacklisted, and died of a heart attack in 1952.

BEST FILMS:
1938 Four Daughters
Michael Curtiz (Warner Brothers)
1941 The Sea Wolf
Michael Curtiz (Warner Brothers)
1943 Air Force
Howard Hawks (Warner Brothers)
1945 Pride of the Marines
Delmer Daves (Warner Brothers)
1945 The Postman Always Rings Twice
Tay Garnett (MGM)
1947 Humoresque
Jean Negulesco (Warner Brothers)
1947 Body and Soul
Robert Rossen (United Artists)
1947 Gentleman's Agreement
Elia Kazan (20th Century Fox)
1948 Force of Evil
Abraham Polonsky (MGM)
1950 The Breaking Point
Michael Curtiz (Warner Brothers)

JUDY GARLAND

Judy Garland combined vitality and vulnerability, gaiety and pain, with an emotional intensity unequalled in the cinema. She was not only one of the greatest musical stars and singers in the history of the movies, but probably the greatest performer. She was almost literally *Born in a Trunk* (as she sang in **A Star Is Born**), the daughter of vaudeville performers who put her on stage at the age of three. Hollywood made her into one of its all-time immortal stars and burned her up in the process; she was fed pills and pumped full of morphine to keep her going non-stop, never allowed to take the time off she needed to cure her addiction, driven to attempted suicide in 1950, and finally finished by an "accidental" overdose of sleeping pills in 1969. One can hardly say that Hollywood wasted her, but it certainly destroyed her while trying to use her full potential. Her personal life was a tragedy, but her greatest films are among the masterpieces of the cinema. Few other stars have achieved so much, but few had to suffer so much to achieve it.

She was born on June 10, 1922, in Grand Rapids, Michigan, with the name Frances Ethel Gumm. The name "Garland" was given her and her sisters by George Jessel, when they were touring and she borrowed "Judy" from the title of a popular song by Hoagy Carmichael. She made her film début in 1936, aged 14, in the short **Every Sunday** with Deanna Durbin ➤, but didn't really capture anybody's attention until she sang her love letter, *Dear Mr Gable,* in **Broadway Melody of 1938.** When Shirley Temple ➤ proved unavailable for the starring role in **The Wizard of Oz** (for which the gods be thanked!), Garland replaced her and immediately became not just a major star but a cinema immortal, forever identified with the film and with the song *Over The Rainbow* MGM then teamed her with Mickey Rooney ➤ in the **Andy Hardy** series and in backstage teenage musicals like **Babes in Arms** and **Strike up the Band,** the best of which were directed by Busby Berkeley. Her life at this time was completely controlled by MGM and by her mother, whom she later described as "the real-life Wicked Witch of the West"; between pep pills, sleeping pills and diet régimes the process of her destruction was begun.

Her next classic musical was the 1944 **Meet Me in St Louis,** one of the most affectionate and effective pieces of Americana ever made, particularly remembered for her singing of *The Trolley Song.* The director was Vincente Minnelli, whom she married the following year (the second of five marriages), and who also directed her in the superb non-musical **The Clock,** the all-star **Ziegfeld Follies,** and the bizarre but beautiful **The Pirate.** She was teamed with Gene Kelly ➤ for the first time in the 1942 **For Me and My Gal;** their work together was even better when swashbuckling in **The Pirate** and getting the show together in **Summer Stock.** Her other great musical partner was Fred Astaire ➤, in one of the happiest of all song-and-dance films, Charles Walters' **Easter Parade,** which included their marvellous duet *We're a Couple of Swells.* She was excellent in **The Harvey Girls** with John Hodiak, in her brief appearance in **Till The Clouds Roll By,** and opposite Van Johnson ➤ in **In the Good Old Summertime.**

By this time, Garland had acquired a reputation for unreli-

ability because of her personal problems, and MGM dumped her in 1950. She made only four films after leaving that studio, but with the help of Sid Luft (whom she later married) she became one of the great concert performers of our time, evoking unrestrained adulation from her fans—especially from the gay community, for whom she was *the* star. When she returned to movies in 1954, she gave her greatest performance ever in **A Star Is Born,** pushing her dazzling but vulnerable show-biz persona to new heights. It was one of the greatest of all screen performances—but the Academy Award that year went to Grace Kelly ➤ for **The Country Girl,** a decision that is incomprehensible. It must have hurt Garland enormously. She returned to concert work and some television, and then made her last films in the '60s. She was good in a small dramatic role in **Judgment at Nuremberg,** touching as a music teacher in **A Child is Waiting,** and very close to autobiography in **I Could Go on Singing,** made in England in 1963. Her reputation has, if possible, risen even higher since her death in 1969. Her daughter, Liza Minnelli ➤, evokes her mother's presence in her films and concerts.

Above: Garland became a film immortal in **The Wizard of Oz** *with fine support from Jack Haley (Tin Woodsman) and Ray Bolger (Scarecrow).*
Left: Judy Garland brought a new emotional intensity to stardom.

BEST FILMS:
1939 The Wizard of Oz
Victor Fleming (MGM)
1939 Babes in Arms
Busby Berkeley (MGM)
1942 For Me and My Gal
Busby Berkeley (MGM)
1944 Meet Me in St Louis
Vincente Minnelli (MGM)
1945 The Clock
Vincente Minnelli (MGM)
1946 The Harvey Girls
George Sidney (MGM)
1948 The Pirate
Vincente Minnelli (MGM)
1948 Easter Parade
Charles Walters (MGM)
1950 Summer Stock
Charles Walters (MGM)
1954 A Star is Born
George Cukor (Warner Brothers)

GREER GARSON

Greer Garson starred in the sleekest, sweetest and most sentimental women's pictures of the '40s. Of their type, they are virtually unbeatable, but because glutinous kitsch is unfashionable now they have won little critical favour. Garson's career was brief, but magnificent in its own way. She came literally out of nowhere, snatched the crown of Queen of MGM from such seasoned troupers as Joan Crawford ➤ and Norma Shearer ➤, won an Academy Award for **Mrs Miniver,** and became a top box-office star in less than four years. She met a popular need for a nobly-suffering but capable and lady-like mother figure for the war years, and then began to fade away almost as soon as the war was over; she was a good actress, but was cast in a mould by Louis B. Mayer, the

Above: Greer Garson as **That Forsyte Woman** *(1949), in which she starred with Errol Flynn, Walter Pidgeon and Robert Young.*

head of MGM, and was never able to break out of it—she acerbically described herself as "Metro's Glorified Mother".

Garson was born in County Down, Northern Ireland, on September 29, 1908, and won a fair reputation on the London stage in the '30s, playing opposite Laurence Olivier ➤ and being directed by Noël Coward ➤. Mayer saw her in a play called *Old Music* (he had thought it was a musical) and signed her for MGM. She made her début in 1939 with the small but meaty role of the young wife who dies in **Goodbye, Mr Chips,** portrayed Elizabeth Bennet opposite Olivier in **Pride and Prejudice,** and began her suffering, self-sacrificing career with Walter Pidgeon ➤ in **Blossoms in the Dust** (the first of eight films they made together). She confronted Joan Crawford ➤ head-on in **When Ladies Meet** (it was considered a tie) and then starred in her most famous film, **Mrs Miniver,** a phoney but beautifully crafted story of wartime Britain. She made the longest acceptance speech in the history of the

Academy Awards when she got her Oscar. She was teamed with Ronald Colman ❯ in **Random Harvest,** sentimentalised history in **Madame Curie,** and kept up her stereotyped but big box-office roles in **Mrs Parkington** and **Valley of Decision.** When Clark Gable ❯ came back from the war, she got him in **Adventure,** but her career was already on the downward slide. She was matched with Errol Flynn ❯ in **That Forsyte Woman** and then re-teamed with Pidgeon in the unfortunate **The Miniver Story** in 1950. That virtually ended her career, but she tried a little more sentiment with him in **Scandal at Scourie,** before quitting the film business in 1955. She has made sporadic reappearances, the most recent being in the 1967 Disney film **The Happiest Millionaire.**

BEST FILMS:
1939 Goodbye, Mr Chips
Sam Wood (MGM)
1940 Pride and Prejudice
Robert Z. Leonard (MGM)
1941 Blossoms in the Dust
Mervyn LeRoy (MGM)
1941 When Ladies Meet
Robert Z. Leonard (MGM)
1942 Mrs Miniver
William Wyler (MGM)
1942 Random Harvest
Mervyn LeRoy (MGM)
1943 Madame Curie
Mervyn LeRoy (MGM)
1944 Mrs Parkington
Tay Garnett (MGM)
1945 Valley of Decision
Tay Garnett (MGM)
1949 That Forsyte Woman
Compton Bennett (MGM)

VITTORIO GASSMAN

Vittorio Gassman has an international reputation as an actor which is relatively unjustified by his actual achievements in the cinema. In his native Italy he has long been a hugely popular stage actor, often in Shakespearean and classical roles, and big cinema box-office because of his satirical comedies. The films for which he is known internationally, however, are relatively few. He first attracted attention carousing with the sensuous Silvana Mangano in the rice fields of Vercelli in the 1948 **Bitter Rice,** a shockingly erotic film for its time. He had another success with Mangano in Alberto Lattuada's 1951 **Anna** and was invited to Hollywood by MGM. There he married Shelley Winters ❯ and made four films, none of which were particularly bad—but then they weren't that interesting either. The most notable were **The Glass Wall** with Gloria Grahame ❯ (he was an illegal immigrant) and **Rhapsody** with Elizabeth Taylor ❯ (romantic love triangle).

Gassman went back to Italy, performed creditably as Anatole in **War and Peace,** and then made

one of his most entertaining films, **I Soliti Ignoti.** Known variously abroad as **Big Deal on Madonna Street** or **The Usual Unknown Persons,** it was a brilliant send-up of **Rififi,** with Gassman as a punchdrunk ex-boxer involved with other incompetents in a ridiculous robbery scheme (their loot finally consists of a bowl of spaghetti). Gassman has made films with Roberto Rossellini (**Anima Nera**) and Francesco Rosi (**Kean**), but it was for sharp-edged satirical and often politically-barbed comedy that he really became popular in the '60s, with such brilliant films as **Il Surpasso (The Easy Life)** and **I Mostri (The Monsters).** He was born in Genoa on September 1, 1922, worked first on the stage, and made his film début in the 1946 **Preludio d'Amore.** He has remained popular in the '70s and had a big success

*Above: Vittorio Gassman won the Best Actor Award at Cannes in 1975 for **Scent of Woman.***

at the Cannes Film Festival in 1975 with **Profumo di Donna (Scent of Woman).** It was directed by Dino Risi, who has made most of Gassman's better comedies, including the 1977 **Anima Persa (The Forbidden Room).** He was also featured in Robert Altman's 1978 **A Wedding.**

BEST FILMS:
1949 Riso Amaro (Bitter Rice)
Giuseppe De Santis (Lux Film)
1951 Anna
Alberto Lattuada (Lux Film)
1953 The Glass Wall
Maxwell Shane (MGM)
1956 War and Peace
King Vidor (Ponti-De Laurentiis)
1958 I Soliti Ignoti (The Usual Unknown Persons)
Mario Monicelli (Lux-Vides)
1959 La Grande Guerra
Mario Monicelli (De Laurentiis)
1962 Barabbas
Richard Fleischer (Columbia-De Laurentiis)
1962 Il Surpasso (The Easy Life)
Dino Risi (Fairfilm)
1963 I Mostri
Dino Risi (Fairfilm)
1975 Profumo di Donna
Dino Risi (Dean Film)

JANET GAYNOR

Janet Gaynor was the first actress to win an Academy Award, which she received for three outstanding films, Murnau's **Sunrise** and Borzage's **Seventh Heaven** and **Street Angel.** She did not have great charisma nor even great acting ability, but she was charming, winsome, wistful and innocent-looking, a large-eyed naive waif who could be used by good directors with wonderful results. She was the direct heir of Mary Pickford ❯ as America's Sweetheart and re-made a number of Pickford's films, including **Daddy Long Legs** and **Tess of the Storm Country.** She was also half of "America's Favourite Lovebirds" duo at this time with Charles Farrell, who starred with her in 12

*Above: Gaynor as cover girl. Below: Janet Gaynor starred as Esther Blodgett in the original version of **A Star Is Born.***

films from the 1927 **Seventh Heaven** to the 1934 **Change of Heart.** She was a Fox star (before Twentieth) and heavily promoted by chief executive Winfield Sheehan, who made her the top Fox female star of the early '30s. In 1937 she was the highest-paid actress in Hollywood (more than $250,000)—not bad for a diminutive, five-foot-nothing girl weighing only 96 pounds.

Janet was born as Laura Gainor in Philadelphia, Pennsylvania, on October 6, 1906. She worked with Hal Roach on comedy shorts and in Universal cowboy pictures until she got her break in Irving Cummings' 1926 **The Johnstown Flood** for Fox. She was immediately developed into a minor star in John Ford's **The Blue Eagle** and other silent pictures, and became a major one with her triple-film Oscar. **Sunrise** is her greatest film (she plays the ideal wife, the image of pure goodness and sacrifice), but she made many good ones. She is best known today for having created the role of Esther Blodgett in the first **A Star is Born** under William Wellman's direction (another Oscar nomination), but she is also charming in her many films for Henry King (notably **State Fair**) and Frank Borzage. She retired

from movies in 1938 and married designer Adrian Gilbert; she has since made only one film, the 1957 **Bernardine,** Pat Boone's mother. She presently lives in California with her third husband.

Her screen partner Charles Farrell (born Onset Bay, Massachusetts, on August 9, 1902) ended his film career in 1941 after his popularity dipped following the ending of their screen romancing. He later turned to professional tennis in Palm Springs, where he now lives.

BEST FILMS:
1927 Sunrise
F. W. Murnau (Fox)
1927 Seventh Heaven
Frank Borzage (Fox)
1928 Street Angel
Frank Borzage (Fox)
1929 Four Devils
F. W. Murnau (Fox)
1929 Sunny Side Up
David Butler (Fox)
1931 Daddy Long Legs
Alfred Santell (Fox)
1933 State Fair
Henry King (Fox)
1934 Carolina
Henry King (Fox)
1937 A Star is Born
William Wellman (Selznick)
1938 The Young in Heart
Richard Wallace (United Artists)

PAULETTE GODDARD

The waterfront waif who wins the heart of Charles Chaplin ➤ in **Modern Times**, the gutter gamin who wins Ray Milland ➤ and nobility in **Kitty**, and the ambitious chambermaid who wins the son of the rich family for whom she works in **Diary of a Chambermaid** —these are Paulette Goddard's best roles and the most representative of her screen persona. She was both pert and very pretty and she usually got her man, both on screen and off. She had excellent taste in husbands, including Chaplin, Burgess Meredith and her present husband Erich Maria Remarque. Like many of the heroines she played, she also became quite wealthy (with one of the most famous jewellery collections in the world). She was a top Paramount star in the '40s, and although her film career faded in the '50s, her best performances certainly haven't; it was a limited screen personality that she created, but it was very much her own, a combination of vivaciousness and stubbornness that is highly attractive.

Paulette was born Pauline Marion Levee in Great Neck, New York, on June 3, 1911 (Goddard was her mother's maiden name), and was on stage as a saucy Ziegfeld girl by 1926. Her film career began in 1929 with Hal Roach shorts, Paramount bit parts and Goldwyn girl glamour (as a blonde), but it wasn't until she met Chaplin in 1932 that she became a success. He starred her with him in **Modern Times** in 1936 (they married the same year) and she was immediately a leading lady. She was good in **The Women** for MGM, but it wasn't until Paramount's **The Cat and the Canary** that her film career really blossomed; she was just right as the frightened girlfriend of Bob Hope ➤ in this light horror classic and was equally good paired with him in the sequel **The Ghost Breakers**. She was a washerwoman romantically involved with barber Chaplin in **The Great Dictator** and became a favourite leading lady for both Cecil B. DeMille (**Northwest Mounted Police, Reap the Wild Wind, The Unconquered**) and Mitchell Leisen (**Hold Back the Dawn, Kitty, Suddenly It's Spring**). She never won any acting awards, but she was a memorable part of '40s cinema and quite outstanding in Jean Renoir's **Diary of a Chambermaid.**

Above right: Betty Grable was the top American female star for most of the 1940s.
Right: Betty Grable, sweetheart of wartime GIs. in her classic pose in a 1942 photo. Her legs were insured for a mind-boggling $1¼ million.

*Above: Paulette Goddard in the 1940 **Northwest Mounted Police**, directed by Cecil B. de Mille, for whom she became a favourite leading lady.*

After her uninteresting films of the '50s, she retired, making only **Gli Indifferenti** in Italy in 1966 (as Claudia Cardinale's ➤ mother) and a TV appearance in *The Snoop Sisters* in 1972.

BEST FILMS:
1936 Modern Times
Charles Chaplin (United Artists)
1939 The Women
George Cukor (MGM)
1939 The Cat and the Canary
Elliot Nugent (Paramount)
1940 The Ghost Breakers
George Marshall (Paramount)
1940 The Great Dictator
Charles Chaplin (United Artists)
1941 Hold Back the Dawn
Mitchell Leisen (Paramount)
1941 Nothing But the Truth
Elliot Nugent (Paramount)
1942 Reap the Wild Wind
Cecil B. DeMille (Paramount)
1945 Kitty
Mitchell Leisen (Paramount)
1946 Diary of a Chambermaid
Jean Renoir (United Artists)

BETTY GRABLE

Betty Grable was the number one pin-up girl of World War II (two million photographs of her in a white swimsuit were sent to GIs), the number one box-office attraction in America in 1943 and a top ten star from 1942 to 1951, and the number one singer for bandleader Harry James (they were married from 1943 to 1965). She was the girl with the million-dollar legs (they were insured at Lloyds for $1,250,000): her gams are as much a part of movie iconography as Fred Astaire's ➤ feet and Lana

Turner's ➤ sweaters. She never got much critical acclaim, however, despite being the second most popular female star of all time, and her kind of slightly brassy, slightly peaches — and — cream, elaborately made-up and coiffured beauty is currently unfashionable. All the same, she is still a delight in her best musicals. It is fascinating to note the change in popular taste as exemplified by 20th Century Fox's leading female stars: Alice Faye ➤, who was tops in the '30s, was replaced by Grable in the '40s (beginning with **Down Argentine Way**), and Grable was then ousted by Marilyn Monroe ➤ in the '50s in **How to Marry a Millionaire,** which featured both of them). The '40s were obviously right for Grable, for she had spent all of the '30s unsuccessfully trying for stardom.

She was born Ruth Elizabeth Grable in St Louis, Missouri, on December 18, 1916, and made her film début at the age of 14 in the 1929 musical **Let's Go Places**. She didn't at all in the '30s, although she tried her hardest and even did a nice number with Edward Everett Horton in **The Gay Divorcée.** Her moment came in 1940, when she was called in to replace a sick Alice Faye in **Down Argentine Way,** and she built up her stardom fast in **Tin Pan Alley, Moon Over Miami** and **Springtime in the Rockies.** The plots of most of her musicals were insipid, normally revolving around backstage romance; she was usually a girl on the make for men or money. She wasn't classy (she was the pin-up of the enlisted men, not the officers), but she was warm and sincere under her brassy exterior and she looked good in period costume as well. She had good songs, which she sang competently in films like **Coney Island, Sweet Rosie O'Grady, The Dolly Sisters** and **Mother Wore Tights,** and her legs were usually highlighted.

After her competition with Monroe in **How to Marry a Millionaire,** she gracefully retired from the scene, making two final films in 1955, **Three for the Show** and **How to Be Very, Very Popular.** She died in 1973.

BEST FILMS:
1940 Down Argentine Way
Irving Cummings (20th Century Fox)
1940 Tin Pan Alley
Walter Lang (20th Century Fox)
1941 Moon Over Miami
Walter Lang (20th Century Fox)
1942 Springtime in the Rockies
Irving Cummings (20th Century Fox)
1943 Coney Island
Walter Lang (20th Century Fox)
1943 Sweet Rosie O'Grady
Irving Cummings (20th Century Fox)
1945 Billy Rose's Diamond Horseshoe
George Seaton (20th Century Fox)
1946 The Dolly Sisters
Irving Cummings (20th Century Fox)
1947 Mother Wore Tights
Walter Lang (20th Century Fox)
1953 How to Marry a Millionaire
Jean Negulesco (20th Century Fox)

GLORIA GRAHAME

Gloria Grahame is one of the cinema's great good-bad girls, usually a cheap slut or a floozie, often hard-boiled, but still touchingly human and always sensual to a degree almost unknown before she came on the scene. She has explained that the powerful sexuality she exudes comes not from what she wears or does on screen, but from the thoughts behind her face when she looks at a man. That rather beautiful face was the recipient of a pot of boiling coffee in **The Big Heat,** one of the most distressing and shocking scenes of violence in the movies. She won a Best Supporting Actress Oscar in 1952 for her performance as the unfaithful Southern belle wife of Dick Powell ❯ in **The Bad and the Beautiful,** but she was even better opposite Humphrey Bogart ❯ in **In a Lonely Place,** matching her toughness against his cynicism. Nicholas Ray, who directed it, was her husband for four years from 1948, and also featured her in his film **A Woman's Secret.** Grahame was essentially a star of the '50s, making almost all her good films between 1950 and 1956, and most regrettably never developed into the major star she should have been with her powerful screen persona.

She was born as Gloria Grahame Hallward in Los Angeles on November 28, 1925, did some stage work, and then began her film career in the 1944 **Blonde Fever** (as a bad girl). She was nice as a platinum tart in Frank Capra's **It's A Wonderful Life,** even better as a bar singer in **Crossfire,** and pursued William Powell ❯ in **Song of the Thin Man. In a Lonely Place** really made her reputation, however, and soon afterwards she was the elephant lady in Cecil B. DeMille's **The Greatest Show on Earth,** tempting Jack Palance ❯ in **Sudden Fear,** and winning her Oscar. After fine performances in Lang's **The Big Heat** and

Above: Gloria Grahame gave one of her greatest tough good-bad girl performances in the 1950 Nicholas Ray film **In a Lonely Place.**

Human desire and Minnelli's **The Cobweb,** she was absolutely delightful in the musical version of **Oklahoma!** singing (naturally) *I'm Just a Girl Who Can't Say No.*

Between marriages and TV work, she did little filming in the '60s, but came back in a small way in the '70s and was starred with Ray Milland ❯ in the TV miniseries **Rich Man, Poor Man** in 1976.

BEST FILMS:
1947 Crossfire
Edward Dmytryk (RKO)
1949 A Woman's Secret
Nicholas Ray (RKO)
1950 In a Lonely Place
Nicholas Ray (Columbia)
1952 The Greatest Show on Earth
Cecil B. DeMille (Paramount)
1952 Sudden Fear
David Miller (RKO)
1952 The Bad and the Beautiful
Vincente Minnelli (MGM)
1953 The Big Heat
Fritz Lang (Columbia)
1954 Human Desire
Fritz Lang (Columbia)
1955 The Cobweb
Vincente Minnelli (MGM)
1955 Oklahoma!
Fred Zinnemann (Magna)

FARLEY GRANGER

Perhaps the brevity of Farley Granger's period as a major star was due to the limitations of his screen personality, a soft, boyish handsomeness, masking weakness and guilt. He made his greatest films between 1948 and 1954 and then virtually faded away; his best movies, however, are dandies. He was outstanding as the weak-willed tennis player trapped into a murder pact by Robert Walker in Alfred Hitchcock's **Strangers on a Train,** brilliant as a weak-willed newlywed terrorised into becoming a criminal in Nicholas Ray's **They Live By Night,** and at his very best as the weak-willed, cowardly lover of Alida Valli in Luchino Visconti's spectacularly beautiful Italian film **Senso.** There are few starring roles of this particular kind, but Granger was perfect for them while they lasted.

Left: Farley Granger created a strange weak-willed persona, almost trapped into murder by Robert Walker in the Hitchcock/Highsmith **Strangers on a Train.**

He was born in San José, California, on July 1, 1925, and made his début as a soldier in Lewis Milestone's 1943 **The North Star.** He had a bigger and better part in **The Purple Heart,** went into the Army, and came out for his short run of outstanding films. Hitchcock featured him as one of the thrill-murderers in the 1948 **Rope** and Anthony Mann used him in a role similar to his **They Live By Night** part in the 1949 **Side Street.** His last major film role was as the vicious Harry Thaw in **The Girl on the Red Velvet Swing** in 1955; afterwards he worked on stage, coming back for less important films in the late '60s. He has mainly worked in minor European films during the '70s.

BEST FILMS:
1943 The North Star
Lewis Milestone (20th Century Fox)
1944 The Purple Heart
Lewis Milestone (20th Century Fox)
1948 They Live By Night
Nicholas Ray (RKO)
1948 Rope
Alfred Hitchcock (Transatlantic)
1949 Side Street
Anthony Mann (MGM)
1951 Strangers on a Train
Alfred Hitchcock (Warner Brothers)
1953 The Story of Three Loves
Vincente Minnelli (MGM)
1954 Senso
Luchino Visconti (in Italy)
1955 Naked Street
Maxwell Shane (United Artists)
1955 The Girl on the Red Velvet Swing
Richard Fleischer (20th Century Fox)

STEWART GRANGER

Stewart Granger became popular in Britain as the star of overheated melodramas like **The Man in Grey,** achieved international stardom as the teeth-flashing hero of '50s swashbucklers like **King Solomon's Mines** and the classic Sabatini role, **Scaramouche,** and says he never made a film that he was proud of. He should be. Perhaps he made few masterpieces (though many critics would rate both **Scaramouche** and **Moonfleet** in that category), but he has made a strong contribution to a number of highly entertaining films that remain likeable. He may not have been a swashbuckler of Errol Flynn ❯ standards but he wields a nice sword in **The Prisoner of Zenda, Beau Brummel** and, especially, in **Scaramouche** under George Sidney's deft direction. He has worked with good action directors, including Roger Corman (**The Secret Invasion**), Robert Aldrich (**Sodom and Gomorrah**), Henry Hathaway (**North to Alaska**), and Richard

Left: Stewart Granger with Liliane Montevecchi in the romantic and undervalued Fritz Lang film **Moonfleet.**

Brooks (**The Last Hunt**); Fritz Lang elicited a fine performance in **Moonfleet** and George Cukor turned him into a notable partner for Ava Gardner ❯ in **Bhowani Junction**. Greater actors have done less.

Granger was born in London, England, on May 6, 1913, with the unfortunate real name (for a potential film actor) of James Stewart. He was on stage from the early '30s, did some film extra work, and made his first film in a leading role in 1939, **So This Is London**. He became a big British star in 1943 with **The Man in Grey**, and made a number of other reasonable British pictures—including Anthony Asquith's **Fanny By Gaslight**, Sidney Gilliat's **Waterloo Road** and Gabriel Pascal's **Caesar and Cleopatra** (as Apollodorus)—before going to Hollywood in 1950 to become a leading MGM star in **King Solomon's Mines**. After his '50s success as a swashbuckler, his career diminished in the '60s, even including three German Westerns as "Old Shatterhand". He has not worked much in the cinema in the '70s, but was featured in the TV film **The Hound of the Baskervilles** in 1971 (as Sherlock Holmes), and in the 1977 adventure film **The Wild Geese**.

BEST FILMS:

1943 The Man in Grey
Leslie Arliss (Gainsborough)
1945 Waterloo Road
Sidney Gilliat (Gainsborough)
1950 King Solomon's Mines
Compton Bennett (MGM)
1952 Scaramouche
George Sidney (MGM)
1952 The Prisoner of Zenda
Richard Thorpe (MGM)
1954 Beau Brummel
Curtis Bernhardt (MGM)
1955 Moonfleet
Fritz Lang (MGM)
1956 Bhowani Junction
George Cukor
1962 Sodom and Gomorrah
Robert Aldrich (Titanus)
1964 The Secret Invasion
Roger Corman (United Artists)

CARY GRANT

Cary Grant has strong claims to being the greatest actor of the American cinema; he has starred in an astonishing number of classic films over a very long period of time and is a consummate master of timing and a performer of such naturalness that critics rarely think of him as acting (he never won a Best Actor Oscar). His screen persona is one of the glories of the Hollywood movie, much imitated but never equalled, always charming but never quite trustworthy, utterly debonair but exceedingly masculine, nonchalant but always aware, seemingly devil-may-care but suspiciously organised. He was the favourite actor of two of the

great American directors, Howard Hawks and Alfred Hitchcock, and his 35-year career has featured him opposite most of the great female stars from Mae West ❯ and Jean Harlow ❯ to Grace Kelly ❯ and Audrey Hepburn ❯—but especially Katharine Hepburn ❯. He seemed virtually never to age and was even more charming in his fifties than he was in his thirties.

He was born in Bristol, England, on January 18, 1904, with the name Alexander Archibald Leach. He began in vaudeville and the theatre, and made his cinema début in 1932 in **This is the Night**. He was an immediate success as a leading man and was soon starred opposite Marlene Dietrich ❯ in Josef von Sternberg's ❯ **Blonde Venus**; Mae West liked what she saw and asked for him as her co-star in **She Done Him Wrong** and **I'm No Angel**. He made his first film with Katharine Hepburn, George Cukor's **Sylvia Scarlett**, in 1935. He was paired with Harlow in **Suzy**, Joan Bennett ❯ in **Big Brown Eyes** and Constance Bennett ❯ in **Topper**, one of his most polished early comedies

(they both play sophisticated ghosts). He was just as delightful opposite Irene Dunne ❯ in **The Awful Truth** and then made his first comedy for Howard Hawks, **Bringing Up Baby**—it teamed him again with Hepburn in one of the most brilliant comedies ever made. For a change of pace he diverted into adventure films and was memorable in the Kipling-derived **Gunga Din** and even better opposite Jean Arthur ❯ in Hawks' **Only Angels Have Wings**, the best of all aviation films. Hawks then starred him as the editor opposite reporter Rosalind Russell ❯ in the brilliant feminist role-reversal remake of **The Front Page** called **His Girl Friday**. Cukor directed him with Hepburn again in the classic "high society" comedy **The Philadelphia Story**. His rich association with Hitchcock began in 1941, frightening then wife Joan Fontaine ❯ in **Suspicion** (it is one of the marvels of his screen persona that we can suspect him of being a murderer even while he charms us). These are only highlights of his career; almost

Above: Cary Grant in **Charade** *(1963), in which he co-starred with Audrey Hepburn.*

Above: Cary Grant and Ginger Rogers deceive the Nazis (and her husband) in the 1942 **Once Upon A Honeymoon.**

every film he made was worthy of attention.

Frank Capra used Grant brilliantly in the black comedy **Arsenic and Old Lace** in 1944, and he should then have been ideal as Cole Porter in the biopic **Night and Day**, but the film wasn't up to its subject. Hitchcock featured him as a secret agent, using Ingrid Bergman ❯ for his own purposes, in **Notorious**, and he made a lot of fun out of **The Bachelor and the Bobby Soxer** and **Mr Blandings Builds His Dreamhouse**. In 1949, Hawks starred him in the quite incredible **I Was a Male War Bride** with Anne Sheridan ❯ (dressing up in women's clothes) and then had him experimenting with a youth serum in **Monkey Business**, a nice part for an actor who never seems to age. He should have been in **Sabrina**, but turned it down and never worked with Billy Wilder, who had always

wanted him (the Grant persona is parodied by Tony Curtis ❯ in Wilder's **Some Like It Hot**). He was teamed with Grace Kelly in Hitchcock's sexy thriller **To Catch a Thief** in 1955, and did a fine job opposite Ingrid Bergman in the less interesting **Indiscreet** and Sophia Loren ❯ in **Houseboat**. He was back with Hitchcock in another classic thriller in 1959, **North by Northwest**, and Blake Edwards teamed him with Tony Curtis in the funny-in-places **Operation Petticoat**. He was very good with Doris Day ❯ in **That Touch of Mink** and even better with Audrey Hepburn in the comedy thriller **Charade**, but his extraordinary career finally began to tail off in the mid-'60s and he retired from screen acting in 1966, after **Walk Don't Run** with Samantha Eggar. He is now primarily a cosmetics executive.

BEST FILMS:

1937 Topper
Norman Z. McLeod (MGM)
1937 The Awful Truth
Leo McCarey (Columbia)
1938 Bringing Up Baby
Howard Hawks (RKO)
1939 Gunga Din
George Stevens (RKO)
1939 Only Angels Have Wings
Howard Hawks (Columbia)
1940 His Girl Friday
Howard Hawks (Columbia)
1940 The Philadelphia Story
George Cukor (MGM)
1941 Suspicion
Alfred Hitchcock (RKO)
1944 Arsenic and Old Lace
Frank Capra (Warner Brothers)
1946 Notorious
Alfred Hitchcock (RKO)
1949 I Was a Male War Bride
Howard Hawks (20th Century Fox)
1955 To Catch a Thief
Alfred Hitchcock (Paramount)
1959 North by Northwest
Alfred Hitchcock (MGM)
1963 Charade
Stanley Donen (Universal)

KATHRYN GRAYSON AND HOWARD KEEL

Kathryn Grayson and Howard Keel are the modern cinema's equivalent of Jeanette MacDonald ❯ and Nelson Eddy, the splendid singing stars of **Kiss Me Kate** and **Showboat**, but unluckily they came at the end of the vogue for musicals and never really got the chance to develop as a duo. From 1950 to 1955 they were the leading stars of the operetta-type musical, both together and separately, and then their cinema careers faded away, but in later years they had a successful nightclub act together. Keel made one great musical without Grayson (**Seven Brides for Seven Brothers**) and a few other good ones, but Grayson was less successful without Keel (in films like **The Desert Song** and **So This Is Love**).

Grayson was the younger (born February 9, 1922, in Winston Salem, North Carolina, as Zelma Kathryn Hedrick), but began her career. Grayson and Keel were then an instant hit in **Showboat**, his big baritone balancing her trilling soprano, just as engaging in **Lovely To Look At,** and at peak form in **Kiss Me Kate,** their last partnership. Keel was good with Doris Day ❯ in **Calamity Jane,** less interesting in **Rose Marie** with Ann Blyth, magnificent in **Seven Brides for Seven Brothers** with Jane Powell, and ended his film musical career with **Jupiter's Darling** and **Kismet.** The rest of his film career was in straight parts, the last being the 1968 **Arizona Bushwackers.** Grayson's career ended in 1956 with the musical failure **The Vagabond King** and she retired from the cinema.

BEST FILMS:
Together:
1951 Show Boat
George Sidney (MGM)
1952 Lovely to Look At
Mervyn LeRoy (MGM)

Below: Howard Keel and Kathryn Grayson in one of their most successful joint efforts, the 1953 **Kiss Me Kate.**

1953 Kiss Me Kate
George Sidney (MGM)
Kathryn Grayson:
1950 The Toast of New Orleans
Norman Taurog (MGM)
1953 The Desert Song
H. Bruce Humberstone (Warner Brothers)
1953 So This Is Love
Gordon Douglas (Warner Brothers)
Howard Keel:
1950 Annie Get Your Gun
George Sidney (MGM)
1953 Calamity Jane
David Butler (MGM)
1954 Seven Brides for Seven Brothers
Stanley Donen (MGM)
1955 Kismet
Vincente Minnelli (MGM)

film career far earlier, in the 1941 **Andy Hardy's Private Secretary.** She was featured in many '40s musicals at MGM, including **Seven Sweethearts, Thousands Cheer** and **The Kissing Bandit** (with Frank Sinatra ❯), but did not really make her breakthrough till the 1951 **Showboat,** despite success with Mario Lanza ❯ in **That Midnight Kiss** and **The Toast of New Orleans.** Keel (born April 13, 1917, in Gillespie, Illinois, as Harold Keel) made his film début in England in the 1948 **The Small Voice** (he didn't sing). His first real success was in the 1950 **Annie Get Your Gun** opposite Betty Hutton ❯, but his next, **Pagan Love Song** with Esther Williams ❯, hardly helped his

SYDNEY GREENSTREET

Sydney Greenstreet, the sinister, chuckling fat man of '40s thrillers at Warner Brothers, is one of the all-time great movie scoundrels. Crafty, calculating, malevolent and cold under his facade of pleasant, quiet politeness, he was a sensation in his first film, **The Maltese Falcon,** nastily involving Humphrey Bogart ❯ in his search for the legendary statue. He was at this time 61 years old, weighed 280 pounds, and had already been a notable stage actor for 40 years. His movie career was brief—he retired in 1950—but while it lasted it was blackly brilliant. He usually played opposite Bogart and Peter Lorre ❯ and his rogue's gallery of memorable villains was astutely directed by the top Warners directors of the time, including Michael Curtiz, Raoul Walsh, John Huston and Jean Negulesco. In **Casablanca** he was Bogart's rival as the owner of the Blue Parrot Café, swatting flies in a fez while handling his black-market activities. In **Across the Pacific** he was a secret fascist, in **Background to Danger** a Nazi colonel, and in **Passage to Marseilles** a Vichy supporter. His finest performance was in **The Mask of Dimitrios,** a film based on a novel by Eric Ambler which could almost have been written with Greenstreet in mind; he

Above: Greenstreet as the black-marketeer in **Casablanca.**

portrays an international criminal with a spiderweb of connections all over Europe. He was also outstanding as the star of Don Siegel's **The Verdict,** tracking down a murderer in foggy London after having hanged the wrong man (even his non-villainous roles had sinister aspects), and as the utterly evil Count Fosco in **The Woman in White.**

Greenstreet was born in Sandwich, Kent, England, on December 27, 1879, and began his acting career in 1902. After 1904 he was based in the USA and was primarily a Shakespearean and comedy actor; John Huston finally coaxed him into the movies for his brilliant run of '40s villains, which culminated splendidly in **Flamingo Road,** as a vicious, corrupt Southern police chief. His last film was the 1950 **Malaya;** he died in 1954.

BEST FILMS:
1941 The Maltese Falcon
John Huston (Warner Brothers)
1942 Across the Pacific
John Huston (Warner Brothers)
1942 Casablanca
Michael Curtiz (Warner Brothers)
1943 Background to Danger
Raoul Walsh (Warner Brothers)
1944 The Mask of Dimitrios
Jean Negulesco (Warner Brothers)
1945 Conflict
Curtis Bernhardt (Warner Brothers)
1946 Three Strangers
Jean Negulesco (Warner Brothers)
1946 The Verdict
Don Siegel (Warner Brothers)
1948 The Woman in White
Peter Godfrey (Warner Brothers)
1949 Flamingo Road
Michael Curtiz (Warner Brothers)

ALEC GUINNESS

Alec Guinness has strong claims to be considered the greatest star of the British cinema. Laurence Olivier ❯ has more prestige, but Guinness has made better films and is a better screen actor, and his career reflects the greatest strength of the British cinema in the post-war period. He began as a brilliant Dickensian actor in **Great Expectations** and **Oliver Twist,** helped attract world attention to the superb Ealing comedies in **Kind Hearts and Coronets,** the **Lavender Hill Mob, The Man in the White Suit** and **The Lady-killers,** moved into the big budget epics of David Lean in **The Bridge**

Below: Alec Guinness won most of the major acting awards in 1957 for his performance in **The Bridge on the River Kwai.**

on the River Kwai and **Lawrence of Arabia,** and recently helped showcase the genius of British technicians in **Star Wars.** Along the way he picked up an Academy Award for his performance in **The Bridge on the River Kwai** and a knighthood for his acting. Without Guinness the British cinema would be far less than it is.

He was born in London on April 2, 1914, and began working on stage from the mid-'30s, despite being told he had no talent. He made his screen début in 1946 as a timorous Herbert Pocket in **Great Expectations,** and then proved himself even more effective as the villainous Fagin of **Oliver Twist.** he attracted international attention for an acting *tour-de-force* playing eight different roles in **Kind Hearts and Coronets** (all of them killed off by Dennis Price to secure a heritage), and won even more fame for **The Lavender Hill Mob** (organising a delightful robbery) and **The Man in the White Suit** (inventing a cloth that won't wear out). He was superb as **Father Brown,** outwitting master criminal Peter Finch ❯, and did a respectable job of portraying a harrowed Cardinal under pressure in **The Prisoner.** He led an even more incredible band of criminals in the blackly comic **The Lady-killers,** and won his Oscar in 1957 as the officer building that bridge in **The Bridge on the River Kwai.** He personally adapted Joyce Cary's novel **The Horse's Mouth** for the screen and starred as the painter hero, was outstanding as the vacuum cleaner salesman who gets tangled up with espionage in **Our Man in Havana,** and turned himself into a vain and convincing martinet in **Tunes of Glory.** Not all of his films up to 1960 were as good as these, but even the weaker ones were strengthened by his performances —for example, **The Mudlark,** in which he was a fine Disraeli. After 1960 his films remained worth-while, but he was no longer the centre of most of them. He was particularly good as Feisal in **Lawrence of Arabia,** well suited to be Marcus Aurelius in **The Fall of the Roman Empire,** cavalier as Charles I in **Cromwell,** and interesting when interpreting Graham Greene again in **The Comedians.** He started the '70s as Marley's Ghost in **Scrooge,** then played Pope to St Francis in **Brother Sun and Sister Moon,** Hitler in **Hitler: The Last Ten Days,** and the blind butler in the detective farce **Murder By Death.** He had another international triumph in 1977 as the old Jedi Knight Ben Kenobi in **Star Wars,** teaching Luke Skywalker how to harness the Force and dying nobly in combat with villainous Darth Vader.

BEST FILMS:
1946 Great Expectations
David Lean (Cineguild)
1948 Oliver Twist
David Lean (Cineguild)

1949 Kind Hearts and Coronets
Robert Hamer (Ealing)
1951 The Lavender Hill Mob
Charles Crichton (Ealing)
1951 The Man in the White Suit
Alexander Mackendrick (Ealing)
1953 The Captain's Paradise
Anthony Kimmins (British Lion)
1954 Father Brown
Robert Hamer (Facet)
1955 The Ladykillers
Alexander Mackendrick (Ealing)
1957 The Bridge on the River Kwai
David Lean (Horizon/Columbia)
1959 The Horse's Mouth
Ronald Neame (Knightsbridge/United Artists)
1959 Our Man in Havana
Carol Reed (Kingsmead/Columbia)
1960 Tunes of Glory
Ronald Neame (Knightsbridge/United Artists)
1962 Lawrence of Arabia
David Lean (Horizon/Columbia)
1964 The Fall of the Roman Empire
Anthony Mann (Samuel Bronston)
1977 Star Wars
George Lucas (20th Century Fox)

OLIVER HARDY
see **Laurel and Hardy**

JEAN HARLOW

Jean Harlow was the first screen tramp to become a heroine and her raw sexuality made her the sex symbol of the '30s, very much in the way Marilyn Monroe ❯ became the sex symbol of the

Above: Jean Harlow as the gold-digging **Red Headed Woman** *(1932). Harlow died tragically at the age of 26 after a sizzling career and three marriages.*

modern cinema. Harlow's screen persona was very different from Monroe's, however; she wasn't vulnerable but impudent, tough, wise-cracking, slatternly and sexually voracious. She gave as good as she got, which made her a wonderful screen partner for Clark Gable ❯ and James Cagney ❯. In her first starring role, in the 1930 **Hell's Angels,** she gave the cinema one of its immortal lines when she asked Ben Lyon to "Pardon me while I slip into something more comfortable", and she gained even more fame in **Red Dust** by taking a bath in a rain barrel and ordering Gable to "Scrub my back". She wore clinging satin dresses without a bra, became known as the Platinum Blonde, and obviously was just as keen on sex as men were. On top of all that she was a fine comedienne and is just as enjoyable to watch today as she was in the '30s. From 1930 to 1937 she was a major star in a delightful series of films, mostly at MGM, and then died tragically of uremic poisoning. She was only 26 years old.

She was born on March 3, 1911, in Kansas City, Missouri, with the name Harlean Carpenter (Jean Harlow was her mother's maiden name). She began her film career as an extra in 1928, worked in Hal Roach comedies (including Laurel and Hardy's ❯

Double Whoopee and **The Unkissed Man),** and became a star when Howard Hughes picked her for **Hell's Angels.** Her screen reputation soared opposite Cagney in **Public Enemy,** Gable in **The Secret Six** and Robert Williams in **Platinum Blonde,** after which MGM took over her contract and built up her reputation even more. She was very funny as a social-climbing secretary in **Red-Headed Woman** and then began her memorable romantic partnership with Gable in **Red Dust,** as a wise-cracking, cheap floozie with a heart of gold. They were back together again in **Hold Your Man,** as lovers in a sparkling tragi-comedy, and then she brilliantly satirised Hollywood in **Bombshell,** portraying a blonde Hollywood sexpot not unlike herself. She more than held her own against the MGM all-stars assembled for **Dinner at Eight** as the bright-and-brassy wife of Wallace Beery ❯, wondering if machinery will take the place of every profession—and being reassured by Marie Dressler ❯ that she will never have to worry.

Harlow was in the musical **Reckless,** back with Gable in the entertaining **China Seas,** and then teamed with Cary Grant ❯ in **Suzy. Libelled Lady** with Spencer Tracy ❯ was one of her funniest films (it was their third and last together), and then she was with Robert Taylor ❯ in **Personal Property.** It was the last film she was to complete. While working on **Saratoga** with Gable, she became ill and died; her mother was a Christian Scientist and this probably prevented her from having the medical treatment that could have helped. At the time of her death, she was romantically involved with William Powell ❯, whom it was expected she would marry. Her three earlier marriages had not been successful, including a brief one to MGM producer Paul Bern, who committed suicide shortly after their wedding. Harlow's life inspired a number of books, and two film biographies in the mid-'60s in which she was portrayed by Carroll Baker ❯ and Carol Lynley.

BEST FILMS:
1930 Hell's Angels
Howard Hughes (Hughes/United Artists)
1931 Public Enemy
William Wellman (Warner Brothers)
1931 Platinum Blonde
Frank Capra (Columbia)
1932 Red-Headed Woman
Jack Conway (MGM)
1932 Red Dust
Victor Fleming (MGM)
1933 Bombshell
Victor Fleming (MGM)
1933 Dinner at Eight
George Cukor (MGM)
1935 Reckless
Victor Fleming (MGM)
1935 China Seas
Tay Garnett (MGM)
1936 Libelled Lady
Jack Conway (MGM)

REX HARRISON

Rex Harrison has become the modern cinema's personification of the most English of Englishmen, more or less replacing Leslie Howard ❯, but with much more egotism in this role. Interestingly, they both portrayed Shaw's Henry Higgins on the screen, Howard in the 1938 **Pygmalion** and Harrison in the musical **My Fair Lady** in 1964. It was this film (and the stage production that preceded it) that made Harrison a star, even though he had been a film actor of importance long before. In fact, he made his cinema début in 1930 in Jack Raymond's **The Great Game**, but he didn't really become famous until 1937, when he played opposite Vivien Leigh ❯ in Victor Saville's charming **Storm in a Teacup**. He was very good in his early films, but more lightweight than he became later with the patina of age and increasing self-confidence in his egotistic screen persona. Among the most notable films of this time were King Vidor's **The Citadel** (as a society doctor) and Carol Reed's **Night Train to Munich** (as a government secret agent). He was excellent if a little brittle in **Major Barbara** before joining the RAF, but it was his two films immediately after the war that really made his reputation: the screen version of Noël Coward's ❯ **Blithe Spirit** and the dated but still effective **The Rake's Progress**.

Rex virtually radiated self-confidence now, and was superbly overbearing in **Anna and the King of Siam** in Hollywood, opposite Irene Dunne ❯ (a role with strong resemblances to his Higgins). He was enjoyable as the ghostly protagonist in **The Ghost and Mrs Muir** and splendidly and outrageously egotistical as the orchestra conductor in Preston Sturges' 1948 **Unfaithfully Yours**, plotting his wife's murder. His '50s films were fairly lightweight again, the best being **The Constant Husband** and **The Reluctant Debutante**, but he had gained great international fame from his 1956 stage performance in *My Fair Lady*, and this led to his being starred in major-budget films. He was a powerful and persuasive Caesar in the blockbuster **Cleopatra** opposite Elizabeth Taylor ❯ and was nominated for a Best Actor Oscar in 1963. He didn't win, however, until the following year, when he re-created his domineering Higgins in the lavish film version of **My Fair Lady** in what is probably the cinema's most convincing and enjoyable portrayal of pure egotism. He maintained this domineering screen image as Pope Julius II in **The Agony and the Ecstasy**, although Charlton Heston's ❯ Michelangelo was rather harder to cow than Audrey Hepburn's ❯ Eliza Doolittle. He returned to the role of knowledgeable, tweedy English-

Above: Rex Harrison became a top star portraying Professor Henry Higgins in the 1964 screen version of **My Fair Lady** *with Audrey Hepburn, having created the role on stage opposite Julie Andrews.*

man in the costly **Dr Dolittle**, enjoyably outrageous but rather less convincing than in **My Fair Lady**. His later films have been slightly disappointing; he was miscast as an elderly homosexual in **Staircase** and weighed down by plot problems, despite his fine performance, in the *Volpone*-derived **The Honey Pot**. He was born as Reginald Carey in Huyton, Lancashire, on March 5, 1908, and published his autobiography, *Rex*, in 1974.

BEST FILMS:
1940 Night Train to Munich
Carol Reed (Gaumont-British)
1945 Blithe Spirit
David Lean (Two Cities)
1945 The Rake's Progress
Sidney Gilliat (Individual Pictures)
1946 Anna and the King of Siam
John Cromwell (20th Century Fox)
1947 The Ghost and Mrs Muir
Joseph L. Mankiewicz (20th Century Fox)
1948 Unfaithfully Yours
Preston Sturges (20th Century Fox)
1963 Cleopatra
Joseph L. Mankiewicz (20th Century Fox)
1964 My Fair Lady
George Cukor (Warner Brothers)
1965 The Agony and the Ecstasy
Carol Reed (20th Century Fox)
1967 Doctor Dolittle
Richard Fleischer (20th Century Fox)

LILIAN HARVEY

Lilian Harvey is an unjustly neglected major star, the sprightly singing-dancing heroine of the best German musical comedies of the 1930s, world renowned in her time. She was the European equivalent of Ginger Rogers ❯ and Jeanette MacDonald ❯, teamed romantically with Willy Fritsch in superb musicals that were also shot in English and French versions. Her popularity became so great that she was brought to Hollywood by Fox and made four American films before becoming dissatisfied and returning to Europe. A retrospective of her movies at the 1974 Berlin Film Festival was wildly successful and has led to reassessment of her importance by world critics. Her best known film, and the only one in wide circulation outside Germany, is Eric Charell's 1931 **Congress Dances**, in which she gives a vivacious performance opposite Fritsch in a kind of operetta set in Vienna at the time of the 1815 Congress. The enormous success of this film made her the gay and capricious fairy-tale princess of the German musical in a series of delightful movies like **Ein Blonder Traum, Ich und die Kaiserin** and **Quick**.

Lilian was born in London in 1907 of an English mother and German father, and she became a dancing star in Germany before making her début in the cinema in 1924 in Robert Land's **Der Fluch**. Director Richard Eichberg devel-

oped her career in the silent cinema with notable success in **Liebe und Trompetenblasen** and **Die Keusche Susanne**, as the European equivalent of a dancing flapper. Her major stardom, however, came with sound, for she could speak three languages perfectly and was ideally suited to making films simultaneously in German, French and English. The 1930 **Liebeswalzer** was a major hit with Harvey and Fritsch, and they were also splendid in **Die Drei von der Tankstelle** and the brilliantly innovative **Einbrecher**. Her Hollywood career was not successful, despite the delights of **My Weakness** and **I Am Suzanne**, and she went back to Germany to make another group of marvellous musicals, including **Black Roses, Gluckskinder, Capriccio** and the ballet star biography **Fanny Elssler**. She returned to England at the outbreak of war and her film career virtually ended; she was unable to make a comeback afterwards and died virtually forgotten in Antibes in 1968.

BEST FILMS:
1930 Die Drei von der Tankstelle
Wilhelm Thiele (Ufa)
1931 Congress Dances
Erik Charell (Ufa)
1932 Quick
Robert Siodmak (Ufa)
1932 Ein Blonder Traum
Paul Martin (Ufa)
1933 Ich und die Kaiserin
Friedrich Hollander (Ufa)
1933 My Weakness
David Butler (Fox)
1934 I Am Suzanne
Rowland V. Lee (Fox)
1935 Black Roses
Paul Martin (Ufa)
1936 Gluckskinder
Paul Martin (Ufa)
1937 Fanny Elssler
Paul Martin (Ufa)

Above: Lilian Harvey, the star of Germany's best '30s musicals, was also featured in four US films, including **My Weakness**. *Another outstanding American production was* **I Am Suzanne**, *but her career there did not sparkle.*

Jack Hawkins

The courageous, stiff upper-lip persona created by Jack Hawkins in the '50s in films like **Angels One Five** and **The Cruel Sea** made him an international star after a very long apprenticeship. He made his film début in the 1930 **Birds of Prey** and was a featured performer in dozens of movies before achieving stardom.

The courage he showed on the screen in these portraits of heroism was reflected in his personal life. He developed cancer of the throat in 1966 and his larynx was removed, but he taught himself to speak using his oesophagus and continued in his film career. Heroism in the cinema is currently unfashionable, but Hawkins represented something very important for the British public in the '50s, despite his stiffness and his unbending acting style.

He was born in London in 1910, made his stage début in 1924 in *St Joan,* and continued to work in the theatre through most of his early film career. He was a colonel in the war and his military bearing made him particularly suited to soldier and police roles. His finest performance was perhaps in **The League of Gentlemen** as a gangleader bringing together his wartime associates for a precisely planned robbery. He was also excellent in villainous roles, notably as the grim interrogater of Cardinal Alec Guinness ≫ in **The Prisoner**. John Ford starred him in his British picture **Gideon's Way** as a police inspector, and David Lean used him very well in his stiffest military manner in **The Bridge on the River Kwai** and **Lawrence of Arabia** (as Allenby). He was superbly naval in **Ben-Hur**, and also starred in the '50s TV series **The Four Just Men**. His last film was the 1973 **Tales That Witness Madness**, and he died the same year. His autobiography, *Anything For a Quiet Life*, was published in 1974.

BEST FILMS:
1950 State Secret
Sidney Gilliat (British Lion)
1952 Angels One Five
George More O'Farrell (Associated British)
1952 The Cruel Sea
Charles Frend (Ealing)
1955 The Prisoner
Peter Glenville (Columbia)
1957 The Bridge on the River Kwai
David Lean (Columbia)
1958 Gideon's Way
John Ford (Columbia)
1959 Ben-Hur
William Wyler (MGM)
1960 The League of Gentlemen
Basil Dearden (Rank)
1962 Lawrence of Arabia
David Lean (Columbia)
1963 Rampage
Phil Karlson (Warner-Seven Arts)
1964 Zulu
Cy Endfield (Paramount)

Above: Jack Hawkins had the perfect jutting jaw and stiff upper lip for heroic British films like **The Cruel Sea**.

Will Hay

Will Hay, one of the glories of British cinema comedy, has never become widely known in America or in other European countries. Whatever is peculiarly British in humour could therefore be said to be incarnate in this superb comedian. In all his films he basically portrays the same character, a variation on an incompetent authority figure; this character evolved from his music hall success as a bogus schoolmaster who knew less than his pupils but would never let on to the fact. So, in his films, he was a floundering schoolmaster in **Boys Will Be Boys,** a ludicrous ship's captain in **Windbag the Sailor,** an anarchic stationmaster in **Oh, Mr Porter!** (probably his finest film), an hilarious prison governor in **Convict 99,** a bumbling policeman in **Ask a Policeman** and an improbable fireman in **Where's That Fire?** His efforts to conceal his ignorance and incompetence invariably lead to deception, disaster and hilarity. Setting off this wonderful, blustering screen character and making it shine even brighter were two other fine comics who had absolutely no faith in Hay's ability to do anything right, the lazy, back-talking fat boy Graham Moffatt and the suspicious, crafty "old codger" Moore Marriott. If anything, they were more corrupt than Hay, whom they invariably involved in some dishonest scheme.

Hay has been compared by critic William K. Everson to W.C. Fields; they are both lazy braggarts involved in dubious schemes—but their characterisations are as different as their physiques. Fields was a big man who usually blustered his way to success; Hay was a small man who was unlikely to emerge victorious. He was born in Stockton-on-Tees in 1888 and became a music hall performer in 1909. He evolved a skit around the "Fourth Form at St Michael's" which was the embryo of the schoolmaster persona which he carried over into radio and films. His first movie was the 1934 **Those Were the Days,** but it was not until **Boys Will Be Boys** that his schoolmaster persona was seen on the screen. He joined forces with Moffat and Marriott in **Windbag the Sailor** and made his best films with them, all directed by Marcel Varnel. His later films, alone, are enjoyable, but lack the zest of the team pictures. He seemed to be developing new possibilities in the black comedy **My Learned Friend** but unfortunately it was his last before illness ended his career. He died in 1949.

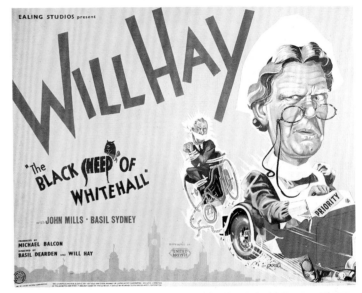

Above: Will Hay was incompetent (as usual) but very funny fighting spies in the 1941 comedy **The Black Sheep of Whitehall**.

BEST FILMS:
1935 Boys Will Be Boys
William Beaudine (Gainsborough)
1936 Windbag the Sailor
William Beaudine (Gainsborough)
1937 Good Morning Boys
Marcel Varnel (Gainsborough)
1937 Oh, Mr Porter!
Marcel Varnel (Gainsborough)
1938 Convict 99
Marcel Varnel (Gainsborough)
1938 Old Bones of the River
Marcel Varnel (Gainsborough)
1939 Ask A Policeman
Marcel Varnel (Gainsborough)
1939 Where's That Fire?
Marcel Varnel (Gainsborough)
1941 The Ghost of St Michael's
Marcel Varnel (Ealing)
1943 My Learned Friend
Basil Dearden (Ealing)

Helen Hayes

Helen Hayes was always primarily a stage actress, but her brief forays into the cinema won her two Academy Awards and a permanent place in film history. She was persuaded to go to Hollywood in the early '30s by her writer-husband Charles Mac-Arthur, after she was already famous in the theatre. Her first film, a woeful weepie called **The Sin of Madelon Claudet,** was a tearful story about a mother and her illegitimate child. Hayes hated it, MGM boss Louis B. Mayer loved it—and the Academy voted her the Best Actress Oscar. She then made some rather good films, including John Ford's **Arrowsmith** with Ronald Colman ≫ and Frank Borzage's **A Farewell to Arms** with Gary Cooper ≫. Her heart was not really in the movies, however, and after only nine pictures she returned to stage work, eventually becoming known as The First Lady of the American Theatre. She later made cameo reappearances in films, including

Above: Helen Hayes' finest film performance as the heroine of the 1932 **A Farewell to Arms**.

the Grand Duchess role in **Anastasia** with Ingrid Bergman ≫, and won a second Oscar as Best Supporting Actress for her dotty old lady stowaway in **Airport**.

She was born as Helen Hayes

Brown in Washington, DC, on October 30, 1900, and became a professional child actress at the age of five. She appeared in some early silent films, like the 1910 **Jean and the Calico Doll,** and became a major Broadway star in 1918 in *Dear Brutus.* She married MacArthur in 1928, became a fringe member of the Algonquin set, and then spent her few years in Hollywood. Among her most recent appearances she was one of **The Snoop Sisters** on television, and Lady St Edmund in the 1977 Disney film **Candleshoe,** with David Niven » and Jodie Foster.

BEST FILMS:
1931 The Sin of Madelon Claudet
Edward Selwyn (MGM)
1931 Arrowsmith
John Ford (Goldwyn/United Artists)
1932 A Farewell To Arms
Frank Borzage (Paramount)
1932 The Son-Daughter
Clarence Brown (MGM)
1933 The White Sister
Victor Fleming (MGM)
1933 Another Language
Edward Griffith (MGM)
1933 Night Flight
Clarence Brown (MGM)
1934 What Every Woman Knows
Gregory La Cava (MGM)
1956 Anastasia
Anatole Litvak (20th Century Fox)
1969 Airport
George Seaton (Universal)

SUSAN HAYWARD

Susan Hayward is primarily known for her highly dramatic portrayals of alcoholics and murderesses in '50s film biographies. She was a pretty, Dresden-doll-like redhead with a penchant for playing aggressive ladies; of one of her early nasty performances, in the 1944 **The Naked Ape,** the perceptive American critic James Agee commented upon the "loathsome" and "vicious" aspects of her screen personality and predicted the histrionic performances to come. Hollywood loves this kind of out-and-out "acting" and gave her five Academy Award nominations, culminating in an Oscar for her role as condemned killer Barbara Graham in the 1958 **I Want To Live.** She was an alcoholic in **Smash-Up,** a singer (Jane Froman) in **With a Song in My Heart,** an alcoholic singer (Lillian Roth) in **I'll Cry Tomorrow,** an evil empress (Messalina) in **Demetrius and the Gladiators,** a seductress in **David and Bathsheba,** and just an ordinary, vicious girl fighting her way to the top of the fashion world in **I Can Get It For You Wholesale.** She was good, gutsy, entertaining fun, and she looks very lovely in her movies, but what she does should not really be labelled good screen acting.

Hayward was born as Edythe Marriner in Brooklyn, New York,

Above: Susan Hayward loved to "act", and built her splendid career on emotional histrionics.

on June 30, 1918, became a model in the '30s, and made her film début in the 1938 **Girls on Probation.** She spent much of the '40s fighting to get bigger and more dramatic roles, won her first

Oscar nomination for the 1947 **Smash-Up,** and had her first big success in **My Foolish Heart,** dallying with Dana Andrews ». She had most of the Bette Davis-type roles of the '50s and starred in some notable Westerns as well, especially **Rawhide** and **The Lusty Men.** Her popularity diminished in the '60s, in films like **Back Street** and **Stolen Hours,** but she was nicely trashy as an ageing star in the trashy **Valley of the Dolls.** She did very little film work in the '70s and died in 1975.

BEST FILMS:
1944 The Naked Ape
Alfred Santell (United Artists)
1947 Smash-Up
Stuart Heisler (Universal)
1949 My Foolish Heart
Mark Robson (Samuel Goldwyn)
1951 I Can Get It For You Wholesale
Michael Gordon (20th Century Fox)
1951 David and Bathsheba
Henry King (20th Century Fox)
1952 With a Song in My Heart
Walter Lang (20th Century Fox)
1952 The Lusty Men
Nicholas Ray (RKO)
1955 I'll Cry Tomorrow
Delbert Mann (MGM)
1958 I Want to Live
Robert Wise (United Artists)
1967 Valley of the Dolls
Mark Robson (20th Century Fox)

Left: Rita Hayworth was the top Hollywood Love Goddess in the 1940s for her vulnerable sexuality as well as her glamour.

RITA HAYWORTH

Rita Hayworth reigned as the Hollywood Love Goddess in the '40s, reached her apotheosis in the 1946 **Gilda** under her most admiring director, Charles Vidor, and then had her screen image literally shattered in the 1948 **The Lady from Shanghai,** directed by her less admiring husband Orson Welles ». She was one of the leading pin-up ladies of World War II, representing for the officers what Betty Grable » symbolised for the enlisted men. She was a superb dancer as well and, for a while, was a top musical star, although her songs were usually dubbed. As a glamour star her screen persona was unusually vulnerable, despite her tempestuous gypsy image and obvious sexual frankness. In the film that first made her famous, Howard Hawks' 1939 **Only Angels Have Wings,** she was a glamour lady who knew she was out of place in a banana republic aviation station with despised husband Richard Barthelmess », unable to revive her old relationship with Cary Grant ». In her last really good role, in the 1958 **Separate Tables,** she was again the glamour lady down on her luck, come to a boarding house to try to revive her old relationship with Burt Lancaster ». She always had trouble with the men in her films, whether tempting bullfighter Tyrone Power » in **Blood and Sand,** fighting with Gene Kelly ≫ over her success in **Cover Girl,** stuck with husband George Macready although she really loves Glenn Ford » in **Gilda;** she was a temptress, but not really evil in her films until Welles took over her image and made her into the vicious Elsa, married to the crippled Everett Sloane, in **Lady from Shanghai.** It was said that the notoriety surrounding her marriage to Prince Aly Khan at this time ruined her film career, but Welles probably toppled her from her throne.

Hayworth was born as Margarita Carmen Cansino in Brooklyn, New York City, on October 17, 1918, to a showbiz family, and made her film début in 1935 in **Under the Pampas Moon.** After her success in **Only Angels Have Wings,** she was the leading star at Columbia in the '40s, in musicals with Gene Kelly and Fred Astaire » as well as in more dramatic roles in films like **Susan and God** and in comedies like **Affectionately Yours.** Her musical **Cover Girl** was one of the best of the '40s and she brought a greater realism to her musicals than her counterparts at Fox. The other highlights were **You'll Never Get Rich** with Astaire, **My Gal Sal** with

Victor Mature ❯ and **You Were Never Lovelier**, again with Astaire. After her marriage to Aly Khan ended, she returned to Hollywood, but she was never again the major star she had been, even in vehicles like **Miss Sadie Thompson**. She was rather splendid, however, fighting for Frank Sinatra's ❯ affections in **Pal Joey** and Lancaster's in **Separate Tables,** at the end of the decade. Her career continued through the '60s and '70s, but there were no more good films and she has not made anything since the 1972 **The Wrath of God.** Her personal life and problems have, however, aroused a great deal of sympathy for her in recent years.

BEST FILMS:
1939 Only Angels Have Wings
Howard Hawks (Columbia)
1941 Blood and Sand
Rouben Mamoulian (20th Century Fox)
1941 You'll Never Get Rich
Sidney Lanfield (Columbia)
1942 My Gal Sal
Irving Cummings (20th Century Fox)
1942 You Were Never Lovelier
William A. Seiter (Columbia)
1944 Cover Girl
Charles Vidor (Columbia)
1946 Gilda
Charles Vidor (Columbia)
1948 The Lady from Shanghai
Orson Welles (Columbia)
1957 Pal Joey
George Sidney (Columbia)
1958 Separate Tables
Delbert Mann (Columbia)

SONJA HENIE

Sonja Henie, who invented, perfected and became the only star of the Hollywood ice musical, was a formidable skater (ten years as world champion) and a smashing success as a movie star (her films made over $25 million). Some film historians seem at a loss to understand her popularity as they search for hints of acting ability and other normal cinematic values. They underrate her audiences; nobody ever thought she could act (she was almost wooden in her emotions), and it wasn't really her sex appeal that attracted (she was nice, not sexy), but she had the magic of a real-life, fairy-tale princess. This somewhat pudgy and rather unremarkable girl had only to put on ice skates and she was transformed into a magical being who could leave dreary reality behind and float and fly into another world of grace and beauty. As she explained before entering movies, "I want to do with skates what Fred Astaire ❯ is doing with dancing." And that, in effect, is what she did. She created a world of form and movement that had very little to do with plot, acting or characterisation, but everything to do with the beauty of movement. She was nearly as good at it as Astaire, too, though her range was very limited.

Above: Sonja Henie, the top ice-skating movie star of all time.

Henie was born in Oslo, Norway, on April 8, 1912, and began skating at the age of eight. She was ice skating champion of Norway by the age of 14 and in 1927, she became world champion, appearing in a Norwegian silent film the same year. She held the title for ten years and was Olympic champion for three consecutive Games, but by then she had determined to become a film star and persuaded Darryl Zanuck to star her in the 1936 **One in a Million.** Like all of her films, it was mostly just a showcase for her skating, but it was a hit. She followed up with more successes, most of them set in winter resorts, with no visible plot except gay and glittering reasons for skating, and remained a top 20th Century Fox star until the very popular **Sun Valley Serenade.** Her films for Fox and other studios after that were less interesting; she left movie-making in 1948 after the failure of **The Countess of Monte Cristo.** She had made only 11 films in her 12 years in Hollywood, and her last screen appearance was portraying herself in the British revue film **Hello London** in 1958. She died in 1969.

BEST FILMS:
1936 One in a Million
Sidney Lanfield (20th Century Fox)
1937 Thin Ice
Sidney Lanfield (20th Century Fox)
1938 Happy Landing
Roy Del Ruth (20th Century Fox)
1938 My Lucky Star
Roy Del Ruth (20th Century Fox)
1939 Second Fiddle
Sidney Lanfield (20th Century Fox)
1939 Everything Happens at Night
Irving Cummings (20th Century Fox)
1941 Sun Valley Serenade
H. Bruce Humberstone (20th Century Fox)
1942 Iceland
H. Bruce Humberstone (20th Century Fox)
1943 Wintertime
John Brahm (20th Century Fox)
1945 It's A Pleasure
William A. Seiter (RKO)

AUDREY HEPBURN
see **Modern Stars**

*Below: Katharine Hepburn, shown here with Spencer Tracy in the 1957 **Desk Set.***

KATHARINE HEPBURN

Katharine Hepburn is probably the greatest "actress" of the American sound cinema and certainly one of its dozen greatest stars. Hollywood has recognised this by giving her more Academy Award nominations (11) and Oscars (3) than any other star—although not for her best performances. She is the only major star of the early '30s who is still a major star today, and she is even more popular now than when she won her first Academy Award in 1933; her 46-year career comprises only 40 films, but the majority of them are of high quality; a consistency matched only by her **Philadelphia Story** co-stars Cary Grant ❯ and James Stewart ❯. And yet, with all this achievement, she has not become a cinema myth in the style of lesser "actresses" like Greta Garbo ❯ and Marilyn Monroe ❯. She is known primarily as an actress—and perhaps she wanted it that way; certainly, she fought to have the best possible parts, to the extent of backing plays for Broadway, buying the movie rights, starring in the stage versions, and then selling them to Hollywood on condition that she starred in the films (which is what happened with **The Philadelphia Story**). This is not to say that she did not create a strong screen persona, which she did, nor that her personality is not a vital part of her screen image, which it certainly is. The difficulty has been that that persona was not a popular one and did not appeal to the mass public because of its affected Bryn Mawr accent, astringent wit, and gauche and gangling beauty. She was too thoroughbred for the masses to identify with (though the intellectuals and the critics have always admired her) and it was really only her later teaming with Spencer Tracy ❯and the softening of her image that won her wide public acceptance. Her second and third Oscars came not in the '30s and '40s, when she was at her greatest, but in the '60s, with relatively lesser films. The high-bred, witty aristocrat of the early years was transformed in the '50s and '60s into a much more stock figure, the stiff-mannered and inexperienced older woman sampling romance—not that Hepburn couldn't take this persona and do wondrous things with it, as she demonstrated so splendidly in **The African Queen,** but the personality suffered a sea-change. The old imperiousness was not lost, as she showed in the 1975 **Rooster Cogburn** opposite John Wayne ❯, but the new character does not have the naturalness it had.

Katharine Houghton Hepburn was born in Hartford, Connecticut, on November 9, 1909, acquired her accent and attitudes from her family and Bryn Mawr, and made her stage début in 1928. There was no long apprenticeship for Hollywood success; she was starred by George Cukor in her first film in 1932, **A Bill of Divorcement,** and won her first Oscar the following year in **Morning Glory** (appropriately portraying a girl with ambitions to become a star). She was suddenly the Queen of the RKO studio (her wilfulness led her detractors to dub her Katharine of Arrogance) and she made a brilliant series of films for Cukor (**Little Women, Sylvia Scarlett**), George Stevens (**Quality Street**), John Ford (**Mary of Scotland**) and others before making her greatest early comedy with Cary Grant, Howard Hawks' **Bringing Up Baby** (baby was a leopard). Despite her critical fame she was not good box-office, and RKO were happy to allow her to buy up her contract. She went to Columbia, made the brilliant stage-derived comedy **Holiday** with Cukor and Grant, and then went back to Broadway success in a play written for her by **Holiday** author Philip Barry, **The Philadelphia Story.** She sold the movie rights to MGM on condition that she star with Grant and James Stewart and gave one of her finest screen performances as the spoiled heroine (no Oscar). She then starred with Spencer Tracy in **Woman of the Year,** which began their long public (and private) association, the first of ten films they made together. MGM put her under contract and starred them in less interesting dramatic films (**Keeper of the Flame, The Sea of Grass**) and superb comedies (**State of the Union, Adam's Rib**). She went back to Broadway again and then found another ideal screen partner in Humphrey Bogart ❯, her co-star in **The African Queen.** She and Tracy were back together in the 1952 **Pat and Mike** and the 1957 **The Desk Set,** and in between she was again the elderly, inexperienced woman in **Summertime** and **The Rainmaker.** In the '60s she played powerful mother figures in **Suddenly Last Summer, Long Day's Journey into Night** and, her last with Tracy, **Guess Who's Coming to Dinner.** He died shortly after it was completed and Hollywood gave Hepburn another Oscar as if to console her. She won the Award again the following year for her fine performance as Eleanor of Aquitaine opposite Peter O'Toole ❯ in **The Lion in Winter.** She then starred in the unfortunate **The Madwoman of Chaillot** and went back to Broadway in the musical *Coco.*

In the '70s she has made **The Trojan Women,** the filmed play **A Delicate Balance,** the stunning theatrical TV film **Love Among the Ruins** with Laurence Olivier ❯ (Cukor directed), **Rooster Cogburn** with John Wayne ❯ and **Olly, Olly, Oxen Free.**

BEST FILMS:
1933 Morning Glory
Lowell Sherman (RKO)
1933 Little Women
George Cukor (RKO)
1938 Bringing Up Baby
Howard Hawks (RKO)
1938 Holiday
George Cukor (Columbia)
1940 The Philadelphia Story
George Cukor (MGM)
1942 Woman of the Year
George Stevens (MGM)
1948 State of the Union
Frank Capra (MGM)
1949 Adam's Rib
George Cukor (MGM)
1951 The African Queen
John Huston (Romulus-Horizon)
1955 Summertime
(Summer Madness)
David Lean (Lopert/Korda)
1960 Suddenly Last Summer
Joseph L. Mankiewicz (Columbia)
1962 Long Day's Journey into Night
Sidney Lumet (Ely Landau)
1968 The Lion in Winter
Anthony Harvey (Avco-Embassy)

CHARLTON HESTON

Charlton Heston used to be described by perceptive French critics as "an axiom of the cinema", while their English and American counterparts were dismissing him as a muscular monolith. Meantime the public, which often recognises quality a lot faster than critics, had made him into the most popular epic star of all time, through films like **Ben-Hur, The Ten Commandments, The Greatest Show on Earth** and **El Cid.** The crunch for honest observers came with the 1966 **Khartoum,** in which Heston easily out-acted the prestigious Laurence Olivier ❯. Had he always been such a fine screen actor? Indeed he had, right back to the beginning of his career—and not only was he outstanding in epics and spectaculars, he was just as fine in smaller films like **Ruby Gentry** or Orson Welles' ❯ masterpiece **Touch of Evil.** He was almost the only screen actor in the world able to portray convincingly, great epic heroes (he won an Oscar for his performance as **Ben-Hur**) and, when epics began to go out of fashion, he was a leading choice for the central role in disaster movies like **Earthquake** and **Two Minute Warning.** His screen presence was such that there was little chance of his being overwhelmed by gigantic sets, masses of extras and spectacular special effects.

Heston was born in Evanston, Illinois, on October 4, 1924, and made his name working on stage and in TV in the late '40s. His first films were 16mm efforts by David Bradley, **Peer Gynt** (1941) and **Julius Caesar** (1948), but he did not make his professional début until the 1950 **Dark City** with Lizabeth Scott. He became a big star when Cecil B. DeMille made him the hero of the hugely successful circus picture **The Greatest Show on Earth** and then made some good smaller-budget films like **Ruby Gentry** and **The Naked Jungle.** Portraying Moses in **The Ten Commandments** made him into a major star, and **Touch of Evil** showed just how good an actor he could be, even up against the formidable talents of Orson Welles. He was then featured in a series of major budget movies, including **The Big Country, The Buccaneer, Ben-Hur, El Cid, 55 Days at Peking** and **The Agony and the Ecstasy,** and gave notable performances in all of them. He was at his very best as a tough major in Sam Peckinpah's western **Major Dundee** and outstanding as a medieval knight in Franklin Schaffner's atmospheric epic **The War Lord.** His confrontation with a prestige "actor" in the 1966 **Khartoum,** playing General Gordon to Olivier's Mahdi, should have proved once and for all what a fine screen actor he had always been. It apparently didn't because, after the excellent **Will Penny** and the hugely commercial **Planet of the Apes,** Heston seemed to feel the need to prove his credentials as a "serious" actor. So he played Mark Antony in both **Julius Caesar** and **Antony and Cleopatra** to demonstrate his long association with Shakespearean theatre; it was almost as if he was underrating his own greatness as a screen actor in his best films. The films were not liked by either critics or public and Heston returned to his real *métier*, holding together such enjoyable disaster romps as **Earthquake, Airport 75, Two Minute Warning** and **Gray Lady Down.**

BEST FILMS:
1952 The Greatest Show on Earth
Cecil B. De Mille (Paramount)
1952 Ruby Gentry
King Vidor (20th Century Fox)
1956 The Ten Commandments
Cecil B. De Mille (Paramount)
1958 Touch of Evil
Orson Welles (Universal)
1958 The Big Country
William Wyler (MGM)
1959 Ben-Hur
William Wyler (MGM)
1961 El Cid
Anthony Mann (Samuel Bronston)
1963 55 Days at Peking
Nicholas Ray (Samuel Bronston)
1965 Major Dundee
Sam Peckinpah (Columbia)

Right: Charlton Heston is the greatest epic star of the modern cinema; one of his most brilliant performances was as the legendary Spanish hero of the 1961 Anthony Mann film **El Cid.** *Few actors have his ability to dominate spectacle.*

WENDY HILLER

Wendy Hiller is a movie actress with a distinct literary bias (most of her films are based on famous plays or novels) who could have become a really major star if she hadn't so drastically curtailed her work in the cinema (only 14 films in 40 years). She has a remarkable screen presence, with a beautifully sharp-edged voice and a steely strength of mind, that makes her screen personality one of memorable impact. Her finest films were at the beginning of her career, as Eliza Doolittle in the 1938 **Pygmalion** opposite Leslie Howard ➤ and in the title role of the 1940 **Major Barbara** with Rex Harrison ➤, but she has been very strong in most of her films. She won a Best Supporting Actress Oscar in 1958 for a beautifully controlled performance as the hotel owner in **Separate Tables** in love with Burt Lancaster ➤ and was powerful playing opposite Geraldine Page in the 1963 **Toys in the Attic.** She was also exceptional in earlier British films like **I Know Where I'm Going** under Powell and Pressburger's direction (as a girl falling in love while stranded on the island of Mull), and Carol Reed's **An Outcast of the Islands** (the resigned wife).

She was born in 1912 in Bramhall, Cheshire, made her reputation on stage in 1934 in *Love on the Dole,* and her film début in the 1937 **Lancashire Luck.** Her two Shaw films made her world famous, but she refused Hollywood offers and stayed in England with her husband, Ronald Gow. She has continued to work in the theatre as much (or as little) as in the cinema and has been seen in only a few recent films, including **A Man for All Seasons** (as the wife of Thomas More, played by Paul Scofield), **David Copperfield** (playing Mrs Micawber to Ralph Richardson) and **Murder on the Orient Express** (using her voice to great effect as the grand Princess Dragomiroff).

BEST FILMS:
1938 Pygmalion
Leslie Howard and Gabriel Pascal (Pascal)
1940 Major Barbara
Gabriel Pascal and Harold French (Pascal)
1945 I Know Where I'm Going
Michael Powell and Emeric Pressburger (GFD)
1951 An Outcast of the Islands
Carol Reed (London Films)

Above: Wendy Hiller in one of her most memorable roles as Eliza Doolittle in the 1938 film version of Shaw's **Pygmalion.**

1958 Separate Tables
Delbert Mann (United Artists)
1960 Sons and Lovers
Jack Cardiff (TCF)
1963 Toys in the Attic
George Roy Hill (United Artists)
1966 A Man for All Seasons
Fred Zinnemann (Columbia)
1970 David Copperfield
Delbert Mann (TCF)
1974 Murder on the Orient Express
Sidney Lumet (EMI)

WILLIAM HOLDEN

William Holden is such a natural, unassuming and unflashy performer that few people think of him as one of the great screen actors, a star for 40 years and a key screen personality. One of the people who has recognised his great talent is director Billy Wilder, who has featured him in four films and described him as the "ideal motion-picture actor". Holden was superb when starring in his first film, the 1939 **Golden Boy** (as a boxer who wants to be a violinist) directed by Rouben Mamoulian, and he was even better in 1978, starring in Wilder's **Fedora.** In between, he has made almost as many important films as stars like James Stewart ➤ or Cary Grant ➤ other top "natural" performers. He served a long apprenticeship in the '40's, assembling his screen persona, but once he had it fashioned, with the help of Wilder

Above: William Holden was never more determined to get his own way than in the 1966 Western **Alvarez Kelly,** *in which he and Richard Widmark clashed head on.*

in the 1950 **Sunset Boulevard,** he was never less than good—and usually brilliant. He is not as showy as Judy Holliday ➤ and Broderick Crawford ➤ in **Born Yesterday,** but he holds the film together.

His screen personality is a long way from being simply a nice guy. He does radiate pleasantness, but he also displays strong self-interest, hardness and a determination to get his own way, whether that aim is seduction (**The Moon Is Blue, Picnic**), power (**Executive Suite, Network**), military achievement (**The Bridge on the River Kwai, The Bridges at Toko-Ri**), or

banditry (**The Wild Bunch**). His performance as the cynical sergeant in Wilder's prison film **Stalag 17** won him the Academy Award for 1953, but he was equally good chasing after Audrey Hepburn ➤ in Wilder's **Sabrina,** or disagreeing with John Wayne ➤ in John Ford's **The Horse Soldiers.** He is capable of playing in almost any kind of film, from comedy to adventure picture, or partnering the most glamorous of actresses (like Sophia Loren ➤ in Carol Reed's **The Key** and Grace Kelly ➤ in **The Country Girl** and **The Bridges at Toko-Ri**). He has also been a potent box office attraction, the No 1 star in 1956 and high-ranked in other years.

Holden was born in O'Fallon, Illinois, on April 17, 1918, with the real name of William Franklin Beedle. Paramount spotted him in a college play in 1937 and put him under contract, but his first real part was in the 1939 **Golden Boy.** His portrayal made him a star, but he was given few roles worthy of his abilities in the '40s and his career did not really take off until 1950, when Wilder showed the depth of his screen personality as the down-and-out screenwriter who gets involved with Gloria Swanson ➤ in **Sunset Boulevard.** Almost every film he made in the '50s was exceptional, and most of them were highly popular with audiences as well. In the '60s he stayed good, but the films were less so—until he came back to prominence as the ageing leader of a gang of outmoded outlaws in the violent Sam Peckinpah film **The Wild Bunch.** In the '70s his career is as strong as ever, with solid performances as the architect in **The Towering Inferno,** the TV executive having an affair with Faye Dunaway ➤ in **Network** and, best of all, as the washed-up producer making one last effort to capture a major star in **Fedora,** a role with fascinating reflections of his portrayal of a writer in **Sunset Boulevard.**

BEST FILMS:
1939 Golden Boy
Rouben Mamoulian (Columbia)
1950 Sunset Boulevard
Billy Wilder (Paramount)
1950 Born Yesterday
George Cukor (Columbia)
1953 Stalag 17
Billy Wilder (Paramount)
1953 The Moon Is Blue
Otto Preminger (United Artists)
1954 Executive Suite
Robert Wise (MGM)
1954 Sabrina
Billy Wilder (Paramount)
1955 Picnic
Joshua Logan (Columbia)
1957 The Bridge on the River Kwai
David Lean (Columbia)
1959 The Horse Soldiers
John Ford (United Artists)
1969 The Wild Bunch
Sam Peckinpah (Warner Brothers)
1976 Network
Sidney Lumet (MGM)
1978 Fedora
Billy Wilder (Geria)

JUDY HOLLIDAY

Judy Holliday became the cinema's most famous dumb blonde with her brilliant, Oscar-winning performance in the 1950 **Born Yesterday**, and she retained that image for the rest of her lamentably short film career. As is obvious from watching her perform in that film, **Adam's Rib** and **It Should Happen to You**, she was in no way dumb, thereby perhaps proving that screen personalities do not necessarily reflect those of the actors—except for the fact that Holliday's "dumb blondes" are actually smarter than anybody else in her movies. Broderick Crawford ≫ may consider her stupid and uncultured in **Born Yesterday**, but she whips the pants off him in gin rummy and completely destroys his political plans with full awareness of what she is doing. In **Adam's Rib** she shoots her husband and gets away with it, as well as almost stealing the film from stars Katharine Hepburn ≫ and Spencer Tracy ≫. In **It Should Happen to You**, she makes herself into an instant celebrity by putting her name up on a billboard

films before she died in 1965. Her entire screen career consists of only 11 films (George Cukor directed five of them), but they assure her of a permanent place as one of the cinema's finest comediennes.

COMPLETE FILMS:
1944 Greenwich Village
Walter Lang (20th Century Fox)
1944 Something For The Boys
Lewis Seiler (20th Century Fox)
1944 Winged Victory
George Cukor (20th Century Fox)
1949 Adam's Rib
George Cukor (MGM)
1950 Born Yesterday
George Cukor (Columbia)
1952 The Marrying Kind
George Cukor (Columbia)
1954 It Should Happen To You
George Cukor (Columbia)
1954 Phffft!
Mark Robson (Columbia)
1956 The Solid Gold Cadillac
Richard Quine (Columbia)
1956 Full of Life
Richard Quine (Columbia)
1960 Bells Are Ringing
Vincente Minnelli (MGM)

Below: Judy Holliday and Jack Lemmon in George Cukor's **It Should Happen To You.**

in New York City, and in **Bells Are Ringing** she wins Dean Martin ≫ through her answer-phone meddling.

She was born as Judith Tuvim in New York City on June 21, 1922, and made her reputation initially in an early '40s nightclub revue. She appeared in small supporting roles in three 1944 films and then went back to New York, where she created the role of Billie Dawn, the junkman's mistress, in *Born Yesterday.* Back in Hollywood after three years in the play, she gave her brilliant performance in **Adam's Rib**, which is said to have convinced Columbia that she should star in the film version of **Born Yesterday.** She won her Oscar over Bette Davis ≫ and Anne Baxter ≫ (nominated for **All About Eve**) and Gloria Swanson ≫ for **Sunset Boulevard,** and then starred in only six more

Above: Bob Hope was a chorus boy who ends up in Arlene Dahl's arms in **Here Come The Girls.**

smug, know-it-all coward who fancies himself, was built more on one-liners and good gag-writers than on characterisation; it worked brilliantly on radio, but did not build well on film. The character worked best in tandem with Crosby (whose mock feud and relaxed manner helped create a continuity) and with strong ladies like Jane Russell ≫ (**The Paleface**) and Lucille Ball ≫ (**The Facts of Life**). No single one of his films is as memorable as Bob Hope himself.

He was born in Eltham, London, on May 26, 1904, as Leslie Town Hope, and came to America at the age of four. He went into vaudeville, then the theatre and finally radio, which made him famous; after a series of shorts and the success of The Big Broadcast of 1938 Paramount rushed him into another feature with Shirley Ross, called **Thanks for the Memory,** and the delightful **College Swing** with George Burns ≫ and Gracie Allen. He was teamed with Martha Raye in two films and then with Paulette Goddard ≫ in what was probably his best non-**Road** film, **The Cat and the Canary.** This old-dark-house-type comedy-thriller was a re-make of the 1927 Paul Leni classic; its strong narrative gave a real basis to his cowardly characterisation. The next year he was teamed with Crosby in the first of the **Road** films, **The Road to Singapore:** the chemistry was wonderful, audiences loved them, and Hope became a top money-making star. There were seven of

BOB HOPE

Bob Hope had the most successful movie career of any of the radio stars of the '30s and '40s and became not only a top box office attraction (fifth in the all-time ratings), but also an American institution. Despite his enormous popularity, most notably in the **Road** films with Bing Crosby ≫ and Dorothy Lamour ≫, he did not make very many outstanding films; the Oscar he was always dreaming about winning in the **Road** pictures he had already won in his very first feature film, **The Big Broadcast of 1938.** It was awarded for the marvellous song he did with Shirley Ross, *Thanks for the Memory,* which later became his theme song on radio and elsewhere. His persona, as a

these films, all hits, all with some fine moments, all slightly dated now. Crosby always got the Sarong-clad Lamour and Hope always got the most gag lines. The best of the series were probably **Morocco, Utopia** and **Rio,** but all have their charm; they are quintessential '40s movies. Hope's solo films were also commercial successes, if less well received by critics; among the better ones were **My Favourite Blonde** (with Madeleine Carroll ≫), **Monsieur Beaucaire** (with Joan Caulfield), and **The Paleface** (his biggest box-office hit outside the **Road** series). He tried Damon Runyon stories (**Sorrowful Jones**), and lots of sequels (**Son of Paleface, My Favourite Spy**), but the films became gradually weaker—they were star vehicles, but they were not well constructed. Hope's last reasonable film was **The Facts of Life** with Lucille Ball; nothing since then has been of more than passing interest. In the meantime, Hope had become the No 1 entertainer of American troops abroad and a best-selling author (*I Never Left Home*), as well as one of the best known show business personalities in the world. His film career continues fitfully, the latest being the 1972 **Cancel My Reservation.**

BEST FILMS:
1938 The Big Broadcast of 1938
Mitchell Leisen (Paramount)
1938 College Swing
Raoul Walsh (Paramount)
1939 The Cat and the Canary
Elliot Nugent (Paramount)
1940 The Ghost Breakers
George Marshall (Paramount)
1942 The Road to Morocco
David Butler (Paramount)

MIRIAM HOPKINS

Miriam Hopkins was one of the most glamorous and intriguing stars of the early 1930's, especially in her three comedies for Ernst Lubitsch, but by the end of the decade she was playing unsympathetic roles opposite Bette Davis » and her film career fizzled out. She came back in the late '40s and early '50s for some fine character portrayals, notably in William Wyler's **The Heiress** and **Carrie,** but the major continuing stardom that should have been hers never happened.

She was born as Ellen Miriam Hopkins in Savannah, Georgia, on October 18, 1902, worked on stage in the '20s, and made her début in the 1931 **Fast and Loose.** She was beautifully matched with Maurice Chevalier » in Lubitsch's delightful **The Smiling Lieutenant** and then won a lot of praise for her barmaid role in **Dr Jekyll and Mr Hyde.** She was in peak form in Lubitsch's **Design for Living,** (loosely based on the Noël Coward » play), as the woman involved with both Gary Cooper » and Fredric March », and equally marvellous in the same director's **Trouble in Paradise** with Herbert Marshall ». In 1935 she starred as Thackeray's heroine in **Becky Sharp,** the first three-colour Technicolor feature film, and was also outstanding opposite Edward G. Robinson » in Howard Hawks' **Barbary Coast.** William Wyler featured her in **These Three,** a cleaned-up version of Lillian Hellman's play about lesbians, The Children's Hour, but her career was beginning to lose impetus—Bette Davis got the praise for the 1939 **The Old Maid,** Hopkins wasn't much liked as **The Lady with Red Hair,** and Davis outclassed her again in **Old Acquaintance.** She went back to the stage and made only occasional films after that, most notably as Laurence Olivier's » nasty wife in **Carrie.** Her last important film was **The Chase** in 1966, and she died in 1972.

BEST FILMS:
1931 The Smiling Lieutenant
Ernst Lubitsch (Paramount)
1932 Dr Jekyll and Mr Hyde
Rouben Mamoulian (Paramount)
1932 Trouble in Paradise
Ernst Lubitsch (Paramount)
1933 Design For Living
Ernst Lubitsch (Paramount)

Above: Miriam Hopkins as the terrified barmaid confronted by Fredric March in the 1932 **Dr Jekyll and Mr Hyde.**

1935 Becky Sharp
Rouben Mamoulian (RKO)
1935 Barbary Coast
Howard Hawks (United Artists/Goldwyn)
1936 These Three
William Wyler (United Artists/Goldwyn)
1939 The Old Maid
Edmund Goulding (Warner Brothers)
1943 Old Acquaintance
Vincent Sherman (Warner Brothers)
1952 Carrie
William Wyler (Paramount)

LESLIE HOWARD

It's nicely ironic that the cinema's ideal Englishman was the son of Hungarian emigrants and that his best known screen role was as an American Southerner in **Gone With The Wind.** The qualities that made Leslie Howard's movie presence ideally English are not now in fashion; men who are romantic, sensitive, poetic, fragile and gentle intellectuals are likely to be dismissed as being simply wet today. Fashions change, of course, but even at the height of his fame he was not everybody's cup of tea. He was as perfectly suited to be the gentlemanly Ashley Wilkes in **Gone With the Wind** as Clark Gable » was to be Rhett Butler, but the characterisation was so disliked by screenwriter Ben Hecht that he wanted to leave Wilkes out of the movie. His off-screen personality appears to have been more or less identical with his screen image and is seen at its fragile best (or worst) as the idealistic poet held prisoner by Humphrey Bogart » in **The Petrified Forest.** Howard was usually a romantic artist/intellectual of one kind or another, vaguely in love, in his Hollywood films, hamstrung by Bette Davis » in **Of Human Bondage** and smitten by Ingrid Bergman » in **Intermezzo.** He looked good in costume and was splendid as the foppish hero of **The Scarlet Pimpernel** and the Shavian mouthpiece Professor Higgins in **Pygmalion.** His excellent speaking voice made him a worthwhile if slightly over-age Romeo to Norma Shearer's » Juliet in the 1936 version of **Romeo and Juliet,** but, surprisingly, it was in Hollywood light comedy that he next found a niche; he was paired delightfully with Bette Davis in **It's Love I'm After,** as battling theatrical lovers, and made a fine bewildered banker involved with a bankrupt studio and Joan Blondell » in **Stand-In** (both 1937).

Howard, who was born in London on April 3, 1893, with the name Leslie Howard Stainer, went on the stage after World War I and became a top theatrical star in both England and America in the mid-'20s. He made his film début in 1930, re-creating his stage success in **Outward Bound,** which was very popular, and he was immediately co-starred with Norma Shearer in **A Free Soul.** He worked on both sides of the Atlantic in the '30s, but concentrated on patriotic films in Britain when the war started. The most notable of these were **Pimpernel Smith, The 49th Parallel** and his last film, **The First of the Few,** in which he portrayed the inventor of the Spitfire. He was killed in 1943, when his plane was shot down returning from Lisbon while he was on a government mission. His death was an enormous shock to both the British and American public, because of his strong identification with the British war effort.

Above: Leslie Howard, with Bette Davis, threatened by Humphrey Bogart in **The Petrified Forest.**

BEST FILMS:
1933 Berkeley Square
Frank Lloyd (Fox)
1934 Of Human Bondage
John Cromwell (RKO)
1934 The Scarlet Pimpernel
Harold Young (London Films)
1936 The Petrified Forest
Archie Mayo (Warner Brothers)
1936 Romeo and Juliet
George Cukor (MGM)
1937 Stand-In
Tay Garnett (Warner Brothers)
1938 Pygmalion
Leslie Howard & Gabriel Pascal (GFD)
1939 Intermezzo
Gregory Ratoff (Selznick/United Artists)
1939 Gone With the Wind
Victor Fleming (Selznick/MGM)
1941 The 49th Parallel
Michael Powell (GFD)

TREVOR HOWARD

Trevor Howard is a good screen actor who has never quite become a major star, possibly because he was not featured in enough good films, but more likely because he lacks the charisma. He has great presence on the screen and has given many beautiful performances, but his sometimes anguished, often sarcastic and always interesting movie image has never been given room to develop. He became an important star in his third film, David Lean's 1946 **Brief Encounter**, finely matched with Celia Johnson in one of the most popular bittersweet love stories. He won the British Film Academy Best Actor Award for his tangy performance in the 1958 **The Key**, with William Holden ❯ and Sophia Loren ❯, and was nominated for an Oscar for his portrayal of the father in the 1960 **Sons and Lovers.** He was very good as Captain Bligh in **Mutiny on the Bounty**, despite unfair comparisons to Charles Laughton ❯ in the earlier version and has continued strong right into the '70s, notably as the priest in **Ryan's Daughter.**

Howard was born in Kent, England, in 1916, began to work on stage from 1934, and made his film debut in **The Way Ahead** in 1944 for director Carol Reed. After his success in **Brief Encounter** and Anthony Asquith's **The Way to the Stars,** he starred in one of the very best British thrillers of the '40s, **Green For Danger,** directed by Sidney Gilliat.

*Left: Trevor Howard as Lt Col Silking in Jack Gold's **Aces High** (1976), the futile-heroic story of World War I pilots.*

Carol Reed and David Lean continued to use him in excellent films like **The Passionate Friends** and **The Third Man,** and he gave outstanding performances even in weak films like **The Heart of the Matter** and **Manuela.** In recent years he has been playing smaller character roles, but was particularly notable as Lord Cardigan in Tony Richardson's **The Charge of the Light Brigade,** as the doctor in Joseph Losey's **The Doll's House,** and as Glenda Jackson's ❯ companion in **Stevie.**

BEST FILMS:
1946 Brief Encounter
David Lean (Cineguild)
1946 Green For Danger
Sidney Gilliat (Rank)
1948 The Passionate Friends
David Lean (GFD)
1949 The Third Man
Carol Reed (British Lion)
1953 The Heart of the Matter
George More O'Ferrall (British Lion)
1958 The Key
Carol Reed (Columbia)
1960 Sons and Lovers
Jack Cardiff (TCF)
1962 Mutiny on the Bounty
Lewis Milestone (MGM)
1968 The Charge of the Light Brigade
Tony Richardson (Woodfall)
1970 Ryan's Daughter
David Lean (MGM)

ROCK HUDSON

The deceptively modest and amiable Rock Hudson seems an unlikely choice to be ranked among the all-time box office stars, but he's up there in the top ten with Wayne ❯, Crosby ❯, Gable ❯ and Cooper ❯. His popularity came through two groups of films: his excellent romantic melodramas of the '50s for Douglas Sirk, and his bubbling sex comedies of the '60s with Doris Day ❯ and other ladies. Hudson was unfairly put down by critics at the time for being simply a chesty leading man, but he was an excellent light comedian, as can be seen in his '60s films, especially **Man's Favourite Sport** directed by Howard Hawks; he may not be as deft as Cary Grant ❯ in light comedy, but he is very good in his own different way, tangling in this film with Paula Prentiss as a fishing expert who has never gone fishing. His image as an amiable personality with hidden resources of courage and knowledge was ably tapped by television in the '70s, with the long-running series *McMillan and Wife* (for which Hudson was paid very large fees).

He was born in Winetka, Illinois, on November 17, 1925, as Roy Scherer, Jr. After the war he worked at odd jobs until agent Henry Willson got him a small part in the 1948 **Fighter Squadron;** he soon became a star for Universal, building his reputation slowly in Westerns and melodramas, notably under the direction of Douglas Sirk in seven films, beginning with the 1954 **Taza, Son of Cochise** (much better than it sounds). He acquired real stardom in two Sirk soap-operas with Jane Wyman ❯, **Magnificent Obsession** and **All That Heaven Allows.** His leading role in **Giant** confirmed his status and two more Sirk films, **Written on the Wind** and **The Tarnished Angels,** helped him make the No 1 box office star in 1957 (he stayed in the top ten, usually first, second or third, until 1965). His popularity continued through his teaming with Doris Day in the 1959 **Pillow Talk,** a frothy but enjoyable comedy, and two more glossily-produced comedies, **Lover Come Back** and **Send Me No Flowers,** then he changed the pace in 1966 with the good science-fiction thriller **Seconds** and the adventure romp **Ice Station Zebra.** Most of his work in the '70s has been for his TV series, but he also starred in **Embryo** and **Avalanche.**

BEST FILMS:
1954 Magnificent Obsession
Douglas Sirk (Universal)
1955 All That Heaven Allows
Douglas Sirk (Universal)
1956 Giant
George Stevens (Warner Brothers)
1957 Written on the Wind
Douglas Sirk (Universal)
1957 The Tarnished Angels
Douglas Sirk (Universal)
1959 Pillow Talk
Michael Gordon (Universal)
1961 Lover Come Back
Delbert Mann (Universal)
1964 Man's Favourite Sport
Howard Hawks (Universal)
1964 Send Me No Flowers
Norman Jewison (Universal)
1966 Seconds
John Frankenheimer (Paramount)

*Below: Rock Hudson, tied up with Maria Perschy in Howard Hawks' brilliant 1964 comedy **Man's Favourite Sport.***

JACK HULBERT

see Cicely Courtneidge

BETTY HUTTON

Betty Hutton was probably the most energetic personality ever to explode on to the screen. She was usually known as the Blonde Bombshell, but she was more like a combination buzzsaw/buzz-bomb, brash, bouncy and almost over-enthusiastic. She was also a very good singer and could even stand the competition of Ethel Merman, with whom she was featured in the Broadway musical *Panama Hattie*. Her film career was as zippy as her personality. She became a star immediately with a featured role in **The Fleet's In** (1942) (her first full-length film, although she had made musical shorts earlier) and quickly became the No 1 musical competitor of Judy Garland ❯, in films like **Star-Spangled Rhythm, And the Angels Sing** and **Here Come the Waves.** She even took over a role from Garland—the lead in MGM's **Annie Get Your Gun**—when Garland became ill, and she could have become a big MGM star in the '50s—but her studio, Paramount, wouldn't part with her. She was excellent in non-musical roles as well, notably in Preston Sturges's **The Miracle of Morgan's Creek** (as an unmarried mother looking for a husband) and Mitchell Leisen's **Dream Girl** (based on the Elmer Rice play). She was featured in a number of biopics, including **Incendiary Blonde** (as Texas "Hello, Sucker" Guinan), **The Perils of Pauline** (as silent serial star Pearl White) and **Somebody Loves Me** (as singer Blossom Seely). She danced with Fred Astaire ❯ in **Let's Dance** and was the lead in the all-star box office blockbuster **The Greatest Show on Earth** (as a trapeze artist in love with Charlton Heston ❯).

Hutton was born as Betty Jane Thornburg in Battle Creek, Michigan, on February 26, 1921, and became a singer with Vincent Lopez's band in the late '30s. Her success on Broadway in *Panama Hattie* led to her Paramount contract. She remained a major star until 1952, when the studio refused to accept her new husband, Charles O'Curran, as the director of her next film; she left the studio and made only one other movie, the 1957 **Spring Reunion.** It was not a success, nor was her television work, but she still apparently hopes to make a comeback.

BEST FILMS:
1942 Star-Spangled Rhythm
George Marshall (Paramount)
1944 The Miracle of Morgan's Creek
Preston Sturges (Paramount)
1944 And the Angels Sing
Claude Binyon (Paramount)

Above: Betty Hutton in **Annie Get Your Gun**. *She took over from Judy Garland, who had suffered a total collapse— one of many disasters which struck before the film was finally produced.*

1944 Here Come the Waves
Mark Sandrich (Paramount)
1945 Incendiary Blonde
George Marshall (Paramount)
1947 The Perils of Pauline
George Marshall (Paramount)
1949 Red, Hot and Blue
John Farrow (Paramount)
1950 Annie Get Your Gun
George Sidney (MGM)
1950 Let's Dance
Norman Z. McLeod (Paramount)
1952 The Greatest Show on Earth
Cecil B. De Mille (Paramount)

VAN JOHNSON

Van Johnson was the average boy-next-door to average girl-next-door June Allyson ❯ in 1940s cinema, fresh-faced, freckled, wholesome, sincere and generally pretty boring. Teenaged girls at the time adored him and he was a top box office star for a short time in the mid-'40s, teamed wet with Esther Williams ❯ when he wasn't dryly wholesome with June Allyson. He wasn't a bad actor, as it turned out, but his screen personality was so vapid that critics and eventually the studios simply dismissed him. He was at his very best in the war film **Battleground** and was also quite appealing in two other Army pictures, **A Guy Named Joe** (which initially made him a star) and **Thirty Seconds Over Tokyo.** The best screen partner he ever had was Judy Garland ❯; their musical **In The Good Old Summertime** is one of the highlights of his career (they play friendly penpals who don't realise that they already know and dislike each other).

He was first teamed with Allyson in the 1944 **Two Girls and a Sailor,** and some of their other (rather forgettable) pictures included **High Barbaree, The Bride Goes Wild, Too Young To Kiss** and **Remains to be Seen;** he was Esther Williams' leading man in **Thrill of a Romance, Easy To Wed, The Duchess of Idaho** and **Easy to Love,** and he was really better in smaller supporting roles, with Spencer Tracy » and Katharine Hepburn » in **State of the Union**, Walter Pidgeon » in **Command Decision**, Humphrey Bogart » in **The Caine Mutiny**, and involved with Lana Turner » in the all-star **Weekend at the Waldorf.**

He was born as Charles Van Johnson in Newport, Rhode Island, on August 25, 1916, worked as an entertainer (especially in nightclubs), and stage actor in the late '30s, and made his film début in the 1942 **Murder in the Big House.** He played opposite Lionel Barrymore in four of the **Dr Gillespie** series (a continuation of the **Dr Kildare** movies) and was second only to Bing Crosby » in box office ratings in 1945; however, his career fizzled out pretty rapidly in the '50s, though he has appeared in occasional movies, and TV films like **Rich Man, Poor Man** in 1976. He is now primarily back in nightclub entertaining and is said to be the "King of Supper Theatre."

BEST FILMS:
1943 A Guy Named Joe
Victor Fleming (MGM)
1944 Two Girls and a Sailor
Richard Thorpe (MGM)
1944 Thirty Seconds Over Tokyo
Mervyn LeRoy (MGM)

Above: Van Johnson as he appeared in **The Last Time I Saw Paris,** *an unconvincing drama based on Scott Fitzgerald's* **Babylon Revisited,** *a story of expatriate Americans centred around VE-Day.*

1945 Weekend at the Waldorf
Robert Z. Leonard (MGM)
1948 State of the Union
Frank Capra (MGM)
1948 Command Decision
Sam Wood (MGM)
1949 In The Good Old Summertime
Robert Z. Leonard (MGM)
1949 Battleground
William Wellman (MGM)
1954 The Caine Mutiny
Edward Dmytryk (Columbia)
1956 Miracle in the Rain
Rudolph Maté (Warner Brothers)

AL JOLSON

"You ain't heard nothing yet," shouted Al Jolson in the 1927 **The Jazz Singer**—and his prophetic words in the first talking picture echo down the years. It seems somehow appropriate that a Russian-Jewish, blackface, vaudeville singer should be the first star of the talkies. The enormous success of **The Jazz Singer** made Jolson the hottest property in movies; his second film, **The Singing Fool** (1928), made more money than any other sound film until **Gone With the Wind.** Jolson was the egotistic, overpowering king of vaudeville before going into films; and he transferred his razzamatazz ability to sell a song on to the screen. His career in the cinema was relatively short, for his range of roles (and songs) was limited, but for a time he was second to none. That his appeal is not simply historical was underlined by the sensational success of the two biopics made about him after the war; Larry Parks played Jolson in the 1946 **The Jolson Story,** but Jolson sang the songs, and it was so popular that Columbia made a sequel in 1949 called **Jolson Sings Again** (in which Jolson meets Parks and

congratulates him). Jolson fan clubs are still active in England and America, although he died in 1950.

Jolson was born as Asa Yoelson in St Petersburg, Russia, on May 26, 1886, and brought to the US as a child. His early life was exactly like the plot of **The Jazz Singer;** his parents wanted him to become a cantor, but he ran away from home and became a vaudeville star. He had hits with songs like *Swanee* as early as 1918, but it was the songs *My Mammy,* in **Jazz Singer,** and *Sonny Boy,* in **Singing Fool,** that were the biggest hits of all. Jolson's style may seem somewhat corny, exaggerated and sentimental to us now, but he can belt out a song as well as Judy Garland », with

Above: Al Jolson, the first star to sing in the movies.

irresistible self-confidence; that combination of vitality and vulgarity is still potent. None of his films is particularly strong simply as cinema, but all of them are good showcases for his talents. In most of them he is a singing star with a problem (egotism, lost voice, etc) and in his later films the characterisation is close to autobiographical. His film persona was primarily a reflection of his own stardom, but it suited him perfectly. His last role, except for **Jolson Sings Again,** was as himself in the 1944 biography of George Gershwin, **Rhapsody in Blue.** The casting was just right.

BEST FILMS:
1927 The Jazz Singer
Alan Crosland (Warner Brothers)
1928 The Singing Fool
Lloyd Bacon (Warner Brothers)
1929 Sonny Boy
Archie Mayo (Warner Brothers)
1930 Mammy
Michael Curtiz (Warner Brothers)
1933 Hallelujah, I'm a Bum
Lewis Milestone (United Artists)
1934 Wonder Bar
Lloyd Bacon (Warner Brothers)
1935 Go Into Your Dance
Archie Mayo (Warner Brothers)
1936 The Singing Kid
William Keighley (Warner Brothers)
1939 Rose of Washington Square
Gregory Ratoff (20th Century Fox)
1939 Swanee River
Sidney Lanfield (20th Century Fox)

JENNIFER JONES

Jennifer Jones won an Oscar in 1943 for her saintliness in **The Song of Bernadette**—and aroused censorial dismay only three years later for her voluptuousness in **Duel in the Sun.** The contrast was extraordinary, but it reflected the good-bad quality of Jones's screen image with Hollywood's usual panache. The unifying personality trait in both performances was a tenacious insistence on having her own way, and this kind of stubbornness was often apparent in her performances. She was never again quite as "good" as the peasant girl with visions of the Virgin convincing an unwilling

Church of their reality, but she was often almost as "bad", as **Madame Bovary, Carrie** and the sexy **Ruby Gentry.** Even when she was nice, there were hints of a passionate nature behind her niceness, romantically pursuing Charles Boyer » in **Cluny Brown** and William Holden » in **Love Is A Many-Splendored Thing,** or destroying everybody's plans as the lovely, lying heroine in **Beat The Devil.** She was a good screen actress and it is unfortunate that she has made only three films since 1961.

She was born as Phyllis Isley in Tulsa, Oklahoma, on March 2, 1919, married actor Robert Walker in 1939, and had roles in two Republic programmers the same year, **New Frontier** and **Dick Tracy's G-Men.** Her real film career began with **The Song of Bernadette,** as David Selznick's discovery; he changed her name, built up her career and married her after she broke up with Walker. She followed **Song** with good performances in **Since You Went Away, Love Letters** and **Cluny Brown,** but **Duel in the Sun** was probably her greatest achievement—there have been few more searingly carnal personifications of sexuality than her performance as the half-breed Pearl Chavez in this film. Her career continued

Above: Jennifer Jones in her greatest and most sensual role as Pearl in **Duel in the Sun.**

strongly through the '50s, with rather fine performances in **The Barretts of Wimpole Street** and **A Farewell to Arms,** in addition to the films mentioned above, but she more or less retired after the 1961 **Tender Is The Night,** and Selznick's death in 1965. Her best recent performance was in the all-star **The Towering Inferno.**

BEST FILMS:
1943 The Song of Bernadette
Henry King (20th Century Fox)
1945 Love Letters
William Dieterle (Paramount)
1946 Cluny Brown
Ernst Lubitsch (20th Century Fox)

1946 Duel in the Sun
King Vidor (Selznick)
1948 Portrait of Jennie
William Dieterle (Selznick)
1949 Madame Bovary
Vincente Minnelli (MGM)
1952 Carrie
William Wyler (Paramount)
1952 Ruby Gentry
King Vidor (20th Century Fox)
1954 Beat the Devil
John Huston (United Artists)
1955 Love Is A Many-Splendored Thing
Henry King (20th Century Fox)

LOUIS JOURDAN

Louis Jourdan is usually cast as a suave, dashing, French charmer, a romantic heart-throb. Despite this limitation, he has made a number of excellent pictures and has been able to extend his screen persona to cover even villainous roles. He is best known for being the bored playboy lover of Leslie Caron ≫ in Vincente Minnelli's MGM musical **Gigi**, in which he had a number of pleasant songs like *Gigi* and *The Night They Invented Champagne*. His other big Hollywood musical, Walter Lang's **Can-Can**, is more or less a repeat performance (and again with Maurice Chevalier ≫).

His straight-forward romantic lover roles have been played in some highly successful films, including **Three Coins in The Fountain, The VIPs,** Minnelli's **Madame Bovary** (with Jennifer Jones ≫) and **The Swan** (with Grace Kelly ≫). His finest performance, however, was in Max Ophuls' masterpiece **Letter from an Unknown Woman,** in which he plays a pianist-playboy unworthy of the obsessive love of Joan Fontaine ≫. He was again a pianist in **Julie,** but much nastier, the insane husband of Doris Day ≫ and trying to kill her. One of his most enjoyable and lesser-known roles was the 1952 **The Happy Time** with Charles Boyer ≫, the

Above: Louis Jourdan in his most famous role as the bored playboy lover of Leslie Caron in Vincente Minnelli's **Gigi**.

story of a French-Canadian family during the 1920s.

Jourdan was born in Marseilles, France, on June 19, 1919, as Louis Gendre. He made his film début in the 1939 French film **Le Corsaire,** but with the arrival of war joined the Resistance. After the war, he was signed by David O. Selznick, who made him a star, and his first American film was for Alfred Hitchcock, the lover/valet in the 1947 **The Paradine Case.** In 1952 he returned to France to make **Rue de l'Estràade** for Jacques Becker, but he has usually worked in Hollywood, continuing to make films in the '60s (**The VIPs, A Flea in Her Ear**) and the '70s (**The Silver Bears**).

BEST FILMS:
1947 The Paradine Case
Alfred Hitchcock (Selznick)
1948 Letter From an Unknown Woman
Max Ophuls (Universal)
1949 Madame Bovary
Vincente Minnelli (MGM)
1952 The Happy Time
Richard Fleischer (Columbia)
1954 Three Coins in the Fountain
Jean Negulesco (20th Century Fox)
1956 The Swan
Charles Vidor (MGM)
1956 Julie
Andrew Stone (MGM)
1958 Gigi
Vincente Minnelli (MGM)
1960 Can-Can
Walter Lang (20th Century Fox)
1977 The Silver Bears
Ivan Passer (EMI)

LOUIS JOUVET

One of the great screen (and theatre) actors, the French equivalent of Laurence Olivier ≫, Louis Jouvet was at his peak in the 1930s, starring in some of the outstanding films of the period. He is the cunning Spanish chaplain in Jacques Feyder's masterpiece **La Kermesse Héroique,** the proud, aristocratic gambler down on his luck in Jean Renoir's **Les Bas-Fonds,** the terrorising bishop in Marcel Carné's **Drôle de Drame** and Arletty's ≫ disdainful pimp in Carné's **Hôtel du Nord.** He still has enormous magnetism on the screen, projecting a kind of cynical worldliness; his persona is that of a sly, shady man-of-the-world, not particularly admirable, but full of sardonic wit and real human qualities. He plays conmen, pimps, seedy detectives, phoney doctors and spies, but he is always smooth-talking and able to get by on his wits. He retains a certain aloof theatricality in his acting, having been a stage actor for 20 years before becoming a movie star.

Jouvet was born in Crozon, Finistère, France, on December 24, 1887, and began his theatre career in 1907. He made his first film appearance in Henri Desfontaines' 1913 **Shylock,** but his cinema career really began in

Above: Louis Jouvet with Annabella in a scene from Marcel Carné's atmospheric 1938 **Hôtel du Nord.**

1933 with **Topaze;** this Marcel Pagnol play adaptation by Louis Gasnier (Jouvet portrays a teacher who becomes the brains of a gang of crooks), and another play-into-film **Doctor Knock** (which he co-directed with Roger Coupillières, portraying a fake doctor), made him instantly popular with movie audiences. He was much admired as a confidence trickster paired with Edwige Feuillère in Robert Siodmak's **Mister Flow** and had an excellent role as a police inspector tracking down Erich von Stroheim ≫ in **L'Alibi.** He worked with great directors (though not always in his best films), including Pabst (**Mademoiselle Docteur, Drame de Shanghai**) and Renoir (**Les Bas-Fonds, La Marseillaise**), but was just as good in works by lesser directors, including Julien Duvivier (**Un Carnet du Bal, La Fin du Jour**) and Maurice Tourneur (**Volpone**). He spent most of the war in Switzerland and South America, returning to Paris in 1945. HIs post-war film career was not nearly as successful, however, the highpoint being Henri-Georges Clouzot's **Quai des Orfèvres** (portraying a seedy detective). He continued to make films until his death in 1951; the last was **Une Histoire d'Amour.** His early films remain just as popular in France as ever.

BEST FILMS:
1933 Topaze
Louis Gasnier (Paramount)
1935 La Kermesse Héroique
Jacques Feyder (Tobis)
1935 Mr Flow
Robert Siodmak (Laver)
1936 Les Bas-Fonds
Jean Renoir (Albatros)
1937 Un Carnet du Bal
Julien Duvivier (Lévy-Strauss Sigma)
1937 Drôle de Drame
Marcel Carné (Corniglion-Molinier)
1938 La Marseillaise
Jean Renoir (Public)
1938 Hôtel du Nord
Marcel Carné (Sedif)
1940 Volpone
Maurice Tourneur (Isle de France/GCT)
1947 Quai des Orfèvres
Henri-Georges Clouzot (Majestic)

BORIS KARLOFF

It seems oddly appropriate that the leading horror star of the movies should have been a gentle English cricket fan whose primary activities off screen were gardening and poetry—horror is founded in the ordinary and the everyday rather than in the mysterious and faraway, and the greatest screen monsters have evoked pity and sympathy as much as fear. Karloff's Frankenstein's Monster is one of the cinema's major myth figures, not because he is gruesome but because behind that horrific, nightmarish face there is a gentle mind forced to behave monstrously because of the world's reaction to

it. Despite the fact that most of Karloff's pictures were cheaply-made, critically-shunned programmers, he brought a quality to them that secures him a place as one of the screen's great actors. It is not his Monster on the rampage that remains in the memory, but the numbing moment in which he plays with a little girl in **Frankenstein,** or the humorous scene when he is taught to smoke in **The Bride of Frankenstein.** These films were made by a great director, James Whale, who was able to show Karloff's skills in a way few of his other directors attempted.

Karloff was born as William Henry Pratt in Dulwich, South London, on November 23, 1887, the son of an Indian civil servant. After attending university in London, he emigrated to Canada and soon joined a theatrical company. He was on stage until 1919, when he began to work in films, starting as an extra and soon working his way up to villainous parts. His slow, deliberate movements seemed always to create a sense of menace, but he achieved little success in the silent era; his reputation as an actor was not established until 1931, when Howard Hawks cast him as the convict butler who becomes a killer in **The Criminal Code,** a role he had already

Above: Boris Karloff began his career as a horror star at the age of nine, playing the demon king in Cinderella, and later became Hollywood's greatest master of the genre, his eyes mirroring the soul's anguish.

performed on stage. Hawks and other directors then began to feature him in gangster films (including **Scarface**), but it was **Frankenstein** that made him famous. Whale cast him after Bela Lugosi ❯ turned down the role, and Karloff's lumbering method of movement was as important to the success of the creation as Jack Pierce's brilliant make-up. He played the monster twice more for Universal (the leading Hollywood horror studio), but was also featured in other '30s horror masterpieces, including Whale's **The Old Dark House** (as the frightening butler) and the remarkable **The Mummy** (another of the great cinematic monsters). He starred in **The Mask of Fu Manchu, The Black Cat** and **The Raven,** all classics of the genre, and found time for some good straight roles, in John Ford's **The Lost Patrol** and opposite George Arliss in **The House of Rothschild.**

Karloff was reduced to pretty negligible films for most of the late '30s and early '40s, but came back strongly in 1945, working with producer Val Lewton at RKO. He made the excellent **The Body Snatchers, Isle of the Dead** and **Bedlam** for Lewton, and played

more straight roles in **The Secret Life of Walter Mitty** and **Unconquered.** He met Abbott and Costello ❯ on film and did a fine job on Broadway as the killer nephew in *Arsenic and Old Lace.* His '50s films were again rather negligible and he returned to live in England in 1955. Roger Corman picked him up in the '60s for some pleasantly tongue-in-cheek horror pictures, including **The Raven** and **The Terror,** and Italian horror specialist Mario Bava featured him in **Black Sabbath.** Peter Bogdanovich provided a beautiful coda to his career by starring him in the 1967 **Targets** as an ageing horror star pitted against a rifle killer in a drive-in (which is showing his film **The Terror**). He died in 1969.

BEST FILMS:
1931 Frankenstein
James Whale (Universal)
1932 The Mummy
Karl Freund (Universal)
1932 The Old Dark House
James Whale (Universal)
1934 The Black Cat
Edgar G. Ulmer (Universal)
1935 The Bride of Frankenstein
James Whale (Universal −)
1939 The Son of Frankenstein
Rowland V. Lee (Universal)
1945 The Body Snatchers
Robert Wise (RKO)
1945 Isle of the Dead
Mark Robson (RKO)
1963 The Raven
Roger Corman (AIP)
1967 Targets
Peter Bogdanovich (AIP)

DANNY KAYE

Danny Kaye was the cinema's master of the tongue-tripping phrase, magical concoctions (usually written by his wife Sylvia Fine) that are sometimes as memorable as lines from Edward Lear or Lewis Carroll. By today's critical standards, his style of humour is forced, full of hammy grimaces and other facial contortions, and his films are no longer widely admired. All the same, he has a way with words and a cleverness with complicated patter songs that ensures him of a lasting place in the affection of cinema-goers. The peak of his popularity was the decade from 1946 to 1956, from his heavy but still amusing interpretation of James Thurber's **The Secret Life of Walter Mitty** to the sometimes brilliant **The Court Jester,** with its delightful mix-up of poisoned pellets in palace chalices (and true brew in dragon flagons). His own favourite film was the 1954 **Knock on Wood,** portraying a ventriloquist mixed up with psychiatrist Mai Zetterling and spies, but the most popular one was **White Christmas,** in which he co-starred with Bing Crosby ❯ as soldiers turned entertainers.

Kaye was born David Daniel Kaminsky in Brooklyn, New York, on January 18, 1913, and had a long career as an entertainer and stage performer before making his feature cinema début in the 1944 **Up in Arms.** The key ingredient to Kaye's later success, and the creator of his word magic, was composer-lyricist Sylvia Fine, whom he married in 1940. She did not write all his good songs (*Tchaikovsky,* for example, was by Ira Gershwin and Kurt Weill, from their musical *Lady in the Dark*), but her contribution was an essential one. **Up in Arms** was a hit and Kaye's movie career continued strong (at different studios) for 20 years. Among his better known films in this period

*Above: Danny Kaye with Glynis Johns in **The Court Jester** (1954), the film in which a pellet of poison becomes a tongue-twister.*

were **The Inspector General** and **Hans Christian Andersen,** but he is probably most associated with **Walter Mitty.**

Kaye's last successful film was the 1959 **The Five Pennies**; his last starring vehicle was the 1963 **The Man from the Diners' Club;** and his last film appearance was in **The Madwoman of Chaillot** in 1969. In 1975 he starred in a TV version of *Peter Pan.*

BEST FILMS:
1946 The Kid from Brooklyn
Norman McLeod (RKO)
1947 The Secret Life of Walter Mitty
Norman McLeod (RKO)
1948 A Song Is Born
Howard Hawks (RKO)
1949 The Inspector General
Henry Koster (Warner Brothers)
1951 On The Riviera
Walter Lang (20th Century Fox)
1952 Hans Christian Andersen
Charles Vidor (RKO)
1954 Knock on Wood
Norman Panama & Melvin Frank (Paramount)
1954 White Christmas
Michael Curtiz (Paramount)
1956 The Court Jester
Norman Panama & Melvin Frank (Paramount)
1959 The Five Pennies
Melville Shavelson (Paramount)

Howard Keel
see **Kathryn Grayson**

Ruby Keeler

Ruby Keeler is the girl we always think of as stepping out of the chorus to replace the sick star and becoming a star herself. It was a strange sort of character to project, but it fitted Miss Keeler perfectly and made her the memorable leading lady of many of choreographer Busby Berkeley's best Warner Brothers extravaganzas of the '30s. Perhaps we believe in her as the extra who makes good because she wasn't too talented to begin with (she later confessed that she couldn't act, had a terrible singing voice, and wasn't the greatest tap dancer in the world either). In her first film, the 1933 smash hit **42nd Street,** she is the chorus girl picked to replace temperamental Bebe Daniels ❯ and, as Warner Baxter ❯ rightly says in the film: "You're going on a youngster, but you've got to come back a star." She did. She was the perfect co-star for Dick Powell ❯ and played opposite him in most of her films. Her face was seared onto the mind of the public in **Dames,** when he sang *I Only Have Eyes For You* in a dream sequence in which her face was literally everywhere.

*Right: Ruby Keeler is about to get her big chance in **42nd Street** as producer Warner Baxter points an accusing finger at stricken star Bebe Daniels.*

Ruby's real life was a little bit like one of her musical comedies, even including the back-stage romance. Born Ethel Keeler in Halifax, Nova Scotia, on August 25, 1909, she was simply a chorus girl and dancer until she met Al Jolson ❯, whom she later married, at Texas Guinan's club. He helped place her in Ziegfeld's 1929 stage production *Show Girl,* and every night after his own show he would walk down the aisle singing *Liza* to her while she tap-danced. After her success in **42nd Street** and its sequel **Gold Diggers of 1933,** she became one of Warner's top musical stars and will always be remembered as one of the quiet focal points of Busby Berkeley's cinematic kaleidoscopes. She made one film with husband Jolson, the 1935 **Go Into Your Dance** (he plays a big-headed star), but after only nine films at Warner's her stardom was cut short. Jolson had a row with the studio and left, taking Ruby with him. She and Jolson were divorced in 1940 and her career foundered after two more films, the last starring movie being the 1941 **Sweetheart of the Campus.** She made a stage comeback in 1971, dancing in the Broadway revival of *No, No, Nanette.* She now lives in Laguna Beach, California. Her last film appearance was as an (unpaid) extra in **They Shoot Horses, Don't They?** in 1969.

BEST FILMS:
1933 42nd Street
Lloyd Bacon (Warner Brothers)
1933 Gold Diggers of 1933
Mervyn LeRoy (Warner Brothers)
1933 Footlight Parade
Lloyd Bacon (Warner Brothers)
1934 Dames
Ray Enright (Warner Brothers)
1934 Flirtation Walk
Frank Borzage (Warner Brothers)
1935 Go Into Your Dance
Archie Mayo (Warner Brothers)
1935 Shipmates Forever
Frank Borzage (Warner Brothers)
1936 Colleen
Alfred E. Green (Warner Brothers)
1937 Ready, Willing and Able
Ray Enright (Warner Brothers)
1938 Mother Carey's Chickens
Rowland V. Lee (RKO)

Gene Kelly

Gene Kelly has contributed more to the development of the screen musical than any other performer, even Fred Astaire , although Astaire was probably the better dancer: The comparison is hardly necessary, however, because their styles were so different: Kelly was a thinker who danced; Astaire was a dancer first and last.

Kelly helped to revolutionise the musical (along with producer Arthur Freed and director Vincente Minnelli), but he was always very conscious of his technique—and sometimes it shows. When it

doesn't, he is unbeatable; the dance-in-the-rain sequence in **Singin' in the Rain** is perhaps the greatest musical number of the movies and many afficionados consider that film as the best of all musicals. Kelly's stunning 20-minute ballet conclusion to **An American in Paris** was the most innovative musical sequence ever filmed up to that time; it still has enormous impact, but seems oddly dated, whereas his more natural dances in **Singin' in the Rain** do not.

His efforts towards a style close to pure ballet in **Invitation to the Dance** are fascinating, but less enjoyable than simpler efforts like **Take Me Out to the Ball Game** or **Summer Stock.**

Kelly's contribution as a choreographer has been as important as his dancing. He was given a special Academy Award in 1951 for his acting, singing, dancing and directing, but "specifically for his brilliant achievements in the art of choreography on film", and **An American in Paris** won the Oscar for the Best Picture.

He was born Eugene Curran Kelly in Pittsburgh, Pennsylvania, on August 23, 1912, and began working on stage in the late '30s. He created the part of the dancer in William Saroyan's *The Time of Your Life* and starred in *Pal Joey* before making his screen début opposite Judy Garland ❯ in the 1942 **For Me and My Gal.** He immediately became an MGM star, but his next big musical role

Left: Gene Kelly and Frank Sinatra as two sailors on shore leave, becoming romantically involved with singer Kathryn Grayson in the 1945 Anchors Aweigh!

was at Columbia with Rita Hayworth ❯ in the delightful **Cover Girl.** MGM didn't loan him out after that, and featured him in the huge hit **Anchors Aweigh,** best remembered for his dance with cartoon mouse Jerry ❯. He was re-teamed with Garland in the bizarre, highly stylised but dazzling **The Pirate,** helped director George Sidney turn **The Three Musketeers** into a delightful romp, and danced splendidly with Vera-Ellen to *Slaughter on Tenth Avenue* in **Words and Music.** After the enjoyable period musical **Take Me Out to the Ball Game** (dancing the title song with Frank Sinatra ❯), he made **On The Town,** one of the all-time classic musicals and his own personal favourite. It is the story of three sailors on leave in New York for 24 hours, and is one of the liveliest, funniest and most entertaining of all musicals. Kelly was at the peak of his career. He subsequently made the charming back-stage musical **Summer Stock** with Garland, followed by **An American in Paris** and **Singin' in the Rain;** then there was nowhere to go but down. He had given the screen musical a zest and a flavour it had never had before, and broken entirely new ground for the dancer-choreographers who would come after. He made some more good, but lesser, musicals (**It's Always Fair Weather, Les Girls**), and directed his ballet film, but by the end of the '50s his dancing career was virtually over. He began appearing in straight acting roles and made his last real dancing appearance in the 1966 French musical **Les Demoiselles de Rochefort,** directed by Jacques Demy. He appeared with Fred Astaire as one of the hosts of the MGM musical compilation film **That's Entertainment Part II,** but it was really just a homage to the Gene Kelly of yesteryear.

BEST FILMS:
1944 Cover Girl
Charles Vidor (Columbia)
1945 Anchors Aweigh!
George Sidney (MGM)
1948 The Pirate
Vincente Minnelli (MGM)
1948 The Three Musketeers
George Sidney (MGM)
1949 Take Me Out to the Ball Game
Busby Berkeley (MGM)
1949 On The Town
Gene Kelly & Stanley Donen (MGM)
1950 Summer Stock
Charles Walters (MGM)
1951 An American in Paris
Vincente Minnelli (MGM)
1952 Singin' in the Rain
Gene Kelly & Stanley Donen (MGM)
1955 It's Always Fair Weather
Gene Kelly and Stanley Donen (MGM)

GRACE KELLY

Grace Kelly has been giving a very good performance since 1956 as the fairytale princess of a never-never land called Monaco, but she was much better as a movie actress. Princesses, even fairy tale ones, are eventually forgotten, but it is unlikely that the star of **Rear Window, To Catch a Thief, Dial M for Murder** and **High Society** will be neglected by future cinema audiences. Admittedly, she was a kind of ice princess in her Hollywood days, but beneath that cool, classy exterior there were hints of unquenchable flames. She held up her transparent nightgown to James Stewart ❯ in **Rear Window** and announced, "Preview of coming attractions", and she offered Cary Grant ❯ a choice of leg or breast in **To Catch A Thief.** Her cool provocation was irresistible to Clark Gable ❯ in **Mogambo** and her other qualities proved irresistible to Hollywood, which gave her a somewhat undeserved Oscar for her performance as Bing Crosby's ❯ bitter wife in **The Country Girl** (over Judy Garland ❯ in **A Star Is Born**). Kelly made her farewell to the cinema with two almost autobiographical films, portraying a princess in **The Swan** and the daughter of a rich socialite Philadelphia family in **High Society.** Her whole Hollywood career consisted of only 11 films.

She was born into a wealthy socialite family in Philadelphia on November 12, 1928, worked first on stage and in television, and made her film début in a small role in the 1951 **Fourteen Hours.** She got slightly more attention as Gary Cooper's ❯ spirited Quaker wife in **High Noon** and was then nominated for an Oscar for her work in **Mogambo.** It was Alfred Hitchcock, however, who made her into a major star with **Dial M For Murder, Rear Window** and **To Catch A Thief.** She was the perfect Hitchcock heroine, the embodiment of what he later called "sexual elegance", and he was never able afterwards to find another blonde who could replace

*Left: Grace Kelly. Her last film was **High Society;** MGM regretted having loaned her out so often and rushed her into the part before she left for Monaco.*

her. Kelly married Prince Rainier in 1956 and has lived happily ever after.
COMPLETE FILMS:
1951 Fourteen Hours
Henry Hathaway (20th Century Fox)
1952 High Noon
Fred Zinnemann (United Artists)
1953 Mogambo
John Ford (MGM)
1954 Dial M For Murder
Alfred Hitchcock (Warner Brothers)
1954 Rear Window
Alfred Hitchcock (Paramount)
1954 The Bridges at Toko-Ri
Mark Robson (Paramount)
1954 The Country Girl
George Seaton (Paramount)
1954 Green Fire
Andrew Marton (MGM)
1955 To Catch A Thief
Alfred Hitchcock (Paramount)
1956 The Swan
Charles Vidor (MGM)
1956 High Society
Charles Walters (MGM)

DEBORAH KERR

Deborah Kerr has a reputation for class and true blue respectability in her film roles, but the actuality of her screen persona is rather more fascinating and has enabled her to remain a star for more than 30 years. Gentle and well-bred she has always been, but there is a strong hint of forbidden sexuality in many of her most famous roles. In **From Here To Eternity** she is a married nymphomaniac having an affair with Burt Lancaster ❯ (and she has another affair with Mr Lancaster in **The Gypsy Moths**); in **Heaven Knows Mr Allison** she is a nun stranded on a desert island with a leering Robert Mitchum ❯; in **Tea and Sympathy**

*Below: Deborah Kerr clinging to a vestige of gentility in the Outback with Robert Mitchum in **The Sundowners.***

she seduces one of her teacher-husband's pupils; in **Bonjour Tristesse** she is the mistress of David Niven ≫; in **Prudence and the Pill** she is having an affair in spite of husband David Niven; in **Beloved Infidel** she is the mistress of F. Scott Fitzgerald, as portrayed by Gregory Peck ≫. And even in **Separate Tables,** she rebels against convention and tough mother Gladys Cooper to befriend dirty-old-man David Niven. The suggestion of refined sensuality behind her screen personality gives an extra edge to her determined governess roles (**The King and I, The Innocents**) and makes even her most ladylike parts (**Edward My Son, The Sun-downers**) more intriguing. Admittedly, she has had many big films in which she is little more than a classy object of beauty (**King Solomon's Mines, Quo Vadis?, The Prisoner of Zenda**), but they do not outweigh films like **The End of the Affair** (repressed wife having an affair with writer Van

Johnson ≫) or **The Proud and the Profane** (Roman Catholic widow seduced by William Holden ≫).

She was born Deborah Kerr-Trimmer in Helensburgh, Scotland, on September 30, 1921, and initially worked in ballet and theatre before getting a small role in the 1940 film **Contraband.** She was good in **Love on the Dole,** but really attracted attention with her triple-role in **The Life and Death of Colonel Blimp** in 1943. MGM tried to make her into another Greer Garson ≫ after the war, but her sensuality in **From Here to Eternity** changed the approach to her casting considerably. Her last screen role was as Kirk Douglas's ≫ wife in **The Arrangement** in 1969; during her career she has had six Academy Award nominations but has not yet won an Oscar.

BEST FILMS:

1943 The Life and Death of Colonel Blimp
Michael Powell & Emeric Pressburger (GFD)

1946 Black Narcissus
Michael Powell & Emeric Pressburger (GFD)
1953 From Here To Eternity
Fred Zinnemann (Columbia)
1956 The King and I
Walter Lang (20th Century Fox)
1956 Tea and Sympathy
Vincente Minnelli (MGM)
1957 Heaven Knows Mr Allison
John Huston (20th Century Fox)
1957 An Affair to Remember
Leo McCarey (20th Century Fox)
1958 Separate Tables
Delbert Mann (United Artists)
1960 The Sundowners
Fred Zinnemann (Warner Brothers)
1962 The Innocents
Jack Clayton (20th Century Fox)

KING KONG

The greatest animal star of the cinema's golden era was not the dog Lassie, nor the horse Flicka, nor even the talking mule Francis —but the giant ape King Kong.

There has never been another film star like Kong, whose impact in his first film, the 1933 **King Kong,** was so huge that he immediately passed into movie mythology. For one thing he was the only movie "monster" who was actually the hero of the film, almost radiating charm as the Beast slain for love of Beauty. His climactic battle with aircraft on top of the Empire State Building is one of the most memorable scenes in cinema history and has become a part of popular folklore.

Kong is really a one-picture star, but like many another movie great he has tried to make comebacks. His first return vehicle was the 1963 Japanese film **King Kong versus Godzilla,** where he gave that monster his come-uppance. He was back again in 1967, battling a mechanical dupli-cate of himself in **King Kong Escapes.** His major attempt to recapture the world's attention, however, was in the big-budget 1976 re-make **King Kong,** pro-

Left: Hairy superstar King Kong with captive Fay Wray in the 1933 classic.

duced by Dino De Laurentiis. He was pretty good in it, too, but not quite as outstanding as on his first appearance 43 years before.

Kong was the brainchild of Merian C. Cooper, a notable documentary film maker who conceived the idea of a giant ape film while working in Africa in 1929. Many people were involved in his ultimate conception, but his actual creator was stop-animation genius Willis O'Brien. It is O'Brien's handiwork that we see on the screen, and his special effects achievements have never been surpassed. There have been many imitations of Kong (the same team made **Son of Kong**), including Konga, Gorgo and even Queen Kong, but none of them has been a patch on the original. Kong was greatly helped by his supporting cast, especially Fay Wray ➤ as his delightfully screaming love interest, and by the music provided by Max Steiner. One of his most successful reappearances in the cinemas was the 1966 **Morgan . . . A Suitable Case for Treatment,** where he inspired David Warner to imitate him.

BEST FILMS:
1933 King Kong
Ernest B. Schoedsack & Merian C. Cooper (RKO)
1963 King Kong versus Godzilla
Inoshiro Honda (Toho)
1966 Morgan . . . A Suitable Case for Treatment
Karel Reisz (British Lion)
1967 King Kong Escapes
Inoshiro Honda (Toho)
1976 King Kong
John Guillermin (Dino De Laurentiis)

MACHIKO KYO

Machiko Kyo was born in Osaka in 1924, began her career as a dancer, and started work for the Daiei film company in 1949. She was the first Japanese star to be built into a sex and glamour star and has remained among the most important actresses in Japan; she was also the first female Japanese movie star to become known in the West, bursting beautifully on to the screen in 1950 at Venice in Akira Kurosawa's **Rashomon,** portraying the Samurai's tempting wife. The film won the Grand Prize and its stars, Kyo and Toshiro Mifune ➤, have remained the Western world's favourite Japanese stars ever since. Kyo was also the star of the astonishingly beautiful colour film **Gate of Hell,** which won the Grand Prize at the Cannes Film Festival in 1954, portraying a woman who sacrifices her life for her husband's. More importantly, she was one of the favourite actresses of the great Japanese director Kenji Mizoguchi, who featured her as the lovely ghost princess in

Above: Machiko Kyo as "Lady Macbeth" in **Throne of Blood.**

Ugetsu Monogatari, as the scullery maid who becomes the emperor's favourite in **The Princess Yang Kwei-Fei** and as the lively Americanised prostitute in **Street of Shame.** She also starred in one of the equally great Yasujiro Ozu's last films, **Floating Weeds.** She has been featured by Kon Ichikawa in the bizarrely sexual **Odd Obsession** and **The Hole,** by Mikio Naruse in **Older Brother, Younger Sister,** and by Hiroshi Teshigahara in **The Face of Another.** She starred in only one American film, **The Teahouse of the August Moon,** playing opposite Marlon Brando ➤.

One of her most recent films was the 1976 **Kenzi Mizoguchi: The Life of a Film Director,** in which she talks about working with the Japanese master.

BEST FILMS:
1950 Rashomon
Akira Kurosawa (Daiei)
1953 Ugetsu Monogatari
Kenji Mizoguchi (Daiei)
1953 Older Brother, Younger Sister
Mikio Naruse (Daiei)
1953 Gate of Hell
Teinosuke Kinugasa (Daiei)
1954 The Princess Yang Kwei-Fei
Kenji Mizoguchi (Daiei)
1956 The Teahouse of the August Moon
Delbert Mann (MGM)
1956 Street of Shame
Kenji Mizoguchi (Daiei)
1959 Odd Obsession (The Key)
Kon Ichikawa (Daiei)
1959 Floating Weeds
Yasujiro Ozu (Daiei)
1966 The Face of Another
Hiroshi Teshigahara (Daiei)

ALAN LADD

The trench-coated figure of Alan Ladd is one of the most enduring myths of '40s cinema, tough, taciturn, never smiling, his cold blue eyes glinting like the gun he always carried, the absolute killer. He had a remarkably successful screen personality from his first starring role in the 1942 **This Gun For Hire;** limited as it was, it

carried him to stardom and a permanent place in movie history. He was tight-lipped, conscience-less, and hard—even when he became the hero of his films he remained a killer. He was equally as good as Dashiell Hammett's tough guy in **The Glass Key** or Raymond Chandler's hero in **The Blue Dahlia,** and was beautifully teamed with Veronica Lake ➤, who helped make his hardness more human. He is best known for his role as the gunfighter trying to give up the trade in **Shane,** finally forced to abandon his plans and kill hired gunman Jack Palance ➤ in order to save the family he lives with. It was brilliant casting by George Stevens, for it used Ladd's screen image to provide the hidden violence needed to make the character credible.

Ladd was a long time arriving at his stardom. He was born on September 3, 1913, in Hot Springs, Arkansas, and his cinema début was a bit part in **Once in a Lifetime** (1932). He had very little success in the '30s and was always in tiny roles (he can be seen as a reporter in **Citizen**

Kane) until he met agent Sue Carol—whom he later married—who began to get him attention. After a minor success in **Joan of Paris** in 1942, he was given the role of the gunman in **This Gun For Hire,** a loose version of Graham Greene's novel *A Gun for Sale.* He became a major star overnight and was billed above the title on virtually every film he made after that. There weren't many good pictures, but his characterisations were strong enough to carry him through even the weaker ones like **Lucky Jordan** and **China.** He was effective in **Salty O'Rourke** and **Two Years Before the Mast** and made a credible gangster hero for F. Scott Fitzgerald's **The Great Gatsby.** After **Shane** he had few good films, but he continued to star in action pictures until the end of his career. Later, jokes about his relative shortness (he was only five-foot-six) and his having to stand on boxes to talk to other actors presumably affected his self-

esteem. He shot himself "accidentally" in 1962 and died in 1964 from an overdose of sedatives and alcohol. His last film, **The Carpetbaggers,** came out the same year; he was in excellent form as the tough, former cowboy film star. The role was later taken over by Steve McQueen ➤, who gave an Alan Ladd-style performance in **Nevada Smith.**

BEST FILMS:
1942 This Gun For Hire
Frank Tuttle (Paramount)
1942 The Glass Key
Stuart Heisler (Paramount)
1945 Salty O'Rourke
Raoul Walsh (Paramount)
1946 The Blue Dahlia
George Marshall (Paramount)
1946 Two Years Before the Mast
John Farrow (Paramount)
1946 OSS
Irving Pichel (Paramount)
1949 The Great Gatsby
Elliot Nugent (Paramount)
1953 Shane
George Stevens (Paramount)
1958 The Proud Rebel
Michael Curtiz (BV)
1964 The Carpetbaggers
Edward Dmytryk (Paramount)

Above: Alan Ladd as the ex-gunfighter of **Shane,** *who has to kill again to protect his new life.*

VERONICA LAKE

Veronica Lake became one of the notable myth figures of '40s cinema because of her trademark hair style, long blonde hair constantly falling over one eye and constantly being brushed back. The style was even featured in a song she did in **Star-Spangled Banner**—"A Sweater, a Sarong and a Peek-a-Boo Bang" (with Dorothy Lamour ➤ as the sarong and Paulette Goddard ➤ as the sweater). Her look was so much imitated by factory girls that the government asked Paramount to change the style until after the war, as it was causing too many accidents.

Lake had much more going for her than just her hair. She had a

husky voice, sultry looks and an off-hand, casual manner that made her the sexiest star of the war years. She was teamed with Alan Ladd ❯ in five films, creating the kind of chemistry later generated by Bogart ❯ and Bacall ❯ (Bacall's hair style was modelled on Lake's). She didn't make many good films—Paramount virtually discarded her after the war—but her best ones are dandies. With Ladd she starred in three key films of the period, **This Gun for Hire** (as a singer-dancer who becomes accidentally involved with killer Ladd), **The Glass Key** (as the daughter of a candidate for governor), and **The Blue Dahlia** (as the wife of a crooked night-club owner), and two lesser ones, **Duffy's Tavern** (in a guest spot with Ladd) and **Saigon** (as an adventuress in Indochina). She was also outstanding as Joel McCrea's ❯ delightful companion on his voyages in Preston Sturges' **Sullivan's Travels** and as an alluring witch in René Clair's **I Married a Witch**. She was also quite extraordinary as a Jap-hating nurse in **So Proudly We Hail**, going to greet Japanese soldiers with a live grenade tucked between her breasts.

She was born in Brooklyn, New York City, on November 14, 1919, with the name Constance Ockleman. She made her film début (as Constance Keane) in the 1939 **Sorority House**, and finally won stardom as a cabaret singer in the 1941 **I Wanted Wings**.

After her Paramount contract came to an end in 1949, her career virtually finished; she declared herself bankrupt in 1951. She did theatre work and then disappeared from sight until 1962, when she was discovered by the press working as a barmaid. The notoriety and extensive newspaper coverage put her back in the public eye; she did two more films (the last was the 1970 horror film **Flesh Feast**) and published her autobiography, *Veronica,* in 1968. She died in 1973.

Above: Alan Ladd and Veronica Lake in their first film together, the 1942 **This Gun For Hire.** *The chemistry of their partnership made them one of the most famous teams of the 1940s.*

BEST FILMS:
1941 I Wanted Wings
Mitchell Leisen (Paramount)
1941 Sullivan's Travels
Preston Sturges (Paramount)
1942 This Gun for Hire
Frank Tuttle (Paramount)
1942 The Glass Key
Stuart Heisler (Paramount)
1942 I Married a Witch
René Clair (United Artists)
1943 So Proudly We Hail
Mark Sandrich (Paramount)
1944 The Hour Before Dawn
Frank Tuttle (Paramount)
1945 Duffy's Tavern
Hal Walker (Paramount)
1946 The Blue Dahlia
George Marshall (Paramount)
1948 Saigon
Leslie Fenton (Paramount)

HEDY LAMARR

Considered the most beautiful woman in the movies in the late '30s, Hedy Lamarr is remembered today for three pictures: the 1932 Austrian production **Ecstasy,** in which her teenage nudity made her world-famous and set standards for sex pictures for decades; the 1938 Walter Wanger production of **Algiers,** in which she became the most alluring lady in American films after Charles Boyer ❯ came out of the Casbah for one last glimpse of her beauty (and the public made a catchline out of "Come wiz me to ze Casbah"); and the 1950 **Samson and Delilah,** in which Cecil B. De Mille had the inspired idea of using her sex appeal straight, and the public loved her as the world's most renowned seductress. Miss Lamarr (who lives today on New York City's Riverside Drive) is famous for other things besides

films, including a sizzling auto-biography (*Ectasy and Me: My Life as a Woman,* over which she sued her collaborators for $21 million); six husbands, most of them millionaires; and a widely-publicised shoplifting incident.

She was born as Hedwig Eva Maria Kiesler in Vienna, Austria, on November 9, 1914, and made her first film in 1931 as an extra in Alexis Granozsky's Austrian **Sturme ein Wasserglas.** Czech director Gustav Machaty (already notorious for his 1929 **Erotikon**), cast her in his film **Symphonie der Liebe (Symphony of Love),** which was later released as **Ecstasy.** In it, Hedy was seen in dappled loveliness taking a nude dip in a lake and running naked through the woods. She was also shown in close-up having an orgasm. The film was extremely daring for its time and not at all bad; it even won the Grand Prize at the 1934 Vienna Film Festival. The part won her her first millionaire husband, from whom she fled to MGM in 1937 (after he tried to buy up and destroy all prints of **Ecstasy**). MGM immediately loaned her to RKO for **Algiers.** Her Hollywood career was not well handled (she was "difficult"), but she was quite pleasant in **Comrade X** with Clark Gable ❯, in

Above: Hedy Lamarr prepares to give Victor Mature an unwel-come haircut in De Mille's **Samson and Delilah.**

H. M. Pulham, Esq with Robert Young and in **Experiment Perilous** with Paul Lukas. She looked stunning in most of her films, most notably as Tondelayo in **White Cargo** and as the Mexican beauty in John Steinbeck's **Tortilla Flat.** Unfortunately, she turned down many good films (Ingrid Bergman ❯ got most of them) and had little understanding of how to best advance her own career. **Samson and Delilah** was her last good film; her last appearance was in **The Female Animal** in 1957.

BEST FILMS:
1932 Ecstasy (Extase)
Gustav Machaty (Universal Elektra)
1938 Algiers
John Cromwell (United Artists)
1940 Boom Town
Jack Conway (MGM)
1940 Comrade X
King Vidor (MGM)
1941 Ziegfeld Girl
Robert Z. Leonard (MGM)
1941 H. M. Pulham, Esq
King Vidor (MGM)
1942 Tortilla Flat
Victor Fleming (MGM)

1942 **White Cargo**
Richard Thorpe (MGM)
1944 **Experiment Perilous**
Jacques Tourneur (RKO)
1950 **Samson and Delilah**
Cecil D. De Mille (Paramount)

DOROTHY LAMOUR

Dorothy Lamour was the No 1 jungle movie actress in the late '30s and early '40s, the undisputed Queen of the Sarong. It must have been grating to have been famous for a costume (she reportedly grew to loathe sarongs), but she was good-humoured and exotically beautiful and built a very nice career out of her drapery. She was put in a sarong in her very first feature film, the 1936 **The Jungle Princess,** became famous

Above: Dorothy Lamour became the exotically beautiful Queen of the Sarong for Hollywood and usually portrayed lovelies with names like Lona or Aloma.

wearing another one in the 1937 John Ford film **The Hurricane,** and became forever associated with the garment in her delightful teaming with Bing Crosby ❯ and Bob Hope ❯ in the **Road** pictures. She didn't make very many good pictures out of a sarong, although she tried hard, but was quite effective as a night club singer in love with Tyrone Power ❯ in **Johnny Apollo** (her own favourite role). She wasn't strong enough to carry pictures on her own, but she was an excellent partner for Hope and others, notably in **My Favourite Brunette.**

Lamour was born Mary Dorothy Stanton in New Orleans on December 10, 1914, and had become reasonably well-known as a singer before she went into movies in 1936. Because of the exotic image that was immediately created for her, however (usually with some dark body make-up), she never really got a chance to become known as a musical star. Her **Road** pictures were her best, beginning with **Road to Singapore** in 1940, and she became as

essential a part of them as the two men, able to match Crosby and Hope as a comedienne as well as being their glamorous love interest. Crosby and Hope made the mistake of not co-starring her in the last one, the 1962 **The Road to Hong Kong** (she had a guest role)—and it was the only flop of the lot.

Her career ran out of steam in the '50s, although she had a nice role in Cecil B. De Mille's circus picture **The Greatest Show on Earth,** so she retired in 1953; John Ford's 1963 **Donovan's Reef** brought her back to the screen and she has made occasional appearances since, including the 1976 TV film *Death at Love House.*

BEST FILMS:
1937 **The Hurricane**
John Ford (Goldwyn/United Artists)
1940 **Johnny Apollo**
Henry Hathaway (20th Century Fox)
1940 **Road to Singapore**
Victor Schertzinger (Paramount)
1941 **Road to Zanzibar**
Victor Schertzinger (Paramount)
1942 **Road to Morocco**
David Butler (Paramount)
1945 **Road to Utopia**
Hal Walker (Paramount)
1947 **My Favourite Brunette**
Elliot Nugent (Paramount)
1947 **Road to Rio**
Norman Z. McLeod (Paramount)
1952 **Road to Bali**
Hal Walker (Paramount)
1963 **Donovan's Reef**
John Ford (Paramount)

BURT LANCASTER

Like all the great screen actors, Burt Lancaster is a "natural" performer who "acts" not only with his words and his actions, but also with the way he moves and the way he looks. He was a circus acrobat before going into films and remains one of the most graceful big men on the screen. He is reported to have said that he was not "acting" at all when portraying the razzamatazz conman evangelist in **Elmer Gantry,** but simply being himself—and he won the Best Actor Oscar for that non-acting performance (which proves something). He has given the modern cinema more pure enjoyment, in films like **The Crimson Pirate** and **The Flame and the Arrow,** than almost any other major star, but his screen persona is much more complex than it appears superficially. He exudes teeth-baring cheerfulness, swaggering vitality and cocksure confidence, but in many ways this is merely an amiable facade masking deeper and sometimes frightening inner drives. There are few more vicious screen characterisations than his gossip columnist in **Sweet Smell of Success,** and he was entirely credible as the general planning

*Above: Burt Lancaster as the marshall in Michael Winner's violent Western **Lawman** (1970). Left: Lancaster in best beefcake style in Siodmak's 1952 **The Crimson Pirate.***

to depose the President in **Seven Days in May.** This steel-hard inner core is seen at its most obvious as Wyatt Earp in **Gunfight at the OK Corral,** but at its most forceful in his three major Italian films, **The Leopard, Conversation Piece** and **1900.** It is also worth noting the flinty determination he shows in such different pictures as **Birdman of Alcatraz, Vera Cruz** and **The Train.**

He was born as Burton Stephen Lancaster in New York on November 2, 1913, became a circus acrobat with his later screen companion Nick Cravat, and worked in many odd jobs before turning to acting. He became a major star in his first film **The Killers** (1946) and after this notable screen début he was featured in a number of excellent late '40s thrillers, including **Brute Force, Criss Cross** and **Sorry, Wrong Number. The Flame and the Arrow** and **The Crimson Pirate,** two of the most enjoyable swashbuckling spoofs ever made, strengthened his position as a star, and his fine performances in **Come Back Little Sheba** and **From Here To Eternity** gave him the acting credentials he needed. His career has never really sagged since it started and he was one of the first actors to set up his own production company. He has had

a long and strong association with certain key directors, most notably Robert Aldrich, who directed him in **Vera Cruz, Apache, Ulzana's Raid** and the 1977 **Twilight's Last Gleaming,** but has also worked very successfully more than once with Luchino Visconti, Robert Siodmak, John Frankenheimer, Richard Brooks and John Sturges. He can give solidity to even such lightweight entertainments as **Airport.** He has made his share of relatively uninteresting films, but the continuing quality of his work is outstanding, and he seems likely to remain a superstar for as long as he wants.

BEST FILMS:
1946 **The Killers**
Robert Siodmak (Universal)
1950 **The Flame and the Arrow**
Jacques Tourneur (Warner Brothers)
1952 **The Crimson Pirate**
Robert Siodmak (Warner Brothers)
1953 **From Here to Eternity**
Fred Zinnemann (Columbia)
1952 **Vera Cruz**
Robert Aldrich (United Artists)
1957 **Sweet Smell of Success**
Alexander Mackendrick (United Artists)
1957 **Gunfight at the OK Corral**
John Sturges (Paramount)
1960 **Elmer Gantry**
Richard Brooks (United Artists)
1962 **Birdman of Alcatraz**
John Frankenheimer (United Artists)
1963 **The Leopard**
Luchino Visconti (20th Century Fox)
1964 **The Train**
John Frankenheimer (United Artists)
1966 **The Professionals**
Richard Brooks (Columbia)
1974 **Conversation Piece**
Luchino Visconti (Rusconi Film)
1976 **1900**
Bernardo Bertolucci (PEA/20th Century Fox)
1977 **Twilight's Last Gleaming**
Robert Aldrich (Lorimer)

MARIO LANZA

Mario Lanza was Hollywood's idea of an opera singer—vain, temperamental and golden-voiced. He immediately began to emulate his own screen persona and become the most difficult and temperamental movie star of his time. He was also the No 1 purveyor of musical culture to the mass public during the '50s. Despite the triteness of the plots of his films, he probably did more than anyone else in recent years to interest a wider public in operatic music. His biggest success (and one of the major commercial hits of the '50s) was **The Great Caruso,** a simplified but not unenjoyable biography of the Italian tenor, filled with operatic tidbits.

Lanza was able to appeal to a mass audience because he took the image of opera singing out of its élitist upper-class ghetto. He showed how an ordinary truck driver (**That Midnight Kiss**) or fisherman (**The Toast of New Orleans**) could have such a glorious voice that he could conquer the musical fortresses of the world. His voice (and it was not a bad one at all) became so popular that when he walked off

Above: Mario Lanza in **Serenade,** *his first and only film for Warners—by 1956 he was becoming too temperamental.*

the set of **The Student Prince** another actor, Edmund Purdom, was hired just to mime to his already-recorded songs; the film was a huge success and made Purdom a (sort of) star.

Lanza was born as Alfred Arnold Cocozza in Philadelphia, Pennsylvania, on January 21, 1921. He studied singing, and while working as a piano-mover (or so his romantic studio once claimed) was discovered by conductor Serge Koussevitzky. He became well-known as a concert and recording star in the late '40s and was signed by MGM to become their new Nelson Eddy ≫. He overshot expectations in his début film, the 1949 **That Midnight Kiss,** belting out *Celeste Aida,* and was even more popular

in **The Toast of New Orleans,** with more Verdi and the specially-written *Be My Love.* His temperament grew more difficult in proportion to his success, co-star Kathryn Grayson ≫ refused to work with him again, and his ego became as swollen as his waistline (he always had weight problems). After the success of **The Great Caruso,** Lanza apparently thought he was a better singer than the subject of the film and soon was virtually impossible to work with. He made **Because You're Mine** for MGM with great difficulty, walked out on **The Student Prince,** and later made **Serenade** for Warners, but no American studio wanted such a difficult artist around so Lanza's last two films were made in Rome by Titanus for distribution by MGM. He died in 1959, aged 38, after various health complications and weakened by continual dieting. His entire cinema career consisted of eight films in ten years.

COMPLETE FILMS:
1949 That Midnight Kiss
Norman Taurog (MGM)
1950 The Toast of New Orleans
Norman Taurog (MGM)
1951 The Great Caruso
Richard Thorpe (MGM)
1952 Because You're Mine
Alexander Hall (MGM)
1954 The Student Prince
Richard Thorpe (MGM)
1956 Serenade
Anthony Mann (Warner Brothers)
1958 The Seven Hills of Rome
Roy Royland (MGM)
1959 For the First Time
Rudolph Maté (MGM)

CHARLES LAUGHTON

Laughton is the greatest character actor star in the history of the cinema, able to portray the most diverse range of personalities with flamboyance or finesse as required. He did not lose himself in his roles (he was too much of the grand actor to do that), but made the roles over to fit himself until they became the definitive versions: after 40 years, he is still the public image of Henry VIII, Captain Bligh, Nero, Rembrandt, Elizabeth Barrett Browning's tyrannical father—even the Hunchback of Nôtre Dame. No other screen actor has created such a range of movie myths, and few others have made as many outstanding films. His power to astonish and delight did not diminish with the years; he was just as effective in 1962 (the year of his death) as he had been in 1932, at the beginning of his Hollywood career, in **The Old Dark House.** His performance in his last film, **Advise and Consent** (as the scheming Southern Senator Seab Cooley), is one of his best and most memorable. The "acting" crown so often awarded to Emil Jannings, in the days

Above: Charles Laughton gave a stunning portrayal as the wily defence attorney in Wilder's **Witness for the Prosecution.**

when critics handed out such laurels, could much more deservedly be given to Laughton. Certainly, nobody has given better "acting" performances on the screen (in the theatrical sense) than Laughton, although this does not necessarily make him the greatest movie actor (over such masters as Gable ≫, Stewart ≫ and Grant ≫ for example). He was also a great director, although he made only one film (and didn't act in it—the terrifying **The Night of the Hunter** in 1955, with Robert Mitchum ≫ and Lillian Gish ≫.

Laughton was born in Scarborough, Yorkshire, on July 1, 1899, studied at the Royal Academy of Dramatic Art in London and was highly successful

in theatre there in the '20s. Elsa Lanchester, whom he married in 1929 (she later portrayed the monster's mate in **The Bride of Frankenstein**), introduced him to comedy shorts; he made his feature début in 1929 in E. A. Dupont's **Piccadilly.** His early British film career was only moderately successful, and it was not until he had a stage hit in New York that Hollywood sought him out. He started out magnificently, with classic performances in two horror films (**The Old Dark House, Island of Lost Souls**) and his great simpering satire of Nero in Cecil B. De Mille's **The Sign of the Cross.** Paradoxically, however, it was back in England that Laughton achieved real stardom— in the first British film to become an international hit, Alexander Korda's **The Private Life of Henry VIII.** His roaring, Rabelaisian, larger-than-life performance stunned cinema audiences everywhere, won him the first Academy Award to be given for a non-American picture, and put his film career into high gear. He was called back to Hollywood for four of his greatest films in 1935 and 1936; he became the personification of a stern Victorian father in **The Barretts of Wimpole Street,** terrorising Norma Shearer ❯ as daughter Elizabeth and Fredric March ❯ as Browning. Next, he was a huge comedy success as a British butler in the American West in Leo McCarey's witty **Ruggles of Red Gap.** Then he was the cruel, implacable police officer Javert, hounding Fredric March as Valjean, in **Les Misérables.** Finally, he gave one of the most famous of all his performances as the sadistic Captain Bligh, in conflict with Clark Gable in **Mutiny on the Bounty;** the film won the Best Picture Oscar and was tops at the box office. Laughton didn't really like the unsympathetic roles he was getting in Hollywood, however, and went back to England to star in Korda's **Rembrandt,** one of the great tragi-comic performances of the cinema. His next film, **I, Claudius,** with Josef von Sternberg directing, could have been his masterpiece (to judge from the remnants shown in the BBC documentary *The Epic That Never Was*), but shooting was abandoned for unclear reasons.

After a series of interesting but relatively unsuccessful British films (including Alfred Hitchcock's **Jamaica Inn**), Laughton returned to America to make **The Hunchback of Notre Dame,** replacing Lon Chaney, Snr ❯ in the popular imagination as the image of Quasimodo. He followed this wonderfully grotesque performance with a series of very different roles, seemingly intent on showing the range of his characterisations: (an Italian immigrant in **They Knew What They Wanted;** a conniving old man in **It Started With Eve;** a patriotic French schoolteacher in Jean Renoir's **This Land Is Mine;** a seventeenth-century ghost in **The Canterville Ghost**). He was brilliant as a henpecked husband planning to kill his wife in Robert Siodmak's thriller **The Suspect,** impressive as a cruel judge in Hitchcock's **The Paradine Case,** and outstanding as a complex editor/murderer being tracked by his own reporter (Ray Milland ❯) in John Farrow's **The Big Clock.** His '50s films were mostly second-rate (he even played opposite Abbot and Costello), except for a revival of his tyrannical father role in David Lean's **Hobson's Choice** and a stunning portrayal of the wily defence attorney in Billy Wilder's **Witness for the Prosecution.** None of these, however, was nearly on a par with his live (and recorded) "reading" as Shaw's Devil in the "Don Juan in Hell" section of **Man and Superman.** He came back strongly in the '60s, however, as a wonderfully

clever Roman patrician in Stanley Kubrick's **Spartacus** and his Machiavellian Southern senator in Otto Preminger's **Advise and Consent.** He died in December, 1962.

BEST FILMS:
1933 The Private Life of Henry VIII
Alexander Korda (London Films)
1934 The Barretts of Wimpole Street
Sidney Franklin (MGM)
1935 Ruggles of Red Gap
Leo McCarey (Paramount)
1935 Les Misérables
Richard Boleslavsky (20th Century Fox)
1935 Mutiny on the Bounty
Frank Lloyd (MGM)
1936 Rembrandt
Alexander Korda (London Films)
1939 The Hunchback of Nôtre Dame
William Dieterle (RKO)
1943 This Land Is Mine
Jean Renoir (RKO)
1948 The Big Clock
John Farrow (Paramount)
1953 Hobson's Choice
David Lean (British Lion)
1957 Witness for the Prosecution
Billy Wilder (Theme Pictures)
1960 Spartacus
Stanley Kubrick (Universal)
1962 Advise and Consent
Otto Preminger (Columbia)

Above: Stan Laurel and Oliver Hardy with James Finlayson in **Way Out West,** *in which they sang the famous* Trail of the Lonesome Pine.

LAUREL AND HARDY

Stan Laurel and Oliver Hardy were the greatest comedy team in the history of the cinema and the gentle, likeable characters they created continue to be the most endearing in the movies. They also made some of the funniest films of all time; Henry Miller considers their 1927 silent **The Battle of the Century** as "the greatest comic film ever made", because it brought custard-pie throwing to its ultimate—pies by the thousand. A single pie had become a cliché by this time, but here every one participates in the "reciprocal destruction" of throwing and receiving pies in the face.

Laurel and Hardy used to be taken for granted. They were

funny, but it was "easy" humour; they were "merely" entertaining without serious purpose or pathos. Now it is generally accepted that their brand of humour is one of the great achievements of the cinema; they were funny without strain, because their characters were so enjoyable—Stan was thin, the eternal innocent, a trusting baby with a child's luck and maliciousness, baffled by the world; and Ollie was fat, a short-tempered Southern gentleman, gallant to ladies, flowery in his language, opinionated in the extreme. Behind the scenes, it was Laurel who created their routines, but on screen Hardy was his equal in every way. They were the only silent comedians able to make the transition to sound without difficulty; their verbal humour is just as enjoyable as their visual gags. Nothing in the movies is as funny as their destruction of James Finlayson's house in **Big Business** (while he destroys their Christmas trees and car)—and nothing is more memorable than Ollie looking reprovingly at Stan in the middle of a disaster and saying: "Here's another fine mess you've gotten me into." In their 1928 **You're**

Darn Tootin', the incredible chaos is caused by Ollie; gradually they drag passers-by into their anarchic world and begin debagging every new arrival in a brilliant, expanding absurdity. In their 1937 feature **Way Out West,** they are revealed to be most enjoyable singers, as the recent hit re-release of their song *The Trail of the Lonesome Pine* proved.

Arthur Stanley Jefferson was born on June 16, 1890, in Ulverston, Lancashire, England, and started out as a vaudeville comedian. He came to America with the Fred Karno .troupe, understudying Charles Chaplin ❯ and began working in movies

in 1918. Norvell Hardy (the Oliver was added later to honour his father) was born on January 15, 1892, in Harlem, Georgia. He began as a singer, then ran a cinema, and finally went into movies in 1914 with Lubin Pictures in Florida (where a barber gave him his nickname "Babe"). Both Laurel and Hardy joined the Hal Roach Studios in 1926, and they came to the notice of comedy genius Leo McCarey, who persuaded Roach to team them together. Their first co-starring film was the 1927 **Putting Pants on Philip.** McCarey, who called them "The Boys", supervised most of their early films, and by 1929 they were famous around the world.

McCarey continued to direct some of their best films, fledgling director George Stevens was an early cameraman, and their supporting actors included such notables as James Finlayson and Edgar Kennedy. Their greatest period was probably 1928-1929, when they made 24 brilliant short films, but their excellence continued all through the '30s. Their superb 1932 **The Music Box** (in which they repeatedly haul a large piano up a long flight of steps—won them an Academy Award (Laurel was given a special Oscar in 1960 for "creative pioneering in comedy"). They made their first feature in 1931 (**Pardon Us**), but continued to make shorts as well until 1935; their features were not as consistently enjoyable as their shorts, with the exception of the superb **Way Out West** and **Sons of the Desert,** but they continued to make them until 1951 when their last film, **Atoll K,** was a disaster.

Hardy died in 1957 and Laurel in 1965. Their best films were re-released in anthology form in the late '60s, and are as enjoyable today as they ever were.

BEST FILMS:
1927 The Battle of the Century
Clyde Bruckman (Roach/MGM)
1928 You're Darn Tootin'
Edgar Kennedy (Roach/MGM)
1928 Early To Bed
Emmett Flynn (Roach/MGM)
1929 Liberty
Leo McCarey (Roach/MGM)
1929 Big Business
James Horne (Roach/MGM)
1929 The Perfect Day
James Parrott (Roach/MGM)
1931 Laughing Gravy
James Horne (Roach/MGM)
1932 The Music Box
James Parrott (Roach/MGM)
1933 Sons of the Desert
William A. Seiter (Roach/MGM)
1937 Way Out West
James Horne (Roach/MGM)

VIVIEN LEIGH

In the Soviet Union they considered Vivien Leigh as the greatest movie star of them all and **Waterloo Bridge** as one of the great films of all time. In America they gave her the plum role of Scarlett O'Hara in **Gone With the Wind** and two Academy Awards. In England she was mainly the wife of Laurence Olivier ≫, the world's greatest stage actor—no wonder she made so few films and had such an odd movie career. She made ten films before **Gone With the Wind**, ambitiously acquiring a reputation, and worked in only eight more after that epic made her world-famous—admittedly she suffered from ill-health and considered herself primarily a stage actress, but it does seem as if a fine screen talent was semi-wasted.

She was born on November 5, 1913, in Darjeeling, India, as Vivien Mary Hartley. Her film début was in the 1934 **Things Are Looking Up,** and although she was very beautiful it wasn't until 1936, when she made **Fire Over England** opposite Laurence Olivier, that she became a star. She was good as a French spy pretending to be a traitor and getting involved with Conrad Veidt ≫ in **Dark Journey** and as the self-centred, ambitious busker using her attractions on Charles Laughton ≫ in **St Martin's Lane.** She went to Hollywood in 1939 simply to see Olivier (they married the next year, after she had divorced her first husband) and was introduced to **Gone With the Wind** producer David Selznick by his brother Myron; every major star in Hollywood wanted the role of Scarlett, but Vivien got it, although she was virtually an unknown in the States.

Her movie persona was a fascinating one. Despite her incredible Dresden doll beauty, she was one of the cinema's great not-very-nice ladies; not quite the bitch type, more the unscrupulous, wily, kittenish beauty who uses

sexual attraction as a weapon to get her own way. The role of Scarlett was the greatest embodiment of this seemingly unsympathetic but actually mesmerising personality, but virtually all her roles were of this type—in **Waterloo Bridge** she becomes a prostitute to get through the war, in **That Hamilton Woman** she

Below: Vivien Leigh and Robert Taylor in one of the cinema's great weepies, the 1940 **Waterloo Bridge** *considered by the USSR to be one of the greatest films ever. She is a ballerina who turns to street-walking when she thinks he has been killed in the war and his family ignores her plight.*

uses her wiles on Nelson, in **Caesar and Cleopatra** she uses her wiles on Caesar, and as Blanche in **A Streetcar Named Desire** she tries to use her wiles on Marlon Brando ≫ in a performance that reportedly stunned even Tennessee Williams. She even played **Anna Karenina,** giving up husband and family for her own gratification.

To what extent these screen characters were a reflection of her own personality would be hard to say, but her last roles were equally fascinating: in **The Deep Blue Sea** she portrayed a fading beauty, cracking up after being jilted by her lover; in **The Roman Spring of Mrs Stone** she was a fading beauty (and former actress) trying a last fling at romance with an Italian gigolo; and in the 1965 **Ship of Fools** she was a fading beauty, disillusioned, divorced and drinking too much.

It was her last film. She was then 52 years old and had been divorced from Olivier five years before. She died in 1967.

BEST FILMS:
1937 Dark Journey
Victor Saville (London Films)
1938 St Martin's Lane
Tim Whelan (Mayflower)
1939 Gone With the Wind
Victor Fleming (Selznick/MGM)
1940 Waterloo Bridge
Mervyn LeRoy (MGM)
1941 That Hamilton Woman (Lady Hamilton)
Alexander Korda (London Films)
1945 Caesar and Cleopatra
Gabriel Pascal (Rank)
1951 A Streetcar Named Desire
Elia Kazan (Warner Brothers)
1955 The Deep Blue Sea
Anatole Litvak (20th Century Fox)
1961 The Roman Spring of Mrs Stone
Jose Quintero (Warner Brothers)
1965 Ship of Fools
Stanley Kramer (Columbia)

Margaret Lockwood

Margaret Lockwood has more claim to movie fame than simply being the "wicked lady" of British '40s cinema, a genre that one critic has aptly described as Gainsborough Gothic. She was born as Margaret Day in Karachi, India, on September 15, 1916, made her stage début in 1928, and her first film in 1934, Basil Dean's **Lorna Doone.** Before she became a villainess and the most popular female movie star in Britain in 1946, she was a delightful ingénue and a favourite heroine for director Carol Reed, who featured her in seven pictures, including **Midshipman Easy** (the first), **Bank Holiday, A Girl Must Live** and **Who's Your Lady Friend?** Her greatest film, however, was Alfred Hitchcock's 1938 **The Lady Vanishes,** in which she was the heroine who becomes disturbed over the disappearance of her elderly travelling companion— although she was also very good in Reed's slightly similar **Night Train to Munich** (both were scripted by Frank Launder and Sidney Gilliat). Even as a pretty young heroine, she had a nice line in ambiguous smiles that sometimes made her motives suspect, an aspect of her screen personality first developed by Reed in **The Stars Look Down** (as a girl who almost destroys coalminer Michael Redgrave). It was the husband-stealing, wife-murdering role in the 1943 **The Man in Grey** that really made her into a major star, however, and under the direction of Leslie Arliss she climbed to new heights of melodramatic kitsch in **Love Story** (as a pianist with a fatal heart ailment,

*Left: Margaret Lockwood in her finest film, Alfred Hitchcock's 1938 **The Lady Vanishes**.*

in love with half-blind pilot Stewart Granger ❯) and **The Wicked Lady** (aristocrat by day, highwaywoman by night). Audiences adored these films in the post-war period (she even won Best Actress awards), and she was never really able to get away from the image. Her career faded quickly in the '50s, despite an excellent performance as a barmaid involved with Dirk Bogarde ❯ in the 1955 **Cast a Dark Shadow**. That was her last film (she has since worked primarily in theatre and TV) until she turned up in 1976 as the wicked stepmother of Cinderella in **The Slipper and the Rose**.

BEST FILMS:
1937 Who's Your Lady Friend?
Carol Reed (20th Century Fox)
1938 Bank Holiday
Carol Reed (Gainsborough)
1938 The Lady Vanishes
Alfred Hitchcock (Gaumont-British)
1939 A Girl Must Live
Carol Reed (Gainsborough)
1939 The Stars Look Down
Carol Reed (Grafton)
1940 Night Train to Munich
Carol Reed (20th Century Fox)
1940 The Girl in the News
Carol Reed (20th Century Fox)
1945 The Wicked Lady
Leslie Arliss (Gainsborough)
1955 Cast a Dark Shadow
Lewis Gilbert (Frobisher)
1976 The Slipper and the Rose
Bryan Forbes (Paradine)

GINA LOLLOBRIGIDA

Gina Lollobrigida's film career was based on big breasts and pneumatic beauty. She was the second of the busty post-war Italian sex stars (following Silvana Mangano) to arouse erotic fantasies on an international scale, and she soon became as closely identified with Italy as spaghetti and opera. La Lolla was a manufactured product, an advertisement for sex rather than the embodiment of it, but during the early '50s she was the queen of the mammaries. She was adequate as an actress (she wasn't called upon to do much), but her screen personality was vapid—although she was usually asked to be tempestuous at some point—and she did not have enough presence to dominate any of her films. In her best pictures she was simply the love interest (**Fanfan la Tulipe, Night Beauties, Trapeze, Beat the Devil**), and even the Italian movies that made her famous (the **Bread, Love and . . .** series) were as much Vittorio De Sica's films as hers. After a while, she became famous for being famous and remains so today, although she seems like an artifact left over from another era.

She was born in Subiaco near

Rome on July 4, 1927, and made her film début in small roles in 1946 films like **Aquila Nera** and **Elisir d'Amore**. She rose to bigger if not necessarily better parts over the next five years and became internationally famous in two French films with Gérard Philipe ❯ **Fanfan la Tulipe** and **Night Beauties**. She looked marvellous —and she looked even better under John Huston's direction in **Beat the Devil** (playing Humphrey Bogart's ❯ wife). Despite these rather good films, it was an Italian village comedy directed by Luigi Comencini, **Bread, Love and Fantasy,** that really made her into a big international star and sex symbol. The world public loves busty village peasant stereotypes —and La Lolla was to be it for some time to come. She was hugely popular in **Women of Rome** and **The Most Beautiful Woman in the World** and then began to work in American films, like **Trapeze** with Burt Lancaster ❯. In the '60s her sex appeal began to diminish, but she got just as much publicity as ever and continued to make forgettable films. Among her better ones were **Come September, Woman of Straw** and **Buona Sera, Mrs Campbell**. In the '70s she began to move away from the cinema and into photo-journalism, pub-

Above: Gina Lollobrigida was the glamorous centre of attention in Carol Reed's 1956 **Trapeze,** *with high-wire artists Burt Lancaster and Tony Curtis forming an aerial triangle.*

lished a book of her work, and held exhibitions in various countries. Her most famous *coup* was an interview with Fidel Castro.

BEST FILMS:
1951 Fanfan la Tulipe
Christian Jaque (Ariane/Rizzoli)
1952 Les Belles de Nuit (Night Beauties)
René Clair (Franco London/Rizzoli)
1953 Beat the Devil
John Huston (United Artists)
1954 Pane, Amore e Fantasia (Bread, Love and Fantasy)
Luigi Comencini (Titanus/Girosi)
1955 La Romana (Woman of Rome)
Luigi Zampa (Ponti/De Laurentiis)
1955 Pane, Amore e Gelosia (Bread, Love and Jealousy)
Luigi Comencini (Titanus)
1955 La Donna più Bella del Mondo (The Most Beautiful Woman In The World)
Robert Z. Leonard (Maleno/Malenotti)
1956 Trapeze
Carol Reed (United Artists)
1961 Come September
Robert Mulligan (Universal)
1969 Buona Sera, Mrs Campbell
Melvin Frank (Universal)

CAROLE LOMBARD

Carole Lombard was the queen of the screwball comedy, a wacky, wonderful, witty, uninhibited prankster whose off-screen personality perfectly fitted her screen image and helped make her one of the top stars of the 1930s. Not only was she blonde and beautiful, but she got to marry Clark Gable ❯ (just after he finished shooting **Gone With the Wind**), became the highest paid film star in the world in 1937 (she earned just under half a million dollars), and starred in some of the best comedies of all time.

Lombard started life as Janice Alice Peters in Fort Wayne, Indiana, on October 6, 1908. She made her film début as a tomboy

Above: Carole Lombard and the highly-educated "tramp" she hires to be the family butler in the crewball comedy **My Man Godfrey** *(but as he's William Powell, all ends zanily well).*

in Allan Dwan's 1921 **A Perfect Crime** and worked in Mack Sennett comedy shorts and other films during the '20s. Paramount put her under contract in 1930 as a romantic comedienne, most notably opposite Gable in **No Man of Her Own,** the only film in which they starred together. She was a big but not a major star until her breezy, free-swinging breakthrough in **Twentieth Century** in 1934; the combination of direction by Howard Hawks, script by Ben Hecht and Charles MacArthur and first-class acting by co-star John Barrymore ❯ hurtled her to major stardom in a story about a producer trying to sign up a star on a luxury train. She sparkled in **Hands Across the Table** (as a gold-digger who digs flat-broke Fred MacMurray ❯), delighted in **Love Before Breakfast** (bickering with Preston Foster), reached new heights of zaniness in **My Man Godfrey** (with ex-husband William Powell ❯ as a suave butler trying to harness her), demonstrated comic genius in **Nothing Sacred** (opposite newspaperman

115

Fredric March ➤ in another Ben Hecht script), and was preposterously funny in **True Confession** (as a murder suspect who can't tell the truth). Her greatest film, however, was her last, the black comedy **To Be or Not to Be,** in which Lubitsch daringly satirised the Nazi invasion of Poland, using Lombard and Jack Benny ➤ as actors caught up in the maelstrom.

At the age of 34 and after making 42 films, she was killed in an air crash in January, 1942; the tragedy was as big an emotional shock for audiences as the suicide of Marilyn Monroe 20 years later.

Lombard was portrayed on screen by Jill Clayburgh ➤ in the 1976 biopic **Lombard and Gable.**

BEST FILMS:
1932 No Man of Her Own
Wesley Ruggles (Paramount)
1934 Twentieth Century
Howard Hawks (Columbia)
1935 Hands Across the Table
Mitchell Leisen (Paramount)
1936 Love Before Breakfast
Walter Lang (Universal)
1936 My Man Godfrey
Gregory La Cava (Universal)
1937 Nothing Sacred
Wiliam Wellman (United Artists)
1937 True Confession
Wesley Ruggles (Paramount)
1940 They Knew What They Wanted
Garson Kanin (RKO)
1941 Mr and Mrs Smith
Alfred Hitchcock (RKO)
1942 To Be or Not To Be
Ernst Lubitsch (United Artists)

PETER LORRE

Peter Lorre is best known to the wider public for his small but unforgettable roles in two Humphrey Bogart ➤ classics, **The Maltese Falcon** (as the sinister gunman Joel Cairo) and **Casablanca** (as the man who killed for the Letters of Transit). "You despise me, don't you?" he asks Bogart, who replies, "Well, if I gave you any thought, I probably would." Lorre was despised, hated and feared in most of his best films, from the child killer of Fritz Lang's 1931 **M** down to the maniacal scientist of his own 1951 directorial effort **Die Verlorene.** He did not often have the lead in films, but even in his lesser roles he was outstanding, one of the screen's greatest villains. Even when he was the hero of the movie, his whispering voice and toadish looks made him oddly menacing, as he was in the eight **Mr Moto** films, portraying a super-cool Oriental detective. Josef von Sternberg starred him as Raskolnikov, the guilt-ridden murderer of **Crime and Punishment;** Alfred Hitchcock used him as a chilling villain in the 1934 **The Man Who Knew Too Much** and in **The Secret Agent;** and Frank Capra directed him as a murderer in the household of two mad old ladies in **Arsenic and Old Lace.**

Above: Peter Lorre portrayed the crafty Japanese detective Mr Moto in eight films, including **Mr Moto's Last Warning** *(1939).*

Twice he was involved in classic horror films about murderous hands, **Mad Love** and **The Beast with Five Fingers.** He was often teamed with Sydney Greenstreet ➤ in the '40s, most notably in **The Mask of Dimitrios,** where he is the writer investigating Greenstreet's villainy.

Lorre was born in Rosenberg, Hungary, on June 26, 1904, as Laszlo Loewenstein, and became an entertainer and stage actor in the '20s. After his success in **M** (he was supposedly Goebbels' favourite actor), he was featured in a number of German pictures, but decided to work elsewhere after 1933 (he was Jewish). The most notable part of his career was in the '30s and '40s, but he continued making good films until his death in 1964. In the '50s he gave excellent performances in **Beat the Devil** and **Silk Stockings,** and in the '60s was highly impressive in films for Roger Corman, including **Tales of Terror** and **The Raven.** His last film was the 1964 **The Patsy,** with Jerry Lewis ➤.

BEST FILMS:
1931 M
Fritz Lang (Ufa)
1934 The Man Who Knew Too Much
Alfred Hitchcock (Gaumont-British)
1935 Mad Love
Karl Freund (MGM)
1935 Crime and Punishment
Josef von Sternberg (Columbia)
1936 The Secret Agent
Alfred Hitchcock (Gaumont-British)
1938 Thank You, Mr Moto
Norman Foster (20th Century Fox)
1941 The Maltese Falcon
John Huston (Warner Brothers)
1943 Casablanca
Michael Curtiz (Warner Brothers)
1944 The Mask of Dimitrios
Jean Negulesco (Warner Brothers)
1962 The Raven
Roger Corman (AIP)

MYRNA LOY

Myrna Loy was John Dillinger's favourite actress. When he came out of hiding to see her latest picture, **Manhattan Melodrama,** in a Chicago cinema on the night of July 22, 1934, he was gunned down by the FBI.

The picture affected Loy's career as well. It was the first time she played opposite William Powell ➤ (he was a DA, Clark Gable ➤ was a gangster, she was the girl in between), and director Woody Van Dyke was so impressed by their chemistry that he cast them immediately in **The Thin Man.** Loy and Powell both became major stars overnight, and in 1937 she was voted the Queen of the Movies when Gable was voted the King. She became known as the Perfect Screen Wife and, when she was a little older, as the Perfect Screen Mother. What she actually was, was one of the finest comediennes ever to light up the screen with a combination of wit and beauty. It took Hollywood a long time to find that out, though; she had already been in movies for ten years and had made some 60 films before she was "discovered" by Van Dyke.

She was born as Myrna Williams in Helena, Montana, on August 2, 1905, and began her film career in 1925. In most of her silent films she was an Oriental, a vamp, or a combination of both. In her early talkies she was a spoiled flirt or daughter and then appeared in a bizarre mixture of all her roles, spoiled, sadistic, Oriental daughter in **The Mask of Fu Manchu.**

The Thin Man changed all that. She became a glamorous leading lady with fabulous clothes, witty lines and an image as a sexy free-thinking wife that made every man in America envy William Powell. They made six **Thin Man** films together between 1934 and 1947 —all of which were enjoyable, although the earliest ones were the funniest—as Nick and Nora Charles; he was a retired detective and she was a rich heiress with a nose for trouble. They loved to drink, and their repartee was as stimulating as a dry martini; they even solved crimes. They did other pictures together as well, almost as funny, like **Love Crazy,** in which they spend their wedding anniversary on the verge of divorce, and **Libelled Lady,** in which he tries to compromise her when she sues a newspaper. She was also very popular co-starring with Clark Gable in films like **Too Hot to Handle** and **Test Pilot.**

Loy semi-retired from films in 1941 but began again as a slightly older perfect screen wife and mother in **The Best Years of Our Lives** in 1946—superb as Fredric March's ➤ wife and Teresa Wright's mother, still witty and sophisticated but a little more like a real housewife. She was also a big hit as a mother to Clifton Webb's brood in **Cheaper By the Dozen** and its sequel.

She moved away from cinema and into UN work in the '50s, but she makes an occasional film when she can find a suitable role. She was last seen in **Airport '75.**

BEST FILMS:
1934 Manhattan Melodrama
W.S. Van Dyke (MGM)
1934 The Thin man
W.S. Van Dyke (MGM)
1934 Broadway Bill
Frank Capra (Columbia)
1936 Libelled Lady
Jack Conway (MGM)
1936 After the Thin Man
W.S. Van Dyke (MGM)

Below: Myrna Loy and William Powell were teamed in 14 movies; one of the most delightful was the 1936 **Libelled Lady.**

BELA LUGOSI

Bela Lugosi should, on the face of it, have become the greatest horror star of them all, for he apparently really believed in his malevolent nonsense, acted with demonic if rather florid conviction, and was actually born in the backwoods of Hungary, where Dracula flourished. His screen image was one of total evil and he never asked (or got) sympathy from the audience. He was, in other words, over the top most of the time, and this lack of everyday human qualities made him (usually) less effective than the gentle Boris Karloff ❯ or the self-mocking Vincent Price ❯❯. At his best, however, he was very good indeed—and his very best was as the original Count Dracula in Tod Browning's 1931 **Dracula**. He really was that mythic figure and no actor since has been able to equal his chilling performance. The role made him a big star (he had already played it on stage in 1927) and during the early '30s he got as much fan mail as the matinée idols.

Most of his good films were made at Universal in the '30s, including **Murders in the Rue Morgue**, **The Black Cat**, **The Raven** (the last two with Karloff), **The Invisible Ray** and **Son of Frankenstein** (as the malevolent hunchback Igor), but he also did some fine work at other studios. **White Zombie**, made for an independent, was one of his most horrific films and started the whole zombie trend in the genre, and he was also excellent in **Chandu the Magician** at Fox and **The Mark of the Vampire** at MGM (again for Browning).

He was born as Béla Lugosi Blasko in Lugos, Hungary, on October 20, 1884, was on stage in Hungary by 1915, and appeared in F. W. Murnau's **Der Januskopf** in Germany in 1920. He made his American screen début in **The Silent Command** in 1923, but didn't become a horror star until **Dracula**. He had a few straight roles in the '30s, notably in Ernst Lubitsch's **Ninotchka**, but in the '40s was reduced to being a horror star for Monogram in B-pictures. He re-created his Dracula superbly for the comedy-horror classic **Abbott and Costello Meet Frankenstein** in 1948, but his '50s films included such Z-pictures as **Bela Lugosi Meets a Brooklyn Gorilla**. He was addicted to drugs at the end of his life and died in 1956.

Above: Bela Lugosi had a truly demonic look which helped to make him one of the most evil of the great horror stars.

BEST FILMS:
1931 Dracula
Tod Browning (Universal)
1932 Murders in the Rue Morgue
Robert Florey (Universal)
1932 White Zombie
Victor Halperin (United Artists/Amusement Securities)
1932 Chandu the Magician
William Cameron Menzies & Marcel Varnel (Fox)
1934 The Black Cat
Edgar G. Ulmer (Universal)
1935 The Mark of the Vampire
Tod Browning (MGM)
1935 The Raven
Lew Landers (Universal)
1936 The Invisible Ray
Lambert Hillyer (Universal)
1939 Son of Frankenstein
Rowland V. Lee (Universal)
1948 Abbott and Costello Meet Frankenstein
Charles Barton (Universal)

IDA LUPINO

Ida Lupino was the great "moll" of '40s cinema, one of the heroines of the American *film noir* genre. She was often a tart or a tramp, sexy but tough, worldly-wise and a little weary. She was only 23 when she starred opposite Humphrey Bogart ❯ in Walsh's powerful **High Sierra**, and one critic described her as the best moll he had ever seen. She had a unique kind of beauty, perfect for gansterish films, but she was also a splendid actress.

Her first film for Warner Brothers was as the flamboyantly insane floozy wife of Alan Hale in **They Drive By Night**. Most of her best films were made at Warner's in the '40s, including her critically acclaimed ambitious older sister in **The Hard Way**; her tough but vulnerable, woman-of-the-world characterisation was seen at its best, however, in **Road House**, as the lady between enemies Richard Widmark ❯ and Cornel Wilde ❯. She also sings in this film, revealing a fine talent for such torch songs as *One for My Baby*. Her screen persona, with its cool mixture of intelligent, good-bad sexiness, was much in vogue at this time and her way of talking was even copied by a Hemingway heroine (in **Across the River and Into the Trees**). Lupino had been in pictures for 15 years by this time.

She was born in London on February 4, 1918, the daughter of star comedian Stanley Lupino. She studied at RADA and was discovered by Allan Dwan, who featured her in his 1933 **Her First Affair**, trapping an older man. She was put under contract by Paramount, but her '30s films were uninteresting except for Rouben

*Above: Ida Lupino had one of her finest roles in Michael Curtiz's 1941 adaptation of Jack London's suspenseful **The Sea Wolf**, with Edward G. Robinson (as the psychopathic freighter captain) and John Garfield.*

*Above left: Ida Lupino, the great "moll" of '40s cinema, in her recent **Junior Bonner** (1972) playing Steve McQueen's mother.*

Mamoulian's **The Gay Desperado**. Warner's signed her in 1940 and the great part of her career began. In the '50s she turned director, making good small-budget films with feminist themes, but also continuing her acting career. She made notable contributions to Aldrich's **The Big Knife** (as Jack Palance's ❯ wife) and Lang's **While the City Sleeps** (as a sob sister on a newspaper). Her career has continued up to the present day, most notably as Steve McQueen's ❯ mother in Peckinpah's 1972 **Junior Bonner**. She lives today in southern California.

BEST FILMS:
1940 They Drive By Night
Raoul Walsh (Warner Brothers)
1941 High Sierra
Raoul Walsh (Warner Brothers)
1941 The Sea Wolf
Michael Curtiz (Warner Brothers)
1941 Out of the Fog
Anatol Litvak (Warner Brothers)
1941 Ladies in Retirement
Charles Vidor (Columbia)
1943 The Hard Way
Vincent Sherman (Warner Brothers)
1948 Road House
Jean Negulesco (20th Century Fox)
1955 The Big Knife
Robert Aldrich (United Artists)
1956 While the City Sleeps
Fritz Lang (RKO)
1972 Junior Bonner
Sam Peckinpah (Cinerama)

JEANETTE MACDONALD (AND NELSON EDDY)

Jeanette MacDonald never liked Nelson Eddy. He didn't much like her either, but they made eight musicals together as "America's Sweethearts" from 1935 to 1942 and the public adored them in large numbers. Most of the critics thought their films were kitsch, which is true—but they are kitsch of high camp appeal and have many admirers still. One is never really sure that MacDonald, a tongue-in-cheek comedienne of great quality, is not sending up the rather wooden Eddy on purpose, but she never let on if she did; MGM studio boss Louis B. Mayer would have had a heart attack—she was his particular favourite and he took kitsch seriously. In fact, MacDonald's greatest films were not made at MGM but at Paramount, and Eddy would not even have been considered for them. Her co-stars there were Maurice Chevalier ➤ and Jack Buchanan ➤, they were directed by Ernst Lubitsch and Rouben Mamoulian, and they are among the most sparkling and delightful musicals ever made.

MacDonald was born in Philadelphia, Pennsylvania, on June 18, 1901, and was on stage in musicals by 1920. Her first film was a dandy, Lubitsch's 1929 **The Love Parade,** the first great screen musical, with MacDonald playing Queen to Chevalier's bored Prince Consort in a wittily-scripted tour-de-force. Europe's waltz king, Ludwig Berger, then put her opposite Dennis King in the Friml operetta **The Vagabond King,** and Lubitsch picked her again as Buchanan's partner in the marvellously inventive **Monte Carlo.** This was even wittier and sexier than the earlier Lubitsch film and included MacDonald singing *Beyond the Blue Horizon* in a brilliantly shot train scene. She was back co-starring with Chevalier in the Lubitsch-George Cukor **One Hour with You,** another delight, and then it was Mamoulian's turn to make musical history with the pair in the stunning **Love Me Tonight.** MacDonald was also making charming comedies during this early '30s period, but when the musical vogue ended Paramount rather shortsightedly dropped her. She got together with Lubitsch and Chevalier one more time, however, at MGM, where they re-made **The Merry Widow** as a satirical musical with great success. And then Nelson Eddy came on the scene.

Eddy, who was born in Providence, Rhode Island, in 1901, had been in films since 1933 but not very successfully until MGM teamed him with MacDonald in the operetta **Naughty Marietta** in

Top: Jeanette MacDonald and Nelson Eddy met for the first time on film in the 1935 smash-hit musical **Naughty Marietta.**
Above: Jeanette MacDonald in the 1930 **The Lottery Bride.**

1935. It was a huge success, as was its sequel **Rose Marie,** and Woody Van Dyke directed them both with a leavening of humour that allowed MacDonald's comedienne qualities to shine through the inane plots. They were both good singers and the public loved them. MacDonald's next movie was not a musical, but the epic disaster film **San Francisco** with Clark Gable ➤, also good fun. It was back to operetta and Eddy again with **Maytime,** and then she was teamed with Allan Jones in **The Firefly.** He wasn't much of an improvement, so she kept on making musicals with Eddy until 1942, the last being **I Married an Angel.** After they split up, both of their careers faded; Eddy was very good, though, as Willie the Singing Whale's voice in Disney's **Make Mine Music** and made his last film in 1947, the Western **Northwest Outpost.** MacDonald's career continued sporadically until 1949, when she made her last film, **The Sun Comes Up,** which also featured Lassie. Their films were revived with remarkable success in the '50s and on television. MacDonald died in 1965; Eddy in 1967.

BEST FILMS:
1929 The Love Parade
Ernst Lubitsch (Paramount)
1930 Monte Carlo
Ernst Lubitsch (Paramount)
1932 One Hour With You
Ernst Lubitsch & George Cukor (Paramount)
1932 Love Me Tonight
Rouben Mamoulian (Paramount)
1934 The Merry Widow
Ernst Lubitsch (MGM)
1935 Naughty Marietta
W.S. Van Dyke (MGM)
1936 Rose Marie
W.S. Van Dyke (MGM)
1936 San Francisco
W.S. Van Dyke (MGM)
1937 Maytime
Robert Z. Leonard (MGM)
1938 Sweethearts
W.S. Van Dyke (MGM)

FRED MACMURRAY

If ever they make "The Richard Nixon Story", Fred MacMurray would be the perfect star. Despite his present day image as the amiable father figure in Disney films and the TV series *My Three Sons* the MacMurray screen image has tended towards being a false front of smiles and goodwill, masking shiftiness and fraudlence. The apotheosis of this personality is seen in MacMurray's two films with Billy Wilder, as the crooked insurance man having an affair with Barbara Stanwyck ➤ in **Double Indemnity** and as the philandering boss who uses both

Jack Lemmon ❯ and Shirley MacLaine ❯ in **The Apartment.** It was also inherent in MacMurray's nine films for Mitchell Leisen in the '30s and '40s, notably in **Remember the Night** (District Attorney involved with shoplifter he is prosecuting, played by Barbara Stanwyck) and **Take A Letter, Darling** (as the male secretary of woman business executive Rosalind Russell ❯). He was normally used by his studio, Paramount, simply as a good, dependable leading man, but it was his hidden untrustworthiness that made him interesting; Wilder could see this quality even in musicals like **And the Angels Sing.** MacMurray could have been one of the great good-bad guys, but was rarely allowed the chance, although he was a fine crooked cop in **Pushover** and nicely unsympathetic in **The Caine Mutiny.**

He was born in Kankakee, Illinois, on August 30, 1908, and in his early years was a saxophonist and singer. He began his movie career as an extra in 1930 and was signed by Paramount in 1934, although his first starring part was at RKO in **Grand Old Girl.** He had a big success with Claudette Colbert ❯ in **The Gilded Lily** and then began his long association with Mitchell Leisen in the 1935 **Hands Across the Table.** He was good as a cowboy for King Vidor in **The Texas Rangers,** outstanding for Leisen in **Swing High, Swing Low,** and worked steadily without ever achieving major stardom. **Double Indemnity** gave a big boost to his career and so did **The Egg and I,** but his career began to go downhill in the '50s. He was rescued by Disney in 1958 with **The Shaggy Dog** and has become a Disney regular, doing his best work under the direction of Robert Stevenson in films like **The Absent-Minded Professor** and **Son of Flubber.** He has continued to work, mainly in TV films, but also in large-budget pictures like **The Swarm.**

BEST FILMS:
1935 Hands Across the Table
Mitchell Leisen (Paramount)
1936 The Texas Rangers
King Vidor (Paramount)
1937 Swing High, Swing Low
Mitchell Leisen (Paramount)
1940 Remember the Night
Mitchell Leisen (Paramount)
1942 Take a Letter, Darling
Mitchell Leisen (Paramount)
1944 Double Indemnity
Billy Wilder (Paramount)
1947 The Egg and I
Chester Erskine (Universal)
1954 The Caine Mutiny
Edward Dmytryk (Columbia)
1954 Pushover
Richard Quine (Columbia)
1956 There's Always Tomorrow
Douglas Sirk (Universal)
1960 The Apartment
Billy Wilder (United Artists)

Left: Fred MacMurray in Disney's **Son of Flubber.**

ANNA MAGNANI

Anna Magnani was the first Italian movie actress to attract international attention since Francesca Bertini in the 1910s. Her powerful performance as the woman shot down by the Nazis in Roberto Rossellini's 1945 **Rome, Open City** stunned world audiences and critics with its fierce, unglamorous vitality. Her characterisation of the earth mother of Italian cinema reached its apogee in the 1955 American film **The Rose Tattoo** opposite Burt Lancaster ❯ (for which she won the Academy Award). Her somewhat frenzied screen acting style in this role, combining vitality and strength of mind with passion and coarseness, was put on display again opposite Anthony Quinn ❯ in **Wild is the Wind** and Marlon Brando ❯ in **The Fugitive Kind,** but was used better by Italian director Pier Paolo Pasolini in **Mamma Roma.**

Magnani's personality came across on the screen with great force, but in many ways she came to embody a cliché-idea of Italian womanhood which was fascinating but not finally convincing. Her long years as a stage actress had made her "actressy" in a way that the greatest screen actresses are not. Jean Renoir realised this, and cast her superbly as an actress in **The Golden Coach,** and then Visconti used her beautifully in **Bellissima,** as a mother with dreams of fame attempting to make her child a movie star, and as an actress in one episode of **Siamo Donne.** Magnani was extremely true to life in her first major appearance in **Rome, Open City,** or so it seemed at the time, but in the end she seemed no

Above: Anna Magnani and Marlon Brando as a love-starved lady and a drifter in **The Fugitive Kind,** *based on Tennessee Williams'* Orpheus Descending.

more realistic than the peasants portrayed by Sophia Loren ❯ and Gina Lollobrigida ❯. She was born (illegitimate) in Alexandria, Egypt, of an Italian mother on April 11, 1905, and became a singer and revue performer as well as a stage actress in the '30s. Her film début was in the 1934 **The Blind Woman of Sorrento (La Cieca di Sorrento),** but her first really important performance was in the 1941 Vittorio De Sica film **Teresa Venerdi,** as a music hall star. She continued to mix theatre and cinema during her

Above: Jean Marais as the poet in Jean Cocteau's **Orphée** *trying to pass through the mirror.*

years as a star, but made relatively few films after the '50s. Her last screen apperance was a cameo performance in Federico Fellini's 1972 **Roma,** and she died the following year.

BEST FILMS:
1945 Rome, Open City (Roma, Cittá Aperta)
Roberto Rossellini (Excelsa)
1947 The Honorable Angelina (L'Onorevole Angelina)
Luigi Zampa (Lux-Ora)
1948 The Miracle (Amore)
Roberto Rossellini (Tevere)
1948 Molti Sogni per le Strade
Mario Camerini (Lux)
1951 Bellissima
Luchino Visconti (Film Bellissima)
1952 The Golden Coach (La Carrozza D'Oro)
Jean Renoir (Panaria Film)
1955 The Rose Tattoo
Daniel Mann (Hal Wallis/Paramount)
1957 Wild is the Wind
George Cukor (Hal Wallis/Paramount)
1960 The Fugitive Kind
Sidney Lumet (United Artists)
1962 Mamma Roma
Pier Paolo Pasolini (Arco-Cineriz)

JEAN MARAIS

Jean Marais used to be the Prince Charming of the movies, the fairytale hero whose extravagantly handsome blond looks were too much like a fantasy to be real. He was the beast magically transformed into a handsome prince in **Beauty and the Beast;** he was the poet Orpheus pursuing his love Eurydice into Hell in **Orphée;** he was Tristan tragically in love with Iseult in **L'Éternel Retour.** He became a top heart-throb of women (and men) around the world. And then he grew a little older and a little overweight (Prince Charming in the fairy tales never does) and lost his hold over the hearts of women and, more importantly, over the heart of poet-playwright-filmmaker Jean Cocteau. The two lived together from 1937 to 1947 and it was Cocteau who made Marais into a star, featuring him in almost every film he made. Marais was his ideal Apollo figure and Cocteau wanted the world to admire him as well.

Marais was born in Cherbourg in 1913 as Jean Marais-Villain, and made his film début in a small part in Marcel L'Herbier's **Épervier** in 1933. He was not much of a success until Cocteau met him in 1937 and began to feature him in plays and even write plays for him (**Les Parents Terribles** is based on Marais' exceedingly close relationship with his mother). In 1943 he became a major film star through two pictures, the Cocteauscripted **L'Éternel Retour** (as a blond tragically in love with Madeleine Sologne) and the smash hit **Carmen** (as a dashing, dark-haired Don José in love with Viviane Romance). Then came **La Belle et la Bête** (with Marais wearing a stunning lion-mask

119

created by Christian Bérard, co-starring Josette Day as the Beauty), Victor Hugo's romantic **Ruy Blas** (adapted by Cocteau and co-starring Danielle Darrieux ❯), and the film version of Cocteau's play **L'Aigle à Deux Têtes** (with Edwige Feuillère). He starred in the film version of **Les Parents Terribles** as well, although he was starting to lose his looks already, and then gave his hypnotic performance in **Orphée,** one of the cinema's most magical films. He made good movies after it, but nothing to match his Cocteau masterpieces. He was especially memorable losing Ingrid Bergman ❯ in Jean Renoir's **Elena et les Hommes,** as Maria Schell's ❯ mysterious sailor lover in Luchino Visconti's Dostoevsky adaptation **White Nights** and in a small role in Cocteau's last film, **Le Testament d'Orphée.** Most of his films after this were swashbucklers or period pieces, among the best being André Hunebelle's **Le Bossu,** with Bourvil, and the Cocteau adaptation of **La Princesse de Clèves.** Prince Charming was soon making the French equivalent of the B-movie, starring as Fantomas or the Saint in cheaper swash-bucklers. He came back wonderfully to the world of fairy tale, however, in 1970, in Jacques Demy's **Peau d'Ane,** portraying a King rather than a Prince as he was now 57 years old, but still trying to win the beautiful Princess (Catherine Deneuve ❯)—a marvellous way to round off a career.

In 1975 he published his autobiography, *Histoires de Ma Vie,* in which he talks about his life with Cocteau.

BEST FILMS:
1943 L'Éternel Retour
Jean Delannoy (Paulvé)
1946 La Belle et la Bête (Beauty and the Beast)
Jean Cocteau (Paulvé)
1947 Ruy Blas
Pierre Billon (Paulvé/Le Grand)
1947 L'Aigle à Deux Têtes
Jean Cocteau (Ariane/Sirius)
1948 Les Parents Terribles
Jean Cocteau (Ariane)
1950 Orphée
Jean Cocteau (Paulvé/Palais Royal)
1956 Elena et les Hommes
Jean Renoir (Franco London/Gibé)
1957 I Notti Bianchi (White Nights)
Luchino Visconti (CIAS)
1961 Le Testament d'Orphée
Jean Cocteau (Editions Cinématographiques)
1970 Peau d'Ane (Donkey Skin)
Jacques Demy (Parc/Marianne)

Fredric March

One of the most respected and distinguished actors in the history of Hollywood, with two Academy Awards (for **Dr Jekyll and Mr Hyde** and **The Best Years of Our Lives**) and 40 years of excellent films, Fredric March paradoxically remained a great stage actor who worked in the cinema. As brilliant

as many of his performances were, he never really had the charisma of a major movie star; like all good stage actors, he lost his personality in his roles and probably for this reason never created a recognisable screen image; the only characteristics he carried with him from film to film were his intelligence and his prestige. All the same, he had a remarkable cinema career, starting in 1929 opposite Ruth Chatterton in **The Dummy** (one of the first stage actors to be brought to Hollywood when sound arrived) and continuing at a high level up to 1973, when he starred opposite Lee Marvin ❯ in **The Iceman Cometh.** In between, he made more than 66 pictures in all genres from comedy to horror, including swashbucklers, epics, romances and heavy drama.

March was born Ernest Frederick McIntyre Bickel in Racine, Wisconsin, on August 31, 1897, and became a stage star in the '20s, marrying (in 1927) and often acting with Florence Eldridge. He appeared opposite most of the glamorous women

stars of the early '30s cinema as his film reputation grew, and he re-created his stage success imitating John Barrymore ❯ in **The Royal Family of Broadway.** His brilliant double performance in Rouben Mamoulian's **Dr Jekyll and Mr Hyde** won him a deserved Oscar and increased his prestige both as an actor and a matinée idol. Cecil B. De Mille cast him as the Roman centurion lead in **The Sign of the Cross,** Ernst Lubitsch brought out his talent for polished comedy in **Design for Living,** and Mitchell Leisen gave him one of his finest roles as Death falling in love in **Death Takes a Holiday.** He was a respectable Robert Browning in **The Barretts of Wimpole**

Street (harassed by Charles Laughton ❯ as Elizabeth's father), a superb Valjean in **Les Misérables** (pursued by Charles Laughton as policeman Javert), and an excellent Vronsky in **Anna Karenina** (with Greta Garbo ❯ leaving her husband for him). This was the peak of his '30s career, starring in one great film after another. He was the hero of Mervyn LeRoy's big budget epic **Anthony Adverse** and the anti-hero of Howard Hawks' **The Road to Glory,** one of the most powerful war films ever made. John Ford cast him as Bothwell in **Mary of Scotland** (with Katharine Hepburn ❯ as Mary and March's wife Florence as Elizabeth), and he then created the role of the fading film star in the first version of **A Star is Born** (the part played by James Mason ❯ and Kris Kristofferson ❯ in the later versions). William Wellman directed and Janet Gaynor ❯ co-starred as the actress on the way up. Wellman immediately starred him again opposite Carole Lombard ❯ in the hilarious Ben Hecht satire **Nothing Sacred,** and Cecil B. De Mille gave him the swash-

Above: Fredric March and his screen wife Myrna Loy in **The Best Years of Our Lives,** *for which he won the 1946 Oscar.*

buckling lead in the spectacular **The Buccaneer** (1938).

March's career faltered at this point, for he was getting too old to be a romantic hero, but he was soon back in major films like René Clair's **I Married a Witch** (with Veronica Lake ❯) and **The Adventures of Mark Twain** (with lots of make-up). He moved definitely to older roles (he was now 49) in William Wyler's **The Best Years of Our Lives,** sensitively portraying the oldest of the three returning veterans and winning

his second acting Oscar. From this point on, his roles were character parts (usually major ones); he portrayed sad Willy Loman in the film version of Arthur Miller's play **Death of a Salesman** and won more acting awards. He was brilliant as one of the power-hungry boardroom in **Executive Suite** in 1954, solidly effective with Grace Kelly ❯ in **The Bridges at Toko-Ri,** and absolutely gripping in **The Desperate Hours** (as an ordinary man who rises to heroic greatness when his family is held hostage by Humphrey Bogart's ❯ gang). He was memorable as the older man in love with Kim Novak ❯ in the film version of Paddy Chayefsky's **The Middle of the Night** (1958), and impressive even in small parts in **Seven Days in May** and **Hombre** in the '60s. He rounded off his career beautifully, playing in the 1973 American Film Theatre production of O'Neill's **The Iceman Cometh** (as the owner of the Last Chance saloon); it was a perfect combination of theatre and cinema that reflected his own best work. He died in 1975.

BEST FILMS:
1932 Dr Jekyll and Mr Hyde
Rouben Mamoulian (Paramount)
1933 Design for Living
Ernst Lubitsch (Paramount)
1934 Death Takes a Holiday
Mitchell Leisen (Paramount)
1935 Les Misérables
Richard Boleslawski (20th Century Fox)
1935 Anna Karenina
Clarence Brown (MGM)
1936 The Road to Glory
Howard Hawks (20th Century Fox)
1937 A Star is Born
William Wellman (Selznick/United Artists)
1937 Nothing Sacred
William Wellman (Selznick/United Artists)
1946 The Best Years of Our Lives
William Wyler (RKO)
1952 Death of a Salesman
Laslo Benedek (Columbia)
1955 The Desperate Hours
William Wyler (Paramount)

Herbert Marshall

Herbert Marshall was too well-bred to become a really major star; he invariably let the most beautiful women in Hollywood movies push him around, deceive him, and generally get the acting accolades they couldn't have won without him. It was Marshall whom Bette Davis ❯ killed by withholding pills in **The Little Foxes,** and whom Greta Garbo ❯ was unfaithful to in **The Painted Veil,** Marlene Dietrich ❯ was unfaithful to in **Angel** and Bette Davis (again) was unfaithful to in **The Letter.** His strong point was being a weak husband, a well-mannered older lover or a polished, immaculate father. Sometimes the image was used imaginatively (as in Alfred Hitchcock's **Foreign Correspondent,** where his sympathetic father turns out to be the Nazi villain), but more often he was starred opposite great actresses because he was such a wonderful, self-effacing reflecting pool for their glory. He began the '30s as a romantic hero and matinée idol, but soon became the older lover and husband, ending up in the '40s as the father figure.

Marshall was born in London on May 23, 1890, lost his right leg in World War I (although this was hardly evident in his walk), and became a stage star in the '20s. His first film was the silent 1927 **Mumsie,** directed by Herbert Wilcox, but it was the 1929 talkie **The Letter,** with Jeanne Eagels, that made his reputation (he was the lover in this first version, not the husband). He was outstanding as a grand actor seeking a killer in Alfred Hitchcock's **Murder,** and then Paramount tried to build him up as a romantic star opposite Marlene Dietrich in **Blonde Venus** and Kay Francis and Miriam

Above: Herbert Marshall is too well bred to cope with Bette Davis's bitchiness in the 1941 **The Little Foxes.**

Hopkins » in **Trouble in Paradise,** two of his finest films. He also made good pictures in England with Victor Saville (**Michael and Mary, I Was a Spy**), while continuing his Hollywood work. His romantic image faltered and he began to play older men, but his best acting was in comedies like the nutty but funny **If You Could Only Cook** with Jean Arthur ». He had a continuing association with Somerset Maugham's work and was at his best as the Maugham narrator in the 1942 **The Moon and Sixpence** and again in **The Razor's Edge.** He was Jennifer Jones' » father in **Duel in the Sun,** but most of his later films were not nearly as good as he was. He continued working, however, until his death in 1966, his last film being **The Third Day** in 1965, directed by Jack Smight.

BEST FILMS:
1930 Murder
Alfred Hitchcock (BIP)
1932 Blonde Venus
Josef von Sternberg (Paramount)
1932 Trouble in Paradise
Ernst Lubitsch (Paramount)
1934 The Painted Veil
Richard Boleslawski (MGM)
1935 The Good Fairy
William Wyler (Universal)
1935 If You Could Only Cook
William A. Seiter (Columbia)
1937 Angel
Ernst Lubitsch (Paramount)
1940 Foreign Correspondent
Alfred Hitchcock (Wanger/United Artists)
1940 The Letter
William Wyler (Warner Brothers)
1941 The Little Foxes
William Wyler (Goldwyn)
1942 The Moon and Sixpence
Albert Lewin (Kramer/United Artists)

THE MARX BROTHERS

The Marx Brothers are even more popular today than they were in the '30s, when they were making their best films. Perhaps anarchy is more fashionable now—certainly, there is nothing dated about their best routines and they are likely to remain popular as long as movies continue to be shown. The basis of their apotheosis as veritable myth figures is not their scripts (although they had excellent writers, including S.J. Perelman, Morrie Ryskind and George S. Kaufman), nor their directors (only Leo McCarey was of any stature), nor even their

zany wit and humour, great as that was. It is the screen characters they created, and which we not only remember but want to see again and again (no matter how relatively poor the film) that have made them immortal. These personae continued from movie to movie, even though the names of the characters they ostensibly portrayed changed with each picture, and they needed to act and react to each other to be truly effective. Like the Beatles of a later era, they were very good separately—but together they were geniuses. There were really only three of them, although another brother, Zeppo, played the love interest in their first five pictures. Groucho was the most quoted, with the funniest lines, incredibly believable in an absurd way, despite his painted-on moustache, loping, crouching stride, and penchant for stuffy, over-sized dowagers in the form of Margaret Dumont. Harpo was the most mythic, almost the heir of the *Commedia dell'Arte* tradition with his pantomime, curly blonde wig, odd hats and mechanical accoutrements, which usually included a horn for honking and a harp for playing. Chico was the slyest, the caricature of an Italian street vendor selling "tootsie-fruitsie ice-a-cream" in his fancy velvet jackets and pointed hat. They did not really set out to destroy the world as we know it; instead they created another bizarre universe that seemed to have an entirely different logic. It was a very great achievement.

They began life in a truly Marxian way. Their mother was named Minnie, their father was

nicknamed "Misfit" (he was an unsuccessful tailor), and they acquired their stage names in a poker game. Chico (Leonard) was born in 1891, Harpo (Adolph Arthur) in 1893, Groucho (Julius Henry) in 1895, and Zeppo (Herbert) in 1910. A fifth brother, Gummo (Milton), did not make movies with them. They were in vaudeville first and then became popular on Broadway in three plays, *I'll Say She Is, The Cocoanuts* and *Animal Crackers.* Their first film was an adaptation of **The Cocoanuts** for Paramount in 1929, followed by a better adaptation of **Animal Crackers** in 1930. The success of these two (filmed in New York) persuaded them to go to Hollywood, where they maintained their zany standards with **Monkey Business** and **Horse Feathers.** They acquired a really good comedy director for the next, **Duck Soup,** a wildly improbable tale which required audiences to believe that Groucho was the president of a banana republic. Director Leo McCarey helped make it their finest film together but it was, incredibly, a box office failure, and Paramount dropped them. Clever Irving Thalberg brought them to MGM, added a little romantic interest to attract female movie-goers, and starred them in two of their greatest (and funniest) films, **A Night at the Opera** and **A Day at the Races.** Thalberg's unfortunate death affected their careers badly; none of their later films was as good as the first seven, (although the

Below: The nucleus of the Marx Brothers—Harpo, Groucho and Chico.

Above: The Marx Brothers—Groucho, Chico, Harpo and Zeppo—were at their best in Leo McCarey's **Duck Soup** *(1933).*

1941 **The Big Store** is pretty funny in its own way). At RKO they made **Room Service,** did two more for MGM (**At the Circus** and **Go West**) and then split up after **Big Store.** They came together again in 1946 for **A Night in Casablanca** and in 1949 for **Love Happy,** but couldn't recapture their old magic. And that was all there was. They made other movie appearances separately and Groucho had considerable success on television, but the Marx Brothers' legacy is only 13 films. Chico died in 1961, Harpo in 1964, and Groucho in 1977.

BEST FILMS:
1929 The Cocoanuts
Robert Florey & Joseph Santley (Paramount)
1930 Animal Crackers
Victor Heerman (Paramount)
1931 Monkey Business
Norman McLeod (Paramount)
1932 Horse Feathers
Norman McLeod (Paramount)
1933 Duck Soup
Leo McCarey (Paramount)
1935 A Night at the Opera
Sam Wood (MGM)
1937 A Day at the Races
Sam Wood (MGM)
1938 Room Service
William A. Seiter (RKO)
1939 At the Circus
Edward Buzzell (MGM)
1941 The Big Store
Charles Reisner (MGM)

Giulietta Masina

For a while in the '50s, it looked as if Giulietta Masina was going to become one of the major stars of international cinema. Her Chaplin-esque performances in Federico Fellini's **La Strada** and **Nights of Cabiria** aroused enthusiasm from critics and audiences around the

Above: Giulietta Masina always seemed to put a great deal into her screen roles, especially the autobiographical **Juliet of the Spirits.**

world who had rarely been so moved by a screen actress. She was a sad-eyed clown, a combination of humour and pathos that had not been so effectively embodied since Chaplin's heyday. And then, suddenly, the magic disappeared. She was in a film scripted by Fellini but directed by Eduardo De Filippo and her screen persona began to seem mannered, and the failure of the 1959 Julien Duvivier film **The Great Life** virtually ended her film career, although she gave one more brilliant performance as the wife with delightful fantasies in Fellini's **Juliet of the Spirits.**

She was born as Giulia-Anna Masina in the village of Giorgio de Piano near Bologna, on February 22, 1920, worked briefly on stage, and then met Fellini through a radio series. They married in 1943 and she stayed away from acting until 1948, when Alberto Lattuada gave her a lovely little slut role in **Without Pity.** When Fellini joined forces with Lattuada to direct his first film, the 1950

Variety Lights, both directors featured their wives in the film.

Masina was usually cast as a good-hearted but much-put-upon woman of not great intelligence or morality, a small-time prostitute, mistress or maid; she was very good in films like **Europa '51** for Roberto Rossellini and **The White Sheik** for her husband. Fellini built **La Strada** around Masina's image, starring her as Gelsomina, the sad-happy companion of travelling strong-man Anthony Quinn »; she finally dies of unhappiness. It was a great and touching performance, and was followed by another good, small one in Fellini's **Il Bidone,** as Richard Basehart's wife.

Masina hit her acting peak as the optimistic, tragi-comic whore smiling through her tears in the 1957 **Cabiria,** the film that was later re-fashioned into the musical **Sweet Charity.** She had nowhere to go but down after that, and her career faded away to nothing in the '60s; her last appearance was in **The Madwoman of Chaillot** in 1969, supporting Katharine Hepburn ».

BEST FILMS:
1948 Senza Pietà (Without Pity)
Alberto Lattuada (Lux)
1950 Luci del Varietà (Variety Lights)
Alberto Lattuada and Federico Fellini (Capitolium)
1952 Lo Sceicco Bianco (The White Sheik)
Federico Fellini (PDC)
1952 Europa '51
Roberto Rossellini (Ponti-De Laurentiis)
1953 Via Padova 45
Giorgio Bianchi (Edo Film)
1955 La Strada
Federico Fellini (Ponti-De Laurentiis)
1955 Il Bidone (The Swindlers)
Federico Fellini (Titanus)
1957 Le Notti di Cabiria (Nights of Cabiria)
Federico Fellini (De Laurentiis)
1958 Fortunella
Eduardo De Filippo (De Laurentiis)
1965 Giulietta degli Spiriti (Juliet of the Spirits)
Federico Fellini (Federiz)

James Mason

James Mason has been a movie star for more than 40 years without ever acquiring the major stardom that seems due to him. He has given us some of the most memorable performances in movies (especially in **A Star is Born, Odd Man Out** and **Lolita**),

*Left: James Mason gave a fine eccentric performance as the villainous river pirate Gentleman Brown in Richard Brooks' **Lord Jim** (1964).*

but his screen personality is apparently not the kind that catches fire with audiences. Basically he portrays good men with damaging or fatal flaws, and movie-goers seem to prefer their heroes to be stronger. In **A Star is Born** he is a drunken has-been, in **Lolita** he is sexually attracted to a very young girl, in **Odd Man Out** he is a weak and dying IRA gunman, in **The Reckless Moment** he is a blackmailer, in two films he is the brilliant but losing General Rommel (**The Desert Fox, The Desert Rats**) and in **Julius Caesar** he is Brutus. Ambition should be made of sterner stuff, as Anthony observed.

Mason was born in Huddersfield, England, on May 15, 1909, and began working professionally in the theatre in 1931. He made his cinema début in 1935 in **Late Extra** and continued with only reasonable success until 1943, when he became a top star in Britain with **The Man in Grey** opposite Margaret Lockwood ➤. His "flawed man" image was almost villainous in his highly popular pictures of this period, being excessively nasty to Phyllis Calvert in **Fanny By Gaslight**, whacking pianist Ann Todd's hands with a stick in **The Seventh Veil**, and joining Lockwood in highwayman activities in **The Wicked Lady**. His first really good film was the 1947 **Odd Man Out**; he left for America shortly afterwards. He did excellent work in Hollywood in films by Max Ophuls (**Caught, The Reckless Moment**), Joseph Mankiewicz (**Five Fingers, Julius Caesar**) and George Cukor (**A Star is Born**), but real stardom remained elusive. He has been good in even his weaker films and outstanding in the stronger ones (**Bigger Than Life, North by Northwest, The Fall of the Roman Empire**), but films have rarely been built around his screen personality. His finest recent performances were in **The Autobiography of a Princess, Cross of Iron** and **Heaven Can Wait**.

BEST FILMS:
1947 Odd Man Out
Carol Reed (Two Cities)
1949 The Reckless Moment
Max Ophuls (Columbia)
1952 Five Fingers
Joseph Mankiewicz (20th Century Fox)
1953 Julius Caesar
Joseph Mankiewicz (MGM)
1954 A Star is Born
George Cukor (Warner Brothers)
1956 Bigger Than Life
Nicholas Ray (20th Century Fox)
1959 North by Northwest
Alfred Hitchcock (MGM)
1962 Lolita
Stanley Kubrick (MGM)

1966 The Deadly Affair
Sidney Lumet (Columbia)
1975 The Autobiography of a Princess
James Ivory (Ivory/Merchant)
1977 Cross of Iron
Samuel Peckinpah (Anglo-EMI)

JESSIE MATTHEWS

Jessie Matthews used to be known as "the lady with the loveliest legs in London". Certainly, she was the loveliest of all British film musical stars, and for a while in the '30s as popular as her American counterparts. She had a high, trilly voice, a vivacious if slightly cool personality, a '30s Mayfair accent, a toothy smile and super legs, and she made some very enjoyable and fondly remembered films. The famous one, of course, was Victor Saville's 1934

Above: Jessie Matthews was the loveliest star in British musicals in the '30s, and was praised by The New York Times as "the counterpart of Fred Astaire".

Evergreen, a delectable piece of froth about a girl pretending to be her own musical comedy star mother, miraculously unaged, and becoming a star herself. The *New York Times* praised the film lavishly in 1935 and described Jessie as "the feminine counterpart of Fred Astaire . . . a joyous and captivating nymph." She made a dozen of these musicals in the '30s and most of them were quite fun, especially those directed by Saville and by her husband, Sonnie Hale. Even Alfred Hitchcock directed her in a musical, the rather extraordinary **Waltzes from Vienna.** She was also good in non-musicals, like Saville's fine adaptation of J.B. Priestley's **The Good Companions** and his all-star bus crash thriller **Friday the Thirteenth,** and Carol Reed's farce **Climbing High.**

She was born in London (Soho, not Mayfair) on March 11, 1907, and was on stage by 1917. She became one of Charles B. Cochran's "Young Ladies" and a stage musical comedy star in the '20s,

after making her film début in a bit part in **The Beloved Vagabond** in 1923. Her first starring film was **Out of the Blue** in 1931, which she followed with **There Goes the Bride.** She was so popular that producer Michael Balcon signed her to a long contract and made her a major star. He thought she could "dance like an angel", and she sang delightfully, making popular such songs as *Dancing on the Ceiling* and *Over My Shoulder.* Her film career virtually ended in 1939, although she went to Hollywood for a brief appearance with 80 other British stars in the fine 1943 **Forever and a Day.** In 1958 she was Tom's mother in **Tom Thumb** (her last film), but she was best known in later years as Mrs Dale on the *Mrs Dale's Diary* radio serial of the '60s. She published her autobiography, *Over My Shoulder,* in 1975.

BEST FILMS:
1933 The Good Companions
Victor Saville (Gaumont-British)
1933 Friday the Thirteenth
Victor Saville (Gaumont-British)
1934 Waltzes from Vienna
Alfred Hitchcock (Tom Arnold)
1934 Evergreen
Victor Saville (Gaumont-British)
1935 First a Girl
Victor Saville (Gaumont-British)
1936 It's Love Again
Victor Saville (Gaumont-British)
1937 Head Over Heels
Sonnie Hale (Gaumont-British)
1937 Gangway
Sonnie Hale (Gaumont-British)
1938 Sailing Along
Sonnie Hale (Gaumont-British)
1938 Climbing High
Carol Reed (Gaumont-MGM)

VICTOR MATURE

Victor Mature may be as bad an actor as the critics who dubbed him "The Hunk" would have us believe, but such a simplification hardly explains his 30-year career as a star and at least a dozen interesting performances. Admittedly he was massive, vulgar and sometimes lurid, but he also had a concealed sense of humour and

the ability to play even his most comic-strip roles with wholehearted directness. He came in handy for filling up the wide spaces of CinemaScope in **The Robe** and supplied ample muscle for **Samson and Delilah,** but there was a time in the late '40s when he was starring in a series of dandy thrillers like **Kiss of Death, Moss Rose** and **Cry of the City.** It is sometimes forgotten that Mature was an excellent Doc Holliday in John Ford's masterpiece **My Darling Clementine,** a superb savage trapper in Anthony Mann's **The Last Frontier,** and a wonderfully hammy has-been movie star in **After The Fox.** If these are the traits of a talentless mountain of meat, then other actors should put on some weight.

Mature was born in Louisville, Kentucky, on January 29, 1916, and acted in more than 60 plays before making his screen début in

*Above: Victor Mature in chains in Cecil B. De Mille's muscular epic **Samson and Delilah** (1949) in which he is surprisingly good, belying criticisms that he is just a hunk of beefcake.*

The Housekeeper's Daughter in 1939. He was immediately cast in a camp classic, **One Million BC,** as a cave-man battling with Hal Roach's prehistoric monsters, and was afterwards accorded star status opposite a series of lovely ladies, including Betty Grable ➤ (**I Wake Up Screaming**), Gene Tierney ➤ (**The Shanghai Gesture**), and Rita Hayworth ➤ (**My Gal Sal**). He stayed a star all through the '40s and '50s, but went into semi-retirement in 1962 (he's a very rich man), although he still makes occasional film appearances, as in **After The Fox** and **Head.** His last role was a cameo in the 1976 **Won Ton Ton.**

BEST FILMS:
1940 One Million B.C.
Hal Roach (United Artists)
1946 My Darling Clementine
John Ford (20th Century Fox)
1947 Moss Rose
Gregory Ratoff (20th Century Fox)
1947 Kiss of Death
Henry Hathaway (20th Century Fox)

1948 Cry of the City
Robert Siodmak (20th Century Fox)
1949 Samson and Delilah
Cecil B. De Mille (Paramount)
1952 The Las Vegas Story
Robert Stevenson (RKO)
1953 The Robe
Henry Koster (20th Century Fox)
1956 The Last Frontier
Anthony Mann (Columbia)
1966 After The Fox
Vittorio De Sica (United Artists)

JOEL McCREA

There is no mystique about Joel McCrea's cinema career. He became a movie star (instead of just another leading man) almost by default; he had the good fortune to work with some very good directors on some outstanding films and he eventually became one of the leading Western heroes, but he never had the ambition to become a major star (as he himself admits). His greatest work was done for three directors: Alfred Hitchcock (as a newspaperman who gets entangled with spies in **Foreign Correspondent**); Preston Sturges (as a Hollywood director on the road in **Sullivan's Travels,** as Claudette Colbert's ❯ husband in **The Palm Beach Story,** and as the inventor of anaesthesia in **The Great Moment**); and Sam Peckinpah (as an old gunman teamed with Randolph Scott ❯ in **Ride the High Country**). His screen personality was never a very strong one, a combination of amiability, strength and lack of understanding of the situations he confronts, but he was a fairish actor and he held up his part of his movies pretty well. He could get overpowered by stronger screen personalities, as he was in **Dead End** (he was the lead but no one noticed, with Humphrey Bogart ❯ and others in the cast), but he was pleasantly forceful with Barbara Stanwyck ❯ in Cecil B. De Mille's epic **Union Pacific** and William Wellman's **Buffalo Bill.**

McCrea was born in Los Angeles on November 5, 1905, became an extra in films during the '20s, and had his first real role in **The Jazz Age** in 1929. He made many good films during the '30s, including **The Most Dangerous Game** with Fay Wray, **The Lost Squadron, Barbary Coast** and **These Three,** but he didn't really make an impression until his '40s films, despite his leading roles. In the '50s he starred in small-budget Westerns and acquired a certain fame in that genre. He retired after the 1962 **Ride the High Country,** making a small comeback in 1976 as a retired rodeo rider in **Mustang Country.**

BEST FILMS:
1932 The Most Dangerous Game
Irving Pichel & Ernest Schoedsack (RKO)
1935 Barbary Coast
Howard Hawks (United Artists)

Above: Joel McCrea was starred in many low-budget Westerns in the '50s like George Sherman's 1953 Lone Hand.

1939 Union Pacific
Cecil B. De Mille (Paramount)
1940 Foreign Correspondent
Alfred Hitchcock (United Artists)
1941 Sullivan's Travels
Preston Sturges (Paramount)
1942 The Palm Beach Story
Preston Sturges (Paramount)
1943 The More the Merrier
George Stevens (Columbia)
1944 Buffalo Bill
William Wellman (20th Century Fox)
1944 The Great Moment
Preston Sturges (Paramount)
1962 Ride the High Country
Sam Peckinpah (MGM)

VICTOR McLAGLEN

Towards the end of his career, Victor McLaglen was featured in the longest and most enjoyable fist fight in screen history, brawling with John Wayne ❯ all over the Irish countryside in John Ford's **The Quiet Man.** He was 66 years old at the time and the fight was a glorious summation of his long life in the movies. He almost always portrayed burly tough guys with soft hearts and warm humour, and more often than not he was involved in fisticuffs (he had been a professional boxer as a young man, hence the broken nose). He is best remembered by movie-goers for his Ford films (their association goes back to the 1925 **The Fighting Heart**), notably as the sergeant in the Cavalry trilogy (**Fort Apache, She Wore a Yellow Ribbon, Rio Grande**), the drunken IRA traitor Gypo in **The Informer** (for which he won the Academy Award in 1935), the sole survivor in the desert in **The Lost Patrol,** and the tough sergeant who befriends Shirley Temple and dies in **Wee Willie Winkie.** He was also notable however, with other directors; it was Raoul Walsh who made him a major star in 1926 in **What Price Glory?,** playing Captain Flagg to Edmund Lowe's Sergeant Quirk, and they repeated their roles in

the even more successful Walsh film **The Cock-Eyed World.** He was excellent as an unusual romantic lead, betrayed by Marlene Dietrich ❯, in Josef von Sternberg's **Dishonored,** married by Jeanette MacDonald ❯ in **Annabelle's Affairs,** bewitched by Mae West ❯ in **Klondike Annie,** and losing Mona Maris to Humphrey Bogart ❯ in **A Devil With Women** — but he was better in action pictures like the superb **Gunga Din** with Cary Grant ❯.

McLaglen was born in Tunbridge Wells, England, on December 10, 1886, and was a highly successful professional boxer, vaudeville performer and Army officer before turning to movies in 1920, with the British picture **The Call of the Road.** After a fair success in England, he went to America, where he began his career with **The Beloved Brute** and made some excellent silents, including Howard Hawks' **A Girl in Every Port** opposite Louise Brooks ❯. His greatest popularity as a leading man was in the early sound period; after the mid-'30s he was mainly a supporting actor. He published his autobiography, *Express to Hollywood,* in 1935. His last film was **Sea Fury** in 1958, and he died the following year. His son Andrew McLaglen has become a film director attempting the Fordian manner.

Below: Victor McLaglen won the Best Actor Oscar in 1935 for his role in The Informer, one of many films he made for John Ford.

BEST FILMS:
1926 What Price Glory?
Raoul Walsh (Fox)
1929 The Cock-Eyed World
Raoul Walsh (Fox)
1934 The Lost Patrol
John Ford (RKO)
1935 The Informer
John Ford (RKO)
1937 Wee Willie Winkie
John Ford (20th Century Fox)
1939 Gunga Din
George Stevens (RKO)
1948 Fort Apache
John Ford (RKO)
1949 She Wore a Yellow Ribbon
John Ford (RKO)
1950 Rio Grande
John Ford (Republic)
1952 The Quiet Man
John Ford (Republic)

ADOLPHE MENJOU

The best-dressed man in Hollywood, the slick, suave and sophisticated ladies' man with the elegant moustache, Adolphe Menjou had one of the longest and most rewarding careers in pictures. At the beginning of his cinema stardom, he gave one of the great performances of the silent cinema in Charles Chaplin's ❯ 1923 **A Woman of Paris** (as the amused and urbane rich protector of Edna Purviance); at the end of his career, he gave an equally memorable performance in Stanley Kubrick's 1957 **Paths of Glory** (as the corrupt General Broulard who ignores Kirk Douglas's ❯ pleas for mercy). In between he made more than 100 films and was featured in many cinema classics; he was the wealthy sophisticate whom Marlene Dietrich ❯ abandons for Gary Cooper ❯ in **Morocco,** he was the fireball editor in the first version of **The Front Page,** he was the seductive impresario who manoeuvres stage-struck Katharine Hepburn ❯ into an affair in **Morning Glory,** and he was the dapper gambler stuck with little Shirley Temple ❯ in **Little Miss Marker.**

Menjou had a remarkable flair for finding his way into good pictures—among them were Ernst Lubitsch's **The Marriage Circle,** Frank Borzage's **A Farewell to Arms** and William Wellman's **A Star is Born.** He was a romantic lead in the '20s, a character lead in the '30s, and a featured performer until the end of his life. He was co-starred with Gloria Swanson ❯ in 1941, when she made her come-back in **Father Takes a Wife,** he was the best criminal lawyer in town, delightfully defending wise-cracking showgirl Ginger Rogers ❯ in **Roxie Hart,** and he was the scheming producer putting the show together with Frank Sinatra ❯ in **Step Lively.**

Menjou was born in Pittsburgh, Pennsylvania, on February 18, 1890, and was on stage before going into films. He began as an extra with Vitagraph in 1912, but did not become a major silent star until the '20s, with **A Woman of Paris.** He appeared in every kind of film in his long career, from musicals in the '30s (**Gold Diggers of 1935, One Hundred Men and a Girl**) to thrillers in the '50s (**The Sniper, Man on a Tightrope**). He published his best-dressed auto-biography in 1952 (*It Took Nine Tailors*) and made his last film in 1960 (**Pollyanna**). He died in 1963.

BEST FILMS:
1923 A Woman of Paris
Charles Chaplin (United Artists)
1924 The Marriage Circle
Ernst Lubitsch (Warner Brothers)
1930 Morocco
Josef von Sternberg (Paramount)

Above: Adolphe Menjou in one of his early films, the 1924 Ernst Lubitsch comedy **The Marriage Circle,** *co-starring Florence Vidor and Marie Prevost.*

1931 The Front Page
Lewis Milestone (United Artists)
1933 Morning Glory
Lowell Sherman (RKO)
1934 Little Miss Marker
Alexander Hall (Paramount)
1937 A Star is Born
William Wellman (United Artists)
1937 Stage Door
Gregory La Cava (RKO)
1942 Roxie Hart
William Wellman (20th Century Fox)
1952 The Sniper
Edward Dmytryk (Columbia)
1957 Paths of Glory
Stanley Kubrick (United Artists)

MICKEY MOUSE

Mickey Mouse was one of the most famous movie stars in the world in the 1930s, right up there with Garbo » and Gable », and he won a special Academy Award for his creator Walt Disney in 1932. He was the first cartoon character to have a real personality and in many ways was the *alter ego* of Disney, who did his voice until the '40s. He starred in the first sound cartoon, **Steamboat Willie** (1928), and it was through his fame that the Disney organisation became truly successful. He starred in 130 films between 1928 and 1953 and although his screen personality is less popular today, in the wake of so many other Disney creations, he remains the first and the greatest of them. He was born in 1927, the joint brainchild of Ub Iwerks (who designed him and animated his first pictures) and Disney (who originally thought him up and created his personality). His first films were **Plane Crazy** (imitating Lindbergh) and **Gallupin' Gaucho** (imitating Douglas Fairbanks Snr »), both made as silents in 1928,

Above: Mickey Mouse was at his most memorable in **The Sorcerer's Apprentice.** *Right: Donald Duck replaced Mickey as Disney's top star.*

but not released until after the success of **Steamboat Willie** (and with added soundtracks). Mickey's rise to fame was extremely rapid; by 1932 he had been featured in *Time* magazine and given an Oscar. Iwerks was enticed away from the studio soon after the Mouse's success, and it was left to other animators and artists to make his greatest films, although the creative mind behind him was always Disney's. Mickey was fairly mischievous in his early films, but soon became a symbol of the ordinary little man, a "representative" American, and had to behave properly. As this also made him a little dull, new characters were created who could behave nastily in ways Mickey couldn't.

By the end of the '30s, Donald Duck had overtaken Mickey in popularity, and in the '40s many of the best Disney cartoons featured Goofy. Minnie had joined Mickey in **Steamboat Willie** (1928) Goofy was first seen in the 1932 **Mickey's Revue,** and Donald made his first appearance in the 1934

The Wise Little Hen. Eventually Mickey became almost the ringmaster of the Disney circus of characters, introducing others and letting the humour revolve around them. He first co-starred with Donald Duck and Goofy in the 1934 **Orpnan's Benefit;** they also appeared together in many later films, including the 1947 feature **Fun and Fancy Free.** The Duck could be much nastier and more temperamental than the Mouse, and Goofy could be much dumber. All three continued to be stars of films for many years. Mickey, who gave his name to the technique of strictly timed rhythmical synchronisation of movement to music originated by the Disney organisation ("mickey mousing"), was seen at his best in the musically-orientated 1935 **The Band Concert**

© Walt Disney Productions

(his first colour film) and in the brilliant 1937 **Clock Cleaners.** He was featured in the 1940 **Fantasia** in the segment directed by James Algar and based on Dukas' *The Sorcerer's Apprentice.* In the '40s, many of his films were supervised by Charles Nichols, who was responsible for the fine 1948 **Mickey and the Seal.**

Donald Duck's rising popularity in the late 1930s continued right through to the '60s, with the addition of his nephews, his Uncle Scrooge and two delightful chipmunks called Chip 'n' Dale. Some of the greatest Disney cartoons were the Goofy "training films" made under Jack Kinney's supervision in the '40s, beginning

with **How To Ride A Horse** in 1941 and including such classics as **Olympic Champ** and **Hold That Pose.** Pluto the Pup also starred in his own films and won a certain popularity. (As Mickey's films were joint efforts under Disney's supervision, the only "director" listed below is Disney himself).

BEST FILMS:
1932 The Whoopee Party
Walt Disney (Disney)
1933 Mad Doctor
Walt Disney (Disney)
1934 Mickey's Steam Roller
Walt Disney (Disney)
1935 The Band Concert
Walt Disney (Disney)
1936 Mickey's Circus
Walt Disney (Disney)
1936 Thru the Mirror
Walt Disney (Disney)
1937 Lonesome Ghosts
Walt Disney (Disney)
1937 Clock Cleaners
Walt Disney (Disney)
1940 Fantasia
Walt Disney (Disney)
1947 Fun and Fancy Free
Walt Disney (Disney)

TOSHIRO MIFUNE

Toshiro Mifune is the No 1 modern star of the Japanese cinema, the leading exponent of the samurai film, and the only Eastern actor to win wide renown in the West. His position is comparable to John Wayne's » in the US: both are primarily stars of action films and no other actors can match them for longevity and popularity. Mifune, however, has a much wider range than Wayne and is entirely satisfactory in films based on Gorky (**The Lower Depths**), Dostoevsky (**The Idiot**) or Shakespeare (**Throne of Blood**). Western audiences first became aware of him through the screening of **Rashomon** at the Venice Film Festival, but he had been an important star since the 1948 **Drunken Angel;** both these films were made by Japan's greatest living director, Akira Kurosawa, who starred Mifune in 16 of his films, one of the greatest relationships in world cinema. Their major international successes together were **Rashomon, The Seven Samurai, Throne of Blood, Yojimbo** and **Sanjuro,** all essentially samurai films despite their different structures. Mifune has become the very embodiment of the samurai swordsman, starring in dozens of other samurai films for lesser-known directors and producing three samurai TV series for his own studio. It would be as difficult to conceive of the films of this genre without his presence as to imagine the Western without John Wayne.

Mifune was born in Tsingtao, China, in 1920 (his parents were doctors), and returned to Japan for war service from 1940 to

125

1945. He made his film début in the 1946 **The Foolish Times** and became a star two years later as a gangster in **Drunken Angel** for Kurosawa. Their collaboration was confirmed the following year with **The Stray Dog** and continued until the 1965 **Red Beard**, though Mifune worked with many other directors, and often on samurai films. He gave outstanding performances in Kobayashi's **Rebellion** and (in a small role) Mizoguchi's **Life of Oharu**. He has occasionally worked in English-language films, including John Frankenheimer's 1966 **Grand Prix**, John Boorman's 1967 **Hell in the Pacific** and Jack Smight's 1976 **Battle of Midway**. His career in the '70s remains strong.

BEST FILMS:
1950 Rashomon
Akira Kurosawa (Daiei)
1954 The Seven Samurai
Akira Kurosawa (Toho)
1957 Throne of Blood
Akira Kurosawa (Toho)
1957 The Lower Depths
Akira Kurosawa (Toho)
1958 The Hidden Fortress
Akira Kurosawa (Toho)
1961 Yojimbo
Akira Kurosawa (Toho)
1962 Sanjuro
Akira Kurosawa (Toho)
1963 High and Low
Akira Kurosawa (Toho)
1965 Red Beard
Akira Kurosawa (Toho)
1967 Rebellion
Masaki Kobayashi (Mifune)

*Below: Toshiro Mifune is the greatest star in the Japanese cinema and by far the best known in the West, especially for his Kurosawa masterpieces. Below right: Toshiro Mifune was literally turned into a human pin cushion at the end of Kurosawa's **Throne of Blood**, a Noh version of Macbeth.*

RAY MILLAND

There was always something weak, insecure, even a little suspect, about Ray Milland's ready smile. It didn't emerge in his earlier films—he was mostly just an ordinary though quite presentable leading man in his '30s pictures—but Mitchell Leisen presumably saw it (he featured him in seven pictures). Billy Wilder brought it to the forefront, however, first in **The Major and the Minor** (with Milland worried about his feelings for a 12-year-old girl who turns out to be grown-up Ginger Rogers ❯ in disguise) and then, for all the world to see, as the alcoholic hiding his booze in **The Lost Weekend** (for which he won the Academy Award). This darker side of his persona was nicely exploited by other directors, too, notably Fritz Lang in **The Ministry of Fear** (fearfully involved with spies); John Farrow in **Alias Nick Beal** (with Milland as an insinuating Devil), Alfred Hitchcock in **Dial M for Murder** (plotting to kill wife Grace Kelly ❯) and Roger Corman in two fine low-budget horror films, **The Premature Burial** and **The Man with the X-Ray Eyes**. The sinister side of his screen image has continued to be important right up to the '70s and can be seen in **Love Story** (as Ryan O'Neal's ❯ father), **The Last Tycoon** (as an East Coast financier in Hollywood), and the TV film series **Rich Man, Poor Man.**

Milland was born in Neath, Wales, on January 3, 1905, with the name Reginald Truscott-Jones. He made his début in a small role in the 1929 British picture **The Plaything** and made a few more films in England, though most of his career was in Hollywood. He quickly established himself as a leading man, notably with Claudette Colbert ❯ in **The Gilded Lily** and Dorothy Lamour ❯ in **The Jungle Princess,** but his most regular director was Leisen, beginning with **Four Hours to Kill** (1935) and continuing with **Easy Living, Arise My Love** and **I Wanted Wings** in the early period. He was excellent as one of the noble brothers in William Wellman's **Beau Geste,** back in Britain in Anthony Asquith's version of **French Without Tears,** and battling a monstrous squid in the Cecil B. De Mille ocean epic **Reap the Wild Wind.** Leisen featured him again in **Lady in the Dark** (with Ginger Rogers), **Kitty** (with Paulette Goddard ❯) and **Golden Earrings** (with Marlene Dietrich ❯). His career has had its ups and downs since the '40s, but he has made many good films, turned director himself (notably on the 1958 **The Safecracker**), and has retained his impetus as a star.

BEST FILMS:
1940 Arise My Love
Mitchell Leisen (Paramount)
1942 Reap the Wild Wind
Cecil B. De Mille (Paramount)
1942 The Major and the Minor
Billy Wilder (Paramount)
1944 Lady in the Dark
Mitchell Leisen (Paramount)
1944 The Ministry of Fear
Fritz Lang (Paramount)
1945 The Lost Weekend
Billy Wilder (Paramount)
1945 Kitty
Mitchell Leisen (Paramount)

*Above: Ray Milland was usually jumpy in his films, but especially in Lang's **The Ministry of Fear.***

1948 The Big Clock
John Farrow (Paramount)
1954 Dial M for Murder
Alfred Hitchcock (Warner Brothers)
1964 The Man with the X-Ray Eyes
Roger Corman (AIP)

ANN MILLER

Ann Miller may not have been as big a musical star as Eleanor Powell ❯, but she certainly took over her position as the most exciting tap dancer in the movies. When she sizzled across the screen in the 1948 **Easter Parade** dancing to *Shakin' The Blues Away,* it seemed as if a new star was about to be born after a very long apprenticeship in B-musicals. Unfortunately, MGM never really used the long-legged Texas lady as they should have; despite her memorable place in the iconography of the screen musical, her film career ended in 1956. She wasn't actually the lead in any of her MGM musicals, but she came

close to being the best thing on view in many of them; her greatest moments were in **On the Town** (singing and tap-dancing *Prehistoric Man* in the Museum of Anthropological History) and **Kiss Me Kate** (four outstanding numbers, but especially the torrid *Too Darn Hot*), although she was also dazzling in **Deep in My Heart**, where her *It* Charleston number is the highlight of the film. One can hardly say that MGM wasted her, but one wishes for much more.

She was born Lucy Ann Collier in Houston, Texas, on April 12, 1919, began dancing at the age of five, and made her screen début in **New Face of 1937.** She was very good as the ballet-mad daughter in **You Can't Take It With You,** joined the Marx Brothers ➤ for **Room Service,** and then had a big success dancing on Broadway in

Above: Ann Miller, the top tap dancer of the '50s, shows off her legs in her last MGM musical, Roy Rowland's 1955 **Hit the Deck.** *She retired in 1956.*

George White's Scandals. She made a lot of musicals in the '40s and was good in them, but little attention was paid to such small-budget delights as **Reveille with Beverly, Jam Session** and **Carolina Blues,** so she didn't really make much of an impact before **Easter Parade.** Even then, she was often thrown away in secondary parts, supporting Red Skelton, Esther Williams ➤ or Jane Powell, but her impact was such that she is remembered as much as the stars. Her last film was **The Great American Pastime** in 1956.

She has been married three times, always to millionaires, and has done some stage and television work in recent years.

BEST FILMS:
1938 You Can't Take It With You
Frank Capra (Columbia)
1943 Reveille with Beverly
Charles Barton (Columbia)
1948 Easter Parade
Charles Walters (MGM)

1949 On The Town
Gene Kelly & Stanley Donen (MGM)
1951 Texas Carnival
Charles Walters (MGM)
1951 Two Tickets to Broadway
James Kern (RKO)
1952 Lovely To Look At
Mervyn LeRoy (MGM)
1953 Kiss Me Kate
George Sidney (MGM)
1953 Small Town Girl
Leslie Kardos (MGM)
1954 Deep in My Heart
Stanley Donen (MGM)
1956 The Opposite Sex
David Miller (MGM)

JOHN MILLS

John Mills has such a self-effacing, quietly heroic and worried screen persona that it is easy to undervalue his contribution to the British cinema over the past 45

Below: John Mills and Dirk Bogarde co-starred in Basil Dearden's 1952 IRA thriller **The Gentle Gunman.** *As usual he was worried, quietly heroic and just a little self-effacing, but his screen persona conceals one of the most continuously successful British actors.*

years. In fact, he was a top ten British box office star for most of the years from 1945 to 1958 and capped his career by winning an Oscar in 1970 as Best Supporting Actor for **Ryan's Daughter.** He hasn't unfortunately, made very many good films, but there are half a dozen that are likely to survive. The film that made him a major star was Gilliat's excellent 1944 **Waterloo Road,** as a British soldier whose wife has been unfaithful to him. He was in top form in the Terence Rattigan-scripted **The Way to the Stars** and then began his long and rewarding association with director David Lean in the 1946 **Great Expectations.** He played Pip in this film and Lean later used him as the much-put-upon cobbler in **Hobson's Choice,** who finally dominates the outrageous Charles Laughton ➤. Finally, Lean cast him as the village idiot in **Ryan's Daughter,** an "acting" job less interesting than his more natural worried hero performances. He was exceptionally good as **Scott of the Antarctic** and as a POW in **The Colditz Story,** and fine in more straightforwardly heroic films like **Above Us the Waves.** He

seems to have been in uniform in a large proportion of his films. His finest performance was probably in the powerful **Tunes of Glory** as a disciplined officer at loggerheads with Alec Guinness ➤.

Mills was born in Felixstowe, Suffolk, England, on February 22, 1908, and was working on stage by 1929. His career was assisted by Noël Coward ➤ and he made his film début in the 1932 **The Midshipmaid;** he appeared in many '30s and early '40s films, including **Goodbye Mr Chips** and **In Which We Serve,** but did not become a major star until 1944. His career has continued right through the '70s, including such films as **The Human Factor, The Big Sleep** and **The Water Babies.** He is married to writer Mary Hayley Bell—their daughters Hayley and Juliet have both become screen actresses—and he was knighted in 1977.

BEST FILMS:
1944 Waterloo Road
Sidney Gilliat (GFD)
1945 The Way to the Stars
Anthony Asquith (Two Cities)
1946 Great Expectations
David Lean (Rank)
1948 Scott of the Antarctic
Charles Frend (Ealing)
1949 The History of Mr Polly
Anthony Pelissier (Two Cities)
1953 Hobson's Choice
David Lean (British Lion)
1954 The Colditz Story
Guy Hamilton (British Lion)
1960 Tunes of Glory
Ronald Neame (United Artists)
1969 Oh! What A Lovely War
Richard Attenborough (Paramount)
1970 Ryan's Daughter
David Lean (MGM)
1973 Oklahoma Crude
Stanley Kramer (Columbia)

CARMEN MIRANDA

If ever there is a Museum of the American Cinema, then a whole display case will have to be devoted to Carmen Miranda and her extravagant costumes in '40s musicals. Hollywood has never had anyone remotely like her before or since. Her head was

Above: Carmen Miranda, a curio of the cinema. Her extravagant costumes helped her to become one of the top stars of the '40s.

usually topped with a turban bearing bananas and other exotic fruits, her body was adorned with outsize outlandish jewellery, and her costumes were riots of flamboyant colour. She was an immediate star from her first American film, the 1940 **Down Argentine Way,** singing *South American Way.* 20th Century Fox immediately exploited her as much as possible in their musicals of the war years (aiming films at the Latin American market, with Europe closed to them), including **That Night in Rio, Weekend in Havana** and **Springtime in the Rockies.** The apotheosis of her style came in Busby Berkeley's incredible production number for her in **The Gang's All Here,** *The Lady with the Tutti Frutti Hat,* with giant bananas and strawberries used as ultimate Freudian kitsch. She had an extraordinary way of gyrating her hips, rolling her eyes and moving her hands, legs and arms all at the same time, while belting out her novelty Brazilian songs non-stop. It was a limited characterisation, but it was fun and no one could ignore it.

Although she came to Hollywood from Brazil, Miranda was born in the small town of Marco de Canavezes in Portugal on February 9, 1909, with the name Maria do Carmo Miranda da Cunha. Her parents emigrated to Brazil and she became a top singing, record and movie star in South America before going to Broadway for a musical. Her success in films obviously had to be limited; she wasn't much use in the plot part of her films, and her vogue died almost as soon as the war was over (and the European markets re-opened). She made only ten films at Fox and four more after she left that studio, dying of a heart attack in 1955 following a TV show.

BEST FILMS:
1940 Down Argentine Way
Irving Cummings (20th Century Fox)
1941 That Night in Rio
Irving Cummings (20th Century Fox)
1941 Weekend in Havana
Walter Lang (20th Century Fox)
1942 Springtime in the Rockies
Irving Cummings (20th Century Fox)
1943 The Gang's All Here
Busby Berkeley (20th Century Fox)
1944 Four Jills in a Jeep
William A. Seiter (20th Century Fox)
1944 Greenwich Village
Walter Lang (20th Century Fox)
1944 Something for the Boys
Lewis Seiler (20th Century Fox)
1945 Doll Face
Lewis Seiler (20th Century Fox)
1946 If I'm Lucky
Lewis Seiler (20th Century Fox)

THOMAS MITCHELL

One of the few character actors to become a star in his own right, Mitchell's performances are memorable in almost every film he made. He was born in Elizabeth, New Jersey, on July 11, 1892, of Irish-American parents, and was a theatre actor, director and writer before starting his film career at the age of 44, in **Craig's Wife** in 1936. His New York theatre roots could be seen in films like **Our Town** and **Angels Over Broadway,** and his greatest period was in the late '30s, when he won a Supporting Actor Academy Award for his unforgettable whisky-soaked Doc Boone in John Ford's **Stagecoach,** had another AA nomination for Ford's **The Hurricane,** and symbolised the best aspects of the old aristocratic South as Scarlett O'Hara's father in **Gone With the Wind.** He was an extremely versatile actor, able to play virtually any kind of role, but he was at his best as worldly-wise and weary professionals, who had seen a lot of life but were still a long way from down. The best embodiment of this was in Howard

Hawks' **Only Angels Have Wings,** as an ageing aviator with failing sight faking his way through eye tests to keep on flying. He was outstanding in newspaper roles (he had himself once been a newspaperman) and was seen at his finest as an honest reporter chasing a killer in Fritz Lang's **While the City Sleeps.** He was superb as the son whom Beulah Bondi has to leave in Leo McCarey's **Make Way for Tomorrow,** as the King of the Beggars in **The Hunchback of Notre Dame,** as the detective after one of Olivia de Havilland's » two manifestations in **The Dark Mirror,** and as an honest man corrupted by Devil Ray Milland » in **Alias Nick Beal.** He made notable contributions to many classic films, especially those directed by Frank Capra (**Lost Horizon, Mr Smith Goes to Washington, It's a Wonderful Life**) and John Ford (**Stagecoach, The Hurricane, The Long Voyage Home**). His last picture was Frank Capra's **A Pocketful of Miracles** in 1961. He died in 1962.

BEST FILMS:
1937 Lost Horizon
Frank Capra (Columbia)
1937 Make Way for Tomorrow
Leo McCarey (Paramount)
1937 The Hurricane
John Ford (Goldwyn/United Artists)
1939 Stagecoach
John Ford (Wanger/United Artists)
1939 Only Angels Have Wings
Howard Hawks (Columbia)
1939 Mr Smith Goes to Washington
Frank Capra (Columbia)
1939 The Hunchback of Notre Dame
William Dieterle (RKO)
1939 Gone With the Wind
Victor Fleming (Selznick/MGM)
1949 Alias Nick Beal
John Farrow (Paramount)
1956 While the City Sleeps
Fritz Lang (RKO)

Below: Thomas Mitchell (front) starred in three John Ford films, including **The Long Voyage Home.**

ROBERT MITCHUM

Robert Mitchum was one of the most important American screen actors to emerge in the 1940s (not that the critics really noticed) and is now beginning to move towards a position analogous to Humphrey Bogart's ». A Mitchum cult like Bogart's has not yet developed, but it is a strong probability for the 1980s. Both actors, interestingly, have portrayed Raymond Chandler's mythical private detective Philip Marlowe (Bogart in the 1946 **The Big Sleep** and Mitchum in the 1976 **Farewell My Lovely** and 1978 **The Big Sleep**), one of the cinema's greatest myth figures. Mitchum, like Bogart, has created one of the great screen personae, sleepy-eyed but watchful, laconic but never lack-lustre, hiding toughness and sometimes menace behind a facade of apparent weariness. Like most other great American screen actors, he denigrates his own ability and hides behind a "natural" performance. Charles Laughton » was not deceived. He described Mitchum as "one of the best actors in the world" and directed him in what is not only Mitchum's greatest performance but one of the cinema's great performances, the crazed and terrifying preacher of **The Night of the Hunter.** This underrated film is surely one of the cinema's major works, and Mitchum's menacing performance is central to it. The letters LOVE and HATE which are tattooed on his hands in this film could well represent the ambiguous source of the power behind his screen personality in his major films, grimly revenging his father's killers in **Pursued** or romantically involved with Shirley MacLaine » in **Two For The Seesaw.** Like Bogart, he is essentially the bad

Above: Robert Mitchum appeared in a large number of fine films like this one, Nicholas Ray's 1952 Western **The Lusty Men,** *in which he co-starred with Arthur Kennedy and Susan Hayward.*

guy turned hero, although his out-and-out villains (**Cape Fear, The Night of the Hunter**) are much more frightening than Bogart's.

Mitchum was born in Bridgeport, Connecticut, on August 6, 1917, and had a long period as labourer, boxer and writer before making his cinema début as an extra in the 1943 **Hoppy Serves a Writ.** He came up through B-pictures and, indeed, many of his finest films were relatively small-budget movies that attracted little critical attention on their release. The first film in which he was really noticed was William Wellman's 1945 **The Story of G.I. Joe,** for which he won an Oscar nomination as the Best Supporting Actor (his only nomination). His films of the late '40s and early '50s were key movies in the development of the cinema of the time, although recognition of that fact has only recently emerged; they include films by Raoul Walsh (**Pursued**), Otto Preminger (**Angel Face, River of No Return**), Edward Dmytryk (**Till The End of Time, Crossfire**), Vincente Minnelli (**Undercurrent**), Don Siegel (**The Big Steal**), Jacques Tourneur (**Out of the Past**), Nicholas Ray (**The Lusty Men**), Robert Wise (**Blood on the Moon**) and many others. His major period of popularity began in the mid-'50s with films like **River of No Return** with Marilyn Monroe » and **Not as a Stranger,** and was confirmed in the '60s with superb performances in **The Sundowners**

Left: Yves Montand has one of the most "lived-in" faces in French (and world) cinema; here he is seen in André Delvaux's acclaimed **Un Soir . . . Un Train.**

and **El Dorado.** Not all of his films, obviously, have been good in themselves, but Mitchum himself is never less than excellent and has often garnered acclaim from critics for films they haven't particularly liked. His '70s career has continued as strong as ever, with notable performances in **The Friends of Eddie Coyle, The Yakuza, Battle of Midway, The Last Tycoon** and the two Philip Marlowe pictures.

BEST FILMS:
1945 The Story of G.I. Joe
William Wellman (United Artists)
1947 Pursued
Raoul Walsh (Warner Brothers)
1947 Crossfire
Edward Dmytryk (RKO)
1947 Out of the Past
Jacques Tourneur (RKO)
1948 Blood on the Moon
Robert Wise (RKO)
1952 Angel Face
Otto Preminger (RKO)
1952 The Lusty Men
Nicholas Ray (RKO)
1954 The Track of the Cat
William Wellman (Warner Brothers)
1954 The Night of the Hunter
Charles Laughton (United Artists)
1960 The Sundowners
Fred Zinnemann (Warner Brothers)
1960 Home From The Hill
Vincente Minnelli (MGM)
1962 Two For The Seesaw
Robert Wise (United Artists)
1967 El Dorado
Howard Hawks (Paramount)
1970 Ryan's Daughter
David Lean (MGM)
1975 Farewell My Lovely
Dick Richards (Avco-Embassy)

MARILYN MONROE
see **Modern Stars**

YVES MONTAND

Yves Montand has a kind of three-in-the-morning, world-weary screen image, sophisticated, self-made and flavoured with political commitment and Gallic nonchalance. He was one of the first French actors to establish an international reputation after the war (in **The Wages of Fear** in 1953) and he remains today one of the most widely-known and highest-paid French film stars. He has worked in the American cinema a number of times (opposite Marilyn Monroe ➤ in **Let's Make Love** and opposite Barbra Streisand ➤ in **On A Clear Day You Can See Forever**), but it is for his French films that he is best known, even outside France. The most famous and the most widely shown have been the political thrillers he made with Costa-Gavras, especially the Oscar-winning **Z.** He first worked with Gavras on **The Sleeping Car Murders,** a nicely complex, non-political thriller in which he portrayed the investigating police inspector. In **Z** he was the socialist politician, victim of the assassination plot; in **The Confession** he was a top party man in Eastern Europe, "persuaded" to make a false confession by Communist officials; and in **State of Siege** he was a CIA agent captured by Tupamaros. His greatest performance, however, was in Alain Resnais' **La Guerre est Finie,** as a tired Spanish revolutionary living in Paris, still struggling for the cause although he knows the war was lost long ago. He was also excellent as a professor in Delvaux' strange **Un Soir . . . Un Train** and as a gangster in Melville's exciting **Le Cercle Rouge.** He has

come to represent French attitudes as much as any other actor working today.

Montand was born in Italy on October 13, 1921, as Ivo Livi, and his Jewish parents moved to Marseilles when he was a child to get away from Mussolini. He left school at 11, worked at odd jobs, started singing in music hall at 18, and became the protégé of Edith Piaf, who got him his first film role in the 1946 **Etoile sans Lumière.** His second film, Marcel Carné's **Les Portes de la Nuit,** led to his becoming famous—but as a singer rather than a film star. His version of the Prévert-Kosma classic *Les Feuilles Mortes* (Autumn Leaves) was a huge hit and he was a major singer by 1951, when he married Simone Signoret ➤. **The Wages of Fear** made his reputation as a film star, and this was reinforced by his performances opposite Michèle Morgan ➤ in **Marguerite**

de la Nuit and with his wife in the Arthur Miller-derived **Les Sorcières de Salem.** His brief stay in Hollywood in the early '60s was not successful (other films included **My Geisha** and **Sanctuary**) and he has mainly worked in France since. He has been willing to act in non-commercial projects like Jean-Luc Godard's **Tout Va Bien,** and to help relatively unestablished directors make big films: Claude Sautet in **César et Rosalie** and Alain Corneau with **Police Python 357.** In 1978 he starred in Joseph Losey's **Les Routes de Sud.**

BEST FILMS:
1953 Le Salaire de la Peur (The Wages of Fear)
Henri-Georges Clouzot (CICC/Film Sonar)
1960 Let's Make Love
George Cukor (20th Century Fox)
1965 Compartiment-Teurs (The Sleeping Car Murders)
Costa-Gavras (PECF)
1966 La Guerre est Finie (The War Is Over)
Alain Resnais (Sotracima-Argos-Europa)
1968 Un Soir . . . Un Train
André Delvaux (Parc-Fox)
1969 Z
Costa-Gavras (Reggane-ONCIC)
1970 L'Aveu (The Confession)
Costa-Gavras (Pomereu-Corona)
1971 Le Cercle Rouge (The Red Circle)
Jean-Pierre Melville (Corona-Selenia)
1973 César and Rosalie
Claude Sautet (Fildebroc-UPF)
1976 Police Python 357
Alain Corneau (Albina-Rizzoli)

MICHÈLE MORGAN

One of the most enduring images of the French cinema is that of Michèle Morgan in beret and trenchcoat as the doom-laden heroine of **Quai des Brumes.** She was only 18 years old when she made this film for Marcel Carné, but it helped make her the most popular of all French film actresses for three decades (she was still tops in 1970). Her partnership with Jean Gabin ➤ in this film was so mesmeric that they were reteamed many times, but the chemistry was never quite as powerful again. She should have become the Garbo ➤ of France (she seemed to have the mysterious allure), but her career was frittered away in too many poor films with only occasional highlights like René Clair's bittersweet **Summer Manoeuvres** (as the object of a bet by Gérard Philipe). She fled to Hollywood

Left: Michèle Morgan stayed a top star in France for 30 years.

from France in 1940, two days before the Nazi occupation, and was given reasonable if hardly outstanding roles in films like **Joan of Paris** (as a Resistance fighter sacrificing herself for Paul Henreid) and **Passage to Marseilles** (more of the same, with Humphrey Bogart »).

Morgan complained later that she was not well used by the American cinema, returning to Europe in 1946 to make **La Symphonie Pastorale.** It won her the Best Actress Award at the Cannes Film Festival and restored her European reputation as a major star. She made **The Fallen Idol** in England (as Ralph Richardson's mistress), and the big budget **Fabiola** in Italy (as an ancient Roman aristocrat, opposite Henri Vidal, whom she later married). She was just as popular as ever in France, despite the fact that most of her films were simply vehicles for the *grande dame* of the French cinema, which she had now become. Among her reasonably interesting recent films are Claude Chabrol's **Landru** and Mark Robson's **Lost Command.** Michèle Morgan began life as Simone Roussel in Neuilly-sur-Seine in 1920, and began to appear in films as an extra in 1935. Her first important roles were opposite Raimu » in **Gribouille** (1937) and Charles Boyer » in **Orage** (1938), both directed by Marc Allégret. Her next film was **Quai des Brumes (Port of Shadows),** as the sad, waif-like ward of Michel Simon », loved by Jean Gabin; she was never to be better during the next 30 years. She published her memoirs in 1976 and is today semi-retired.

BEST FILMS:
1937 Gribouille
Marc Allégret (Lauer)
1938 Quai des Brumes
Marcel Carné (Rabinovich)
1941 Remorques
Jean Grémillon (Sedif)
1942 Joan of Paris
Robert Stevenson (RKO)
1944 Passage to Marseilles
Michael Curtiz (Warner Brothers)
1946 La Symphonie Pastorale
Jean Delannoy (Gibe)
1948 The Fallen Idol
Carol Reed (British Lion)
1949 Fabiola
Alessandro Blasetti (Universalia)
1953 Les Orgueilleux
Yves Allégret (CICC-Chrysaor-Lana)
1955 Les Grandes Manoeuvres
René Clair (Filmsonor-Rizzoli)
1975 Le Chat et la Souris
Claude Lelouch (Films 13)

PAUL MUNI

The "great actor" of '30s films, fawned over by critics, adored by audiences and showered with acting prizes for his boring biographies of "important" people like Pasteur, Zola and Juarez. He is remembered today, however, for being one of the first great

screen gangsters, in Howard Hawks' **Scarface,** and for his convincing man-on-the-run in Mervyn LeRoy's **I Am a Fugitive from a Chain Gang.** His best period was during his earlier years at Warner Brothers, before he was weighed down with prestige, when he also made tough social melodramas like Michael Curtiz's **Black Fury** (about the situation of coal miners) and emotional melodramas like **Bordertown** (involved in a love triangle with Bette Davis » and Eugene Pallette). Muni carried the theatrical baggage of his earlier stage career into the movies with him (including an excessive love of make-up and a propensity for the "old men" roles that he had specialised in in Yiddish theatre), but under the control of a good director he could be outstanding. His thinly-disguised

portrayal of Al Capone in **Scarface** is one of the great gangster portraits of the cinema, arrogant and power hungry, ruthless enough to murder his rivals, vainly ambitious and too insensitive to realise his own incestuous feelings for his sister. Film gangsters after Muni could grow in characterisation because he had shown the way.

Muni was born in Lemberg, Austria, on September 22, 1895, as Muni Weisenfreund, and came to the US as a child with his actor parents. He was in Yiddish theatre for most of his stage career, before making his film début in 1929 in William K. Howard's **The Valiant** (portraying a murderer and getting an Oscar nomination). He was both a big prestige actor and a top box office attraction in the '30s and won an Academy Award for **The Story of Louis**

Left: Paul Muni as the man on the run who steals to survive in Mervyn LeRoy's 1932 **I Am a Fugitive from a Chain Gang.**

Pasteur in 1935. He was also the star of **The Life of Emile Zola** (best picture Oscar) and **Juarez,** and helped Luise Rainer get an Academy Award by portraying her Chinese husband in **The Good Earth.** He was much better as a married doctor in love with a young girl in the 1940 **We Are Not Alone.** His career tailed off after that, but he was enjoyably awful in one of the great kitsch movies, teaching Chopin to play the piano in **A Song to Remember.** His last film, and one of his strongest performances, was the 1959 **The Last Angry Man,** in which he plays an ageing slum doctor. He died in 1967.

BEST FILMS:
1932 Scarface
Howard Hawks (Hughes/United Artists)
1932 I Am a Fugitive from a Chain Gang
Mervyn Leroy (Warner Brothers)
1935 Bordertown
Archie Mayo (Warner Brothers)
1935 Black Fury
Michael Curtiz (Warner Brothers)
1935 The Story of Louis Pasteur
William Dieterle (Warner Brothers)
1937 The Good Earth
Sidney Franklin (MGM)
1937 The Life of Emile Zola
William Dieterle (Warner Brothers)
1939 Juarez
William Dieterle (Warner Brothers)
1940 We Are Not Alone
Edmund Goulding (Warner Brothers)
1959 The Last Angry Man
Daniel Mann (Columbia)

ANNA NEAGLE

Anna Neagle has a rather special place in British cinema. She didn't make any really good films, she had no screen persona of any importance and she was never popular outside Britain. Yet she was warmly loved by her public, was the top female star in England for seven years, and brought a kind of gaiety and glamour to the British cinema when it most needed it, during the Depression and post-war years. She was most popular teamed with Michael Wilding in the late '40s, in such escapist romances as **Piccadilly Incident, Spring in Park Lane** and **Maytime in Mayfair.** Much of her career consisted of impersonating famous ladies, notably Queen Victoria (**Victoria the Great, Sixty Glorious Years**), **Nell Gwynn,** Peg Woffington (**Peg of Old Drury**) and **Nurse Edith Cavell** in the '30s, and Amy Johnson (**They Flew Alone**), Florence Nightingale (**The Lady with the Lamp**) and **Odette** in the

Left: Anna Neagle and Michael Wilding in Herbert Wilcox's 1952 **Derby Day**; *gaiety and glamour in postwar Britain.*

'40s and '50s. Her best films are probably her musicals, however, teamed with Jack Buchanan ❯ in **Goodnight Vienna**, Ray Milland ❯ in **Irene** and Ray Bolger in **Sunny.** Her career was masterminded by Herbert Wilcox, who directed all her films from 1932 on and married her in 1943.

She began life as Marjorie Robertson in Forest Gate, London, in 1904, was a Cochran "Young Lady" and show girl in the '20s, and made her film début in 1930 in **Should a Doctor Tell?** She was briefly in Hollywood at the beginning of the war, but was not popular and returned to the UK for the rest of her career.

Her cheerful gentility lost its attraction in the '50s and she made her last film in 1959, **The Lady is a Square,** opposite Frankie Vaughan. She went back on stage in the '60s for the long-running musical *Charlie Girl,* spryly kicking up her heels to help Wilcox out of a difficult financial situation (he died in 1977). She published her autobiography, *There's Always Tomorrow,* in 1974.

BEST FILMS:
1932 Goodnight Vienna
Herbert Wilcox (B & D)
1934 Nell Gwynne
Herbert Wilcox (B & D)
1937 Victoria the Great
Herbert Wilcox (British Lion)
1938 Sixty Glorious Years
Herbert Wilcox (Imperator)
1940 Irene
Herbert Wilcox (RKO)
1941 Sunny
Herbert Wilcox (RKO)
1946 Piccadilly Incident
Herbert Wilcox (ABP)
1948 Springtime in Park Lane
Herbert Wilcox (British Lion)
1950 Odette
Herbert Wilcox (Wilcox)
1951 The Lady with the Lamp
Herbert Wilcox (British Lion)

PATRICIA NEAL

Patricia Neal is not only one of the best actresses of the modern cinema but also one of the most courageous. She won an Academy Award for her performance in the 1963 **Hud,** experienced three strokes in 1965, fought back from semi-paralysis affecting both speech and movement when most people considered her career was over, returned to the screen in 1968 in **The Subject Was Roses**—and got another Oscar nomination. Neal's intriguing screen persona reflects this courage, but it also reflects her much-publicised relationship with Gary Cooper ❯ in the late '40s, when they fell in love but couldn't marry because of his Catholic wife's refusal to agree to a divorce. In most of her films, Neal portrays a tough-minded independent woman who has a relationship problem with a man. In **The Fountainhead** the man was architect Gary Cooper; she

Above: Patricia Neal with Paul Newman in **Hud** *(1963).*

was rich and secretly in love with him. In **Bright Leaf** she was again rich and in love with Cooper. In **A Face in the Crowd** she discovers and promotes TV personality Andy Griffiths and is cast aside by him on his rise to fame. In **Breakfast at Tiffany's** she is the rich lady who keeps (and is rejected by) George Peppard. In **Hud** she was at her very best as the once-bitten-twice-shy housekeeper resisting the advances of Paul Newman ❯ because she knows that ultimately he is not serious. It was a very moving performance and one could suspect that some of it was based on Neal's own experience.

Patricia Neal was born in Packard, Kentucky, on January 20, 1926, studied at Northwestern University, and began acting on Broadway in *The Voice of the Turtle* and *Another Part of the Forest.* Warner Brothers decided to make her into a star, beginning with the 1949 **John Loves Mary** and **The Fountainhead,** but fame was a long time coming; it didn't really arrive until after she left Warners, partially because of adverse affects of the Cooper relationship.

She married British writer Roald Dahl in 1953 and afterwards worked much less in the cinema. Following **Hud,** she was excellent as a navy nurse opposite John Wayne ❯ in **In Harm's Way** and battling with Jack Albertson in **The Subject Was Roses.** She has acted very little in the '70s, but was notable in the British **Baxter!,** the Spanish **B Must Die** and the horror film **Happy Mother's Day, Love George.**

BEST FILMS:
1949 The Fountainhead
King Vidor (Warner Brothers)
1950 The Breaking Point
Michael Curtiz (Warner Brothers)
1951 The Day the Earth Stood Still
Robert Wise (20th Century Fox)
1952 Diplomatic Courier
Henry Hathaway (20th Century Fox)
1957 A Face in the Crowd
Elia Kazan (Warner Brothers)
1961 Breakfast at Tiffany's
Blake Edwards (Paramount)
1963 Hud
Martin Ritt (Paramount)
1965 In Harm's Way
Otto Preminger (Paramount)
1968 The Subject Was Roses
Ulu Grosbard (MGM)
1972 Baxter!
Lionel Jeffries (EMI)

DAVID NIVEN

The impeccable, unflappable, urbane, sophisticated (and some-

times frivolous or slightly brittle) "Englishman" of world cinema for more than 40 years, Niven has starred in over 70 American, British and Italian movies since he began his career in 1935 (as an extra in **Mutiny on the Bounty**), with a goodly number of enjoyable films and some excellent ones. His image as the epitome of the civilised Englishman abroad is most memorable in **Around the World in 80 Days** (1956), in which he plays London club member Phileas Fogg, travelling the globe for a wager but never losing his impeccable coolness even in the most difficult situations. The film won a Best Picture Oscar, and Niven got his own Academy Award two years later for Best Actor in **Separate Tables.** This was a variation on his urbane Englishman role (revealed as not only a bogus Major but also a molester of ladies in cinemas), but he carried it through bravely in true stiff-upper-lip fashion. He was excellent, heroically climbing up the cliffs in **The Guns of Navarone,** surprisingly credible as the doubly-loved father in **Bonjour Tristesse** (1958), and the ultimate in sophisticated charm as the gentleman cat burglar in **The Pink Panther.** He attracted enormous notoriety (of a nice kind) after his role as the suave seducer in **The Moon is Blue,** which contained such naughty words as "virgin" and "mistress". The film had widely publicised censorship problems (it was the first film of importance to be refused an MPA seal and was condemned by the Legion of Decency, amongst others), so it was naturally a popular success. It was fun, but really very innocent—and important for Niven as it put his career back into high gear after a low period.

Born James David Graham Niven in Kirriemuir, Scotland, on March 1, 1910, he began working in movies in Hollywood in 1935, without prior experience. He was, and still is, immensely entertaining company, and was soon signed up by Samuel Goldwyn. He played Bertie Wooster in the 1936 **Thank You, Jeeves** (with Arthur Treacher as Jeeves), but is best remembered from this time for his gallant officer role in **The Charge of the Light Brigade.** He was a delight as Fritz in **The Prisoner of Zenda** (1937) and charmingly debonair opposite French star Annabella ❯ in **Dinner at the Ritz** the same year. His co-star in the 1939 **Bachelor Mother** under Garson Kanin's direction was Ginger Rogers ❯. It was a good comedy, but he was not up to Ronald Colman's ❯ standard when he starred in **Raffles** the following year. He then joined the British Army (serving impeccably

Left: David Niven in urbane top form as Sir James Bond in the spy spoof **Casino Royale** *(1967), whose all-star cast included Deborah Kerr.*

as a major in the Commandos) and was let out to make **The First of the Few** in 1942 (with Leslie Howard ≫ as co-star and director) and **The Way Ahead** (excellent propaganda from Carol Reed). He was in fine form in Michael Powell's post-war **A Matter of Life and Death,** but his career started sputtering after two spectacular failures, **Bonnie Prince Charlie** and **The Elusive Pimpernel. The Moon is Blue** restored his suave, unflappable image, and he has coasted ahead with it superbly ever since. He is always likeable, even in less interesting films, and makes a good job out of the unlikeliest of roles, for example as James Bond in the send-up **Casino Royale** in 1967. None of his recent films has been particularly outstanding, though he did a fine job in Jerzy Skolimowski's flawed **King, Queen, Knave** (1972), had a chance to be Dracula (in **Vampira,** in 1974), and helped Neil Simon mock the murder mystery (in **Murder by Death** in 1975). He has also made TV series and written two best-selling autobiographies (*The Moon's a Balloon* in 1972; *Bring on the Empty Horses* in 1975), which have helped to solidify his witty, urbane image, as did his role in **Death on the Nile.**

BEST FILMS:
1936 The Charge of the Light Brigade
Michael Curtiz (Warner Brothers)
1937 The Prisoner of Zenda
John Cromwell (United Artists)
1938 The Dawn Patrol
Edmund Goulding (Warner Brothers)
1939 Wuthering Heights
William Wyler (United Artists)
1944 The Way Ahead
Carol Reed (Rank)
1946 A Matter of Life and Death
Michael Powell (Rank)
1953 The Moon is Blue
Otto Preminger (United Artists)
1956 Around the World in 80 Days
Michael Anderson (United Artists)
1958 Separate Tables
Delbert Mann (United Artists)
1961 The Guns of Navarone
J. Lee Thompson (Columbia)
1964 The Pink Panther
Blake Edwards (United Artists)

DONALD O'CONNOR

Donald O'Connor was one of the cinema's best musical comedy stars, matching leaps and dances with Gene Kelly ≫ in **Singin' in the Rain,** proving he could be as energetic as Ethel Merman in **Call Me Madam** and holding his own against Bing Crosby ≫ in **Anything Goes.** That he never became one of the major stars of the genre is inexplicable, for he had untapped reserves of singing and dancing talent and an entertaining personality to go with it. It certainly wasn't for lack of trying. He began his cinema career aged 12, in the 1938 **Sing You Sinners** with

Crosby, and was a featured child star long before his great '50s musicals. It's possible that his screen image was damaged by his association with Francis, the Talking Mule, with whom he co-starred in six Universal films in the '50s. They were entertaining, but critically disliked, aimed at the less sophisticated end of the movie audience (O'Connor had to portray a nice but very stupid young man, 647th in his class of 647 at West Point).

He was born as Donald David Dixon Ronald O'Connor in Chicago, Illinois, on August 30, 1925, the son of an acrobat. He joined the family act and then became a very popular teenage film star after his début in **Sing You Sinners.** He was in **On Your Toes, Beau Geste, Mister Big, Follow the Boys** and **Patrick the Great** in his earlier years; in the late '40s he was featured in two minor Universal musicals, **Feudin', Fussin' and A-Fightin'** and **Yes, Sir, That's My Baby,** before making his first **Francis** film in

Above: Donald O'Connor had more than enough energy to cope with any other musical comedy star, as he vividly demonstrated to Gene Kelly and Debbie Reynolds in possibly the greatest of all MGM musicals, **Singin' in the Rain,** *made in 1952.*

1950. It was directed by Arthur Lubin, with the mule's voice supplied by Chill Wills, but O'Connor backed out after six of them when he discovered the mule was getting more fan mail than he was (Mickey Rooney ≫ starred in the last one). The peak of O'Connor's career came in 1952, when he showed himself almost as talented as Kelly in **Singin' in the Rain,** especially in his athletic *Make 'em Laugh* solo. He was good in a series of lesser musicals after that, including **Walking My Baby Back Home** and **I Love Melvin,** and outstanding in both **Call Me Madam** and **There's No Business Like Show Business.** His career faded at the end of the '50s and his last film was opposite Sandra Dee in the 1965 **That Funny Feeling.** He has mainly worked in nightclubs since.

BEST FILMS:
1938 Sing You Sinners
Wesley Ruggles (Paramount)
1948 Feudin', Fussin' and A-Fightin'
George Sherman (Universal-International)
1949 Yes, Sir, That's My Baby
George Sherman (Universal-International)
1950 Francis
Arthur Lubin (Universal-International)
1952 Singin' in the Rain
Gene Kelly & Stanley Donen (MGM)
1953 Call Me Madam
Walter Lang (20th Century Fox)
1953 Walking My Baby Back Home
Lloyd Bacon (Universal-International)
1953 I Love Melvin
Don Weis (MGM)
1954 There's No Business Like Show Business
Walter Lang (20th Century Fox)
1956 Anything Goes
Robert Lewis (Paramount)

MAUREEN O'HARA

Maureen O'Hara was known as the Queen of Technicolor in the 1940s when her flashing green

Above: Maureen O'Hara battled and bickered with John Wayne for many years, to the delight of movie audiences. In Andrew V. McLaglen's **McLintock** *(1963), a kind of Western version of* The Taming of the Shrew, *they are married but still fighting.*

eyes and blazing red hair made her the cinema's most beautiful demonstration of the colour process. She adorned countless swashbucklers in the '40s and '50s—her hot-tempered Irish personality enlivened even drab pictures and colourless leading men—but her screen reputation really rests on her outstanding films for director John Ford and her long screen partnership with John Wayne ≫. It is O'Hara that Wayne fights for all over the Irish countryside in Ford's **The Quiet Man**—and because of her the longest fight in screen history seems worth it. Her screen relationship with Wayne was never an easy one. They had the strength of personality to stand up well to each other, whether battling in the West (**Rio Grande, Big Jake**) or over aviation matters

(**The Wings of Eagles**), in a relationship nicely summed up by Wayne's comment to her in the Western **McLintock**: "Who put that burr under your saddle?"

She was born as Maureen Fitzsimmons near Dublin, Ireland, on August 17, 1920, and gave up the opportunity to become an Abbey Theatre star for the cinema. She made her film début in the 1938 **Kicking the Moon Around**, had an important role in Alfred Hitchcock's 1939 **Jamaica Inn**, and became a big star playing Esmeralda to Charles Laughton's ❯ Quasimodo in **The Hunchback of Notre Dame**. In 1941 she made her first film for John Ford, chasing after parson Walter Pidgeon ❯ in **How Green Was My Valley**, and then starred in her first and best swashbuckler (opposite Tyrone Power ❯❯), **The Black Swan**. She was good in many kinds of film, from serious drama (Jean Renoir's **The Land Is Mine**) to women's pictures (her **Sentimental Journey** has been called "the apotheosis of the weepie"), to light comedy (**Miracle on 34th Street, Sitting Pretty**). She remained a major star right through the '50s and '60s, giving especially notable performances in Carol Reed's **Our Man In Havana** and Sam Peckinpah's **The Deadly Companions**. Her last film was the 1971 **Big Jake** with Wayne.

BEST FILMS:
1939 The Hunchback of Notre Dame
William Dieterle (RKO)
1941 How Green Was My Valley
John Ford (20th Century Fox)
1942 The Black Swan
Henry King (20th Century Fox)
1948 Sitting Pretty
Walter Lang (20th Century Fox)
1950 Rio Grande
John Ford (Republic)
1952 The Quiet Man
John Ford (Republic)
1955 The Long Gray Line
John Ford (Columbia)
1957 The Wings of Eagles
John Ford (MGM)
1959 Our Man in Havana
Carol Reed (Columbia)
1962 The Deadly Companions
Sam Peckinpah (Pathé-American)

LAURENCE OLIVIER

Laurence Olivier may well be the greatest stage actor in the world today, but he is a long way from being the greatest movie actor. What he is, in fact, is the great prestige actor of the cinema, a movie star of major proportions whose appearance in any film attracts wide attention because of his awesome theatrical reputation. Very few top stage actors have become outstanding film actors, as the qualities required for greatness are different, but Olivier has done better than most. His French equivalent as a theatrical genius, Louis Jouvet ❯, never equalled Olivier's screen achievements. He has himself said that he did not wish to be "just a film star like Cary Grant" and it is certain that his prime interest has never been in the cinema. Although his reputation has continued to grow with the years, it is for his '40s films that he is best known and is most likely to be remembered by cinema audiences. From 1939 to 1948 he starred in (and sometimes directed) a series of classic movies that are still shown and admired. In Wyler's **Wuthering Heights** he became many people's idea of Heathcliffe. In Hitchcock's **Rebecca** he was word perfect as Joan Fontaine's aristocratic husband (helping her win an Oscar nomination). In **Pride and Prejudice** he became the personification of Darcy, and he was much liked as Nelson in **Lady Hamilton** opposite Vivien Leigh ❯. With **Henry V** and **Hamlet** he made Shakespeare popular as no one else ever had.

He was a "great actor" in all these films, as he was in the '50s in **Carrie, Richard III** and even

The Prince and the Showgirl, but perhaps that is the problem; we are always aware that this is Olivier "acting" and are full of admiration for his ability to look different, speak with foreign accents, and show his marvellous understanding of what the role demands. The greatest movie actors are not like that at all—they are so natural that we don't consider they are acting. They are Cary Grant ❯ or Gary Cooper ❯ or James Stewart ❯, and their personalities are a necessary part of their greatness; Olivier, as a stage actor, likes to submerge his personality in the role. The difference between these two approaches to acting is best seen in **Khartoum**, which matched Olivier as the Mahdi against Charlton Heston ❯ as General Gordon. Heston acted Olivier off the screen by being "natural", while Olivier was lost in black face and voice mannerisms. This is no denigration of Olivier's ability, but a necessary observation if one is to understand his contribution to the cinema. He doubtless realises

*Below: Laurence Olivier is considered the greatest **Hamlet** of modern times; his 1948 film version of the Shakespeare classic became the first foreign film to win an Oscar.*

this himself, for most of his parts in recent years have been character roles, in which he can use his acting skills in chameleon ways, or simply filmed stage plays. He "acts" very enjoyably as a music hall comedian in **The Entertainer,** as lordly officers in **Oh! what a Lovely War** and **The Battle of Britain,** as a conjurer of mystification in the stage-derived **Sleuth,** as the Nazi war criminal-dentist in **Marathon Man,** and as the sly automobile tycoon in **The Betsy.** The cinema would have been less rich without his presence as an actor, but he does not hold a central place in the development of screen acting.

Olivier was born in Dorking, Surrey, on May 22, 1907, and was on stage by 1922. His film career began as a light romantic hero in 1930, opposite German musical comedy star Lilian Harvey ❯ in **The Temporary Widow,** the English version of a German film in which his role had been played by Willi Fritsch. He went to Hollywood in 1931 and made films at Fox and RKO, including Raoul Walsh's **The Yellow Ticket** and Victor Schertsinger's **Friends and Lovers.** He made no great impression, however, and his film career did not really advance until he returned to England and starred opposite Elisabeth Bergner in **As You Like It** and Vivien Leigh in **Fire Over England.** Back in America, he achieved major stardom in 1939 with **Wuthering Heights** and the greatest part of his cinema achievement began. He has been nominated for Academy Awards eight times and won it for his performance in **Hamlet,** which he also directed; he was knighted in 1948 and received a peerage in 1970, primarily for his work in the theatre and especially with the National Theatre. One of his finest major roles in recent years was opposite Katharine Hepburn ❯ in the outrageously romantic and delightfully theatrical **Love Among the Ruins,** directed by George Cukor for television but shown at the London Film Festival. He also won praise for **The Boys from Brazil.**

BEST FILMS:
1939 Wuthering Heights
William Wyler (Goldwyn/United Artists)
1940 Rebecca
Alfred Hitchcock (Selznick/United Artists)
1941 Pride and Prejudice
Robert Z. Leonard (MGM)
1944 Henry V
Laurence Olivier (Rank/Two Cities)
1948 Hamlet
Laurence Olivier (Rank/Two Cities)
1951 Carrie
William Wyler (Paramount)
1955 Richard III
Laurence Olivier (London Films)
1960 The Entertainer
Tony Richardson (Woodfall/British Lion)
1972 Sleuth
Joseph L. Mankiewicz (Palomar)
1974 Love Among the Ruins
George Cukor (ABC-TV)

Our Gang

"Our Gang" was a movie star as an entity, the most famous of all child groups. It lasted for 23 years, the longest-running series in movie history, and is still popular today on television as the *Little Rascals*. It even won an Oscar in 1936 for **Bored of Education**. There was no individual star of the group: the average age of the players was seven and they had to leave the show by their 12th birthday. There were more than 176 of them between 1922, when the series was started by Hal Roach, and 1944, when it was ended by MGM. The most famous performer in the sound era was undoubtedly George "Spanky" McFarland, who was featured in 89 of the shorts and around whom Roach shot a feature film in 1936, **General Spanky**. Other famous '30s performers included Billie "Buckwheat" Thomas, Carl "Alfalfa" Switzer and Mickey Gubitosi (who grew up to be Robert Blake, the star of **In Cold Blood**). Other famous alumni included Jackie Coogan (Oscar nominee for **Skippy**), Nanette Fabray and Eddie Bracken.

The first film of the group was the 1922 **One Terrible Day,** directed by Robert McGowan, who wrote and directed most of the films in the series until 1934. The combination of small fry, pathos, humour, charm, anarchy and even tiny tot sex appeal was an immediate hit; there were always pretty girls, black kids, mischievous boys and an animal or two. The original Gang consisted of Mickey Daniels, Peggy Cartright, Jackie Condon and Ernie "Sunshine Sammy" Morrison. They were quickly joined by Mary Kornman of the golden hair, Jackie "Tuffy" Davis, "Fat Joe"

Cobb, Allen Clayton "Farina" Hoskins and Pete, the dog with a black ring around his eye. "Our Gang" went from silent to sound films with no trouble at all and MGM took over production from Roach in 1938.

Among the directors who worked on the series were George Sidney, Cy Endfield, Gordon Douglas and James Horne. Former gang member Jacquie Lyn (Taylor) has written a biography of "Our Gang" called *The Turned-On Hollywood.*

BEST FILMS:
1924 Jubilo Jr
Robert McGowan (Roach/MGM)
1925 The Sundown Limited
Robert McGowan (Roach/MGM)
1926 Free Wheeling
Robert McGowan (Roach/MGM)
1939 When The Wind Blows
James Horne (Roach/MGM)
1931 Readin' and Writin'
Robert McGowan (Roach/MGM)
1932 Spanky
Robert McGowan (Roach/MGM)
1934 Washee Ironee
James Parrott (Roach/MGM)
1935 Our Gang Follies of 1936
Gus Meins (Roach/MGM)
1936 Bored of Education
Gordon Douglas (Roach/MGM)
1938 Practical Jokes
George Sidney (MGM)

Jack Palance

The taut, tortured, cruel face of Jack Palance conveys menace even when he smiles and, despite its unfortunate origins, has been the key to his rapid rise to stardom. The deadly, black-clad killer who confronts Alan Ladd ➤ in **Shane**, the new husband out to kill Joan Crawford ➤ in **Sudden Fear** and the plague-bearing criminal-on-the-run in **Panic in the Streets** are among the most

Above: Jack Palance gave one of his greatest performances as the smiling killer gunman of George Stevens' 1953 **Shane**.

chilling villains of the cinema. The cruelly-stretched face is also perfectly able to convey anguish and torment, as it does in Palance's three superb films for director Robert Aldrich: **The Big Knife** (as a depressed and angry movie star); **Attack!** (as a doomed officer in the Battle of the Bulge, whose arm is run over by a tank); and **Ten Seconds to Hell** (as a bomb disposal expert in Berlin). Palance acquired his face during World War II service, when he was badly burned and had to have extensive plastic surgery.

He was born of Russian immigrants in Lattimer, Pennsylvania, on February 18, 1920, with the name Walter Jack Palanuik. He was a boxer and a writer before turning to stage acting and meeting Elia Kazan, who featured him in his devastating début in the 1950 **Panic in the Streets.** He received Oscar nominations for his performances in **Sudden Fear** and **Shane,** and then began to branch out into ethnic roles in **Sign of the Pagan** (as a Hun), **The Mongols**

(as a Mongol) and **Barabbas** (as a Slavic gladiator). Among his best performances in the '60s, often working in Europe, were the villainous film producer in Jean-Luc Godard's **Contempt** and the Mexican bandit who kidnaps Claudia Cardinale ➤ in **The Professionals.** In the '70s he has begun to dabble with horror roles, notably in the TV films **Dr Jekyll and Mr Hyde** and **Dracula,** and the SF thriller **Welcome to Blood City.**

BEST FILMS:
1950 Panic in the Streets
Elia Kazan (20th Century Fox)
1952 Sudden Fear
David Miller (RKO)
1953 Shane
George Stevens (Paramount)
1954 Sign of the Pagan
Douglas Sirk (Universal)
1955 The Big Knife
Robert Aldrich (United Artists)
1956 Attack!
Robert Aldrich (United Artists)
1959 Ten Seconds to Hell
Robert Aldrich (United Artists)
1962 Barabbas
Richard Fleischer (Columbia/
De Laurentiis)
1963 Contempt (Le Mépris)
Jean-Luc Godard (Rome-Paris Films)
1966 The Professionals
Richard Brooks (Columbia)

Lilli Palmer

Lilli Palmer should have become a much bigger star than she did. Her sophisticated, cosmopolitan, mysterious, woman-of-the-world persona was ideally suited for the American film *film noir* of the '40s, as can be seen in her two best films, Fritz Lang's **Cloak and Dagger** and Robert Rossen's **Body and Soul.** Unfortunately, she only made four films in Hollywood at this time and spent much of her life living up to her

Below: The most famous group star of children was the anarchic Our Gang.

Above: Lilli Palmer with Gary Cooper in Fritz Lang's 1946 film noir masterpiece **Cloak and Dagger,** *probably her best film.*

own image, travelling from country to country and making films in German, Spanish, French and Italian which did not do much for her screen reputation. Her 1975 autobiography was aptly titled *Change Lobsters and Dance.*

She was born as Lillie Peiser in Posen, Germany, on May 21, 1914, was on stage in Germany by 1932, and went to England in 1934. She made her film début in the 1935 British film **Crime Unlimited** and had a mixed career in the '30s, even playing opposite Will Hay ≫ in **Good Morning, Boys.** She made her first real impact as a Hungarian in Carol Reed's 1939 **A Girl Must Live** and a bigger one as a ghost in Roy Boulting's 1942 **Thunder Rock.** She married Rex Harrison ≫ in 1943 (they divorced in 1957) and was very good opposite him as a Jewish girl in **The Rake's Progress;** she went to Hollywood with him in 1946 and made her best films in the late '40s: **Cloak and Dagger, Body and Soul, My Girl Tisa** and **No Minor Vices.** After that she went back to the stage, returning to Hollywood in 1952 with Harrison for the screen version of their hit play **The Fourposter.** From then on she made films all over the world, but came back to Hollywood for two more good ones, **But Not For Me** with Clark Gable ≫ and **The Pleasure of Her Company** with Fred Astaire ≫. Her best non-English language films were probably the elegant French **Le Rendez-vous de Minuit** and the horrific Spanish **La Residencia,** but she was also excellent in the 1977 East German film **Lotte in Weimar.**

BEST FILMS:
1942 Thunder Rock
Roy Boulting (Charter)
1945 The Rake's Progress
Sidney Gilliat (GFD)
1946 Cloak and Dagger
Fritz Lang (Warner Brothers)
1947 Body and Soul
Robert Rossen (United Artists)
1948 My Girl Tisa
Elliot Nugent (Warner Brothers)
1948 No Minor Vices
Lewis Milestone (MGM)
1952 The Fourposter
Irving Reis (Columbia)
1959 But Not For Me
Walter Lang (Paramount)
1961 The Pleasure of Her Company
George Seaton (Paramount)
1962 Le Rendez-vous de Minuit
Roger Leenhardt (Argos-Editions Cinégraphiques)

GREGORY PECK

The "reality" of movie images was emphasised not long ago, when it was discovered that Gregory Peck was high on Richard Nixon's list of

Below and left: Gregory Peck in two rather different roles: romancing Ann Blyth in Raoul Walsh's 1952 **The World in His Arms** *and seeking revenge for the murder of his wife in Henry King's 1958* **The Bravados.**

dangerous enemies. Peck has been the Great Liberal of the American cinema for more than 30 years, radiating integrity, sincerity and concern with great skill. He is also, it should be stressed, one of the great screen actors, with an extraordinary record of outstanding performances in major films. His screen personality is not an exciting one, because he usually conveys conflicts in social values, but he is certainly never dull, as some critics erroneously insist. The strength of his "liberal" personification is that he is almost always flawed in some critical way and forced to act in a manner disturbing to his inner morality. This conflict is seen at its most open in **Twelve O'Clock High,** when he literally freezes into immobility because of having to send his men to possible death on an air mission, but it can also be seen in films as different as **The Gunfighter** (forced to kill to survive, despite his efforts to avoid it), **MacArthur** (having to disobey the President and lose his command because of his beliefs), and **The Omen** (forced to try to kill his own diabolical son).

Peck has been the star of every movie he has made since his début in the 1944 **Days of Glory,** and he has made an amazing number of good films. He has had five Academy Award nominations and he won the Oscar for his beautifully modulated perfor-

mance in **To Kill A Mockingbird.** The liberal values he represented in that film were so evident that a lesser actor would have been boringly "good", whereas Peck made the small-town lawyer of the film not only likeable but imperfect enough to be convincing.

He was born in La Jolla, California, on April 5, 1916, as Eldred Gregory Peck. He was a stage actor in the early '40s, but his screen acting ability was so evident in his first film that he instantly became not only a major star but one who was able to pick his own films. Peck denigrates his own acting ability (like all the great screen actors) and claims that he is only as good as his scripts; the falseness of this judgement is most apparent in his weak films because, despite their badness, he is still good. In his second film he had to portray a missionary priest of incredible nobility, but his performance makes **The Keys of the Kingdom** still watchable. One of the amazing things about his film acting is that he can play dullish good men in such a way that they become memorable instead of ciphers. His roles as a good-hearted father in **The Yearling,** a good-natured journalist escorting princess Audrey Hepburn ≫ in **Roman Holiday,** and a high-principled officer in **The Guns of Navarone** could not have been portrayed as well by any other screen actor. He is equally fine, although in some ways less interesting, in nastier roles, like the ne'er-do-well brother battling sensually to the death with Jennifer Jones ≫ in **Duel in the Sun** or the obsessed Captain Ahab in **Moby Dick.** He has made many of his best films over the years with director Henry King, who specialises in Americana, but he has worked just as well with other top American directors, including William Wellman, Alfred Hitchcock, Robert Mulligan, William Wyler, John Huston and Elia Kazan. His contribution to the American cinema has been immense and will endure.

BEST FILMS:
1945 Spellbound
Alfred Hitchcock (Selznick)
1946 The Yearling
Clarence Brown (MGM)
1946 Duel in the Sun
King Vidor (Selznick)
1947 The Macomber Affair
Zoltan Korda (United Artists)
1949 Twelve O'Clock High
Henry King (20th Century Fox)
1950 The Gunfighter
Henry King (20th Century Fox)
1953 Roman Holiday
William Wyler (Paramount)
1958 The Big Country
William Wyler (United Artists)
1961 The Guns of Navarone
J. Lee Thompson (Columbia)
1962 To Kill A Mockingbird
Robert Mulligan (Universal)
1976 The Omen
Richard Donner (20th Century Fox)
1977 MacArthur
Joseph Sargent (Universal)

GÉRARD PHILIPE

Gérard Philipe could be considered the James Dean » of France, embodying the ideals of France in the postwar period and dying young (aged 36) in 1959, after becoming one of the major myth figures of the French cinema. They represented very different ideas and Philipe had a longer period as a major star (12 years), but they both created screen images that tapped profound currents of feelings in their own countries. Philipe's screen personality embodied the conflicting attitudes of the French post-war generation—gay, light-hearted and ambitious, but usually flawed by inner conflicts expressed in moodiness and turbulence—almost a gentle paranoia. He portrayed the distraught heros of novels by Stendhal (**La Chartreuse de Parme, Le Rouge et le Noir**) and Dostoevsky (**The Idiot, The Gambler**) and re-interpreted other classics for a new generation. He was much more than simply a jeune premier, as could be seen in the film that first made him famous, the 1947 **Le diable au Corps**; he plays an adolescent having an affair with a woman (Micheline Presle) whose husband is away during World War I, and is the inadvertent cause of her death—she becomes pregnant by him and she dies in childbirth. This kind of unintentional betrayal of the loved one is a prominent feature in his persona: in **Les Grandes Manoeuvres** he loses the love of Michèle Morgan »

Above: Gérard Philipe dreamed for many years of filming the Till Eulenspiegel *legend and finally directed himself in* **Les Aventures de Till l'Espiègle (The Bold Adventure)** *in 1957.*

when she discovers that he had earlier made a bet he could seduce her. In **La Ronde** he tells actress Isa Miranda that there is no happiness and then seeks it in the arms of prostitute Simone Signoret ». In **Les Liaisons Dangereuses** he destroys the lives of both Jeanne Moreau » and Annette Stroyberg by being in love with them both. His most famous performance was probably that of the swashbuckling hero of **Fanfan la Tulipe**, with his persona at its most frivolous and light-hearted, but he was also brilliant in his English comedy **Knave of Hearts**, as a philanderer confessing his misdeeds to his wife.

He was born as Gérard Philip (without the "e") in Cannes in 1922, and his first screen role was a small one in the 1943 **La Boîte aux Rêves**. His first starring role was as the Dostoevsky protagonist of **The Idiot**, Prince Myshkin, whose "goodness" destroys those around him. Most of his great films were based on literary works, ranging from Dostoevsky, Stendhal, Laclos, Zola and Radiguet, to retellings of the Faust and Till Eulenspiegel legends. His reputation as a theatre actor equalled his cinema renown, especially in plays by Corneille and Racine. He died in 1959 after becoming ill during shooting of his last film (**La Fièvre Monte à El Pao**).

BEST FILMS:
1947 Le Diable au Corps
Claude Autant-Lara (Transcontinental)
1947 La Chartreuse de Parme
Christian-Jaque (Discina-Scalera)
1950 La Beauté du Diable
René Clair (Universalia)
1950 La Ronde
Max Ophuls (Sacha Gordine)
1951 Fanfan la Tulipe
Christian-Jaque (Ariane-Rizzoli)
1952 Les Belles de Nuit
René Clair (Franco-London Films)
1954 Knave of Hearts
René Clement (Transcontinental)
1954 Le Rouge et le Noir
Claude Autant-Lara (Franco-London Films)
1955 Les Grandes Manoeuvres
René Clair (Filmsonor)
1959 Les Liaisons Dangereuses
Roger Vadim (Les Films Marceau)

WALTER PIDGEON

The solid, authoritative, pipe-smoking image of Walter Pidgeon is probably the cinema's best-known personification of experienced, reliable maturity. There was reality behind that persona as well, for he had a 15-year apprenticeship as a leading man before he finally became a major star teamed with Greer Garson »

the Waldorf, a re-make of **Grand Hotel.**

Pidgeon was born in East St John, New Brunswick, Canada, on September 23, 1897, and began his career as a singer and stage actor. He made his film début in the 1926 **Mannequin**, had a brief flurry as a Romberg musical star of the early '30s, but had to wait for maturity to give him screen stardom in the '40s. He was actually quite good as **Nick Carter—Master Detective** for Jacques Tourneur in 1939, but it was a 60-minute programmer. His films with Garson filled cinemas in the '40s, as did his strong teaming with Clark Gable » in **Command Decision.**

In the '50s his mature image was mostly used in character parts, notably in **The Bad and the Beautiful** and **Executive Suite**, and he was exceptionally good as the Senate majority leader in the 1962 **Advise and Consent.** He has continued working right up to the present time, his recent films including **Two Minute Warning** and **Murder at 40,000 Feet.** He considers his best films to be those with Garson.

Below: Walter Pidgeon and Ginger Rogers in **Weekend at the Waldorf,** *a stylish re-make of* **Grand Hotel.**

in the '40s. The insecurity of the war years obviously required just such a stalwart father-husband figure, and Pidgeon fitted it beautifully; his partnership with Garson, beginning in 1941 with **Blossoms in the Dust** and continuing through such sentimental but beautifully crafted films as **Mrs Miniver, Madame Curie** and **Mrs Parkington**, made him one of the top male stars of the period. He lent his authority to other, better, films as well, most notably as the man-on-the-run from Hitler's minions in Fritz Lang's **Man Hunt**, as the strong village minister in John Ford's Welsh coalmining saga **How Green Was My Valley,** and rather charmingly involved with Ginger Rogers » in **Weekend at**

BEST FILMS:
1941 Man Hunt
Fritz Lang (20th Century Fox)
1941 How Green Was My Valley
John Ford (20th Century Fox)
1941 Blossoms in the Dust
Mervyn LeRoy (MGM)
1942 Mrs Miniver
William Wyler (MGM)
1943 Madame Curie
Mervyn LeRoy (MGM)
1944 Mrs Parkington
Tay Garnett (MGM)
1945 Weekend at the Waldorf
Robert Z. Leonard (MGM)
1948 Command Decision
Sam Wood (MGM)
1952 The Bad and the Beautiful
Vincente Minnelli (MGM)
1962 Advise and Consent
Otto Preminger (Columbia)

DICK POWELL

Dick Powell must be ranked as one of the male superstars of the Hollywood musical, even though his simple no-nonsense screen personality makes this seem unlikely. He was the star of virtually all the great Warner Brothers musicals of the '30s, the counterpart of Fred Astaire ❯ at RKO and Bing Crosby ❯ at Paramount. His abilities, of course, were entirely different. He did not dominate his films like Astaire and Crosby, but he was exactly right for the ensemble style of musical that Warners developed with Busby Berkeley, bevies of beautiful girls and a brilliant supporting cast. If his personality had been too strong, he would have clashed with this style, but his amiable, boyish good nature and ability to work with rather than above the rest of the performers made him one of the busiest of all the '30s musical stars. Powell made 31 films between 1931 and 1939—and most of them were musicals featuring this curly-haired tenor from Mountain View, Arkansas. He didn't like being a musical star and fought to get out of what he considered bad type-

casting, but even after he left Warners in 1940 he was forced to go on singing, despite his efforts to become a dramatic actor. He succeeded in breaking the pattern in 1944, when Edward Dmytryk let him play hard-boiled private eye Philip Marlowe in a superb version of Raymond Chandler's *Farewell My Lovely* (retitled **Murder My Sweet**). After that he was good in a number of hard-boiled roles, but ironically his last film, Frank Tashlin's **Susan Slept Here** in 1954, required him to sing once again, to Debbie Reynolds ❯.

Richard E. Powell was born on November 14, 1904, and worked as a band singer and theatre emcee before going to Hollywood

for his first film in 1931, **Blessed Event** (as a down-and-out bandleader, crooning three songs). He was a hit, and quickly began working on his great series of Warners musicals, from **Gold Diggers of 1933** and **42nd Street**, through **Dames** and **Page Miss Glory**, down to **Naughty But Nice** in 1939. He was teamed with Ruby Keeler ❯ in seven of the best of these, but there was also ample support from Joan Blondell ❯ (whom he married), Ginger Rogers ❯, Hugh Herbert, Guy Kibbee and even James Cagney ❯. He was usually the writer/composer trying to get his songs into a big show and singing many of the best ones himself, including *By a Waterfall, I Only Have Eyes For You* and *Lullaby of Broadway* He didn't have the greatest voice in the movies, but it wears well and his songs are still enjoyable. He was so well liked that other studios asked to borrow him for their musicals; he joined Fred Allen and Ann Dvorak at Fox for **Thanks a Million** and returned to that studio to star with Madeleine Carroll ❯ in the superb Irving Berlin musical **On the Avenue**. When he left Warners for Paramount, he started off with a brilliant Preston Sturges comedy **Christmas in July** (spending

money he mistakenly thinks he has won in a contest), but was soon back singing again with Mary Martin in **Star Spangled Rhythm** and Dorothy Lamour ❯ in **Riding High**. René Clair gave him a good role in his fantasy **It Happened Tomorrow**, but there was still another musical with Lucille Ball ❯, **Meet the People**. After Dmytryk let him be a tough guy in **Murder My Sweet** and its excellent *film noir* follow-up **Cornered**, he was pretty tough

and pretty good in the rest of his films, including **Johnny O'Clock** for Robert Rossen and **The Tall Target** for Anthony Mann. He was outstanding as a writer involved with Hollywood tycoon Kirk Douglas ❯ in Vincente Minnelli's **The Bad and the Beautiful** in 1952. After that he was mainly concerned with TV, including the *Four-Star Playhouse* and *The Dick Powell Show,* married June Allyson ❯ in 1945 (after divorcing Joan Blondell the same year) and became a successful producer and director of movies as well as a TV executive and star. He died in 1963, a rich man.

BEST FILMS:
1933 42nd Street
Mervyn LeRoy (Warner Brothers)
1933 Gold Diggers of 1933
Lloyd Bacon (Warner Brothers)
1933 Footlight Parade
Lloyd Bacon (Warner Brothers)
1934 Dames
Ray Enright (Warner Brothers)
1935 Gold Diggers of 1935
Busby Berkeley (Warner Brothers)
1937 On The Avenue
Roy Del Ruth (20th Century Fox)
1940 Christmas in July
Preston Sturges (Paramount)
1944 It Happened Tomorrow
René Clair (United Artists)
1944 Murder My Sweet
Edward Dmytryk (RKO)
1952 The Bad and the Beautiful
Vincente Minnelli (MGM)

ELEANOR POWELL

Eleanor Powell was promoted as the World's Greatest Female Tap Dancer and, from 1935 to 1943, was one of MGM's greatest musical stars. Her tapping was truly spectacular and her elaborate dance numbers are among the most memorable in musicals, but her talent was strictly limited to dancing. She did for tapping what Sonja Henie ❯ did for ice skating and Esther Williams ❯ for swimming; their acting abilities were roughly equivalent and the attractions of their films were in the elaborate production numbers rather than in plot or personality. As a screen actress, Powell was simply amiable, but as a dancer she was unbeatable, a long-legged whirlwind whose wondrous work has never been bettered. She had some great partners in her films, including Fred Astaire ❯ in **Broadway Melody of 1940** (in which they dance *Begin the Beguine* together), but her finest achievements were by herself: in **Broadway Melody of 1936** she was simply stunning in top hat and spangled tux doing *Broadway Rhythm;* in **Born to Dance** she danced aboard an incredible battleship with sequined cannons to *Swingin' the Jinx Away;* in **Broadway Melody of 1938** she was back in top hat and tux doing *Your Broadway, My Broadway* In

Rosalie she had West Point Cadets backing her big number and was nicely teamed with Ray Bolger. In her later films she was often teamed with comedian Red Skelton and even got a chance to tap dance a morse code message in **Ship Ahoy**.

Powell was born in Springfield, Massachusetts, on November 21, 1912. By 1929 she was on stage, dancing in the revue *Follow Through,* and she made her film début in 1935 in a guest spot in the Fox musical **George White's Scandals**. MGM then built a series of spectacular musicals around her, with fine humorous support that included Robert Benchley ❯, George Burns ❯, Gracie Allen ❯, Una Merkel, etc. In her last Skelton film, the 1943 **I Dood It,** (a re-make of Buster Keaton's ❯ Spite Marriage), the focus was on him rather than her, and she left MGM after a guest spot in **Thousands Cheer**. She made one further musical at United Artists, **Sensations of 1945,** and then guested in the 1950 **The Duchess of Idaho,** her last film. Amazingly, her career consisted of only 13 movies. She starred in a TV religious series in the '50s (winning five Emmys) and made a brief comeback as a dancer in 1961, after her divorce

Above: Dick Powell became one of the cinema's finest tough guys after he shed his musical comedy image. Here he is with Lee J. Cobb in Robert Rossen's **Johnny O'Clock.**

Above: Eleanor Powell dancing with Fred Astaire to Cole Porter's Begin the Beguine *in their only musical together,* **Broadway Melody of 1940,** *the last of a famous MGM series.*

from Glenn Ford ❯, her husband from 1943 to 1959. She hasn't danced since 1964, but her best film work was featured in the MGM compilation **That's Entertainment** in 1974.

BEST FILMS:
1935 Broadway Melody of 1936
Roy Del Ruth (MGM)
1936 Born to Dance
Roy Del Ruth (MGM)
1937 Broadway Melody of 1938
Roy Del Ruth (MGM)

1937 Rosalie
W.S. Van Dyke (MGM)
1939 Honolulu
Edward Buzzell (MGM)
1940 Broadway Melody of 1940
Norman Taurog (MGM)
1941 Lady Be Good
Norman Z. McLeod (MGM)
1942 Ship Ahoy
Edward Buzzell (MGM)
1943 I Dood It
Vincente Minnelli (MGM)
1944 Sensations of 1945
Andrew L. Stone
(United Artists)

WILLIAM POWELL

William Powell is remembered today primarily for his two greatest comedy roles: Nick Charles, the detective in the **Thin Man** series, and the cantankerous but good-hearted father in **Life With Father**. These are only two of many outstanding performances he gave in 94 films over a 33-year cinema career. He was an impeccable comedian who created one of the most durable and enjoyable screen personalities of any '30s star—one that has dated surprisingly little. Basically, he was a slightly villainous good-guy, a suave and charming cad, a combination of fine manners with a mocking sense of superiority, voguishly dressed, urbanely witty and not really nice. And yet he was so much fun to be with.

Powell's best comedies are likely to be classics for years to come; he was the perfect butler to Carole Lombard ➤ in the brilliant **My Man Godfrey**, the ultimate in adulterous mixed quartets with Jean Harlow ➤, Myrna Loy ➤ and Spencer Tracy ➤ in **Libelled Lady**, and the most sophisticated of detectives with Ginger Rogers ➤ in **Star of Midnight** and Jean Arthur ➤ in **The Ex-Mrs Bradford**. But no creation was more enjoyable than his tandem with Myrna Loy as Nick and Nora Charles in the **Thin Man** films. There were six of them and they were probably the best series ever made in Hollywood, full-fledged studio productions, not cheapies. Powell and Loy were first used together by director W.S. Van Dyke in the 1934 **Manhattan Melodrama**; the chemistry worked so well that he persuaded MGM boss Louis B. Mayer to team them in **The Thin Man** the same year. They immediately became the most successful husband-wife team in the movies, changing the way married couples were portrayed on the screen and starting the screwball comedy vogue. Between dry martinis and wisecracks, the couple solved crimes; they were the ultimate in sophistication and wit, and they even had an urbane wire-haired terrier called Asta. Powell was a retired detective, Loy was a rich heiress. The Thin Man was actually the

murder victim in the first film, but the name became associated with Powell and was used in all the sequels. They were all good films, the last being made in 1947 and titled **Song of the Thin Man**. That was also the year Powell starred in **Life With Father**, a great role he had wanted to play for years; the film was based on a hugely successful stage play, which in turn was based on an autobiographical book by Clarence Day about his own father. Powell's incredibly convincing performance won him an Academy Award acting nomination and finally proved to the unconverted that he was a matchless comedian.

Powell was born in Pittsburgh, Pennsylvania, on June 29, 1892. He came to films from the stage and made his cinema début as a villain in **Sherlock Holmes** in 1922. He was a baddie in nearly all of his silent pictures, but never a star until Josef von Sternberg gave him two great roles: the cruel film director of **The Last Command** and the underworld boss in **Dragnet**. His voice was ideally suited to sound, and by combining elements of his silent villainy with his suave looks, voice and manner, he very quickly built up a new

Below: William Powell and Myrna Loy in their fifth reprise as Nick and Nora Charles in **The Thin Man Goes Home** *(1944).*

screen persona, notably as Philo Vance in the 1929 **The Canary Murder Case.** Aside from his **Thin Man** films and witty comedies, Powell's biggest '30s success was as Ziegfeld in **The Great Ziegfeld** in 1936; it won the Best Picture Oscar and co-star Luise Rainer won the Best Actress award.

After 1947, Powell settled down to white-haired character parts, but there weren't many despite his skill. His last film was the 1955 **Mr Roberts** in which he played Doc superbly.

BEST FILMS:
1928 The Last Command
Josef von Sternberg (Paramount)
1934 Manhattan Melodrama
W.S. Van Dyke (MGM)
1934 The Thin Man
W.S. Van Dyke (MGM)
1935 Star of Midnight
Stephen Roberts (RKO)
1936 The Great Ziegfeld
Robert Z. Leonard (MGM)
1936 The Ex-Mrs Bradford
Stephen Roberts (RKO)
1936 My Man Godfrey
Gregory LaCava (Universal)
1936 Libelled Lady
Jack Conway (MGM)
1936 After the Thin Man
W.S. Van Dyke (MGM)
1947 Life With Father
Michael Curtiz (Warner Brothers)

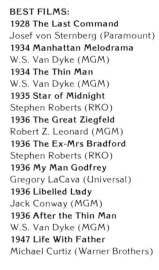

TYRONE POWER

Tyrone Power was 20th Century-Fox's top male star from 1938 to 1948 and for a time was among the most popular stars in America. There was something quintessentially American about him, or at least what Americans like to think is American. He was boyish, modest, likeable, natural and exceedingly handsome. Fox studio chief Darryl Zanuck considered him "the truest, handsomest, best of the lot", and director Henry King (who specialised in Americana in his movies) starred Power in ten of his films. It was King who made Power famous in his 1937 picture **Lloyds of London,** and it was King who

Left: Tyrone Power in his best film, duelling with villain Basil Rathbone at the climax of Mamoulian's **The Mark of Zorro.**

directed many of his best pictures, including **In Old Chicago, Alexander's Ragtime Band, Jesse James, The Black Swan, Captain from Castile** and **Prince of Foxes.** Power had a very malleable screen persona (ie, it wasn't very strong and mostly consisted of being handsome, nice and American) and was a fair actor, so he was able to star in everything from musicals and Westerns to historical epics and swashbucklers. His forte was as a swashbuckler, however, and he was almost as good as Errol Flynn ≫ in his best films, notably his masterpiece, the 1940 **The Mark of Zorro.** Director Rouben Mamoulian was able to play upon some of Power's weaker, hidden character traits and make him into a delightful, witty swordsman pretending to be a fop in nineteenth-century Spanish California, duelling brilliantly with villain Basil Rathbone ≫. In **The Black Swan** he was a seventeenth-century adventurer in Jamaica, duelling this time with villain George Sanders ≫, who was also the bad man of the eighteenth-century epic **Son of Fury.** The buckles were less shiny in **Captain from Castile** and **Prince of Foxes,** but Power still swashed entertainingly.

Power, who was born into a theatrical family on May 5, 1913, in Cincinnati, Ohio, began in films with a bit part in the 1932 **Tom Brown of Culver.** His finest moment as a serious screen actor, as far as the critics were concerned, came late in his career, in the *film noir* bleakness of Edmund Goulding's 1947 **Nightmare Alley.** He portrayed a fake spiritualist fighting his way to success in a truly American way, but getting his just desserts in the end. His last film was a good one, too, Billy Wilder's 1957 **Witness for the Prosecution,** in which he was a clever murderer on trial for his life. Power died a true swashbuckler's death in 1958 while duelling with George Sanders on the set of **Solomon and Sheba** in Madrid. It was a heart attack and not a sword thrust that killed him, but Zorro himself could not have devised a more memorable exit.

BEST FILMS:
1939 Jesse James
Henry King (20th Century Fox)
1939 The Rains Came
Clarence Brown (20th Century Fox)
1940 Johnny Apollo
Henry Hathaway (20th Century Fox)
1940 The Mark of Zorro
Rouben Mamoulian (20th Century Fox)
1941 Blood and Sand
Rouben Mamoulian (20th Century Fox)
1942 The Black Swan
Henry King (20th Century Fox)
1946 The Razor's Edge
Edmund Goulding (20th Century Fox)

Above: Anthony Quinn usually plays ethnic roles, often Indians, as in Carol Reed's 1970 **Flap** (**The Last Warrior**).

1947 Nightmare Alley
Edmund Goulding (20th Century Fox)
1949 Prince of Foxes
Henry King (20th Century Fox)
1957 Witness for the Prosecution
Billy Wilder (United Artists)

VINCENT PRICE
see Modern Stars

ANTHONY QUINN

Anthony Quinn has come to represent a kind of elemental life force in the cinema, swaggering, leering and uncouth, but somehow rooted in the essentials of nature; he is also uncommonly vicious and self-centred in his best roles.

It would be strange indeed if his 16-year apprenticeship in small and usually villainous ethnic roles were not reflected in his screen personality when he became a major star. Quinn has a limited talent, but it is effective when he is properly controlled by good directors. His most famous performances were for European film makers who restrained his tendency to go over the top: Quinn has rarely been better than as the lusty **Zorba the Greek** or the insensitive strong-man of **La Strada.**

He was born in Chihuahua, Mexico, on April 15, 1915, of an Irish father and a Mexican mother, and dragged himself to superstardom by dogged persistence. He made his début in a bit part in the 1936 **Parole** and for the next 16 years played a variety of Mexicans, Indians, Chinese and other small roles deemed suitable for his ethnic mix. He began to despair of ever having real success, and perhaps this was the key to his eventual rise, portraying despairing villainy. The breakthrough

came with Elia Kazan's **Viva Zapata!** as Marlon Brando's ≫ disgruntled brother who wants to get some rewards for their heroics. He won the Oscar for Best Supporting Actor, went to Italy to make a few films, and came back with an even greater performance as the vicious strong-man of **La Strada** (and it won the Oscar for Best Foreign Film). Another Best Supporting Actor Oscar for his vigorous portrayal of Gauguin opposite Kirk Douglas's ≫ Van Gogh in the 1956 **Lust for Life** confirmed his stature.

Quinn wasn't quite a major star yet, but he was outstanding in two superb Westerns, **Last Train from Gun Hill** and **Warlock,** giving almost manic performances in both. He became a big star with **The Hunchback of Notre Dame** and **Wild is the Wind,** even though the films were nothing to speak of, and then gave rather better performances for George Cukor in **Heller in Pink Tights** and Nicholas Ray in **The Savage Innocents** (back once again in an ethnic role as an eskimo). The possibility of major stardom began to emerge with strong performances in three grandiose epics, **The Guns of Navarone, Barabbas** and **Lawrence of Arabia,** and finally arrived with his internationally popular **Zorba the Greek** in 1965. He was very good the same year as the pirate captain betrayed by children in **A High Wind in Jamaica,** but then started to believe rather too much in his own histrionic abilities; the critics turned cool when he began almost to parody his own acting style. His star continues to shine just as brightly, however, and he has recently been featured in two major religious productions, the Moslem film **The Message** and the TV epic **Jesus of Nazareth.** In 1972 he published his autobiography, *The Original Sin.*

In 1978 he gave fabulous performances as the Onassis-like protagonist of the trashy-but-fun **The Greek Tycoon** and as a poor Mexican father in **The Children of Sanchez.**

BEST FILMS:
1952 Viva Zapata!
Elia Kazan (20th Century Fox)
1954 La Strada
Federico Fellini (Ponti-De Laurentiis)
1956 Lust For Life
Vincente Minnelli (MGM)
1959 Warlock
Edward Dmytryk (20th Century Fox)
1961 The Guns of Navarone
J. Lee Thompson (Columbia)
1962 Barabbas
Richard Fleischer (Columbia-De Laurentiis)
1962 Lawrence of Arabia
David Lean (Columbia)
1965 Zorba the Greek
Michael Cacoyannis (20th Century Fox)
1965 A High Wind in Jamaica
Alexander Mackendrick (20th Century Fox)
1978 The Greek Tycoon
J. Lee Thompson (Universal)

GEORGE RAFT

George Raft is one of the Big Four movie gangsters (along with Cagney ≫, Robinson ≫ and Bogart ≫). Sober, solemn, almost expressionless, his hat pulled down low over his eyes, he is mean, tough and a real killer. His image was fixed for all time in Howard Hawks' 1932 **Scarface,** as a coin-flipping thug bumped off by Paul Muni ≫. It was the coin that made him a star (Hawks said it came to symbolise a new kind of cool defiance and hostility), but it was Raft's own sleek menace, especially when dressed in incongruous spats and gloves in his early films, that kept him a big name; that and his real life association with the underworld. He insisted that he came into films because he was sent as a protection racket heavy to Texas Guinan's night club, and she put him into her 1929 movie **Queen of the Night Clubs.** His ambition, he said, was to become a big-shot gangster. British Home Office officials, at least, accepted his screen image as being a reflection of his real life, because they refused him entry to Britain because of his supposed "associations"; whatever the truth, Raft seems more like a genuine gangster than any other of the Big

Above: George Raft as a gangster up against Pat O'Brien in the somewhat autobiographical **Broadway** *(1942).*

Four, probably because there is very little about him that is nice—even when he's on the side of the law, he's vicious.

Raft was not a great screen actor by any means—he is usually quite wooden—and he starred in few good films (the best were directed by Raoul Walsh), but he did succeed in creating a strong and memorable screen personality which he carried through all his films from 1929 to the 1972 **Hammersmith is Out.** The relative thinness of this characterisation was brilliantly satirised in Billy Wilder's 1959 **Some Like It Hot,** where Raft portrays an ageing gangster called Spats and bawls out one of his own men for the "cheap trick" of coin-tossing. But as Raft so rightly said when he was teamed with Bogart in **They Drive by Night,** "We're tougher than any truck." He was, too, and teamed with the great Warner Brothers gangsters from 1939 to 1943, he held his own astonishingly well.

Raft was with Cagney in the 1939 **Each Dawn I Die,** leading a prison break and dying to save pal Cagney (Raft made over 100 films and was killed in most of them). He was teamed with Bogart in **Invisible Stripes,** playing an ex-con trying to go straight. He tried to go straight again in **I Stole a Million** after falling in love with Claire Trevor, but was back menacing the hell out of Walter Pidgeon ❯ in **The House Across the Bay.** His best starring film was probably **They Drive by Night,** teamed with Bogart and Ida Lupino ❯ in a story about truckers fighting crooked bosses. He joined up with Robinson in **Manpower** to fight over Marlene Dietrich ❯ and he almost seemed autobiographical playing a prohibition gangster in **Broadway,** with Pat O'Brien as his rival.

Raft was born in a rough neighbourhood in New York City (the Hell's Kitchen area) in 1903 and did a little bit of everything, including dancing, in his early years. After he became a star and Paramount deftly featured him opposite Mae West ❯, the studio tried to make him into a dancing star with films like **Bolero** and **Rumba.** It didn't work, as his screen persona was already set.

After his satisfactory '30s films for Paramount and his better work for Warners, he became a floating star, impersonating George Raft (and sometimes playing himself by name) in dozens of films. Some of the early small budget pictures made by Edwin Marin (**Johnny Angel, Nocturne**)— are not bad at all, but the Raft image did not, probably could not, develop. Raft may not have made a big contribution to the art of cinema, but he made an unforgettable one.

BEST FILMS:
1932 Scarface
Howard Hawks (Hughes/United Artists)
1932 Night After Night
Archie Mayo (Paramount)
1933 The Bowery
Raoul Walsh (20th Century Fox)
1939 Each Dawn I Die
William Keighley (Warner Brothers)
1939 Invisible Stripes
Lloyd Bacon (Warner Brothers)
1940 The House Across the Bay
Walter Lang (Wanger/United Artists)
1940 They Drive By Night
Raoul Walsh (Warner Brothers)
1941 Manpower
Raoul Walsh (Warner Brothers)
1942 Broadway
William Seiter (Universal)
1959 Some Like It Hot
Billy Wilder (United Artists)

RAIMU

Raimu used to be considered the greatest actor in the world by rather good judges, including Orson Welles ❯, Marlene Dietrich ❯ and Zero Mostel, and was much praised by perceptive critics like Parker Tyler and James Agee. That he is little talked about today is probably due to the fact that he made his best films in the 1930s for Marcel Pagnol, a fine director currently out of favour.

Raimu's greatest role was as the Marseilles café owner César in the trilogy, **Marius, Fanny** and **César,** written and produced by Pagnol, but he was also outstanding in Pagnol's **La Femme du Boulanger.** His great, sad face with its tiny little moustache,

Above: Raimu in Pagnol's **La Femme du Boulanger.**

his continually dishevelled appearance and his remarkably expressive way of slouching were well known to French (and world) audiences in the '30s in a series of highly popular and delightful films. He rarely worked with important directors (he did not like being told what to do), which is probably another reason for his relative neglect, but he turned in exceptional performances even in weak films. His persona was essentially that of the pathetic clown, the comedian able to mix sentiment with humour, tears with laughter. Unlike most of the other great French actors of the period, who tended to be rather stylish, Raimu's trademark was being non-stylish, a warm-hearted, ordinary man of the people.

He was born Jules Muraire in Toulon in 1883 and began as a singer and vaudeville artist. He made his first film, **L'Homme Nu,** in 1910, but his real entry into the cinema did not come until he was already a stage star in plays by Guitry, Feydeau and Pagnol. His first feature film was the 1931 **Le Blanc et le Noir,** but it was **Marius** in the same year that made his screen reputation. He had already played the role of César on stage in 1929, and essentially the same cast was assembled for the film. The story of the trilogy is simple: Marius (César's son, played by Pierre Fresnay) loves Fanny (Orane Demazis) who gets preg-

nant after he goes away to sea, so César has to make respectable arrangements. Its unmatched portrait of the Marseilles waterfront world inspired other films and the musical **Fanny.** Among Raimu's other best-remembered roles: the baker who refuses to make more bread until his unfaithful wife returns in **La Femme du Boulanger;** the captain stuffed with vanity and hypocrisy in **Les Gâités de l'Escadron;** the village mayor who marries his maid in **Un Carnet de Bal;** and the well-digger with a pregnant unmarried daughter in **La Fille du Puisatier.** He made few films during the Occupation, but ended his career on a high point with an effective, Dostoevsky-inspired portrayal of an alcoholic cuckold in **L'Homme au Chapeau Rond.** He died in 1946.

BEST FILMS:
1931 Le Blanc et le Noir
Robert Florey (Billancourt)
1931 Marius
Alexander Korda (Paramount)
1932 Les Gâités de l'Escadron
Maurice Tourneur (Pathé-Nathan)
1932 Fanny
Marc Allégret and Pierre Prevert
1936 César
Marcel Pagnol (Paramount)
1937 Un Carnet de Bal
Julien Duvivier (Lévy-Strauss-Sigma)
1938 La Femme du Boulanger (The Baker's Wife)
Marcel Pagnol (Pagnol)
1940 La Fille du Puisatier (The Well-Digger's Daughter)
Marcel Pagnol (Pagnol)
1942 Les Inconnus dans la Maison
Henri Decoin (UGC)
1946 L'Homme au Chapeau Rond
Pierre Billon (Alcina)

CLAUDE RAINS

Claude Rains was one of the great character-actor stars, with a memorable mellifluous voice (sometimes edged with steel), a commanding but pleasurable presence, and a neat line in epigrams and eyebrow movements (he could raise the right one to express everything from amusement to scorn). His most famous screen line comes at the end of **Casablanca,** as the politically ambiguous French police chief: he watches Humphrey Bogart ❯ shoot down the Nazi villain and then order his minions to "round up the usual suspects." His voice made him famous (in his first film, **The Invisible Man**), but his intelligent acting made him a star.

Above: Claude Rains gave one of his most memorable performances as the police chief in **Casablanca** *(1943).*

He was Bette Davis's ❯ perfect partner in three classic films (**Now Voyager, Mr Skeffington, Deception**) and the musical father of the **Four Daughters** series. He created one of the great screen villains as wily Prince John opposing Errol Flynn ❯ in **The Adventures of Robin Hood,** was even more villainous for Alfred Hitchcock as the Fascist leader in **Notorious,** and turned suavely into a radio star-murderer in **The Unsuspected.** He was also excellent in horror films like **The Invisible Man** and **The Phantom of the Opera** (as the pathetic, tortured Erik). He was the representative of heaven in **Here Comes Mr Jordan** and the representative of hell (as a corrupt senator) in **Mr Smith Goes to Washington.** He was nominated for an acting Oscar four times, but never won it despite the enormous admiration his acting skills aroused in Hollywood.

Rains was born in London on November 10, 1889, and was an English stage star before going to America. After his screen début in **The Invisible Man,** he was shown to audiences for the first time in the Ben Hecht-Charles MacArthur picture **Crime Without Passion.** He was much praised for it and became a screen regular at Warner Brothers, but kept up his work in the theatre. He made films in England as well, notably as Ceasar in **Caesar and Cleopatra** (Shaw asked for him) and in David Lean's **The Passionate Friends.**

His last film role was as Herod the Great in the 1965 **The Greatest Story Ever Told,** and he died two years later.

BEST FILMS:
1933 The Invisible Man
James Whale (Universal)
1938 The Adventures of Robin Hood
Michael Curtiz & William Keighley (Warner Brothers)
1939 Mr Smith Goes to Washington
Frank Capra (Columbia)
1942 Now Voyager
Irving Rapper (Warner Brothers)
1943 Casablanca
Michael Curtiz (Warner Brothers)
1943 The Phantom of the Opera
Arthur Lubin (Universal)
1944 Mr Skeffington
Vincent Sherman (Warner Brothers)
1945 Caesar and Cleopatra
Gabriel Pascal (Rank)
1946 Notorious
Alfred Hitchcock (RKO)
1947 The Unsuspected
Michael Curtiz (Warner Brothers)

Basil Rathbone

Basil Rathbone has to be considered the greatest villain in the history of the cinema, hawkish, cunning and suave, his lean face with a cutting edge like a razor. That he is also the best Sherlock Holmes of the movies only shows how well his persona matched the dark-light, slightly sinister aspects of Conan Doyle's famous detective. Among his other roles, there are no more memorable scenes in the cinema than Rathbone toying with the foppish Tyrone Power ≫ in **The Mark of Zorro** before their duel to the death, sardonically mocking Robin Hood before the screen's greatest sword fight in **The Adventures of Robin Hood,** or radiating absolute evil as Mr Murdstone in **David Copperfield.** He received only two Oscar nominations for his film work, as Tybalt in **Romeo and Juliet** and as the hunchbacked Louis XI in **If I Were King,** but his fame will

endure longer than that of many actors who won that prize.

He was born with the (appropriately villainous) name of Philip St John Basil Rathbone in Johannesburg, South Africa, and was educated in England, where he made his stage début in 1911. He made his first British film in 1921 (**The Fruitful Vine**) and his first Hollywood picture in 1924 (**Pity the Chorus Girl**). He was a romantic lead in his early years, but after his frightening success in **David Copperfield** in 1935 he was usually nasty. He was Greta Garbo's ≫ unsympathetic husband in **Anna Karenina,** aristocratically evil as the Marquis St Evremonde in **A Tale of Two Cities,** and brilliantly matched against Errol Flynn ≫ for the first time in **Captain Blood.** He began his career as Sherlock Holmes in

1939 in **The Hound of the Baskervilles** and played the role to perfection in 14 films with Nigel Bruce as his beloved, bumbling Watson. One of the villainous highpoints of his '40s career was being stabbed to death by Joan Fontaine ≫ in **Frenchman's Creek,** but he left the cinema soon after for stage work, making only a few films in the '50s. He was nicely vicious in John Ford's 1958 **The Last Hurrah,** but made mostly horror films in the '60s. He died in 1967. His autobiography, *In and Out of Character,* was published in 1962.

BEST FILMS:
1935 David Copperfield
George Cukor (MGM)
1935 Anna Karenina
Clarence Brown (MGM)
1935 Captain Blood
Michael Curtiz (Warner Brothers)
1936 Romeo and Juliet
George Cukor (MGM)
1938 The Adventures of Robin Hood
Michael Curtiz (Warner Brothers)
1938 If I Were King
Frank Lloyd (Paramount)
1939 The Hound of the Baskervilles
Sidney Lanfield (20th Century Fox)
1939 The Adventures of Sherlock Holmes
Alfred Werker (20th Century Fox)
1940 The Mark of Zorro
Rouben Mamoulian (MGM)
1944 Frenchman's Creek
Mitchell Leisen (Paramount)

*Below: Basil Rathbone portrayed Sherlock Holmes in 14 films (with Nigel Bruce as his bumbling Watson) and is the actor most identified with the role; this is **The Scarlet Claw.***

Fernando Rey
see **Modern Stars**

Debbie Reynolds

Debbie Reynolds was the bouncy, bright-eyed, singing-dancing star of '50s musicals, who hit her peak in the 1952 **Singin' in the Rain** with Gene Kelly ≫ and Donald O'Connor ≫ and stayed a top box office attraction until the mid-'60s. She was good in light comedy, too, especially in films liked **The Catered Affair, Susan**

Slept Here and **The Tender Trap,** but she is most famous for her musical numbers. In **Three Little Words** she energetically mimed and Charlestoned to boop-boop-a-doo girl Helen Kane's words, and in **Two Weeks With Love** she stole the show with her infectious *Aba Daba Honeymoon* routine with Carleton Carpenter. In **Singin' in the Rain,** probably the best and certainly the most liked of all Hollywood musicals, she was the girl that Kelly and O'Connor make into a star by pulling back a curtain (revealing that she is Jean Hagen's tuneful voice). She sang the title song and the peppy *Good Morning* with them and contributed a good deal to the film's charm. She continued to star in smaller-scale musicals, but didn't have another big one until **The Unsinkable Molly Brown** in 1964,

*Above: Debbie Reynolds and Gregory Peck were among the many stars featured in the 1963 **How the West Was Won.***

as the hustling, bustling, Molly.

She was born as Mary Frances Reynolds in El Paso, Texas, on April 1, 1932, and got into films by the unlikely route of being elected a beauty queen (Miss Burbank of 1948). Her first film was a bit part in the 1948 **June Bride,** and she made a good impression in the 1950 **The Daughter of Rosie O'Grady** (both with Warner Brothers of Burbank) before becoming a (dubbed) star in **Three Little Words** for MGM. She was teamed with O'Connor again in **I Love Melvin,** but was better with Frank Sinatra ≫ in **The Tender Trap.** She reached her peak of box office popularity at the end of the '50s, at the same time as she was losing husband Eddie Fisher to Elizabeth Taylor ≫ , but her '60s career was less successful despite the brilliant comedy **Divorce American Style** and the musical **The Unsinkable Molly Brown.** She had a short-lived TV series in 1969, *Debbie,* and starred in an excellent horror film in 1971, **What's The Matter With Helen?** She lent her voice to the animated cartoon feature **Charlotte's Web** in 1972 and was on Broadway in 1973 in the musical *Irene.*

THELMA RITTER

Thelma Ritter was the star of character actresses. She was nominated six times for the Best Supporting Actress Oscar (a record, even though she never won) and in most of the pictures she made she was as popular as, and usually more amusing than, the leads. Ritter's screen persona was as the barbed-tongued, Brooklyn-accented adviser-friend-maid-landlady who could see things more clearly than the heroine and comment scathingly. In **All About Eve** she was Bette Davis's ❯ sceptical maid, undeceived by Ann Baxter's sad story ("everything but the bloodhounds yappin' at her behind"). In **The Mating Season** she has acid comments by the score, posing as the servant of her son's new socialite bride, Gene Tierney ❯. In **Rear Window** she looks wittily after the invalid James Stewart ❯ and in **Daddy Long Legs** she looks sniffily after Fred Astaire ❯. Her finest performance was in a straight role in Sam Fuller's 1952 **Pickup on South Street,** in which she plays an underworld stoolpigeon who refuses to inform on pickpocket Richard Widmark ❯, although she knows she will be killed if she doesn't. As she showed in this film, she could have been a brilliant dramatic actress, but she became a prisoner of her (admittedly superb) screen image and was never really able to break out of it.

Ritter was born in Brooklyn, New York City, on February 14, 1905, made her acting début on Broadway in 1926, and didn't appear in her first film until 1947. That was **Miracle on 34th Street** and her delightful performance as a mother bawling out a department store Santa for promising her son a pair of skates made her a character star overnight. In **A Letter to Three Wives** she was a talkative, heavy-drinking cynic, in **Father Was a Fullback** she was a servant in a household with a spoiled teenage daughter ("she needs a good clip in the chops"), and in **The Model and the Marriage Broker** she got star

Above: Thelma Ritter joins James Stewart in voyeuristic viewing in Hitchcock's **Rear Window.**

billing with Jeanne Crain ❯ whom she wisecracks into marriage. In **Pillow Talk** she was Doris Day's ❯ drunken maid and in **The Misfits** she was Marilyn Monroe's ❯ friendly landlady. Her last film was the 1967 **The Incident;** she died two years later of a heart attack.

BEST FILMS:
1949 A Letter to Three Wives
Joseph L. Mankiewicz (20th Century Fox)
1950 All About Eve
Joseph L. Mankiewicz (20th Century Fox)
1951 The Mating Season
Mitchell Leisen (Paramount)
1951 The Model and the Marriage Broker
George Cukor (20th Century Fox)
1952 With a Song in My Heart
Walter Lang (20th Century Fox)
1953 Pickup on South Street
Samuel Fuller (20th Century Fox)
1954 Rear Window
Alfred Hitchcock (Paramount)
1959 Pillow Talk
Michael Gordon (Universal)
1961 The Misfits
John Huston (United Artists)
1962 Birdman of Alcatraz
John Frankenheimer (United Artists)

EDWARD G. ROBINSON

One of the great screen actors, Robinson is remarkable not only for being one of the four major gangster figures of the cinema (most notably in 1930 with his brilliant Rico in **Little Caesar**), but also for being able to escape from that image and take on dozens of different types of roles. Because of his short stature and bulbous features he could never become a romantic hero, but he was a dynamic character star; his versatility was as impressive as Charles Laughton's ❯, with whom he bears comparison—both Robinson and Laughton were non-romantic, at their best in domineering roles and greatly aided in their careers by highly individual and beautifully modulated voices.

Robinson was born on December 12, 1893, in Bucharest, Romania, with the name Emmanuel Goldenberg. His family came to the US in 1902 and he was on stage in New York by the age of 20; he appeared in his first film in 1923 (portraying an old man in **The Bright Shawl**), but his film career did not really start until 1929 when he was asked to play a gangster in **The Hole in the Wall,** directed by Robert Florey. Within a year he was the cinema's leading gangster, mainly through his work with director Mervyn Le Roy on **Little Caesar** and **Two Seconds,** but avoided being typecast and appeared in films by other major directors—he was a fisherman for Howard Hawks in

Left: Edward G. Robinson with Fred MacMurray in Billy Wilder's 1944 thriller **Double Indemnity.**

Tiger Shark, the editor of a sensational newspaper for Le Roy again in **Five Star Final,** a fight manager for Michael Curtiz in **Kid Galahad,** and a mild-mannered bank clerk with a gangster double in John Ford's **The Whole Town's Talking.** Good as his '30s films were, the '40s ones were even better. He worked with Julien Duvivier on two good episode films (**Tales of Manhattan, Flesh and Fantasy**) and then made five great films, with Billy Wilder (**Double Indemnity,** as a persistent investigator), Fritz Lang (as an ordinary little man mixed up in murder in **The Woman in the Window** and **Scarlet Street**), Orson Welles (investigating once more in **The Stranger**) and Joseph L. Mankiewicz (**House of Strangers,** as a ruthless financier using his own sons in his schemes). He made more gangster films and murder mysteries in the '50s, with pictures like **Tight Spot, The Glass Web** and **Black Tuesday,** and then expanded his range in the '60s, from delightful diamond smuggler in Africa for Alexander MacKendrick in **Sammy Going South** to outrageous movie mogul in Rome in Vincente Minnelli's **Two Weeks in Another Town.**

His power to astonish and to dominate films, even in comparatively small roles, continued right up to the end of his career; he may not have been on screen for much of the time in the 1965 **The Cincinnati Kid,** but his performance as the greatest poker player of them all subdued even Steve McQueen ❯. He was the great professional.

In his last film, the bleakly futuristic **Soylent Green** with Charlton Heston, he was as remarkable as ever. For all his brilliance he was never even nominated for an Academy Award, but a posthumous Oscar was given for his whole career shortly after he died in 1973. His autobiography, *All My Yesterdays,* was published the same year.

BEST FILMS:
1930 Little Caesar
Mervyn Le Roy (Warner Brothers)
1931 Five Star Final
Mervyn Le Roy (Warner Brothers)
1935 The Whole Town's Talking
John Ford (Columbia)
1938 A Slight Case of Murder
Lloyd Bacon (Warner Brothers)
1941 The Sea Wolf
Michael Curtiz (Warner Brothers)
1944 Double Indemnity
Billy Wilder (Paramount)
1944 The Woman in the Window
Fritz Lang (RKO)
1945 Scarlet Street
Fritz Lang (Universal)
1945 The Stranger
Orson Welles (RKO)
1948 Key Largo
John Huston (Warner Brothers)
1965 The Cincinnati Kid
Norman Jewison (MGM)

GINGER ROGERS

Ginger Rogers was not only the best dancing partner Fred Astaire ≫ ever had, she was also one of the most delightful, wise-cracking showgirls to grace Hollywood comedies in the '30s and '40s. Some of the most memorable quips in movies came out of her brasher characterisations. In her first feature film in 1930, **The Young Man of Manhattan,** she tossed off the never-to-be-forgotten request, "Cigarette me, Big Boy." In **42nd Street** she was the flip-talking Anytime Annie, of whom it was memorably said that the only time she ever said no was when she didn't hear the question. She was the brazenest of tarts with a heart of gold in her major gum-snapping, wise-cracking role as **Roxie Hart,** but it was Robert Benchley ≫ who got to say the most quoted line of them all to her in **The Major and the Minor,** advising her: "Why don't you step out of those wet clothes and into a dry martini?" Rogers herself likes to be remembered as a more serious actress; her favourite roles are **Kitty Foyle** (progressing from innocent schoolgirl to knowing businesswoman), which won her an Academy Award, and **Primrose Path** (as the 17-year-old daughter of a prostitute, who decides to become a prostitute herself). Most filmgoers, however, usually think of her as the prettier half of the greatest dancing team in the movies; she didn't particularly want to be a musical comedy star, but she accepted the teaming gracefully and Astaire was never able to find another partner who complemented him so well. He was far the superior dancer, but her brashness gave his airiness substantiality and they danced their way through ten of the finest musicals of all time. The first was almost an accident and they were only billed third and fourth in the bizarre **Flying Down to Rio,** but they stole the show, so RKO rushed them into **The Gay Divorcée, Roberta** and **Top Hat.** They quickly became top box office stars in movies which had plots and even good directors, but which they dominate so totally that the films seem to run together into one long Fred-and-Ginger story. They stand up remarkably well today and are still being revived.

Nobody, it should be pointed out, was more pleased with Ginger's success than her mother. She had given birth to this brassy star on July 16, 1911, in Independence, Missouri, and named her Virginia Katherine McMath (the nickname "Ginger" was given to her by a cousin, and "Rogers" came from her mother's second marriage). Lela Rogers has often been ranked first in the ambitious stage mother stakes, but Ginger

didn't seem to mind, feeling it was necessary to have somebody pushing her. She became a singing vaudevillean and then went into musical comedy before going to Hollywood. In her early years (ie, in the 19 films before she was teamed with Astaire) she was mostly cast as a worldly-but-witty flapper type; after the success of the musicals she was able to persuade the studio to give her meatier roles. She was deftly teamed with William Powell ≫ in the sophisticated murder mystery **Star of Midnight,** still wisecracking but showing the insecurity underneath as Katharine Hepburn's ≫ room-mate in **Stage Door** (directed by Gregory La Cava), and a brassy nightclub singer who marries shy professor James Stewart ≫ in **Vivacious Lady** (directed by George Stevens). After the dissolution of her partnership with Astaire following the 1939 **The Story of Vernon and Irene Castle,** she launched

Above: Ginger Rogers wasn't the greatest hoofer in the movies, but she was still the best dancing partner Astaire had.

herself eagerly into her solo career. Her greatest '40s films were Billy Wilder's **The Major and the Minor** (an astonishing predecessor of **Lolita;** in it she becomes romantically involved with Ray Milland ≫ while posing as a 12-year-old), **Roxie Hart** (as a chorus girl out to make her reputation during a murder trial), **Once Upon a Honeymoon** (as a gold-digger involved with a Nazi and rescued by Cary Grant ≫, a black political comedy ahead of its time), **Tom, Dick and Harry** (in which she has a triple daydreaming role), and finally **Lady in the Dark** (a lavish version of the Kurt Weill musical with extraordinary Freudian dream sequences). In 1949 she joined up with Astaire again for one last dance together in **The Barkleys of Broadway.**

Her '50s films were also entertaining, the best being **Monkey Business** (a wacky Howard Hawks comedy about a rejuvenation serum, with Cary Grant) and **Dream Boat** (as a former silent film star whose old films embarrass former co-star Clifton Webb). Her film career began to tail off in the '60s and her last role was as Jean Harlow's ≫ mother in the 1965 **Harlow,** but she was back on stage in 1969 in London, as *Mame.*

BEST FILMS:
1934 The Gay Divorcée
Mark Sandrich (RKO)
1935 Top Hat
Mark Sandrich (RKO)
1936 Swing Time
George Stevens (RKO)
1940 Kitty Foyle
Sam Wood (RKO)
1941 Tom, Dick and Harry
Garson Kanin (RKO)
1942 Roxie Hart
William Wellman (20th Century Fox)
1942 The Major and the Minor
Billy Wilder (Paramount)
1942 Once Upon a Honeymoon
Leo McCarey (RKO)
1944 Lady in the Dark
Mitchell Leisen (Paramount)
1952 Monkey Business
Howard Hawks (20th Century Fox)

ROY ROGERS

Roy Rogers was truly the "King of the Cowboys", the undisputed Number One B-Western star for some 12 years from 1943, far surpassing Gene Autry ≫, who was on top for only six years. Just to make his superlatives complete, he had "The Smartest Horse in the Movies" (Trigger, a palomino which could do 52 separate tricks and often rescued Roy), and he married the "Queen of the West" (Dale Evans, who appeared with him in 20 pictures). He also had one of the most humorous side-

Top: Roy Rogers tames a bronc in the 1976 **Mackintosh & T.J.** *Above: Rogers with his partner Trigger, The Smartest Horse in the Movies.*

kicks in the cinema, George "Gabby" Hayes, who stole every scene he was in. Roy was not a number one actor, however, but he had a pleasant, boyish, happy-go-lucky style, he could sing well (and did so in all his films) and he wore fancy cowboy garb almost naturally.

Rogers was born Leonard Slye in Cincinnati, Ohio, on November 5, 1912, and began in the movies in 1935 with his singing group, the Sons of the Pioneers. He began acting under the name Dick Weston and was turned into Roy Rogers by Republic Pictures' boss Herbert J. Yates in the 1938 film **Under Western Stars.** It was directed by Joseph Kane, who handled the next 42 Rogers pictures, and was a notable success. It was followed by an even better action-packed **Billy the Kid Returns,** but Rogers remained less popular than Autry until the rival Republic singing cowboy went into the Army in 1942. Rogers became tops the next year

Left: Will Rogers. His greatest films were made for John Ford and Henry King during the depths of the Depression.

His dexterity with a lariat led to a career spinning ropes and joke-telling in vaudeville and with the Ziegfeld Follies. He began as a silent movie actor in 1918 for Samuel Goldwyn, in **Laughing Bill Hyde**, but never really became a success in movies until the arrival of sound. Borzage directed him in the 1929 **They Had to See Paris** (the unimpressed American abroad) and he immediately became a major star for Fox. He was in many way the Mark Twain of his day and was a huge success in Twain's **A Connecticut Yankee**, in which most of his dialogue was his own. His finest and most folksy films (his screen roles were simply versions of his rustic persona) were for King (**Lightnin'** and **State Fair**) and Ford (**Doctor Bull, Judge Priest** and **Steamboat 'Round the Bend**); Ford thought highly of Rogers and their pictures together. Rogers' last released film was the 1935 **In Old Kentucky,** for George Marshall. He died in an air crash in August, 1935, but his reputation has not diminished; his popular syndicated newspaper columns were recently re-released and a biopic, **The Will Rogers Story,** was made in 1952, with Will Rogers, Jr, portraying his father.

BEST FILMS:
1931 Lightnin'
Henry King (Fox)
1931 A Connecticut Yankee
David Butler (Fox)
1933 State Fair
Henry King (Fox)
1933 Doctor Bull
John Ford (Fox)
1934 David Harum
James Cruze (Fox)
1934 Handy Andy
David Butler (Fox)
1934 Judge Priest
John Ford (Fox)
1935 Life Begins at Forty
George Marshall (Fox)
1935 Steamboat 'Round the Bend
John Ford (Fox)
1935 In Old Kentucky
George Marshall (Fox)

MICKEY ROONEY

Mickey Rooney has been making movies for longer than most other major stars, well over half a century. He appeared in his first film in 1926, portraying a midget in **Not To Be Trusted,** and in 1978 he was featured in **The Magic of Lassie.** In between he has been at the top and the bottom of the acting profession, the No 1 box office star in the world from 1939 to 1941—and low-billed on the cheapest films in the 1960s. He earned more than $12 million during his long career, but he was a bankrupt in 1962; in 1975 he

still owed the government $250,000 in back taxes.

His film work, like his personal life, is a mass of extraordinary contradictions. He acquired his greatest fame in the dated **Andy Hardy** series as what MGM considered the average American teenager, but gave his finest film performance as a cocky gangster in Don Siegel's low-budget **Baby Face Nelson.** He seemed just as talented as Judy Garland ≫ in their joint teenage musicals, but he never made one musical afterwards as good as her best films. His aggressive, energetic, brash screen persona is closest in pint-sized style to that of James Cagney ≫, but unlike Cagney he has rarely had directors able to

Above: Mickey Rooney in Busby Berkeley's 1939 **Babes in Arms,** co-starring Judy Garland.

channel that energy into good films. He is the classic example of a great but directionless talent, never properly harnessed by Hollywood.

Rooney was born as Joe Yule, Jr, in Brooklyn, New York City, on September 23, 1920. His parents were vaudevilleans and he was on stage at the age of two. After his movie début in two feature films, he was starred in a series of comedy shorts in the late '20s, using the name Mickey McGuire (from a comic strip character). He changed his name to Mickey Rooney in 1932 and began working in small roles in many films. His reputation began to grow after he portrayed Clark Gable ≫ as a boy in the 1934 **Manhattan Melodrama** and then had a wonderful success as Puck in the lavish 1935 version of **A Midsummer Night's Dream,** created by Max Reinhardt. He was excellent as the young brother in Clarence Brown's film version of Eugene O'Neill's play **Ah Wilderness!** and was much admired as the tough kid contrasted to Freddie Bartholomew in **Little Lord Fauntleroy.** In 1937 he made the first of the **Andy Hardy** series, **A Family Affair,** a small town saga which quickly became the favourite project of MGM

and stayed that way until the death of the B-Western in the '50s.

During the early '40s, Rogers' films became overly musical, but by the end of the decade they turned back to action with stronger films like **Springtime in the Sierras.** Rogers made his last B-Western in 1951 (**Pals of the Golden West**), turned up in rather splendid form the following year, assisting Bob Hope ≫ in **Son of Paleface,** and then retired to television for most of the '50s. He made a very enjoyable comeback in 1976 as an old drifter helping a young boy in **MacKintosh and T.J.**

BEST FILMS:
1938 Billy the Kid Returns
Joseph Kane (Republic)
1939 In Old Caliente
Joseph Kane (Republic)
1940 Dark Command
Raoul Walsh (Republic)
1942 Heart of the Golden West
Joseph Kane (Republic)
1944 San Fernando Valley
John English (Republic)
1945 Don't Fence Me In
John English (Republic)
1946 My Pal Trigger
Frank McDonald (Republic)
1947 Springtime in the Sierras
William Witney (Republic)
1950 Trail of Robin Hood
William Witney (Republic)
1952 Son of Paleface
Frank Tashlin (Paramount)

WILL ROGERS

One of the great American humorists and a major film star in the early '30s, Will Rogers was quintessentially American. English critics have never really understood his appeal, but then the Americans have never really appreciated Will Hay ≫ or Gracie Fields ≫. Rogers was the screen's greatest personification of the cracker-barrel philosopher, the folksy, homespun humorist who could deflate the pretences of politicians and "explain" international events in ways that even the ordinary person could understand. "All I know is just what I read in the papers every day," was his usual prefatory remark, and his amiable warmth was conveyed in his famous phrase, "I never met a man I didn't like." He acted as the representative of the people to the powers that be, most of whom also knew and admired him. From 1931 to 1935 he was a top box office star (number one in 1934) and his persona was used to fine effect in populist films directed by John Ford, Henry King, George Marshall and Frank Borzage.

Rogers was born in Cologah, Oklahoma (then Indian Territory), on November 4, 1879, and worked in his early years as a ranch hand.

mogul Louis B. Mayer, and had a fine, small role in **Captains Courageous** with Spencer Tracy ». In 1938 he was teamed for the first time with Judy Garland in **Thoroughbreds Don't Cry,** MGM began to turn **Andy Hardy** into one of their most profitable series of films, but Rooney's best film of that year was Norman Taurog's **Boys' Town.** He played a tough delinquent to Spencer Tracy's Father Flanagan and helped Tracy win his second Oscar in a row. Rooney also got an Oscar, a miniature one for "bringing to the screen the spirit and personification of youth". The next year he became the top star in the world and began his pleasant series of teenage musicals with Judy Garland in **Babes in Arms,** later to be followed by **Strike Up the Band, Babes on Broadway** and **Girl Crazy.** He was a star in capital letters now, dominating his films to a degree that would soon become impractical. He made notable appearances in **The Human Comedy** and **National Velvet,** spent a short time in the Army, and then came back to a career that was suddenly headed downhill, despite good films like Rouben Mamoulian's musical **Summer Holiday.** He left MGM and his star started to burn out in bad films and bad roles. He began to get lower billing, and even superb performances like his gangster in **Baby Face Nelson** and his soldier in **The Bold and the Brave** did little to improve his career. Mostly, he was good in his films, but mostly the films weren't very good. He was funny as the Japanese who lives upstairs in **Breakfast at Tiffany's,** but it was a silly role for him to play. His subsequent films were often forgettable, but he kept on working as energetically as ever; given his talent and his drive he may yet come back. Among his more memorable recent roles, he was splendid as a ham comedian in **The Comic,** as a convict in **The Domino Principle,** as a lighthouse keeper in **Pete's Dragon** and as a diminutive Mafioso in **Pulp.**

BEST FILMS:
1935 A Midsummer Night's Dream
Max Reinhardt & William Dieterle (Warner Brothers)
1938 Boys' Town
Norman Taurog (MGM)
1939 Babes in Arms
Busby Berkeley (MGM)
1940 Strike Up the Band
Busby Berkeley (MGM)
1941 Babes on Broadway
Busby Berkeley (MGM)
1943 The Human Comedy
Clarence Brown (MGM)
1943 Girl Crazy
Norman Taurog (MGM)
1948 Summer Holiday
Rouben Mamoulian (MGM)
1956 The Bold and the Brave
Lewis R. Foster (RKO)
1957 Baby Face Nelson
Don Siegel (United Artists)
1972 Pulp
Mike Hodges (United Artists/Klinger)

JANE RUSSELL

Hollywood sex stars usually turn out to be far more interesting (and talented) than their publicity would lead you to expect. Jane Russell was publicised primarily for having big breasts (from the censors' reaction one would have thought cleavage was about to destroy the moral fibre of the American nation), but she proved to have a nice line in scepticism and wry wit as well, making her an excellent comedienne. Her screen début in Howard Hughes's **The Outlaw** was probably the most heavily promoted in the history of the cinema, so much so that no one could have lived up to the promise of unbridled passion. The film turned out to be just a goodish version of the Billy the Kid story, with Russell having to climb into the Kid's bed to keep him warm during a fever bout. At the time, the movie was considered the ultimate in licentiousness and was banned for over two years after its initial release in 1943.

Russell finally recovered from its inhibiting effect on her career by going into comedy, first with Bob Hope » in **The Paleface** and **Son of Paleface** and then brilliantly as Marilyn Monroe's » partner in **Gentlemen Prefer Blondes.** She was pretty good in some small-budget RKO thrillers as well,

Above: Jane Russell, protégé of eccentric millionaire Howard Hughes, created a furore in the 1940s with her sexuality in **The Outlaw** *(1943). A complete contrast was the 1948 comedy* **The Paleface** *with Bob Hope.*

opposite Robert Mitchum » in **His Kind of Woman** and **Macao** and Victor Mature » in **The Las Vegas Story.** She was a strong partner for Clark Gable » in **The Tall Men,** excellent as a gypsy involved with Cornel Wilde » in **Hot Blood,** and likeable as a singing dance hall girl in **The Revolt of Mamie Stover.** Her career virtually ended in the late '50s; she has made only five unimportant films since then, her last appearance being in the 1970 **Darker Than Amber.**

Jane Russell was born as Ernestine Jane Geraldine Russell in Bemidji, Minnesota, on June 21, 1921, worked as a chiropodist's assistant for a time, and then turned to modelling and acting. Howard Hughes promoted her breasts into a national fetish in 1943 and apparently had genuine faith in her abilities, for he kept her under contract until his death. She now works primarily in dinner theatre shows, as well as advertising big-breasted bras on television.

BEST FILMS:
1943 The Outlaw
Howard Hughes (RKO)

1948 The Paleface
Norman Z. McLeod (Paramount)
1951 His Kind of Woman
John Farrow (RKO)
1952 Macao
Josef von Sternberg (RKO)
1952 Son of Paleface
Frank Tashlin (Paramount)
1953 Gentlemen Prefer Blondes
Howard Hawks (20th Century Fox)
1955 The Tall Men
Raoul Walsh (20th Century Fox)
1955 Gentlemen Marry Brunettes
Richard Sale (United Artists)
1956 Hot Blood
Nicholas Ray (Columbia)
1956 The Revolt of Mamie Stover
Raoul Walsh (20th Century Fox)

ROSALIND RUSSELL

The cinema's No 1 career woman, competing with men on their own ground and doing very well at it long before women's lib became fashionable. The highpoint of Rosalind Russell's screen career was the 1940 **His Girl Friday;** director Howard Hawks took the Ben Hecht-Charles MacArthur play, *The Front Page,* filmed earlier by Lewis Milestone, and gave her the part of the tough reporter originally played by Edmund O'Brien. With Cary Grant » as her editor, she turned in a superb performance, competing with men on their own turf—and winning. This role-reversal was again used well by Mitchell Leisen in **Take a Letter, Darling,** in which she is the business executive and Ray Milland » is her secretary. She later complained that she had been typecast as a boss lady (in 23 films), but the role suited her rather dominant, no-nonsense persona perfectly, as can be seen in her later film hits **Auntie Mame** and **Gypsy.**

Rosalind Russell was born in Waterbury, Connecticut, on June 4, 1908, worked on stage in the '20s and early '30s, and made her film début in 1934 in **Evelyn Prentice.** There were rather too many talented ladies at MGM at

Above: Rosalind Russell as she appeared in the 1940 **No Time for Comedy.**

that time for her own career to advance quickly, but she did excellent work in Dorothy Arzner's **Craig's Wife** and opposite axe-murderer Robert Montgomery in **Night Must Fall.** She first attracted real attention in **The Women** in 1939, going right over the top and more or less stealing the film from her co-stars. Her films remained fun in the '40s, especially **My Sister Eileen** and **No Time for Comedy,** but she bit off rather more than she could chew dramatically with **Mourning Becomes Electra** and her film career faded. She was an enormous success on Broadway in a musical version of **My Sister Eileen** called *Wonderful Town* and returned to Hollywood with good performances in **Picnic** and **Auntie Mame.** She was in her best, dominant form pushing Gypsy Rose Lee (Natalie Wood ») to rebellion in the delightful musical **Gypsy,** and continued to work occasionally in the cinema. She was last seen in the TV movie **The Crooked Hearts** with Douglas Fairbanks, Jr » in 1972. She died in 1976.

BEST FILMS:
1939 The Women
George Cukor (MGM)
1940 His Girl Friday
Howard Hawks (Columbia)
1940 No Time for Comedy
William Keighley (Warner Brothers)
1942 Take a Letter, Darling
Mitchell Leisen (Paramount)
1942 My Sister Eileen
Alexander Hall (Columbia)
1943 What a Woman
Irving Cummings (Columbia)
1945 Roughly Speaking
Michael Curtiz (Warner Brothers)
1955 Picnic
Joshua Logan (Columbia)
1958 Auntie Mame
Morton da Costa (Warner Brothers)
1962 Gypsy
Mervyn Le Roy (Warner Brothers)

Margaret Rutherford

Margaret Rutherford is one of the great screen comediennes, despite the fact that she rarely had starring roles and that most of her films were not good in themselves. She was always delightful, even in the weakest movie, and her multiple chins, baggy face and shapeless figure projected an endearing dottiness unlike that of any other screen personality. She should have become a major star, but never had the luck to find a director to develop her screen persona to its full potential; all the same, she won a Best Supporting Actress Oscar at the age of 72 for her brilliant performance in the 1963 **The VIPs,** was made a Dame of the British Empire in 1966, created an unforgettable Miss Marple (Agatha Christie's spinster detective) and enlivened every movie she was in.

She was born in London in 1892, began to work on stage in 1925, and made her cinema début in the 1936 **Dusty Ermine.** Her wonderful scattiness came to the forefront in such early '40s films as **Yellow Canary, The Demi-Paradise** and **English Without Tears,** and she achieved international recognition as the spiritualist in **Blithe Spirit.** She was terrific as a medieval expert in **Passport to Pimlico,** superb as a headmistress matched against Alastair Sim in **The Happiest Days of Your Life,** and perfection as Miss Prism in **The Importance of Being Earnest.** She was brilliantly cast as Miss Marple in four films (**Murder She Said, Murder at the Gallop, Murder Most Foul** and **Murder Ahoy**), although the films themselves could have been a lot better. She was possibly at her very best as Mistress Quickly in Orson Welles' » 1966 **Chimes at Midnight,** and was one of the most likeable aspects of Charles Chaplin's » **A Countess from Hong Kong.** *An Autobiography* was published in 1972, the year she died.

Above: Margaret Rutherford in Anthony Kimmins' 1954 **Aunt Clara** *with Henry Markin; she plays a nice little old lady who inherits a brothel.*

BEST FILMS:
1945 Blithe Spirit
David Lean (Two Cities)
1949 Passport to Pimlico
Henry Cornelius (Ealing)
1950 The Happiest Days of Your Life
Frank Launder (British Lion)
1952 The Importance of Being Earnest
Anthony Asquith (Rank)
1957 The Smallest Show on Earth
Basil Dearden (British Lion)
1961 Murder She Said
George Pollock (MGM)
1963 The Mouse on the Moon
Richard Lester (United Artists)
1963 Murder at the Gallop
Basil Rayburn (MGM)
1963 The VIPs
Anthony Asquith (MGM)
1966 Chimes at Midnight
Orson Welles (Internacional Films)

Robert Ryan

Robert Ryan was a very fine and intelligent screen actor with a long period of stardom in many excellent movies—but he never quite became a major star. The reason for this was not lack of presence, nor even the lack of an identifiable screen persona, but because he was really best at being a nasty villain. Ryan was born in Chicago, Illinois, on November 11, 1909, studied at Dartmouth College, where he was a champion boxer, and began to work on stage in the late '30s. He made his film début in 1940 in small roles in **Golden Gloves** and **Queen of the Mob;** his first really important role came in 1947 as Joan Bennett's » lover, urged to murder her blind husband, in Jean Renoir's **Woman on the Beach.** He went on to play heroic and unvillainous roles, and played them well, but as a pleasant character he seemed slightly weak, while as a villain he was terrifyingly strong. It is probable that this nastiness interfered with his charisma, because major stars always have sympathetic screen personas—even when they play gangsters and horror roles—while there were no redeeming features in Ryan's heavies. He was a vicious, Jew-hating murderer in **Crossfire,** a sadistic gunfighter in **Return of the Badman,** a paranoid husband in **Caught,** a pursuing fury in **Act of Violence,** a bitter lover in **Clash By Night,** a pitiless killer tracked down by James Stewart » in **The Naked Spur,** and a killer hunting Spencer Tracy » in **Bad Day at Black Rock.**

These were early films, but that frightening image did not change with the years. In **House of Bamboo** he headed a criminal group in Tokyo, and he stayed the chief of violent and sinister organisations in the '70s, in films like **Executive Action** and **The Outfit.** His pure, unadulterated nastiness was seen at its most disturbing in **Odds Against Tomorrow,** as a nigger-hating psychopath, viciously baiting Harry Belafonte, and in **Billy Budd** as the horrifically nasty Claggart. He was very strong on pursuing missions, as the chief bounty-hunter in **The Wild Bunch,** the detective in pursuit of a killer in **On Dangerous Ground,** and the hired gunman chasing Jack Palance » in **The Professionals.** Obviously, he had to be one of the stars of **The Dirty Dozen.** Ryan's sympathetic roles pale into insignificance beside these performances, but he was outstanding as

Below: Robert Ryan turns in his badge in the 1956 Western **The Proud Ones,** *directed by Robert D. Webb. Even when he was on the right side of the law, Ryan retained a certain nastiness.*

a washed-up boxer making a crooked comeback in **The Set-Up,** as a Georgian farmer looking for gold in **God's Little Acre,** and as Larry Slade in **The Iceman Cometh,** his last film. He died of cancer in 1973.

BEST FILMS:
1947 Woman on the Beach
Jean Renoir (RKO)
1947 Crossfire
Edward Dmytryk (RKO)
1948 Act of Violence
Fred Zinnemann (MGM)
1949 Caught
Max Ophuls (MGM)

1951 On Dangerous Ground
Nicholas Ray (RKO)
1952 Clash By Night
Fritz Lang (RKO)
1955 House of Bamboo
Samuel Fuller (20th Century Fox)
1957 Men in War
Anthony Mann (United Artists)
1962 Billy Budd
Peter Ustinov (Allied Artists)
1967 The Dirty Dozen
Robert Aldrich (MGM)
1969 The Wild Bunch
Sam Peckinpah (Warner Brothers/
Seven Arts)

GEORGE SANDERS

Any man who could marry both Zsa Zsa and Magda Gabor, write an autobiography called *Memoirs of a Professional Cad,* and finally kill himself through sheer boredom, has to be one of the most extraordinary personalities ever to become a movie star. In fact,

Sanders was the cinema's greatest incarnation of the suave, silky scoundrel, the ultimate *roué,* with casual disdain for lesser mortals fairly emanating from him. He won an Academy Award for the greatest demonstration of this persona, the utterly superior drama critic/narrator of **All About Eve,** but he was the suavest of snobs and iciest of villains in dozens of good films. Leslie Charteris's sophisticated adventurer "The Saint" fitted his personality perfectly and he played the role (and its twin brother "The Falcon") in a number of enjoyable films.

Like that other great screen Englishman, Leslie Howard », Sanders was actually of foreign descent. He was born in St Petersburg, Russia, on July 3, 1906 (his mother was British), and came with his family to England during the Russian Revolution. He began his acting career on stage, made his British

film début in the 1936 **Find the Lady,** and made his first American picture, **Lloyds of London,** in 1937. He was very quickly successful, making his first "Saint" movie in 1939 (**The Saint in London**) and starting a nice line in villains in the '40s with such swashbucklers as **Son of Fury** and **The Black Swan.** He was featured by Alfred Hitchcock in **Rebecca** and **Foreign Correspondent,** was the Nazi pursuing Walter Pidgeon » in Fritz Lang's **Man Hunt,** and was excellent as the Gauguin character in **The Moon and Sixpence.** He worked steadily right into the '50s, when he starred in his two greatest films, **All About Eve,** and Roberto Rossellini's **Voyage in Italy,** with Ingrid Bergman ».

He made so many films that there had to be bad ones, but there were also a remarkable number of excellent ones, including Lang's **While the City Sleeps** and **Moonfleet,** and three films for Douglas Sirk (**Summer Storm, A Scandal in Paris, Lured**). Among his notable later pictures were

Above: George Sanders and Ingrid Bergman in Roberto Rossellini's 1954 **Viaggio in Italia,** *one of the key films of the modern cinema and one of Sanders' finest performances. It is the story of an English couple whose marriage is in trouble.*

Village of the Damned, The Quiller Memorandum and **The Kremlin Letter.**

He died in Barcelona in 1972 of an overdose of sleeping pills, leaving a very George Sanders-ish farewell note.

BEST FILMS:
1939 The Saint in London
John Farrow (RKO)
1940 Rebecca
Alfred Hitchcock (United Artists)
1940 Foreign Correspondent
Alfred Hitchcock (United Artists)
1941 Man Hunt
Fritz Lang (20th Century Fox)

1942 Son of Fury
John Cromwell (20th Century Fox)
1942 The Moon and Sixpence
Albert Lewin (United Artists)
1944 The Lodger
John Brahm (20th Century Fox)
1950 All About Eve
Joseph L. Mankiewicz (20th Century Fox)
1953 Viaggio in Italia (Voyage in Italy)
Roberto Rossellini
1953 Call Me Madam
Walter Lang (20th Century Fox)

RANDOLPH SCOTT

Randolph Scott is one of the icons of the cinema's West, long, lean and leather-faced, forever riding tall in the saddle. He is more identified with the genre than any of the other major Western stars and appeared almost exclusively in cowboy films from 1946 until his retirement in 1962. He is best remembered now for the out-

standing Westerns he made in the '50s, especially the seven directed by Budd Boetticher, and for his brilliant swansong, Sam Peckinpah's 1962 **Ride the High Country,** but in his earlier career he starred in a great variety of films. He was featured in musicals like **Roberta** (with Fred Astaire » and Ginger Rogers ») and **High, Wide and Handsome** (with Irene Dunne »), comedies like **Go West, Young Man** (with Mae West ») and **My Favourite Wife** (with Cary Grant »), war pictures like **To the Shores of Tripoli** and **Gung Ho!,** and even opposite Shirley Temple

» in **Rebecca of Sunnybrook Farm.**

Scott was born in Orange County, Virginia, on January 23, 1903, to a wealthy family (he was once married to one of the Dupont heiresses), and made his film début as an extra in the 1928 **Sharpshooters.** He became a Western star very quickly and was featured in ten Zane Grey-derived films in the early '30s, as well as big budget Western productions like **The Last of the Mohicans** and **Frontier Marshall.** He starred in good adventure films like **She** and was an important star all through World War II, in such memorable pictures as **Western Union** and **The Spoilers.** The 1946 **Badman's Territory** was such a big hit that he decided to concentrate on cowboy pictures from that point.

Below: Randolph Scott became one of the myths of the movie West during the 1950s and a top box-office star, especially in seven outstanding films with director Budd Boetticher.

It was an astute decision. From 1950 to 1953 he was among the top ten box office stars in the US, with films like **Colt .45, Sugarfoot** and **Carson City.** In 1956 he began the series of Boetticher-directed pictures that won him cinematic immortality, older and more rugged now, with the kind of hard-earned integrity that only years in the saddle could bestow. These seven films (**Seven Men From Now, The Tall T, Decision at Sundown, Buchanan Rides Alone, Ride Lonesome, Westbound** and **Comanche Station**) are unique achievements in the genre, as austere and bleak as the landscapes in which they are made, without sentimentality and entirely focused upon the persona of Scott as the essential man of the West. After this stunning conclusion to his career, Scott made only one more film, **Ride the High Country,** a superb farewell portraying an ageing gunfighter on his last job.

BEST FILMS:
1940 My Favorite Wife
Garson Kanin (RKO)
1941 Western Union
Fritz Lang (20th Century Fox)
1956 Seven Men From Now
Budd Boetticher (Warner Brothers)
1957 The Tall T
Budd Boetticher (Columbia)
1957 Decision at Sundown
Budd Boetticher (Columbia)
1958 Buchanan Rides Alone
Budd Boetticher (Columbia)
1959 Ride Lonesome
Budd Boetticher (Columbia)
1959 Westbound
Budd Boetticher (Warner Brothers)
1960 Comanche Station
Budd Boetticher (Columbia)
1962 Ride the High Country
Sam Peckinpah (MGM)

NORMA SHEARER

Norma Shearer was the ultra-chic Joan Crawford ➤ of her day, the glamorous movie star to her fingertips, promoted by MGM as the First Lady of the Screen. She was regal, almost the Queen of Hollywood, married to MGM production chief Irving Thalberg, and admired by women everywhere for her sophisticated, woman-of-the-world image. She was one of the few major silent stars to become a top sound star, and after winning an Academy Award in 1930 for **The Divorcée** was a top box office attraction during the early '30s. Her acting ability and her beauty seem less impressive today, but there is no denying her charisma. She was born in Montreal, Canada, on August 10, 1900, as Edith Norma Shearer, and made her film début in tiny parts in 1922. She made her greatest films in the silent era, notably Victor Sjöström's **He Who Gets Slapped** with Lon Chaney ➤ (as the bareback rider) and Ernst Lubitsch's **The Student Prince** (as the barmaid Kathi), but she made some good ones in sound as well. After joining MGM in 1923 and being built up as a star by Thalberg, Clarence Brown starred her opposite Clark Gable ➤ in **A Free Soul,** in which he knocks her about, and **Idiot's Delight,** as an old flame. George Cukor turned her into a passable if slightly old Juliet in **Romeo and Juliet** and gave her the central role in **The Women** (tears a-plenty, with an all-star cast). Her own favourite role was as Elizabeth in **The**

Right: Norma Shearer as Elizabeth Barrett and Fredric March as Robert Browning in **The Barretts of Wimpole Street,** *terrorised by Mr. Barrett.*

Barretts of Wimpole Street, opposite Charles Laughton ➤ and Fredric March ➤, but she also turned in an enjoyable performance as the star of the opulent **Marie Antoinette.** In the '30s, as is evident, she tended to favour adaptations of famous stage plays, and even tried Noël Coward's ➤ **Private Lives.**

Shearer was in many ways the epitome of MGM gloss and glamour and was much admired for a not currently fashionable personality trait—she had class. What she most wanted to be in the world was a glamorous movie star; she worked hard at becoming and remaining one. She reputedly knew as much about lighting and camera angles as the cameramen, and she certainly knew what was right for her—she remained a major MGM star for 18 years, from 1924 to 1942, although after Thalberg's death her career faltered slightly. She made some more successful films, but after two failures in 1942, **We Were Dancing** and **Her Cardboard Lover,** she retired permanently from the cinema. She lives today in California with her second husband and does not involve herself in the film world.

BEST FILMS:
1924 He Who Gets Slapped
Victor Sjöström (MGM)
1927 The Student Prince
Ernst Lubitsch (MGM)
1930 The Divorcée
Robert Z. Leonard (MGM)
1931 A Free Soul
Clarence Brown (MGM)
1934 Riptide
Edmund Goulding (MGM)
1934 The Barretts of Wimpole Street
Sidney Franklin (MGM)
1936 Romeo and Juliet
George Cukor (MGM)
1938 Marie Antoinette
W.S. Van Dyke (MGM)
1939 Idiot's Delight
Clarence Brown (MGM)
1939 The Women
George Cukor (MGM)

ANN SHERIDAN

Ann Sheridan was touted by Warner Brothers as the "Oomph Girl" in the early '40s in a bid to make her a sexy pin-up star, but she was really best as a brassy, down-to-earth waitress, dance hall girl or gangster's moll. She was just as good with a memorable wisecrack as toughie male screen partners like James Cagney ➤ and Humphrey Bogart ➤ and proved herself a brilliant comedienne in films like **I Was a Male War Bride,** opposite Cary Grant ➤. She was superb as a hash-

Above: Ann Sheridan with her screen husband Cary Grant in WAC disguise in Howard Hawks' amazing **I Was a Male War Bride.**

house waitress with Bogart ➤ and George Raft ➤ in **They Drive by Night,** equally strong opposite Ronald Reagan in **King's Row** and unforgettable as the saloon girl who sings in **Dodge City** with Errol Flynn ➤. She sang even better as a night club performer in **Torrid Zone** with Cagney and Pat O'Brien and had sparkling dialogue as well, so Warners made her into a minor musical star with films like **Shine On Harvest Moon.** Her screen personality was flexible and very enjoyable and her style of playing has hardly dated.

Ann Sheridan was born as Clara Lou Sheridan in Denton, Texas, on February 21, 1915, and made her film début in the 1934 **Search for Beauty** as the result of winning a beauty contest. She did well in a varied series of late '30s films, but first really attracted attention in **Angels with Dirty Faces.** She was teamed with John

Garfield ➤ in **They Made Me a Criminal** and starred in a musical with Dick Powell ➤, **Naughty But Nice;** she had Bogart as her co-star in the comedy **It All Came True** and got together with Cagney again in **City for Conquest.** She was in splendid form as the actress who visits **The Man Who Came to Dinner** and very funny with Jack Benny ➤ in **George Washington Slept Here.** After leaving Warners in 1948 she made two of her best films, **Good Sam** with Gary Cooper ➤, and that masterpiece of sex reversal, **I Was a Male War Bride.**

She remained an outstanding performer in '50s films like **Take Me to Town, Come Next Spring** and **The Opposite Sex,** but retired from the screen after the 1957 **Woman and the Hunter.** She spent the rest of her life in theatre and television and died in 1967.

BEST FILMS:
1939 Dodge City
Michael Curtiz (Warner Brothers)
1940 Torrid Zone
William Keighley (Warner Brothers)

1940 They Drive By Night
Raoul Walsh (Warner Brothers)
1940 City for Conquest
Anatole Litvak (Warner Brothers)
1941 The Man Who Came to Dinner
William Keighley (Warner Brothers)
1941 King's Row
Sam Wood (Warner Brothers)
1944 Shine On Harvest Moon
David Butler (Warner Brothers)
1948 Good Sam
Leo McCarey (RKO)
1949 I Was a Male War Bride
Howard Hawks (20th Century Fox)
1953 Take Me to Town
Douglas Sirk (Universal)

SIMONE SIGNORET

Simone Signoret is today a bloated, overweight character actress whose superb performance as an aged prostitute in **Madame Rosa** helped that French film win the 1978 Oscar as Best Foreign Film. It is difficult to see in her ravaged face the incredibly beautiful woman of 20 years ago, who was considered one of the most sensual females in the world. It was for that sensuality that she was brought to England in 1958 to star opposite Laurence Harvey in **Room at the Top** (loving him too much for her own good, as he cynically discarded her on his way up), becoming the first actress to win the Academy Award in a non-American film and the only French Actress ever to get it.

Signoret was born in Wiesbaden, Germany, on March 21, 1921, as Simone-Henriette-Charlotte Kaminker, and started using her mother's name of Signoret in 1945, after the Liberation. She made her film début as an extra in the 1942 **Le Prince Charmant**, married film director Yves Allégret in 1945, and became a star under his direction as the street girl with a cigarette always in her mouth in the 1947 **Dédée d'Anvers**. Her stardom was enhanced portraying a slut in his **Manèges** (she usually plays sluts, whores and loose women), and she became an international star with a sexy image in 1950, as the tart who begins and ends Max Ophuls' **La Ronde**, completing the ring of liaisons. Her international stature as a radiantly beautiful woman and a great actress was confirmed as the ill-fated courtesan in **Casque d'Or** (1951) and the star-crossed lover in **Thérèse Raquin** (1953); her popularity with international audiences increased when she starred as one of the two murderesses in **Les Diaboliques** and was featured by Luis Buñuel in his lesser-known **La Mort en ce Jardin**. She had great success with second husband Yves Montand in **The Witches of Salem** based on Arthur Miller's *The Crucible* and then made **Room at the Top**.

After the '50s her star dimmed slightly as she refused Hollywood

Above: Simone Signoret with Laurence Harvey in the 1958 British film **Room at the Top,** *in which she portrayed an older married woman in love with an ambitious opportunist.*

offers and began to put on weight. She gave fine performances in **Adua et le Compagne** (as an ex-whore starting a restaurant), **Term of Trial** (as Laurence Olivier's wife), **Ship of Fools** (her first American picture, romancing with Oscar Werner), **The Deadly Affair** (a former concentration camp inmate living in England), and **The Seagull** (as Arkadina). She was excellent, but she was no longer the centre of attention. In the '70s she began to move back into the limelight again, playing women much older than herself, although she looked old enough for the roles. She was especially notable opposite Jean Gabin ❯ in **Le Chat**—two sacred monsters of the French cinema in beautiful harmony—Alain Delon ❯ in **Le Veuve Couderc,** and (especially) the Oscar-winning **Madame Rosa.** The French cinema industry awarded her the Best Actress Cèsar (their equivalent of the Oscar) for that last film. The exterior may be ravaged, but the interior is still pure gold.

BEST FILMS:
1947 Dédée d'Anvers
Yves Allégret (Sacha Gordine)
1950 La Ronde
Max Ophuls (Sacha Gordine)
1951 Casque d'Or
Jacques Becker (Speva-Paris)
1953 Thérèse Raquin
Marcel Carné (Paris-Lux)
1954 Les Diaboliques (The Fiends)
Henri-Georges Clouzot (Filmsonar)
1957 Les Sorcières de Salem (The Witches of Salem)
Raymond Rouleau (CICC/Borderie/Pathé)
1958 Room at the Top
Jack Clayton (Remus)
1965 Ship of Fools
Stanley Kramer (Columbia)
1966 The Deadly Affair
Sidney Lumet (Columbia)
1974 Le Chat
Pierre Granier-Deferre
1977 La Vie Devant Soi (Madame Rosa)
Moshe Mizrahi (Lira)

JEAN SIMMONS

A girl who can be as good or better than Laurence Olivier ❯ in **Hamlet,** Spencer Tracy ❯ in **The Actress,** Burt Lancaster ❯ in **Elmer Gantry** and Marlon Brando ❯ in **Guys and Dolls** must be ranked as one of the cinema's great actresses, and yet there are not really enough good films in Jean Simmons' career. She has been very beautiful in some very big and successful epics (**Spartacus, The Big Country**), and she has been brilliant in some small and less popular movies (**Angel**

Narcissus, even without dialogue. Her performance as a blonde Ophelia in Olivier's star-studded **Hamlet** was natural and real and won her an Oscar nomination; her greatest period of stardom, however, was in Hollywood in the '50s, culminating in her finest performance as the white-robed evangelist in **Elmer Gantry.** She was almost as good playing the wife and mother in **All The Way Home,** a fine adaptation of James Agee's *A Death in the Family,* and

Below: Jean Simmons in the 1967 **Divorce American Style.** *In recent years she has unfortunately made only rare movie appearances.*

Face, All The Way Home), but she has never created the recognisable screen personality that would have carried her to major stardom. As Katharine Hepburn ❯ once said, "Show me an actress who isn't a personality and I'll show you an actress who isn't a star." Simmons is a very fine actress indeed, but the baffling lack of continuing achievement in her film career can only be explained by this lack of a full-blown persona. Not that she is colourless on the screen, far from it, but the strong-willed femininity that she projects becomes a part of her role-playing rather than the roles becoming a part of her personality. She has appeared only rarely in movies in the past ten years (the last was the 1975 **Mr Sycamore**), and it is the cinema's loss.

Simmons was born in Crouch Hill, London, on January 31, 1929, and made her film début in the 1944 **Give Us The Moon.** She was superb as the spoiled Estella in **Great Expectations** and excellent as the Indian girl in **Black**

in 1969 received an Oscar nomination for her role as a disillusioned wife in **The Happy Ending.**

She has been married twice, first to actor Stewart Granger ❯ and, since 1960, to director Richard Brooks.

BEST FILMS:
1948 Hamlet
Laurence Olivier (Rank)
1952 Angel Face
Otto Preminger (RKO)
1953 The Actress
George Cukor (MGM)
1953 Young Bess
George Sidney (MGM)
1955 Guys and Dolls
Joseph L. Mankiewicz (Goldwyn/MGM)
1958 Home Before Dark
Mervyn Le Roy (Warner Brothers)
1960 Spartacus
Stanley Kubrick (Universal-International)
1960 Elmer Gantry
Richard Brooks (United Artists)
1963 All The Way Home
Alex Segal (Paramount)
1969 The Happy Ending
Richard Brooks (United Artists)

MICHEL SIMON

Michel Simon's gross corpulence was the disturbing embodiment of an overwhelmingly anarchistic spirit and dominated some of the masterpieces of the French cinema. What was particularly upsetting (and memorable) about his fat, sly, truculent screen image was its sexual aspect: he often portrayed men obsessively in love with beautiful girls—and loved in return. He is an ugly, middle-class bank clerk in love with a prostitute in

Above: Michel Simon was 75 years old when he starred as a jealous baron with a lovely young wife in Borowczyk's **Blanche** in 1971.

Jean Renoir's 1931 **La Chienne** (he kills her after she deceives him and gets away with it, becoming a wandering tramp). Forty years later he was the grizzled old medieval baron with an extremely beautiful young wife in Walerian Borowczyk's 1971 **Blanche** (his obsession with her leads to her death). In one of the classic, fatalistic Marcel Carné films of the late '30s, **Quai des Brumes,** he is the villainous "guardian" of beautiful young orphan Michèle Morgan ➤ and is killed by Jean Gabin ➤. One of the extraordinary things about Simon was that he became an old man (and one of the great ones) so young; he was only 39 years old when he gave his magnificent portrayal of the grizzled old mate on the barge in Jean Vigo's **L'Atalante.** He is ugly but likeable, helping to smooth over a newly-wed's quarrel and maintaining a bizarre collection of mementos in his cabin, including pictures of prostitutes and the pickled hand of a long-dead friend. It is one of the most memorable performances in all cinema, combining lyricism with horror, beauty with ugliness, surrealism with reality. He was nearly as outstanding two years earlier in Renoir's **Boudu Sauvé des Eaux,** as a scruffy old

tramp saved from suicide in the Seine, who insists his rescuer must now take care of him (he goes to live with him and seduces his wife before once more falling into the river and returning to the freedom of a tramp).

Simon was born in Geneva, Switzerland, in 1895 (baptized François) and became a music hall entertainer and acrobat in the 1910s. He began his stage and film career in the '20s, making his cinema début in Marcel L'Herbier's classic **Feu Mathias Pascal.** He had a small role in Carl Dreyer's **La Passion de Jeanne d'Arc** (as Jean Lemaître) and his first major role in Renoir's 1928 **Tire-au-Flanc** as the valet of an aristocrat, drafted into the army at the same time as his master. He was much liked in Jean Choux's comedy **Jean de la Lune** with Madeleine Renaud and in Renoir's **On Purge Bébé**; in fact, he was extremely popular throughout the '30s, appearing in films by Marc Allégret, Sacha Guitry and other minor directors in addition to his major work with Renoir, Carné and Vigo. He was outstanding as one of three old men in a retired actors' home in Julien Duvivier's **La Fin du Jour** (with Louis Jouvet ➤) and good cracking jokes with Arletty ➤ and Fernandel ➤ in Claude Autant-Lara's **Fric Frac.** His career in the '40s continued strong, especially as an old man in love with a young woman in Duvivier's 1946 **Panique** and as both old Faust and Mephistopheles in Jean Cocteau's **La Beauté du Diable** in 1949 (a stunning performance, matched by Gerard Philipe ➤ at his best as the young Faust).

Simon appeared in many good films and roles after that (including John Frankenheimer's **The Train**), but his next big personal success was as a lovable, anti-semitic bigot in Claude Berri's **The Two of Us,** looking after and loving a small boy during the war, unaware that the child is Jewish. He was in peak form again in **Blanche** in 1971, now aged 75 and looking excessively old. He died in Paris in 1975, after 50 years of screen stardom.

BEST FILMS:
1928 Tire-au-Flanc
Jean Renoir (Neo-Films/Braunberger)
1931 La Chienne
Jean Renoir (Braunberger/Richebé)
1932 Boudu Sauvé des Eaux
Jean Renoir (Simon/Gehret)
1934 L'Atalante
Jean Vigo (Nounez/Gaumont)
1938 Quai des Brumes
Marcel Carné (Rabinovich)
1939 La Fin du Jour
Julien Duvivier (Régina)
1939 Fric Frac
Claude Autant-Lara (Lehman)
1949 La Beauté du Diable
René Clair (Universalia/ENIC)
1968 Le Vieil Homme et l'Enfant (The Two of Us)
Claude Betri (PAC/Valoria/Renn)
1971 Blanche
Walerian Borowczyk (Telepresse/Abel & Chartan)

FRANK SINATRA

Frank Sinatra's reputation as one of the greatest popular singers of the twentieth century has diverted attention from the fact that he is also one of the great screen actors. His chip-on-the-shoulder, pugnacious, happy-go-lucky personality has been as impressive in non-musicals as in his fine singing roles, and he probably could have been a major movie star without singing a note.

Above: Frank Sinatra became the star of excellent action films as well as musicals; here he is in **Von Ryan's Express** (1965).

Musicals came first, of course (he made his début singing with the Tommy Dorsey Band in the 1941 **Las Vegas Nights**), and include such masterpieces of the genre as **Anchors Aweigh, Take Me Out to the Ball Game** and **On The Town** (all with Gene Kelly ➤), **Guys and Dolls** (with Marlon Brando ➤), **High Society** (with his one-time idol Bing Crosby ➤) and **Pal Joey** (in which he is the central attraction). His dramatic roles have been in such classics as **From Here To Eternity** (which won him the Best Supporting Actor Oscar in 1953), **The Man With The Golden Arm** (superb as a drug addict; it won him an Oscar nomination), **Some Came Running** and **The Manchurian Candidate.** He made a series of highly entertaining films with his Hollywood "Clan" group—Dean Martin ➤, Sammy Davis, Jr, Peter Lawford, etc—which have been unfairly dismissed by critics despite the first-class directors who made them, including John Sturges (**Sergeants Three**), Lewis Milestone (**Ocean's Eleven**), Robert Aldrich (**Four For Texas**) and Gordon Douglas (**Robin and the Seven Hoods**). Douglas also directed a trilogy of films in which Sinatra portrayed a tough,

cynical detective with compelling force: **Tony Rome, The Detective** and **Lady in Cement.** Sinatra's screen personality is "natural" (like that of every other great screen actor) and has been reflected in his widely-publicised off-screen life, including rows with press and photographers, four wives—including Ava Gardner ➤ and Mia Farrow ➤— and associations with underworld figures.

Sinatra was born in Hoboken, New Jersey, on December 12, 1915, and became an important band singer in the late '30s, especially with Tommy Dorsey. He was the crooning idol of the bobby-soxers in the early '40s and had an effect similar to Presley's in the '50s. He was regarded as only a musical phenomenon until his acting breakthrough in **From Here To Eternity** in 1953, at a very low ebb in his career; his huge personal success in that film helped him bounce back to even greater stardom as both a singer and an actor. The '50s were the years of his great recordings for Capitol Records and he was a top ten box office star from 1956 to 1960. Unfortunately, his aggressiveness on screen was reflected in his private behaviour; it probably had an adverse effect on his movie career when he gained a reputation as being difficult to work with. All the same, he continued to make enjoyable films in the '60s, including his "Clan" and detective films as well as **The Manchurian Candidate** and **Von Ryan's Express.** He retired from screen acting after **Dirty Dingus Magee** in 1970.

ALBERTO SORDI

see **Modern Stars**

BARBARA STANWYCK

Barbara Stanwyck is one of the great Hollywood screen actresses. She perfected the screen persona of the gutsy, independent woman, hard-boiled on the outside, tender on the inside, who is self-assured and self-reliant, able to run the show when necessary. This characterisation developed from an early '30s working-girl-on-the-make in a man's world to its greatest sophistication in her '40s films like **Double Indemnity** and **Ball of Fire**: pushy, jaded, amoral, fierce and willing to kill if necessary to get what she wants. But this screen character was also enormously attractive, with a warm, husky voice and a personality you had to like. Stanwyck never gave a bad performance, redeeming even lesser films with her charisma: her popularity can be gauged by the fact that in 1944 she was the highest-paid woman in the USA. She received four Academy Award Best Actress nominations: for **Stella Dallas** (as a mother sacrificing everything for her daughter); **Ball of Fire** (as a stripper on the run, teaching slang to encyclopedist Gary Cooper »); **Double Indemnity** (as a double-crossing wife luring Fred MacMurray » to murder); and **Sorry, Wrong Number** (as a woman who learns of a plot to murder her). She gave brilliant comedy performances (**The Lady Eve**), was highly sexy (**Lady of Burlesque, The Bitter Tea of**

General Yen), a powerful board-room executive (**Executive Suite**), and a memorable Western star (**Union Pacific, Forty Guns**).

Stanwyck's tough, down-to-earth screen persona was very much a reflection of her own early life. Born as Ruby Stevens in Brooklyn on July 16, 1907, and orphaned young, she supported herself by getting a job wrapping packages at 13 and dancing in speakeasies at 15. She became a dancing star on Broadway and married comic Frank Fay, who helped her get into movies—she made her first cinema appearance

Above: Barbara Stanwyck, one of Hollywood's great actresses.

(as a dancer) in the 1927 **Broadway Nights** and her break-through came at the beginning of the '30s. She appeared in many films directed by Capra and Wellman in these early years, and she was a major star by 1933. Her first marriage broke up and in 1939 she married co-star Robert Taylor.

She continued to be a big star until the mid-'50s, but made only occasional films after that (her last was the 1964 **The Night Walker**). She had a hit TV series (*The Big Valley*) in the '60s, but now lives in semi-retirement in Beverly Hills.

BEST FILMS:
1933 The Bitter Tea of General Yen
Frank Capra (Columbia)
1937 Stella Dallas
King Vidor (United Artists)
1939 Union Pacific
Cecil B. De Mille (Paramount)
1941 The Lady Eve
Preston Sturges (Paramount)
1941 Ball of Fire
Howard Hawks (RKO)
1943 Lady of Burlesque
William Wellman (United Artists)
1944 Double Indemnity
Billy Wilder (Paramount)
1948 Sorry, Wrong Number
Anatole Litvak (Paramount)
1952 Clash by Night
Fritz Lang (RKO)
1957 Forty Guns
Samuel Fuller (20th Century Fox)

JAMES STEWART

James Stewart has starred in more recognised masterpieces of the American cinema than any other actor, and must be a top contender for the ranking of best American screen actor. He has appeared in more than his share of notable films because of the versatility of his screen personality; he became a great Western star in classics directed by John Ford and Anthony Mann, but he was

*Above: James Stewart starred in a series of great Westerns for director Anthony Mann in the '50s, including **The Far Country**.*

equally outstanding in non-Westerns made by Alfred Hitchcock, Otto Preminger, Frank Capra, George Cukor and Henry Hathaway. While at first sight his drawling, gangling screen personality appears limited, it is actually incredibly flexible, ranging from the honest idealist fighting corruption in **Mr Smith Goes to Washington** to the voyeur with a telescope in **Rear Window**, from the engaging young reporter in **The Philadelphia Story** to the cold, hard bounty hunter of **The Naked Spur**. He can be believable as a good-natured drunk who believes in a giant rabbit (**Harvey**), an opportunist cashing in on other men's deeds (**The Man Who Shot Liberty Valance**), or a romantic of frightening obsessiveness (**Vertigo**). These are the marks of a very intelligent actor indeed—one whom at least one respected American critic, Andrew Sarris, considers "the most complete actor-personality in the American cinema". More often, however, movie critics simply consider him as a "natural"

performer and reserve their accolades for lesser stars who can be seen to be "acting". Stewart's greatness, however, has always been recognised by the people who matter—the directors.

James Maitland Stewart was born in Indiana, Pennsylvania, on May 20, 1908, and was on stage in New York by 1932. He made his film début in 1935 in **The Murder Man** and became a top star very quickly. By 1936 he was co-starring at MGM with Eleanor Powell » in **Born to Dance** (and singing *Easy to Love* and in 1938 he was featured by Capra in his delightful comedy **You Can't Take It With You**. Almost every film he made at this time was of real interest, but it was Capra's **Mr Smith Goes to Washington** which really made him famous and got him an Oscar nomination. He was superb with Claudette Colbert » in the comedy **It's A Wonderful World**, even better as the son of a famous gunslinger with Marlene Dietrich » in **Destry Rides Again**, outstanding when teamed with Margaret Sullavan in Lubitsch's **The Shop Around the Corner** and Borzage's **The Mortal Storm**, and given an Academy Award for his performance in **The Philadelphia Story** (over Cary Grant » and Katharine Hepburn »). He spent the war as an Air Force officer and came back to Capra's whimsical **It's A Wonderful Life**, then starred in one of the great thrillers of the post-war period, Hathaway's **Call Northside 777**. His first film with Hitchcock was the technically fascinating **Rope**, and he then made even a sentimental baseball picture, **The Stratton Story**, seem appealing. His rich association with Anthony Mann began in 1950 with the powerful revenge Western **Winchester 73**, hunting down his own brother; he starred in another good Western by

Delmer Daves, **Broken Arrow**, and then made his likeable **Harvey** and the big-budget **The Greatest Show on Earth** (hiding under clown make-up). His great run of Westerns for Mann continued in the '50s with **Bend of the River, The Naked Spur, The Far Country** and **The Man from Laramie**. He was also very popular in Mann's biopic **The Glenn Miller Story** and in **Strategic Air Command**. Hitchcock featured him in three of his finest films, **Rear Window, The Man Who Knew Too Much** and **Vertigo**, and Billy Wilder starred him in **The Spirit of St Louis** (as Lindbergh). He made another good film with Kim Novak, **Bell, Book and Candle**, and gave a brilliant performance as the defence lawyer in **Anatomy of a Murder**. In the '60s he gave the Hoover organisation a boost with **The FBI Story** and then starred in three John Ford classics in a row, **Two Rode Together, The Man Who Shot Liberty Valance** and **Cheyenne Autumn**.

He relaxed a little after that, with some minor Westerns and adventure pictures, but has continued working right through the '70s. He gave particularly fine performances in Don Siegel's 1976 **The Shootist** and Michael Winner's 1978 **The Big Sleep** as General Sternwood.

BEST FILMS:
1938 You Can't Take It With You
Frank Capra (Columbia)
1939 Mr Smith Goes to Washington
Frank Capra (Columbia)
1939 Destry Rides Again
George Marshall (Universal)
1940 The Philadelphia Story
George Cukor (MGM)
1948 Call Northside 777
Henry Hathaway (20th Century Fox)
1950 Winchester 73
Anthony Mann (Universal)
1950 Harvey
Henry Koster (Universal)
1954 Rear Window
Alfred Hitchcock (Paramount)
1956 The Man Who Knew Too Much
Alfred Hitchcock (Paramount)
1958 Vertigo
Alfred Hitchcock (Paramount)
1959 Anatomy of a Murder
Otto Preminger (Columbia)
1961 Two Rode Together
John Ford (Columbia)
1962 The Man Who Shot Liberty Valance
John Ford (Paramount)

Tarzan

Tarzan must be one of the most popular movie stars of all time, although the same cannot be said of any of the 15 actors who portrayed him on screen. Tarzan films have earned an estimated $500 million around the world and have been seen by more than two billion people. The most famous Tarzan was Johnny Weissmuller, but even he was never very popular in other roles. In a delightful 1977 German film called

Above: Johnny Weissmuller was the most famous screen Tarzan and his best films, like **Tarzan's Secret Treasure**, *were at MGM.*

Jane is Jane Forever, a slightly dotty old lady tries to persuade a reporter that she is Tarzan's widow and points at photographs on the wall of her husband. But which one, he asks; Weissmuller, Gordon Scott, Lex Barker? All of them, she astutely replies—they are all Tarzan. As they truly are, in 40 cinema films and in the TV series featuring Ron Ely.

Tarzan was the brainchild of writer Edgar Rice Burroughs, who published *Tarzan of the Apes* in the 1912 *All-Story Magazine* and immediately captured the attention of the world. He wrote 26 Tarzan books in all, although the actual plots of them were rarely used in the movie versions. The first Tarzan was brawny, 200-pound Elmo Lincoln, who starred in the 1918 **Tarzan of the Apes,** a huge success earning over $1 million; Lincoln starred in a sequel the same year, **The Romance of Tarzan,** with Enid Markey portraying Jane in both films. More Tarzan movies were made during the '20s, with Gene Pollar, P. Dempsey Tabler, James Pierce and Frank Merrill as the African ape-man.

MGM began its rather more glossy series with Weissmuller in 1932, with **Tarzan the Ape Man.** Weissmuller (born in Chicago in 1907) was the world's greatest swimmer at that time, a two-time Olympic champion with 67 world records to his name. His mate Jane in the first six films was Maureen O'Sullivan; afficionados feel that these were the best Tarzan pictures ever. Tarzan swam rather more than in the books and his vocabulary was reduced to around 60 words, but he appealed enormously to the mass public and these years marked the peak of his popularity. Weissmuller never actually got a chance on film to say "Me Tarzan—you Jane", but was wonderful screaming "ahh-eee-oow", which aroused

cheers of delight from audiences. MGM abandoned the series in 1942, but Weissmuller went on playing the role at RKO until 1948, when he switched to his "Jungle Jim" series. The Tarzan series continued with other actors, including Lex Barker, Gordon Scott (whose **Tarzan's Greatest Adventure** was among the best of the later films), Denny Miller, Jock Mahoney, Mike Henry, and Ron Ely on TV. During the '30s, other actors also played the role at other studios, including Buster Crabbe, Glen Morris and Herman Brix, the last in films with which Burroughs was himself involved. Tarzan has continued to be a star into the '70s, a longevity unequalled by any other screen character.

BEST FILMS:
1918 Tarzan of the Apes
Scott Sidney (National General)
1932 Tarzan of the Apes
W.S. Van Dyke (MGM)
1934 Tarzan and His Mate
Cedric Gibbons (MGM)
1936 Tarzan Escapes
Richard Thorpe (MGM)
1938 Tarzan and the Green Goddess
Edward Kull (Principal)
1939 Tarzan Finds a Son
Richard Thorpe (MGM)
1941 Tarzan's Secret Treasure
Richard Thorpe (MGM)
1942 Tarzan's New York Adventure
Richard Thorpe (MGM)
1946 Tarzan and the Leopard Woman
Kurt Neumann (RKO)
1959 Tarzan's Greatest Adventure
John Guillermin (Paramount)

Elizabeth Taylor
see **Modern Stars**

Robert Taylor

Robert Taylor was the last of the matinée idols and was under contract to MGM for 25 years, longer than any other major star. His heyday as a ladies' man was in the late '30s, when he squired Irene Dunne » in **Magnificent Obsession,** Greta Garbo » in **Camille,** Barbara Stanwyck » (whom he later married) in **His Brother's Wife,** and Joan Crawford » in **The Gorgeous Hussy,** among others. His best performance in this manner, however, was opposite Vivien Leigh » in **Waterloo Bridge.** He was a solid, steady performer, a heart-throb rather than a notable actor, but on occasion he could be very impressive on screen, as he was as a gangster in **Johnny Eager,** with Lana Turner » and as Katharine Hepburn's » maniacal husband in **Undercurrent.** His finest screen performance was as the Shoshone Indian of Anthony Mann's **Devil's Doorway,** a war hero who finds he can't even homestead his own land. In the '50s he became the popular star of costume epics, beginning with the blockbuster **Quo Vadis?** and continuing with an enjoyable trilogy of medieval romps, **Ivanhoe, Knights of the Round Table** and **Quentin Durward.**

Taylor was born in Filley, Nebraska, on August 5, 1911, with the memorable name of

Below: Robert Taylor was the last of the matinée idols and versatile enough to work in all kinds of pictures, including epic war films like **D-Day, The Sixth of June** *(1956).*

Spangler Arlington Brough. He began as an MGM contract star in 1934, but his first film, **Handy Andy,** was made at Fox. He was teamed with Eleanor Powell >> in **Broadway Melody of 1936,** but it was **Magnificent Obsession** that really made him a big star —and a favourite of female movie-goers. He was nicely American in **A Yank at Oxford,** even better in love with Margaret Sullavan in **Three Comrades,** and quite adequate in action pictures like **The Crowd Roars** and **Bataan.** He turned often to Westerns in the '50s (**Ride, Vaquero!** was a good one) and finally left MGM in 1959. His films after that were of less importance, and during the '60s he was featured in the TV series *The Detectives.* He died in 1969 after completing his last film, **The Day the Hot Line Got Hot.**

BEST FILMS:
1935 Magnificent Obsession
John Stahl (Universal)
1936 Camille
George Cukor (MGM)
1938 A Yank at Oxford
Jack Conway (MGM)
1938 Three Comrades
Frank Borzage (MGM)
1940 Waterloo Bridge
Mervyn Le Roy (MGM)
1942 Johnny Eager
Mervyn Le Roy (MGM)
1946 Undercurrent
Vincente Minnelli (MGM)
1950 Devil's Doorway
Anthony Mann (MGM)
1951 Quo Vadis?
Mervyn Le Roy (MGM)
1952 Ivanhoe
Richard Thorpe (MGM)

SHIRLEY TEMPLE

The greatest, or at least the most popular, child star in the history of the cinema, Shirley Temple was the No 1 American box office attraction from 1935 to 1938 (Clark Gable >> was merely second). She became a major star in 1934 at the age of six and won a special Academy Award for the eight big-grossing films she made that year. She was a phenomenon not only in her success but in her acting ability; Adolphe Menjou >>, her experienced co-star in the delightful Damon Runyon story **Little Miss Marker,** considered her knowledge of acting techniques and tricks so incredible as to be frightening and compared her to child prodigies in chess and music. She was so good that Graham Greene suggested she might be an adult masquerading as a child (and was sued for suggesting it). His implication that she was coquettish was correct, but coquetry in miniature becomes charming rather than sexy. She wasn't "cute"—she was rather too knowing and wise—but her films were fun because she was the most sensible person in

Above: Shirley Temple's best film (and her own favourite) was John Ford's 1937 re-working of Kipling, **Wee Willie Winkie.**

them, and made things turn out right in the end. Every mother may have thought she wanted her little girl to be like Shirley, but really she herself wanted to be like the child star.

She was born in Santa Monica, California, on April 23, 1928, and was pushed into films by her mother at the age of four, making **Baby Burlesk** shorts. She had her first bit part in a feature film in 1932 (**The Red-Haired Alibi**), but did not have much success until she appeared in the 1934 **Stand Up and Cheer.** She sang and danced (in a polka-dot pinafore) a song called *Baby Take a Bow* and she was a sensation. Fox signed her to a seven-year contract, and she walked away with her first starring vehicle, called, naturally, **Baby Take a Bow.** One of her big hits that first year was **Bright Eyes,** in which she sang her trademark song *On the Good Ship Lollipop.* Shirley Temple dolls, colouring books and associated merchandise became a multi-million-dollar business and she was acclaimed as the greatest film star in the world. She hadn't even made her best films yet. They began in 1935 with **The Little Colonel** (in which she danced for the first time, most splendidly, with Bill "Bojangles" Robinson) and continued in 1936 with **Captain January** (where she danced with Buddy Ebsen and sang *At the Codfish Ball*) and **Poor Little Rich Girl** (where she danced with Alice Faye >> and Jack Haley). Her best film, and her own favourite, is the 1937 **Wee Willie Winkie,** with John Ford giving form to her charm in a re-telling of the Kipling story. Matching her against Victor McLaglen and C. Aubrey Smith, this sentimental story concerns a brave little girl stationed with the British Army in nineteenth-century India. Allan Dwan did very well the same year in remaking

the classic **Heidi,** but after that she was over the hill (aged 10) and headed down. There were still three interesting films to come, the nicely showbiz **Little Miss Broadway** and the Walter Lang fairy tales **The Little Princess** and **The Blue Bird**—but then her stardom ended. She left Fox for MGM and Selznick and appeared as a teenager in movies like **Since You Went Away,** but the magic was gone.

She went on making movies, however, until 1949 (the last was **A Kiss for Corliss**), and then retired at the ripe old age of 21 (having married three years earlier). As Shirley Temple Black she later became a Republican politician, but any resemblance between this woman, protesting about immoral Swedish movies, and the worldly-wise child star of long ago is purely chronological.

BEST FILMS:
1934 Little Miss Marker
Alexander Hall (Paramount)
1934 Bright Eyes
David Butler (Fox)
1935 The Little Colonel
David Butler (Fox)
1936 Captain January
David Butler (20th Century Fox)
1936 Poor Little Rich Girl
Irving Cummings (20th Century Fox)
1937 Wee Willie Winkie
John Ford (20th Century Fox)
1937 Heidi
Allan Dwan (20th Century Fox)
1938 Little Miss Broadway
Irving Cummings (20th Century Fox)
1939 The Little Princess
Walter Lang (20th Century Fox)
1940 The Blue Bird
Walter Lang (20th Century Fox)

GENE TIERNEY

Gene Tierney was sleek, svelte and breathtakingly beautiful, and she became one of the most popular '40s stars primarily because of the way she looked. In the film that really made her an important star, the 1944 **Laura,** her incredible beauty is talked

about for half an hour before she makes an appearance—few actresses could have lived up to the expectation of loveliness in the way that Tierney did.

She was born in Brooklyn, New York City, on November 19, 1920, worked briefly in the theatre and as a model, and made her film début in the 1940 Fritz Lang picture **The Return of Frank James** (as Henry Fonda's > sweetheart). Most of her early roles were in Westerns or exotica (**Tobacco Road, Belle Starr, Sundown, The Shanghai Gesture**), but she was better used by Rouben Mamoulian in the comedy **Rings on Her Fingers** and by Ernst Lubitsch in the fantasy **Heaven Can Wait.** After **Laura** made her a major star, she had better and more sophisticated roles. Not that her screen persona was necessarily a nice one; behind that beautiful mask there were often selfish demons at work—in **Leave Her to Heaven** she is so obsessed by husband Cornel Wilde >> that she drowns his brother, kills their unborn child and commits suicide, and in **The Razor's Edge** she is the heartless, parasitic society girlfriend of Tyrone Power >.

Her emotional situations were also usually complicated and disruptive. She falls in love with Rex Harrison > in **The Ghost and Mrs Muir**—but he's the ghost. She marries Vincent Price > in **Dragonwyck,** but it turns out he murdered his last wife. She marries John Lund in **The Mating Season** and then hires his mother as her servant. The ill-luck that was a feature of many of these films finally caught up with her in real life; she had a breakdown in 1955 and went into a mental home for three years. It was virtually the

Above: Gene Tierney started off her career in Westerns like **Belle Starr** *(1941) with Dana Andrews and Randolph Scott.*

end of her film career, although she returned to the screen in 1962 in a small but splendid part in **Advise and Consent** as Walter Pidgeon's > mistress. She worked in only two subsequent films, **Toys in the Attic** and **The Pleasure Seekers.** She has been happily married to a Texas millionaire since 1960, following an earlier marriage to designer Oleg Cassini.

BEST FILMS:
1943 Heaven Can Wait
Ernst Lubitsch (20th Century Fox)
1944 Laura
Otto Preminger (20th Century Fox)
1945 A Bell For Adano
Henry King (20th Century Fox)
1945 Leave Her To Heaven
John Stahl (20th Century Fox)
1946 Dragonwyck
Joseph L. Mankiewicz (20th Century Fox)
1946 The Razor's Edge
Edmund Goulding (20th Century Fox)
1947 The Ghost and Mrs Muir
Joseph L. Mankiewicz (20th Century Fox)
1949 Whirlpool
Otto Preminger (20th Century Fox)
1951 The Mating Season
Mitchell Leisen (Paramount)
1953 Never Let Me Go
Delmer Daves (MGM)

TOM AND JERRY

Tom and Jerry have won more Academy Awards than any other movie stars, taking home seven of the coveted statuettes. Tom (a mean-spirited cat who often turns out to have a heart of gold) and Jerry (an endlessly inventive mouse with a nice sense of humour) are both great performers, but Jerry is the slight favourite, if only because he did

Above: Tom and Jerry, winners of seven Oscars for their brilliant films.

such a superb dance with Gene Kelly ≫ in **Anchors Aweigh.** They are the joint creation of Fred Quimby, who produced all except their first picture, and animators William Hanna and Joseph Barbera, who directed them for their first 17 years on the screen. They were the greatest MGM cartoon stars, beginning in 1940 with **Puss Gets the Boot,** produced by Rudy Ising. Being MGM products, they often had a little more class than their cartoon rivals (in the

1946 **Cat Concerto,** for example, Tom is a concert pianist trying to perform Liszt while Jerry is asleep in his piano on stage), but most of their films consist of wonderfully anarchic chases. They were always antagonistic, but they couldn't have survived without each other.

Their Oscar-winning films were **The Yankee Doodle Mouse, Mouse Trouble, Quiet Please, The Cat Concerto, The Little Orphan, The Two Mouseketeers** and **Johann Mouse.** After leaving MGM, Hanna and Barbera went on to create some of the most famous television cartoon characters, including Huckleberry Hound and The Flintstones. Fred Quimby died in 1957.

BEST FILMS:
1943 The Yankee Doodle Mouse
William Hanna & Joseph Barbera (MGM)
1944 Mouse Trouble
Hanna & Barbera (MGM)
1944 Anchors Aweigh
George Sidney (MGM)
1945 Quiet Please
Hanna & Barbera (MGM)
1945 Tee for Two
Hanna & Barbera (MGM)
1946 The Cat Concerto
Hanna & Barbera (MGM)
1948 The Little Orphan
Hanna & Barbera (MGM)
1951 The Two Mouseketeers
Hanna & Barbera (MGM)
1952 Johann Mouse
Hanna & Barbera (MGM)
1956 Mucho Mouse
Hanna & Barbera (MGM)

SPENCER TRACY

Spencer Tracy has acquired a reputation as Hollywood's greatest actor. Extravagant praise has been lavished on him by critics and fellow actors, he has had more Academy Award nominations than any other male performer (winning the Award twice), and he is often referred to as "the actors' actor". A close look at his screen career tells a slightly different story: he did not make nearly as many great films in his 37 years in the movies as did James Stewart ≫ and Cary Grant ≫, and in none of them did he have the kind of impact that was made by Humphrey Bogart ≫, Clark Gable ≫ and John Wayne ≫. Many of his best films were made with long-time associate and sparring partner Katharine Hepburn ≫, and in his later years (when he could have been making his finest movies) he became extremely difficult to work with and almost undirectable. This is not to deny that he is one of the great stars and one of the best screen actors—but he cannot be considered the best. He won his Academy Awards for two somewhat dated films, although he himself is excellent as the Portuguese fisherman in **Captains Courageous** and the strong-minded Nebraska priest Father

Flanagan in **Boys' Town.** His persona as the gruff, no-nonsense man of integrity with natural strength is seen at its best in six films: **Man's Castle** (struggling to survive in the Depression), **The Power and the Glory** (as a railroad president), **Fury** (innocent man involved with lynch mob), **Father of the Bride** (delightfully funny, marrying off Elizabeth Taylor ≫), **Bad Day at Black Rock** (outstanding as a one-armed stranger in a hostile town), and **The Last Hurrah** (exceptionally strong as a Boston political boss on his way out). Tracy was good in almost all his other films as well, but he did not usually work with major directors more than once; he had a long association with George Cukor, who directed Tracy and Hepburn in three of their best films (**Keeper of the Flame, Adam's Rib, Pat and Mike**), although the couple were first teamed brilliantly by George Stevens in the 1942 **Woman of the Year.**

Tracy was born in Milwaukee, Wisconsin, on April 5, 1900, worked on stage in the '20s, and made his film début in John Ford's 1930 **Up the River.** He became a star pretty quickly for Fox, with a big success in his second film, **Quick Millions,** and an even bigger one in Michael Curtiz's **20,000 Years in Sing Sing.**

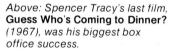
Above: Spencer Tracy's last film, **Guess Who's Coming to Dinner?** *(1967), was his biggest box office success.*

He was difficult even at this time and Fox reluctantly sacked him in 1935, whereupon he went to MGM, became an even bigger star, and won his two Oscars. He was a delight in the screwball comedy **Libelled Lady,** impressive as a tough cab-driver in **The Big City,** and good opposite Joan Crawford ≫ in **Mannequin.** MGM gave him the best possible parts, but few of his films in the '40s were memorable, except for King Vidor's **Northwest Passage** and his comedies with Hepburn. Frank Capra directed the pair superbly in **State of the Union,** and Tracy's '50s career was quite strong with **Father of the Bride, Bad Day at Black Rock** and **The Last Hurrah. The Old Man and the Sea** should have been a good film (it wasn't), and most of his later films were directed by Stanley Kramer, who got on well with him. He was the Clarence Darrow figure in **Inherit the Wind,** the judge in **Judgement at Nuremberg,** and the police chief in **It's a Mad, Mad, Mad, Mad World,** before retiring because of poor health. He returned for the 1967 **Guess Who's Coming to Dinner?,** with Hepburn, and died two weeks after it was completed.

BEST FILMS:
1933 The Power and The Glory
William K. Howard (Fox)
1933 Man's Castle
Frank Borzage (Columbia)
1936 Fury
Fritz Lang (MGM)
1937 Captains Courageous
Victor Fleming (MGM)
1938 Boys' Town
Norman Taurog (MGM)
1942 Woman of the Year
George Stevens (MGM)
1948 State of the Union
Frank Capra (MGM)
1949 Adam's Rib
George Cukor (MGM)
1950 Father of the Bride
Vincente Minnelli (MGM)
1952 Pat and Mike
George Cukor (MGM)
1955 Bad Day at Black Rock
John Sturges (MGM)
1958 The Last Hurrah
John Ford (Columbia)

LANA TURNER

Lana Turner is more a part of movie mythology than many greater stars. It was Lana who was "discovered" sitting on a stool in Schwab's Drugstore (in reality in an ice cream parlour), and it was Lana who became the "Sweater Girl" of World War II. She may not have been a great actress, but she was one of the best cheap broads in the movies. Kirk Douglas ❯ summed it up beautifully in **The Bad and the Beautiful** when he told her: "You acted badly and you moved clumsily, but the point is every eye in the audience was on you." She had screen charisma right from her first role in a tight sweater, walking out of a drugstore in the 1937 **They Won't Forget.** She was marvellous as a cheap showgirl in **Ziegfeld Girl**, developed real chemistry with Clark Gable ❯ in **Honky Tonk** and **Somewhere I'll Find You,** and was nicely matched with gangster Robert Taylor ❯❯ in **Johnny Eager.** Her finest performances, however, were as the broad persuading John Garfield ❯ to murder her husband in **The Postman Always Rings Twice,** as the alcoholic actress in **The Bad and the Beautiful,** as the neurotic mother Constance McKenzie in **Peyton Place** (which won her an Academy Award nomination), and as the actress with daughter trouble in **Imitation of Life.**

Lana Turner's off-screen life was as lurid as her screen one. She was born Julia Jean Turner in Wallace, Idaho, on February 8, 1920. Her father was murdered when she was ten, her mother went to work in a beauty parlour, and she had a difficult time with foster-parents. She married seven times (including Artie Shaw and Lex Barker) and was the centre of one of Hollywood's great scandals in 1958 when her 15-year-old daughter Cheryl stabbed Lana's gangster boyfriend Johnny Stom-

panato to death while protecting her. It didn't harm her career, for it matched her screen image, and she had a huge box office success with her next film, **Imitation of Life.** She has since made other soap-operas (**Madame X** was a tearjerking highspot) and was still working in the '70s in such films as the 1976 **Bittersweet Love.**

BEST FILMS:
1941 Ziegfeld Girl
Robert Z. Leonard (MGM)
1941 Honky Tonk
Jack Conway (MGM)
1942 Johnny Eager
Mervyn Le Roy (MGM)
1942 Somewhere I'll Find You
Wesley Ruggles (MGM)

Above: Lana Turner was a sexy, wicked high priestess corrupting Edmund Purdom in Richard Thorpe's **The Prodigal** *(1955).*

1945 Weekend at the Waldorf
Robert Z. Leonard (MGM)
1946 The Postman Always Rings Twice
Tay Garnett (MGM)
1947 Cass Timberlane
George Sidney (MGM)
1953 The Bad and the Beautiful
Vincente Minnelli (MGM)
1957 Peyton Place
Mark Robson (20th Century Fox)
1959 Imitation of Life
Douglas Sirk (Universal)

PETER USTINOV

see **Modern Stars**

CONRAD VEIDT

Veidt's career was truly remarkable. He was one of the first great international stars, with major careers in Germany, America and England, as well as occasional work in France, Italy, Sweden and Austria. His sinister, nightmarish figure stalked the German silent era with Expressionist fever and cast its shadow over world cinema.

He then became a romantic anti-hero villain in the British cinema of the 1930s and was, despite this, extremely popular with women. He ended his career as one of the most memorable German villains in the movies, the arrogant Major Strasser, shot by Humphrey Bogart ❯ in **Casablanca.** For devotees of

the silent cinema, however, he will always be remembered as the enigmatic, tortured, noble hero of **The Cabinet of Dr Caligari;** pale, tall, gaunt, ill, anxious and disconcerting, he set a standard for horror-fantasy acting that is still emulated today.

Veidt was born in Potsdam, near Berlin, in 1893, and studied under Max Reinhardt as a stage actor. He made his screen début in 1917 and starred in two lost F.W. Murnau films, including a

version of **Dr Jekyll and Mr Hyde.** He appeared in many nightmarish German Expressionist classics, including Wiene's **The Hands of Orlac,** Leni's **Waxworks** and Galeen's **The Student of Prague.** This last film made him world famous, and he was invited to Hollywood to star opposite John Barrymore ❯ in **The Beloved Rogue;** his best Hollywood silents, however, were Leni's **The Man Who Laughs** and Fejos' **The Last Performance,** but they were not popular successes. His German accent ended his first American career when sound arrived, so he returned to Germany, but his having a Jewish wife meant trouble with the Nazis there. He finally settled permanently in Britain, where he had great success, especially in Walter Forde's **Rome Express,** Victor Saville's **I Was a Spy** and Michael Powell's **The Spy in Black** and **Contraband.** He returned to America on the magic carpet of **The Thief of Bagdad** (he was the wizard) and even got to be Joan Crawford's ❯ beloved in George Cukor's **A Woman's Face.** He died in Hollywood in 1943 after completing Richard Thorpe's **Above Suspicion,** still a star after 25 years.

Below: Conrad Veidt gave one of his greatest performances as the hideously smiling victim of Paul Leni's 1928 **The Man Who Laughs,** *with Mary Philbin, but it was not a popular film.*

BEST FILMS:
1919 The Cabinet of Dr Caligari
Robert Wiene (Decla-Bioscop—Germany)
1924 Waxworks
Paul Leni (Neptun Film—Germany)
1924 The Hands of Orlac
Robert Wiene (Pan Film—Austria)
1926 The Student of Prague
Henrick Galeen (Sokal Film—Germany)
1927 The Man Who Laughs
Paul Leni (Universal—USA)
1931 Congress Dances
Erick Charell (Ufa—Germany)

ERICH VON STROHEIM

Von Stroheim the director was allowed to show his genius only during the silent era, but von Stroheim the actor, "The Man You Love to Hate", had a long and successful career in sound films. His greatest acting achievement, however, was not in any single film but in the creation of his persona, a living legend, both as the extravagant, genius director destroyed by the moguls of Hollywood and as the menacing personification of the Hun (in the silent period) and the Nazi (in sound films). He was immediately recognisable to all, with his closely-cropped bullet head, penetrating eyes and air of aristocratic evil. The finest embodiment of this persona was in Renoir's **La Grande Illusion**, where he portrays the ramrod German aristocrat von Rauffenstein, in charge of a prisoner of war camp; chivalrous and cultured, his metal neck-support reflecting his way of thinking, he is both Hun and gentleman, but regretfully shoots his French aristocrat friend, whom he thinks is trying to escape. Almost as fine was his personification of himself in Billy Wilder's **Sunset Boulevard**; he portrays faded silent star Gloria Swanson's ➤ former director (which he actually was—the film incorporates a scene from **Queen Kelly**, in which he directed her) and present butler. Von Stroheim was so good at being himself that he got his only Academy Award nomination for the part, after acting in films for 35 years.

Stroheim's "von" was probably invented. He appears to have been born in Vienna as Erich Oswald Stroheim in 1885. He acquired military experience and punctiliousness as an Austrian Army officer and emigrated to the US in 1906, working at various odd jobs before making his film début in 1914 in **Captain McLean**. He had tiny roles in several D.W. Griffith films, including **The Birth of a Nation** and **Intolerance**, and began gradually to get larger parts as a Prussian officer; the persona he created in later roles became so famous that comedians like Ben Turpin based satires around it.

He turned director and starred himself in three of his best films, **Blind Husbands**, **Foolish Wives** and **The Wedding March**. **Queen**

Kelly sank his directing career, but he continued to star in important films, including the memorable ventriloquist taken over by his dummy in **The Great Gabbo**, the fanatical film director (Erich von Furst) of **The Lost Squadron** (sending men to their deaths in aircraft in order to get realistic shots), and Garbo's ➤ bizarre protector in **As You Desire Me**. In 1936 he went to France to make **La Grande Illusion** and other French films, but later returned to Hollywood for more Hun roles. He was brilliant as Rommel in Wilder's **Five Graves to Cairo** and superb as the murderous sharpshooter in Mann's **The Great Flamarion**. After the war he worked mostly in France, except for his stunning appearance in **Sunset Boulevard**. He died in Paris in 1957.

*Above: Erich von Stroheim gave one of his best performances as Rommel in **Five Graves to Cairo**.*

BEST FILMS:
1918 Blind Husbands
Erich von Stroheim (Universal)
1921 Foolish Wives
Erich von Stroheim (Universal)
1928 The Wedding March
Erich von Stroheim (Paramount)
1929 The Great Gabbo
James Cruze (Sono-Art)
1932 The Lost Squadron
George Archainbaud (RKO)
1932 As You Desire Me
George Fitzmaurice (MGM)
1937 La Grande Illusion
Jean Renoir (France)
1943 Five Graves to Cairo
Billy Wilder (Paramount)
1945 The Great Flamarion
Anthony Mann (Republic)
1950 Sunset Boulevard
Billy Wilder (Paramount)

JOHN WAYNE

John Wayne has great claims to being the greatest movie star of all time. Polls of exhibitors going back to 1932 indicate clearly that he is the No 1 box office attraction of the sound cinema, achieving top ten stardom in 1949 and remaining there almost every year until 1974. He is the biggest money-earner in movie history, too—way over $400 million—and

has starred in more classic Hollywood films than anyone else, except Cary Grant ➤ and James Stewart ➤, mostly directed by John Ford and Howard Hawks: he is without doubt the No 1 Western star. And yet there are still critics who consider that he is not a good actor, simply a "natural" performer. In fact, he is nearly as great a screen actor as he is a star, a consummate master of timing, with personality nuances that have made his screen persona one of the most interesting in the cinema. Admittedly, his range is limited, but within those limits he has used his abilities to extraordinary effect—the shy, almost

diffident Ringo Kid of the 1939 **Stagecoach** is a far cry from the stubborn and fatally-flawed trail boss of **Red River**. His screen personality has never stopped developing, as can be seen in his recent portrayal of a resigned and dying gunfighter in Don Siegel's **The Shootist**. There has been great misunderstanding of Wayne's screen work because of his supposedly right-wing Republican attitudes in real life, but what is actually seen in the cinema is not a reactionary but a great individualist. He is more than just a man of action in these films: he is a study in the glories and failings of self-sufficiency, some-

Left: John Wayne is easily the most popular and biggest money-earning star of the sound era, especially for his Westerns.

*Above: John Wayne finally won an Academy Award in 1969 for his portrayal of a one-eyed gunfighter in **True Grit**.*

times arrogant and harsh, usually impatient but good-humoured, always leathery, tough and masculine. Perhaps he has been underrated as an actor because he works in action films, but his movies include some of the great masterpieces of world cinema.

Wayne was born in Winterset, Iowa, on May 26, 1907, with the name Marion Michael Morrison. He began his long association with John Ford in 1928, working on the sets of **Mother Macree** and with a bit part in **Hangman's House.** His first starring role was in Raoul Walsh's 1930 **The Big Trail,** but he did not have the solidity he gained in later years and was soon reduced to being the star of B-Westerns. He was pretty good at this and was one of the most popular heroes of these sagebrush sagas throughout the '30s. He was re-introduced to a wider public by Ford in the 1939 **Stagecoach** and was a major star from that point onward, first in Walsh's **Dark Command** and then again with Ford in **The Long Voyage Home.** He starred opposite Marlene Dietrich ❯ in Tay Garnett's **Seven Sinners,** gave a strong performance in Cecil B. De Mille's **Reap the Wild Wind,** and had a wonderful fight with Randolph Scott ❯ over Dietrich in **The Spoilers.** He began his long career as a war film hero with **The Fighting Seabees** in 1944 and made such classics of the genre as Ford's **They Were Expendable** and Allan Dwan's **Sands of Iwo Jima.** In 1948 he began to be truly great, in Ford's **Fort Apache** and Hawks' **Red River.** He completed Ford's famous Cavalry trilogy with **She Wore a Yellow Ribbon** and **Rio Grande** and then made one of his most likeable and good-natured pictures, **The Quiet Man.** It may be the best film ever made by Republic Studios, the B-picture outfit which he had almost carried with him to major status.

Even the lesser films he was making now were big box-office, and the great ones were magnificent, particularly Ford's **The Searchers** and Hawks' **Rio Bravo** (rated by many critics as the best Western of all time). In 1960 he turned director with his epic **The Alamo,** a critically-maligned but enjoyable film. His screen personality continued to develop in Ford's **The Horse Soldiers** and especially in **The Man Who Shot Liberty Valance,** in which the limitations of his kind of individual pioneer fighter were finely shown. He completed his western trilogy with Hawks by starring in **El Dorado** and **Rio Lobo,** as well as their enjoyable **Hatari!**

He received a lot of political flak in 1968 for his patriotic Vietnam film **The Green Berets,** released at the height of the anti-war movement, but the public went to see it in large numbers. He finally won an Academy Award in 1969 for his portrayal of the cantankerous, one-eyed gunfighter in **True Grit,** possibly a show of solidarity from the Hollywood community and a gesture for his having conquered cancer. Wayne later reprised the role opposite Katharine Hepburn ❯ in **Rooster Cogburn** in 1975, but his greatest performance in the '70s was as the old gunfighter dying of cancer in **The Shootist.** He died (of cancer) on 11 June 1979.

BEST FILMS:
1939 Stagecoach
John Ford (United Artists)

1940 The Long Voyage Home
John Ford (United Artists)
1945 They Were Expendable
John Ford (MGM)
1948 Red River
Howard Hawks (United Artists)
1948 Fort Apache
John Ford (RKO)
1949 Sands of Iwo Jima
Allan Dwan (Republic)
1949 She Wore a Yellow Ribbon
John Ford (RKO)
1950 Rio Grande
John Ford (Republic)
1952 The Quiet Man
John Ford (Republic)
1956 The Searchers
John Ford (Warner Brothers)
1959 Rio Bravo
Howard Hawks (Warner Brothers)
1961 The Man Who Shot Liberty Valance
John Ford (Paramount)
1962 Hatari!
Howard Hawks (Paramount)
1967 El Dorado
Howard Hawks (Paramount)
1969 True Grit
Henry Hathaway (Paramount)
1976 The Shootist
Don Siegel (Dino De Laurentiis)

JOHNNY WEISSMULLER
see **Tarzan**

ORSON WELLES

It is often forgotten that Orson Welles got an Academy Award nomination for Best Actor for **Citizen Kane,** as well as receiving acclaim for writing and directing it. He is, in fact, one of the major stars of world cinema, as well as being the most influential filmmaker alive. He has appeared in a large number of good, bad and indifferent movies, but he has never been less than impressive on screen. He has been at his best in his own films, which are among the masterpieces of the cinema, but he has also been outstanding in others—his relatively small role as Harry Lime was the focus of **The Third Man,** he was superb as the Clarence Darrow-like lawyer in **Compulsion,** and he was outstanding as Cardinal Wolsey in **A Man For All Seasons.** He has been delightfully involved in hocus-pocus in several movies, sawing Marlene Dietrich ❯ in half in **Follow The Boys,** as the magician Cagliostro in **Black Magic,** as a man who makes things vanish in **A Safe Place,** and as the king of cinematic illusions and frauds in his own **F for Fake.** He was eerily persuasive in costume drama, as the mysterious Mr Rochester in **Jane Eyre,** the

*Left: Orson Welles is almost as good an actor as he is a director, as he showed playing Harry Lime in **The Third Man** (1949), in which he upstaged Trevor Howard and Joseph Cotten.*

terrifying Cesare Borgia in **Prince of Foxes,** the swaggering Genghis Khan of **The Black Rose** and the sermonising Father Mapple in **Moby Dick.** None of these, however matches up to his performances as the newspaper magnate in **Citizen Kane,** the police colonel in **Journey into Fear,** the Nazi in disguise in **The Stranger,** the seaman involved with Rita Hayworth ❯❯ in **The Lady from Shanghai,** the unscrupulous financier in **Mr Arkadin,** or the bloated police chief in **Touch of Evil,** all directed by himself. He has been impressively individual in Shakespearean roles, in his **Macbeth, Othello** and **Chimes at Midnight** (as Falstaff), and is particularly effective as himself in films like **F for Fake** and **Filming Othello.**

Welles was born in Kenosha, Wisconsin, on April 6, 1915, and was accorded genius status while still a young man, acting at the Gate Theatre in Dublin at the age of 16 and appearing on stage with Katharine Cornell before he was 20. He founded the Mercury Theatre with John Houseman in 1936, when he was only 21, and became a radio star (he was "The Shadow" for a while), culminating in the production of *The War of the Worlds,* probably the most famous radio drama ever—it was so effective that thousands of Americans thought they were listening to a bulletin about a real Martian invasion, and there was widespread panic.

On the strength of his theatre reputation, RKO invited him to make any film he wanted—**Citizen Kane** was the result. Unfortunately, that movie aroused the wrath of newspaper magnate William Randolph Hearst (on whose life it was loosely based) and Hearst's antagonism virtually destroyed Welles' Hollywood career. Since the '40s he has been a drifter, primarily based in Spain, making films whenever he could get the finance and acting in others. As he grew older and larger, his screen persona changed from the edginess of Kane and Rochester to the grosser portrayals of Falstaff and the **Touch of Evil** police chief, but he has always retained complete control of his characterisations, aided by one of the most remarkable voices in the movies.

BEST FILMS:
1941 Citizen Kane
Orson Welles (RKO)
1946 The Stranger
Orson Welles (RKO)
1946 The Lady from Shanghai
Orson Welles (Columbia)
1948 Macbeth
Orson Welles (Republic)
1949 The Third Man
Carol Reed (British Lion)

1952 Othello
Orson Welles (United Artists)
1955 Mr Arkadin
Orson Welles (Warner Brothers)
1958 Touch of Evil
Orson Welles (Universal)
1962 The Trial
Orson Welles (Paris Europa)
1966 Chimes at Midnight
Orson Welles (Internacional Films)

Mae West

Mae West was once described as "an outrageous female impersonator"; certainly, the persona she evolved on stage and in the cinema must be considered as the ultimate sex satire: splendidly vulgar, ostentatiously overdressed, and not so much licentious as laughable. She is one of the great screen comediennes and the object of her mockery is not sex at all, but our attitudes towards it. Her first stage play was called simply *Sex* and gained her a ten-day jail sentence for its naughtiness. She could be considered the Lenny Bruce of the '30s, daring to talk about the unmentionable—how else can one explain the fact that a rather full-bodied 41-year-old woman could become not only a major movie star but a sex symbol?—that 37½-29½-37½ figure on a mere five-foot-four frame was 126 pounds of pure fun. She was also a brilliant writer, as clever at coining epigrams as Oscar Wilde and probably just as often quoted. Among her most famous lines are her reply to the hat-check girl who says, "Goodness, what beautiful diamonds"—"Goodness had nothing to do with it" (in her first film, the 1932 **Night After Night**); "Beulah, peel me a grape" (Mae's order to her maid in **I'm No Angel**, probably her best film); and "Why don't you come up sometime, see me" (spoken to Salvation Army man Cary Grant ➤ in **She Done Him Wrong** and slightly altered in popular usage). Her whole attitude to life could be summed up in her statement: "Whenever I'm caught between two evils, I take the one I've never tried before."

Mae West was born on August 17, 1892, in Brooklyn, New York, and began to work on stage and in vaudeville as a teenager. She introduced the shimmy to Broadway in the musical *Sometime* and then began to write her own plays. Her biggest stage hit was *Diamond Lil* and it made her both famous and notorious (it became the basis for her film **She Done Him Wrong**). After nearly 30 years in show business, she made her cinematic début in **Night After Night**; it was really a vehicle for George Raft ➤, but she rewrote her part and, as Raft laconically observed afterwards, "She stole everything but the camera". She was such a hit that Paramount immediately signed her to make *Diamond Lil* into a film. It earned $2 million in a few months and she

was soon hailed as the financial saviour of the studio, which was close to bankruptcy. Most of the films she made at Paramount were a delight. It didn't really matter who directed them—and there were major names like McCarey, Walsh and Hathaway—for she dominated them with her scripts and performances. Her delightful bawdiness had unexpected effects, including causing a clampdown by the censorious Hays Office and leading to the foundation of the Legion of Decency; some things, after all,

are sacred. Mae kept right on flaunting her caricature of a sex goddess, but censorship cuts and changes affected **Belle of the Nineties** (in which she has an amazing series of tableaux as a rose, a butterfly, a bat—and even the Statue of Liberty). Audiences and critics were beginning to get used to her new ways of slipping *double-entendres* past the censors (notably in **Goin' to Town**), but she remained popular for a few more years.

Mae West's star had been so brilliant that it had to burn out

quickly. She made her last film at Paramount in 1938—**Every Day's a Holiday** with Mae as a confidence trickster selling the Brooklyn Bridge—but it was not well received, and she moved to Universal to join W.C. Fields ➤ in **My Little Chickadee**. Both she and Fields wrote their own lines, which never quite seem to match up in this story of a shady lady and a conman in the Old West, but it is still highly entertaining.

Her last film of this period, the independently-made **The Heat's On** in 1943, was criticised for being dated in mannerism and style, so she returned to the theatre, notably in *Catherine Was Great* and, again, *Diamond Lil*. She returned to movies in 1970, as a Hollywood agent opposite Raquel Welch ➤ in the not very successful **Myra Breckinridge**, and in 1978 in **Sextette**, a bad parody of her own earlier films, in campily awful taste. She recently summarised her own career most succinctly: "There'll never be another star like me."

BEST FILMS:
1932 Night After Night
Archie Mayo (Paramount)
1933 She Done Him Wrong
Lowell Sherman (Paramount)
1933 I'm No Angel
Wesley Ruggles (Paramount)
1934 Belle of the Nineties
Leo McCarey (Paramount)
1935 Goin' to Town
Alexander Hall (Paramount)
1936 Klondike Annie
Raoul Walsh (Paramount)
1936 Go West, Young Man
Henry Hathaway (Paramount)
1938 Every Day's a Holiday
Edward Sutherland (Paramount)
1940 My Little Chickadee
Edward Cline (Universal)
1943 The Heat's On
Gregory Ratoff (Columbia)

Richard Widmark

Richard Widmark started his film career giggling, laughing hysterically and shoving a little old lady down a flight of stairs. That was in 1947 in **Kiss of Death**, as a psychotic killer, and although he has done a lot of outstanding work since then, he has never been better. If he'd stayed a villain, it might have kept him from becoming a major star, so he cleverly incorporated some rather nasty traits into an heroic persona and is still going strong. In the 1977 **Twilight's Last Gleaming** he was the SAC General who

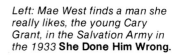

*Left: Mae West finds a man she really likes, the young Cary Grant, in the Salvation Army in the 1933 **She Done Him Wrong**.*

*Left: Richard Widmark portrayed Jim Bowie, inventor of a famous frontier knife, in John Wayne's $12 million patriotic epic **The Alamo** (1960).*

orders his men to shoot the President, along with rebel general Burt Lancaster ❯. He was the first of the really brutal modern cops in Madigan, and he was drunken and vicious but still heroic as Jim Bowie in The Alamo. One of his finest roles was as the amoral pickpocket of Samuel Fuller's Pickup on South Street, not at all sure that he wants to cooperate with the authorities when he lifts a message from a Communist spy ring. His good-nasty persona is ideal for Westerns and he made two excellent ones for John Ford, Two Rode Together (joining forces with James Stewart ❯ to rescue Comanche prisoners) and Cheyenne Autumn (a moving depiction of the great Cheyenne trek north).

Widmark was born in Sunrise, Minnesota, on December 26, 1914, began his acting career in radio, and then moved on to stage work before his Kiss of Death début. His truly frightening performance made him a star overnight and he was top-billed in vicious roles in two more superb thrillers, Road House and The Street With No Name. He turned nice guy for Elia Kazan's Panic in the Streets (hunting down plague-bearing Jack Palance ❯, who was making his horrific début) and generally played men on the right side of the law after that. He was good in war films (Hell and High Water), psychological dramas (The Cobweb), and even as the weak Dauphin in Otto Preminger's St Joan. He was very strong with Henry Fonda ❯ in the psychological Western Warlock, but not at his best as the prosecuting attorney in Judgement at Nuremberg. He was convincing again as the ruthless warship commander of The Bedford Incident (describing himself as "a mean bastard"), and made two more fine Westerns, Death of a Gunfighter and When the Legends Die. He starred in a TV series based on Madigan in 1972 and was the deserving murder victim in Murder on the Orient Express. His other recent films include Rollercoaster, The Swarm and Coma.

BEST FILMS:
1947 Kiss of Death
Henry Hathaway (20th Century Fox)
1948 Road House
Jean Negulesco (20th Century Fox)
1948 The Street With No Name
William Keighley (20th Century Fox)
1950 Panic in the Streets
Elia Kazan (20th Century Fox)
1953 Pickup on South Street
Samuel Fuller (20th Century Fox)
1960 The Alamo
John Wayne (United Artists)
1961 Two Rode Together
John Ford (Columbia)
1964 Cheyenne Autumn
John Ford (Warner Brothers)
1965 The Bedford Incident
James B. Harris (Columbia)
1968 Madigan
Don Siegel (Universal)
1977 Twilight's Last Gleaming
Robert Aldrich (Lorimar)

CORNEL WILDE

Wilde became famous making "miracles of music in Majorca" in one of the great Hollywood kitsch films, the 1945 A Song to Remember, playing Chopin to Merle Oberon's Georges Sand, who advised him in the never-to-be-forgotten phrase: "Discontinue that so-called Polonaise jumble you've been playing for days". He got an Oscar nomination for dying over his piano keys, female audiences adored him and the critics had a lot of fun sending him up ("as infuriating and funny a misrepresentation of an artist's life and work as I have ever seen", noted James Agee). Wilde never made such an impact again, but he made better films. He was quite an intelligent actor in a limited way, he looked good on

Above: Cornel Wilde directed and starred in **The Naked Prey** *(1966), as a safari guide in Africa captured by a hostile tribe and allowed to live only if he can evade their hunters.*

the screen, and his previous experience as a champion fencer made him a rather good swash-buckling hero in films like The Bandit of Sherwood Forest. He became cultural again as a famous author married to possessive Gene Tierney ❯❯ in Leave Her to Heaven, he was Linda Darnell's true love in the then-sensational Forever Amber, and he enjoyed himself with Ginger Rogers ❯ in the comedy It Had To Be You. He was better in tough noir films like the remarkable Road House (as a paroled convict in love with Ida Lupino ❯❯) and the powerful Shockproof (as a parole officer in love with Patricia Knight). He had a major role as a star trapeze artist in the all-star The Greatest Show on Earth and was good as one of the husbands in Woman's World. His present-day reputation, however, mainly rests on films which he both directs and stars in, most

notably The Naked Prey (hunted through the African jungle) and Beach Red (a brutal anti-war film). His recent films include Shark's Treasure and The Norseman (supporting Lee Majors). Cornel Wilde was born in New York City on October 13, 1915, became a stage actor (he was Tybalt in Laurence Olivier's ❯ 1940 production of Romeo and Juliet), and made his film début in The Lady with Red Hair, in 1940.

BEST FILMS:
1945 A Song to Remember
Charles Vidor (Columbia)
1945 Leave Her to Heaven
John Stahl (20th Century Fox)
1946 The Bandit of Sherwood Forest
George Sherman (Columbia)
1946 Centennial Summer
Otto Preminger (20th Century Fox)
1947 Forever Amber
Otto Preminger (20th Century Fox)
1948 Road House
Jean Negulesco (20th Century Fox)
1949 Shockproof
Douglas Sirk (Columbia)
1952 The Greatest Show on Earth
Cecil B. De Mille (Paramount)
1966 The Naked Prey
Cornel Wilde (Paramount)
1967 Beach Red
Cornel Wilde (United Artists)

ESTHER WILLIAMS

She couldn't act, she couldn't dance, she couldn't sing—but, boy, could she swim! And in the water she became a major movie star for MGM for 11 years, from 1944 to 1955, directed in dazzling water ballet sequences by Busby Berkeley, Vincente Minnelli and others. She was big box-office and her appeal has not diminished a whit, as was seen from the rapturous reception given to her sequences in the MGM compilation That's Entertainment in 1974. She did for swimming what Sonja Henie ❯ did for ice-skating and Eleanor Powell ❯ for tap-dancing, and the most interesting parts of her pictures are the spectacular swimming numbers. Her career was succinctly summed up by Fanny Brice in the famous comment: "Wet she's a star, dry she ain't".

Williams was born in Los Angeles on August 8, 1921, and after becoming a champion swimmer and being featured in Billy Rose's Aquacade, she was lured to movies, swimming onto the screen in 1942 opposite Mickey Rooney ❯ in Andy Hardy Steps Out. Her first swimming spectacular came two years later with Bathing Beauty, staged by John Murray Anderson. She was reluctant to go into films at first (she knew she was no actress), but when she capitulated she did wondrous things with her limited talent. Her films include On an Island With You, Neptune's Daughter and Million Dollar

Mermaid (extravagantly choreographed by Busby Berkeley); her best is probably Take Me Out to the Ball Game, with Gene Kelly ❯ and Frank Sinatra ❯, but it's hardly typical of her usual vehicles —she only swam once in it. In Easy to Love she leads one hundred water skiers in the elaborate climax, in Ziegfeld Follies Minnelli kept her underwater for a fascinating ballet number. Her last cinematic breaststroke was the 1955 Jupiter's Darling, but it was a failure. She tried a few straight roles and then retired; her last released film was The Big Show in 1961, with present husband Fernando Lamas.

Below: Esther Williams could not act, sing or dance, but she was a magnificent swimmer for MGM for 11 years in musical extravaganzas. She's seen here (underwater) in **Skirts Ahoy!**

BEST FILMS:
1944 Bathing Beauty
George Sidney (MGM)
1945 Thrill of a Romance
Richard Thorpe (MGM)
1946 Ziegfeld Follies
Vincente Minnelli (MGM)
1948 On an Island With You
Richard Thorpe (MGM)
1949 Take Me Out to the Ball Game
Gene Kelly & Stanley Donen (MGM)
1949 Neptune's Daughter
Edward Buzzell (MGM)
1950 Duchess of Idaho
Robert Z. Leonard (MGM)
1952 Million Dollar Mermaid
Mervyn Le Roy (MGM)
1953 Dangerous When Wet
Charles Walters (MGM)
1953 Easy to Love
Charles Walters (MGM)

SHELLEY WINTERS

Shelley Winters has progressed from being a tough and rather pretty floozy to being a tough and rather blowsy mother, in a series

of memorable film roles that have won her two Best Supporting Actress Oscars and warm affection from a lot of moviegoers. Despite her often unsympathetic parts and the brashness of her screen persona, she usually conveys a romantic vulnerability under her brassy facade that has made her particularly endearing. She has continually been put into victim roles, trying very hard indeed but fated to be a loser: she was the waitress murdered by Ronald Colman ❯ in **A Double Life**, the pregnant girlfriend drowned by Montgomery Clift ❯ in **A Place in the Sun**, the new wife killed by preacher Robert Mitchum ❯ in **The Night of the Hunter**, the starlet murdered for her black-mailing activities in **The Big Knife**, and the new wife of James Mason ❯, run over by a car, in **Lolita**. One of the most effective things in **The Poseidon Adventure** was her over-the-hill Jewish mama swimming champion, rescuing Gene Hackman ❯ but then dying from exhaustion. Her unpleasant mother roles won her Oscars in **The Diary of Anne Frank** and **A Patch of Blue**, reaching a glorious kind of culmination in **Bloody Mama**, and she also has a nice line in madames, including **The Balcony** and **A House is Not a Home**.

Shelley Winters was born Shirley Schrift in St. Louis, Missouri, on August 18, 1922, and borrowed her first name from her favourite (Romantic) poet and her last name from her mother (adding an "s"). She aggressively fought her way into stage roles in the early '40s and made her screen début in a bit part in the 1943 **What a Woman!**

Her career has had its ups and downs, but she has astutely elected to take even small roles in films—if they are good roles. She has alternated film work with theatre and has retained her stardom while other contemporaries have faded. Among her

Above: Shelley Winters won two Oscars for her fine acting.
Top: Shelley Winters and Jack Palance in Robert Aldrich's **The Big Knife** *(1955) in which she is once again a murder victim.*

best recent films were Paul Mazursky's **Next Stop Greenwich Village** and Roman Polanski's **The Tenant**. She can also be seen in **Pete's Dragon**, the Italian **An Average Man**, **Tentacles** and **City on Fire**.
BEST FILMS:
1947 A Double Life
George Cukor (Universal)
1951 A Place in the Sun
George Stevens (Paramount)
1955 I Am A Camera
Henry Cornelius (DCA)
1955 The Night of the Hunter
Charles Laughton (United Artists)
1955 The Big Knife
Robert Aldrich (United Artists)
1959 The Diary of Anne Frank
George Stevens (20th Century Fox)
1962 Lolita
Stanley Kubrick (MGM)
1963 The Balcony
Joseph Strick (Continental)
1965 A Patch of Blue
Guy Green (MGM)
1970 Bloody Mama
Roger Corman (AIP)

FAY WRAY

"When I'm in New York I look at the Empire State Building and feel as though it belongs to me . . . or is it vice versa?" said Fay Wray recently. The heroine of **King Kong** ❯ will be forever identified with that building and with the giant ape who lovingly carried her to its top before gently putting her down to fight his Nemesis. Fay Wray added enormously to the effectiveness of the movie, because she really was beautiful enough in the film to make Kong's obsession with her believable.

She was born on September 16, 1907, in Alberta, Canada, on her father's ranch, but the family moved to Los Angeles when she was a child. After a short stage career she began working in Hal Roach comedies and as a leading lady for Universal Westerns, then Erich von Stroheim ❯ picked her out of a line of bathing beauties in 1926 to be his co-star as Mitzi in his last extravagant studio production, **The Wedding March.** She is the poor girl with whom the prince falls in love. The film, even in its mutilated form, remains one of

Above: Fay Wray watches her awesome admirer dispose of an annoyance in **King Kong,** *her most memorable film and one which made her immortal as the Beauty who killed the Beast.*

the masterpieces of the silent cinema. Fay was also picked to co-star with Gary Cooper ❯ (in **The Texan**), with Ronald Colman ❯ (in **The Unholy Garden**), and with Richard Arlen (in **Sea God**). She was the favourite leading lady of **King Kong** director Ernest B. Schoedsack, who also starred her in **The Four Feathers** and **The Most Dangerous Game.** She made a wonderful screaming victim in horror films, most notably opposite Lionel Atwill in the early two-colour Technicolor film **The Mystery of the Wax Museum,** in which she claws off his false face to reveal the horribly scarred features beneath.

Her career tailed off in the late '30s after more than 50 films, and she was reduced to playing in B-pictures. She continued making films until 1958 (**Drag Strip Riot** was the last). Her first two marriages were to top Hollywood screenwriters, John Monk Saunders (who wrote **Wings**) and

Robert Riskin (**It Happened One Night**), and she wed Dr Sanford Rothenberg in 1971. They live in Brentwood, California, where she still gets fan mail from new TV viewers of **King Kong**.

BEST FILMS:
1928 The Wedding March
Erich von Stroheim (Paramount)
1929 The Four Feathers
Ernest B. Schoedsack, Merian C. Cooper and Lothar Mendes (Paramount)
1930 The Texan
John Cromwell (Paramount)
1932 Dr X
Michael Curtiz (Warner Brothers)
1932 The Most Dangerous Game (The Hounds of Zaroff)
Ernest B. Schoedsack and Irving Pichel (RKO)
1932 The Mystery of the Wax Museum
Michael Curtiz (Warner Brothers)
1933 King Kong
Ernest B. Schoedsack and Merian C. Cooper (RKO)
1934 Viva Villa!
Jack Conway (MGM)
1934 The Affairs of Cellini
Gregory La Cava (United Artists)
1935 Bulldog Jack
Walter Forde (Gaumount-GB)

JANE WYMAN

One of Hollywood's great suffering actresses, Jane Wyman is remembered for being tearful, noble and plucky with a charming, rounded face like a worried baby squirrel. She suffered her way to an Academy Award in 1948 as a deaf-mute rape victim in **Johnny Belinda** and won acting nominations for her patient, tired wife and mother in **The Yearling**, self-sacrificing nanny in **The Veil**, and suffering blind woman in **Magnificent Obsession**. She also brought tears to many eyes as the club-footed heroine of **The Glass Menagerie** and as the widow in love with a younger man in **All That Heaven Allows**. Her most enjoyable film, however, was the delightfully light-hearted musical **Here Comes the Groom**, in which she teamed up with Bing Crosby ≫ to win a Best Song Oscar for *In the Cool, Cool, Cool of the Evening,* under the deft direction of Frank Capra. It reminded her admirers that Wyman had actually had a long career at Warner Brothers as a peppy blonde comedienne, with appearances in many musicals.

She was born as Sarah Jane Fulks in St Joseph, Missouri, on January 4, 1914, and spent her early years as a singer and dancer before going into films in 1936. Her oft-quoted first movie line was as a chorus girl auditioning for Dick Powell ≫ in **Stage Struck**: "My name· is Bessie Fuffnik. I swim, ride, dive, imitate birds and play the trombone". It's small wonder that she was stuck in dumb blonde parts for years, the sidekick to the heroine or to Jack Carson, or a substitute for

Above: Jane Wyman suffered her way to stardom, but she could also look very elegant.

Joan Blondell ≫. She was pleasant but unmemorable; Warners might never have developed her tearful potential if Billy Wilder hadn't borrowed her for the role of alcoholic Ray Milland's ≫ worried fiancée in the 1945 award-winner **The Lost Weekend**. Her new screen persona was developed at MGM in **The Yearling** and RKO in **Magic Town**, and finally capitalised on by Warner's in 1948 in **Johnny Belinda**. That film made her the hottest property in Hollywood and her career continued strong until the mid-'50s; since then she has made only a few films, the last being the 1969 **How To Commit a Marriage**. She also starred in her own television series. Four times married (once to Ronald Reagan), she now lives alone in Carmel, California.

BEST FILMS:
1945 The Lost Weekend
Billy Wilder (Paramount)
1946 The Yearling
Clarence Brown (MGM)
1947 Magic Town
William Wellman (RKO)
1948 Johnny Belinda
Jean Negulesco (Warner Brothers)
1950 Stage Fright
Alfred Hitchcock (Warner Brothers)
1950 The Glass Menagerie
Irving Rapper (Warner Brothers)
1951 Here Comes the Groom
Frank Capra (Paramount)
1951 The Blue Veil
Curtis Bernhardt (RKO)
1954 Magnificent Obsession
Douglas Sirk (Universal)
1955 All That Heaven Allows
Douglas Sirk (Universal)

LORETTA YOUNG

Loretta Young was the most beautiful clothes-horse ever to become a major Hollywood star. She was lovely to look at and a fair actress, but it was for glamour and high fashion that she was most renowned (sometimes her ward-

robe got better reviews than she did). She was the epitome of cinema fashions through the '30s and '40s—and in the '50s she turned to television to model her clothes. The TV series opened and closed with her wearing the latest *haute couture;* she won a lawsuit in 1971 to keep the programmes from being repeated, as the fashions had dated and would damage her image. She also made some good movies along the way (not many, considering she starred in nearly 100). She even won an acting Oscar for **The Farmer's Daughter** in 1947, in what was considered the biggest upset in Academy history (she gave a charming performance as a Swedish farm girl who becomes a Congresswoman). She may have looked virginal and delicate, but she was nicknamed the "iron butterfly" and seemed intensely aware of lighting and make-up as well as costumes.

Young was born Gretchen Michaela Young in Salt Lake City on January 6, 1913, and broke into movies while very young, her first picture being the 1927 **Naughty But Nice**. Her first important role was as the high-wire artiste loved by Lon Chaney ≫ in **Laugh, Clown, Laugh**. She worked first at Warners and then at Fox in the '30s, making a number of films with director William Wellman (who had a famous fight over her with Spencer Tracy ≫ in a nightclub in 1935). Her best films of this time were **Zoo in Budapest** (as a

*Below: Loretta Young, looking elegant even in bedclothes, puzzles over her sleepwalking gear in the 1951 **Half Angel.***

refugee from an orphanage, loved by a zookeeper) and **Man's Castle** (poverty-stricken love with Spencer Tracy). She was popular, especially in the fan/fashion magazines, but never a top box-office draw. The acting highpoint of her career came in the late '40s in **The Stranger** (opposite Orson Welles ≫ and Edward G. Robinson ≫), the Oscar-winning **Farmer's Daughter**, and the Dieterle thriller **The Accused** (as a sex-obsessed murderess). She also liked to appear eternally young (**Mother is a Freshman**) or wearing a nun's habit (**Come to the Stable**). Her film personality went out of fashion in the early '50s (her last film was the 1953 **It Happens Every Thursday**), when she turned very successfully to TV. She wrote her autobiography in 1962 (*The Things I Had to Learn*), and lives as glamorously as ever in Beverly Hills, California.

BEST FILMS:
1928 Laugh, Clown, Laugh
Herbert Brenon (MGM)
1931 Platinum Blonde
Frank Capra (Columbia)
1932 Taxi
Roy Del Ruth (Warner Brothers)
1933 Zoo in Budapest
Rowland V. Lee (20th Century Fox)
1933 Man's Castle
Frank Borzage (Columbia)
1938 Four Men and a Prayer
John Ford (20th Century Fox)
1938 Suez
Allan Dwan (20th Century Fox)
1946 The Stranger
Orson Welles (RKO)
1947 The Farmer's Daughter
H. C. Potter (RKO)
1948 The Accused
William Dieterle (Paramount)

3 THE MODERN MOVIE STARS

The modern cinema can be said to have begun in the mid-'50s at the confluence of a number of different sociological and cinematic currents. The decline of the cinema as an industry reached its nadir at this time, and then began the upturn which led to its revived prosperity in the '60s and its boom in the '70s. The decline was due primarily to the growth of television as entertainment, but also to the break-up of the production-distribution-exhibition chains in the US, increased taxes on foreign films in most countries and the weakening of the long-established studio system. One major American studio, RKO, disappeared entirely, and Senator McCarthy's notorious anti-Communist witch hunt lowered Hollywood's credibility just when the strength of European production began to increase. The nouvelle vague which emerged in France in 1959 was the most visible sign of Europe's new prestige.

As studio power went down, star power went up. Former RKO star Lucille Ball bought RKO through her TV production company Desilu and many other star/producers became of major importance in the '50s. Stars no longer had to be manufactured in Hollywood; Brigitte Bardot became a box office attraction in the US and elsewhere through French films. The biggest stars, however, were men. John Wayne was the top box office attraction throughout the '50s and the '60s, and Clint Eastwood was top in the '70s. Doris Day was the most popular actress, followed by Elizabeth Taylor.

New kinds of stars emerged in the mid-'50s. Many female stars were variations of the girl-woman: Bardot was a sex kitten, Carroll Baker a baby doll, Audrey Hepburn a waif and Marilyn Monroe an innocent. In the '60s "swinging" blondes like Julie Christie and Faye Dunaway became prominent while the '70s seemed to lean towards dark-haired model types like Jacqueline Bisset. A new style of acting also became noticeable in the '50s, especially among the male performers; the Stanislavsky-derived Method spread from New York's Actors' Studio to Hollywood, with Marlon Brando its first notable exponent. Montgomery Clift pioneered the brooding intro-spection typical of the technique and James Dean gave the style its first myth figure. Dean and Brando, who can be considered the first modern stars, influenced most of the actors who came after them including especially Paul Newman, Dustin Hoffman and other theatre-trained performers.

The stars in this modern section mostly became known after 1955 (and include more non-Americans than the previous sections). The few exceptions are either those who didn't become important stars until the modern era or who changed in an important way; for example, Dean Martin and Jerry Lewis were stars as a team before 1955, but their solo careers did not begin until 1956. Not all of the actors and actresses of note in the modern cinema have been included, but certainly all the major stars and many of those of medium magnitude. Some new "stars" have been left out because the extent and durability of their star-dom is still unclear (Nick Nolte, for example), some older stars excluded because their movies and their screen personalities seem of only minor interest today (ie Sandra Dee) and some excellent actors and actresses because they have not yet created and maybe never will create the personality and charisma that a star requires.

ANOUK AIMÉE

Anouk Aimee was at the peak of her fame as an international movie star in the '60s, portraying a nymphomaniac for Federico Fellini in **La Dolce Vita,** an enchanting cabaret dancer for Jacques Demy in **Lola** and a chic and glamorous woman who finds the man. she wants in Claude Lelouch's romantic **A Man and a Woman**—she was nominated for an Oscar for her performance in this picture and it won the Academy Award for Best Foreign Film. She then became one of the most sought-after stars in Europe and was starred opposite Omar Sharif in **The Appointment** and as the central character in the Lawrence Durrell adaptation **Justine;** then she married Albert Finney ❯ in 1970 (her third husband) and her career stopped. She did not return to film-making until 1977, working with Lelouch again in **Second Chance** opposite Catherine Deneuve ❯ (finding happiness with Deneuve's young son) and then with Lelouch's ex-assistant (and her new companion) Elie Chouraqui in **My First Love,** a tearful story about a son getting to know his dying mother. Neither film seemed likely to restore Aimée to international stardom but as her earlier career had also contained many low periods, she will probably climb to the top again.

She was born in Paris in 1932 as Françoise Sorya and made her début as a servant in the 1947 **La Maison sous la Mer.** Writer Jacques Prévert was so impressed that he wrote **Les Amants de Vérone** for her and she was expected to become a British star in the '50s after **The Golden Salamander** with Trevor Howard ❯. She didn't, but she began to

Below: Anouk Aimée in André Delvaux's mysterious **Un Soir... un Train** *(1968), in which she portrays Yves Montand's mistress.*

make excellent French films with emerging new directors; Alexandre Astruc starred her first in the medium-length **The Crimson Curtain** as an enigmatic girl who seduces a soldier and dies in his arms, and then in **Les Mauvaises Rencontres** as a girl remembering her relationships with men while being interrogated by the police. Georges Franju gave her a good role in his first feature **La Tête Contre les Murs** in 1958 and she became an international star in 1960 through her sexy performance in **La Dolce Vita.** Fellini starred her again in **8½** as film director Marcello Mastroianni's wife and she was featured in a number of other fine Italian films, including **Il Terrorista** and **Il Successo.** After her major success in **A Man and a Woman,** she worked with Jacques Demy in the role of Lola once more in **Model Shop,** made the big-budget **Justine** and **The Appointment** and worked with André Delvaux in his mysterious **Un Soir . . . Un Train.**

BEST FILMS:
1952 Le Rideau Cramoisi (The Crimson Curtain)
Alexandre Astruc (Argos/Como)
1955 Les Mauvaises Rencontres
Alexandre Astruc (Les Films Marceau)
1958 La Tête Contre les Murs
Georges Franju (Sirius/Atica)
1960 La Dolce Vita
Federico Fellini (Riama/Pathé)
1960 Lola
Jacques Demy (Rome-Paris Films)
1963 8½
Federico Fellini (Cineriz)
1966 Un Homme et une Femme (A Man and a Woman)
Claude Lelouch (Les Films 13)
1968 Model Shop
Jacques Demy (Columbia)
1969 Justine
George Cukor (20th Century-Fox)
1978 Mon Premier Amour (My First Love)
Élie Chouraqui (7 Films/Gaumont)

WOODY ALLEN

Woody Allen represents for the modern cinema what Charlie Chaplin ❯ stood for in the silent era. Though Allen is a long way as yet from Chaplin's popularity, both can be seen as the symbolic underdogs of their very different societies. Chaplin's insecurities were usually based on money and work problems while Allen's are founded in himself: his persona, which he perfected as a stand-up night club comic, derives from his Jewishness, physical appearance, slight build, emotional hang-ups and sexual inadequacies. He is the modern educated urban man who knows enough about everything to be worried about it. Allen, himself the writer-director behind the actor, appears to have many of the characteristics of his screen persona and while the two are certainly not the same their insecurities seem to grow from the same source. Given the somewhat intellectual, urban basis of Allen's humour and his obvious middle-class attitudes, it seems improbable that he will ever have the mass popularity of Chaplin, or even Mel Brooks ❯ (whose films attract audiences three times the size of Allen's). All the same, Allen's writing/acting, in the guise of comedy, has created some of the most perceptive and revealing cinema of our time; the four Oscars given in 1978 to his **Annie Hall** (best film, director, screenplay and actress) indicate the growing recognition of his importance and his contribution to the cinema.

Allen was born in Brooklyn, New York City, on December 1, 1935 (real name Allen Stewart Konigsberg). He began writing comedy professionally at the age of 17, contributing to newspaper columns and TV shows, and was

Left: Woody Allen has become the greatest "little man" of the modern cinema with a "cowardly" persona resembling Bob Hope's.

soon working for Sid Caesar and Herb Shriner. His material was featured in the stage revue *From A to Z* in 1960 and he was persuaded to make his début as a stand-up comic in 1961 at the Duplex Club in Greenwich village by his agents Jack Rollins and Charles Joffe (who later became the producers of his films). It took him a year to perfect his persona and he had his first notable success at the Bitter End in November 1962; he began to write stories and essays for *The New Yorker* and other magazines and then wrote and made his film début in **What's New, Pussycat?** (1965). The following year he took a Japanese spy film acquired by AIP, added a few sequences with a new soundtrack and music by the Lovin' Spoonful, and created a very odd but funny film called **What's Up, Tiger Lily?** He had a success with the stage play *Don't Drink the Water* and was "Jimmy Bond" in the disastrous James Bond spoof **Casino Royale.**

His real cinema career began in 1969 when he wrote, directed and starred in the amusing gangster romp **Take the Money and Run** and appeared on stage in the production of his play *Play It Again, Sam* with Diane Keaton ❯ and Tony Roberts. In 1971 he directed and starred in **Bananas,** an anarchic story about a mad New York inventor becoming a Latin American revolutionary leader. His skills as a film actor, however, were seen at their best in the screen adaptation of **Play It Again, Sam,** directed by Herbert Ross and all the funnier for its greater disciplines. Allen directed himself and others in the sketch film **Everything You've Always Wanted to Know About Sex,** which was very good in parts; then came **Sleeper** (science-fiction satire) and **Love and Death** (mainly Tolstoy but with a strong flavouring of Bergman) starring himself and both also featuring Diane Keaton. He returned to straight acting with **The Front,** portraying a loser who lends his name to a blacklisted writer.

His myriad comic writing-directing-acting skills came together in his finest film in 1977, **Annie Hall,** in which he shared the limelight with Keaton in what was seen as a semi-biographical film. He portrayed a famous comedian with many of Allen's own attitudes and foibles. He did not appear in his next film, the Bergman-esque non-comedy **Interiors,** but then co-starred with Keaton again in **Manhattan** in 1979.

Allen's essays and stories have been published in two volumes, *Getting Even* and *Without Feathers;* he has also made three records and is the subject of a comic strip. His hobby is playing clarinet with a Dixieland jazz band called The Ragtime Rascals—he did not attend the Academy Award ceremony for **Annie Hall** because it conflicted with his regular night for playing with his band.

BEST FILMS:
1965 What's New, Pussycat?
Clive Donner (United Artists)
1967 What's Up, Tiger Lily?
Woody Allen & Senkichi Taniguchi (Benedict/Toho)
1969 Take the Money and Run
Woody Allen (Palomar)
1971 Bananas
Woody Allen (United Artists)
1972 Play It Again, Sam
Herbert Ross (Paramount)
1972 Everything You've Always Wanted to Know About Sex
Woody Allen (United Artists)
1973 Sleeper
Woody Allen (United Artists)
1975 Love and Death
Woody Allen (United Artists)
1976 The Front
Martin Ritt (Columbia)
1977 Annie Hall
Woody Allen (United Artists)

BIBI ANDERSSON
see **Ingmar Bergman Stars**

HARRIET ANDERSSON
see **Ingmar Bergman Stars**

URSULA ANDRESS

Ursula Andress is a striking example of photogenic stardom. She has never claimed to be an actress and in her films she is usually aloof, cold and humourless, unapproachable and not very interesting—but she photographs fabulously, her skin quality is magically luminous and the camera loves her. She is the nth degree of statuesque voluptuousness but her reserve and non-emotionality have won her the title of the Ice Maiden.

She made her initial impact on world cinema audiences in the first James Bond movie, **Dr No**, emerging from the sea like Botticelli's Venus clothed only in a white bikini with a knife at her waist, deeply tanned, gloriously beautiful and bewildered. The icy glamour of her screen persona—beauty without emotion—was immediately established and has hardly varied in her later pictures. It was encapsulated in what is probably her most interesting role, the hunter in the science-fiction thriller **The Tenth Victim** who shoots down men with a double-barrelled bra—she seduces victim Marcello Mastroianni ⟩, then drugs him and hauls him off

*Below: Ursula Andress emerging from the sea, to the delight of James Bond, in Terence Young's **Dr No** (1962).*

to the Roman Colosseum to be shot dead on live TV for a tea commercial. In most of her other films she is essentially decor, but her statuesque glamour is good value all the same.

She was born in Berne, Switzerland, in 1936 of German parents, was spotted by talent scouts while on holiday in Rome at the age of 16 and began appearing in Italian films from 1953. Her first major role was in **Dr No**; she soon become one of the best-known sex symbols of the '60s in films like **Four for Texas** (with Frank Sinatra ⟩), **Fun in Acapulco** (with Elvis Presley ⟩) and rather appropriately as the aloof demi-goddess star of **She**. She was married to actor/director John Derek for ten years from 1956, and he used her in the small-budget **Once Before I Die**, a story about American soldiers and a girl in the Philippines during World War II. She was featured in several British films of the late '60s including **The Southern Star, Casino Royale, Perfect Friday** and **The Blue Max**, but her career has lost its impetus in the '70s with appearances restricted mostly to minor Italian films.

BEST FILMS:
1962 Dr No
Terence Young (Eon/United Artists)
1963 Four for Texas
Robert Aldrich (Warner Brothers)
1964 Fun in Acapulco
Richard Thorpe (Paramount)
1964 She
Robert Day (Hammer/ABP)
1965 What's New, Pussycat?
Clive Donner (United Artists)
1965 The Tenth Victim
Elio Petri (CC Champion)
1966 The Blue Max
John Guillermin (20th Century Fox)
1968 The Southern Star
Sidney Hayers (Columbia)
1970 Perfect Friday
Peter Hall (London Screenplays)
1971 Red Sun
Terence Young (National General Pictures)

JULIE ANDREWS

Julie Andrews was the Queen of Hollywood in the mid-'60s: she was given the Best Actress Oscar for her performance as the governess in **Mary Poppins, The Sound of Music** became the most popular film of all time and she was named the No 1 box office star by exhibitors in 1966 and 1967. Yet by the end of the decade her movie career had ground to a halt and her films had become box office disasters. During the '70s she has made only one film, the unsuccessful 1974 **The Tamarind Seed,** and has worked mainly in television.

Her ten-year career in films is one of the most extraordinary in the history of the medium. She has been a professional entertainer for more than 30 years, although she is still a relatively young

*Above: Julie Andrews was the top box office star for two years following the astounding success of **The Sound of Music** in 1965.*

woman, born in Walton-on-Thames in 1934 as Julia Elizabeth Wells. Her family were in music hall; they promoted her superb four-octave voice and she made her London début in 1947 in the revue *Starlight Roof* She became a principal girl in pantomime, was invited to New York in 1954 to star in the stage production of *The Boy Friend,* and was given the plum role of Eliza Doolittle in the original 1956 production of *My Fair Lady* (after Mary Martin turned it down). She was an incredible international hit in her three years in the musical, worked in television, and starred in the stage production of *Camelot* in 1960. But Warner Brothers decided not to trust the film version of **My Fair Lady** to the little-known Andrews and gave the role to Audrey Hepburn ⟩. It was an unfortunate error: Disney immediately starred Andrews as **Mary Poppins** and not only did she win the Best Actress Oscar (Hepburn wasn't even nominated, although most of the other Academy Awards went to **My Fair Lady**), but her film made more money than the Warners' picture and became the most popular Disney film of all time.

Her next film role was a far cry from the wholesome, scrubbed, no-nonsense innocence of her usual screen persona; she was the war widow who sleeps with James Garner ⟩ in **The Americanization of Emily** on condition that he won't get himself heroically killed. She was superb, but the film was not a big hit. Her third film was **The Sound of Music,** the most popular musical up to then, and until quite recently the most popular film. Andrews was excellent as the most tuneful member of the Trapp Family Singers; in its clean-cut, sentimental way **The Sound of Music** was an extremely well-made romp through the Austrian hills. After such success there was nowhere to go but down, but first she was well received as the missionary's wife in **Hawaii,** the secret agent's wife in **Torn Curtain** and the delightful flapper in **Thoroughly Modern Millie.** At the end of 1967 she was voted the most popular star in the world.

Andrews' only film in 1968 was **Star!,** the life story of Gertrude Lawrence; it was very expensive and very unpopular, for audiences did not feel that the role matched her persona. Studios began to have second thoughts about expensive musicals, MGM cancelled the already costly **Say It With Music,** and Andrews' next film was the big-budget Paramount musical **Darling Lili,** as a Mata Hari-style spy in World War I. It flopped—and suddenly she was box office poison instead of guaranteed success. It was not her fault; she was as good a singer and performance as ever, given the right vehicle, but Hollywood seemed to have lost faith in her. Since then she has worked only in the 1974 romantic intrigue **The Tamarind Seed** with Omar Sharif ». These last two pictures were directed by Blake Edwards, whom she married during the filming of **Darling Lili** (following an earlier marriage to designer Tony Walton). Edwards is a very fine director, but he is probably not the best director for his wife, although they made a third film, **10,** in late 1978.

COMPLETE FILMS:
1964 Mary Poppins
Robert Stevenson (Disney)
1964 The Americanization of Emily
Arthur Hiller (MGM)
1965 The Sound of Music
Robert Wise (20th Century Fox)
1966 Hawaii
George Roy Hill (United Artists)
1966 Torn Curtain
Alfred Hitchcock (Universal)
1967 Thoroughly Modern Millie
George Roy Hill (Universal)
1968 Star!
Robert Wise (20th Century Fox)
1970 Darling Lili
Blake Edwards (Paramount)
1974 The Tamarind Seed
Blake Edwards (Jewel)
1979 10
Blake Edwards (Warner Brothers)

CARROLL BAKER

Carroll Baker became famous sucking her thumb in 1956, portraying the wilful child bride of Karl Malden in Elia Kazan's **Baby Doll.** She was terribly erotic doing it, the film won censorial fame, and the vulgar, trashy, blonde sexpot image it created for her has remained her screen persona ever since. She is actually at her

Above: Carroll Baker in Joseph E. Levine's production of **The Carpetbaggers.**

best in trashy movies, gloriously revelling in her Jean Harlow-like role in **The Carpetbaggers** or portraying the star herself in **Harlow.** She has appeared in some rather good big movies, like **Giant, The Big Country** and **Cheyenne Autumn,** but because they weren't vulgar she didn't stand out in them. Since the mid-'60s she has worked mainly in Italy, where she made one rather fine film, **The Harem,** under the direction of Marco Ferreri, a good film maker who can turn trash into art. Most of her other films there, like **Orgasmo,** are not quite good enough to be called trash, although she did make a neat little **Les Diaboliques**-type thriller called **The Sweet Body of Deborah.**

Baker was born in Johnstown, Pennsylvania, on May 28, 1931, worked in nightclubs for a while, and made her film début with a bit part in an Esther Williams » film, the 1953 **Easy to Love.** She then returned to New York, studied at the Actors' Studio, worked on Broadway, and returned to Hollywood for a better role in **Giant.** Kazan made her famous as Tennessee Williams' fantasy child in **Baby Doll,** but afterwards her career went wildly downhill, although she was satisfactory in husband Jack Garfein's **Something Wild,** as an emotionally disturbed girl saved from suicide by Ralph Meeker, and quite agreeable tempting the frustrated men of **Station Six Saraha.** Then **The Carpetbaggers** made her a big star again and she followed it with a good thriller, **Sylvia.** She has maintained her sex image by displaying her body in *Playboy* and elsewhere, and in 1977 achieved a kind of trash apotheosis by starring in **Andy Warhol's Bad,** a bizarre black comedy described

by *Variety* as "the sleaziest trash imaginable".

BEST FILMS:
1956 Giant
George Stevens (Warner Brothers)
1956 Baby Doll
Elia Kazan (Warner Brothers)
1958 The Big Country
William Wyler (United Artists)
1963 Station Six Sahara
Seth Holt (British Lion)
1964 The Carpetbaggers
Edward Dmytryk (Paramount)
1964 Cheyenne Autumn
John Ford (Warner Brothers)
1965 Harlow
Gordon Douglas (Paramount)
1967 The Sweet Body of Deborah
Romolo Guerrieri (Zenith-Flora)
1967 The Harem
Marco Ferreri (Sancro International)
1977 Andy Warhol's Bad
Jed Johnson (New World)

ANNE BANCROFT

Anne Bancroft is a great screen actress, one of the very best, yet she has not become a major movie star because she has chosen to remain a character actress rather than a personality. Like other stage-orientated stars, she becomes the roles she portrays rather than creating a fusion between personality and part— there is an enormous difference between Helen Keller's teacher in **The Miracle Worker,** the oft-pregnant wife in **The Pumpkin Eater,** the sexy Mrs Robinson of **The Graduate,** the trapped housewife of **The Prisoner of Second Avenue** and the ageing ballerina of **The Turning Point.** Bancroft is magnificent in all these roles but she doesn't exhibit star personality; great as she is, there is no screen "Anne Bancroft". The most consistent thread binding her roles together is steely-minded deter-

mination; to teach a deaf-mute to respond in **The Miracle Worker,** to seduce Dustin Hoffman » in **The Graduate** (and keep him from marrying her daughter), to achieve justice for rape victims in **Lipstick** and to retain her position as a ballet star in **The Turning Point.** This iron will seems to be a reflection of the real Bancroft personality. She was born in the Bronx, New York City, on September 17, 1931, as Anna Maria Luisa Italiano. She studied acting at the AADA in New York, made her professional début in a TV play and began her film career in 1952 playing Richard Widmark's » girlfriend in **Don't Bother To Knock.** She worked steadily in movies until 1956 but her early Hollywood career was a relative failure: she didn't make it as a star and she attracted little attention from critics or producers. Among her better films were **The Last Frontier** (outstanding as a cavalry colonel's wife in love with Victor Mature »), **Nightfall, The Restless**

Above: Anne Bancroft as the not-so-nice Mrs Robinson in **The Graduate** *(1968).*

Breed and **Tonight We Sing.** The less notable ones included **Gorilla At Large, Demetrius and the Gladiator** and **Treasure of the Golden Condor.** Discouraged, she went back to New York and immediately became a major stage star in *Two For the Seesaw* and *The Miracle Worker,* both written by William Gibson and directed by Arthur Penn. She was so good that Penn insisted on her playing Annie Sullivan to Patty Duke's Helen Keller in the 1962 film version; Bancroft gave one of the most complex, powerful and moving performances ever seen on film and deservedly won the Academy Award for Best Actress (Duke was voted Best Supporting Actress). The strength and intensity of her acting did not make her (or the film) big box-office, however.

After starring in a Broadway production of *Mother Courage* she went to Britain to make **The Pumpkin Eater,** portraying the constantly-pregnant and insecure

wife of Peter Finch ❱. Again it was a performance of stunning power and complexity and gained her many awards, including an Oscar nomination and the Best Actress prize at the Cannes Film Festival. She was then off screen for two years before reappearing in 1966 as the suicidal wife saved by Sidney Poitier ❱ in **The Slender Thread** and the strong-willed, self-sacrificing heroine of John Ford's farewell film **Seven Women.** Her brilliant performance as Dustin Hoffman's sexual educator in **The Graduate** won her a third Oscar nomination and even wider fame, but she stayed away from films for four years, finally returning as Churchill's mother in **Young Winston.** She shared Jack Lemmon's ❱ miseries in **The Prisoner of Second Avenue,** appeared in the disastrous **The Hindenberg,** played the feminist lawyer in **Lipstick** and won more acting honours in **The Turning Point.** She was married for four years (from 1953) to real estate agent Martin May, and since 1964 has been married to Mel Brooks; he featured her in one of the funniest scenes in his **Silent Movie.**

BEST FILMS:
1956 The Last Frontier
Anthony Mann (Columbia)
1962 The Miracle Worker
Arthur Penn (United Artists)
1964 The Pumpkin Eater
Jack Clayton (Columbia)
1966 Seven Women
John Ford (MGM)
1966 The Slender Thread
Sydney Pollack (Paramount)
1968 The Graduate
Mike Nichols (Avco-Embassy)
1972 Young Winston
Richard Attenborough (Columbia)
1975 The Prisoner of Second Avenue
Melvin Frank (Warner Brothers)
1976 Lipstick
Lamount Johnson (Paramount)
1977 The Turning Point
Herbert Ross (20th Century Fox)

BRIGITTE BARDOT

Brigitte Bardot created one of the major myths of the modern cinema but found it difficult to be one of the most desirable dreamed-about women in the world. Marilyn

Left: Brigitte Bardot and Jeanne Moreau in **Viva Maria!** *as two music hall girls caught up in a revolution in Mexico.*

Monroe ❱ killed herself in 1962; Bardot made a near thing of it in 1960. They were the greatest sex stars of the '50s; indeed, of the whole modern cinema, but their screen personas were very different. Bardot represented uninhibited sex, the fantasy liberation of desire, a new openness about sexuality and especially a freedom to be casual, barefoot and naked. Her appeal was not just to men—women imitated her everywhere—but she was certainly a male wish fulfilment, an experienced and slightly older Lolita who was cleverly publicised as a "sex kitten". Criticisms of her acting ability entirely miss the point; Bardot "acted" merely by projecting her naturalness on to the screen, pouting, smiling, walking, dressing and undressing, taking showers and baths, displaying her sleek body and fantastic hair, and almost (if not quite) making love—and thus achieving some of the most exciting and erotic "acting" ever to take place in the cinema.

She was initially the creation of husband-director Roger Vadim, who developed and showcased her physical and emotional traits, beginning in 1956 with the sensationally successful **And God Created Woman.** Bardot had been making films since 1952 without much impact, but after her fully-developed screen persona (and nude body) were put on display in that film, she became the biggest European star in the world. In 1958 she became the only foreign star ever to make the American top box office ratings and her films were seen by people who normally never went to see "foreign" films. Her immense popularity did not last long after the world was flooded with rather inferior Bardot pictures, but while she was on top there was nothing else like her. Her private life, if her goldfish-bowl existence off screen could be called that, reflected her movie image and was followed avidly by fans around the world; the little fishing village of St Tropez in the south of France became the "in" holiday resort because Bardot stayed there, and even today retains its position as a trendsetter for beach nudity.

Bardot soared in four years from being a virtual nobody to being the most famous woman in the world—and her 1960 suicide attempt, on her 26th birthday, was probably a scream for help. She got it in a back-handed way: Louis Malle made a highly autobiographical film with her, **Private Life,** the story of a sexy star trying to cope with her fame. Her popularity began to decline almost immediately; by 1963 she was no longer even the most popular female star in France (Sophia Loren was) and the American

producers who had been chasing her so assiduously decided she was over-exposed and looked elsewhere. That diminution of attention probably saved her life.

Bardot was born Camille Javal on September 28, 1934, in Paris, to a middle class family. She began to work as a model as a teenager and it was through a photograph that she first attracted the attention of director Marc Allégret and his assistant Roger Vadim. She made her film début (not very sexily) in the 1952 **Le Trou Normand** and then had a series of relatively unimportant parts, building up to better ones in **Helen of Troy** and the British **Doctor at Sea** with Dirk Bogarde ❱. She had a good supporting role in René Clair's marvellous **Les Grandes Manoeuvres** and then starred sexily in **The Light Across the Street,** as the unfaithful wife of a truck driver. She was still not the "sex kitten" that she was to become, but husband Vadim was busy building up her myth with adroit publicity. He wrote **En Effeuillant la Marguerite** for her (variously known as **Please Mr Balzac** and **Mam'selle Striptease**) and then unveiled her fully-developed mythical screen persona in **And God Created Woman.** She was, he said, a "phenomenon of nature", but in fact her image had been carefully built by Vadim, including even the appellation "sex kitten" and the use of the initials "BB". Vadim was the creator, but his creation now had a life and a vitality of its own and by the end of the shooting of **And God Created Woman** Bardot had taken charge of her own image.

The films that followed developed her mythical status, although none had the same impact as **Woman.** Bardot had become something new in the cinema, a woman who could enjoy sex apparently without guilt, parade playfully in the nude and yet not be cheapened by it. She made a half-hearted stab at becoming a "serious actress" in **La Verité** (the film she was working on when she made her suicide attempt) but quickly realised that her métier was of a different and not necessarily inferior kind. She increasingly lived up to her image while offscreen, made the the film **Private Life,** and was very sexy again in Vadim's **Warrior's Rest.** In 1963 she made her greatest film, Jean-Luc Godard's **Le Mépris** (**Contempt**), although this was not the greatest celebration of Bardot's particular screen virtues. She was rather fun opposite Jeanne Moreau ❱ in **Viva Maria,** if absurdly nervous at having to co-star with a real "actress", and then did a presentable job in English in the Western **Shalako** with Sean Connery ❱. She semi-retired in the '70s (although she did make another film for Vadim, the 1973 **If Don Juan Were a Woman**), devoting herself to animals and hedonism. She is past 40 now, but she still looks as sex kittenish as ever in the nude. Her popularity may have diminished, but her myth is still potent.

BEST FILMS:
1955 Les Grandes Manoeuvres (Summer Manoeuvres)
René Clair (Filmsonor-Rizzoli)
1956 Et Dieu Créa la Femme (And God Created Woman)
Roger Vadim (Iéna-UCIL-Cocinor)
1957 Une Parisienne
Michel Boisrond (Iéna)
1958 Les Bijoutiers du Clair de Lune
Roger Vadim (Iéna-UCIL-CEIAP)
1958 En Cas de Malheur
Claude Autant-Lara (Iéna)
1960 La Verité
Henri-Georges Clouzot (Iéna-CFIAP)
1962 Vie Privée
Louis Malle (Progefi-Cipra-CCM)
1962 Le Repos du Guerrier (Warrior's Rest)
Roger Vadim (Francos-Incei)
1963 Le Mépris (Contempt)
Jean-Luc Godard (Concordia-Champion-Rome-Paris)
1965 Viva Maria
Louis Malle (NEF-Dancigers-UA)

ALAN BATES

Alan Bates is probably the most prestigious British actor of his generation but he has not yet become a major film star despite leading roles in a number of important and popular movies. Although he has been making films since 1960 (**The Entertainer**, as Laurence Olivier's pacifist son) and has starred in films like **Zorba the Greek** and **Women in Love**, he has devoted as much or more attention to the stage as to the cinema; he became a major theatrical star in England but did not develop a memorable screen personality or persona for some time. Despite Bates' brilliant performances it is Anthony Quinn » that audiences remember for **Zorba the Greek**, Lynn Redgrave whom they think of in **Georgy Girl** and Glenda Jackson » (or even Oliver Reed ») in **Women in Love**. Bates perhaps realises this, and during the late '70s he has begun to develop a screen persona which could carry him to major stardom—he has, in essence, become a male sex symbol combining obvious masculinity with acute intelligence, brawn and brains. Thus in **An Unmarried Woman** he is the ideal man, the tough (he fights for her) and artistic (he's a famous painter) lover of Jill Clayburgh ». In **The Shout** he is again the virile stranger/ideal lover hypnotising Susannah York with his masculinity. This developing Bates persona actually goes back to 1966 and **Georgy Girl** where he was the lover of both Lynn Redgrave and Charlotte Rampling. He was again the sexual male in the nude wrestling sequence with Oliver Reed in **Women in Love** (1969), and as the virile farmer and lover of Julie Christie » in

The Go-Between (1971).

Bates was born in Allestree, Derbyshire, on February 17, 1934, studied at RADA and made his stage début in 1955 in Coventry with *You and Your Wife*. He was Cliff in the original production of *Look Back in Anger* in London and New York and his work at the Royal Court led to Tony Richardson casting him in **The Entertainer**. He was the criminal on the run in **Whistle Down the Wind** and became a star with his brilliant performance as the trapped husband in **A Kind of Loving**. He re-created his stage role in the film version of Harold Pinter's **The Caretaker**, starred in **The Running Man** and **Nothing But the Best**, and then was cast as the young Englishman who learns how to dance from Anthony Quinn in **Zorba the Greek**. This perform-

Below: Alan Bates in one of his most brilliant film (and stage) performances in **Butley** *(1973), from the play by Simon Grey.*

ance should have made him a major star but Quinn's more showy performance attracted all the attention. **Georgy Girl** and **King of Hearts** (in France) were fine, but even better was the 1967 **Far From the Madding Crowd** with Bates giving a superb performance as Julie Christie's steadfast lover in this Thomas Hardy adaptation.

His impressive playing of a Russian Jewish peasant victimized by anti-semitism in **The Fixer** the following year (from the Bernard Malamud novel) won him an Oscar nomination but he lost to Cliff Robertson in **Charly**. After **Women in Love**, he made a number of filmed stage plays, acting impressively in **Three Sisters**, **A Day in the Death of Joe Egg**, **Butley** and **In Celebration**. He also starred in John Frankenheimer's unsuccessful **Impossible Object** and had a supporting role in **Royal Flash**. Bates has recently become as popular on television as in the theatre, most notably in the adaptation of Thomas Hardy's *The Mayor of Casterbridge*.

BEST FILMS:
1962 A Kind of Loving
John Schlesinger (Anglo-Amalgamated)
1964 Zorba the Greek
Michael Cacoyannis (20th Century Fox)
1966 Georgy Girl
Silvio Narizzano (Columbia)
1967 Far From the Madding Crowd
John Schlesinger (EMI)
1968 The Fixer
John Frankenheimer (MGM)
1969 Women in Love
Ken Russell (United Artists)
1971 The Go-Between
Joseph Losey (EMI)
1973 Butley
Harold Pinter (Landau)
1978 An Unmarried Woman
Paul Mazursky (20th Century Fox)
1978 The Shout
Jerzy Skolimowski (Rank)

THE BEATLES

The importance of the Beatles as movie stars is sometimes overlooked in considering their impact on contemporary culture. Their first two films **A Hard Day's Night** and **Help!** completely changed the approach to making, and the public's attitude towards, pop/rock films, while the Beatles themselves were able to create on-screen "natural" personas unlike any rock performers before; the influence of these films and the Beatles' style of performance had a strong and continuing influence on rock movies as well as animation and semi-documentaries. Backed by the genius of director Richard Lester and script-writers Alun Owen and Charles Wood, the Beatles were able to create highly entertaining screen personalities which were just as much the subject of their films as the plot, and which could be seen reflected in their songs. Before **A Hard Day's Night**, no pop music film had been considered important as a film in itself, so its impact was stunning when it was released in 1964—even those who were not interested in the Beatles' music were entertained by their films, as their chemistry created a sense of zany fun reminiscent of the Marx Brothers ».

None of the later Beatles films had nearly as much impact but some were important in other ways. Their animated feature **Yellow Submarine** set new standards of design and invention for world animators and even the somewhat disorganised **Magical Mystery Tour** was a rewarding experience, especially when considered as a TV film made by the Beatles themselves. The last joint Beatles film was the documentary **Let It Be** in 1970, which is almost a record of the Beatles splitting up.

The members of the group have also appeared individually in films, in important if lesser ways. John Lennon (born Liverpool, October 9, 1940) was the non-singing star of Lester's 1967 anti-war picture **How I Won the War**, and he and wife Yoko Ono were the main performers in their own surrealistic collage film **Imagine** in 1973. Ringo Starr (born Liverpool, July 7, 1940 as Richard Starkey) has acted in a number of films including **Candy, The Magic Christian, Blindman** and the rock movies **That'll Be The Day** and **200 Motels**, as well as directing Marc Bolan in **Born to Boogie**. He also appears with George Harrison (born Liverpool, February 25, 1943) in the Harrison-produced 1972 documentary **The Concert for Bangladesh,** one of the very

Left: The Beatles revitalised pop music films with their new anarchistic approach in two movies for Richard Lester, the second of which was **Help!**

best of rock concert films. Finally, odd man out as always, Paul McCartney (born Liverpool, June 18, 1942) has not yet appeared solo in a film though he filmed his Wings tour of America and a documentary movie of it is expected to be released eventually.

Beatles-based films have become virtually a sub-genre of the rock movie boom. Among the more notable examples are the big-budget musical **Sergeant Pepper's Lonely Hearts Club Band,** based on their album and featuring the Bee Gees and Peter Frampton; **All This and World War II,** which features Beatles songs performed by other musicians to a collage of war footage; and **I Wanna Hold Your Hand,** a film about teenagers trying to meet the Beatles during their first appearance on the Ed Sullivan show, February 9, 1964, in which the Beatles are only glimpsed from behind.

BEATLES' FILMS:
1964 A Hard Day's Night
Richard Lester (United Artists)
1964 The Beatles in New York
Albert and David Maysles (TV)
1965 Help!
Richard Lester (United Artists)
1967 Magical Mystery Tour
The Beatles (TV/Apple)
1968 Yellow Submarine
George Dunning (King/Apple)
1970 Let It Be
Michael Lindsay-Hogg (United Artists)
1976 All This and World War II
Susan Winslow (20th Century Fox)
1978 I Wanna Hold Your Hand
Robert Zemeckis (Universal)
1978 Sergeant Pepper's Lonely Hearts Club Band
Michael Schultz (Robert Stigwood)

WARREN BEATTY

Warren Beatty has a reputation for portraying sexual smoothies with an unfailing attraction for women. His actual screen persona, while incorporating his sexual charisma, is much more complex and contemporary and is probably the reason he has become a major star. Basically he portrays maladjusted heroes out of synch with society, fighting against an evil establishment and a soured American dream—a highly suitable identification figure for our rebel age. This persona is seen at its most obvious in **Bonnie and Clyde,** the film that made him into a top star. He portrays a limping, impotent but successful crook who steals from the banks hated by the poor farmers in the '30s, gets the beautiful girl and becomes a mythic hero. In **McCabe and Mrs Miller** he is the small entrepreneur who refuses to sell out to the big mining company even when they send gunmen after him. In **The Parallax View** he is a newspaperman trying to expose a murderous, sinister right-wing conspiracy which operates through a sleek corporation. In **Heaven Can Wait** he is so far out of synch that he "dies" at the wrong time and has to be put back in the body of a hated millionaire industrialist so that he can oppose pollution and other inefficient business practices. It is worth noting that Beatty is killed in all four of these films and actually shot down by establishment representatives in three of them.

Beatty (real name Beaty), the younger brother of Shirley MacLaine ≫, was born in Richmond, Virginia, on March 30, 1937. He began acting in radio and TV, made his Broadway début in William Inge's 1959 *A Loss of Roses* and was picked by Elia Kazan to star opposite Natalie Wood ≫ in the 1961 **Splendour in the Grass.** As Brando ≫ and Dean ≫ had both made their first films for Kazan, his debut was widely publicised, but it took a time for Beatty to get his screen persona together. He was an Italian gigolo

Above: Warren Beatty played around with his own public image in **Shampoo** *(1975), and found that the audience loved it.*

opposite Vivien Leigh ≫ in **The Roman Spring of Mrs Stone** and was good as the narcissistic young man loved by Eva Marie Saint·≫ in **All Fall Down,** both roles emphasising his sexual magnetism. His persona really took form, however, in the 1963 **Lilith** in which he portrays a man going against an institutionalised establishment for the first time, in this case a mental institution where he becomes involved with patient Jean Seberg. He came even more fully into his own in **Mickey One,** a brilliant Arthur Penn film about a nightclub entertainer on the run from an unknown organisation, probably the mob but also American institutionalised society. He was a porn film-maker in **Promise Her Anything** and a gambler in **Kaleidoscope,** and then made his big breakthrough with **Bonnie and Clyde.** He slipped back a bit with the unsuccessful **The Only Game in Town** opposite Elizabeth Taylor ≫, but all his '70s films have been of value. In addition to the movies mentioned earlier he had a big hit with **Shampoo** as a sexually amoral hairdresser flaunting alternate values on the night of Nixon's election, November 4, 1968. In **The Fortune** he went against establishment sexual ideas, flouting the Mann Act by marrying his runaway heiress Stockard Channing to dumb friend Jack Nicholson ≫ before deciding to murder her for her money.

Beatty's continuing opposition to establishment values is likely to keep him a major star for as long as the anti-establishment likes movies.

BEST FILMS:
1961 Splendour in the Grass
Elia Kazan (Warner Brothers)
1962 All Fall Down
John Frankenheimer (MGM)
1963 Lilith
Robert Rossen (Columbia)
1965 Mickey One
Arthur Penn (Columbia)
1967 Bonnie and Clyde
Arthur Penn (Warner Brothers-Seven Arts)
1971 McCabe and Mrs Miller
Robert Altman (Warner Brothers)
1974 The Parallax View
Alan J. Pakula (Paramount)
1974 The Fortune
Mike Nichols (Columbia)
1975 Shampoo
Hal Ashby (Columbia)
1978 Heaven Can Wait
Warren Beatty & Buck Henry (Paramount)

JEAN-PAUL BELMONDO

Jean-Paul Belmondo, who became the symbol of the French *nouvelle vague* as the Bogart ≫-worshipping hoodlum of **Breathless,** is one of the three top box-office stars in France and one of the few non-Hollywood stars whose screen persona is internationally famous: He has taken over the position of the late Jean Gabin ≫ in the French cinema, and seems likely to remain a star for as many years as his predecessor.

Although most of his great films were made in the early years of his stardom, his popularity and box-office appeal have stayed high in his less-demanding commercial films of recent years. His persona as an ebullient introvert/extrovert outlaw with an appealing manner, beaten-up face and pain-concealing eyes has been used in some films without much value but Belmondo is Belmondo in even a weak picture. The persona was created by director Jean-Luc Godard in **Breathless** (1959) where it is seen at its most complex, as a combination of sensitivity and hardness, brusque-ness and gentleness, not so much anti-social as asocial, an instinctive existential hero who became the myth figure of the '60s. This persona obviously drew on aspects of Belmondo's own personality, including his admiration for Bogart and Gabin, but it also included many of Godard's haphazard and impulsive ideas about life and love. The film was one of the most influential ever made and it catapulted Belmondo into major international stardom. Belmondo is a superb actor, and though he has come more and more to rely on his screen persona, his ability to create other characterisations without losing his own personality was shown in a number of fine early '60s films. In **Leon Morin, Priest** he is a priest trying to convert former Communist Emmanuele Riva and disturbed by her emotional involvement with him. In **La Viaccia** he is a rich peasant's son besotted by Claudia Cardinale ≫ in nineteenth-century Florence. In **Two Women** he is a

Above: Jean-Paul Belmondo became famous imitating Bogart in **Breathless** *in 1959, and is now his French equivalent.*

bookish teacher and admirer of Sophia Loren ≫, and in **Moderato Cantabile** a shy workman and admirer of Jeanne Moreau ≫. There was no doubt that he could play many different roles, but he was best (and audiences liked him best) in outlaw, criminal and gangster parts. The variation within this kind of role was large and impressive. For Jean-Pierre Melville he was brilliant as the gangster informant of **Le Doulos,** for Philipe de Broca he was a delightful soldier-adventurer in **That Man From Rio;** working again with Godard he was the slightly mad hero of **Pierrot le Fou** and for Louis Malle he was marvellous as a romantic period housebreaker in **Le Voleur.** He scaled new heights of criminality with Alain Delon ≫ as they became the gangsters controlling

Marseilles in **Borsalino**, and then he gave one of his greatest performances for Alain Resnais as the super-swindler protagonist of **Stavisky**.

Belmondo was born in Neuilly-sur-Seine, France, on April 9, 1933, the son of sculptor Paul Belmondo. He studied acting at the Conservatoire d'Art Dramatique under Raymond Girard and Pierre Dux for three years and made his professional début in 1950. He began working in films in 1957 with tiny parts in **A Pied, à Cheval et en Voiture** (his scene was cut) and **Sois Belle et Taistoi**. After a reasonable role in Claude Chabrol's **A Double Tour**, he became a major star overnight in **A Bout de Souffle** (**Breathless**). He was excellent in a gangster role in Claude Sautet's **Classe Tous Risques**, less interesting in **Les Distractions** (**Trapped by Fear**) as a reporter and fine in Alberto Lattuada's Italian **Letters from a Novice** as a poor double-dealing aristocrat. Godard featured him as a friend who fancies married Anna Karina in **Une Femme est une Femme**, and he showed what a good swashbuckler he could be in de Broca's delightful **Cartouche**. He and Jean Gabin were co-starred in **A Monkey in Winter** and worked splendidly together as a young alcoholic and an old ex-alcoholic.

Belmondo made up to six films a year during the '60s, apparently fearing. his star would fade, and though there were as many poor ones as good ones he remained popular through them all. He rather intelligently decided to avoid the American film scene, knowing that his persona worked best in the French cinema, and in the '70s cut down his schedule to one or two films a year. He worked again with Chabrol on **Docteur Popaul** and de Broca on **L'Incorrigible** and **Le Magnifique**. Other films include three for Henri Verneuil including **Le Corps de Mon Ennemi**, **Peur sur la Ville** and **Le Casse**. His best '70s film, however, remains the magnificent **Stavisky**. He published his autobiography in 1963, *30 Ans et 25 Films*.

BEST FILMS:
1959 A Bout de Souffle (Breathless)
Jean-Luc Godard (SNC/de Beauregard)
1960 Classe Tous Risques
Claude Sautet (SNC)
1961 La Viaccia
Mauro Bolognini (Arco/Titanus)
1961 Une Femme est une Femme
Jean-Luc Godard (Rome-Paris Films)
1961 Leon Morin, Prêtre
Jean-Pierre Melville (Rome-Paris Films)
1963 Le Doulos
Jean-Pierre Melville (Rome-Paris Paris)
1964 L'Homme de Rio (That Man From Rio)
Philipe de Broca (Lapert)
1965 Pierrot le Fou
Jean-Luc Godard (Rome-Paris Films)
1967 Le Voleur (The Thief of Paris)
Louis Malle (United Artists)

1969 La Sirène du Mississippi (Mississippi Mermaid)
François Truffaut (United Artists)
1970 Borsalino
Jacques Deray (Adel)
1974 Stavisky
Alain Resnais (Cerito/Ariane)

INGMAR BERGMAN'S "STARS"

Ingmar Bergman's "repertory company" of Swedish actors and actresses is the greatest group star in the history of the cinema and embodies the highest achievements of serious screen acting. Liv Ullmann ❯ and Bibi Andersson ❯ in **Persona**, Ingrid Thulin and Gunnel Lindblom in **The Silence**, Max von Sydow ❯ in **The Seventh Seal**, and Harriet Andersson in **Through A Glass Darkly**, represent an intensity of acting unparalleled elsewhere in the cinema. Each member of the company is a fine individual actor and some of them have worked extensively in international films, but all owe their reputation and their greatness to Bergman. He has moulded their screen personas into objective correlatives of his own pain and experience, distressingly real representatives of his ideas and feelings. The intense emotion of Liv Ullmann, the bubbly innocence of Bibi Andersson and mental anguish of Max von Sydow have all been created by Bergman, and the actors who embody these personae have not really succeeded in carrying them into their international films. Hollywood's enormous respect for the achievements of Bergman through his actors has led time and again to his stars being featured in American movies, but it has never really worked, because they cannot convey Bergman characteristics in non-Bergman films.

The Bergman repertory company consists essentially of four men and seven women; it would almost be possible to trace the evolving history of Bergman's ideas through his changing use of star actresses during the last 30 years. The repertory group began in 1949, when three of its members made their first appearance in a Bergman movie, the 1949 **To Joy**; Maj-Britt Nilsson (born 1924 in Stockholm, and his first continuing leading lady) was the quiet, sensitive, transitional youth-to-maturity star. Her greatest achievement was in **Summer Interlude** the following year, Bergman's finest early film, portraying a hedonistic ballerina facing up to old age and death. She also starred in the 1952 **Waiting Women**.

Also featured in **To Joy** was Erland Josephson, a personal friend of Bergman and occasional co-scripter. He usually portrays husbands whose failings and insensitivity cause intense pain:

Above: Max von Sydow has become a popular international Bergman star. Right: Bibi Andersson and Gunnel Lindblom in Bergman's **Wild Strawberries** *(1957) which stars six of his "company". Below: Liv Ullmann and Erland Josephson in Bergman's superb* **Scenes from a Marriage** *(1973). Below right: Ingrid Thulin as the Baroness Sophie in* **Cries and Whispers** *(1972).*

his greatest achievement was as Liv Ullmann's husband in the magnificent **Scenes from a Marriage** (1973), but he also made important contributions to **Face to Face**, **A Passion**, **Hour of the Wolf**, **Now About These Women**, **The Devil's Eye**, **So Close to Life** and **Autumn Sonata**. The third actor appearing in **To Joy** was Victor Sjöström, only nominally a member of the Bergman stock company as he appeared in only one other film, **Wild Strawberries**; he gave a central performance in that film which is one of the greatest achievements of the Bergman group. He portrays an old man on the brink of death, looking for the meaning of life (he died three years after making the film). Sjöström (born in 1879), a director whose work in the silent period was as important as Bergman's has been in the sound cinema, is one of the fathers of Swedish cinema as well as an important figure in the American film (directing Lillian Gish ❯ in

The Wind, Lon Chaney ❯ in **He Who Gets Slapped**, etc).

Eva Dahlbeck and Harriet Andersson co-starred or alternated as stars of Bergman's films from 1952 to 1955. Andersson (born 1932 in Stockholm and married to director Jörn Donner), more sensual and earthy than other Bergman actresses, first appeared in **Summer With Monika** and was featured in **Sawdust and Tinsel**, **Lesson in Love**, **Journey into Autumn** and **Smiles of a Summer Night**. She later returned to give great performances as the schizophrenic heroine of **Through a Glass Darkly**, as one of the ladies in **Now About These Women** and as one of the sisters in **Cries and Whispers**. Eva Dahlbeck, born 1930 in Stockholm, represented a more mature and intelligent personality than Andersson and was balanced against her in the films of the mid-'50s. She made her first appearance in the last episode of the 1952 **Waiting Women** and was starred in Bergman's happiest

and harrowed knight in **The Seventh Seal** (1957), playing chess with Death in plague-stricken medieval Sweden. His persona as the embodiment of anguish, as well as Bergman's alter ego, has made his presence slightly stronger than Björnstrand's but neither is as central as the actresses. Von Sydow's other featured roles include **The Face** (as the magician), **The Virgin Spring** (as the avenging father of the murdered girl), **Hour of the Wolf** (as the painter) and **Shame** (as the musician Jan). He was also in **So Close to Life, Wild Strawberries, Through a Glass Darkly, Winter Light, A Passion** and **The Touch.** He has had a strong career in other Swedish films, including Alf Sjöberg's 1951 **Miss Julie** and Jan Troell's two-part epic **The Emigrants** and **The New Land.** In recent years he has been prominently featured in American films, including **The Exorcist** (as the exorcist priest who dies of a heart attack), its sequel **Exorcist II, Three Days of the Condor, The Voyage of the Damned, March or Die, The Greatest Story Ever Told** (as Christ) and **Hurricane.**

Bibi Andersson (born 1935 in Stockholm) was the symbol of optimism, hope and youthful innocence in her early Bergman films, beginning with **Smiles of a Summer Night** and continuing through **The Seventh Seal, Wild Strawberries, The Face** and **The Devil's Eye.** She was remarkable as the girl expecting an illegitimate child in **So Close to Life,** good in **Now About These Women,** outstanding as the nurse in **Persona,** and very fine as Elliot Gould's ➤ wife in **The Touch** and in one episode of **Scenes from a Marriage.** Her films outside Sweden include the 1966 Western **Duel at Diablo** with James Garner ➤ and the 1978 Ibsen adaptation **An Enemy of the People** with Steve McQueen ➤.

Gunnel Lindblom (born 1931 in Göteborg) made her first appearance in **The Seventh Seal** and was also seen in **Wild Strawberries, The Virgin Spring, Winter Light** and **Scenes from a Marriage.** Her major Bergman film, however, was **The Silence,** as the sensual, seductive sister Anna. She has acted in a number of other important Scandinavian films, including **Hunger** in Denmark, and turned very successfully to directing in 1977 with **Games of Love and Loneliness.**

Ingrid Thulin (born 1929 in Solleften) entered Bergman's world in 1957, playing the daughter-in-law in **Wild Strawberries,** and was featured prominently in his films over the next 15 years. She was the expectant mother who has a miscarriage in **So Close to Life,** the magician's wife in **The Face,** and the mistress in **Winter Light, Hour of the Wolf** and **The Rite.** Her two greatest performances were in "sister" roles, as the lesbian sister in **The Silence**

and one of the trio in **Cries and Whispers.** Thulin, who is married to Harry Schein, founder of the Swedish Film Institute, has had a reasonably strong film career outside Sweden, with notable appearances in Alain Resnais' **La Guerre est finie,** Vincente Minnelli's **The Four Horsemen of the Apocalypse,** Luchino Visconti's **The Damned** (as the Baroness Sophie) and Mauro Bolognini's **Agostino.**

The youngest and probably the greatest of the Bergman actresses is Liv Ullmann, born in Tokyo in 1938, brought up in Canada during the war, but actually a Norwegian. She made her first stunning appearance in 1966 in **Persona,** as an actress who has lost the ability to speak, dominating the film without saying a word. Since then she has been Bergman's favourite leading actress and was featured in **Hour of the Wolf, Shame, A Passion, Cries and Whispers, Scenes from a Marriage, Face to Face, The Serpent's Egg** and **Autumn Sonata.** Her ability to convey emotion through her face and movements alone is unmatched even by Bergman's other great actresses and makes her "acting" so natural as to be sometimes painful to experience. This ability to convey intense emotion has made her much in demand in other Swedish films, but the only notable ones are Jan Troell's **The Emigrants** (for which she was nominated for an Academy Award in 1972) and its sequel **The New Land.** A major effort was made in the mid-'70s to make her into an international star; she was featured in such films as **Pope Joan, Cold Sweat, 40 Carats, The Abdication** and **A Bridge Too Far,** but her work without Bergman simply confirmed his greatness as a creator. It is unlikely that any Bergman actress or actor can remain a major star away from his creative force.

BEST FILMS AND THEIR STARS:
1950 Summer Interlude
Nilsson
1955 Smiles of a Summer Night
Dahlbeck, H. Andersson, Björnstrand'
1956 The Seventh Seal
Von Sydow, Björnstrand, B. Andersson, Lindblom
1957 Wild Strawberries
Sjöström, B. Andersson, Thulin, Björnstrand, von Sydow, Lindblom
1959 The Virgin Spring
Von Sydow, Lindblom
1961 Through a Glass Darkly
H. Andersson, von Sydow, Björnstrand
1963 The Silence
Thulin, Lindblom
1966 Persona
B. Andersson, Ullmann, Björnstrand
1968 Hour of the Wolf
Ullmann, von Sydow, Björnstrand, Josephson, Thulin
1972 Cries and Whispers
Ullmann, H. Andersson, Thulin, Josephson.
1973 Scenes from a Marriage
Ullmann, Josephson, B. Anderson, Lindblom

films, the comedies **A Lesson in Love** and **Smiles of a Summer Night.** She was also featured in **Journey into Autumn, So Close to Life** and **Now About These Women.** Her international films include George Seaton's 1961 **The Counterfeit Traitor.**

Dahlbeck's co-star in these two comedies was Gunnar Björnstrand, who made his first appearance with her in **Waiting Women.** Björnstrand, born in Stockholm in 1909, has been in most of Bergman's films since 1952, usually representing a projection, alter ego or mouthpiece of the director (alternating or co-starring with Max von Sydow). He was particularly central to **Winter Light, The Devil's Eye** and **Journey into Autumn,** in addition to the comedies, and was featured in **The Seventh Seal** (as a knight's squire), **The Face, Through a Glass Darkly, Persona, Shame, Face to Face** and **Autumn Sonata.**

Von Sydow made his first Bergman appearance as the gaunt

JACQUELINE BISSET

Jacqueline Bisset has become the class sex star of the '70s, the beautiful, elegant and willing woman who is usually rich, but if not is striving to get money as well as men. She is exceptionally photogenic (she was a photographic model before going into films) and her breathtaking loveliness and vulnerability were the focus of François Truffaut's **Day for Night.** Her persona is seen at its most open in **The Greek Tycoon,** a thinly disguised portrayal of Jackie Kennedy Onassis opposite Anthony Quinn's ➤ tycoon, and in **The Thief Who Came to Dinner,** as a beautiful but bankrupt heiress who latches on to thief Ryan O'Neal ➤ as a source of sex and revenue. In **The Grasshopper** she is supported by a series of men in her attempts to get ahead, while in **The Deep** she swims around half-naked in her efforts to wrest treasure from the bottom of the sea.

Bisset was born in Weybridge,

Above: Jacqueline Bisset played a sexy double role in Philippe de Broca's 1973 spy fantasy adventure **Le Magnifique.**

Surrey, on September 13, 1944, studied at the French Lycée in London, worked for a time as a model and made her film début in the 1965 **The Knack.** She was a non-speaking sex object in **Cul de Sac,** had the role of Giovanna Goodthighs in the James Bond spoof **Casino Royale** and was starred opposite Tony Franciosa in **The Sweet Ride.** She had a leading role opposite Frank Sinatra ➤ in **The Detective** and was the girl in Steve McQueen's ➤ life in **Bullitt.** She made a terrific impact as the very beautiful but slightly pregnant air hostess in **Airport;** she was excellent as the object of the affections of a disturbed French boy in **The Secret World** and she superficially explored the women's liberation movement in

Stand Up and Be Counted. She was a Hungarian countess to Michael York's Count in **Murder on the Orient Express** and a sexual wheeler-dealer opposite Charles Bronson ❯ in **St Ives.** She was very good as an enigmatic and unsatisfied rich woman involved in a murder case in the Italian **Sunday Woman** with Marcello Mastroianni ❯ and she starred opposite Maximilian Schell ❯ in another Italian film **I Love You, I Love You Not.** The Greek Tycoon showed her at her most elegantly beautiful after the clinging wet costumes of **The Deep.**

BEST FILMS:
1968 Bullitt
Peter Yates (Warner Brothers)
1969 Airport
George Seaton (Universal)
1970 The Grasshopper
Jerry Paris (National General Pictures)
1972 Stand Up and Be Counted
Jackie Cooper (Columbia)
1973 Day For Night (La Nuit Américaine)
François Truffaut (Warner Brothers)
1973 The Thief Who Came to Dinner
Bud Yorkin (Warner Brothers)
1976 St Ives
J. Lee Thompson (Warner Brothers)
1976 Sunday Woman (La Donna della Domenica)
Luigi Comencini (20th Century Fox)
1977 The Deep
Peter Yates (Columbia/EMI)
1978 The Greek Tycoon
J. Lee Thompson (Universal)

GUNNAR BJÖRNSTRAND

see Ingmar Bergman Stars

CLAIRE BLOOM

Claire Bloom, who became internationally famous as the ballerina loved by clown Charlie Chaplin ❯ in **Limelight,** has always concentrated more on theatre than on cinema and probably for this reason has never become a top movie star. She has continued to work in starring roles into the '70s (she was George C. Scott's ❯ wife in the 1976 **Islands in the Stream**) but like other stage actresses has never really created the continuing persona necessary for major screen success. She is, all the same, a superb actress and has given some notable film performances.

Bloom was born in London on February 15, 1931, made her stage début in 1946 in Oxford, became a Rank starlet and made her film début in a small role in the 1948 **The Blind Goddess.** She made her stage reputation at Stratford-upon-Avon and it was because of this that she was picked by Chaplin as his beautiful co-star in the 1952 **Limelight.** It was a great performance in a great film, a ballerina sent on her

way to stardom by a dying clown, and she has never surpassed it. Her other '50s films were minor efforts (**Innocents in Paris, The Man Between, Alexander the Great, The Brothers Karamazov**) though she was always good. Her '60s films were of a much higher standard, including **Charly** and **The Spy Who Came in From the Cold** as well as **The Haunting** (a taunting lesbian), **The Chapman Report** (a pitiful nymphomaniac), **Il Maestro di Vigevano** in Italy (as the money-orientated wife of teacher Alberto Sordi ❯) and **The Outrage** (as the outraged wife).

Above: Claire Bloom with co-star Laurence Olivier in 1955 version of **Richard III,** *which he directed.*

She married actor Rod Steiger ❯ in 1959 and they worked together in two pictures, **The Illustrated Man** and **Three Into Two Won't Go,** just before they divorced. She married producer Hillard Elkins in 1969 and he produced the 1973 film version of **A Doll's House.** Her other '70s films include **A Severed Head** and **Red Sky at Night** and she has also worked steadily in TV in England, including *The World of Emily Dickenson, The Legacy* and *Love for Lydia.*

BEST FILMS:
1952 Limelight
Charles Chaplin (United Artists)
1959 Look Back in Anger
Tony Richardson (Woodfall)
1961 The Chapman Report
George Cukor (Warner Brothers)
1963 The Haunting
Robert Wise (MGM)
1964 The Outrage
Martin Ritt (MGM)
1966 The Spy Who Came in From the Cold
Martin Ritt (Paramount)
1968 Charly
Ralph Nelson (Selmur)
1969 Three Into Two Won't Go
Peter Hall (Universal)
1973 A Doll's House
Patrick Garland (Elkins Productions)
1976 Islands in the Stream
Franklin J. Schaffner (Paramount)

DIRK BOGARDE

Dirk Bogarde was saved from a cinematic fate worse than death, slowly fading out of existence in **Doctor** films and other British trivia, by expatriate American director Joseph Losey, although one of Bogarde's more notable achievements was the first screen portrayal by a major star of a "real" homosexual in the courageous but dated 1962 **Victim.** Losey made Bogarde into an international star of stature with

Above: Dirk Bogarde made two of his greatest films for Italian director Luchino Visconti, **Death in Venice** *and* **The Damned.**

four '60s films (**The Servant, King and Country, Modesty Blaise** and **Accident**), after he had been a "British star" for 15 years in films like **The Blue Lamp** and **The Sea Shall Not Have Them.** After Losey's transformation, Bogarde became one of the major actors of the new European cinema, featuring brilliantly in films by Luchino Visconti (**The Damned, Death in Venice**), Liliana Cavani (**The Night Porter**), Alain Resnais (**Providence**) and Rainer Werner Fassbinder (**Despair**).

He was born in Hampstead, London, on March 28, 1921, as Dirk van der Bogaerde. He began to work on stage in 1939, had a bit part in a 1940 George Formby ❯ film and began his cinema career in earnest in 1947 with **Esther Waters.** He had a fair success as a crook in the 1950 **The Blue Lamp,** first of the noble police films, made an early film for Losey in 1954 (**The Sleeping Tiger**), and achieved real popularity as a movie star with the 1954 **Doctor in the House** and its sequels. He was a top box office star by the mid-'50s, making many films, good and bad; two of the better ones were Michael Powell's **Ill Met by Moonlight** and Anthony Asquith's **The Doctor's Dilemma.**

In 1963 an article about Bogarde

in the magazine *Films and Filming* was titled "A Great Actor Who Has Never Appeared in a Great Film". The situation changed that same year with his magnificent performance in a great film, **The Servant,** and his career rose to a new level: in addition to his Losey films, he was starred in **Darling** with Julie Christie ❯, **The Fixer** with Alan Bates ❯, and the all-star adaptation of Lawrence Durrell's **Justine.**

Bogarde now lives permanently in France and his career has never been stronger. In 1977 he published his autobiography, *A Postillion Struck By Lightning* and continued it with *Snakes and Ladders* in 1978.

BEST FILMS:
1963 The Servant
Joseph Losey (Elstree)
1964 King and Country
Joseph Losey (BHE)
1965 Darling
John Schlesinger (Anglo-Amalgamated)
1966 Modesty Blaise
Joseph Losey (20th Century Fox)
1967 Accident
Joseph Losey (London Independent Producers)
1968 The Fixer
John Frankenheimer (MGM)
1969 The Damned
Luchino Visconti (Warner Brothers)
1970 Death in Venice
Luchino Visconti (Warner Brothers)
1974 The Night Porter
Liliana Cavani (Avco-Embassy)
1977 Providence
Alain Resnais (Action Film)
1978 Despair
R.W. Fassbinder (Geria)

JAMES BOND

James Bond is the biggest "screen character" star of the modern cinema in much the same way that Tarzan was the most important "screen character" star of the classic era. The differences between their personalities probably says a lot about the differences between the '30s and the '60s, but basically they are both superheroes with phenomenal strength, intelligence and power—not too far removed from the comic strips. Both are also enormously good fun and entertainment value. The charisma of Bond has made important stars out of two actors whose reputations were negligible before they portrayed 007; Sean Connery and Roger Moore now seem likely to become major stars in their own right though it is doubtful if they will ever lose their association with Bond. This was not true of the actors who played Tarzan; none of them became major stars in other films.

James Bond was the creation of thriller writer Ian Fleming (1908-1964), who featured British Secret Agent 007 in a number of fine spy novels that became best-sellers in the '50s and '60s. Turning the books into films was a slow process that accelerated when the rights to all but one of them were bought by Harry Saltzman and Albert Broccoli, who have produced all the Bond pictures except the spoof **Casino Royale**. Several actors were considered for Bond but the relatively inexperienced Connery was finally chosen, possibly because he did not cost much (£15,000). The first film was the 1962 **Dr No** with Joseph Wiseman as the villainous Dr No and Ursula Andress ⟩ as the stunning sex interest. Its popularity was slow in building, but it kept on

Connery made another film, the 1967 **You Only Live Twice,** and then tried to break away from the Bond image. The $4 million parody film **Casino Royale** was released the same year with a whole host of jokey James Bonds including David Niven ⟩ and Woody Allen ⟩, but was a huge flop both as entertainment and as commerce. Producers Saltzman and Broccoli eventually found themselves another Bond, Australian-born (1939) TV commercials star George Lazenby, and they featured him in the 1969 **On Her Majesty's Secret Service** with

role but in his own amiably mocking way he is very good. The latest and most expensive film is the 1978 **Moonraker**. All the Bond films have featured Bernard Lee as Bond's Secret Service boss M and Lois Maxwell as the secretary, hopelessly in love with Bond, Miss Moneypenny. The villains change continually; Blofeld was featured in three films, portrayed by three different actors (Telly Savalas ⟩, Charles Gray, Donald Pleasence). The original theme music was composed by Monty Berman, but John Barry has written most of the music since.

Marlon Brando

Marlon Brando is a great screen actor, but whether he is the greatest actor of the modern American cinema is open to question. Many critics think he is; Pauline Kael has described him as "the most exciting American actor on the screen", and his colleagues have voted him acting Oscars for **On the Waterfront** and **The Godfather,** with five other nominations. He is certainly one of the biggest movie stars of the past 30 years and has a wider range than almost any other American movie actor, from southern slob (**A Streetcar Named Desire**) to Shakespearean aristocrat (**Julius Caesar**), from Japanese interpreter (**The Teahouse of the August Moon**) to Mafia boss (**The Godfather**).

In a very different way from Olivier ⟩ and other classical stage actors, Brando is a "theatrical" film performer. His style is derived from the Stanislavsky "Method", which he learned at the Actor's Studio in the '40s and applied to stage acting from 1943 and cinema acting from 1950. Method theatricality is less noticeable than the classical kind and far more suited to the cinema, but it is ultimately just as studied and technique-orientated — and so, finally, "unnatural". It is ironic that Brando became the prisoner of his early screen persona as a mumbling, inarticulate slob in **A Streetcar Named Desire** (reprised in slightly different form in **Viva Zapata!, The Wild One** and **On the Waterfront**), because this was no more a reflection of Brando's natural personality than **Julius Caesar** or **Guys and Dolls.** These performances, powerful and effective as they are, remain incredible technical feats which no other actor could duplicate— but which more natural stars would not attempt.

The mechanisms behind Brando's acting became retrospectively apparent in later years, when he gave performances that seemed to reflect his introspective personality more genuinely: the tortured and masochistic protagonists of **One-Eyed Jacks, The Chase, Reflections in a Golden Eye** and, above all, **Last Tango in Paris.** These fine performances were still theatrically-based (ie, Method-orientated) but they also seemed to come from the well springs of Brando's own being. His performance in **Last Tango in Paris** is one of his most awe-inspiring and this kind of great acting makes his Oscar-winning performance in **The Godfather** seem excessively studied and theatrical, a brilliant exercise rather than a reality.

Brando was born in Omaha, Nebraska, on April 3, 1924, studied acting after being kicked

Above: Roger Moore has taken over the role of James Bond in recent years and made it his own after a career mainly in television, notably as The Saint. The Bond image has helped boost his stardom in other films. Left: Sean Connery was the original James Bond, and the role made him the No 1 box office star in America in 1965. Since he disassociated himself from the part his star rating has been less, despite good films.

snowballing and the follow-up **From Russia With Love** became a big hit almost immediately. **Goldfinger** was an even bigger success, the books became huge sellers and the Bond phenomenon began to roll with juggernaut force. In 1965 the "unknown" Connery was named the biggest box office attraction in both the US and England; what the exhibitors really meant was James Bond, but they couldn't vote for a screen character. The 1965 Bond film **Thunderball** was the most successful ever and has earned about $29 million, $6 million more than the second most successful **Goldfinger**. This was the peak of Bond's popularity but he has remained a box office hit right up to the present time.

Diana Rigg. He had little screen charisma so Connery was persuaded to make one more Bond film for a very high fee (over a million dollars), the 1971 **Diamonds Are Forever.** After that he permanently ended his association with the series.

Portraying Bond in the last four films, and doing it rather well, has been ex-TV "Saint" Roger Moore (born London, October 14, 1928). Although the emphasis has now gone over more to the gadgetry and the production designs of Ken Adam, Moore is a solid screen personality with the strength to keep the Bond character functioning for a good many more films. He doesn't have the edge that Connery brought to the

BEST FILMS:
1962 Dr No
Terence Young (Eon/United Artists)
1963 From Russia With Love
Terence Young (Eon/United Artists)
1964 Goldfinger
Guy Hamilton (Eon/United Artists)
1965 Thunderball
Terence Young (Eon/United Artists)
1967 You Only Live Twice
Lewis Gilbert (Eon/United Artists)
1971 Diamonds Are Forever
Guy Hamilton (Eon/United Artists)
1973 Live and Let Die
Guy Hamilton (Eon/United Artists)
1974 The Man with the Golden Gun
Guy Hamilton (Eon/United Artists)
1977 The Spy Who Loved Me
Lewis Gilbert (Eon/United Artists)
1978 Moonraker
Lewis Gilbert (Eon/United Artists)

out of a military academy, and made his Broadway début in 1943. He became a major Broadway star in 1947, as Stanley Kowalski in *A Streetcar Named Desire* under Elia Kazan's direction. His first film, **The Men,** in 1950, was an acting tour-de-force (or a theatrical exercise); he played a paraplegic in a wheelchair and had to act with limited movements. Kazan then directed him in **Streetcar** and **Viva Zapata!** and he

BEST FILMS:
1951 A Streetcar Named Desire
Elia Kazan (Warner Brothers)
1952 Viva Zapata!
Elia Kazan (20th Century Fox)
1953 The Wild One
Laslo Benedek (Columbia)
1954 On the Waterfront
Elia Kazan (Columbia)
1961 One-Eyed Jacks
Marlon Brando (Paramount)
1966 The Chase
Arthur Penn (Columbia)
1967 Reflections in a Golden Eye
John Huston (Warner Brothers)
1968 Queimada!
Gillo Pontecorvo (PEA)
1971 The Godfather
Francis Ford Coppola (Paramount)
1972 Last Tango in Paris
Bernardo Bertolucci (United Artists)

Above: Marlon Brando won his second Academy Award for a fine but studied performance in **The Godfather** (1972), though he would not accept the Oscar.

became the most important star in the movies: every kid in America was imitating his mumbling as Kowalski and Zapata, and when he made **The Wild One** he became their leather-jacketed, motorcycle-riding idol. Brando insisted that he wasn't really like that (even if he did wear blue jeans and tee shirts), but the vast public had taken him to their hearts as one kind of screen personality and he was to have a very hard time breaking out of that mould. **On the Waterfront** was right for the persona (and won him an Oscar), but **Guys and Dolls** (as a Damon Runyon gambler), **Desirée** (as Napoleon) and **Teahouse of the August Moon** (as a Japanese) weren't. Gradually and reluctantly, movie audiences gave up their insistence that Brando remain an inarticulate oaf, but even in the '60s his early persona dogged critical acceptance of his work in films as different as **Mutiny on the Bounty** and **Reflections in a Golden Eye.** After his critical rehabilitation with **The Godfather** and his magnificence in **Last Tango in Paris,** the '70s seemed open to great new achievements from Brando, but have so far resulted only in the studied Western **The Missouri Breaks** and the epic comic-strip **Superman.**

CHARLES BRONSON

Charles Bronson began making American movies in 1951 and achieved minor stardom in the late '50s and early '60s. In 1968 he began making European movies and very quickly became one of the most popular film stars in the world—except in the USA. His overseas fame soon filtered back to the States, though, and in 1973 he entered the American top ten box office star listings for the first time on the strength of films like **The Mechanic, The Valachi Papers** and **The Valdez Horses.** His major breakthrough, however, came with the 1974 **Death Wish,** which aroused huge controversy over its apparent approval of vigilante action and made Bronson's name universally known. The *New York Daily News* had already run a cover story titled "Charles Bronson: The New King of the Movies" noting that he was considered the top box office star in Europe and was equal in popularity to Toshiro Mifune ❯ in the Far East.

Bronson has not yet had a blockbuster success in the US (the most popular are **The Valachi Papers** and **Death Wish,** at just under $10 million in earnings), but his films have been consistently successful in the action market in most countries. They are popular largely for Bronson's screen persona rather than their own merits; by and large, his films have not been of remarkable quality. Bronson is a rock-hard, macho tough guy, usually a morose and mysterious stranger with an uncertain past, a loner who can be very dangerous when aroused. This persona was seen in its first real flowering in Sergio Leone's **Once Upon a Time in the West,** in which Bronson portrayed the mysterious Harmonica, the eventual good guy who kills villain Henry Fonda ❯. Bronson's greatest solo starring vehicle, however, is Walter Hill's début film **Hard Times** (called **The Streetfighter** in England), in

which Bronson portrayed a tough pugilist of the Depression era with remarkable finesse. Under the right directors, it is possible that Bronson will make important movies in the '80s.

He was born as Charles Dennis Buchinsky in Ehrenfeld, Pennsylvania, on November 3, 1921, into a poor coalmining family. He became a miner himself in 1939 and worked in the pits until he was drafted into the Army in 1949; he swore never to return underground and began studying art and dabbling in acting after the Korean war. Eventually he studied at the Pasadena Playhouse and made his screen début in the 1951 **You're in the Navy Now** as Charlie Buchinski (the family had changed the spelling). He also began to work regularly in television, adopting the name Bronson in 1954 in time for the film **Drum Beat.** He was soon being featured in good parts in films like **Big House USA** and Samuel Fuller's **Run of the Arrow,** and starred in low-budget films like **Gang War** and **Showdown at Boot Hill.** His first important starring role was in Roger Corman's 1958 **Machine Gun Kelly;** Bronson's European popularity probably began to take off from that point. He was very good as one of **The Magnificent Seven** (befriending the Mexican kids) and equally good as the Tunnel King in **The Great Escape,** both for director John Sturges. He was a star, but not a very big one—although he was extremely potent in Robert Aldrich's **The**

Above: Charles Bronson became a major star internationally before achieving stardom in the USA; the breakthrough film was Michael Winner's **Death Wish.**

Dirty Dozen as one of the three survivors of the mission.

While making **Villa Rides** in Spain, Bronson agreed to co-star with Alain Delon in **Adieu l'Ami,** the first of his European films. It was followed by Leone's **Once Upon a Time in the West** and René Clément's **Rider in the Rain,** the two films that did most to make him a major star. Thereafter he rarely stopped working. He began a successful collaboration with English director Michael Winner in 1972 with **Chato's Land** and continued with **The Mechanic, The Stone Killer** and **Death Wish.** Terence Young co-starred him with Toshiro Mifune in **Red Sun** and then directed him again in **The Valachi Papers,** while John Sturges made **The Valdez Horses** and Richard Fleischer shot **Mr Majestyk.** After the brilliant **Hard Times** and Tom Gries's **Breakout,** Bronson spoofed his own image in **From Noon Till Three,** was directed by J. Lee Thompson in **St Ives** and **White Buffalo,** and then starred in his first major-budget American film **Telefon.** He was also featured in the film **Raid on Entebbe** as General Shomron, head of the rescue group. Bronson has been married to Jill Ireland since 1958, and she has appeared with him in a number of his films.

BEST FILMS:
1958 Machine Gun Kelly
Roger Corman (AIP)
1960 The Magnificent Seven
John Sturges (United Artists)
1963 The Great Escape
John Sturges (United Artists)
1967 The Dirty Dozen
Robert Aldrich (MGM)
1969 Once Upon a Time in the West
Sergio Leone (Paramount)
1969 Rider in the Rain
René Clément (Avco-Embassy)
1972 The Valachi Papers
Terence Young (Euro-France)
1974 Death Wish
Michael Winner (Paramount)
1975 Hard Times
Walter Hill (Columbia)
1977 Telefon
Don Siegel (MGM)

MEL BROOKS

An American comic genius who made bad taste respectable in a series of films that satirise film genres from an outrageous (usually Jewish) point of view, Brooks, short, stocky and absurdly energetic, is a sane maniac who makes people laugh as an actor, director and writer by shotgunning gags unmercifully until the toughest audiences surrender.

Born June 28, 1926, as Melvin Kaminsky in the poorest part of Brooklyn, he was a stand-up comic by the age of 14 and a top TV gag writer (for Sid Caesar) at 21. Long an underground hero and comic's comic, he began to acquire a wider reputation through the record *The 2000-Year-Old Man.* His first film was the cartoon **The Critic**, which he wrote and narrated off-screen as an anti-modernist attacking abstract art. Then came **The Producers** (an hilarious account of the production of the musical *Springtime for Hitler*), and **The Twelve Chairs** (a Yugoslav-made adaptation of a famous Russian novel), neither of which he acted in. His first two films had been critical successes but commercial failures.

He became internationally famous in 1973 with **Blazing Saddles**, a parody of cowboy films that also poked fun at cinematic clichés about blacks, farting and other memorable aspects of the West. Brooks appeared as Governor William J. Lepetomane and an Indian chief. With **Young Frankenstein**, his satire of the James Whale horror picture, he again stepped back from acting. In his recent films, however, he is the undisputed star. In **Silent Movie**, sending up Hollywood and the silent era, he is the drunken director Mel Funn. In **High Anxiety**, a satiric homage to Alfred Hitchcock's thrillers, he is the vertigo-afflicted psychiatrist in charge of a mental home.

Brooks tends to pull out all the stops and heavily underline jokes in his acting-writing-directing style, but he is a truly funny man whom good taste will never be able to keep down. He is the only film comedian whose work is mainly focused on the audiences' knowledge of cinema and its conventions.

COMPLETE FILMS:
1962 The Critic
Ernest Pintoff (short)
1967 The Producers
Mel Brooks (MGM)
1970 The Twelve Chairs
Mel Brooks (UMC)
1973 Blazing Saddles
Mel Brooks (Warner Brothers)
1974 Young Frankenstein
Mel Brooks (20th Century Fox)
1976 Silent Movie
Mel Brooks (20th Century Fox)
1978 High Anxiety
Mel Brooks (20th Century Fox)

Above: Mel Brooks has become the most popular film comedian in America today, satirising aspects of the cinema itself in films like **Silent Movie** *(1976).*

YUL BRYNNER

Yul Brynner has become a top movie star by vaunting arrogance and baldness. This may not seem like much of a screen persona, but it works surprisingly well when Brynner is cast in the right role in the right film. His reputation is based primarily on two movies. He was absolutely right as the proud and supercilious King of Siam in the 1956 **The King and I** (sparring with governess Deborah Kerr ❯ in this musical version of *Anna and the King of Siam*) and played the role with such autocratic power that the Academy gave him the Best Actor Oscar. His other great role was as the leader of that extraordinary group of major movie stars in the making known as **The Magnificent Seven.** Dressed all in black, Brynner was the entirely credible power house of this classic Western (and it took some doing to be arrogant to Steve McQueen ❯, Charles Bronson ❯, James Coburn ❯ and Robert Vaughn, among others).

Brynner has been good (ie, nicely arrogant and shinily bald) in other films, including **The Ten Commandments** (as the nasty Pharaoh), **Anastasia** (as the General on the side of Ingrid Berg-

man ❯), **Invitation to a Gunfighter** and **Return of the Seven** (back in his black Western garb), and **Romance of a Horsethief** (as a Cossack), but has never matched his success nor his performances in his two major films. In the '70s he has turned to science fiction with fair success, especially as the robot gunfighter in **Westworld** (and its sequel **Futureworld**) and the superman hero of **The Ultimate Warrior.**

Brynner's origins are as mysterious as that shiny pate image would suggest (he shaved his head for the stage version of *The King and I* and has—mostly—stayed bald ever since). He was probably born in Sakhalin, an island off the coast of Siberia, on July 11, 1915, was probably a trapeze artist, and probably studied at the Sorbonne in Paris—but he definitely came to the US in 1941 and began to act for a living. He made his screen début in the 1949 thriller **The Port of New York,** but it was his stage stardom in *The King and I* in 1951 that led to Hollywood renown., His bald arrogance is likely to last for a good few years yet.

BEST FILMS:
1956 The King and I
Walter Lang (20th Century Fox)
1956 The Ten Commandments
Cecil B. De Mille (Paramount)
1956 Anastasia
Anatole Litvak (20th Century Fox)
1959 Solomon and Sheba
King Vidor (United Artists)
1960 Once More with Feeling
Stanley Donen (Columbia)
1960 The Magnificent Seven
John Sturges (United Artists)
1962 Taras Bulba
J. Lee Thompson (United Artists)
1964 Invitation to a Gunfighter
Richard Wilson (United Artists)
1973 Westworld
Michael Crichton (MGM)
1975 The Ultimate Warrior
Robert Clouse (Warner Brothers)

Above: Yul Brynner gave one of his greatest performances as the leader of **The Magnificent Seven,** *with Steve McQueen as his No 2.*

GENEVIEVE BUJOLD

Genevieve Bujold has been described by the trade newspaper *Variety* as "that unique category of actress who can be forgiven any botched job of casting and performance". She has certainly had her share of unsuccessful films, but even in the bad ones she looks good and she is growing in star charisma every year. Her biggest successes have been in suspense thrillers like **Coma** and **Obsession,** where her screen persona of strong-willed intelligence combined with sensual beauty becomes a magnetic focal

Above: Genevieve Bujold made her film début in 1966 in Alain Resnais's **La Guerre est Finie** *as the young left-wing student mistress of Yves Montand.*

point for complicated plots. She actually became an international star in the 1969 **Anne of the Thousand Days** playing strong-minded and beautiful Anne Boleyn to Richard Burton's ❯ Henry VIII; her superb performance won her an Oscar nomination.

Bujold was born in Montreal, Canada, on July 1, 1942, studied at the Montreal Conservatory of Drama and once worked as an usherette in a Montreal cinema. Alain Resnais featured her as the young left-wing student lover of Yves Montand ❯ in La Guerre est Finie in 1966, and her cinema career blossomed because of her photogenic looks and acting ability. Her husband Paul Almond directed her in three slightly bizarre but reasonably successful films: the 1968 **Isabel** (as a girl returning home to weird and mysterious goings-on), the 1970 **The Act of the Heart** with Donald Sutherland ❯ (as a farm girl with religious hysteria falling in love with a priest) and the 1972 **Journey** (about a girl's attempt to find herself through a journey back in time). Bujold's cinema career developed slowly until she was featured opposite Charlton Heston ❯ in the 1974 **Earthquake** as his young actress-mistress. The commercial success of that film boosted her stardom, which was confirmed in 1976 with a magnificent double performance as Cliff Robertson's ❯ wife/daughter in **Obsession**, a Hitchcockian thriller which revelled in its incestuous overtones. She did as well as she could with the flop pirate film **Swashbuckler**, opposite Robert Shaw ❯, better with the odd melodrama **Alex and the Gypsy** with Jack Lemmon ❯ and very well as a French woman out West in **Another Man, Another Chance** opposite James Caan ❯. In the 1978 **Coma** she was at her best as a doctor investigating suspicious happenings in a hospital and opposed by hospital superiors Richard Widmark ❯ and Rip Torn.

BEST FILMS:

1966 La Guerre est Finie
Alain Resnais (Sofracima)
1966 King of Hearts
Philippe de Broca (NEF)
1968 Isabel
Paul Almond (Quest)
1969 Anne of the Thousand Days
Charles Jarrott (Universal)
1970 The Act of the Heart
Paul Almond (Quest)
1974 Earthquake
Mark Robson (Universal)
1976 Obsession
Brian de Palma (Columbia)
1976 Swashbuckler
James Goldstone (Universal)
1977 Another Man, Another Chance
Claude Lelouch (United Artists)
1978 Coma
Michael Crichton (MGM)

ELLEN BURSTYN

Ellen Burstyn is a superb screen actress whose short career as a star has been recognised with an Academy Award (**Alice Doesn't Live Here Anymore**), a New York Critics award (**The Last Picture Show**, as the disillusioned mother of Cybill Shepherd) and two Oscar nominations (**The Last Picture Show**, and **The Exorcist** as the actress mother of the possessed Linda Blair). Not only has she given fine performances in these films, but they have also been big box-office pictures, especially **The Exorcist**, which is one of the five biggest-grossing films of all time. And yet for all that Burstyn has not yet become a really major star because she has not created a recognisable screen personality. She is a character actress who loses her own personality (brilliantly) through identifying herself with her screen roles (she usually portrays women having a difficult time) but has therefore not created a continuity between her roles. That said, she is still one of the best film actresses now working, and a pleasure to watch in everything from exotic Paris society in Henry Miller's **Tropic of Cancer** (opposite Rip Torn as Miller, in the role of his wife Mona) to the winter desolation of Atlantic City in **The King of Marvin Gardens** (as the girlfriend of Bruce Dern ❯). Her ability to carry a film by herself has only really been tested in **Alice Doesn't Live Here Anymore**; she succeeded wonderfully as a woman trying to recapture a lost dream of becoming a singer, and showed that her personality was quite strong enough for major stardom. It is possible that her starring role in the 1978 **Same Time, Next Year** opposite Alan Alda, re-creating her Tony award role as a woman involved in a happy long-term affair, will increase her star charisma.

Burstyn was born in Detroit, Michigan, in 1932 as Edna Gilhooley. She left home at 18 to become a fashion model in Texas, then went to Montreal where she worked as a dancer and finally settled in New York and took up acting. She started in TV commercials, became a regular on the Jackie Gleason show and made her Broadway début opposite to Sam Levene in *Fair Game*. She made her first films in 1964 using the name Ellen McRae in **Goodbye Charlie** and **For Those Who Think Young**, then returned to New York to study at the Actors' Studio and work in the TV series *The Doctors*. In 1969 director Joseph Strick heard her making a political speech in California and asked her to star in **Tropic of Cancer**; her film career took off immediately. Paul Mazursky featured her as Donald Sutherland's ❯ wife in **Alex in Wonderland** in 1970 and then again as Art Carney's daughter in the 1974 **Harry and Tonto**. One of her best recent performances was as John Gielgud's daughter in Alain Resnais' literary fantasy **Providence**.

Above: Oscar-winning Ellen Burstyn was teamed with Melina Mercouri in Jules Dassin's **Dreams of Passion**.

BEST FILMS:

1969 Tropic of Cancer
Joseph Strick (Paramount)
1970 Alex in Wonderland
Paul Mazursky (MGM)
1971 The Last Picture Show
Peter Bogdanovich (Columbia)
1972 The King of Marvin Gardens
Bob Rafelson (Columbia)
1973 The Exorcist
William Friedkin (Warner Brothers)
1974 Thursday's Game
Robert Moore (TV-ABC)
1974 Harry and Tonto
Paul Mazursky (20th Century Fox)
1974 Alice Doesn't Live Here Anymore
Martin Scorsese (Warner Brothers)
1977 Providence
Alain Resnais (Action Film)
1978 Same Time, Next Year
Robert Mulligan (Universal)

RICHARD BURTON

As a screen actor Richard Burton is rather like that famous little girl with a curl on her forehead; when he is good, he is very, very good, but when he is bad, he is horrid. The bad films easily outweigh the good ones, despite his magnificent voice and his genuine acting ability. Part of the trouble is his stage background and his tendency to be the "great actor with a voice" when working in movies. When he allows himself to be more natural, he can be outstanding, especially in recent years when arrogance and widely publicised dissipation have combined to make his screen persona that of the faded hero. This was seen at its best as the weary, experienced secret agent of **The Spy Who Came in from the Cold**, and also contributed mightily to his performances in **The Night of the Iguana** and **Who's Afraid of Virginia Woolf?** His long, gaudy and very public relationship with Elizabeth Taylor ❯, one of the great kitsch romances of all time, began as off-screen gossip during the shooting of **Cleopatra** in Rome and reached its cinematic apotheosis in their highly entertaining on-screen battles in **Who's Afraid of Virginia Woolf?** and **The Taming of the Shrew**.

Burton was born as Richard Jenkins on November 10, 1925, in Pontrhyfen, Wales, the twelfth child of a miner. He won a scholarship to Oxford and made his reputation as a potential "great actor" on stage in the late '40s and '50s. He made his film début in 1949 in **The Last Days of Dolwyn** in England, and first really established himself as a film star in Hollywood in Daphne du Maurier's romance **My Cousin Rachel** with Olivia de Havilland ❯. He was pretty awful in **The Robe**, a little better in **Alexander the Great** and pretty good as Jimmy Porter in **Look Back in Anger**, even if the film had less impact than the stage production. After making world headlines for his offscreen indiscretions with Taylor during **Cleopatra**, he began the best decade of his screen career with a fine performance as **Becket**, and then made **Spy**, **Virginia Woolf** and **Shrew**.

He ended the '60s with the enjoyable adventure romp, **Where Eagles Dare**, and his '70s films have been a mixed lot, again demonstrating what a great voice artist he is. This was stressed in his credible but static film version of Dylan Thomas's radio play **Under Milk Wood** and his powerful but very word-centred perform-

Left: Richard Burton and his then wife Elizabeth Taylor were co-stars in the Graham Greene adaptation **The Comedians** (1967).

ance as the psychiatrist in the adaptation of the stage hit **Equus.** He gave a reasonable impersonation of Trotsky in Joseph Losey's **The Assassination of Trotsky** and was very strong as the priest losing his faith in **Exorcist II-The Heretic.** He was **Bluebeard** in the trashy film by Edward Dmytryk and a mercenary soldier in the slightly better adventure film **The Wild Geese.** Burton's image as the "great actor" who hasn't quite succeeded yet has had·its effect on his colleagues in the industry: he has received six Academy Award nominations for Best Actor.

Died 1984.

BEST FILMS:
1953 My Cousin Rachel
Henry Koster (20th Century Fox)
1958 Look Back in Anger
Tony Richardson (Warner Brothers)
1963 Cleopatra
Joseph L. Mankiewicz (20th Century Fox)
1964 Becket
Peter Glenville (Paramount)
1964 The Night of the Iguana
John Huston (MGM)
1965 The Spy Who Came in from the Cold
Martin Ritt (Paramount)
1966 Who's Afraid of Virginia Woolf?
Mike Nichols (Warner Brothers)
1967 The Taming of the Shrew
Franco Zeffirelli (Columbia)
1977 Exorcist II-The Heretic
John Boorman (Warner Brothers)—
1977 Equus
Sidney Lumet (United Artists)

JAMES CAAN

James Caan has a reputation for being macho when what his screen persona really reflects is heroic masochism. He has become a major star by portraying perplexed tough guys striving to win, getting beat up and shot up for being one step behind the villains, and very rarely "winning" in the broader sense. This persona is particularly on view in **The Gambler,** where he seems subconsciously to strive to lose at gambling so that he can be physically hurt, and in **Rollerball,** where as a top sports hero he creates a situation where he "wins" only at the cost of death for all his teammates and terrible punishment for himself. In **The Godfather** he is the hothead Sonny Corleone whose attitudes cause the gang warfare in which he is eventually killed. In **The Killer Elite** he is shot and crippled by partner Robert Duvall and fights to rehabilitate himself, only to quit his profession when he has done so. In **A Bridge Too Far** he is a sergeant who forces a doctor at gunpoint to attend to a seemingly dead superior. In **Freebie and the Bean,** all his efforts to save a man are wasted and in **Slither** all his efforts to retrieve the loot from a robbery come to nought. In **Cinderella Liberty** he is a sailor whose records are lost and who

Above: James Caan has created a star persona around a mixture of macho and masochism which reflects aspects of "winning."

loses out on his plans to gain revenge and get a girl. In **Funny Lady** he loses Fanny Brice (Barbra Streisand ») and in **Rabbit, Run** he has an alcoholic wife and a semi-prostitute girlfriend.

Sometimes he ends up a winner after a long losing sequence. In **Harry and Walter Go to New York** he and Elliot Gould » rob a bank successfully after many misadventures, and in **Another Man, Another Chance** he eventually wins Genevieve Bujold » after his wife has been raped and killed. Whether his appearance in Mel Brooks' » **Silent Movie** is winning or losing is hard to say.

Caan was born in the Bronx, New York City, on March 26, 1939. He worked in various jobs including beach lifeguard and athletic coach before becoming a professional actor; he was in the off-Broadway production of *La Ronde* in 1961 and made his film debut in 1963 in **Irma La Douce,** uncredited. He had support roles all through the '60s, notably as a sadistic thug in **Lady in a Cage** keeping Olivia De Havilland » penned up in a lift in her home, and backing up John Wayne » in **El Dorado.** In 1969 he became a star playing a retarded former football hero picked up by Shirley Knight in **The Rain People** and then was exceptional in **Rabbit, Run** and the TV film **Brian's Song;** his other '60s films include **The Glory Guys, Red Line 7000, Countdown, Games** and **Journey to Shiloh.** **The Godfather** made him into a major star and won him a nomination for an Academy life, shopping in the local super-Award.

BEST FILMS:
1969 The Rain People
Francis Ford Coppola (Warner Brothers-Seven Arts)
1970 Rabbit, Run
Jack Smight (Warner Brothers)
1972 The Godfather
Francis Ford Coppola (Paramount)
1973 Slither
Howard Zieff (MGM)
1974 Cinderella Liberty
Mark Rydell (20th Century Fox)
1975 Freebie and the Bean
Richard Rush (Warner Brothers)
1975 The Gambler
Karel Reisz (Paramount)
1975 Funny Lady
Herbert Ross (Columbia)
1975 Rollerball
Norman Jewison (United Artists)
1975 The Killer Elite
Sam Peckinpah (United Artists)

MICHAEL CAINE

Michael Caine was the most interesting British movie hero to emerge in the '60s: his screen persona was unashamedly based on working class Cockney origins and he made no attempt to disguise his South London accent —his background was neither vaunted nor hidden, but merely a part of his very appealing mild-mannered but basically arrogant personality. The persona is seen at its best in his most popular film, **Alfie,** in which he portrays a Cockney Casanova, charming but unscrupulous as he beds a series of "birds" without letting himself get involved. The hint of self-mockery in his style of acting is an important part of his screen appeal and is very much to the forefront in his delightful portrait of a small-time Cockney crook involved in a big-time robbery in **The Italian Job.**

Three of his best pictures starred him as Harry Palmer, the

*Below: Michael Caine in frozen Finland as British secret agent Harry Palmer in **Billion Dollar Brain,** flamboyantly directed by Ken Russell.*

working man's answer to James Bond, beginning with **The Ipcress File** and continuing with **Funeral in Berlin** and **Billion Dollar Brain.** Unlike Bond he lived an ordinary life shopping in the local supermarket, delighting in gourmet cookery and becoming one of the few, cinema heroes to wear glasses.

Caine was born in South London on March 14, 1933, as Maurice Micklewhite, started acting as a teenager and learned his craft working with a repertory company in Horsham, Sussex. He began getting bit parts in TV and cinema in 1953, usually uncredited, though by 1957 he was able to get as high as tenth billing in **How To Murder a Rich Uncle.** His rise to film stardom came when he was spotted by Stanley Baker in the 1963 London production of *Next Time I'll Sing To You;* he was given a leading role in **Zulu** (but as an aristocratic officer, not a Cockney soldier) and won wide praise. After playing Horatio in a TV film of **Hamlet,** he was cast as Harry Palmer in **The Ipcress File** from a spy thriller by Len Deighton, and that film made him a star. **Alfie,** the following year, made him an international name (it earned $9 million in the USA alone and won him a Best Actor Oscar nomination) and led to such miscast roles as that of a nasty landowner in the American South in **Hurry Sundown.** He was much better in thrillers like **Gambit** and **Deadfall,** war films like **Play**

Dirty, **The Battle of Britain** and **Too Late the Hero** and comedies like **The Wrong Box** and even dramas like **The Magus.** His '70s career has continued strong; he was exceptionally fine in two British gangster films directed by Mike Hodges, **Get Carter** and **Pulp,** and as a strange Kipling adventurer in **The Man Who Would Be King.** He won another Academy Award nomination for his two-handed game of deception with Laurence Olivier in **Sleuth,** did a fine job of playing the down-to-earth fantasy writer of **The Romantic Englishwoman** and seemed to enjoy himself trying to kidnap Churchill in **The Eagle Has Landed.** He was good as a big-time safecracker in **Harry and Walter Go to New York,** even if the film wasn't, and the same could be said about his roles as a mobster's banker in **Silver Bears** and a scientist coping with bees in **The Swarm.** Caine seems never to stop working; his other '70s films include **The Last Valley, The Black Windmill, The Marseilles Contract, The Wilby Conspiracy** and **A Bridge Too Far.**

BEST FILMS:
1964 Zulu
Cy Endfield (Paramount)
1965 The Ipcress File
Sidney J. Furie (Rank/Universal)
1966 Alfie
Lewis Gilbert (Paramount)
1966 Funeral in Berlin
Guy Hamilton (Paramount)
1969 The Italian Job
Peter Collinson (Paramount)
1971 Get Carter
Mike Hodges (MGM)
1973 Sleuth
Joseph L. Mankiewicz (20th Century Fox)
1975 The Romantic Englishwoman
Joseph Losey (Dial Films)
1976 The Man Who Would Be King
John Huston (Allied Artists)
1977 The Eagle Has Landed
John Sturges (ITC)

CLAUDIA CARDINALE

Claudia Cardinale was originally intended to be Italy's answer to Brigitte Bardot » (CC versus BB) and as her only training for acting was winning "the most beautiful Italian girl in Tunisia" contest in 1957 this seemed like a reasonable kind of competition. In the end Cardinale never became as big a star as Bardot at her height, but she has lasted a lot longer and starred in far better pictures. BB's films are memorable only because she is in them; CC's films, on the other hand, are memorable not only because she looks lovely but because they were directed by such major figures as Visconti, Fellini, Bolognini and Comencini, not to mention Sergio Leone, Blake Edwards and Richard Brooks. It helps to be promoted by a major producer (Franco Cris-

Above: Claudia Cardinale, one of Italy's most popular and exotic stars, in a characteristic pose from Ferreri's **L'Udienza.**

taldi, whom she later married) but Cardinale actually did very well indeed so she can hardly be dismissed as a mere beauty contest winner.

She was born in Tunis, Tunisia, on April 15, 1939, and began her film career in 1957 after being sent to the Venice Film Festival as her beauty contest prize. She made her début in a small role in the Tunisian-made 1957 film **Goha** and her first impact in the delightful **I Soliti Ignoti (Big Deal on Madonna Street).** She was then taken up by major Italian directors for a fine series of films beginning with Bolognini: **Il Bell' Antonio** (worrying Marcello Mast-troianni » about his virility), **La**

Viaccia (driving Jean-Paul Bel-mondo » to despair in 19th century Florence) and **Senilità** (disturbing Anthony Franciosa in turn-of-the-century Trieste); and then Zurlini: **The Girl with the Suitcase** (involved with Jacques Perrin). Her association with Visconti began in 1960 with **Rocco and His Brothers** (playing the fiancée of the oldest brother) and continued through **The Leopard** (as the beautiful bourgeois Angelica whom Alain Delon » marries), **Sandra/Of a Thousand Delights** as the ambiguous protagonist Sandra around whom the film revolves) and finally **Conversation Piece** (as Burt Lancaster's » wife). Luigi Comencini featured her as the star of **La Ragazza di Bube** and then Fellini used her splendidly as the famous actress and beauty Claudia Cardinale in 8½, the stimulus for film

director Marcello Mastroianni's fantasies. She looked equally fabulous in **The Pink Panther** romancing with jewel thieves David Niven » and Robert Wagner; in **The Professionals** she was the object of so much passion, jealousy and double-dealing by a hefty crew of top stars that her beauty was essential to the credibility of the plot. She was also fine as the heroine of Sergio Leone's Western **Once Upon a Time in the West,** the love interest in Jerzy Skolimowski's historical romp **The Adventures of Gerard** and paired with Bardot in **The Legend of Frenchie King.** She has also been teamed with Monica Vitti in two popular Italian films, **Midnight Pleasures** and **Lucky Girls.** Among her recent Italian films are Alberto Sordi's **A Common Sense of Decency** and Alan Bridges' **The Little Girl in Blue Velvet.** Her box office appeal seems as strong as ever.

BEST FILMS:
1960 La Ragazza con la Valigia (The Girl with the Suitcase)
Valerio Zurlini (Titanus)
1960 Rocco e i Suoi Fratelli (Rocco and His Brothers)
Luchino Visconti (Titanus)
1961 La Viaccia
Mauro Bolognini (Arco)
1962 Senilità
Mauro Bolognini (Zebra)
1963 8½
Federico Fellini (Cineriz)
1963 Il Gattopardo (The Leopard)
Luchino Visconti (Titanus/20th Century Fox)
1963 The Pink Panther
Blake Edwards (United Artists)
1965 Vaghe Stelle dell'Orsa (Sandra/Of a Thousand Delights)
Luchino Visconti (Vides)
1966 The Professionals
Richard Brooks (Columbia)
1969 Cera Una Volta il West (Once Upon A Time in the West)
Sergio Leone (Rafran)

LESLIE CARON

Leslie Caron became the Cinderella of Hollywood musicals in the '50s after dancing her way to stardom in the 1951 **An American in Paris.** She had been a professional ballet dancer in Paris in the late '40s, but her off-beat looks and awkward girlishness were as important to her cinema success as her dancing ability. She usually portrayed gauche orphans, not too bright but very captivating, and there was always a Prince Charming in there somewhere.

In **Lili** she is an unsophisticated orphan with a travelling carnival whose closest friend is a puppet (but the puppeteer gets her in the end). In **The Glass Slipper** she plays Cinderella for real, with Michael Wilding as her Prince

Left: Leslie Caron dancing her way to an uneven career in the climactic ballet of Minnelli's **An American in Paris.**

Charming. In **Daddy Long Legs** the unknown benefactor whom she loves (she's a poor orphan again) turns out to be Fred Astaire ❯—who could want a more charming prince? In **Gigi** she is an orphan wooed and won by Louis Jourdan ❯ while Maurice Chevalier ❯ thanks Heaven for little girls. And finally, in the quirky non-musical film **Fanny**, based on the stage musical of the same name, she is left holding the baby while lover Horst Buchholtz goes off to sea. Despite the charm of her personality, the highlights of her films were the song-and-dance sequences, elaborately balletic with Gene Kelly ❯ in **An American in Paris**, wonderfully fantastic with Astaire in **Daddy Long Legs** and delightfully simple singing *Hi-Lili, Hi-Lo* with Mel Ferrer in **Lili.**

She was born Leslie Claire Margaret Caron in Paris, France, on July 1, 1931; her mother was American. She began studying ballet from the age of ten, and would probably have continued in that profession if Kelly hadn't seen her dancing and persuaded her to join him in **An American in Paris**. Since the '50s she has concentrated on straight roles, giving quite effective performances in **The L-Shaped Room** and **Is Paris Burning?** and was married to National Theatre director Peter Hall from 1956 to 1966. She has continued working in the '70s, including a thriller (**Chandler**), a Western (**Madron**), a small role in a pleasant François Truffaut film (**The Man Who Loved Women**), and a brilliant, ambiguous performance as a mysterious housekeeper in the French film **Sérail**. She was also fascinating, if rather grotesque, as Nazimova in Ken Russell's flamboyant **Valentino.**

BEST FILMS:
1951 An American in Paris
Vincente Minnelli (MGM)
1953 The Story of Three Loves
Vincente Minnelli (MGM)
1953 Lili
Charles Walters (MGM)
1955 The Glass Slipper
Charles Walters (MGM)
1955 Daddy Long Legs
Jean Negulesco (20th Century Fox)
1958 Gigi
Vincente Minnelli (MGM)
1959 The Doctor's Dilemma
Anthony Asquith (MGM)
1961 Fanny
Joshua Logan (Warner Brothers)
1963 The L-Shaped Room
Bryan Forbes (Columbia)
1976 Sérail
Eduard de Gregorio (Filmoblic)
1977 Valentino
Ken Russell (United Artists)

CARRY ON STARS

The most popular group star in English cinema history, a comedy collective that has starred in 29 **Carry On** films and virtually become a British institution.

Although none of its individual members have become major stars, the combination of Sid James, Kenneth Williams, Charles Hawtrey and the others is a veritable superstar. In 1968, for example, **Carry On Camping** was the No 1 box office film in Britain and **Carry On Up the Khyber** was No 2; audiences loved these films right from the beginning, and lately even some critics have grown fond of them. The National Film Theatre in London has organised an evening of tribute to them and critic Kenneth Eastaugh has written an excellent biography, *The Carry-On Book.*

The slightly risqué comedy series was born in 1957, the combined brainchild of producer Peter Rogers and director Gerald Thomas, who have made all 29 films; the first five were scripted by Norman Hudis, the rest by Talbot Rothwell. The first in the series was **Carry On Sergeant**, which became the third most popular film in Britain in 1957. It set standards of double entendre and vulgar suggestiveness that became the pattern for the series. The humour is always of the anticipated type; like Greek

Above: Kenneth Connor intrepidly defending Kenneth Williams and Jim Dale in one of the best of the comedy series, **Carry on Cleo.**

tragedy, the audience knows what to expect and is not disappointed. In the words of its creators, "familiarity breeds laughter", and there is no escaping the fact that the best of the series (like **Carry On Up the Khyber**) are very funny indeed despite (or because of) their vulgarity. They were sexily suggestive before permissiveness became the vogue, and they have remained suggestive rather than explicit, though with a bit more nudity. The **Carry On** stars number about 15 actors. The first film featured Kenneth Williams, Charles Hawtrey, Hattie Jacques, Kenneth Connor and Terry Scott, who all continued to work regularly in the series. Sid James, who

became the focal point of the films, made his first appearance in **Carry On Constable** and Barbara Windsor, who became the sexual mainstay of them, first bounced into view in **Carry On Spying.** Joan Sims turned up in the second film, **Carry On Nurse;** she and Hawtrey appeared in 24 of the films, bettered only by Williams with 25. James (who died in 1976) starred in 19; his last was **Carry On Dick.**

Other actors who have made important contributions include Frankie Howerd (who starred in two), Leslie Phillips (who starred in three), Peter Butterworth (16), Bernard Bresslaw (14), Jim Dale (10), and Jack Douglas (6). The series was enormously profitable, originally costing only £200,000 and usually earning that amount back in a few days. They were made very quickly; Rogers once joked that he could make a **Carry On Cleo** in the time it took 20th Century Fox to set up the scenery for **Cleopatra.** He then did so, and the result was very amusing. The latest film, **Carry On Emmannuelle**, was made in 1978 and it looks as though the series may continue for years.

BEST FILMS:
1958 Carry On Sergeant
Gerald Thomas (Peter Rogers)
1958 Carry On Nurse
Gerald Thomas (Peter Rogers)
1959 Carry On Teacher
Gerald Thomas (Peter Rogers)
1959 Carry On Constable
Gerald Thomas (Peter Rogers)
1964 Carry On Cleo
Gerald Thomas (Peter Rogers)
1965 Carry On Doctor
Gerald Thomas (Peter Rogers)
1967 Carry On Doctor
Gerald Thomas (Peter Rogers)
1968 Carry On Up the Khyber
Gerald Thomas (Peter Rogers)
1968 Carry On Camping
Gerald Thomas (Peter Rogers)
1970 Carry On Loving
Gerald Thomas (Peter Rogers)

JULIE CHRISTIE

Julie Christie, who became the international image of the "swinging London" of the '60s after her extraordinary success as a fashion model in **Darling**, has survived into the '70s with surprising strength. Her reputation as a screen actress is probably just as high now as it was in 1965 when she won both the Oscar and the New York Film Critics' award for her performance in **Darling**, setting a trend for look-alikes for the rest of the decade. She has not made many films in the '70s but all six of them are worthwhile in various ways, for she has shown remarkable skill in picking good directors. Her biggest commercial success has been **Shampoo** with Warren Beatty ❯; its $22 million earnings make it one of the biggest box-office movies of all time, along with her '60s film **Doctor Zhivago**,

Above: The beautiful Julie Christie as Hardy's impetuous heroine Bathsheba Everdene in the hillside love scene with wastrel Captain Troy in **Far From the Madding Crowd.**

which earned $46 million. Three of her '70s films can be considered as important artistic achievements: Robert Altman's **McCabe and Mrs Miller**, with Christie as the madam of a brothel in partnership with Warren Beatty, is one of the best portraits of the Old West ever filmed; Joseph Losey's **The Go-Between**, with Christie as the aristocratic lover of Alan Bates ❯, is a superbly realised adaptation of an L. P. Hartley novel; and Nicolas Roeg's **Don't Look Now**, with Christie as a mother mourning a lost daughter in Venice, and co-starring Donald Sutherland ❯, is one of the eeriest evocations of mental anguish and despair on film. Her recent **Heaven Can Wait**, with long-time friend Warren Beatty directing as well as co-starring, has also proved to be a box-office bonanza. During this decade, only Donald Cammell's **Demon Seed** has been a relative failure.

Christie was born in Assam, India, on July 14, 1941, studied drama at the Central School in London and worked with a theatrical repertory company from 1957 to 1960. She made her initial reputation with a TV serial *A for Andromeda* in 1962 and made her film début the same year with bit parts in **Crooks Anonymous** and **The Fast Lady**. John Schlesinger made her name as the dream girl of **Billy Liar**, the symbol of freedom, and it was also Schlesinger who turned her into a major star in **Darling**. He directed her a third time in a fine performance in **Far From the Madding Crowd**, based on the Thomas Hardy novel with Alan Bates, Terence Stamp and Peter Finch ❯ as the men in her life. Her performance as Lara in **Doctor Zhivago** helped that film to its success, and she was excellent in **Petulia**, as a kookie girl in San Francisco involved with George C. Scott. Her weakest films were in the late '60s, François Truffaut's Ray Bradbury adaptation, **Fahrenheit 451**, in a double role which never seemed quite real, and the pretentious **In Search of Gregory**, but on average her movies have been of a higher quality than most other stars.

BEST FILMS:
1963 Billy Liar
John Schlesinger (Vic Films)
1965 Darling
John Schlesinger (Anglo-Amalgamated)
1965 Doctor Zhivago
David Lean (MGM)
1967 Far From the Madding Crowd
John Schlesinger (EMI)
1968 Petulia
Richard Lester (Warner Brothers)
1970 McCabe and Mrs Miller ·
Robert Altman (Warner Brothers)
1971 The Go-Between
Joseph Losey (EMI)
1973 Don't Look Now
Nicolas Roeg (British Lion)
1975 Shampoo
Hal Ashby (Columbia)
1978 Heaven Can Wait
Warren Beatty and Buck Henry (Paramount)

Jill Clayburgh

Jill Clayburgh has created an intriguing contemporary screen persona which is likely to make her into a major star. She is tough but nervous, independent but vulnerable, full of energy and fun and casually willing to sleep around without worrying too much about it. She is a Sarah Lawrence girl grown into a movie star. Clayburgh made her biggest impact in 1978 with her superb portrayal in **An Unmarried Woman** of an abandoned wife trying to create a new life for herself; it was one of the most effective and sensitive performances of the new American cinema, and won her the Best Actress award at the Cannes Film Festival. The persona, however, had been developing for some years in some notable roles. In **Semi-Tough** she is the much-married roommate of professional football players Burt Reynolds ❯ and Kris Kristofferson ❯, sleeping with one but eventually going off with the other. In **Silver Streak** she sleeps with Gene Wilder on a luxury train, and what he sees that night is the basis of the comedy thriller plot. In **Gable and Lombard** her affair (as Lombard) with the already-married Gable creates a scandal, but she refuses to behave "properly". In

the TV film **Hustling** she is a tough-minded New York hooker, in **The Terminal Man** she is a stripper and in the TV film **Griffin and Phoenix: A Love Story** she and Peter Falk are both dying of incurable diseases and get together to do all the things they didn't dare do before.

Clayburgh was born in New York on April 30, 1944, and studied (naturally) at Sarah Lawrence College. Brian De Palma filmed his **The Wedding Party** at Sarah Lawrence in 1964 and starred Clayburgh in it, but the film was not released until five years later. In the meantime, she worked in off-Broadway plays like *The Next* and was featured in the Broadway productions of *The Rothschilds* and *Pippin,* while her début in the commercial cinema came in the 1972 **Portnoy's Com-**

*Above: Jill Clayburgh, destined to be one of the major actresses of the '80s, in the stylish comedy thriller set aboard the express train **Silver Streak**.*

plaint. Her latest film is Bernardo Bertolucci's important **The Moon**, made in Italy; her star seems likely to continue to rise in the next few years.

BEST FILMS:
1969 The Wedding Party
Brian De Palma (De Palma)
1973 The Thief Who Came to Dinner
Bud Yorkin (Warner Brothers)
1974 The Terminal Man
Mike Hodges (Warner Brothers)
1975 Hustling
Joseph Sargeant (TV)
1976 Gable and Lombard
Sidney J. Furie (Universal)
1976 Griffin and Phoenix: A Love Story
Daryl Duke (TV)
1976 Silver Streak
Arthur Hiller (20th Century Fox)
1977 Semi-Tough
Michael Ritchie (United Artists)
1978 An Unmarried Woman
Paul Mazursky (20th Century Fox)
1979 The Moon (La Luna)
Bernardo Bertolucci (Fiction Films)

Montgomery Clift

Montgomery Clift must be considered one of the first of the "modern" style film actors, along with James Dean ❯ and Marlon Brando ❯. He was apparently as tortured in his private life as he usually was in his screen performances, but this inwardness gave an intensity to his acting which has rarely been equalled. His screen persona was a mixture of suffering, ambition and thwarted desire which seemed to reflect not only his personality but his film career (only 17 films in 18 years). He was a fortune hunter after Olivia de Havilland's ❯ money in **The Heiress**, plotted to kill his fiancée to further his social climbing in **A Place in the Sun**, was tortured by his vow of a silence when a murderer confessed to him as a priest in **I Confess**, and played a highly introverted cowboy in **Red River** (his first and best film). He was usually a loser, victimised by the Army system in **From Here to Eternity**, by his own conscience in **Lonelyhearts**, and by Elizabeth Taylor in **Raintree County**. His career was oddly abortive; he should have become a really major star but he almost wilfully prevented it from happening.

He was born in Omaha, Nebraska, on October 17, 1920, as Edward Montgomery Clift and became an actor as a teenager. He was regularly on stage in New York from 1935 until Howard Hawks introduced him to the cinema in 1948 with **Red River**. He made a dozen good films between 1948 and 1962 and was one of the hottest properties in Hollywood during that time, although drink, drugs, depression and other problems made him increasingly difficult to work with, especially after a severe car accident in 1957. He was, however, still outstanding in five more films after that. After making **Freud** in 1962 he was offscreen until the 1966 **The Defector**. He died of a heart attack the same year. One of his last and most likeable performances was in the strangely tragic 1960 **The Misfits** with Clark Gable ❯ and Marilyn Monroe ❯, both of whom died shortly after it was completed.

BEST FILMS:
1948 Red River
Howard Hawks (United Artists)
1948 The Search
Fred Zinnemann (MGM)
1949 The Heiress
William Wyler (Paramount)
1951 A Place in the Sun
George Stevens (Paramount)
1952 I Confess
Alfred Hitchcock (Warner Brothers)
1953 From Here to Eternity
Fred Zinnemann (Columbia)
1958 The Young Lions
Edward Dmytryk (20th Century Fox)

*Above: Montgomery Clift in a flashback sequence with Anne Baxter in Alfred Hitchcock's religious thriller **I Confess**.*

1959 Suddenly Last Summer
Joseph L. Mankiewicz (Columbia)
1960 Wild River
Elia Kazan (20th Century Fox)
1960 The Misfits
John Huston (United Artists)
1962 Freud: The Secret Passion
John Huston (Universal)
Died 1966

James Coburn

James Coburn is lazy, relaxed, easy-going and amiable but ultimately as tough as nails. This persona first made an impression on cinema audiences in 1960 in **The Magnificent Seven** where he was the quiet but deadly knife expert. It was developed in Don Siegel's war film **Hell Is For Heroes**, seen to excellent effect in **The Great Escape** (as an easygoing Australian) and then as a villain in **Charade**. Coburn was still improving on his screen personality in the excellent **The Americanization of Emily** and **Major Dundee**, more or less got it together in pirate form in **A High Wind in Jamaica** and then achieved fame with a fully-fledged persona in the spy/secret agent films **Our Man Flint** and **In Like Flint**; this combination of laconic humour and professional expertise appealed to a wide audience and made Coburn a viable star (rather than supporting actor) for the first time. In fact, it is a difficult persona for stardom as basically it is not that of a leader but an opportunist; most of Coburn's films place him in situations where he takes advantage of or plays against the actions of other stars. Thus in **Pat Garrett and Billy the Kid** the way he behaves is conditioned by the way Billy (Kristofferson ❯) acts; in **Hard Times** his behaviour as a fight promoter is only valid in correlation to the achievements of streetfighter Charles Bronson ❯; in A

friendly weapon), not strong enough to hold together **The President's Analyst** or **Duffy** but at his best as a rodeo performer in **The Honkers**. Westerns suit him particularly well, and he was fine with Charlton Heston ➤ in **The Last Hard Men** and Gene Hackman ➤ in **Bite the Bullet**. Among his other recent films he was a hang-gliding pilot out to rescue Susannah York in **Sky Rider**, and Captain Vinton Maddox in the big-budget Navy film **Midway**.

BEST FILMS:
1960 The Magnificent Seven
John Sturges (United Artists)
1963 The Great Escape
John Sturges (United Artists)
1965 Major Dundee
Sam Peckinpah (Columbia)
1965 Our Man Flint
Daniel Mann (20th Century Fox)

the wrong target: within four years of **Black Shield**, Curtis won an Academy Award nomination for his fine performance in **The Defiant Ones** and international praise for his brilliant portrayal of an ambitious press-agent in **Sweet Smell of Success**. That film also had a much-quoted line, "Match me, Sidney," spoken to the fawning Curtis by Burt Lancaster ➤. Curtis was never to give a better dramatic performance, but he equalled it in comedy the following year, teamed with Jack Lemmon ➤ and Marilyn Monroe ➤ in **Some Like It Hot**. He portrays a musician on the run from an Al Capone-type gangster in the Prohibition era, disguised (quite believably) as a girl and delightfully imitating Cary Grant ➤ when he woos Monroe. After his success in this film Curtis was

The Great Imposter and **The Boston Strangler** in dramatic parts, and **Sex and the Single Girl, Goodbye Charlie** and **The Great Race** in comedy parts. His film career in the '70s appeared to be faltering, despite his TV series *The Persuaders* with Roger Moore and his fine performance as a movie star worried about his impotence in **The Last Tycoon**. Other recent films include the gangster picture **Lepke**, the supernatural thriller **The Manitou** and **The Bad News Bears Goes to Japan**.

Below: Tony Curtis spent most of Alexander Mackendrick's 1967 **Don't Make Waves** *chasing Claudia Cardinale and Sharon Tate around Malibu and finding the hunt more interesting than the capture.*

Above: James Coburn, as the tough hired killer in **Hard Contract**, *mugs up with Berlitz in order to track down three business men in Belgium and Spain.*

Fistful of Dynamite/Duck You Sucker he is an IRA explosives expert, but what he does is shaped throughout by bandit-bankrobber Rod Steiger ➤; in **Cross of Iron** his actions as the brave but undisciplined German Sergeant Steiner are wholly in relation to the actions of Maximilian Schell's ➤ Captain Stransky. His persona is effective and enjoyable—but it's too lazy to work alone. Even in the **Flint** films he is goaded into action by Lee J. Cobb ➤.

He was born in Laurel, Nebraska, on August 31, 1928, established a career in the theatre and TV after studying with Stella Adler and made his film début in the 1959 Randolph Scott ➤ Western **Ride Lonesome**. He stayed in supporting roles until **Our Man Flint** and has mostly been paired with another star in his films since. He was very good as an amiable gambler/rapist in **Waterhole Three** (excusing himself by saying that his rape was assault with a

1967 Waterhole Three
William Graham (Paramount)
1971 Giù La Testa (A Fistful of Dynamite/Duck You Sucker)
Sergio Leone (United Artists)
1971 The Honkers
Steve Ihnat (United Artists)
1973 Pat Garrett and Billy the Kid
Sam Peckinpah (MGM)
1975 Hard Times (The Streetfighter)
Walter Hill (Columbia)
1977 Cross of Iron
Sam Peckinpah (EMI)

Sean Connery

see **James Bond**

Tony Curtis

Tony Curtis became a film immortal in 1954, portraying a cultured English knight in **The Black Shield of Falworth**, and proclaiming (in an inimitable Bronx accent), "Yonder lies da castle of my fahder". At the time Curtis was a whipping-boy for critics who wanted to show how talentless Hollywood movie stars were, but they picked

good in many more comedies, although none was up to the same standard.

He was born as Bernard Schwartz in New York City (the Bronx, of course) on June 3, 1925, and worked briefly on stage before signing a contract with Universal Pictures. He was groomed for stardom in a series of bit parts, beginning with the 1948 **Criss Cross**, and made his début as a star in the 1951 Arabian Nights swashbuckler **The Prince Who Was a Thief** with Piper Laurie. It was ordinary-awful, but enough people went to see it (the kids loved his long, greasy hair) for a sequel to be made—**Son of Ali Baba**. Curtis won more favourable notice with an energetic performance in **Houdini**, made the memorably corny **Black Shield of Falworth** and quite a few less noteworthy pictures, and then took a giant stride forward in his career by starring opposite Burt Lancaster in **Trapeze**. He was good, so Lancaster astutely cast him as the unprincipled Sidney Falco in **Sweet Smell of Success**.

Among Curtis's more notable films of the '60s were **Spartacus**,

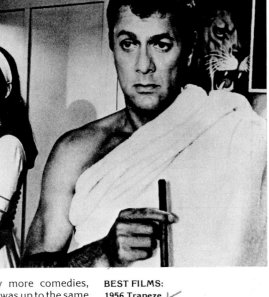

BEST FILMS:
1956 Trapeze
Carol Reed (United Artists)
1957 Sweet Smell of Success
Alexander Mackendrick (United Artists)
1958 The Defiant Ones
Stanley Kramer (United Artists)
1959 Some Like It Hot
Billy Wilder (United Artists)
1960 Spartacus
Stanley Kubrick (Universal)
1960 The Great Imposter
Robert Mulligan (Universal)
1964 Sex and the Single Girl
Richard Quine (Warner Brothers)
1965 The Great Race
Blake Edwards (Warner Brothers)
1968 The Boston Strangler
Richard Fleischer (20th Century Fox)
1976 The Last Tycoon
Elia Kazan (Paramount)

Peter Cushing

Peter Cushing, one of the all-time great horror film stars, is an excellent screen actor whose persona is one of the glories of the Gothic cinema. Essentially he is the arrogant aristocratic mastermind, a combination of scientist and priest, a man who is knowledgeable about the unknown. His greatest screen creations are variations of this hero/anti-hero figure. In the Hammer **Frankenstein** films he is Baron Frankenstein, elegant and authoritative, a combination of cruelty and creativity; he is the protagonist of these films, not the Monster as was true with the Universal/Boris Karloff versions. In the Hammer **Dracula** films he is Van Helsing, the continuing opponent and Nemesis of the Count, equally knowledgeable about the secrets of life and eath, and in **The Hound of the Baskervilles** he is Sherlock Holmes. Cushing's importance and popularity have been underestimated about the secrets of life and death, by most critics (with the notable exception of David Pirie, who analyses Hammer films in his fine study *A Heritage of Horror*). He was born in Purley, Surrey, on May 26, 1913, and began his acting career in a Worthing repertory company. He made his film début in Hollywood in 1939 in **The Man in the Iron Mask,** working appropriately for James Whale, director of the original **Frankenstein.** He acted in many films over the next 18 years, including even the role of Osric in Olivier's **Hamlet,** but he did not become a star until 1957; that was the year of the release of **The Curse of Frankenstein,** an enormous international success that cost £65,000, earned £1 million in the US alone and helped make Hammer the major modern horror studio. Cushing based his brilliant portrayal of the Baron on the original novel and on the character of pioneer anatomist Dr Robert Knox, becoming more ruthless and satanic as the series progressed. The contributions of

Above: Peter Cushing as the evil doctor meshing together human spare parts in the witty and gory **Frankenstein and the Monster from Hell.**

director Terence Fisher and designer Bernard Robinson were crucial to the success of these Hammer films, but the acting of Cushing and co-star Christopher Lee ➤ was equally important. Cushing played Van Helsing, the

implacable opponent of vampires, for the first time in the 1958 **Dracula.** He continued to play both roles over the years with great skill, but was equally good as Sherlock Holmes in **The Hound of the Baskervilles;** unfortunately Hammer could not get the rights for further stories and had to drop plans for a series. Cushing has worked in many other horror and science-fiction films, including portraying Dr Who in two film versions of the TV series, and usually carried his persona into them. One of his best non-horror pictures is **Cash on Demand** about a bank robbery.

His understanding of the basis of good screen acting is worth noting: "The greatest compliment is that it all looks easy".

BEST FILMS:
1957 The Curse of Frankenstein
Terence Fisher (Hammer)
1958 Dracula (Horror of Dracula)
Terence Fisher (Hammer)
1958 The Revenge of Frankenstein
Terence Fisher (Hammer)
1959 The Hound of the Baskervilles
Terence Fisher (Hammer)
1959 The Mummy
Terence Fisher (Hammer)
1960 The Brides of Dracula
Terence Fisher (Hammer)
1966 Frankenstein Created Woman
Terence Fisher (Hammer)
1966 The Skull
Freddie Francis (Amicus)
1969 Frankenstein Must Be Destroyed
Terence Fisher (Hammer)
1972 Dracula A.D. 1972
Don Houghton (Hammer)

ZBIGNIEW CYBULSKI

Zbigniew Cybulski was the James Dean ➤ of Eastern Europe, the symbolic rebel figure who embodied the feelings of the Polish post-war generation and then died tragically in an accident. The tinted glasses he wore in the film that made him famous, Andrzej Wajda's **Ashes and Diamonds,** became his trademark, inspiring imitation in Poland and other Communist countries. Although he made 37 films and was a legend in his own lifetime, his achievements as a cinema actor are limited to half a dozen films directed by Wajda, Has and Aleksander Ford. Many of his films are what Hollywood would call programmers, but he was really as famous for what he represented as for what he did.

Not that he wasn't a very fine actor in his best films: **Ashes and Diamonds** remains one of the strongest portraits of disillusionment made anywhere after the war, and Cybulski's performance is as complex and rich as the Hamlet personality it appears to have been modelled on. Cybulski appeared in a small part in Wajda's earlier **A Generation** and starred in Wajda's segment of the

Above: Eastern Europe's answer to James Dean—Zbigniew Cybulski in Andrzej Wajda's **Ashes and Diamonds.**

French episode film **L'Amour à Vingt Ans,** but his only other leading role for Poland's major director was **Innocent Sorcerers.** He made two important films for Has, **How To Be Loved** (which again seemed to question the meaning of heroism) and, more importantly, the magnificent **The Saragossa Manuscript,** a complex but rewarding adaptation of a famous novel by Jan Potocki.

Cybulski was born in the Ukraine, USSR, in 1927, and made a notable contribution to the Polish theatre before making his film début in **A Generation.** His rapid rise to a position as the leading actor of his generation in Poland and symbolic rebel figure seemed to disillusion him, as was reflected in his screen persona.

He began to drink heavily in the '60s and his accidental death while trying to board a train seemed almost predetermined. The accident was the focal point of Wajda's brilliant film homage to Cybulski in 1968, **Everything For Sale,** starring Daniel Olbrychski.

BEST FILMS:
1954 A Generation
Andrzej Wajda (Film Polski)
1957 The Eighth Day of the Week
Aleksander Ford (Film Polski)
1958 Ashes and Diamonds
Andrzej Wajda (Film Polski-Kadr)
1960 See You Tomorrow
J. Morgenstern (Film Polski-Kadr)
1960 Innocent Sorcerers
Andrzej Wajda (Film Polski-Kadr)
1962 L'Amour à Vingt Ans
Andrzej Wajda & others (Roustang)
1963 How To Be Loved
Wojciech Has (Film Polski-Kamer)
1964 To Love
Jörn Donner (Sandrews)
1964 The Saragossa Manuscript
Wojciech Has (Film Polski-Kamer)
1967 The Murderer Leaves a Clue
Aleksander Schibor-Ryski (Film Polski)

EVA DAHLBECK
see Ingmar Bergman Stars

JAMES DEAN

Cinema myths are often based on the tragic early deaths of actors who embody certain ideas of their time, like Rudolph Valentino ➤ and Marilyn Monroe ➤. James Dean was just such a myth, and his violent death now appears to

be the inescapable destiny of a legendary figure. Like a Greek mythological hero, he was brought up by foster parents, ran away to make his own way in the world, achieved fame and fortune, became a spiritual and moral leader, imparted his message, was struck down by jealous gods and then was accorded virtual Pantheon status. Edgar Morin, one of the critics who has noted this parallel, believes that Dean's kind of stardom could not have been fabricated but had to be revealed, like a religious happening. This is only partially true, for Dean's screen personality was as manufactured as any other cinema persona; admittedly, it reflected a great deal of Dean's own personality (as all personas do), but it was really built up in two films (**East of Eden, Rebel Without a Cause**) after Dean had appeared in small parts in three other movies without being noticed. The essentials of the persona were created by Dean, but it was shaped for public consumption (and eventual adulation) by directors Elia Kazan and Nicholas Ray. In **East of Eden** he was a young man craving for his parents' understanding, and in **Rebel** he was again an anguished son crying out against adult insensitivity—a cry recognised by every teenager of the time.

In 1956 came the good but less interesting **Giant** (the youthful myth figure has to age in the film)—and died the day after its completion when he crashed his new white Porsche at 115 miles per hour. Death turned him into a legend: a year afterwards his studio, Warner Brothers, was still receiving thousands of fan letters every week. A movie of his life was made from available documentary material and released with great success as **The James Dean Story** in 1957, and the adulation, the admiration, the myth has never really ended. In 1975 (20 years after his death) another documentary film, **James Dean—The First American Teenager,** was brought out and in 1976 Robert Butler directed a good fictional re-creation **James Dean.**

Dean was born on February 8, 1931, in Fairmont, Indiana. His mother died when he was nine and he was brought up by an uncle and aunt. He ran away from university, worked at all kinds of odd jobs, joined a drama group, and had bit parts in three films, **Sailor Beware, Fixed Bayonets** and **Has Anybody Seen My Gal?** He went to New York to work with the Actors' Studio, made his name on stage in *See the Jaguar* and *The Immoralist*—and returned to California to become a legend. Mythological heroes always go West, into the land of the setting sun.

Left: James Dean with Natalie Wood in the 1955 **Rebel Without a Cause.**

COMPLETE FILMS:
1951 Sailor Beware
Hal Walker (Paramount)
1951 Fixed Bayonets
Samuel Fuller (20th Century Fox)
1952 Has Anybody Seen My Gal?
Douglas Sirk (Universal)
1955 East of Eden
Elia Kazan (Warner Brothers)
1955 Rebel Without a Cause
Nicholas Ray (Warner Brothers)
1956 Giant
George Stevens (Warner Brothers)
1957 The James Dean Story
George W. George & Robert Altman (Warner Brothers)
1975 James Dean—The First American Teenager
Ray Connolly (VPS)

ALAIN DELON

Alain Delon, who has come to personify the French gangster to international cinema audiences, is one of the three top box-office stars in France (along with Jean-Paul Belmondo ➤ and Louis de Funes). Although he is now best known for his criminal roles on screen, a persona intensified by his much-publicised off-screen gangster associations, Delon actually began his career as the star of major "art" movies. He was the Rome stockbroker involved with Monica Vitti in Antonioni's **The Eclipse,** the honest Rocco in Visconti's **Rocco and His Brothers,** the talented Mr Ripley in Clément's **Plein Soleil (Purple Noon)** from the novel by Patricia Highsmith, and the revolutionary Tancredi in Visconti's **The Leopard.** Delon's tight-lipped, quiet-mannered, tough gangster persona first began to emerge in Henri Verneuil's 1963 **Mélodie en Sous-Sol,** in which he co-starred with Jean Gabin ➤, but it was director Jean-Pierre Melville who perfected it in three films: he adapted the cinema's gangster mythology to the French underworld and featured Delon brilliantly as a ruthless killer in the 1967 **Le Samourai,** later directing two more, **Le Cercle Rouge** (1970) and **Un Flic** (1972); the persona was so obviously right for Delon that he continued being a gangster for Verneuil in the hugely successful **The Sicilian Clan** in 1968, again opposite Jean Gabin. In 1969 Delon was the centre of a major scandal when his bodyguard was found shot dead in a garbage dump and his underworld relationships were widely publicised. He was cleared of complicity in the killing, and his real-life association with gangster activities made his tough screen image even more credible and popular to audiences. After Delon's second film for Melville, Jacques Deray co-starred him with Jean-Paul Belmondo in the extremely popular **Borsalino,** where they became kingpins of Marseilles crime. Belmondo was killed at the end of the film but the Delon character survived to come back for revenge in Deray's sequel

Above: Alain Delon, the star of films as great as L'Eclisse *and a mediocre as* **Girl on a Motorcycle.**

Borsalino and Co. Delon's best non-gangster film of the '70s was a superb Joseph Losey picture, **Mr Klein,** in which he portrays an art dealer making immoral profits out of Jews forced to flee France in 1942 and who is himself gradually forced into assuming the identity of a mysterious Jewish double.

He was born in Sceaux, outside Paris, on November 8, 1935, and had a difficult childhood. He served in the French Marines in Indo-China and when he returned got to know the criminal underworld of Marseilles. His film career grew out of a visit to the Cannes Film Festival in 1957 with actor Jean-Claude Brialy, after which he got a bit part in the film **Quand la Femme s'en Mêle.** By 1959 he was starring opposite Romy Schneider ➤ in **Christine, and then Plein Soleil** made him a star. His recent films include another gangster picture with Deray called **Le Gang,** the elaborate thriller **Armaguedon** by Alain Jessua and the melodramatic **L'Homme Pressé** again portraying an art dealer. An attempt to become a Hollywood star in the mid-'60s did not work out, though he starred in such films as **Texas Across the River** with Dean Martin ➤, **The Lost Command** with Anthony Quinn ➤ and **The Yellow Rolls-Royce** with Shirley MacLaine ➤.

BEST FILMS:
1959 Plein Soleil (Purple Noon)
René Clément (Paris Film)
1960 Rocco e i Suoi Fratelli (Rocco and His Brothers)
Luchino Visconti (Titanus)
1962 L'Eclisse (The Eclipse)
Michelangelo Antonioni (Interopa)
1963 Il Gattopardo (The Leopard)
Luchino Visconti (Titanus)
1967 Le Samourai
Jean-Pierre Melville (Filmel)
1968 Le Clan des Siciliens (The Sicilian Clan)
Henry Verneuil (Fox-Europa)
1970 Le Cercle Rouge (The Red Circle)
Jean-Pierre Melville (Corona)

1970 Borsalino
Jacques Deray (Adel)
1972 Un Flic (Dirty Money)
Jean-Pierre Melville (Corona)
1972 The Assassination of Trotsky
Joseph Losey (de Laurentiis)
1976 Mr Klein
Joseph Losey (Lira)

CATHERINE DENEUVE

Catherine Deneuve has been compared to Greta Garbo ➤ because of her extraordinary beauty and her ability to act as a reflecting pool for the audience's emotions. Like Garbo at the end of **Queen Christina,** Deneuve often does more simply by allowing herself to be a cypher than most other actresses can express by "acting." This quality has made her one of the most popular modern French actresses and a leading international star in American, English and Spanish films as well.

Her screen persona is one of icy sensuality, a beautiful and seemingly innocent girl driven by an intense sexuality which sometimes frightens and repels her. She often portrays call girls or mistresses and sex is almost always the focal point of her relationships. Her greatest performances have been for Luis Buñuel, first in **Belle de Jour** as the housewife who works during the day as a whore because she enjoys the job, and then in **Tristana** as a willing young innocent seduced by her elderly guardian. In Roman Polanski's **Repulsion** she is a young girl so obsessed by and frightened of sex that she barricades herself in

Above: The ice-cold but erotic Catherine Deneuve as the part-time prostitute in Luis Buñuel's 1967 surrealist masterpiece of repressed desire (and biggest commercial success) **Belle de Jour.**

her flat with her fantasies, and in Robert Aldrich's **Hustle** she is again a call girl as well as being the mistress of police officer Burt Reynolds ➤. In **Benjamin** she seduces the virginal hero because she doesn't want to give away her own virginity to an elderly roué whom she loves, in **Dirty Money** she is the mistress of a Marseilles gangster, in **Mayerling** she is the mistress of the Austrian crown prince and in the fairy tale **Donkey Skin** it is her own father who wants to get her into bed. Even in lighthearted musicals like **The Umbrellas of Cherbourg** she jumps into bed and becomes pregnant. Deneuve's screen persona appears to reflect some of her real-life independent attitudes about men and sexual morality: she has had two children outside marriage (refusing to wed Roger Vadim when he offered) and has maintained a strong-minded feminist attitude. She was married to photographer David Bailey in 1965-68 but decided marriage did not suit her. She was born in Paris in 1943 as Catherine Dorléac, (the younger sister of Françoise Dorléac). She began working in bit parts in films like **Les Collégiens** in 1956 while still at school but considers her film career actually began in 1960 when she played Françoise's sister in **Les Portes Claquent.** Vadim tried to make her a star in the 1963 **Le Vice et la Vertu** and **Et Satan Conduit le Bal . . .** but it was Jacques Demy's **The Umbrellas of Cherbourg** that really made her well-known. She co-starred with her sister in the sequel **The Young Girls of Rochefort** shortly before Françoise was killed in a car accident. **Belle de Jour** made her internationally famous (it was Buñuel's biggest commercial success), and she was excellent in films like **Benjamin** and **La Chamade.** Her American picture with Jack Lemmon ≫ **The April Fools**, was not very good but she was very much better with Jean-Paul Belmondo ≫ under François Truffaut's direction in **Mississippi Mermaid.** Her films in the '70s have not been as impressive, but she has remained one of France's top female stars in films like **L'Argent des Autres, 129, Zig-Zag** and **La Femme aux Bottes Rouges.**

BEST FILMS:
1964 Les Parapluies de Cherbourg
(The Umbrellas of Cherbourg)
Jacques Demy (Parc)
1965 Repulsion
Roman Polanski (Compton)
1966 Les Créatures
Agnes Varda (Parc)
1967 Belle de Jour
Luis Buñuel (Paris)
1968 Benjamin
Michel Deville (Parc)
1969 La Sirène du Mississippi
(Mississippi Mermaid)
François Truffaut (United Artists)
1970 Tristana
Luis Buñuel (Epoca)
1970 Peau d'Ane (Donkey Skin)
Jacques Demy (Parc)
1972 Un Flic (Dirty Money)
Jean-Pierre Melville (Corona)
1976 Hustle
Robert Aldrich (Paramount)

ROBERT DE NIRO

Robert De Niro became one of the major stars of the American cinema in the mid-'70s after an apprenticeship in semi-underground movies and supporting roles. Although he is usually thought of as a symbol of contemporary violence (**Taxi Driver, The Godfather Part II, Mean Streets**), his screen persona is actually much more complex and existential. His usual role is that of a man caught in a private hell, angry and resentful because he is unable to change his situation, his environment or his society and invariably losing the girl he loves. In **Taxi Driver** the horrors and squalor of New York City which he sees every day create so much resentment after he loses the girl he wants that he explodes into violence. In **1900** he is a rich Italian landowner trapped into traditional behaviour patterns and unable either to oppose Fascism or to

Above: Robert De Niro in **The Deer Hunter**, *the story of three friends from a small community drafted to serve in Vietnam.*

become a Socialist and losing his wife because of it. In **The Last Tycoon** he is a '30s studio production chief who fails to recapture his lost love in the shape of a new girl or to wrest control of the studio from its real boss. In **New York, New York** he is a band musician unable to compromise his ideals and play the kind of music that changing tastes demand, nor again to keep the girl he loves. In **The Deer Hunter** his private hell is as much the steel town in which he works as the Vietnamese prison camp he ends up in as a soldier. In **Bang the Drum Slowly**, the film that made his name in 1973, he is a baseball player with an incurable disease striving to play one more season before he dies; in **Mean Streets** he is happy-go-lucky debtor Johnny Boy trapped in Little Italy and

taking out his resentment by blowing up mailboxes; in **Godfather Part II** he is the young "godfather" escaping from Sicily and building an empire of violence in the US. De Niro has been highly praised by critics for the intensity of his performances. He has won the Best Supporting Actor Oscar for **The Godfather Part II** and the New York Film Critics Best Actor award for **Taxi Driver** and Best Supporting Actor award for **Bang the Drum Slowly.**

De Niro was born in New York City in 1945, studied acting with Stella Adler and Lee Strasberg and appeared in many relatively unsuccessful off-Broadway plays in the '60s. He began his cinema career with Brian De Palma, giving outstanding performances in such semi-underground classics as **The Wedding Party, Greetings** and **Hi, Mom!** He also built up his reputation as a solid commercial actor in films like **Bloody Mama,** and **Born to Win.** He was again outstanding in **The Gang That Couldn't Shoot Straight,** a not very successful adaptation of a Jimmy Breslin novel, portraying an illegal Italian immigrant in New York who refuses to betray his girlfriend even when he is deported. His association with director Martin Scorsese, begun in 1973 in the low-budget **Mean Streets,** eventually made him a major star through **Taxi Driver** and **New York, New York.** De Niro brings remarkable grace and power as well as intensity to his acting, and is likely to continue to grow in magnitude as a star in the '80s.

BEST FILMS:
1969 Greetings
Brian De Palma (De Palma)
1971 Bloody Mama
Roger Corman (AIP)
1973 Bang the Drum Slowly
John Hancock (Paramount)
1973 Mean Streets
Martin Scorsese (Warner Brothers)
1974 The Godfather Part II
Francis Ford Coppola (Paramount)
1976 1900
Bernardo Bertolucci (PEA/20th Century Fox)
1976 Taxi Driver
Martin Scorsese (Columbia)
1976 The Last Tycoon
Elia Kazan (Paramount)
1977 New York, New York
Martin Scorsese (United Artists)
1978 The Deer Hunter
Michael Cimino (Universal/EMI)

GERARD DEPARDIEU

Gerard Depardieu is the most important new actor in France and appears likely to overtake Jean-Paul Belmondo ≫ and Alain Delon ≫ in popularity. He became a huge success on the basis of **Les Valseuses (Making It)** in 1974, and has been starring in three or four films every year since. His

status is such that he was co-starred with Robert De Niro ≫ in **1900**, but he is equally at home in difficult "art" movies like Marguerite Duras' **Le Camion** or straightforward commercial pictures like **7 Morts sur Ordonnance.** American critic Molly Haskell has described him in *Film Comment* as "one of the most exciting and important new actors in the movies today" and he is rapidly becoming the new male sex symbol of the European cinema, taking over the position once held by Marcello Mastroianni ≫. His rugged, virile image, however, is used in extraordinary ways. Marco Ferreri pushes his macho behaviour into a psychological trap in **The Last Woman,** ending with him emasculating himself with an electric knife, while in **Bye Bye Monkey** he is raped by a feminist theatre group in a bizarre New York of the future.

Depardieu was born in Chateauroux, France, on December 27, 1948, spent a tough childhood as a petty criminal and odd-job

Above: Gerard Depardieu as the peasant hero of **1900**, *Bernardo Bertolucci's four-hour political epic on Italian fascism.*

labourer and became interested in acting while working as a beach boy during the Cannes Film Festival. He went to Paris to study, made his film début in 1965 in a short by Roger Leenhart titled **Le Beatnik et le Minet,** and began to work in TV and the theatre on a regular basis. Marguerite Duras featured him in her 1972 **Nathalie Granger** and he worked steadily in films after that, including **Le Tueur, Au Rendez-vous de la Mort Joyeuse** and **La Scoumoune.** **Les Valseuses** made him a big star as a charismatic petty criminal and sexual athlete, a persona strikingly similar to his early real-life exploits. He showed great ability as an actor portraying the hold-up man in **The Wonderful Crook** and was exceptionally powerful as the peasant who becomes a partisan hero in **1900.**

The strength of his natural screen presence was magnificently demonstrated by Marguerite Duras in the two-person tour-de-force **Le Camion**.

BEST FILMS:
1974 Les Valseuses (Making It)
Bertrand Blier (CAPAC)
1975 Pas Si Méchant Que Ça (The Wonderful Crook)
Claude Goretta (Gasser)
1976 1900
Bernardo Bertolucci (PEA/20th Century Fox)
1976 Baxter, Vera Baxter
Marguerite Duras (Sunchild)
1976 L'Ultima Donna (The Last Woman)
Marco Ferreri (Flaminia)
1977 René La Canne (René the Cane)
Francis Girod (President)
1977 Le Camion
Marguerite Duras (Cinema 9)
1977 Dites Lui Que Je L'Aime (This Sweet Sickness)
Claude Miller (Filmoblic)
1978 Bye Bye Monkey
Marco Ferreri (Prospectacle)
1978 Preparez Vos Mouchoirs (Get Out Your Handkerchiefs)
Bertrand Blier (CAPAC)

BRUCE DERN

Bruce Dern has specialised in portraying wide-eyed psychotics and obsessively driven fanatics, which is presumably the reason for his growing stardom in the '70s. As he rarely plays heroic characters it is unlikely that he will become a true superstar, but he has certainly become one of the best-known and most-admired "sympathetic" villains of the cinema. In **Black Sunday** he is the vengeful Vietnam veteran prepared to kill a football stadium full of people. In **Silent Running** he kills the other human beings on his space station in his obsessive desire to preserve mankind's last forest. In **Posse** he is the manic Western gang leader whose crazed determination upsets the political plans of sheriff Kirk Douglas ⟩. In **The King of Marvin Gardens** he is the wildly-scheming brother of Jack Nicholson ⟩, and his mad dreams end in his own death. In **Coming Home** he is Jane Fonda's ⟩ crazed husband fresh back from Vietnam, prepared to kill her but finally doing away with himself. In **The Driver** he is an obsessed detective out to capture Ryan O'Neal ⟩. In **Bloody Mama** he joins Shelley Winters' ⟩ murderous gang and is shot by her in the end, in **The Cowboys** he is the mad cattle rustler who shoots John Wayne ⟩ in the back, in **The Great Gatsby** he is the unpleasant wealthy husband of Daisy, in **Smile** he is "Big Bob" the car dealer, prime organiser of the beauty contest, and in **Family Plot** he is just an ordinary crook supplying information to fake spiritualist Barbara Harris. Dern's "villains" are unusual in that they are almost always men whose evil

or obsessive behaviour can be understood and sympathised with.

Dern was born in Winnetka, Illinois, on June 4, 1936, into a wealthy family, studied at the University of Pennsylvania, going on to the Actors' Studio and beginning his professional career working off-Broadway. He began his screen work in 1960 with **Wild River** and **The Trip**, and his quick-tempered manic persona grew through the '60s in many good films including **Castle Keep** and **They Shoot Horses, Don't They?** He achieved stardom in 1972 with **Silent Running** and **The King of Marvin Gardens** and his career is likely to continue to accelerate if he has the right parts.

BEST FILMS:
1972 Silent Running
Douglas Trumbull (Universal)
1972 The King of Marvin Gardens
Bob Rafelson (Columbia)
1973 The Laughing Policeman
Stuart Rosenberg (20th Century Fox)
1974 The Great Gatsby
Jack Clayton (Paramount)

Above: Bruce Dern as the police detective obsessed with nailing Ryan O'Neal in Walter Hill's existentialist thriller **The Driver**.

1974 Smile
Michael Ritchie (United Artists)
1975 Posse
Kirk Douglas (Paramount)
1976 Family Plot
Alfred Hitchcock (Universal)
1976 Black Sunday
John Frankenheimer (Paramount)
1978 Coming Home
Hal Ashby (United Artists)
1978 The Driver
Walter Hill (20th Century Fox/EMI)

RICHARD DREYFUSS

Richard Dreyfuss is a new kind of cinema hero, a worried introvert with a tendency to become obsessed about an idea and follow it through, no matter what

the consequences. In **Close Encounters of the Third Kind** his obsession focuses on flying saucers, in **Jaws** on sharks, in **The Goodbye Girl** on acting (a gay Richard III!), in **The Apprenticeship of Duddy Kravitz** on obtaining a piece of land, and in **American Graffiti** on a beautiful girl in a white sports car. He struggles with these obsessions in a peculiarly '70s way which obviously has a widespread appeal: it can't be pure coincidence that most of his starring films have been hugely successful at the box office. He has created an identifiable persona in a very short time.

Dreyfuss was born in Brooklyn, New York, in 1949, studied at Beverly Hills High School, and began his professional acting career at the Gallery Theatre in Los Angeles. He has worked on and off Broadway and in TV, making his film début in 1967 in bit parts in **The Graduate** and **Valley of the Dolls**. He had slightly bigger roles in **Hello Down There** and **The Young Runaways**, but it was his performance as a larger-than-life Baby Face Nelson in **Dillinger** in 1973 that first attracted attention. In the same year he was the central figure in **American Graffiti**, as the introverted poet who flies off to college at the end of the film without ever meeting the lovely vision in the white Thunderbird. That film made him a star and he became a bigger one in **The Apprenticeship of Duddy Kravitz**, the most successful film ever made in Canada, playing a Jewish boy in Montreal, a hustler who betrays even his best and oldest friends to get what he wants.

Jaws made Dreyfuss a major star, playing the shark expert Hooper, but the British film **Inserts**, in which he played a has-been film director named Boy Wonder, was not box office des-

Above: Richard Dreyfuss in his Oscar-winning role as an out-of-work actor involved with Marsha Mason, in Neil Simon's comedy **The Goodbye Girl** *(1977).*

pite his fine performance. In **Victory at Entebbe** he was the Colonel leading the Israeli rescue party, and in **Close Encounters of the Third Kind** (his second film with Steven Spielberg) he was a workman whose contact with an alien spaceship changes his life. In **The Goodbye Girl** he was histrionically worried by Marsha Mason and her daughter, as well as his acting career; it was a brilliant performance, justly rewarded with the 1977 Academy Award for Best Actor.

BEST FILMS:
1973 Dillinger
John Milius (AIP)
1973 American Graffiti
George Lucas (Universal)
1974 The Apprenticeship of Duddy Kravitz
Ted Kotcheff (ICC)
1975 Inserts
John Byrum (FGP/UA)
1975 Jaws
Steven Spielberg (Universal)
1976 Victory at Entebbe
Marvin J. Chomsky (Wolper)
1977 Close Encounters of the Third Kind
Steven Spielberg (Columbia)
1977 The Goodbye Girl
Herbert Ross (MGM/Warner Brothers)

FAYE DUNAWAY

Faye Dunaway burst into the American cinema in 1967 with a style and a face that looked refreshingly different. **The Happening** and **Hurry Sundown** were minor achievements, but **Bonnie and Clyde** was a major film and made Dunaway an international

ROBERT DUVALL

Robert Duvall is a ruthless, balding wheeler-dealer organiser, often a smooth company director, usually a criminal. It is not a screen persona likely to make him into a major star, but he is stunningly good at what he does and should remain an important name for many years. Duvall became known in **The Godfather** portraying the deceptively mild-mannered "consigliere" legal adviser and right-hand man of Mafia boss Marlon Brando ≫, and he received an Oscar nomination for it. He played the same role again in **The Godfather Part II**. In **The Betsy** he is the tough and efficient managing director of a Detroit car manufacturing company intent on retaining control and revenging himself on his grandfather Laurence Olivier ≫. In **Network** he is the director of the TV company who first exploits mad Messiah Peter Finch ≫ and then arranges for him to be killed. In **The Conversation** he portrays a company director who hires Gene Hackman ≫ to bug a couple whom Hackman suspects he plans to kill. In **The Eagle Has Landed** he is the German officer who organises the kidnapping of Winston Churchill, and in **The Killer Elite** he is the CIA-sponsored killer who turns villain and cripples his own partner, played by James Caan ≫. In **Joe Kidd** he is an evil cattle baron who hires Clint Eastwood ≫ and in **M*A*S*H** he is the much-disliked Major Burns. He is not always unsympathetic even when he is on the other side of the law. He portrays a criminal out to destroy the Mob in **The Outfit**, in **Breakout** he is an American in a Mexican jail whom Charles Bronson ≫ finally succeeds in rescuing, in **The Great Minnesota Raid** he is Jesse James opposed to the much more criminal railway barons and in **THX-1138** he is the rebel against a computer-dominated future society who finally succeeds in escaping. Even as an historic "heroic" figure like Dr Watson in **The Seven Per Cent Solution** he is very much a behind-the-scenes organiser.

Duvall was born in San Diego, California, in 1931, the son of a Rear Admiral. He worked on stage and in TV and made his cinema début superbly as the simpleton Boo Radley in **To Kill a Mockingbird** in 1962. His television programmes include *Route 66* and *The FBI* and he starred in the 1965 off-Broadway production of *A View From the Bridge*. He worked steadily in films all through the '60s, most notably in **Captain Newman MD, The Chase, The Detective, Bullitt** and **True Grit** (as John Wayne's ≫ opponent). He also began a strong and continuing association with director Francis Ford Coppola in **The Rain People** in 1969 which continued through his stardom-

Above: Robert Duvall plays a criminal just out of prison who tangles with the Mafia in John Flynn's **The Outfit**.

achieving performances as Tom Hagen in **The Godfather** and its sequel, **The Conversation** and the Coppola-produced **THX-1138**.

BEST FILMS:
1969 The Rain People
Francis Ford Coppola (Warner Brothers-Seven Arts)
1971 THX-1138
George Lucas (Warner Brothers)
1971 The Great Minnesota Raid
Philip Kaufman (Universal)
1972 The Godfather
Francis Ford Coppola (Paramount)
1973 The Outfit
John Flynn (MGM)
1974 The Godfather Part II
Francis Ford Coppola (Paramount)
1975 The Killer Elite
Sam Peckinpah (United Artists)
1976 Network
Sidney Lumet (MGM/United Artists)
1976 The Eagle Has Landed
John Sturges (ITC Entertainment)
1978 The Betsy
Daniel Petrie (Allied Artists)

CLINT EASTWOOD

Clint Eastwood is the No 1 star of the '70s and is close to overtaking Paul Newman ≫ as the most popular modern star. It seems probable that he will soon have a superstar status equivalent to John Wayne ≫, from whom he has already taken over as the major Western and action film

---

star. She seemed to have fashioned a screen persona out of beauty, naive sexuality and frustration at the world around her (which reflected the feelings of the 1967 young), expressed in the anti-establishment violence of the '30s bank robber she portrayed. It was not realistic but mythical/romantic; Faye Dunaway/Bonnie Parker became an instant myth.

As it turned out, the persona was more director Arthur Penn's creation than Dunaway's; she was simply a very good actress able to adapt chameleon-like to the demands of her directors and her roles. The disappointment aroused by her very interesting performances as the detective pursuing Steve McQueen ≫ in **The Thomas Crown Affair** or consoling Kirk Douglas ≫ in **The Arrangement** was not because of her acting but because of the discovery that her persona would not and probably could not be carried over into other movies. Dunaway was a fine, glamorous actress—but she was not a myth. Good as she has been in many films since **Bonnie and Clyde**, she has never again had such impact, although the combination of sexuality and ambition she displayed as a power-hungry TV executive in **Network** was very impressive.

Dunaway was born in Bascom, Florida, on January 14, 1941, and began her acting career on stage with the Lincoln Center Repertory Company in New York. Her work in the '70s has made her one of the big box-office female stars and she has made a valuable contribution to such financial blockbusters as **The Towering Inferno, Three Days of the Condor, The Three Musketeers** and **The Four Musketeers** (as

Above: Warren Beatty and Faye Dunaway fighting the cops (and finally losing) in Arthur Penn's critically acclaimed celebration of the gangster movie era. **Bonnie and Clyde** *(1967).*

Milady de Winter), and **Voyage of the Damned**. Her best work has been as a complex '30s *femme fatale* to Jack Nicholson's private eye in **Chinatown** for Roman Polanski, as Katie Elder in Frank Perry's **Doc**, and in an excellent smaller role for Penn as a minister's amorous wife in **Little Big Man**. Her romantic Italian fling with Marcello Mastroianni ≫ in Vittorio De Sica's **A Place for Lovers** is best forgotten, but she was clever and stylish as a high-fashion model with emotional problems in **Puzzle of a Downfall Child** and rather splendid as a lady with an oil well in **Oklahoma Crude**. Her glamour was very much to the fore in her recent thriller **Eyes of Laura Mars**.

BEST FILMS:
1967 Bonnie and Clyde
Arthur Penn (Warner Seven Arts)
1968 The Thomas Crown Affair
Norman Jewison (United Artists)
1969 The Arrangement
Elia Kazan (Warner Brothers)
1970 Little Big Man
Arthur Penn (Warner Brothers)
1970 Puzzle of a Downfall Child
Jerry Schatzberg (Universal)
1971 Doc
Frank Perry (United Artists)
1973 Oklahoma Crude
Stanley Kramer (Columbia)
1974 Chinatown
Roman Polanski (Paramount)
1975 Three Days of the Condor
Sydney Pollack (Paramount)
1976 Network
Sidney Lumet (MGM/United Artists)

hero. His persona is not the same as Wayne's, but there are enough similarities to make it seem likely that Eastwood has assumed Wayne's No 1 mantle. (In 1971 Wayne was listed as the top box office star with Eastwood second; in 1972 and 1973 Eastwood was the top star and Wayne was fourth and ninth.) The parallels in their screen images include the essential heroic values of toughness, strength, power and self-sufficiency used with intelligence and knowledge, charismatic, dominating personalities, and a no-nonsense, professional approach to their usual screen roles as skilled gunmen on the right side of the law. Eastwood once said his credo was "I just believe that everybody ought to know his job and do it well, or find something else to do", and this exactly echoes the professionalism stressed by directors Howard Hawks and John Ford in the Wayne movie persona.

Neither director worked with Eastwood, whose screen image was created by Sergio Leone and Don Siegel, with Eastwood himself as an active participant. It was Leone who made him an international star after he had achieved a measure of fame portraying Rowdy Yates for eight years in the TV series *Rawhide:* Leone made Eastwood into the "Man with No Name", the cynical, nihilistic avenging angel of death in the brutal Western trilogy **A Fistful of Dollars, For a Few Dollars More** and **The Good, the Bad and the Ugly.** In these films Eastwood spoke little, thought a great deal, and killed ruthlessly and superhumanly fast, dressed in poncho and flat black hat and smoking a black cheroot. That image, as much as the films, aroused international response; it was soon apparent that the persona was as much Eastwood's as Leone's, for Eastwood successfully re-created it in an American Western **Hang 'em High,** directed by Ted Post. One of the more fascinating aspects of Eastwood's persona was the puzzlement he expressed at the complexities of what was happening around him. Don Siegel had the brilliant idea of transferring that persona into an urban environment where there was an equal amount of violence and even more complexities to be puzzled out. He did this very cleverly for the first time in **Coogan's Bluff,** bringing Western sheriff Eastwood to New York to track down a killer in an alien and hostile environment with no sympathy for an unbureaucratic loner. He was then able to take Eastwood completely away from his Western background and feature him as **Dirty Harry,** the toughest cop in San Francisco, who operates just as individualistically as a frontier marshall—when the red tape doesn't trip him up. The wisdom of Siegel's move was shown by the box-office success of the film's sequels, **Magnum**

Force and **The Enforcer,** which made even more money than **Dirty Harry** itself (all three are among the biggest grossing films of all time).

Eastwood was born in San Francisco on May 31, 1930, had a lot of success as an athlete in school, served his time in the Army as a swimming instructor, and began to work in films as an extra for Universal in the mid-'50s. He made 14 films for that company, his first noticeable roles being in Jack Arnold's 1955 horror pictures **Revenge of the Creature** and **Tarantula.** Stardom came at last through the TV series *Rawhide* and with Leone in Italy.

After the success of **Coogan's Bluff,** Eastwood was starred by Siegel in **Two Mules for Sister Sara** (tough cowboy involved with nun Shirley MacLaine », who turns out be a whore), **The Beguiled** (wounded Northern soldier hiding in Southern girls' school) and the key **Dirty Harry.** He was featured by director Brian Hutton in two splendid World War II adventure pictures, **Where Eagles Dare** and **Kelly's Heroes,** and less successfully in an odd, tough musical, **Paint Your Wagon** with Lee Marvin ». In the '70s Eastwood turned director and proved to be exceptionally skilled at manipulating his own screen persona as a Western hero (**The Outlaw Josey Wales, High Plains Drifter**), city cop (**The Gauntlet**), and even as a disc jockey (**Play Misty for Me**). It is probable that

*Above: Clint Eastwood directed himself as **The Outlaw Josey Wales,** one of the greatest Westerns of the modern cinema.*

Eastwood's superstar status will continue to grow in power and achievement.

BEST FILMS:
1964 A Fistful of Dollars
Sergio Leone (Jolly/UA)
1965 For a Few Dollars More
Sergio Leone (PEA/UA)
1966 The Good, the Bad and the Ugly
Sergio Leone (PEA/UA)
1968 Coogan's Bluff
Don Siegel (Universal)
1970 Kelly's Heroes
Brian G. Hutton (MGM)
1971 The Beguiled
Don Siegel (Universal)
1971 Play Misty for Me
Clint Eastwood (Universal)
1971 Dirty Harry
Don Siegel (Warner Brothers)
1973 High Plains Drifter
Clint Eastwood (Universal)
1976 The Outlaw Josey Wales
Clint Eastwood (Warner Brothers)
1977 The Gauntlet
Clint Eastwood (Warner Brothers)

Mia Farrow

Mia Farrow is the haunted waif of the contemporary cinema, so fragile in body and insecure in emotions that the audience worries about her all the time she's on screen. Her persona is remarkably

effective when used in the right film by a good director, because Farrow has the ability to transfer her hurts and worries to the viewer. In **Rosemary's Baby** the diabolical horror of what is happening is conveyed by Farrow's terror as much as by the plot. In **John and Mary** her insecurity about being a one-night lay for Dustin Hoffman » is projected to the audience as much as it is to him. In **Secret Ceremony** she is a seemingly innocent girl trying to make Elizabeth Taylor » into her mother—and Taylor's (and the audience's) discovery of the hidden aspect of her nature causes her suicide. In **Full Circle** it is necessary for the viewer to empathise with the supernatural horrors that befall the woman she portrays, and in

*Above: Mia Farrow, whose ethereal beauty has been effectively used in thrillers, notably **Full Circle.***

Blind Terror her position as the threatened victim is again transferred.

Farrow is the daughter of Tarzan's most memorable Jane, Maureen O'Sullivan, and the director John Farrow. She was born in Los Angeles on February 9, 1945, was educated partly at a Catholic boarding school in London and began her acting career with a small role in the 1964 British film **Guns at Batasi.** That led to her being cast as Alison MacKenzie in the TV series *Peyton Place* from 1964 to 1967. Her unconventional life style (it was called kookiness then) attracted a lot of publicity, as did her marriage to Frank Sinatra in 1966 and its break-up two years later. She appeared in Anthony Mann's last film **A Dandy in Aspic,** but it was **Rosemary's Baby,** a huge critical and box office success, which made her a major star. In 1970 she got more off-screen publicity when she gave birth to twins while she and composer André Previn were waiting for his divorce so they could get married. She starred opposite Jean-Paul Belmondo » in Claude Chabrol's bizarre **Docteur Popaul** and then was the focus of activity in **The Great Gatsby** as Daisy, the girl Gatsby loves. After a lull in the mid-'70s, she starred in three films in 1978: as the jilted lover in the big-budget Poirot mystery **Death on the Nile,** the fascinating silent sister of the bride in Robert Altman's **A Wedding** and the sexy former wife of Rock Hudson ≫ in the disaster film **Avalanche.**

BEST FILMS:
1968 Rosemary's Baby
Roman Polanski (Paramount)
1969 Secret Ceremony
Joseph Losey (Universal)
1969 John and Mary
Peter Yates (20th Century Fox)
1971 Blind Terror
Richard Fleischer (Columbia)
1972 Docteur Popaul
Claude Chabrol (Les Films la Boétie)
1974 The Great Gatsby
Jack Clayton (Paramount)
1976 Full Circle
Richard Loncraine (Fetter)
1978 Avalanche
Corey Allen (New World)
1978 A Wedding
Robert Altman (20th Century Fox)
1978 Death on the Nile
John Guillermin (Paramount/EMI)

PETER FINCH

Peter Finch was one of those thoughtful, intelligent actors who begin their careers slowly but get better and better as the passing years give them greater experience, maturity and authority. His death in 1977 was a great loss to the cinema, for he had only really begun to reach peak form; the posthumous Oscar he received for **Network** was partial recognition of this. His screen performances in the last seven years of his life were among the strongest he had given, and helped give

stature to films like **Sunday, Bloody Sunday** (as a highly intelligent, homosexual doctor), **Bequest to the Nation** (as Nelson), **The Red Tent** (as the Arctic explorer General Nobile), **England Made Me** (as a corrupt German industrialist), and even the unfortunate musical version of **Lost Horizon** (in Ronald Colman's ≫ old role). Finch's career stretched back to the Australian cinema of the '30s and he had received his share of acting prizes in the '50s for films like **A Town Like Alice,** but his continuing development makes it seem that he was cut off in his prime.

He was born in London on September 28, 1916, as William Mitchell, and was brought up in France, India and Australia, where he settled. His film début was in the 1936 Australian film **Dad and Dave Come to Town;** he became well known in Australia as a theatre and radio actor before returning to England in 1948. He soon won popularity in '50s war films like **The Battle of the River Plate,** attention from Hollywood in films like **The Nun's Story,** and acclaim as an actor for films like **The Trials of Oscar Wilde.** He made a number of good films in the '60s, including **The Girl with Green Eyes, The Pumpkin Eater** and **The Flight of the Phoenix,** and ended the decade with superb performances in **Far From the Madding Crowd** and **The Legend of Lylah Clare.** He ended his career sadly but gloriously as the crazed television Messiah of **Network.**

Below: Peter Finch takes a rest during the filming of the 1966 **Judith,** *which was set in the Israel of 1948.*

BEST FILMS:
1956 A Town Like Alice
Jack Lee (Rank)
1960 The Trials of Oscar Wilde
Ken Hughes (Warwick)
1961 No Love For Johnnie
Ralph Thomas (Rank)
1964 The Pumpkin Eater
Jack Clayton (Columbia)
1967 Far From the Madding Crowd
John Schlesinger (EMI)
1968 The Legend of Lylah Clare
Robert Aldrich (MGM)
1971 The Red Tent
Mikhail Kalatozov (Paramount)
1971 Sunday, Bloody Sunday
John Schlesinger (United Artists)
1972 England Made Me
Peter Duffell (Hemdale)
1976 Network
Sidney Lumet (MGM/United Artists)

ALBERT FINNEY

Albert Finney created one of the British cinema's great screen personas in his first starring role, the working class hero of **Saturday Night and Sunday Morning** in 1960. He expanded the persona with his Rabelaisian performance in **Tom Jones** in 1963, winning Best Actor awards in New York and Venice and an Oscar nomination, as well as making a personal fortune from his percentage on the film (it made $17 million in the US alone). He could have become Britain's top film star, but said, "I don't give a damn whether I am a star or not", and so has made very few films—only 13 in 18 years. His primary interest has always

been the stage, and though he has continued to be regarded as a movie star in spite of himself, his importance to the British cinema has now become peripheral. His only starring role in recent years was as Hercule Poirot in the 1974 **Murder on the Orient Express,** a performance of great theatricality by an actor who does not need to "act" in this way to be a star. He also took a supporting role in the British film **The Duellists,** portraying the intriguing Fouché, starred in a respectable film version of his stage hit **Alpha Beta** and seemed to enjoy himself in the big-budget musical **Scrooge.** His finest role in the '70s was in the small-budget **Gumshoe,** a brilliant performance as a Liverpool bingo caller who fantasises about becoming a Bogart-type private eye and then finds himself caught up in the real thing.

Finney was born in Salford, Lancashire, on May 9, 1936, studied at RADA, worked in repertory in Birmingham and made his West End stage début in 1958 in *The Party.* Tony Richardson gave him a small role as Olivier's son in the 1960 **The Entertainer** and Reisz cast him as the factory worker hero of **Saturday Night and Sunday Morning.** Finney could have had any film role after that, but he turned down even **Lawrence of Arabia** to go back on stage in *Billy Liar* and *Luther.* **Tom Jones** made him wealthy enough not to have to worry about future film roles. He was good as the psychopath in **Night Must Fall** but the film was

Left: Albert Finney downing a pint with Rachel Roberts, one of his two mistresses, in **Saturday Night and Sunday Morning,** *Karel Reisz' study of a Northern England factory worker.*

laboured. He was excellent opposite Audrey Hepburn in **Two for the Road,** but even better directing himself in the neglected **Charlie Bubbles,** playing a successful writer bored with his lot. Its brilliance did not get it wide distribution and Finney has regrettably not directed since. He married French actress Anouk Aimée in 1970—although they have now split up.

BEST FILMS:
1960 Saturday Night and Sunday Morning
Karel Reisz (Woodfall)
1963 Tom Jones
Tony Richardson (United Artists)
1967 Two for the Road
Stanley Donen (20th Century Fox)
1968 Charlie Bubbles
Albert Finney (Memorial)
1969 The Picasso Summer
Serge Bourguignon (Warner Brothers-Seven Arts)
1970 Scrooge
Ronald Neame (Cinema Center)
1972 Gumshoe
Stephen Frears (Memorial)
1973 Alpha Beta
Anthony Page (Memorial)
1974 Murder on the Orient Express
Sidney Lumet (EMI)
1977 The Duellists
Ridley Scott (Enigma)

JANE FONDA

The intensity of Jane Fonda's off-screen political commitment has been reflected in her screen performances (and persona), especially since her adoption of a left-wing stance in the late '60s, and has helped her gain a deserved reputation as the finest American film actress of her generation. She won a Best Actress Oscar for her highly intelligent performance as the call girl under threat of death in **Klute** and received nominations for her equally brilliant performances as a desperate marathon dancer in **They Shoot Horses, Don't They?** and as writer Lillian Hellman in **Julia.**

In the early '60s Fonda was a good, new-style glamorous, slightly "Method" actress in films like **The Chase, Cat Ballou** and **The Chapman Report.** She was transformed into a very sexy star indeed by Brigitte Bardot's former Svengali and husband Roger Vadim; he married her in 1965 and featured a lot of her in **Barbarella, La Ronde** and **La Curée.** After she split with Vadim four years later, her screen roles became more directly connected with her political ideas, including aspects of feminism (**Klute, A Doll's House**) and opposition to the Vietnam conflict (**Vietnam**

Journey, Coming Home). Her present activities with, and marriage to, radical Tom Haydon have not prevented her from working in comedy, but films like **Fun with Dick and Jane** can also be read as attacks on establishment values. The protest is upfront in the amusing **Steelyard Blues** and the more propagandist **Tout Va Bien.**

Jane Seymour Fonda is the daughter of Margaret Seymour Brokaw and actor Henry Fonda ≫ and was born in New York City on December 21, 1937. Her brother Peter, also well known as a movie actor, was born in 1940, and their mother died ten years

Above: Jane Fonda as writer Lillian Hellman in Fred Zinnemann's **Julia** *(1977).*

later. She was mostly raised by her grandmother in Connecticut after that, studied at Vassar and worked at the Actors' Studio, making her professional stage début with her father in *The Country Girl* in 1955 and appearing in her first film, Joshua Logan's **Tall Story,** in 1960. Her early persona was explored by Richard Leacock and Robert Drew in the 1963 documentary **Jane,** and other interesting '60s films include **Barefoot in the Park** with Robert Redford ≫ and **Hurry Sundown** with Michael Caine ≫ as well as the films mentioned above. She made a very good thriller for René Clement in France in 1964, **The Love Cage (Les Félins)** with Alain Delon ≫, but her most enjoyable French film was undoubtedly Vadim's comic-strip-in-motion **Barbarella.**

Her resolute, aggressive and always intelligent attitude to film making in the '70s makes it probable that she will have a career as important and as enduring as that of Katharine Hepburn ≫, the older generation actress whose work Fonda's most resembles.

BEST FILMS:
1965 Cat Ballou
Elliot Silverstein (Columbia)
1967 Barefoot in the Park
Gene Saks (Paramount)
1968 Barbarella
Roger Vadim (Paramount)

1969 They Shoot Horses, Don't They?
Sydney Pollack (Palomar)
1971 Klute
Alan J. Pakula (Warner Brothers)
1972 Tout Va Bien
Jean-Luc Godard & Jean-Pierre Gorin (Anouchka)
1972 Steelyard Blues
Alan Myerson (Warner Brothers)
1976 Fun with Dick and Jane
Ted Kotcheff (Columbia)
1977 Julia
Fred Zinnemann (20th Century Fox)
1978 Coming Home
Hal Ashby (United Artists)

JAMES GARNER

James Garner has one of the friendliest and most engaging "hero" personalities in the cinema, good-natured, easy-going, humorous, sometimes a little bumbling and cowardly but able to cope with difficult situations with courage and competence when absolutely required. In **The Americanization of Emily** he is a World War II officer in London willing to use every cowardly means to survive the war, but reluctantly forced to become a D-Day war hero. In **Support Your Local Sheriff** he tames the rougher elements of a boom town, keeping a gunman prisoner in his new jail even though it doesn't have bars yet. In **The Great Escape** he is the scrounger able to barter or steal anything needed by the escape committee. In **Move Over, Darling** his easy-going nature is considerably stretched when his presumed-dead wife Doris Day returns after five years, just as he is planning to marry Polly Bergen. In **Marlowe** he succeeded in taking the Raymond Chandler

private eye role and fitting it very nicely over his own screen personality, watching bemused as Bruce Lee smashed his office to bits. In **They Only Kill Their Masters** he is a casual easy-going police chief looking for a killer in a small California town. In **The Skin Game** he's a good natured con man with a black partner in the bad old days of slavery.

Garner was born in Norman, Oklahoma, on April 7, 1928, as James Baumgarner. A producer friend got him a stage job in 1954 after war service in Korea and he was soon working in TV and cinema; his film début was in a small role in the 1956 **Toward the Unknown,** but he became a star through his Western TV series *Maverick* from 1957 to 1961. He had his first starring role in the 1958 **Darby's Rangers,** made a strong impression in **Cash McCall** in 1960 and became a fully-fledged star in 1963 with a series of pictures that included **The Great Escape,** two Doris Day films and **The Wheeler Dealers** with Lee Remick. He was good in thrillers like **36 Hours,** Westerns like **Duel at Diablo** and odes to the racing car like **Grand Prix.** One of his finest performances was as Wyatt Earp in **Hour of the Gun,** John Sturges' fascinating sequel to **Gunfight at the OK Corral.** Sadly, his amiable persona seems to be out of fashion in the cinema of the '70s; he has been doing his best work as the investigator of the TV series *The Rockford Files.*

Below: James Garner as the jocular lawman in **Support Your Local Sheriff,** *here emulating Henry Fonda as Wyatt Earp in Ford's* **My Darling Clementine.**

ANNIE GIRARDOT

Annie Girardot is probably the most popular actress in France today, the star who has come to represent the typical French woman, especially to the French. She certainly features in far more films than her rivals Jeanne Moreau » and Simone Signoret » and her screen persona has emerged more recently—where Signoret is most identified with her '50s roles in **Casque d'or** and **Thérèse Raquin** and Moreau with such '60s films as **Les Amants** and **Jules et Jim**, Girardot is thought of as the tragic middle-aged heroine of such '70s films as **Mourir d'Aimer, La Vieille Fille** and **Docteur Françoise Gailland**. She has the most expressive "everyday" face in French movies, and her combination of vitality, sensuality, vulnerability and humour have helped her to win numerous acting awards. In 1977 she was given the French equivalent of the Oscar, the César, for her performance in **Docteur Françoise Gailland** as a doctor with family and professional problems who finds she has an incurable illness; in 1972 she was justly acclaimed Best Actress at the Berlin Film Festival for her touching portrayal of a shy, middle-aged spinster tentatively coming out of her shell in **Le Vieille Fille**; and in 1965 she was the recipient of the Volpi Cup at the Venice Film Festival for her role as a sentimental, neurotic woman finding life difficult in **Trois Chambres à Manhattan**. Her most extraordinary performance, however, was as a woman covered with hair in Marco Ferreri's **The Ape Woman**, one of the most memorable and sad "outsiders" of the modern cinema.

Girardot was born in Paris in 1931, raised in Normandy during the war and studied acting at the Paris Conservatoire before working at the Comédie Française. She made her film début in the 1956 **L'Homme aux clés d'or** (winning the Suzanne Bianchetti prize) and

was featured in 1960 by Alexandre Astruc in his **La Proie pour l' ombre** as a woman torn between rich husband and poor lover. Luchino Visconti invited her to Italy to appear opposite Renato Salvatori in the 1960 **Rocco and His Brothers**; Salvatori rapes her in the film, but their real-life relationship was such that she married him and joined the Italian film world (they are still married, though separated, and have a daughter Giulia). Girardot appeared in Mario Monicelli's **I Compagni (The Organiser)** and three films for Ferreri, **The Ape Woman, Dillinger Is Dead** (as the maid seduced by Michel Piccoli) and **The Seed of Man** (as a kind of Lilith in a postholocaust Eden). She made two bitter-sweet romantic films for Claude Lelouch, **Vivre pour Vivre** with Yves Montand » and **Un Homme Qui Me Plait** with Jean-Paul Belmondo ». She has been extremely busy in the '70s, appearing in three films for director André Cayatte based on real events: in **Mourir d'Aimer** she portrays a thirty-ish schoolteacher who falls in love with a 17-year-old student and is eventually

*Above: Annie Girardot, one of the leading ladies of the French cinema with films like **Vice and Virtue** and **Vivre Pour Vivre**.*

hounded to death, in **Il n'y a pas de fumée sans feu** she is a political candidate's wife and the target of a fake scandal and in **A Chacun son Enfer** she is the mother of a kidnapped child. Other '70s films are **La Mandarine** (a married woman having an affair with an English teenager), **Elle boit pas, elle fume pas, elle drague pas... mais elle cause** (as a gossipy charwoman causing a lot of blackmail activity), **Le Dernier Baiser** (as a female taxi driver who dislikes male passengers) and **Le Point de Mire** (as a photographer involved in an assassination plot).

ELLIOTT GOULD

Elliot Gould's screen persona is one of wry disillusionment, sometimes anxious, more often amused and never cowed by the rules and regulations that "they" have established. He obviously has no faith in the people in charge and prefers to create a direct one-to-one relationship. He made his screen début in 1968 in **The Night they Raided Minsky's** and made a strong impression as Billy Minsky, owner of the burlesque house. In almost all his films he is paired with another iconoclast: thus his persona was first seen in developed form in the hugely successful **M*A*S*H** where, as Trapper John, he teamed up with Hawkeye (Donald Sutherland ») to flout Army regulations and get their jobs as doctors done all the quicker. The pair were re-teamed

in **S*P*Y*S**, to go against the CIA establishment and rules, but far less successfully. In **Busting** Gould was in partnership with Robert Blake as cynical Los Angeles vice-squad cops breaking the rules because they know their superiors are being paid off by the real criminals. In **California Split** Gould joins up with George Segal » to take on the laws of chance, eventually winning a bundle at a casino. In **Harry and Walter Go to New York** he joins forces with James Caan » in a successful attempt to outwit big-time safecracker Michael Caine ». In **Little Murders** he is so disillusioned with society that he has become totally apathetic, but he teams up with Marcia Rudd and eventually becomes a sniper like the one that kills her. His lack of faith in "them" is nicely confirmed in **Capricorn One**, where (as a reporter) he discovers that the first manned space flight to Mars is a hoax, and at the end of the film superbly joins forces with Telly Savalas. Through all these adventures Gould is almost always amusing; even in the big-budget war epic **A Bridge Too Far** he is a wisecracking officer. In **Bob and Carol and Ted and Alice**, the film that first made him known, he is the most amusing of the four, even stopping off to brush his teeth before the climactic orgy.

Gould was born as Elliot Goldstein in Brooklyn, New York, on August 29, 1938. He worked mainly in the theatre in the '60s and appeared with Barbra Streisand » in *I Can Get It For You Wholesale;* he was the leading man, she had a small part and they were both from Brooklyn so they got married, staying together until the late '60s.

Left: Elliott Gould and George Segal have their eyes set on a poker game in Robert Altman's California Split (1974), a rambling, deceptively casual study of the highs and lows of compulsive gambling in Las Vegas.

After the hugely successful **M*A*S*H** he was fifth on the box office popularity list and the film made $37 million. Robert Altman, who directed it, has remained Gould's most sympathetic and expert director and his best performances have been in Altman pictures, including **The Long Goodbye** (as Raymond Chandler's detective Philip Marlowe, but modernised) and **California Split**. Gould also became the first American actor to work with Ingmar Bergman starring opposite Bibi Andersson ➤ in **The Touch**, though it wasn't one of the director's best. His recent films include the multi-prize-winning Canadian picture **The Silent Partner** (his "partner" in this case being bank robber Christopher Plummer, whom he tricks out of his loot) and a boxing-kangaroo movie called **Matilda** with Robert Mitchum ➤.

BEST FILMS:
1969 Bob and Carol and Ted and Alice
Paul Mazursky (Columbia)
1970 M*A*S*H
Robert Altman (20th Century Fox)
1970 The Touch
Ingmar Bergman (ABC)
1971 Little Murders
Alan Arkin (20th Century Fox)
1973 The Long Goodbye
Robert Altman (United Artists)
1973 Busting
Peter Hyams (United Artists)
1974 California Split
Robert Altman (Columbia)
1978 The Silent Partner
Daryl Duke (Carolco)
1978 Capricorn One
Peter Hyams (ITC)
1978 Matilda
Daniel Mann (AIP)

GENE HACKMAN

Gene Hackman has created one of the most interesting screen personae of the '70s as the nail-hard, dedicated professional whose dedication and skill make him seem heroic, but whose confidence in that professionalism often betrays him. He became a major star as the dogged, grim and violent New York narcotics detective Popeye Doyle in the hugely successful thriller **The French Connection** and deservedly won the 1971 Best Actor Academy Award. He was equally skilled as a surveillance expert in **The Conversation**, but here his screen personality crumbled upon learning that he was as vulnerable to his techniques as anyone else. Hackman repeated his tough Popeye role with variations in **French Connection Number 2**, proving that most of his starring screen roles have empha-

sised the complexities and difficulties of being "tough": the private eye in **Night Moves**, the hired assassin convict in **The Domino Principle** and the Foreign Legion major of **March or Die** find that professionalism and toughness create as many problems as they resolve. As the villainous pimp and dope pedlar Mary Ann in **Prime Cut** he is destroyed by his own brutality after outraging gangster Lee Marvin ➤, and as a Polish Parachute Brigade commander in **A Bridge Too Far** he finds that courage and skill are not enough when his troops are decimated in an attack. His tough-minded clergyman leading the escape party in **The Poseidon Adventure** discovers that even positive actions and determination can lead to tragedy. One of the most fascinating variations on Hackman's persona was in the undervalued **Scarecrow**, where his toughness combines with his temper to nullify his determination to open his own car wash business. Hackman's films may sometimes look like simple man-of-action pictures, but they are not.

Born in 1930 in San Bernardino, California, he began his career as

Above: Gene Hackman, a bent narcotics cop blakmailing Kris Kristofferson in Cisco Pike.

a stage actor with the off-Broadway revue *The Premise*, made his name opposite Sandy Dennis in the Broadway production of *Any Wednesday*, and acquired a certain fame in TV work. He made a brilliant film début in 1963 in the role of a small-town husband in Robert Rossen's **Lilith**, slowly established himself as an excellent character actor in films like **Hawaii**, and made his first real impact as Warren Beatty's ➤ brother, Buck Barrow, in **Bonnie and Clyde**. His career took off in films like **Downhill Racer** and **Marooned**, but it was his brilliant performance as the distressed son in **I Never Sang For My Father** which really revealed the greatness of his acting talent (he was nominated for a Best Supporting Actor Oscar for it, as he had also been for **Bonnie and Clyde**).

The French Connection then gave him unexpected and deserved stardom.

BEST FILMS:
1967 Bonnie and Clyde
Arthur Penn (Warner Brothers-Seven Arts)
1969 I Never Sang For My Father
Gilbert Cates (Columbia)
1971 The French Connection
William Friedkin (20th Century Fox)
1972 Prime Cut
Michael Ritchie (Cinema Center)
1972 The Poseidon Adventure
Ronald Neame (20th Century Fox)
1973 Scarecrow
Jerry Schatzberg (Warner Brothers)
1974 The Conversation
Francis Ford Coppola (Paramount)
1975 French Connection Number 2
John Frankenheimer (20th Century Fox)
1975 Night Moves
Arthur Penn (Warner Brothers)
1977 The Domino Principle
Stanley Kramer (ITC)

RICHARD HARRIS

Richard Harris started off the '60s as a working class Irishman in **A Terrible Beauty** and ended the decade as an English aristocrat in **A Man Called Horse**; but his screen persona as a rumbustious rebel hardly changed. He was Marlon Brando's ➤ chief mutineer in **Mutiny on the Bounty**, Rachel Roberts' loud-mouth footballer-on-the-way-up in **This Sporting Life**, Charlton Heston's ➤ confederate Nemesis in **Major Dundee**, a Norwegian Resistance leader at loggerheads with Kirk Douglas ➤ in **The Heroes of**

Above: Richard Harris as the inarticulate rugby-football player in love with widow Rachel Roberts in This Sporting Life.

Telemark and even Britain's top historical rebel in **Cromwell**. Harris's off-screen personality seemed at times to be modelled on his screen persona when he made headlines for brawls and disputes but the working actor was well aware of what he was doing—by the end of the decade Harris had become one of Britain's top male stars and had begun to shift his image from rebel to hero. His biggest box-office success was as King Arthur in the musical **Camelot**, but he was also much admired as a detective infiltrating the Irish rebels headed by Sean Connery ➤ in **The Molly Maguires** and as an English lord teaching the American Indians courage in **A Man Called Horse**.

Harris was born in Limerick, Ireland, on October 1, 1930, studied at the London Academy of Music and Dramatic Art, and made his acting début for Joan Littlewood in her stage production of *The Quare Fellow*. He was an Irishman in his first film, the 1958 **Alive and Kicking**, but it wasn't until the 1960 **The Long and the Short and the Tall** that he really attracted attention. He quickly became a star through films like **The Guns of Navarone** and **This Sporting Life**, and even did a good job in the service of Antonioni and alienation in **The Red Desert**. He made big films like **The Bible** and **Hawaii** and Doris Day comedies like **Caprice** and then turned director himself. The film was called **Bloomfield**, it was made in Israel and it wasn't very good despite its fantasy football elements. He had a big personal success in the TV film of Paul Gallico's **The Snow Goose**—the later film **Echoes of a Summer** had similarities of sentiment—and he also achieved success in the pop music field: he sold over a million copies of his recording of *MacArthur Park* in 1968.

In the '70s his career has not been as strong as it should have been, for he has chosen to star in too many weak adventure films, the best of which are **Juggernaut, The Wild Geese** and **Orca . . . Killer Whale**. The rebel image on screen and off has dissipated but a new Harris persona has not yet been fully achieved, although he was good playing an English king again, Richard the Lion-Hearted in **Robin and Marian** (1976).

BEST FILMS:
1963 This Sporting Life
Lindsay Anderson (Rank)
1964 Il Deserto Rosso (The Red Desert)
Michaelangelo Antonioni (Duemila)
1965 Major Dundee
Sam Peckinpah (Columbia)
1965 The Heroes of Telemark
Anthony Mann (Rank)
1967 Camelot
Joshua Logan (Warner Brothers-Seven Arts)
1969 The Molly Maguires
Martin Ritt (Paramount)
1970 A Man Called Horse
Elliot Silverstein (Cinema Center)
1970 Cromwell
Ken Hughes (Columbia)
1974 Juggernaut
Richard Lester (United Artists)
1977 The Wild Geese
Andrew V. McLaglen (Richmond)

LAURENCE HARVEY

Laurence Harvey was a major star in the late '50s and early '60s, despite a relatively unsympathetic screen personality and carping critical comments on his acting ability. His icy portrayals of ambitious cads with charm was epitomised by his fine performance as Joe Lampton in **Room at the Top**, one of the key British realist films of the '50s—his role of a man willing to use his charm and good looks to get ahead and marry for money and position was so naturalistic that the persona became identified with him off screen. He had, it was said, advanced his career considerably by relationships with established older women, including Hermione Baddeley, Margaret Leighton and Joan Cohn, the widow of the Columbia studio boss. In the end this identification probably harmed his career, which is a shame because at his best he was a fascinating screen actor with a kind of nice nastiness all his own. Two of his best parts were in **The Manchurian Candidate**, in the role of a brain-washed war hero "zombie" primed for assassination

Above: Laurence Harvey was in peak form portraying a phoney revivalist in **WUSA** *(1970), a political thriller directed by Stuart Rosenberg and based on a novel by Robert Stone.*

—a chillingly effective performance—and **The Alamo,** as the stiff and priggish Colonel Travis, the commander of the 187 Texans resisting the Mexican assault; brilliantly unlikeable, unbending and, in the end, oddly heroic.

Harvey was born in Yoniskis, Lithuania, on October 1, 1928, as Larushka Mischa Skikne. His Jewish family emigrated to South Africa when he was six, but he began his acting career in England after a short period of study at RADA. He made his film début in the 1948 **House of Darkness** but did not really attract attention until Renato Castellani starred him opposite Susan Shentall in the 1954 Italian-British **Romeo and Juliet**. His career was promoted by producer James Woolf of Romulus films, who gave him good starring roles in **I Am A Camera** opposite Julie Harris ≫ (the film of the play of the stories which later became **Cabaret**) and **Three Men in a Boat** with Jimmy Edwards, an adaptation of the book by Jerome K. Jerome. Woolf then bought the rights to John Braine's novel *Room at the Top;* Harvey's performance in the film version made him internationally famous and gained him his only Academy Award nomination for Best Actor (co-star Simone Signoret ≫ won the Best Actress award for her performance). Harvey was nearly as good as the ambitious promoter in **Expresso Bongo** and then went to Hollywood to work in **The Alamo** with John Wayne ≫, **Butterfield 8** with Elizabeth Taylor ≫ (she won the Best Actress Oscar as well, so Harvey must have been doing something right despite the critics), **Two Loves** with Shirley MacLaine ≫, **Summer and Smoke** with Geraldine Page, and **Walk on the Wild Side** with Jane Fonda ≫. He was also the star of the goodish British film-of-the-play **The Long and the Short and the Tall**.

Harvey unfortunately appeared in as many bad films as good

ones, and even the best like **The Manchurian Candidate** and **The Running Man** were not popular successes. His luck began to run out in the late '60s after playing a good supporting role to Julie Christie in **Darling** (she was actress No 3 to win the Oscar playing opposite him) and **Life at the Top,** the sequel to **Room at the Top**. Director Anthony Mann died during the shooting of **A Dandy in Aspic,** then Harvey was down the bill in a good performance as a con-man revivalist in **WUSA**. His last pictures were poor ones, culminating in his cannibal horror picture **Welcome to Arrow Beach,** which he himself directed. It was released after his death from cancer on November 25, 1973, at the age of 45. He was married three times, to Margaret Leighton (1957-1961), Joan Cohn (1968-1972) and model Paulene Stone (1972-1973). His supposed lack of popularity at the end of his career is belied by the appearance of three biographies since his death.

BEST FILMS:
1955 I Am A Camera
Henry Cornelius (Romulus)
1956 Three Men in a Boat
Ken Annakin (Romulus)
1958 Room at the Top
Jack Clayton (Remus)
1959 Expresso Bongo
Val Guest (British Lion)
1960 The Alamo
John Wayne (United Artists)
1960 Butterfield 8
Daniel Mann (MGM)
1962 The Manchurian Candidate
John Frankenheimer (United Artists)
1963 The Running Man
Carol Reed (Columbia)
1965 Darling
John Schlesinger (Anglo-Amalgamated)
1965 Life at the Top
Ted Kotcheff (Columbia)

AUDREY HEPBURN

In the '50s and '60s Audrey Hepburn could do no wrong: she was given an Oscar for her first starring role in a film (**Roman Holiday**), adored by audiences and worshipped by critics. She was the chic, fashion-plate princess, the Cinderella of elegance, the impish gamine with the big and very expressive brown eyes. Then in 1967 she grew up and retired from the screen for ten years; when she returned in **Robin and Marian** she was older, still beautiful and still a fine actress, but the gamine was gone. Her future is uncertain, but her past career has already established her as one of the screen's great actresses.

She was born in Brussels on May 4, 1929, as Audrey Hepburn-

Ruston, daughter of the second marriage of Baroness Ella van Heemstra. She was educated in London, studied ballet and worked as a model, made her film début in a bit part in the 1951 **One Wild Oat,** and became famous in the Broadway production of *Gigi* after author Colette selected her as the ideal child-woman for the part. **Roman Holiday,** her first film in a starring part, was exactly suitable for her persona, portraying a princess on the loose for a day in Rome with journalist Gregory Peck ❯; she won the Academy Award and almost every other prize going. Nearly every film she made during the following 14 years was worthwhile, and many were masterpieces of their kind. She was as good in epics like **War and Peace** (playing Natasha to perfection) as she was in musicals (**Funny Face** with Fred Astaire ❯). She became a favourite actress of Billy Wilder, who starred her in **Sabrina** as a chauffeur's daughter romantically involved with William Holden ❯ and Humphrey Bogart ❯, and in **Love in the Afternoon,** in which she fascinated Gary Cooper ❯.

Hepburn was usually loved by much older men in her films, a reflection of her child-woman image. She wasn't a Lolita or a Baby Doll, she had far too much class for that, but her sex appeal seemed to have the same kind of roots. She was a kookie young girl on the lookout for a rich husband in **Breakfast at Tiffany's** (while dallying with George Peppard), and in **Charade** she became involved with Cary Grant ❯ and spy problems in Paris (she was 34 at the time and he was 59, but they still made a nice romantic couple). Hepburn also did very creditable jobs off the usual track, portraying a nun in **The Nun's Story,** a South American jungle child-of-nature in **Green Mansions** and a Red Indian girl in **The Unforgiven.** Her most famous role of the '60s, and in an odd way the most unfortunate, was as Eliza Doolittle in the lavish film version of **My Fair Lady;** Hepburn was good in the role, but most people felt the part should have gone to Julie Andrews ❯, so she was almost thought of as being miscast.

After making the brilliant **Two for the Road** with Stanley Donen (who had directed her so well in **Funny Face** and **Charade** and the exciting thriller **Wait Until Dark,** she retired. She and her husband Mel Ferrer divorced in 1968 and she married psychiatrist Andrea Dotti the following year (unlike her movie leading men, he was younger than her). Hepburn had received five Oscar nominations for her films and most of them had been commercially successful. She emerged from retirement in 1976 with **Robin and Marian** and, as

Left: The enchanting and beautiful Audrey Hepburn, a major star of the '50s and '60s but now in semi-retirement.

always, had excellent reviews for her performance as the now-older love of Robin Hood (Sean Connery ❯).

BEST FILMS:
1953 Roman Holiday
William Wyler (Paramount)
1954 Sabrina
Billy Wilder (Paramount)
1956 War and Peace
King Vidor (Paramount)
1957 Funny Face
Stanley Donen (Paramount)
1957 Love in the Afternoon
Billy Wilder (Allied Artists)
1959 The Nun's Story
Fred Zinnemann (Warner Brothers)
1961 Breakfast at Tiffany's
Blake Edwards (Paramount)
1963 Charade
Stanley Donen (Universal)
1964 My Fair Lady
George Cukor (Warner Brothers)
1967 Two for the Road
Stanley Donen (20th Century Fox)
1976 Robin and Marian
Richard Lester (Columbia)

DUSTIN HOFFMAN

Dustin Hoffman became a major star literally overnight in 1968 as the confused hero of **The Graduate.** The film made $50 million, Hoffman shot into the top ten box office stars and won an Oscar nomination, and cinema-goers young and old seemed to be willing to accept him as the symbolic representative of the new generation. He was baffled, bewildered and uncertain, repelled by the standards of success and morality established by the older generation and unsure what he wanted in its place. He was also a very fine actor who felt he was completely different from the character he played in the film and tried to show it by portraying a crippled tubercular con-man in his next film, **Midnight Cowboy.** He was just as good in this role and just as popular, but even more surprisingly the Hoffman personality came through in this "character role" as much as it had in **The Graduate;** Hoffman, despite his background in theatre, had screen charisma and a projectable personality that would remain evident in every role he played, good or bad. Aside from the way he looks, acts, talks and moves, the ineluctable components of the screen personality, he has also created a somewhat ambiguous screen persona; a man confused and baffled by a situation but trying desperately hard to find answers and willing in the last resort to use force if necessary to resolve it. His amiable uncertainty is deceptive because he is not usually what he appears to be on the surface in his films. In **The Graduate** he deceives first Mr Robinson, and then Mrs Robinson. In **Midnight Cowboy** he is a con-man, in **John and Mary** he tries to deceive Mia Farrow ❯ after their

night together so he won't get involved and in **Straw Dogs** he is not after all a weak person who can be continually pushed around. In **Little Big Man** he is possibly a fraud but a very good storyteller about his involvement with General Custer, and in **Papillon** he is a convicted forger who in the end does not really want to escape from Devil's Island. His persona of the baffled searcher for truth is very much to the forefront as the eager investigative reporter Carl Bernstein in **All the President's Men,** as the clear-sighted prober of social ills through comic insight Lenny Bruce in **Lenny** and even as the young man trying to find out what the hell is going on in **Marathon Man** (where his bland helplessness again proves deceptive when he becomes an avenging killer).

Hoffman was born in Los Angeles on August 8, 1937, and was named by his Hollywood-obsessed mother after silent film star Dustin Farnum. Hoffman's off-beat comic style seems to have emerged while he was still at school (he would pass the word around class for everyone to

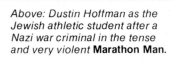
*Above: Dustin Hoffman as the Jewish athletic student after a Nazi war criminal in the tense and very violent **Marathon Man.***

cough at exactly 2:05 and eventually the teachers blamed every cough on him) but he originally intended to be a concert pianist. He began acting at the Pasadena Community Playhouse and then went to New York, sharing a flat with Gene Hackman ❯ and Robert Duvall ❯ and making his Broadway début in *A Cook for Mr General.* His first film part was a tiny role in the 1967 **The Tiger Makes Out** from Murray Schisgal's play and he then starred in a poor Italian film **Madigan's Millions (Un Dollaro per Sette Vigliacchi)** as an Internal Revenue agent in Rome. He was essentially an unknown when Mike Nichols picked him to play opposite Anne Bancroft ❯ and Katharine Ross ❯ in **The Graduate,** and he shot to major star status. He is a very craftsmanlike actor, building up his role in tiny details, as shown by the portrayal of Ratso in **Midnight Cowboy.** He was worried about his "real" personality being too boring for the straightforward young-lover role in **John and Mary** but his hesitations and uncertainties were excellent, even if the film wasn't. After **Little Big Man** and **Straw Dogs**, he made a kind of sub-**Graduate** film in Italy with Pietro Germi, **Alfredo, Alfredo,** playing an insecure man involved with the wrong woman and trying to get involved with the right one. Hoffman's two least successful films have been made with his old theatre friend and director Ulu Grosbard, who directed him in the 1971 **Who is Harry Kellerman and Why Is He Saying Those Terrible Things About Me?** (as a pop song writer) and the 1978 **Straight Time** (as a paroled criminal). Hoffman was in the top ten box office popularity list from 1969 to 1972 but dropped out because of weaker films and did not return until 1976 after the success of **Lenny, All the President's Men** and **Marathon Man.** His latest 1979 film was Robert Benton's **Kramer vs Kramer.**

BEST FILMS:
1968 The Graduate
Mike Nichols (Embassy/United Artists)
1969 Midnight Cowboy
John Schlesinger (United Artists)
1969 John and Mary
Peter Yates (20th Century Fox)
1970 Little Big Man
Arthur Penn (Cinema Center/Warner Brothers)
1971 Straw Dogs
Sam Peckinpah (Talent Associates)
1971 Alfredo, Alfredo
Pietro Germi (Rizzoli)
1973 Papillon
Franklin Schaffner (Allied Artists)
1975 Lenny
Bob Fosse (United Artists)
1976 All the President's Men
Alan J. Pakula (Warner Brothers)
1976 Marathon Man
John Schlesinger (Paramount)

GLENDA JACKSON

Glenda Jackson became one of the most sought-after female stars in the world after winning two Academy Awards for Best Actress, a third Oscar nomination and other notable acting prizes in the short period of three years. She was refreshingly different, good to look at though not beautiful in the ordinary sense, equipped with a razor-sharp intelligence, a strong personality, the ability to articulate her feelings, a dry, witty, clipped manner of speaking—and a powerful sex drive. She was also a fine actress, as she showed in superb performances as "free woman" Gudrun Brangwen in **Women in Love** (an Oscar and the New York Critics Award), as the nymphomaniac wife of gay Tchaikovsky in **The Music Lovers,** as the woman forced to share an AC-DC lover with a homosexual in **Sunday,**

Bloody Sunday (British Film Academy Best Actress Award) and as a divorced career woman enjoying sex with a married man in **A Touch of Class** (another Oscar). By 1973 it looked as if her screen personality, the strongest since the heyday of Bette Davis ❯ and Joan Crawford ❯, would sweep her easily to superstardom. Instead her directors rather overstressed that personality in a series of sometimes theatrical and often only semi-successful films that diminished her reputation. Not that she wasn't very good indeed, and working as intensely as ever—but audiences grew used to her style, which could sometimes seem mannered and rather theatrical. Many of her recent films have, in fact, had a direct stage connection, including the excellent biography **Stevie** (based on a play about poet Stevie Smith), **Hedda** (based on the Ibsen play *Hedda Gabler*),

Bequest to the Nation (based on the play about Nelson by Terence Rattigan), **The Incredible Sarah** (the story of stage actress Sarah Bernhardt) and **The Maids** (based on the Genet play).

Jackson was born in Birkenhead, Cheshire, in 1937, studied at RADA and learned her craft in repertory in Worthing and Crewe. She joined the Royal Shakespeare Company in 1964 and was featured as Charlotte Corday in *The Marat-Sade* play and the film made of it in 1966, both directed by Peter Brook. She also appeared in his film-play **Tell Me Lies** and then made her first real film, the appropriately titled **Negatives,** directed by Peter Medak. Her next was for Ken Russell, Larry Kramer's

excellent adaptation **Women in Love,** and her sexy, free-thinking woman persona was born in this film. It made her world famous, and perhaps her next for Russell, **The Music Lovers,** made her world infamous. The film was a bizarre musical homage but Jackson was good even rolling around in the nude in garish lighting on a night train with a homosexual husband. She was better, however, in **Sunday, Bloody Sunday,** directed by John Schlesinger, a finely nuanced performance as a woman fighting to keep the young man she loves (Murray Head), even though she has to share him with a man. Her performance was beautifully balanced by that of Peter Finch's as the boy's other lover in one of the best British films of the '70s. Jackson was an obvious candidate to play the strong-minded Queen Elizabeth and did so both on film in **Mary**

*Above: Glenda Jackson as the woman whose lover is also gay in the award-winning 1971 **Sunday, Bloody Sunday.***

Queen of Scots and in a very popular TV series, *Elizabeth R.* She did a small bit in **The Boy Friend** for Russell and then joined George Segal ❯ for the hugely popular bittersweet comedy **A Touch of Class,** showing that adultery can be fun and witty when two excellent actors engage in it.

Jackson's films were rarely as interesting and popular after that. She joined Oliver Reed ❯ once more in the sex-change melodrama **Triple Echo,** was back with Peter Finch playing Lady

Hamilton to his Nelson in **Bequest to the Nation** and teamed in **The Maids.** She was at her best again as an adulterous wife (although we're never really sure if she is or not) with an imaginative writer husband (Michael Caine ❯) in Joseph Losey's **The Romantic Englishwoman.** She has been exceptionally busy recently and released three films in 1978: the excellent **Stevie** with Trevor Howard ❯, the hospital-orientated comedy **House Calls** with Walter Matthau ❯ (as a woman looking for a man who can be faithful) and **The Class of Miss MacMichael** with Oliver Reed (as a dedicated schoolteacher).

BEST FILMS:
1969 Women in Love
Ken Russell (United Artists)
1970 The Music Lovers
Ken Russell (United Artists)
1971 Sunday, Bloody Sunday
John Schlesinger (United Artists)
1972 A Touch of Class
Melvin Frank (Avco-Embassy)
1972 Triple Echo
Michael Apted (Hemdale)
1973 Bequest to the Nation
James Cellan Jones (Universal)
1975 The Romantic Englishwoman
Joseph Losey (Dial)
1976 The Incredible Sarah
Richard Fleischer (Readers Digest)
1978 House Calls
Howard Zieff (Universal)
1978 Stevie
Bob Jones (First Artists)

ERLAND JOSEPHSON
see Ingmar Bergman Stars

ANNA KARINA

Anna Karina was the key star of the French *nouvelle vague* in the '60s, the centrepiece of directorhusband Jean-Luc Godard's major films. Many of the seven feature films he made with her can be considered as documentaries about their relationship (they were married from 1961 to 1967). As he was at this time probably the most influential director in the world and in his period of greatest achievement, her stardom was primarily of his making (or their collaboration) and has not survived their break-up. On the other hand, his films since she stopped being his star actress have been lesser achievements.

Karina looked and sounded different from the other *nouvelle vague* stars because she was Danish rather than French. She was born in Copenhagen in 1940 as Hanne Karin Blarke Bayer. She left school at 16, studied painting for a while, worked as a photographic model and made her film début in a 1957 Danish short **Pigin Och Skoene.** She went to

Paris in 1958, was employed by fashion magazines and Pierre Cardin and then appeared in advertising films where Godard spotted her. She turned down the role played by Jean Seberg in **Breathless** but then made her feature début for Godard in the 1960 **Le Petit Soldat**; although the central character is a French Army deserter working for the OAS, the film includes a photographic session to display Karina's beauty. The next film, **Une Femme est une Femme,** is almost a pure "documentary" study of Karina's looks, feelings, reactions and movements—in short, her whole personality—as projected through a slight story about a stripper eager to have a baby and getting co-operation from two men. **Vivre sa Vie** stars her as a girl who drifts casually into prostitution, and can be read as a portrait of Karina and her approaches to various aspects of life in Paris in 1962. **Bande à Part** has slightly more story line in a detached, dreamy way, with Karina portraying a student involved in a plot to rob an old lady. **Alphaville** has the strongest narrative of any Godard film with Karina guiding secret agent Lemmy Caution (Eddie Constantine) through a futuristic city where his assignment is to kill her

lead in Jacques Rivette's **La Religieuse,** and also starred in big international films including Luchino Visconti's **The Stranger,** Guy Green's **The Magus,** George Cukor's **Justine** and Tony Richardson's **Laughter in the Dark.** She was fine, but the strange Karina-Godard personality was no longer there. It has reappeared in shadowy form only twice since, as the mysterious woman who boards and beds Mathieu Carrière in André Delvaux's enigmatic **Rendez-vous à Bray** and in Karina's own attempt to direct herself, **Vivre Ensemble.**

BEST FILMS:
1960 Le Petit Soldat
Jean-Luc Godard (SNC/de Beauregard)
1961 Une Femme est une Femme
Jean-Luc Godard (Rome-Paris Films)
1962 Vivre sa Vie
Jean-Luc Godard (Films de la Pléiade)
1964 Bande à Part
Jean-Luc Godard (Anouchka Films)
1965 Alphaville
Jean-Luc Godard (Chaumiane/ Filmstudio)
1965 Pierrot le Fou
Jean-Luc Godard (Rome-Paris Films)
1965 La Religieuse
Jacques Rivette (Rome-Paris Films)
1966 Made in USA
Jean-Luc Godard (Rome-Paris/ Anouchka Films)
1971 Rendez-vous à Bray
André Delvaux (Parc Film/Cinevog)
1973 Vivre Ensemble
Anna Karina

DIANE KEATON

Diane Keaton and the kooky girl she won an Academy Award for portraying in **Annie Hall** are not the same, but the similarities are close enough to be revealing. Her screen persona appears to be the joint creation of Keaton and her writer-director-mentor Woody Allen ❯, who has featured her in six films and a stage play and been the impetus to her stardom. Apart from Allen she has had some success, most notably in **Looking for Mr Goodbar** and the two **Godfather** films, but she is a star because of Allen's films and seems likely to remain closely associated with his work in the future.

Like Annie, Keaton's real name is Hall. She was born in Los Angeles on January 5, 1946, grew up in Santa Anna, California, and began her acting career in summer stock in upstate New York. She made her Broadway début in 1968 in the musical *Hair,* and her association with Allen began in 1969 when she co-starred with him in the Broadway production of *Play It Again, Sam.* She made her cinema début the same year in the relatively small role of a would-be divorcée in **Lovers and Other Strangers,** but did not make another film appearance until 1972 when she starred in the film version of **Play It**

Again, Sam as the best friend's wife that Allen gives up just like Bogart ❯ in **Casablanca.** In the same year she played the WASP wife of Al Pacino ❯ in **The Godfather,** repeating the part with more prominence in **The Godfather Part II,** where she has an abortion and leaves Pacino to keep the Corleone dynasty from continuing. The kooky, quirky, nervous, incoherent and fascinating Keaton screen persona was further developed in **Sleeper** (set in the future) and **Love and Death** (set in nineteenth-century Russia) and proved itself the perfect foil and balance for Allen's own persona.

Two efforts to make films away from Allen, **Harry and Walter Go to New York** and **I Will, I Will . . . For Now,** both with Elliott Gould ❯ proved unsuccessful. The pair were then reunited in their finest

collaboration, **Annie Hall.** The seemingly biographical nature of this love story comes as much from its tone and emotional rightness as in its factual detail; even the distancing necessary to portray a relationship is satirised within the film. Keaton portrays a WASP from the West who becomes involved with a famous New York Jewish comedian who tries to educate her as well as love her. Like Keaton her hobby is photography and her ambition is to be a singer, and like Keaton and Allen the couple eventually break up and stay friends. In the film the Allen character writes a play about their relationship, putting himself in the best light, a kind of mocking warning about inter-

preting the film too autobiographically.

Keaton was more successful in her next film away from Allen, the movie version of the best-selling novel **Looking for Mr Goodbar,** portraying a sexually confused girl with some of the kookiness and most of the insecurities of Keaton's established screen persona. In 1978 Keaton starred in Allen's first "serious" film, **Interiors,** with Bergman-esque attitudes and Allen directing but not acting. The pair were reunited on screen early in 1979 in the Allen-directed **Manhattan.**

Below: Diane Keaton trying to take seriously Woody Allen's attempts to behave like Humphrey Bogart. The film was Play It Again Sam which, with The Godfather, launched her increasingly successful career.

BEST FILMS:
1969 Lovers and Other Strangers
Cy Howard (ABC Pictures)
1972 Play It Again, Sam
Herbert Ross (Paramount)
1972 The Godfather
Francis Ford Coppola (Paramount)
1973 Sleeper
Woody Allen (United Artists)
1974 The Godfather Part II
Francis Ford Coppola (Paramount)
1975 Love and Death
Woody Allen (United Artists)
1976 I Will, I Will . . . For Now
Norman Panama (Brut)
1977 Annie Hall
Woody Allen (United Artists)
1977 Looking for Mr Goodbar
Richard Brooks (Paramount)
1978 Interiors
Woody Allen (United Artists)

Above: Anna Karina, a key star of '60s French cinema.

father. **Pierrot le Fou** is the most complex of the Karina-Godard films with the Karina screen persona/personality at its fullest development, Godard at the peak of his cinematic form and their relationship (ie, its imminent break-up) the actual subject of the film. She worked twice more for Godard but not in such an open, personal way, first in **Made in USA** where she is investigating the death of her former lover and then in the episode titled **In The Year 2000** from **Le Plus Vieux Metier du Monde.** Karina played other interesting roles in French films in the '60s, including the

KRIS KRISTOFFERSON

Kristofferson, the only rock star who has succeeded in becoming an important film actor in a way that even Presley didn't, displays a renegade image in both his careers; whether he plays a truck driver (**Convoy**) or a footballer (**Semi-Tough**) or a pop star (**A Star Is Born**), he is essentially as outlaw as he is in **Pat Garrett and Billy the Kid**, playing the Kid, and until his recent reform his reputation in the music field was as a rowdy hard-drinker.

He began his film career in 1971 as an outlaw pop star (**Cisco Pike**), was a singer again in **Blume in Love** and found time for a song in **Alice Doesn't Live Here Anymore**. He has been villainous in two films (a nasty motorcyclist/rapist in **Bring Me the Head of Alfredo Garcia** and a vicious Vietnam veteran in **Vigilante Force**), although his screen persona is usually working-class heroic with quiet but rugged charm. His background, however, is upper middle class—he is the son of a retired Air Force general, born in Brownsville, Texas, on June 22, 1936, and brought up in California. After graduating from Pomona College, he studied at Oxford as a Rhodes Scholar and then spent five years in the Army, mostly flying helicopters in Germany. He left the Army in 1965 and went to Nashville where he worked as a recording studio janitor, among other things, before his songs began to be recorded by people like Roger Miller, Johnny Cash and Janis Joplin. He made his record début in 1970 and his film début in 1971, portraying a pop singer in **Cisco Pike**. *Me and Bobby McGee* became an international hit for Janis Joplin and the song was also featured in Dennis Hopper's film **The Last Movie**, in which Kristofferson had a cameo role. Another hit song, *Help Me Make It Through the Night,* was featured in John Huston's **Fat City**. Sam Peckinpah choose Kristofferson to star as Billy opposite James Coburn in the excellent 1973 **Pat Garrett and Billy the Kid**, and his film career took off from that part. Also in the film was singer Rita Coolidge, whom he married that same year. Kristofferson was especially good as the love interest at the end of the road for Ellen Burstyn ❯ in **Alice Doesn't Live Here Anymore**, but says he was very dissatisfied with the violence in his next film, **Vigilante Force**. The following year, nude photographs of Kristofferson and co-star Sarah Miles in lovemaking scenes from **The Sailor Who Fell From Grace With the Sea** were featured in *Playboy* and gained him a certain notoriety, then his selection by Barbra Streisand ❯ to play opposite her in **A Star Is**

Above: Kris Kristofferson as 'Rubber Duck', the truck driver in Sam Peckinpah's **Convoy** *who becomes a national celebrity after a bar-room brawl.*

Born finally made him a major star. He was excellent as a pop star in decline, re-creating a role played in earlier versions of the film by Fredric March ❯ and James Mason ❯, and if the heavy drinking required by the role seemed natural, he himself recognised it. He quit drinking after seeing himself in the film and began touring again with his wife, whose popularity was now equal to his.

Kristofferson's performances in **Semi-Tough** and **Convoy** showed the growing strength of his screen personality but as he is now beardless and abstemious, it remains to be seen whether the image will change.

BEST FILMS:
1971 Cisco Pike
Bill L. Norton (Columbia)
1973 Pat Garrett and Billy the Kid
Sam Peckinpah (MGM)
1973 Blume in Love
Paul Mazursky (Warner Brothers)
1974 Bring Me the Head of Alfredo Garcia
Sam Peckinpah (United Artists)
1975 Alice Doesn't Live Here Anymore
Martin Scorsese (Warner Brothers)
1975 Vigilante Force
George Armitage (United Artists)
1976 The Sailor Who Fell From Grace With the Sea
Lewis John Carlino (Avco Embassy)
1976 A Star Is Born
Frank Pierson (First Artists/Warner Brothers)
1977 Semi-Tough
Michael Ritchie (United Artists)
1978 Convoy
Sam Peckinpah (EMI/United Artists)

JEAN-PIERRE LÉAUD

Jean-Pierre Léaud is one of the key stars of the modern French cinema, the disconcerting wide-eyed alter ego of François Truffaut, Jean-Luc Godard, Jean Eustache and other major directors in a number of films. He is probably best known to the wide international public as the obsessive filmmaker of **Last Tango in Paris** and the selfish film star of **Day For Night,** but his persona and personality are really products of the French *nouvelle vague* of the '60s. He usually portrays obsessive failures, young men who desperately want something, don't quite know how to go about getting it and finally fail because they have no true directions. The Léaud personality combines shyness and insecurity with brashness

and egotism, alert intelligence and verbal wit with emotional imbalance and furtive naïvety—and usually an overwhelming passion for the cinema. This persona/personality is most associated with Truffaut films, but is evident in almost every film Léaud has made.

He was born in Paris in 1944, the son of an actress and an assistant film director. He became a star at the age of 14 in 1959 in Truffaut's **The 400 Blows**, a role he secured through answering an advertisement in *France-Soir*. He portrayed an unloved juvenile delinquent with a passion for the cinema who finally runs away from his remand home. The final freeze-frame of Léaud staring at the ocean (and the audience) became the most famous image of the New Wave. The character he portrayed, Antoine Doinel, has been featured by Truffaut in four further films, but the character is now based as much on Léaud as it is on Truffaut. In these films Doinel has an unsuccessful love affair with Marie-France Pisier (**Love at Twenty**), works as a private detective and courts Claude Jade (**Stolen Kisses**), marries her and then breaks up with her (**Bed and Board**) and finally re-establishes a relationship with old love Marie-France Pisier (**Love on the Run**). Truffaut also featured Léaud as the vain and egotistic actor who seduces Jacqueline Bisset ❯ in **Day For Night** (and tells her husband) and as the writer who loves and is loved by both sisters in **Anne and Muriel** (and who ends up with neither).

The other director with whom he has most often worked is Jean-Luc Godard, who starred him in **Masculin-Féminin** as a revolutionary without a mission who falls to his death after moving in with the girl he loves. He was also featured in smaller roles in **Made in USA, Le Plus Vieux Metier du Monde, La Chinoise, Weekend** and **Le Gai Savoir**. His ability to become the alter ego of directors other than Truffaut was notable in Jean Eustache's autobiographical **The Mother and the Whore** (Eustache had earlier featured him in **Le Père a les Yeux Bleus**) where his obsessions are women and philosophy, Jerzy Skolimowski's **Le Départ** (where he struggles desperately to get a car to compete in a rally and then oversleeps and misses the start) and even Jacques Rivette's **Out One: Spectre** (where he is as obsessed with the film's puzzles as the director himself).

BEST FILMS:
1959 Les 400 Coups (The 400 Blows)
François Truffaut (Les Films du Carrosse)
1966 Masculin-Féminin
Jean-Luc Godard (Anouchka/Argos)

Left: Jean-Pierre Léaud gets to grips with his life as Antoine Doinel in the third of François Truffaut's largely autobiographical series, **Baisers Volés**.

BRUCE LEE

Bruce Lee was one of the major movie phenomena of the '70s, the first Chinese superstar and a major factor in the growth of interest in martial arts and Hong Kong movies. Lee came at just the right time to attract world attention following US President Richard Nixon's visit to China, the growing influence of Mao and the spreading Kung Fu vogue, but there is no doubt that he had the screen charisma of a major star. Like James Dean », his impact was felt on the screen instantly and like Dean he died tragically almost as soon as he became a star. His first starring film was released in 1971, he completed three more and then died mysteriously at the age of 32 in seemingly perfect health when a blood vessel burst in his brain. An enormous cult like Dean's sprang up immediately and has continued to the present time.

Lee was born in San Francisco on November 27, 1940, to a touring Hong Kong vaudeville family. He was named Lee Yeun Kam by his mother but a hospital nurse gave him the more American name of Bruce Lee. Back in Hong Kong he made his film début at the age of six in **The Beginning of a Boy.** He appeared in twenty films as a child and a teenager and studied martial arts from the age of 13. He became a hot-headed street fighter nicknamed The Little Dragon and began to perfect his own form of karate, Jeet Kune Do, a professional attacking style based on street fighting techniques. In 1958 he returned to the US and found out about anti-Chinese prejudice. He started his own martial arts school and was eventually picked to play Kato in *The Green Hornet* television series in 1966 and 1967. He was featured in four episodes of TV's *Longstreet* and made his American film début in **Marlowe,** smashing up James Garner's »

office with flying fists and feet. By this time he was famous in Hong Kong film circles for his earlier movies like **The Long and Winding Road** and his TV work. He was then signed to star in two films for $10,000 each by Raymond Chow of Golden Harvest films; the first was the 1971 **The Big Boss** (released in the US as **Fists of Fury**); it established the Lee screen persona as the No 1 Kung Fu star and was a huge commercial success. The follow-up, **Fist of Fury** (released in the US as **The Chinese Connection**) was even more popular. It made Lee into a hero for downtrodden Chinese, as its plot revolves around anti-Chinese prejudice on the part of the Japanese. He directed his third film himself, **The Way of the Dragon,** and it became his most successful film ever, earning $25 million in America alone. Shot in Europe, it features Lee as a country boy in Rome hired by a Chinese restaurateur to help him deal with the local syndicate. His last completed film was the Warner Brothers-backed **Enter the Dragon** with an all-star cast of karate champions and Lee as a Government agent tracking down

Above: Bruce Lee displays the physique which literally cata-pulted him to kung-fu stardom which was all too brief.

and destroying a master criminal and his men.

Lee was working on a new film, **Game of Death,** when he died. The few minutes of film in which he appeared were later incorporated into a feature (using a double for the new material) and released in 1978 as **Bruce Lee's Game of Death.** A documentary about Lee's life and death and was produced in 1974, **Bruce Lee: The Man and the Legend,** as well as a fiction film called **The Bruce Lee Story.** Many books have been written about him, including one by his wife Linda, but the best is probably Alex Ben Block's *The Legend of Bruce Lee.*

BEST FILMS:
1967 The Green Hornet
(TV series compilation)
Norman Foster (20th Century Fox)
1969 Marlowe
Paul Bogart (MGM)

1970 The Way of the Intercepting Fist
(from TV series **Longstreet**)
1971 The Big Boss (US title: Fists of Fury)
Lo Wei (Golden Harvest)
1972 Fist of Fury (US: The Chinese Connection)
Lo Wei (Golden Harvest)
1972 The Way of the Dragon
Bruce Lee (Concord)
1973 Enter the Dragon
Robert Clouse (Concord/Warner Brothers)
1974 Bruce Lee: The Man and the Legend
(compilation biography) (Concord)
1974 The Bruce Lee Story
Shih ti (Pacific Group)
1978 Bruce Lee's Game of Death
Robert Clouse (Golden Harvest)

CHRISTOPHER LEE

Christopher Lee is considered the king of the British horror film; he has portrayed most of the great horror characters for Hammer

Above: Christopher Lee in one of his many incarnations as **Dracula,** *a role for which his tall, satanic presence is tailor made.*

including Dracula, Frankenstein's Monster, the Mummy, Fu Manchu and Rasputin. His greatest creation is Dracula, a part he has taken in ten films and imbued with such sinister brilliance that he is considered the screen's finest-ever personification of the Bram Stoker vampire. He no longer likes to be thought of as solely a horror film star and has succeeded in getting good roles in non-horror films, but his greatest work remains in the genre. He is usually the villain or the monster and is horrifically good at it, already larger than life at six-foot-four. Recent non-horror films star him in villainous roles, including the evil Rochefort in **The Three Musketeers** and James Bond's opponent Scaramanga in **The Man with the Golden Gun,** and even in non-villainous roles he is somewhat sinister as, for example, in **The Devil Rides Out,** in which he stars as the Duc fighting the Satanists, or in **The Private Life of Sherlock Holmes** in which he portrays Sherlock's brother Mycroft.

Lee was born in London on May 27, 1922, as Christopher Frank Caradini Lee, the son of an Army officer. He served in the RAF from 1940 to 1946, signed a contract with Rank the following year and made his film début in a small part in **Corridor of Mirrors**. He continued in relatively minor roles until 1957, when he starred as the Monster in Hammer's **The Curse of Frankenstein** opposite Peter Cushing ➤ as the Baron, beginning one of the great partnerships of the horror cinema. That role led to his becoming **Dracula** in 1958, again opposite Cushing, and his rapid rise to pre-eminence in the British horror film. He seemed worried about being too closely identified with certain roles and didn't play Dracula again for Hammer until 1965, though he played almost every other villain. He has also starred in first-class horror films for other companies, notably **The Skull** for Amicus and **The Wicker Man** for British Lion, but he has never surpassed his performance as Dracula.

BEST FILMS:
1957 The Curse of Frankenstein
Terence Fisher (Hammer)
1958 Dracula (Horror of Dracula)
Terence Fisher (Hammer)
1959 The Mummy
Terence Fisher (Hammer)
1965 The Face of Fu Manchu
Don Sharp (Hallam)
1965 The Skull
Freddie Francis (Amicus)
1965 Rasputin, the Mad Monk
Don Sharp (Hammer)
1965 Dracula, Prince of Darkness
Terence Fisher (Hammer)
1967 The Devil Rides Out
Terence Fisher (Hammer)
1970 The Private Life of Sherlock Holmes
Billy Wilder (United Artists)
1973 The Wicker Man
Robin Hardy (British Lion)
1973 The Three Musketeers
Richard Lester (20th Century Fox)

JACK LEMMON

Jack Lemmon is probably the best light comedian working in the cinema today, but his screen persona as an honest neurotic, the representative man of our time, is beginning to become restrictive and mannered. He has been the favourite actor of satire master Billy Wilder, who has featured him in six films (**Some Like It Hot, The Apartment, Irma la Douce, The Fortune Cookie, Avanti!** and **The Front Page**). He is the ideal Wilder protagonist, essentially good-hearted and resilient but easily distressed and pained by the ways of the world. In **The Apartment** the persona is seen at its best, gradually turning

against his business superiors as he realises the effects of lending his apartment for love trysts. The Lemmon screen personality usually starts out nice but disintegrates under pressure; he finally becomes the mugger he is afraid of in **The Prisoner of Second Avenue**. He becomes worried and neurotic, not because of other people but because of modern society: he is destroyed by the conspiracy known as New York City in **The Out-of-Towners**. He is not exactly faultless himself; a lecher in **Mister Roberts**, an alcoholic in **Days of Wine and Roses**, a chauvinist would-be murderer in **How To Murder Your Wife**, and bankrupt in his Oscar-winning **Save the Tiger**. He goes along with a shyster lawyer's plan to swindle an insurance company in **The Fortune Cookie** and he becomes an annoyingly fastidious "housewife" in **The Odd Couple**. He presumably sees himself as the representative "little man" of the modern cinema, the heir of Chaplin's screen hero, but Lemmon's middle-class persona is far less universal.

He was born in Boston, Massachusetts, on February 8, 1925, as John Uhler Lemmon III, was educated at Harvard, worked for

Above: Jack Lemmon, as ace reporter Hildy Johnson, in Billy Wilder's 1974 version of Hecht and MacArthur's **The Front Page.**

more than six years in theatre and TV, and made his film début (magnificently) opposite Judy Holliday ➤ in the 1954 **It Should Happen To You**. His screen persona was probably based on his characterisation in this film, but he continued to develop it in **Mister Roberts** (for which he won a Best Supporting Actor Oscar) and especially **Some Like It Hot**, the film that began his long association with Wilder. His popularity as a movie star probably reached its peak in the late '60s, but his career in the '70s has been equally notable. He has become a favoured interpreter of Neil Simon's New York comedies (including **The Odd Couple, The Out-of-Towners** and **The Prisoner**

of Second Avenue), and formed a brilliant partnership with Walter Matthau in **The Front Page, The Fortune Cookie** and **The Odd Couple**. His recent films include **Alex and the Gypsy** with Genevieve Bujold, and **Airport 77**.

BEST FILMS:
1954 It Should Happen To You
George Cukor (Columbia)
1955 Mister Roberts
Mervyn Le Roy & John Ford (Warner Brothers)
1959 Some Like It Hot
Billy Wilder (United Artists)
1960 The Apartment
Billy Wilder (United Artists)
1962 Days of Wine and Roses
Blake Edwards (Warner Brothers)
1963 Irma la Douce
Billy Wilder (United Artists)
1966 The Fortune Cookie
Billy Wilder (United Artists)
1968 The Odd Couple
Gene Saks (Paramount)
1970 The Out-of-Towners
Arthur Hiller (Paramount)
1972 Save the Tiger
John G. Avildsen (Paramount)
1972 Avanti!
Billy Wilder (United Artists)
1974 The Front Page
Billy Wilder (Universal-International)
1975 The Prisoner of Second Avenue
Melvin Frank (Warner Brothers)

JERRY LEWIS

Jerry Lewis may or may not be one of the all-time great clowns of the cinema—it's probably too early to judge—but he was certainly very funny when he was at the peak of his zany, inventive form. He was goofy, mad, idiotic and demented, whether teamed with Dean Martin ➤ in his early films, or solo in his later ones, which he often wrote and directed. He was the ultimate boob (Martin always treated him in their films as an utter jerk) who could find a wrong way to do anything if he tried. His persona obviously struck responsive chords in the American public, because both with Martin and without he was a top ten box-office star throughout the '50s and into the early '60s. The Martin and Lewis films were less inventive and less interesting cinematically than Lewis's solo pictures, but they were no less funny for that; they made audiences laugh despite intellectual reservations and people literally rolled in the aisles when they were released. The cult of Lewis as an *auteur,* founded in France and cautiously taken up in the English-speaking world, insists that Lewis is a genius worthy of comparison to Robert Bresson. No such mocking evaluation is necessary: Lewis is good as he is.

He was born as Joseph Levitch in Newark, New Jersey, on March 16, 1926, to a show business family, began entertaining while still in his teens, and first teamed with Martin in a night club act in Atlantic City in 1946. They soon became immensely popular in

cabaret and were brought to Hollywood by Hal Wallis, who featured them in supporting roles in the 1949 **My Friend Irma**. They were an immediate hit and were first starred in the 1950 **At War with the Army**. In the many films that followed, Martin always sang and chased women while Lewis was a dumb slob and victim who somehow won through in the end (the smoothie and the rough, as compared to the fat and the thin of Abbott and Costello). The best of the duo's films were **Sailor Beware, Living It Up**, and the two at the end of their partnership directed by Frank Tashlin, **Artists and Models** and **Hollywood or Bust**. After they split up (no reason given, but probably just the strain of working together continually for ten years), Lewis made the successful **The Delicate Delinquent** and had a further ten years as a highly popular solo artist. Tashlin and Lewis directed the best of the solo films, which were sometimes bizarre (**The Nutty Professor**) but always entertaining, and even included self-satire (**The Bellboy**). Lewis's popularity began to diminish in the late '60s and he has made no films since the 1970 **Which Way to the Front?**

Above: Jerry Lewis demonstrates to TV viewers his Jekyll and Hyde transformation in the 1963 **The Nutty Professor.**

BEST FILMS:
1954 Living It Up
Norman Taurog (Paramount)
1955 Artists and Models
Frank Tashlin (Paramount)
1956 Hollywood or Bust
Frank Tashlin (Paramount)
1960 The Bellboy
Jerry Lewis (Paramount)
1960 Cinderfella
Frank Tashlin (Paramount)
1961 The Ladies' Man
Jerry Lewis (Paramount)
1963 The Nutty Professor
Jerry Lewis (Paramount)
1964 The Patsy
Jerry Lewis (Paramount)
1965 The Disorderly Orderly
Frank Tashlin (Paramount)
1965 The Family Jewels
Jerry Lewis (Paramount)

GUNNEL LINDBLOM
see Ingmar Bergman Stars

SOPHIA LOREN

Sophia Loren has a wonderful screen presence, remarkable physical endowments, statuesque beauty and a leading Italian producer as a husband, so it's no wonder that she became a major Italian movie star. What is surprising is that she became a major international star as well, despite limited acting ability and very few good films. There are two probable reasons: her screen personality is highly likeable—warm, sympathetic, a little mischievous and a little mocking— and she personifies a certain kind of Italian female stereotype which seems to be required by the international public. Loren has worked hard at advancing her career and, with the help of producer/husband Carlo Ponti, has converted her assets into golden achievements. She also improved her looks and screen style considerably as she went along. In 1961 she became the first actress to win an acting Oscar in a foreign-language film when she got the prize for her rather emotive performance in Vittorio De Sica's **Two Women,** and in 1967 she gave her greatest ever screen performance in Francesco Rosi's delightful fairy tale **Once Upon a Time . . .,** portraying a Neapolitan Cinderella, a role that seemed to reflect her own life.

She was born Sofia Scicolone, an illegitimate child, in Rome on September 20, 1934, and was brought up in poverty by her mother in Pozzuoli near Naples. She won second prize in a beauty contest when she was 14 and her mother took her back to Rome to try to break into the movie business. They both got extra parts in May, 1950, in **Quo Vadis?** and Loren's film career began. A meeting with Ponti led to bigger and bigger roles (including **Aida,** miming to Renata Tebaldi's voice) until she was given the part of a Neapolitan pizza seller in De Sica's **The Gold of Naples** in 1955. This was the part that gained her international attention and helped create her screen persona. Ponti followed it with the very successful **Woman of the River,** good box-office probably because of wet, clinging clothes. She began to appear in international productions like **Boy on a Dolphin** (more wet, clinging clothes) and **The Pride and the Passion** (fiery peasant) and then went to Hollywood to confirm her world stardom.

She was good with Cary Grant ➤ in **Houseboat** and Anthony Quinn ➤ in **Black Orchid,** and beautiful with Quinn in **Heller in Pink Tights** and Clark Gable ➤ in

It Started in Naples. They weren't outstanding films, but they made a wide public aware of her. She also made reasonable films in Britain: **The Key** with Trevor Howard ➤ and William Holden ➤ and **The Millionairess** with Peter Sellers ➤. By this time she was so beautiful that she just had to win that acting Oscar for emoting as a distressed and banged-about mother in wartime Italy in **Two Women.** She worked in international epics (**El Cid, The Fall of the Roman Empire**), comedies (**Arabesque**) and melodramas (**Judith**), but was best in films with a "genuine" Italian background, lovely and charming with Marcello Mastroianni ➤ in **Yesterday, Today and Tomorrow** and **Marriage, Italian Style** (another

*Above: Sophia Loren as the daughter of the Roman Emperor Marcus Aurelius in **The Fall of the Roman Empire,** Anthony Mann's 1964 spectacular epic. Loren's statuesque beauty was particularly suitable for big-budget international movies.*

Oscar nomination) and at her very best as the Neapolitan peasant loved by Prince Charming Omar Sharif ➤ in **Once Upon a Time** (known as **Cinderella, Italian Style** in England and **More Than a Miracle** in the USA). Her career has continued strongly if not very excitingly in the '70s, with films like **White Sister, The Cassandra Crossing** and **Man of La Mancha.** She made a considerable impact at the 1977 Cannes Festival,

"acting" with all stops out as a plain housewife turned on by homosexual Mastroianni in **A Special Day,** set in Fascist Italy.

BEST FILMS:
1958 The Key
Carol Reed (Columbia)
1958 Houseboat
Melville Shavelson (Paramount)
1960 Heller in Pink Tights
George Cukor (Paramount)
1960 The Millionairess
Anthony Asquith (20th Century Fox)
1961 La Ciociara (Two Women)
Vittorio De Sica (Champion)
1961 El Cid
Anthony Mann (Allied Artists)
1963 Ieri, Oggi e Domani (Yesterday, Today and Tomorrow)
Vittorio De Sica (Champion)
1964 Matrimonio all'Italiana (Marriage, Italian Style)
Vittorio De Sica (Champion)
1966 Arabesque
Stanley Donen (Universal)
1976 C'era Una Volta . . . (More Than a Miracle/Cinderella, Italian Style)
Francesco Rosi (MGM)

ALI MacGRAW

Ali MacGraw can be defined in film terms only in relation to men, as her screen persona is that of a "partner" whose presence necessitates the other half of an equation. In **Love Story** it's Ryan O'Neal ➤, in **The Getaway** it's Steve McQueen ➤, in **Goodbye Columbus** it's Richard Benjamin and in **Convoy** it's Kris Kristofferson ➤. The way she behaves, her very existence, is formulated in terms of these relationships. Off screen, her life has strangely paralleled this "partner" behaviour: as a Wellesley College student she married a Harvard man; as a fledgling film star she married Paramount production chief Robert Evans, who made her into a superstar in **Love Story,** then she split up with him and married fellow superstar Steve McQueen. After that she virtually retired from movies for five years. Now that she and McQueen have divorced, she is making films again.

MacGraw was born in Pound Ridge, New York, in 1938, and after studying at Wellesley worked on a fashion magazine. She turned to modelling and finally to the cinema in 1969 when, at the age of 30, she was starred as a 21-year-old Jewish girl in **Goodbye Columbus.** She was good, so Evans produced **Love Story** for her—she played a poor baker's daughter studying classical music at Radcliffe and O'Neal was an ultra-rich man's son studying law at Harvard. She gives up her plans to study in Europe to marry him, works to pay his way through law school when his dad won't, and then dies without ever having to say she was sorry, all to music by Francis Lai. It was sentimental women's magazine stuff, even if it was written by

Above: Ali MacGraw hitches a ride with trucker Kris Kristofferson in Sam Peckinpah's 1978 knockabout **Convoy,** *her comeback film after five years of virtual retirement with fellow-superstar husband Steve McQueen.*

a Yale professor, but it was very slick and engrossing and it became one of the biggest money-making movies of all time. **The Getaway,** two years later, with the MacGraw-McQueen love-hate relationship as the centre of an ostensible thriller, didn't do quite as well but MacGraw's first three films still made over $100 million. She was the hottest female property in Hollywood when she chose to become a virtual hermit with McQueen. She finally came back with **Convoy,** keeping Kristofferson company in a trucking epic, and then got together with ex-husband Evans once more when he produced the tennis-orientated film **Players** in 1979.

BEST FILMS:
1969 Goodbye Columbus
Larry Peerce (Paramount)
1970 Love Story
Arthur Hiller (Paramount)
1972 The Getaway
Sam Peckinpah (First Artists)
1978 Convoy
Sam Peckinpah (EMI/United Artists)
1979 Players
Anthony Harvey (Paramount)

SHIRLEY MacLAINE

When Shirley MacLaine first appeared on the screen, in **The Trouble With Harry** in 1955, she was the most unusual movie personality to have emerged for a long time. She was kookie before that word came into vogue, impish, off-beat, disconnected

Above: Shirley MacLaine in the all-star (but not very successful) comedy **Woman Times Seven** *in which she portrays seven types of female allure.*

and beautiful in her own way. She never improved on that performance and after a while audiences grew used to her unusual screen persona; as she got better known, she became a very big star and the kookiness began to seem mannered. She was still very good with a good script, but with a weak one was no longer interesting.

MacLaine hit her peak in the late '50s and early '60s in **The Sheepman** (naive cowgirl befriending Glenn Ford » as the sheep farmer), **Some Came Running** (naive small-town floozie friend of Frank Sinatra »), **Ask Any Girl** (naive girl on her own in New York with David Niven ») and especially in **The Apartment** (naive liftgirl used by Fred MacMurray » and rescued by Jack Lemmon »). **The Apartment** won the Best Picture Oscar and MacLaine got an Oscar nomination plus acting prizes in Venice and England. She had a kookie part ideally suited for her persona in

Two For The See-Saw, playing opposite Robert Mitchum », and then joined Jack Lemmon in another Billy Wilder satirical comedy, a non-musical version of **Irma la Douce** with MacLaine as a street walker. Her films after that were less successful, but her career revived in 1968 with the musical **Sweet Charity;** she was excellent in the role that Giulietta Masina » had created in the original (Fellini's **Nights of Cabiria**). She moved into the '70s with reasonable films like **Desperate Characters** and **The Possession of Joel Delaney** and her career had another terrific boost in 1977 with the ballet-orientated **The Turning Point,** portraying a former dancer who meets old rival Anne Bancroft ».

MacLaine is the sister of Warren Beatty » and was born Shirley MacLean Beaty in Richmond, Virginia, on April 24, 1934. She was discovered by producer Hal Wallis after she replaced Carol Haney in the stage musical *The Pajama Game* . She published her autobiography, *Don't Fall Off The Mountain,* in 1970, and in 1975 wrote a book based on her well-publicised visit to the Republic of China, *You Can't Get There From Here,* and produced a movie based on the visit and titled **The Other Half of the Sky: A China Memoir.**

BEST FILMS:
1955 The Trouble With Harry
Alfred Hitchcock (Paramount)
1956 Around the World in 80 Days
Michael Anderson (United Artists/Mike Todd)
1958 The Sheepman
George Marshall (MGM)
1958 Some Came Running
Vincente Minnelli (MGM)

1959 Ask Any Girl
Charles Walters (MGM)
1960 The Apartment
Billy Wilder (United Artists)
1962 Two For The See-Saw
Robert Wide (United Artists)
1963 Irma la Douce
Billy Wilder (United Artists)
1968 Sweet Charity
Bob Fosse (Universal)
1977 The Turning Point
Herbert Ross (20th Century Fox)

JAYNE MANSFIELD

"If she's a girl, then I don't know what my sister is," says a character in **The Girl Can't Help It.** Jayne Mansfield was the cinema's favourite sex joke in the late '50s, the walking-talking-bouncing embodiment of the breast fetish, the girl with the 40-18-36 measurements who was too much like a parody to be real. Her greatest desire in life was to be a glamorous movie star; by allowing press and film-makers to satirise her image as a sex object, she actually achieved her aim for a brief period from 1956 to 1960. Despite her over-sized mammaries she was not a dumb blonde as far as her career was concerned, and she parlayed a modicum of talent and a maximum of flesh to international fame. Along the way she made some surprisingly good films, including Frank Tashlin's delightful **The Girl Can't Help It,** the film version of her stage hit *Will Success Spoil Rock Hunter?*, a nice little thriller called **The Burglar** and an enjoyable adaptation of John Steinbeck's **The Wayward Bus.** It was easy to laugh at

Left: Jayne Mansfield has a routine bubble bath and takes Peyton Place with her to read: no finer choice for a statuesque queen of Hollywood froth.

Mansfield, but today her achievements look greater than her detractors allowed at the time.

She was born as Vera Jayne Palmer at Bryn Mawr, Pennsylvania, on April 19, 1933. She married Paul Mansfield in 1950 at the age of 16, had her first child the following year and began to study for stardom as well as win beauty contests like "Miss Photoflash of 1952". Her appearance at the première of the film **Underwater** in half a red bikini upstaged its bosomy star Jane Russell ➤, and led to her getting small parts in the 1955 films **Pete Kelly's Blues, Illegal** and **Hell on Frisco Bay** under a Warner Brothers contract. She was given the female lead opposite Dan Duryea in the fine small-budget **The Burglar** and then became a stage star wearing a Turkish towel in *Will Success Spoil Rock Hunter?* 20th Century Fox were having problems with Marilyn Monroe ➤ so they signed Mansfield as an alternative; she was at her best in **The Girl Can't Help It**, so sexy that spectacle lenses crack from seeing her and blocks of ice melt as she passes by. She was nearly as good playing an actress very like herself in the film version of **Will Success Spoil Rock Hunter?** which also featured her second husband, Mickey Hargitay, a former Mr Universe. Mansfield and Hargitay together were the ultimate satire on sex and muscles, and for a while were one of the most famous couples in the world.

Mansfield's film career faded out nearly as fast as it began after the commercial failure of her film with Cary Grant ➤, **Kiss Them for Me.** She went to England to make **The Sheriff of Fractured Jaw, The Challenge** and **Too Hot to Handle**, had reasonable roles in **The George Raft Story** and **It Happened in Athens** and was washed up as a movie star by 1962. She tried to revive her popularity by becoming the first Hollywood star to do a nude scene in the 1963 **Promises, Promises,** but the latter part of her career was mostly stage work. Third husband Matt Cimber made one of her last films, the 1967 **Single Room Furnished**, about three stages in the life of a prostitute. She was killed in a car accident on June 29, 1967, driving from Biloxi to New Orleans.

BEST FILMS:
1956 The Girl Can't Help It
Frank Tashlin (20th Century Fox)
1957 The Burglar
Paul Wendkos (Columbia)
1957 Will Success Spoil Rock Hunter?
Frank Tashlin (20th Century Fox)
1957 The Wayward Bus
Victor Vicas (20th Century Fox)
1957 Kiss Them for Me
Stanley Donen (20th Century Fox)
1959 The Sheriff of Fractured Jaw
Raoul Walsh (20th Century Fox)
1960 Too Hot to Handle
Terence Young (Associated British Pictures)
1961 The George Raft Story
Joseph Newman (Allied Artists)
1961 It Happened in Athens
Andrew Marton (20th Century Fox)
1967 Single Room Furnished
Matt Cimber (Musto)

DEAN MARTIN

In 1964 Dean Martin starred in a film in which he portrayed an easy-going popular singer named Dino who liked to drink a lot and who got a headache if he didn't have sex every night. This mocking portrait of Martin's screen persona as a lazy, drinking womaniser was presented by Billy Wilder in his savagely satirical **Kiss Me Stupid** and is, ironically, probably Martin's

Above: Dean Martin with another "Clan" member, Frank Sinatra, in the highly enjoyable **Sergeants Three,** *a Western re-working of* **Gunga Din.**

greatest movie performance. That same image was exploited to greater popular success in the Matt Helm secret agent series, beginning in 1966 with **The Silencers,** not so much a parody of Bond as of Martin's own persona. Obviously, there is something about this image that audiences admire, envy and enjoy laughing at. How close that persona is to Martin's real personality is debatable; no lazy, lecherous drunk could have had such a highly successful, well-organised and enduring career as a movie star, both in comedy (especially with Jerry Lewis ➤) and in drama (**Some Came Running, Rio Bravo**). Martin is, in fact, very professional; behind that I'm-no-actor-just-an-amiable-drunk façade is a first-class actor.

He was born Dino Crocetti in Steubenville, Ohio, on June 17, 1917, began working as a singer in nightclubs in the early '40s and formed his partnership with comedian Jerry Lewis in 1946. They were so popular in clubs that Hal Wallis brought them to Hollywood in 1949 and featured them in **My Friend Irma.** By 1952 they were the top box office attraction in America; they were in 18 films together before they split up in 1956, taking over from Abbott and Costello ➤ as America's favourite comedy team, with more developed but not totally dissimilar personae: where Costello was a smooth-talking con-man, Martin was a smooth womaniser; where Costello was a gullible fool, Lewis was a demented idiot. The best of the Martin and Lewis films were the late ones directed by Frank Tashlin, **Artists and Models** and **Hollywood or Bust,** although Martin never really had much chance to develop his screen personality in any of them.

Martin's box office potential dropped without Lewis, but he came back strongly with superb acting performances as a soldier in **The Young Lions,** an easy-going, small-town gambler in **Some Came Running,** and a drunken gunfighter rehabilitated by John Wayne ➤ in **Rio Bravo.** This last was one of his finest screen peformances and he gave another good one opposite Judy Holliday in **Bells Are Ringing,** as a lazy writer. He joined Frank Sinatra's ➤ "Clan" off screen and on, in such enjoyable romps as **Ocean's Eleven** and **Sergeants Three,** and made it back into the box office top ten with his Matt Helm films just when Lewis was beginning to fade. His career has continued strongly since, with films like **Airport** (still womanising), and he has become a regular star of easy-going Westerns like **Showdown** and **Something Big.**

BEST FILMS:
1955 Artists and Models
Frank Tashlin (Paramount)
1958 The Young Lions
Edward Dmytryk (20th Century Fox)
1959 Some Came Running
Vincente Minnelli (MGM)
1959 Rio Bravo
Howard Hawks (Warner Brothers)
1960 Bells Are Ringing
Vincente Minnelli (MGM)
1961 Ocean's Eleven
Lewis Milestone (Warner Brothers)
1964 Robin and the Seven Hoods
Gordon Douglas (Warner Brothers)
1964 Kiss Me Stupid
Billy Wilder (Lopert)
1966 The Silencers
Phil Karlson (Columbia)
1969 Airport
George Seaton (Universal)

LEE MARVIN

Lee Marvin introduced a new kind of violence to the cinema in 1953 in **The Big Heat,** stubbing out his cigarette on Carolyn Jones's hand and throwing boiling coffee into Gloria Grahame's ➤ face. His casual, brisk, business-like violence, without warning or gloating, was more terrifying than anything seen on the screen up to that time. Marvin quickly became the leading bad guy of the cinema, more vicious than Marlon Brando ➤ in **The Wild One,** utterly despicable when threatening one-armed Spencer Tracy ➤ in **Bad Day at Black Rock.** Throughout the '50s, he occupied a central place in the development of violence on the screen, even in ostensibly less villainous roles like the Army colonel in Robert Aldrich's **Attack!**

This lethal, professional persona was seen at its most disturbing and effective in Don Siegel's **The Killers** (an immaculately-dressed, unfussy executive, casually eliminating people as he goes after a big haul); John Boorman's **Point Blank** (briskly killing off members of a crime syndicate as he goes after money owed to him); and Aldrich's **The Dirty Dozen** (leading a group of condemned Army criminals on a suicide mission, where casual killing can be

Above: Lee Marvin, in the 1967 **Point Blank,** *discovers that the Mafia man who owed him money has only a string of credit cards.*

considered patriotic). These were great performances in key films of the modern cinema, but Marvin's official major stardom actually came through parodying his killer image. In John Ford's **The Man Who Shot Liberty Valance** he is the icy murderer finally shot down by John Wayne ➤, and that portrayal was the basis of a double role in **Cat Ballou,** as a vicious killer with a silver nose and as his twin, a drunk who befriends Jane Fonda. It was a hammy but amusing performance and Marvin was given the 1965 Academy Award for Best Actor. His comedy talents as a drunk were utilised again in the big-budget musical **Paint Your Wagon,** but despite the forays into comedy he was far more interesting in straightforward, unpretentious gunslinger roles in films made around the same time, especially **The Professionals** and **Monte Walsh.**

Marvin was born in New York City on February 19, 1924, a

maverick from an old and respected family, who was kicked out of a number of schools, enlisted in the Marines and served in the South Pacific. He made his film début for director Henry Hathaway in the 1951 **You're in the Navy Now** and soon established himself as a heavy of real intensity; he had leading roles as a killer in films like **A Life in the Balance** (as a religious maniac), **Violent Saturday** (afflicted with a heavy cold), and **Seven Men From Now** (arrogantly nasty to Randolph Scott ❯). He was nicely matched with John Wayne ❯ in rather more sympathetic brawling roles in **The Comancheros** and **Donovan's Reef** and was a heavy drinker once more in **Ship of Fools**, making passes at Vivien Leigh ❯. His career in the '70s has so far not matched his '60s work, although he was notable as a mob enforcer in **Prime Cut** and a tough railway bum in **Emperor of the North Pole**. He tried serious theatrical film acting with only minor success '(**The Iceman Cometh**) and returned to his forte, the nasty war film, in 1979 with Samuel Fuller's long-awaited **The Big Red One**.

BEST FILMS:
1953 The Big Heat
Fritz Lang (Columbia)
1954 Bad Day at Black Rock
John Sturges (MGM)
1956 Attack!
Robert Aldrich (United Artists)
1962 The Man Who Shot Liberty Valance
John Ford (Paramount)
1964 The Killers
Don Siegel (Universal)
1965 Cat Ballou
Elliot Silverstein (Columbia)
1966 The Professionals
Richard Brooks (Columbia)
1967 The Dirty Dozen
Robert Aldrich (MGM)
1967 Point Blank
John Boorman (MGM)
1969 Paint Your Wagon
Joshua Logan (Paramount)
1972 Prime Cut
Michael Ritchie (Cinema Center)
1973 Emperor of the North Pole
Robert Aldrich (20th Century Fox)
1979 The Big Red One
Samuel Fuller (Lorimer)

MARCELLO MASTROIANNI

Marcello Mastroianni has become the modern cinema's personification of the Latin Lover, which is not at all what it might appear to be.

His screen persona is one of inexpressible weariness, sometimes worried, usually tired to the point of impotence, yet always incredibly attractive to women.

Federico Fellini made Mastroianni world-famous as the bored and hedonistic journalist of **La Dolce Vita** and then as the film

Above: Marcello Mastroianni as a notorious playboy ignoring the affections of Sophia Loren in **Marriage—Italian Style.**

director who has run out of ideas in **8½**. Michelangelo Antonioni beautifully matched him with Jeanne Moreau ❯ as her bored husband in **La Notte**, the ideal partnership of the most lived-in faces of the modern cinema. Luchino Visconti, who had earlier featured him as Maria Schell's ❯ doomed suitor in **White Nights**, used him to portray Camus' existential hero in **The Stranger**. Vittorio De Sica gave him international popular appeal as Sophia Loren's ❯ bedmate in **Yesterday, Today and Tomorrow** and **Marriage, Italian Style**. He was nicely teamed with Brigitte Bardot ❯ in her semi-biographical **Vie Privée**, Ursula Andress in the science-fiction tale **The Tenth Victim**, and best of all with Claudia Cardinale ❯ in **Il Bell'Antonio**, where he was totally impotent. Mastroianni's unbroken string of great films in the '60s offered him a wide variety of roles, despite the seeming limits of his screen personality: he was superbly crafty as a turn-of-the-century union man in **The Organizer**, brilliantly weak-minded as a philanderer suspected of murder in **The Assassin**, delightfully funny as a Sicilian preparing to bump off his wife in **Divorce, Italian Style** and touchingly sad as Jacques Perrin's brother in **Family Chronicle**.

Mastroianni was born in Fontane Liri near Rome on September 28, 1923, and first began to act on stage in the late '40s. He was soon working with Visconti's theatre company and made his film début in the 1947 **I Miserabili** directed by Ricardo Freda. He rose slowly to stardom

in the '50s in some excellent if relatively minor Italian films. The 1960 **La Dolce Vita** made him into a major European and world star and his popularity continued strong through the decade.

In 1970 he began another group of remarkable films with John Boorman's **Leo the Last** (rich, weary and ineffectual in London) and Roman Polanski's bizarre sex comedy **What?** (doing odd things with whips to that Latin Lover image). He went brilliantly over the top in 1973 in Marco Ferreri's grotesque satire on the consumer society **La Grande Bouffe** (**Blow-Out**), but was less successful with the same director and co-stars in the Western send-up **Don't Touch the White Woman**. His great strength as a weak but still sympathetic protagonist was put to magnificent use by the Taviani brothers in their studies of failed revolutionaries **Allonsanfan**. In 1977 he portrayed a homosexual seduced by Sophia Loren in **A Special Day**, but the Latin Lover persona had not basically changed.

BEST FILMS:
1958 Le Notti Bianchi (White Nights)
Luchino Visconti (CIAS-Vides-Intermondia)
1960 La Dolce Vita (The Sweet Life)
Federico Fellini (Rlama-Pathé)
1960 Il Bell'Antonio
Mauro Bolognini (Del Duca-Arco)
1961 La Notte
Michelangelo Antonioni (Nepi-Sofitedi-Silver)
1961 L'Assassino (The Assassin)
Elio Petri (Titanus-Vides)
1961 Divorzio all'Italiana (Divorce, Italian Style)
Pietro Germi (Lux-Vides-Galatea)
1962 Cronaca Familiare (Family Chronicle)
Valerio Zurlini (Titanus)

1963 8½
Federico Fellini (Cineriz)
1963 I Compagni (The Organizer)
Mario Monicelli (Lux-Vides)
1964 Ieri, Oggi et Domani (Yesterday, Today and Tomorrow)
Vittorio De Sica (Champion)
1964 Matrimonio all'Italiana (Marriage, Italian Style)
Vittorio De Sica (Champion)
1967 Lo Straniero (The Stranger)
Luchino Visconti (De Laurentiis)
1970 Leo the Last
John Boorman (United Artists)
1973 La Grande Bouffe (Blow-Out)
Marco Ferreri (Mara-Films 66)
1974 Allonsanfan
Paolo & Vittorio Taviani (Italnoleggio)

WALTER MATTHAU

Walter Matthau was a boxing instructor before turning to acting, and a good deal of that art has gone into his screen persona. He is always sparring with someone in his movies; in **The Odd Couple** he's the slob "husband" battling with obsessively neat "wife" Jack Lemmon ❯, in **The Sunshine Boys** he and George Burns ❯ continue their squabbling from youth in vaudeville through to old age. In **The Bad News Bears**, his most successful film in box-office terms, he battles with his juvenile baseball team, in particular with star pitcher Tatum O'Neal ❯. In **House Calls** he bickers with prospective spouse Glenda Jackson ❯, in **The Secret Life of an American Wife** with prospective bed partner Anne Jackson, in **Pete 'n' Tillie** with patient nutty wife Carol Burnett and in **A New Leaf** with rich clumsy wife Elaine May. In **Hello Dolly!** his running dispute is with husband-hunter Barbra Streisand ❯, in **Kotch** as a cantankerous grandfather with his children and in **The Front Page**, once again with Jack Lemmon, as an editor trying to keep his star reporter. Even in a non-comedy role like the bank robber in **Charley Varrick**, he has a running battle with an opponent, in this case most dangerously the Mafia whose loot he has unwittingly stolen. His screen persona is matched with one of the most enjoyable of all modern screen personalities, a wry New Yorkerish self-mocking, sour-faced, wise-cracking derisive know-it-all who never quite takes himself or life seriously. His style of acting is uniquely his own; he is basically an over-reactor who hams his actions so knowingly while yet remaining in character that his hamminess becomes a part of his screen personality. Normally this exaggeration is used with extreme care and subtlety; occasionally it becomes just plain hammy as in his exaggerated drunkard role in **Earthquake**. Perhaps that was because **Earthquake** was the only film in which he used his real name—Walter Matuschanskayasky.

He was born in New York City on October 1, 1923, the son of a Russian Orthodox priest. After working in many jobs (including boxing instructor) and serving in the Air Force during World War II, he turned actor and started appearing on stage in 1946. He made his film début as a villain opposite Burt Lancaster ➤ in the 1955 **The Kentuckian,** and played mostly villains during his first ten years in the movies. He was exceptionally good as one of the three baddies after Audrey Hepburn ➤ in **Charade** and as the cynical reporter in **A Face in the Crowd.** He also built up a high reputation on Broadway which climaxed in 1965 in his multi-award-winning performance in *The Odd Couple.* Billy Wilder then starred him in **The Fortune Cookie (Meet Whiplash Willie)** in his first real verbal-pugilist role as a shyster lawyer who fast-talks Jack Lemmon into cashing in on

STEVE McQUEEN

Steve McQueen has combined icy cool, casual insolence and a delinquent grin into a charismatic screen persona which began in 1960 in **The Magnificent Seven.**

It progressed in **Hell is for Heroes** and **The Honeymoon Machine,** and was seen at its clearest in **The Great Escape,** when all his qualities were on show as the "Cooler King" of the prison camp, including his essential loner status, his unique brand of jaunty, insolent rebellion, and his love for motorcycles. His kind of outsider status has been described as "existential cool". In **The Thomas Crown Affair** he appears on the surface to be a wealthy, respectable businessman, but underneath he is the same rebel, masterminding bank robberies. His most Establishment role was as the cop in **Bullitt,** but he was just as aggressive and rebellious in this as in his other films, again demonstrating his preoccupation with racing cars and climactic cycles in the central chase sequence; he has established a symbiotic relationship between the power of his persona and the power of racing engines.

He was born as Terence Stephen McQueen in Beach Grove, Indiana, on March 24, 1930. He was "difficult", spent two years in a California reform school, ran away from home and drifted, working as a merchant seaman, oil-field labourer and carnival barker. He joined the Marines (and spent 41 days of his service in detention) and then, after more odd jobs, began to study acting. He was in the 1956 Broadway production of *A Hatful of Rain* (replacing Ben Gazzara) and made his film début the same year as an extra in **Somebody Up There Likes Me.** He was featured in his next film, **Never Love a Stranger,** as the friend of protagonist John Drew Barrymore, and began to build his screen personality in **The Blob** and **The Great St Louis Bank Robbery.** He came on strong with Frank Sinatra ➤ in the war film **Never So Few** and finally got it all together in **The Magnificent Seven.**

Not all his films since then have been good, but most of them have used his personality to fine

Above: Walter Matthau, pictured in **Casey's Shadow,** *specialises in portraying laconic con-men and reluctant husbands.*

an injury. He won the Best Supporting Actor Oscar and then gained even more kudos under Gene Saks in the film version of **The Odd Couple.** It was a very big box-office film and although the musical **Hello Dolly!** that followed it was a flop, in 1970 and 1971 he was listed among the top ten box office stars. He has remained popular, whether portraying grandfathers or gangsters, and has had two further Oscar nominations for **Kotch** and **The Sunshine Boys.** In 1978, apart from **House Calls** as a middle-aged lecher/doctor, he has appeared in **Casey's Shadow** as a poor man with a fine racing horse.

BEST FILMS:
1966 The Fortune Cookie
Billy Wilder (United Artists)
1968 The Odd Couple
Gene Saks (Paramount)
1968 The Secret Life of an American Wife
George Axelrod (20th Century Fox)

Above: Steve McQueen as the San Francisco detective **Bullitt,** *the film that shot the Ford Mustang to world fame.*

effect. It is a limited persona, with little more versatility than that of John Wayne ➤, but these very restrictions make it extremely powerful when properly showcased, as it was in **The Cincinnati Kid:** McQueen played a top-notch poker player challenging the King, Edward G. Robinson ➤. He was excellent as a cowboy obsessed with revenge in **Nevada Smith** and won his only Oscar nomination in 1967 for **The Sand Pebbles,** as a loner sailor-engineer on a US gunboat in China in the 1920s. McQueen was first listed among the top ten box office stars in 1967 and stayed there until 1976.

McQueen's recent films have been a mixed bag, beginning with **The Reivers** (hired hand in the Faulkner South) and **Le Mans** (all cars and no characters), and improving under Sam Peckinpah's direction in **Junior Bonner** (rodeo performer) and **The Getaway** (bank robber). His role as the fire

Above: Steve McQueen dreams of escaping Devil's Island and his diet of stale bread and insects in the gruelling 1972 **Papillon.**

chief in **The Towering Inferno** was credible if unexciting, but his performances in two "serious" films makes one wish he would leave them alone: in 1973 he starred as the real-life convict escapee hero of **Papillon** (showing that his forté is not in playing historical characters, even if they are escape heroes) and then, after a very long delay, in the Ibsen adaptation **An Enemy of the People** (showing that his forté is not classic theatre).

BEST FILMS:
1960 The Magnificent Seven
John Sturges (United Artists)
1962 Hell is for Heroes
Don Siegel (Paramount)
1963 The Great Escape
John Sturges (United Artists)
1963 Love with the Proper Stranger
Robert Mulligan (Paramount)
1965 The Cincinnati Kid
Norman Jewison (MGM)
1966 The Sand Pebbles
Robert Wise (20th Century Fox)
1968 The Thomas Crown Affair
Norman Jewison (United Artists)
1968 Bullitt
Peter Yates (Warner Pathé)
1972 Junior Bonner
Sam Peckinpah (Cinerama)
1972 The Getaway
Sam Peckinpah (Cinerama)

Melina MERCOURI

Melina Mercouri is the leading star of the Greek cinema, the internationally popular heroine of the 1960 **Never On Sunday,** an actress of great talent but extravagant tendencies. Her long stage career has made her liable to over-act in the cinema, with broad gestures and fire-eating enthusiasm, but properly restrained she is splendid. The Oscar-winning **Never On Sunday** remains her best film, a paean of praise to the life force, in which she portrays a Greek prostitute who takes Sundays off for other pursuits and resists intellectual "improvement". The fine music by Manos Hadjidakis helped the film to world popularity and it made the reputation of director Jules Dassin, a black-listed American residing in Europe because of the political witch hunts of the period.

Mercouri was born in Athens in 1923 as Maria Amalia Mercouri (Melina is a nickname meaning honey) and worked on stage for some years before making her cinema début in the 1955 **Stella,** under the direction of Michael Cacoyannis. The film was shown at the Cannes Film Festival, where Mercouri met Dassin and formed a partnership (they were married a few years later) that continues today. Dassin featured her in his religious allegory **He Who Must Die** and in **La Loi,** and she had a part in Joseph Losey's **The Gypsy and the Gentleman** before the world success of **Never**

Above: Melina Mercouri, star of numerous films directed by her husband Jules Dassin (**Never on Sunday, Phaedra**) *which explore her volatile character.*

On Sunday. Dassin and Mercouri were never to repeat that success, although Mercouri was very good as one of the robbery gang in **Topkapi.** Her tendency to go over the top when acting for the cinema has not lessened with either the years or her political involvement (she is now in the Greek Parliament, following active opposition to the Colonels' régime). Her most recent picture was Dassin's 1978 **A Dream of Passion** with Ellen Burstyn, a variation on the theme of Medea and very theatrical in conception and execution.

BEST FILMS:
1955 Stella
Michael Cacoyannis (United Artists)
1957 He Who Must Die
Jules Dassin (United Artists)
1958 The Gypsy and the Gentleman
Joseph Losey (Rank)
1960 Never On Sunday
Jules Dassin (United Artists)
1962 Phaedra
Jules Dassin (United Artists)
1963 The Victors
Carl Foreman (Columbia)
1964 Topkapi
Jules Dassin (United Artists)
1966 10.30 pm Summer
Jules Dassin (United Artists)
1969 Gaily, Gaily
Norman Jewison (United Artists)
1978 A Dream of Passion
Jules Dassin (Dassin)

Liza MINNELLI

Liza Minnelli's relatively stunted career as a Hollywood musical comedy star illustrates graphically the difference between the old studio-dominated system and the new freelance methods. In 1978 Minnelli was 32 years old, and despite her incredible singing, dancing and acting talents had starred in only two musicals, had

Above: Liza Minnelli, the daughter of Judy Garland, has built a spectacular career that alternates films with cabaret.

sung in two other films, and had been featured in a total of seven movies. Her mother, Judy Garland », whose great talent Minnelli has inherited, was 32 in 1954, by which time she had made all her great musicals and had been featured in 30 films.

Minnelli has the ability to become a great musical star, but it seems unlikely that Hollywood will give her the opportunity. All the same, she has done a superlative job with what little chance she has had. Her first musical was the 1972 **Cabaret;** she was outstanding as Sally Bowles, winning the Best Actress Oscar (something her mother never achieved) over such formidable competition as Liv Ullmann » and Diana Ross », and helping the film to become a huge box office success. Her other musical, Martin Scorsese's 1977 **New York, New York,** has been less well received, although her work in it was widely admired. She also had songs in the non-musicals, **Lucky**

Lady and **A Matter of Time,** and received an Oscar nomination for her role as Pookie Adams in **The Sterile Cuckoo.**

Minnelli was born in Los Angeles on March 10, 1946; her father was MGM's great musical director Vincente Minnelli. After studying in private schools she began work in various forms of theatre from the age of 15, and made her Broadway début at 19 in *Flora the Red Menace* (winning a Tony award). She quickly made a name for herself singing in clubs and working in TV; her first LP, *Liza Minnelli,* was released in 1968. She made her film début under Albert Finney's direction in the much under-rated **Charlie Bubbles** in 1967, was excellent as a talkative girl involved in her first sexual adventure in **The Sterile Cuckoo,** and did her best as the disfigured member of the strange trio that featured in **Tell Me That You Love Me, Junie Moon.** Her concert, record and TV work has been as successful as her film career.

COMPLETE FILMS:
1967 Charlie Bubbles
Albert Finney (Universal)
1969 The Sterile Cuckoo (Pookie)
Alan J. Pakula (Paramount)
1969 Tell Me That You Love Me, Junie Moon
Otto Preminger (Paramount)
1972 Cabaret
Bob Fosse (ABC)
1975 Lucky Lady
Stanley Donen (20th Century Fox)
1977 A Matter of Time
Vincente Minnelli (AIP)
1977 New York, New York
Martin Scorsese (United Artists)

Marilyn MONROE

Marilyn Monroe is the greatest myth figure of the modern cinema. Her life reads like a traditional legend: beautiful blonde goddess born to a crazy mother from unknown father becomes the most famous sex star in the world, mates with greatest heroes of brawn and intellect, and then sacrifices herself in atonement for her culture's sins. Certainly, Monroe's death had a shattering effect on people around the world; a far greater effect than the death of a movie star, however charismatic, could have had—she had become a symbolic figure, but it is a simplication to say she was a sex symbol. Audiences liked her because she had what Billy Wilder described as "flesh impact" on the screen, but her sexiness was combined with innocence and her glamour with vulnerability.

Monroe projected the image of someone who needed to be protected and every seemingly scandalous revelation about her life only reinforced this feeling in her public. She was illegitimate, her mother was confined to

Above: The incredible and tragic Marilyn Monroe singing to a potential sugar-daddy in the 1954 **There's No Business Like Show Business.**

mental institutions, she had been brought up in foster homes and orphanages, and she had married when barely 16, but these facts were accepted as if they were only to be expected of the personality she displayed on screen. No one could condemn her because she had posed for a nude calendar to earn money, just as no one could condemn her for the failures of her marriages. What one could see on the screen, through her incredible beauty, was that she was already condemned.

Monroe was born as Norma Jeane Mortenson in Los Angeles on June 1, 1926. She grew up with dreams of becoming a movie star to escape from her unhappy life; she began to stammer at the age of nine and in her stays at various foster homes experienced child molestation, religious fanaticism, persecution and a more or less complete lack of love and affection.

At the age of 16 she married a 21-year-old aircraft worker named Jim Dougherty; the marriage lasted four years, by which time Marilyn had become a model and was on the fringe of the film world.

Her film début was the 1948 **Scudda-Hoo! Scudda-Hay!**, but her part was cut and she was not seen on screen until **Dangerous Years**, later in the same year. She had the lead in a small-budget film called **Ladies of the Chorus**, playing a stripteaser, and sang two songs.

Her real film career began with two fine, small roles, as a gangster's moll in **The Asphalt Jungle** and as George Sanders' » girl friend in **All About Eve**. Monroe had at this time become good friends with 60-year-old Joseph M. Schenck, chairman of her studio, 20th Century Fox, and with Johnny Hyde, a 53-year-old executive vice president of her agency, William Morris. More than anyone else, Hyde promoted her career and boosted her to success, but she refused to marry him, even when he offered her $1 million. She attracted attention in films like **Clash by Night** and **Don't Bother To Knock**, but her first important starring role was in the 1952 **Monkey Business** opposite Cary Grant ». Her tight red satin dress made her world famous in **Niagara** and pressure groups began complaining about her sexiness. She was superb in **Gentlemen Prefer Blondes** with Jane Russell », proving that she was a fine light comedienne able

to guy her own sex image and singing the splendid *Diamonds Are a Girl's Best Friend*. She was now a top ten box office star, and pictures like **How to Marry a Millionaire** and **River of No Return** were hugely successful. She married baseball star Joe DiMaggio in January, 1954; they divorced in October the same year.

Monroe was beginning to have studio troubles because of tardiness and temperament, but she continued to make popular films, including **The Seven Year Itch.** Her confidence in her acting was boosted by working at the Actors' Studio, and she starred in a good version of the play **Bus Stop** and married playwright Arthur Miller in June, 1956. She then went to England to star in **The Prince and the Showgirl**, with Laurence Olivier » co-starring and directing; it didn't really work, but her next film, for Billy Wilder, did. This was **Some Like It Hot**, in some ways the best film of her career; she matched Tony Curtis » and Jack Lemmon » with a lovely, breathy performance. **Let's Make Love**, with George Cukor directing her and Yves Montand », was not as good.

Her next and last film was the 1961 **The Misfits**, written by her husband, a strange but powerful film about a group involved with wild horses. The doomed cast included Clark Gable » and Montgomery Clift ». Miller and Marilyn were divorced in January, 1961 and she did not work again until April 1962, when she started on **Something's Got To Give** for Fox; she was fired on June 19, after having shown up for work on only 12 of the 32 days of production—for a total of 7½ minutes of film. Many people in Hollywood considered this to be the end of her career, that no one would risk employing her again. On August 5, 1962, she was found dead in bed from an overdose of barbiturates.

BEST FILMS:
1952 Monkey Business
Howard Hawks (20th Century Fox)
1952 Niagara
Henry Hathaway (20th Century Fox)
1953 Gentlemen Prefer Blondes
Howard Hawks (20th Century Fox)
1953 How to Marry a Millionaire
Jean Negulesco (20th Century Fox)
1954 River of No Return
Otto Preminger (20th Century Fox)
1955 The Seven Year Itch
Billy Wilder (20th Century Fox)
1956 Bus Stop
Joshua Logan (20th Century Fox)
1959 Some Like It Hot
Billy Wilder (United Artists)
1960 Let's Make Love
George Cukor (20th Century Fox)
1961 The Misfits
John Huston (United Artists)

Died 1962

ROGER MOORE
see **James Bond**

JEANNE MOREAU

Jeanne Moreau is considered by some critics to be the finest actress of the modern cinema; she has certainly starred in more outstanding films by major directors than any other contemporary female star. She is the woman with the lived-in face, the weary-eyed, worldly-wise personification of sophisticated sensuality. She represents mature eroticism in most of her classic films.

Moreau is indeed a very great actress but, like Marlon Brando

Above: Jeanne Moreau directed herself superbly in **Lumière** *(1976), a sensitive portrayal of a star.*

», whose career resembles hers, she came from a very successful theatre career, was hailed for a time as the greatest performer of them all, and then began to lose her pre-eminent position, and weaker films have revealed the framework on which the illusion was built. She is not a natural screen actress, but a sensitive and finely-trained theatre performer who "acts" rather than "is". She is extremely good at it, but as the years go by one can begin to see the thought and the mechanism—effective but studied —behind her performances in the films that made her famous, most especially **The Lovers.**

Moreau was born in Paris in 1928, of a French father and an English showgirl mother. She became a top stage actress in the postwar period, first at the Comédie Française (1945-1952) and then at the TNP, made her film début in the 1949 **Dernier Amour**, but didn't really make an impact until after her stage success in *Cat on a Hot Tin Roof* in 1956. This was the genesis of her sexy, worldly screen persona, which first made an impact in Louis Malle's

Ascenseur pour l'Échafaud (Lift to the Scaffold/Elevator for the Gallows) in 1957. The following year she became world famous in The Lovers, as a wife and mother who abandons her family for a man she has just met. The film had a lot of censorship problems because of its bath scene and Moreau came to be considered, rather ironically, as the naughtiest actress on the screen.

The next six years were the most creative of her career. She was superb as Gérard Philipe's ➤ sophisticated partner in sexual games in Les Liaisons Danger-euses, fascinating as a Marguerite Duras heroine in Moderato Can-tabile and bleakly pessimistic about her marriage to Marcello Mastroianni ➤ in La Notte. Jules et Jim was her most charming film; she was the centre of it as a delectable woman loved by and loving two men. She became bitchier and harder in Eve, Bay of Angels and Diary of a Chamber-maid, but returned to gaiety in Viva Maria! She did two excellent small roles for Orson Welles in The Trial (as Fraulein Becker) and Chimes at Midnight (as Doll Tearsheet) and then became the focus of his 1968 The Immortal Story as a prostitute hired to enact a legend. She was less satis-factory as the avenging woman of The Bride Wore Black and the wandering woman of A Sailor From Gibraltar. Her '70s movies have been relatively weak, al-though she gave excellent per-formances for Duras in Nathalie Granger and Losey in Mr Klein.

BEST FILMS:
1958 Les Amants (The Lovers)
Louis Malle (Nouvelles Editions)
1959 Les Liaisons Dangereuses
Roger Vadim (Films Marceau)
1960 Moderato Cantabile
Peter Brooks (Real Levy)
1961 La Notte
Michelangelo Antonioni (Nepi Film)
1961 Jules et Jim
François Truffaut (Les Films du Carrosse)
1962 Eve
Joseph Losey (Paris Film)
1963 La Baie des Anges
Jacques Demy (Sud-Pacifique)
1964 Le Journal d'une Femme de Chambre
Luis Buñuel (Speva/Dear)
1965 Viva Maria!
Louis Malle (United Artists)
1968 The Immortal Story
Orson Welles (ORTF/Albina)
1972 Nathalie Granger
Marguerite Duras (Moullet et Cie)
1976 Mr Klein
Joseph Losey (Lira-Adel-Nova)

PAUL NEWMAN

Paul Newman is the defiantly casual, thumb-on-nose imperti-nent, No 1 star of the modern cinema by box office and most other measurements. He has been listed among the top ten

stars almost continually since 1963 and topped the rankings in 1969 and 1970, while three of his films (The Sting, The Towering Inferno, Butch Cassidy and the Sundance Kid) are among the 15 most popular movies of all time. What is it that is so appealing about the Newman screen per-sona? More than anything it's that thumb on the nose. He has the rugged good looks, charm, like-ableness and acting skill of the other superstars; but what is uniquely his own is that imperti-nence.

This unifying trait of his screen personality can be seen to continue from his earliest films (The Rack, Somebody Up There Likes Me, The Long Hot Summer), through '60s Westerns (Hud, Hombre, Butch Cassidy) and films about loners (The Hustler, Harper, Cool Hand Luke), to the individualist heroes of the '70s (The Sting, Buffalo Bill and the Indians, Slap Shot). Newman is almost never a part of the establishment in his films and on the rare occasions when he seems to be (ie, the architect in The Towering Inferno) he is strongly opposed to the ideas of real establishment mem-bers.

Newman was born in Shaker Heights, Ohio, on January 26, 1925, and after war service studied at Kenyon College and the Yale School of Drama. He

Above: Paul Newman as a foul-mouthed, over-the-hill ice-hockey star who violently bends the rules to win in George Roy Hill's Slap Shot.

began to work in TV and on stage, studied at the Actors' Studio, and made his Broadway début in 1953 in *Picnic.* His first film was a starring role in the 1954 The Silver Chalice, a very expensive failure in which Newman was mistakenly promoted as another Brando ➤. Although Newman and Brando share some of the Method mannerisms, Newman absorbed them into his personality; he can therefore be much more "natural" on the screen than Brando.

Newman's second film was two years later and he was much better in The Rack, already outside society as a Korean war veteran on trial for collaborating with the enemy. He became a star in his third film, portraying boxer Rocky Graziano in Somebody Up There Likes Me and confirmed his popularity in 1958 in The Long Hot Summer, which was probably the key film in Newman's life and career. In it, he established his drifter, outsider image, met Joanne Woodward ➤, whom he later married, and began a valuable collaboration with Martin Ritt (who also directed him in Hud, Hombre, Adventures of a Young

Man and The Outrage). Newman was very fine as Billy the Kid in Arthur Penn's The Left-Handed Gun and then began his rise to superstardom with the very suc-cessful Cat on a Hot Tin Roof, playing Elizabeth Taylor's ➤ husband. After From the Terrace, Exodus and The Hustler, he was one of the major stars. Many people felt he should have won an Oscar for his superb performance as the hustling pool player in the last film: he has been nominated for Cat on a Hot Tin Roof, The Hustler, Hud and Cool Hand Luke, but has never won an Academy Award.

Newman's popularity continued to rise in the '60s with films like Hud, The Prize, Torn Curtain, Cool Hand Luke and especially the phenomenally successful Butch Cassidy and the Sundance Kid, which became the most popular Western of all time. It started a new trend in male buddy films which clicked again for Newman when he rejoined co-star Robert Redford ➤ in The Sting. Both films were directed by George Roy Hill, who also made Newman's excellent ice hockey film Slap Shot. Newman has been replaced as the No 1 box office star in recent years by Redford and Clint Eastwood ➤, but neither has yet surpassed him in con-tinuing popularity.

BEST FILMS:
1958 The Left-Handed Gun
Arthur Penn (Warner Brothers)
1958 Cat on a Hot Tin Roof
Richard Brooks (MGM)
1961 The Hustler
Robert Rossen (20th Century Fox)
1963 Hud
Martin Ritt (Paramount)
1966 Harper
Jack Smight (Warner Brothers)
1967 Cool Hand Luke
Stuart Rosenberg (Warner Brothers)
1969 Butch Cassidy and the Sundance Kid
George Roy Hill (20th Century Fox)
1973 The Sting
George Roy Hill (Universal)
1974 The Towering Inferno
John Guillermin (20th Century Fox/ Warner Brothers)
1976 Buffalo Bill and the Indians
Robert Altman (De Laurentiis)
1977 Slap Shot
George Roy Hill (Universal)

JACK NICHOLSON

Jack Nicholson has created one of the most disconcerting per-sonas in the cinema, an off-centre, non-conformist personality which can be considered crazy but in which '70s audiences recognise a reflec-tion of their own thoughts and worries. It is as if the world were a little mad and Nicholson its rebellious mirror.

In One Flew Over the Cuckoo's Nest, Nicholson is the mocking, madcap McMurphy, a "sane" man in a madhouse, eventually lobotomised into mental death for his non-conformity. In **The Passenger** he exchanges identities with a corpse and then follows the dead man's appointment schedule to his own death. In **Five Easy Pieces** he is a short-tempered classical pianist working as a manual labourer, dissatisfied with his way of life but not knowing what he .wants instead; in **The King of Marvin Gardens** he invents bizarre fantasies for radio broadcasts but is unable to cope with the even more bizarre "real life" fantasies of his brother; in **The Last Detail** he is the "bad-ass" sailor-turned-shorepatrolman, creating another rebel against the system and then knocking down his own creation; in **The Missouri Breaks** he is a rustler who buys a farm for a cover and then disgusts his gang by becoming involved in making it a success; in **Chinatown** he is a '30s investigator crazily fighting the system; and in **Easy Rider,** the film that first attracted attention to him as an actor, he is the non-conformist, small-town lawyer who drops out with Peter Fonda and Dennis Hopper. The power he generated in these performances was reflected in five Oscar nominations in eight years, culminating in an Academy Award for his stunning performance in **One Flew Over the Cuckoo's Nest.**

Nicholson was born in Neptune, New Jersey, on April 22, 1936, and began his cinema career in the cartoon department at MGM. He worked on TV and stage, where he was noticed by Roger Corman, who cast him as the lead in the 1958 low-budget **Cry Baby Killer** (as a teenager who thinks he's a killer). He was then featured in a number of early '60s films, including **Studs Lonigan, The Wild Ride** and **The Wild Land;** Corman directed him again in **The Little Shop of Horrors, The Raven** and **The Terror.** Then Nicholson turned writer as well as actor, co-scripting **Thunder Island,** writing **Flight to Fury** (in which he also acted) and teaming up with director Monte Hellman to co-produce two low-budget Westerns, **Ride the Whirlwind** and **The Shootist.** Next was **Hell's Angels on Wheels** and then he wrote the drug-orientated **The Trip** for Corman and Peter Fonda and the bizarre **Head** for Bob Rafelson and The Monkees.

Easy Rider won Nicholson an Oscar nomination; his performance was so powerful that stardom was merely a matter of time. He was Barbra Streisand's ≫ strange brother in **On A Clear Day You Can See Forever** and became a real star with the somewhat auto-biographical **Five Easy Pieces.** Nicholson then turned to directing himself in 1970 with **Drive, He Said,** but it was not a very successful film. He was superb in the sexual explorations of **Carnal Knowledge** with Ann-Margret,

had a small role opposite Tuesday Weld in **A Safe Place,** and continued his brilliant partnership with Rafelson in **The King of Marvin Gardens.**

In addition to the '70s films mentioned above, he had a good small role as a doctor in **Tommy,** a strange one as the dim-witted partner of Warren Beatty ≫ in **The Fortune,** and a strong one as a union organiser in **The Last Tycoon.** Stanley Kubrick's new epic **The Shining** stars him opposite Shelley Duval; Nicholson has also directed himself in the comedy adventure film **Goin' South.**

Above: Jack Nicholson as the tough marine who foul-mouths his way through the very witty **The Last Detail.**

BEST FILMS:
1969 Easy Rider
Dennis Hopper (Columbia)
1970 Five Easy Pieces
Bob Rafelson (Columbia)
1971 Carnal Knowledge
Mike Nichols (Avco Embassy)
1972 The King of Marvin Gardens
Bob Rafelson (Columbia)
1973 The Last Detail
Hal Ashby (Columbia)
1974 Chinatown
Roman Polanski (Paramount)
1975 The Passenger
Michelangelo Antonioni (MGM)
1976 One Flew Over the Cuckoo's Nest
Milos Forman (Fantasy/United Artists)
1976 The Fortune
Mike Nichols (Columbia)
1976 The Missouri Breaks
Arthur Penn (Kastner/United Artists)

Kim Novak

Kim Novak was one of the last manufactured glamour stars of the studio system and was very beautiful indeed in late '50s films like **The Eddie Duchin Story, Bell, Book and Candle** and **Vertigo.**

Her Svengali was Columbia boss Harry Cohn, who regulated every detail of her make-up, hair style and wardrobe and made her one of the top box office stars of the '50s. The critics, always wary of being taken in by manufactured products, were relatively dismissive of her acting talent. They should look again—she was a fine screen actress, combining ethereal beauty with nervous insecurity and creating a screen persona of fragile loveliness that reflected a devastating lack of confidence in the reality of her own image.

In **Bell, Book and Candle,** portraying an immortal witch, she

Above: Kim Novak playing the hooker Polly the Pistol in Billy Wilder's satire on American ·morals, **Kiss Me Stupid.**

is so unsure of her ability to win the love of a human being that she cries and thereby proves her love for him (witches don't cry). In Hitchcock's **Vertigo** she has the double role of the woman loved, lost, "remanufactured" and lost again by James Stewart ≫, again without faith in her own beauty. In **Jeanne Eagels** she was perfectly cast as a doubt-ridden actress and in **Picnic** she was equally insecure as a small-town girl seduced by William Holden ≫. She usually had a lot of trouble with the men in her films, especially Frank Sinatra ≫ as a drug addict in **The Man with the Golden Arm** and as the louse anti-hero of **Pal Joey.**

Like the manufactured star she was, Kim Novak was always aware that underneath the glamour was plain Marilyn Pauline Novak, the daughter of a railway labourer, who had worked in dime stores and as an elevator girl before becoming a star. She was born in Chicago, Illinois, on February 13, 1933, and broke into films with a bit part in the 1954 musical **French Line.** Columbia pushed her to stardom quickly, but in the '60s her career went downhill, despite a superb performance in

Billy Wilder's **Kiss Me Stupid.** Her last good film was Robert Aldrich's 1968 **The Legend of Lylah Clare,** in which she portrays a star manufactured by Peter Finch ≫ to resemble his lost love of the '30s. She has been in semi-retirement during the '70s, except for appearances in **Tales That Witness Madness, The White Buffalo** and **Just a Gigolo.**

BEST FILMS:
1954 Pushover
Richard Quine (Columbia)
1956 The Man with the Golden Arm
Otto Preminger (United Artists)
1956 Picnic
Joshua Logan (Columbia)
1957 Pal Joey
George Sidney (Columbia)
1957 Bell, Book and Candle
Richard Quine (Columbia)
1958 Vertigo
Alfred Hitchcock (Paramount)
1959 Middle of the Night
Delbert Mann (Columbia)
1960 Strangers When We Meet
Richard Quine (Columbia)
1964 Kiss Me Stupid
Billy Wilder (Lopert)
1968 The Legend of Lylah Clare
Robert Aldrich (MGM)

Ryan O'Neal

Ryan O'Neal has an undeserved reputation for portraying decent, honest young men with boyish appeal. In fact, his screen characters are usually criminals, or at least not what they seem under their veneer of charm: in **Paper Moon** (co-starring daughter Tatum ≫) he is a swindler in the American mid-west during the Depression; in **Barry Lyndon** he is a gambling rogue in eighteenth-century Ireland and Europe; in **The Thief Who Came to Dinner** he is a computer programmer whose sideline is cat burglary; in **The Driver** he is a master getaway driver; and in **Wild Rovers** he is a bank robber in the Old West. Peter Bogdanovich's 1972 **What's Up, Doc?** has him causing havoc as a nice young musicologist who, amongst other things, has to "innocently" set fire to his hotel bedroom to conceal the presence of the half-naked Barbra Streisand ≫, and in the 1976 **Nickelodeon** (Bogdanovich again) he is a pioneer film director, pursued by the Patents Trust, making movies illegally. If this slightly deceptive persona is the real one, then perhaps Oliver, the bland and wealthy hero of **Love Story,** isn't that straightforward after all.

He was born Patrick Ryan O'Neal in Los Angeles on April 20, 1941. He began his acting career in 1959 in Germany as a stand-in, then as a stuntman, and finally as an actor in the TV series *Tales of the Vikings.* He made his acting reputation back in the States playing Rodney Harrington, the "decent, honest, charming young man" of the TV series *Peyton Place* from 1964 to 1968. His film début was in **The Big**

Above: Ryan O'Neal and Ali MacGraw turned a simple young romance into a multi-million-dollar **Love Story** *in 1970.*

Bounce (1969) as an ex-GI with a criminal record, getting into trouble at a motel, and bounded to stardom the following year in **The Games** and **Love Story**.

His latest movie is **Oliver's Story**, a sequel to **Love Story** and scripted again by Erich Segal.

BEST FILMS:
1970 The Games
Michael Winner (20th Century Fox)
1970 Love Story
Arthur Hiller (Paramount)
1971 Wild Rovers
Blake Edwards (MGM)
1972 What's Up, Doc?
Peter Bogdanovich (Warner Brothers)
1973 The Thief Who Came to Dinner
Bud Yorkin (Warner Brothers)
1973 Paper Moon
Peter Bogdanovich (Paramount)
1975 Barry Lyndon
Stanley Kubrick (Warner Brothers)
1976 Nickelodeon
Peter Bogdanovich (Columbia)
1977 A Bridge Too Far
Richard Attenborough (Joseph E. Levine)
1978 The Driver
Walter Hill (20th Century Fox)

TATUM O'NEAL

Tatum O'Neal has become the leading child star of the modern cinema, the only juvenile in many years to appear on the top ten box

---

she was equally good as a tomboy whizz-kid pitcher named Amanda Whurlizer whom Walter Matthau ≫ persuades to join his baseball team of misfit kids in exchange for ballet lessons.

While there is no overt sexuality in either of these films, the relationships are definitely those of woman-to-man equality with elements of sexual jealousy (eg getting rid of Ryan O'Neal's floozy girlfriend in **Paper Moon**). The 1976 **Nickelodeon** was less successful for Tatum—the characterisation and plot were underdeveloped—but she came back strong in 1978 as the teenage star of **International Velvet**. This updated sequel to **National Velvet** features her as an American girl (once again an orphan) in England being brought up by the National Velvet girl, now a childless woman (played by Nanette Newman) and eventually winning the Olympic riding competition. She also gets

Above: Physically diminutive but a powerhouse of energy, Tatum O'Neal in **Paper Moon** *(1973) with real-life father Ryan.*

office popularity list (eighth in 1976) and to win an Academy Award (Best Supporting Actress in 1973 for **Paper Moon**). She has made only four films, but they have been extremely popular ones and both **The Bad News Bears** and **Paper Moon** are among the biggest money-making films of the modern cinema. She is exceptionally good at projecting a "natural" screen personality, and the tough-minded independent free-thinking little girls of **Paper Moon** and **Bad News Bears** are memorable creations.

Tatum is the daughter of Ryan O'Neal ≫ and Joanna Moore and was born in Los Angeles in 1964. Her début film was the 1973 **Paper Moon** where her fine portrayal of the foul-mouthed, cigarette-smoking, sharp-thinking "orphan" Addie Pray stole most of the attention from her co-star father. In **The Bad News Bears**

---

a husband, which could signal the end of Tatum O'Neal's reign as a child star.

COMPLETE FILMS:
1973 Paper Moon
Peter Bogdanovich (Paramount)
1976 The Bad News Bears
Michael Ritchie (Paramount)
1976 Nickelodeon
Peter Bogdanovich (Columbia/EMI)
1978 International Velvet
Bryan Forbes (MGM)

PETER O'TOOLE

Peter O'Toole, despite the outdoor adventurer image he acquired with **Lawrence of Arabia**, is actually one of the most theatre-orientated of movie stars. Not only has he worked on stage as much as in the cinema but most of his better-known films are adaptations of plays; **Becket**, in which he played Henry II opposite Richard Burton's ≫ Becket, was derived from the play by Jean Anouilh, while **The Lion in Winter**, in which

---

he was Henry II again with Katharine Hepburn ≫ as his Queen, was from the play by James Goldman. The musical version of **Goodbye Mr Chips** with Petula Clark was the work of playwright Terence Rattigan, the musical **Man of La Mancha**, with O'Toole as Don Quixote opposite Sophia Loren ≫, was a stage production written by Dale Wasserman, and **Under Milk Wood** was based on Dylan Thomas's radio/stage play. **The Ruling Class**, in which he portrayed a mad baronet who switches from being Jesus Christ to being Jack the Ripper, was an adaptation of a play by Peter Barnes, while poet/playwright Adrian Mitchell wrote the Defoe satire **Man Friday**. O'Toole's other films mostly have literary sources, from **The Bible** and **Lord Jim** to **The Night of the Generals** and **Rogue Male**.

The O'Toole screen persona has emerged as an intense,

Above: Peter O'Toole contemplates his loneliness in Jack Gold's ambitious revision of Defoe, **Man Friday**.

introspective character involved in a situation of stress that causes obsessive, neurotic and sometimes psychotic behaviour. This is particularly notable in **Lawrence of Arabia**, where despite the epic grandeur of landscape and story, the focus of the film was on O'Toole's personality. It can be seen in various forms in most of his films, but is particularly evident in his performances as the mad aristocrat in **The Ruling Class**, the psychotic Nazi killer in **The Night of the Generals**, the obsessed mystic of **Lord Jim**, the crazed Don Quixote of **Man of La Mancha** and the neurotic ladies' man of **What's New, Pussycat?** In his latest film **Power Play** he is a tank commanding officer who double-crosses his associates in a *coup d'etat* and then slaughters even his fellow colonels.

O'Toole was born in Connemara, Galway, Ireland, in 1932, and brought up in the north of England. He was a drama student at RADA, worked with the Bristol Old Vic in the late '50s and made his stage reputation in *The Long and the Short and the Tall* in 1959 (but was passed over for Laurence Harvey ≫ for the film version). He made his screen début in the 1960 Disney version of **Kidnapped**, directed by Robert Stevenson, and then appeared in **The Savage Innocents** and **The Day They Robbed the Bank of England** before becoming famous in **Lawrence of Arabia**. His popularity remained strong throughout the '60s despite the commercial and critical failure of films like **Lord Jim** and **Great Catherine**, because **Lawrence of Arabia**, **Becket**, **What's New, Pussycat?** and **The Lion in Winter** were huge box-office successes. His '70s film career has faltered, with no big hits and a lot of stage work. His finest recent performance was in the TV film of Geoffrey Household's classic thriller **Rogue Male**, playing a British sportsman who is hunted down by Nazis after trying to shoot Hitler.

BEST FILMS:
1962 Lawrence of Arabia
David Lean (Columbia)
1964 Becket
Peter Glenville (Paramount)
1965 What's New, Pussycat?
Clive Donner (United Artists)
1967 The Night of the Generals
Anatole Litvak (Columbia)
1968 The Lion in Winter
Anthony Harvey (Avco Embassy)
1969 Goodbye Mr Chips
Herbert Ross (MGM)
1971 The Ruling Class
Peter Medak (Keep Films)
1972 Man of La Mancha
Arthur Hiller (United Artists)
1976 Rogue Male
Clive Donner (TV)
1978 Power Play
Martyn Burke (Magnum)

AL PACINO

Al Pacino won four Oscar nominations in his first five years as a star, and has been listed among the top ten box-office stars since 1974. He is very much a contemporary-style star with a cynical, tough persona, the kind of person who is only too aware of what the world is really like today. In **Serpico** he's the hippy-style but honest New York cop who finds out that the system is even more corrupt than he thought when he tries to do his job the way he feels it should be done. In **The Panic in Needle Park** he is a New York drug addict betrayed by the girl he loves and without much faith in any aspect of society. In **The Godfather** and its sequel he is Michael Corleone, the cynical son who revenges Marlon Brando ≫ and takes over control of the Mafia family, acting with cold-blooded precision. In **Dog Day Afternoon** he is the bank robber trying to steal enough

money to pay for a sex change operation for his second transvestite "wife". In **Scarecrow** he is the partner of Gene Hackman ≫ trying to convince him that it is better to make people laugh than to fight them, but he stills gets beaten nearly to death. In **Bobby Deerfield** he is again cynical, a Formula I racing champion who distrusts the behaviour of mysterious Marthe Keller until he discovers that she has an incurable illness.

Pacino's screen personality seems particularly suitable for continuing stardom. He was born in New York City in 1939 as Alfredo Pacino, studied at the Actors' Studio and began his professional career working off-Broadway. He won a number of theatrical awards, including two Tonys and an Obie, and made his film début in the small role of Tony in the 1969 **Me Natalie** with Patty Duke. His first important

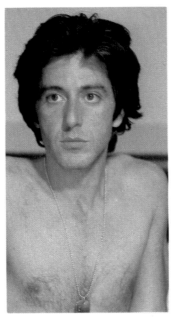

*Above: Al Pacino as the racing driver in the 1977 **Bobby Deerfield**, directed by Sydney Pollack.*

role came in his second film, **The Panic in Needle Park**, and he became a star with his performance in **The Godfather**. Pacino has made remarkably few films for a major star and has worked primarily with three directors: Jerry Schatzberg (who launched him), Francis Ford Coppola (who made him a star) and Sidney Lumet (who gave him his finest roles).

COMPLETE FILMS:
1969 Me Natalie
Fred Coe (Cinema Center)
1971 The Panic in Needle Park
Jerry Schatzberg (20th Century Fox)
1972 The Godfather
Francis Ford Coppola (Paramount)
1973 Scarecrow
Jerry Schatzberg (Warner Brothers)
1973 Serpico
Sidney Lumet (Paramount)
1974 The Godfather Part II
Francis Ford Coppola (Paramount)

1975 Dog Day Afternoon
Sidney Lumet (Warner Brothers)
1977 Bobby Deerfield
Sydney Pollack (Columbia)

ANTHONY PERKINS

Anthony Perkins transmuted the friendly, anxious, sincere, boy-next-door screen persona into the friendly, smiling, psychotic/ schizophrenic/paranoid boy-next-door. It was a bizarre change, initiated in a masterfully chilling way by Alfred Hitchcock in **Psycho** —nervous, nice young men have never been the same since.

Perkins began his film career being as nice as he seemed, first as Jean Simmons' ≫ awkward boyfriend in the 1953 **The Actress** and then as Gary Cooper's ≫ worried Quaker son in **Friendly Persuasion**. He began to crack under the strain in the 1957 **Fear Strikes Out**, having a nervous breakdown because of his father fixation, learned all about killing from father-figure bounty hunter Henry Fonda ≫ as a nervous, inexperienced young sheriff in **The Tin Star**, and then fell anxiously in love with his father's wife in **Desire Under the Elms**. The screen personality was ripe for exploitation by Hitchcock after he began to behave waywardly in **The Matchmaker** and worried about the death of the world in **On The Beach**. In **Psycho** he was more anxious to make friends than ever, smiling, nervous, and

*Above: Anthony Perkins as the motel owner Norman Bates in Hitchcock's **Psycho**. Here he chats innocently with new guest Janet Leigh before murdering her in her shower, in one of the most horrific scenes ever.*

obviously distressed by his unsympathetic mother—then Hitchcock peeled back the smiling face to reveal the horrific madman hiding behind it. Other directors quickly took advantage of Perkins' new screen image: in **Five Miles to Midnight** he faked his own death to collect insurance; in **The Trial** he was accused of nameless crimes; in **Pretty Poison** he was a psychotic arsonist; in **WUSA** he was a do-gooder who turns into a political assassin. The boy-next-door had grown up to be the man-of-his-times.

Perkins was born in New York City on April 4, 1934, the son of actor Osgood Perkins (who died when he was five). After his screen début in **The Actress**, an Oscar nomination for **Friendly Persuasion** and late '50s stardom in the US, he became one of the first American stars to work regularly in Europe, where his movies included two films for Claude Chabrol, **The Champagne Murders** and **Ten Days Wonder**.

His well-meaning anxiety/ madness does not always turn nasty, as his fine performance as the chaplain in **Catch-22** showed. He has worked regularly in the '70s, including notable roles in **Lovin' Molly** and **Remember My Name**.

BEST FILMS:
1953 The Actress
George Cukor(MGM)
1956 Friendly Persuasion
William Wyler (Allied Artists)
1957 Fear Strikes Out
Robert Mulligan (Paramount)
1957 The Tin Star
Anthony Mann (Paramount)
1960 Psycho
Alfred Hitchcock (Paramount)
1962 The Trial
Orson Welles (Gibraltar)
1968 Pretty Poison
Noel Black (20th Century Fox)
1970 Catch-22
Mike Nichols (Paramount)
1970 WUSA
Stuart Rosenberg (Paramount)
1978 Remember My Name
Alan Rudolph (Columbia)

SIDNEY POITIER

Sidney Poitier was the first black American to become a major movie star; while this stardom has caused him to be attacked by radicals who don't like his liberal image, he is actually much cleverer than most of his critics. Admittedly his screen persona can seem bland—the pleasant, soft-spoken, well-educated, well-dressed Negro with integrity, understanding and a sense of humour; the kind of person you would want your sister to marry—but this exterior masks a much more complicated and fascinating screen personality, with quirks, edginess, egotism, anger and driving intelligence. It was seen at its most open in Poitier's brilliant performance in **In the Heat of the Night,** as a Northern detective stuck in a small Southern town with a bigoted but not dumb police chief (Rod Steiger ❯). All the resentments that Poitier and other middle-class American blacks have had to repress boiled under the performance.

Poitier was born in Miami, Florida, of West Indian parents on February 20, 1927. He began to work on stage in 1946, made a film for the US Army Signal Corps in 1949 **(From Whence Cometh My Help),** and made his commercial début for Joseph Mankiewicz in the 1950 **No Way Out.** He was a doctor (nice, well-dressed, middle-class) threatened by racialist Richard Widmark ❯; the film has dated, but it was a major step forward in its time, breaking stereotypes of what kind of parts blacks could play in Hollywood films. Poitier made even more of an impression as one of the rebellious (but not too rebellious) students in Glenn Ford's ❯ school in **The Blackboard Jungle** (1955). His career began to boom, and really took off after the success of Martin Ritt's directorial début **Edge of the City,** which featured Poitier and John Cassavetes as longshoremen friends threatened by racialist Jack Warden.

Poitier was nominated for an Oscar for his strong performance in 1958 in **The Defiant Ones,** as an escaping convict chained to another racialist, Tony Curtis ❯. The symbolism was over-obvious and was pounded home by director Stanley Kramer, but it was a very important film in its time. Poitier did as well as he could in **Porgy and Bess,** considering that he had to mime the songs, did better in **Paris Blues,** and had a fair success in the film version of Lorraine Hansberry's all-black play **A Raisin in the Sun.** He won international acclaim for his next picture, **Lilies of the Field,** a sentimental but still enjoyable story about a handyman who helps East German refugee nuns in Arizona build a chapel. He was

Below: Hollywood's first major black star Sidney Poitier as the New York dock worker in Martin Ritt's **Edge of the City** *(UK:* **A Man Is Ten Feet Tall***).*

named Best Actor at the Berlin Film Festival and then won the Academy Award, the first black actor ever to win the main award (although Hattie McDaniel won a Best Supporting Actress Oscar for **Gone With the Wind**). Poitier was still breaking fresh ground; it didn't really matter whether the character in the film was black or not.

The next frontier he crossed was the inter-racial sex barrier, first befriending a blind girl (Elizabeth Hartman) in **A Patch of Blue,** despite opposition from bigoted mother Shelley Winters ❯, and then actually marrying Katharine Houghton in **Guess Who's Coming to Dinner?** In the same year, 1967, Poitier married Canadian film actress Joanna Shimkus and starred in two other major films, **In the Heat of the Night** and **To Sir With Love.** In 1968 he was listed as the No 1 box office star in America and he began producing and directing films as well as acting in them. The breakthrough he had made meant that other black stars could and did emerge in the '70s with other kinds of screen personas. None of them has yet come near the degree of stardom attained by Poitier.

During the '70s Poitier has done some interesting work as a director-star, especially in his trilogy with Bill Cosby (**Uptown Saturday Night, Let's Do It Again, A Piece of the Action**).

BEST FILMS:
1955 The Blackboard Jungle
Richard Brooks (MGM)
1957 Edge of the City
Martin Ritt (MGM)
1958 The Defiant Ones
Stanley Kramer (United Artists)
1961 A Raisin in the Sun
Daniel Petrie (Columbia)
1963 Lilies of the Field
Ralph Nelson (United Artists)
1965 A Patch of Blue
Guy Green (MGM)
1967 To Sir With Love
James Clavell (Columbia)
1967 In the Heat of the Night
Norman Jewison (United Artists)
1967 Guess Who's Coming to Dinner?
Stanley Kramer (Columbia)
1975 Let's Do It Again
Sidney Poitier (Warner Brothers)

ELVIS PRESLEY

Elvis Presley was a major movie star as well as being the King of Rock 'n' Roll; he was high among the top ten box office actors for seven years. Although most non-Presley fans have ignored his movies, he was not at all bad as a film actor. The majority of his pictures were musical vehicles and introduced hit title songs (*Jailhouse Rock, King Creole, Love Me Tender*), but they were mainly directed by highly qualified Hollywood professionals, including Michael Curtiz, Phil Karlson, Gordon Douglas, Richard Thorpe and (most often) Norman Taurog. His

greatest film simply as a film, however, was the non-musical Western **Flaming Star** directed by Don Siegel; Presley sings one song at a birthday party and another over the credits, but the film itself (originally written for Marlon Brando ❯) is concerned with the relationship between Indians and whites (Presley plays a half-breed). The film was, unfortunately, not a big commercial success; it didn't have enough music for the fans, and the non-fans ignored it.

Presley was born in Tupelo, Mississippi, on January 8, 1935, and made his first commercial record, *That's Alright, Mama,* in 1954. He had his first No 1 hit song, *Heartbreak Hotel,* in 1956 and made his film début the same year in **Love Me Tender.** One year

Above: Elvis Presley gyrating in one of his later formula movies, **Girl Happy,** *in which he is in love with the daughter of a Chicago mobster.*

later he was rated the fourth biggest box office star in the US; few other stars have done as well. Presley was the first rock star to become a movie star, and his entry into films with this new music must be considered as one of the starting points of the modern cinema. His raunchy, thrusting "Pelvis" image was toned down for the cinema by manager Colonel Tom Parker until it offended virtually no one and aroused no criticism. It also made his screen persona surprisingly bland in most of his films. The best Presley fiction films are the early ones, up to 1963, but the best projections of him as a performer are two later documentaries, **Elvis—That's the Way It Is** and the even better **Elvis on Tour.** He died on August 16, 1977, at his Gracelands mansion in Memphis, Tennessee. In addition to his importance as the first rock star and a major movie star, he was also one of the all-time greats of popular music. He became the modern equivalent of Bing Crosby

», with whom he shares honours in various measurements of highest record sales.

BEST FILMS:
1957 Jailhouse Rock
Richard Thorpe (MGM)
1958 King Creole
Michael Curtiz (Paramount)
1960 GI Blues
Norman Taurog (Paramount)
1961 Flaming Star
Don Siegel (20th Century Fox)
1961 Wild in the Country
Philip Dunne (20th Century Fox)
1962 Blue Hawaii
Norman Taurog (Paramount)
1962 Kid Galahad
Phil Karlson (United Artists)
1962 Follow That Dream
Gordon Douglas (United Artists)
1970 Elvis—That's the Way It Is
Denis Sanders (MGM)
1972 Elvis on Tour
Pierre Adidge & Robert Abel (MGM)

VINCENT PRICE

That Vincent Price has become the King of the Modern Horror Film, taking over the crown from the late Boris Karloff », only confirms that this cinematic genre is rather different than most critics and non-horror fans believe for there is certainly nothing overtly horrific about the gentle-voiced, subtly-mocking Price, whose off-screen interests are pre-Columbian art and gourmet cookery. His central position in the field of contemporary horror is primarily due to his silky-smooth voice, which conveys menace in the suavest of gentlemanly tones, and to his ability to stand back slightly from the supernatural environments in which he moves, ever so quietly disdainful of the horrible actions he is involved in. Price's horror reputation is based on his brilliant collaboration with director Roger Corman in the '60s, when they made a series of Poe-derived classic horror pictures culminating in the brilliant atmospherics of **The Masque of the Red Death** and **The Tomb of Ligeia.** The most truly frightening and malevolent character Price portrayed on screen, however, was not based on fiction but on history—the terrifying witch-burner of Michael Reeves' disturbing **Witchfinder General.**

Price actually came to the horror field rather late in his career, after a long period of semi-stardom in movies stretching back to 1938. He was born in St Louis, Missouri, on May 27, 1911 into a wealthy family, studied at Yale and the University of London, and began working on stage in the mid-'30s. He made his screen début in the comedy **Service de Luxe** (rather appropriately at Universal, the horror studio) and quickly became a character star in films like **The Private Lives of Elizabeth and Essex** (as Raleigh) and **Tower of London** (as Clarence). He soon began to veer towards more villainous roles, viciously opposing Jennifer Jones » in **The Song of Bernadette** and sadistically tormenting Gene Tierney » in **Dragonwyck.** He was very good as one of Tierney's admirers in **Laura,** but even better in Samuel Fuller's underrated **The Baron of Arizona,** as a suave swindler who very nearly takes possession of that territory. His entry into the horror field came through the 1953 3-D film **House of Wax,** re-creating Lionel Atwill's old role from **The Mystery of the Wax Museum.** It was a huge commercial success and Price began to appear in more and more films of this type, notably **The Fly** and **The Tingler.**

Price's collaboration with Roger Corman began in 1960 with **The House of Usher,** an adaptation of

*Above: Vincent Price with a typical collection of roommates, in Corman's Edgar Allan Poe satire **The Raven.***

the Poe story by the science-fiction writer Richard Matheson. This film, and its Poe-derived sequels like **The Pit and the Pendulum, The Raven,** etc, were made for the low-budget company AIP, but despite their miniscule costs they rank among the most imaginative films of the genre. Price also began to work with other horror directors in Italy and England. The mocking humour of his style of horror came very much to the fore in **The Abominable Dr Phibes** and its sequel, and in **Theatre of Blood** he gained the actor's ultimate revenge on critics by killing them with Shakespearian devices. His career has continued strong up to the present time. He published his autobiography in 1958, *I Like What I Know.*

BEST FILMS:
1950 The Baron of Arizona
Samuel Fuller (Lippert)
1953 House of Wax
André de Toth (Warner Brothers)
1960 The House of Usher
Roger Corman (AIP)

1961 The Pit and the Pendulum
Roger Corman (AIP)
1962 The Raven
Roger Corman (AIP)
1963 The Haunted Palace
Roger Corman (AIP)
1964 The Masque of the Red Death
Roger Corman (AIP)
1964 The Tomb of Ligeia
Roger Corman (AIP)
1968 Witchfinder General
Michael Reeves (Tigon)
1971 The Abominable Dr Phibes
Robert Fuest (AIP)

ROBERT REDFORD

Robert Redford became the No 1 box office star in America in the mid-'70s, topping the annual popularity charts in 1974, 1975 and 1976 on the strength of such films as **All the President's Men, Three Days of the Condor, The Sting** and **The Way We Were.** In a period when the other top male stars represented various forms of violence and rebellion (Clint Eastwood », Paul Newman », Charles Bronson », Steve McQueen »), it was surprising to have a clean-cut, all-American good guy suddenly emerging as the most popular star. The reasons are complex, but reflect Redford's own interest in exploring the American myth of "winning", with all the moral and emotional ambiguities that involves.

Redford is sardonic and playful, the nonchalant golden boy whose well-scrubbed good looks and charm can sometimes mask ugly moral characteristics without los-

ing audience sympathy. He portrays ambitious men who strive to win whatever the cost: in **The Candidate** the arena is politics, in **Downhill Racer** it's sport, and in **All the President's Men** it's journalism. In **The Great Waldo Pepper** his driving desire to show he is a better fighter pilot than a German World War I ace leads to a real dogfight. In **Jeremiah Johnson** he tries to become the king of the wilderness, while in **The Way We Were** he will make any compromises to get ahead as a writer. In **Three Days of the Condor** he takes on the whole CIA in his fight to protect himself, and in **A Bridge Too Far** he succeeds in a dangerous daylight raid across the Rhine. He doesn't always succeed in his ambitions, but he makes superlative efforts, becoming a rich man so he can woo a girl in **The Great Gatsby** and escaping from prison to get back to wife Jane Fonda » in **The Chase.**

Redford's greatest commercial successes have been in tandem with Paul Newman in **Butch Cassidy and the Sundance Kid** and **The Sting,** films which started a male bonding syndrome. The chemistry between Redford and Newman is extraordinarily effective because they compensate for the weaknesses in each other's screen personas and together become "good guy rebels". They are bank robbers in **Butch Cassidy** and swindlers in **The Sting,**

*Below: Robert Redford, known to the world as The Sundance Kid, the outlaw who couldn't swim and died in Bolivia full of holes (**Butch Cassidy and the Sundance Kid,** 1969).*

but there is little that is nasty about their characterisations and everything that is sympathetic. The charismatic power of their combined personas is so effective that a third film seems certain. In the meantime, Redford is likely to remain a top star as long as the public loves a golden boy.

Redford was born in Santa Monica, California, on August 18, 1937, and spent his youth very much in the way his screen image reflects, becoming a star athlete and winning a baseball scholarship to the University of Colorado. He eventually dropped out, worked in an oil field to earn money and went to Europe for a year. When he came back he became interested in acting and by 1959 was appearing on Broadway. He made his film début in 1962 in the small-budget, independent **War Hunt,** made by Terry and Dennis Sanders, but it did not advance his career much—nor did the 1965 **Situation Hopeless but Not Serious** with Alec Guinness ➤. **Inside Daisy Clover** gave him a better chance as a star who marries rising singer Natalie Wood ➤ but runs away on their wedding night because he is gay. He was good as the escaped convict trying to get home in **The Chase,** and adequate as a Southern railway boss in **This Property is Condemned,** but he was a long way from being a big star.

Redford then had a notable success with Jane Fonda ➤, recreating his stage success in **Barefoot in the Park,** but his judgement seemed off when he turned down starring roles in **Who's Afraid of Virginia Woolf?** (George Segal ➤ did it), **The Graduate** (it made Dustin Hoffman ➤ a star) and **Rosemary's Baby** (in John Cassavetes' part). He accepted **Blue,** then backed out one week before shooting began and was sued. His promising career seemed suddenly to have become very unpromising, until Paul Newman picked him as his partner in **Butch Cassidy;** he became a major star overnight. Redford has fought hard against being absorbed into the star system but his reticence has only made him more sought-after. He has worked consistently with the same directors (George Roy Hill, Sydney Pollack, Michael Ritchie) and has shown an admirable willingness to act in relatively non-commercial films if he likes the subject matter and the director. He married in 1958 and he and his wife Lola have three children.

BEST FILMS:
1967 Barefoot in the Park
Gene Saks (Paramount)
1969 Butch Cassidy and the Sundance Kid
George Roy Hill (20th Century Fox)
1969 Tell Them Willie Boy is Here
Abraham Polonsky (Universal)
1969 Downhill Racer
Michael Ritchie (Paramount)
1972 The Candidate
Michael Ritchie (Warner Brothers)

1973 The Sting
George Roy Hill (Universal)
1974 The Great Gatsby
Jack Clayton (Paramount)
1975 The Great Waldo Pepper
George Roy Hill (Universal)
1975 Three Days of the Condor
Sydney Pollack (Paramount)
1976 All the President's Men
Alan J. Pakula (Warner Brothers)

VANESSA REDGRAVE

Vanessa Redgrave is a constantly evolving screen actress whose off-camera political activities have attracted as much attention as her film work. Her stardom was probably greater in the mid-'60s following the success of **Morgan** and **Blow Up** than it is now, but her reputation has risen since her Academy Award for her perform-

Above: Vanessa Redgrave, one of Britain's best actresses and certainly the most politically active, in **Yanks,** *set in Northern England during WW2.*

ance in **Julia.** As this role, portraying a politically aware woman fighting fascism in Europe in the '30s, is very much a reflection of Redgrave's off-screen persona, it is to be expected that this type of "committed" role will be much more in evidence in her future films. On the other hand, Redgrave's present radical stance can also be seen as merely a component of the persona she has been creating on screen and off since the mid-'60s—a quirky, eccentric and talented individualist whose sexuality is not lessened by commitment. The epitome of this persona is seen on screen in **Isadora,** where Redgrave portrayed the sexually-liberated but utterly obsessive dancer Isadora Duncan. In **Camelot** she was Guinevere, loyal to Arthur but unable to resist creating political

turmoil by having an affair with Lancelot. In **Blow Up** she is willing to engage in half-naked sexual games with photographer David Hemmings, but never forgets her aim of retrieving an incriminating photo. In **The Devils** she is the sex-starved mother superior of a seventeenth-century French convent brought to a lewd frenzy by dreams of Oliver Reed ➤. In **Mary, Queen of Scots** her political involvement is undermined by her amorous relationships with Darnley and Bothwell. Even in **Julia** she leaves an illegitimate child behind when she is killed.

Redgrave was born in London in 1937, the daughter of Sir Michael Redgrave and sister of Lynn and Corin. She began working on stage in 1957 and made her film début in 1958 in **Behind the Mask,** portraying her father's daughter. She made her initial reputation as a stage actress with the Royal Shakespeare Company and became a film star in 1966 with her second picture, **Morgan . . . A Suitable Case for Treatment.** Then she had a tiny role as Anne Boleyn in **A Man For All Seasons,** starred in **Blow Up** and appeared in two films for Tony Richardson (whom she married and divorced during the '60s), **The Sailor from Gibraltar** and **The Charge of the Light Brigade.** Her Italian films with Franco Nero, the father of one of her children, included Elio Petri's **A Quiet Place in the Country** and two films for Tinto Brass, **Drop Out** (shot in London) and **La Vacanza.** They did not enhance her reputation, nor did the stolid **The Trojan Women** or the frenetic **The Devils.** Her political radical persona was seen in its most open form in her self-financed documentary **The Palestinian,** in which she interviews Arabs in Lebanon. Her anti-Zionist speech at the 1978 Academy Award ceremonies caused controversy but she has continued to star in important films including **Yanks** and **Agatha.** She has also been nominated for Oscars for her performances in **Morgan, Isadora** and **Mary, Queen of Scots.**

BEST FILMS:
1966 Morgan . . . A Suitable Case for Treatment
Karel Reisz (British Lion)
1966 Blow Up
Michelangelo Antonioni (MGM)
1967 Camelot
Joshua Logan (Warner Brothers)
1968 Isadora
Karel Reisz (Universal)
1968 The Seagull
Sidney Lumet (Warner Brothers)
1971 The Devils
Ken Russell (Warner Brothers)
1972 Mary, Queen of Scots
Charles Jarrott (Universal)
1975 Out of Season
Alan Bridges (EMI)
1977 Julia
Fred Zinnemann (20th Century Fox)
1977 The Palestinian
Roy Battersby (Vanessa Redgrave Productions)

OLIVER REED

Oliver Reed exudes a masculine virility that is unusual in the British cinema, where most of the actors have come up through the theatre. Reed skipped stage training, going straight into film extra roles after doing his Army service as a medical orderly. He never lost his youthful vitality and his dynamism made him into a star within a year of starting, portraying the werewolf in Hammer's **The Curse of the Werewolf.** This kind of animalistic persona has stayed with him in most of his later roles whether he portrays the brutish Bill Sikes in **Oliver!,** the sexually "possessed" priest in **The Devils** or gangster Eddie Mars in **The Big Sleep.** Reed has become a bigger star in the '70s than he was in the '60s but the limitation of his screen personality will probably prevent him from becoming a major international star.

Reed was born in Wimbledon on February 13, 1938, the nephew of film director Carol Reed. He made his film début as an extra in 1959 in **Beat Girl,** and his burly animalism made him a werewolf star by late 1960. Hammer featured him in other horror films, including Joseph Losey's notable **The Damned** (as the leader of a motor bike gang), and he was then taken up by director Michael Winner who made him into a bigger star in **The System, The Jokers** and **I'll Never Forget What's 'is Name.** He acquired more renown under his uncle's direction as Sikes in the musical **Oliver!** (Academy Award for Best Picture of 1968) and then real

1974 **The Four Musketeers**
Richard Lester (Film Trust)
1975 **Royal Flash**
Richard Lester (20th Century Fox)
1975 **Tommy**
Ken Russell (Robert Stigwood Organisation)

LEE REMICK

The screen persona built around Lee Remick in her early years in films was oddly at variance with her actual background. On screen she was an overheated Southern girl with a fondness for sex, drink and difficult men, and seemed to have a predilection for getting raped. Someone apparently thought these were ideal characteristics for a Churchill, so she ended up playing *Jennie* on British television.

Remick's real background is

Above: Oliver Reed as Athos in **The Four Musketeers—The Revenge of Milady** *(Faye Dunaway)* which showed off Reed's capacity for toughness and comedy. Beginning in low-budget horror, Reed has built a dynamic career.

fame wrestling in the nude with Alan Bates **>** in Ken Russell's **Women in Love.** Russell's **The Devils** added to his notoriety, and the sexually strange **Triple Echo** enhanced his critical reputation. In 1973 he began working for his best director, Richard Lester, who featured him as Athos in **The Three Musketeers** and its fine sequel **The Four Musketeers,** and then as the evil Bismarck in **Royal Flash.** Russell also gave him another good role as the villainous stepfather in **Tommy.** His recent films, not his best, include **Burnt Offerings** (supernatural nastiness with Karen Black), **The Prince and the Pauper** (as a soldier of fortune befriending the prince) and **The Class of Miss MacMichael** (as the mean and hypocritical head of a school where Glenda Jackson **>** teaches).

BEST FILMS:
1960 **The Curse of the Werewolf**
Terence Fisher (Hammer)
1961 **The Damned**
Joseph Losey (Hammer)
1964 **The System**
Michael Winner (British Lion)
1968 **Oliver!**
Carol Reed (Columbia)
1969 **Women in Love**
Ken Russell (United Artists)
1971 **The Devils**
Ken Russell (Warner Brothers)
1973 **The Three Musketeers**
Richard Lester (Film Trust)

loving, suffering wife of Steve McQueen **>** in Texas, and finally turned firmly against alcohol as a temperance campaigner in **The Hallelujah Trail.** She went to Broadway for a year to break the mould, starring as the blind protagonist in *Wait Until Dark,* and then featured brilliantly as George Segal's **>** girlfriend in **No Way to Treat a Lady.** She was Frank Sinatra's **>** wife in **The Detective,** sexy again, and then moved to London, where she starred in **A Severed Head** and **Loot.** She went to Oregon to work with Paul Newman **>** in the enjoyable **Sometimes a Great Notion,** was featured in the filmed play **A Delicate Balance,** and starred in the IRA thriller **Hennessy.** Her biggest commercial success was **The Omen,** in which she plays the adoptive mother of the devil-child, in 1976; the following year she was a secret agent in partnership with Soviet agent Charles Bronson **>** in **Telefon.**

BEST FILMS:
1959 **Anatomy of a Murder**
Otto Preminger (Columbia)
1960 **Wild River**
Elia Kazan (20th Century Fox)
1962 **Days of Wine and Roses**
Blake Edwards (Warner Brothers)
1965 **Baby the Rain Must Fall**
Robert Mulligan (Columbia)
1968 **No Way to Treat a Lady**
Jack Smight (Paramount)
1968 **The Detective**
Gordon Douglas (20th Century Fox)
1971 **Sometimes a Great Notion**
Paul Newman (Universal)
1975 **A Delicate Balance**
Tony Richardson (Ely Landau)
1976 **The Omen**
Richard Donner (20th Century Fox)
1977 **Telefon**
Don Siegel (MGM)

FERNANDO REY

Fernando Rey is the leading Spanish star of the international cinema and more and more the anarchistic screen alter ego of director Luis Buñuel. Although Rey is probably best known to most filmgoers as the ruthless and elusive drugs baron of **The French Connection** and **French Connection Number 2,** his greatest achievements have been in Buñuel's films. Despite his age and his portly, bearded appearance, Rey's roles in these pictures invariably turn on a sexual relationship with a young, innocent and extremely beautiful girl; in **Viridiana** he is the uncle who drugs and attempts to seduce innocent Silvia Pinal and then hangs himself; in **Tristana** he is the guardian of virginal Catherine Deneuve **>** who he seduces and eventually marries; in **The Discreet Charm of the Bourgeoisie** the object of his seductive charm is Delphine Seyrig **>**; in **That Obscure Object of Desire** his love-hate sexual relationship is with lovely young Carole Bouquet. In all of these

films sexual desire is explicit and disruptive, making the 62-year-old Spanish actor probably the oldest sex star in the movies.

He was born in La Coruñu, Spain, in 1917, as Fernando Casada D'Armbillet. His architectural studies were ended by the Civil War and after it finished he began working as an extra in films. His first important role was in the 1944 **Eugenia de Montijo** and his magnificent voice, imposing presence and fine acting ability soon made him a top Spanish star. He starred in **Reina Santa** in 1947, **Don Quijote de la Mancha** in 1948 and **Mare Nostrum** in 1949. Buñuel saw him working on a film in Mexico in 1959 and gave him his first great role in **Viridiana** in 1961. In the '60s he was featured in many international productions including Orson Welles' **>** **Chimes at Midnight** (as Worcester), Laurence

Above: Fernando Rey as he was seen in Lewis Gilbert's 1970 **The Adventurers,** portraying a South American patriot hero who fathers a famous playboy.

Harvey's **>** **The Ceremony, The Return of the Seven, Navajo Joe** and **Villa Rides.** His greatest period of international stardom, however, has been in the '70s with the **French Connection** films and the Buñuel pictures. He was starred opposite Catherine Deneuve once more in a second sexual duel, **La Femme aux Bottes Rouges,** directed by Buñuel's son Juan, and gave good performances in **Seven Beauties** (as an anarchist), **The Voyage of the Damned** and **This Kind of Love.**

BEST FILMS:
1961 **Viridiana**
Luis Buñuel (Alatriste/Uninci Films)
1966 **Chimes at Midnight**
Orson Welles (Internacional Films Española)
1970 **Tristana**
Luis Buñuel (Epoca/Talia Films)

Above: Lee Remick posing as a nurse in Don Siegel's strong 1977 spy thriller **Telefon.** The American Miss Remick lives permanently in London.

that of a dyed-in-the-wool Yankee, born in Boston, Massachusetts, on December 14, 1935, educated at Barnard College, and entering the cinema from (Northern) stage and TV. Elia Kazan started her on the road to Southern degradation by casting her as the sexy drum-majorette in the 1958 **A Face in the Crowd.** She was the supposed rape victim in **Anatomy of a Murder,** the Tennessee widow attracted to Montgomery Clift **>** in **Wild River** and the heavy-drinking rape victim Temple Drake in **Sanctuary.** In **Days of Wine and Roses** she was alcoholic Jack Lemmon's **>** amiable wife who starts drinking to keep him company and becomes an alcoholic herself; her performance won her an Oscar nomination. She was back in the South again in **Baby the Rain Must Fall,** playing the

213

BURT REYNOLDS

Burt Reynolds seems likely to become one of the biggest box office stars of the cinema on the basis of such huge commercial successes as **Smokey and the Bandit** and **Hooper.** Reynold's loveable con artist persona, the brash off-hand wise guy who claims to be the best at whatever he does (and more often than not proves it), obviously has very wide appeal and has made Reynolds one of the most "bankable" stars in the business. There is no doubt that it is the Reynolds personality that makes his films popular, for even the critical failures are among *Variety's* all-time box office champs.

Reynolds has been making films since 1961, but his stardom goes back only to 1972 when he was (1) the first male nude centrefold for *Cosmopolitan* magazine and (2) the Oscar-nominated star of **Deliverance.** His career soared from that point. In 1973 he was listed as fourth in the top ten box office stars, he has stayed in the top ten every year since, and he has made an average of two or three popular films a year. All these films stress the Reynolds charm and personality, though they are certainly not all light-hearted. In **Hooper** he is the world's greatest stuntman performing one last super-stunt before passing on the title. In **Smokey and the Bandit** he is out to set a new record by transporting beer illegally from Texas faster than it's ever been done before. In **W.W. and the Dixie Dance Kings** he is the greatest Country and Western promoter there is (he says) and surprises himself by living up to his word. In **The Longest Yard** he is a top professional football player trapped into playing ball as a prison convict and finally winning the game despite vicious threats. In **Semi-Tough** he is again a professional footballer, conning his way into the arms of Jill Clayburgh ⟩ and winning her from Kris Kristofferson ⟩ literally at the altar.

Reynolds, of course, was a real-life professional footballer. He was born in West Palm Beach, Florida, on February 11, 1936 (with a Cherokee grandmother of whom he is particularly proud) and educated at Florida State University where he played football; he played pro ball with the Baltimore Colts until a car accident forced him to quit; he then turned to studying drama. He began working in television in 1959 on the *Riverboat* series and made his film début in the 1961 **Angel Baby.** His other '60s films included **Armored Command, Operation CIA, Navajo Joe, Impasse** and the drastically-cut Sam Fuller film **Shark.**

By this time Reynolds was a minor star and was featured in two TV series, *Hawk* and *Dan August,* as well as reasonable Westerns like **Sam Whiskey** and **100 Rifles.** After he became a major star in 1972 with **Deliverance,** the police film **Fuzz** and the private eye movie **Shamus,** he began to develop his Southern loveable wise guy persona in **White Lightning.** This led to a sequel, **Gator,** as well as films like **W.W. and the Dixie Dance Kings** and **Smokey and the Bandit.** He starred in two of Peter Bogdanovich's less successful films, the Cole Porter musical **At Long Last Love** and the film pioneer comedy **Nickelodeon,** and two of Robert Aldrich's best films, **The Longest Yard** and **Hustle.** The $12 million **Lucky Lady,** with Stanley Donen directing him, Liza Minnelli ⟩ and Gene Hackman ⟩ was unlucky but his guest appearance in **Silent Movie** was fun.

Above: Burt Reynolds as the macho leader of a group of businessmen who take a canoe-trip to death and disaster in the haunting **Deliverance.**

BEST FILMS:
1972 Deliverance
John Boorman (Warner Brothers)
1972 Fuzz
Richard A. Colla (United Artists)
1972 Shamus
Buzz Kulik (Columbia)
1973 White Lightning
Joseph Sargent (United Artists)
1974 The Longest Yard/The Mean Machine
Robert Aldrich (Paramount)
1975 W.W. and the Dixie Dance Kings
John G. Avildsen (20th Century Fox)
1976 Hustle
Robert Aldrich (Paramount)
1977 Smokey and the Bandit
Hal Needham (Universal)
1977 Semi-Tough
Michael Ritchie (United Artists)
1978 Hooper
Hal Needham (Warner Brothers)

JASON ROBARDS

Jason Robards has become a major movie star because of television—after 20 years of outstanding films, enormous critical acclaim as an actor and two Academy Awards. His icy-edged portrayal of President Monkton in the TV mini-series *Washington: Behind Closed Doors* made him into a hot property in a way that his fine film and stage career never could. It helps, of course, to win the Best Supporting Actor Oscar two years in a row—in 1976 as *Washington Post* editor Ben Bradlee in **All The President's Men** and in 1977 as Dashiell Hammett in **Julia**—but Robards' career was already full of brilliant performances. He was as forceful as a gangster (Al Capone in **The St Valentine's Day Massacre**) as he was amusing as an eccentric comedy writer (**A Thousand Clowns**), able to switch from heightened theatrical drama (**A Long Day's Journey into Night**) to plush period romance (**Isadora**), and mix meaningful message films (**Johnny Got His Gun**) with entertaining burlesque (**The Night They Raided Minsky's**). Unusually for an actor with a strong theatre background, Robards has also been highly effective in Westerns, from **The Hour of the Gun** (as Doc Holliday) and **Pat Garrett and Billy the Kid** (as Governor Lew Wallace) to the brutalities of Sergio Leone's Italian West (**Once Upon a Time in the West**) and the fantasies of Sam Peckinpah's bizarre West (**The Ballad of Cable Hogue**).

To confirm his present-day achievement of real stardom, Robards has finally dropped the "Jr" from his name. He is the son of Jason Robards, Sr, a famous theatre and cinema star of the '20s and early '30s, and was born in Chicago, Illinois, on July 26, 1922. Dismayed by the speed with which his father's star dimmed, Robards originally planned a different kind of career, but ended up treading the same path from stage to screen. He made his Broadway début in 1951 in *Stalag 17* and his first film, **The Journey,** in 1959. He was officially a star by 1961, playing opposite Jennifer Jones ⟩ in the adaptation of F. Scott Fitzgerald's novel **Tender Is the Night,** but his career is only now reaching its zenith.

BEST FILMS:
1961 Tender Is the Night
Henry King (20th Century Fox)
1962 Long Day's Journey into Night
Sidney Lumet (United Artists/Ely Landau)
1965 A Thousand Clowns
Fred Coe (United Artists)

Left: Jason Robards as the hard drinking writer Dashiell Hammett, living with Lillian Hellman in Fred Zinnemann's **Julia.**

1985 attorney in; "The Atlanta Child Murders"
2/11,13/85 - 2 nights

1967 The Hour of the Gun
John Sturges (United Artists)
1967 The St Valentine's Day Massacre
Roger Corman (20th Century Fox)
1968 The Night They Raided Minsky's
William Friedkin (United Artists)
1969 Once Upon a Time in the West
Sergio Leone (Paramount)
1970 The Ballad of Cable Hogue
Sam Peckinpah (Warner Brothers)
1976 All the President's Men
Alan J. Pakula (Warner Brothers)
1977 Julia
Fred Zinnemann (20th Century Fox)

CLIFF ROBERTSON

Cliff Robertson is an ambitious, talented, obsessive, persevering actor: he finally won an Oscar in 1968 for **Charly** and starred in a big box-office movie in 1975, **Three Days of the Condor**, but he has not yet become a major star and probably never will. On screen he usually portrays ambitious, talented, obsessive men who often achieve their aim only to discover it wasn't worth it.

The most ambitious and successful person Robertson ever portrayed on screen was John F. Kennedy in his war hero days in the film **PT 109**. In **The Best Man** Robertson is a political candidate ruthlessly battling Henry Fonda for the presidential nomination. In **J. W. Coop** he is a rodeo star fighting obsessively for success after coming out of prison, and eventually finding that success can have a bitter taste. In **Obsession** he is tormented by the tragic death of his wife, tries to re-create her in the form of a mysterious girl who may just be his own daughter, and then finds the tragedy repeating itself. In **Three Days of the Condor** he is a CIA section chief who succeeds in becoming the top man in the organisation, but it backfires on him. In **Charly** he is a mentally retarded floorsweeper who becomes a genius through the aid of an operation—only to find that what goes up must come down, even mentally.

Robertson was born in La Jolla, California, on September 9, 1925, as Clifford Parker Robertson III. He attended Antioch College, served in the merchant marine and began acting with theatre groups in 1947. He worked on stage with Joshua Logan, who gave him a good role in the 1956 film **Picnic**. Then Robert Aldrich gave him an even better one opposite Joan Crawford ➤ in **Autumn Leaves**, portraying her young, unstable husband. He was also good in **The Girl Most Likely** and the film version of Norman Mailer's **The Naked and the Dead**, but then had a run of weak films before giving a brilliant performance as an obsessive revenge-seeking hood in Sam Fuller's **Underworld USA**. He was enjoyable in the hospital soap

opera **The Interns**, the political **The Best Man** and the all-star Ben Jonson-derived **The Honey Pot**. He worked exceptionally hard to win his 1968 Academy Award for **Charly**, a good if somewhat "acted" performance, through intensive promotion activity but his films still remained mixed in quality. He was good as a tough officer leading a suicide mission in World War II in **Too Late the Hero**, excellent in a ruthless personification of old West bandit Cole Younger in **The Great Northfield Minnesota Raid**, and at his very best directing himself as a rodeo man on the rise in **J. W. Coop**. He was a cop tracking down a sex murderer in Frank Perry's **Man on a Swing** and then was one of the naval officers involved in **Midway**, which together with **Three Days of the Condor** has been his biggest commercial success, the two films having earned $20 million in the US alone. His 1978 films include **The Pilot**, portraying an international airlines captain suffering from alcoholism, and **Good Times, Bad Times**, again directing.

Below: Cliff Robertson as the cynical and corrupt Presidential candidate in the Gore Vidal scripted **The Best Man.**

BEST FILMS:
1956 Autumn Leaves
Robert Aldrich (Columbia)
1958 The Naked and the Dead
Raoul Walsh (Warner Brothers)
1961 Underworld USA
Samuel Fuller (Columbia)
1964 The Best Man
Franklin Schaffner (United Artists)
1967 The Honey Pot
Joseph L. Mankiewicz (United Artists)
1968 Charly
Ralph Nelson (Cinerama)
1970 Too Late the Hero
Robert Aldrich (Palomar)
1971 J. W. Coop
Cliff Robertson (Columbia)
1975 Three Days of the Condor
Sydney Pollack (Paramount)
1976 Obsession
Brian De Palma (Columbia)

DIANA ROSS

Diana Ross is one of the three or four biggest female movie stars in the world, as far as the film industry is concerned, even if she has only made three films. Both she and Barbra Streisand ➤ are superstars because their huge reputations as singers have transferred to the screen with equal potency, and their films are big box-office. Ross surprised the critics, if not her fans, by giving a superb performance in her first film, **Lady Sings the Blues**, portraying jazz singer Billie Holiday.

Above: Diana Ross, the Motown star, in her acclaimed début as Billie Holliday in the biopic **Lady Sings the Blues.**

She won an Oscar nomination and the film made $10 million in the US alone. The critics were less kind to her about the film **Mahogany**, in which she plays a chic fashion designer, but the film still made $7 million in the States and the theme song (*Do You Know Where You're Going To*) was a No 1 hit. Her latest performance as Dorothy in **The Wiz**, based on a stage musical derived from **The Wizard of Oz**, will certainly invoke comparison with Judy Garland's ➤ performance in the earlier film version and possibly help make Ross just as popular.

Ross was born in Detroit, Michigan, on March 26, 1944, to a poor family. At the age of 14 she joined high school friends Florence Ballard and Mary Wilson in a singing group that eventually became The Supremes; under the guidance of Motown record chief Berry Gordy they became one of the most popular groups in the world during the '60s, following the No 1 *Baby Love* with many other top hits. Ross went solo in 1969, continued to make hit records, starred in the TV special *Diana* in 1971 and made her film début in 1972 in **Lady Sings the Blues**. Gordy was the executive producer and, though the film skipped over some aspects of Holiday's career, it was still one of the most effective film biographies ever made in Hollywood. Ross did a fine job of singing the Lady's songs and an even better one of

acting her unhappy life. Gordy took over the directorial chores from Tony Richardson on the next film, **Mahogany**, with Ross wearing beautiful clothes and singing nice songs in a piece of enjoyable high-fashion trash. **The Wiz**, with Ross as a 24-year-old Harlem school teacher, showed her at her very best, dancing as well as singing, and "easing on down the road" to what should prove to be her biggest commercial success.

COMPLETE FILMS:
1972 Lady Sings the Blues
Sidney J. Furie (Paramount)
1975 Mahogany
Berry Gordy (Paramount)
1978 The Wiz
Sidney Lumet (Universal)

KATHARINE ROSS

Katharine Ross has come to represent the free-thinking liberated woman in contemporary Hollywood cinema, desirable and amoral but still vulnerable, sensitive about her sexual status and insistent that relationships be on an equal basis. She is, of course, very beautiful and decorative but it is the mind behind her expressive

Above: Katharine Ross in **The Graduate** *as Elaine Robinson, just married but about to run away with Dustin Hoffman.*

face, her screen personality, which has made her one of the major young female stars of today's cinema.

Ross was born on January 29, 1943, in Hollywood, studied at Santa Rosa College and worked with the San Francisco Workshop. She made her TV début in 1962 and her first film, **Shenandoah**, in 1965. Her persona was first seen in developed form in the movie that made her famous, **The Graduate**, for which she received an Oscar nomination, where she portrayed the daughter of Anne Bancroft ❯. In **Butch Cassidy and the Sundance Kid** she shares her favours between Robert Redford ❯ and Paul Newman ❯, agrees to go off to South America with them but insists on leaving before they get themselves killed. The same year, in **Tell Them Willie Boy Is Here**, she was a beautiful Indian girl who runs off with Robert Blake when her father opposes their marriage.

Her '70s career started slowly, but since the middle of the decade has been going strong; in **The Stepford Wives** (1974) she was a career-woman photographer trying to raise the consciousness of the housewife zombies in her new Connecticut home and discovering a sinister plot by the local men. Two years later she played the role of Etta Place again in the TV movie **Wanted: The Sundance Woman,** which shows her adventures after Butch's and the Kid's deaths, when the Pinkerton men get on her trail, and then portrayed a strong-minded whore in **Voyage of the Damned.**

She made three films in 1978; after the rather unfortunate **The Swarm, The Betsy** showed her seducing father-in-law Laurence Olivier ❯, whom she prefers to her own weak and, it is later revealed, homosexual husband, and in **The Legacy** she inherited the magic powers of a dying warlock and herself becomes a potent witch.

BEST FILMS:
1967 The Graduate
Mike Nichols (United Artists)
1969 Butch Cassidy and the Sundance Kid
George Roy Hill (20th Century Fox)
1969 Tell Them Willie Boy Is Here
Abraham Polonsky (Universal)
1972 They Only Kill Their Masters
James Goldstone (MGM)
1974 The Stepford Wives
Bryan Forbes (Palomar)
1976 Voyage of the Damned
Stuart Rosenberg (ITC Entertainments)
1976 Wanted: The Sundance Woman
Lee Philips (TV)
1978 The Swarm
Irwin Allen (Warner Brothers)
1978 The Betsy
Daniel Petrie (Allied Artists/United Artists)
1978 The Legacy
Richard Marquand (EMI)

TELLY SAVALAS

Telly Savalas has been making movies since 1959, but has only become a real star since the stunning international success of his TV series *Kojak*. The tough, bald New York cop with a lollipop in his mouth and a wisecrack on his lips has made Savalas famous literally around the world, and has opened the way for bigger and more sympathetic film roles. His finest achievements in the cinema before *Kojak,* with the exception of his Oscar-nominated performance in **Birdman of Alcatraz,**

have been as doubled-dyed villains: in **The Dirty Dozen** he was a brutal Southern racist and rapist; in **The Scalphunters** a renegade killer; in **Battle of the Bulge** a black marketeer; and in **On Her Majesty's Secret Service** James Bond's ❯ arch-foe Blofeld. He was a little nicer (but not much) in the Army chasing after gold with Clint Eastwood ❯ in **Kelly's Heroes,** but was really sadistic again as a bandit chief in **A Town Called Bastard.** What is interesting about Savalas's success with his new persona as a good guy is that he had retained much of his vicious power and toughness but has gained charisma by channelling it into anti-villainous nastiness.

*Above: Telly Savalas, in his pre-*Kojak *days, as a narcotics agent who exploits a Vietnam veteran in the tough thriller* **Clay Pigeon**

Savalas was born as Aristotle Savalas in Garden City, New York, on January 21, 1924, studied at Columbia University, and worked in executive capacities for the State Department and ABC Television before sidling into acting. He made his TV début playing a European judge when no one more suitable for the role could be found, and his film début came in 1959 in **The Young Savages** with Burt Lancaster ❯. Lancaster brought him back again for a good role in **Birdman of Alcatraz** and his movie career took off. Among his recent films are **Capricorn One, Inside Out** and **Killer Force (The Diamond Mercenaries).** He played a Greek for the first time in the movies in the 1978 **Escape to Athens** and is making **Beyond the Poseidon Adventure.**

BEST FILMS:
1961 Birdman of Alcatraz
John Frankenheimer (United Artists)
1965 Battle of the Bulge
Ken Annakin (Warner Brothers)
1967 The Dirty Dozen
Robert Aldrich (MGM)
1968 The Scalphunters
Sydney Pollack (United Artists)
1968 The Assassination Bureau
Basil Dearden (Paramount)
1970 Kelly's Heroes
Brian Hutton (MGM)

1971 A Town Called Bastard (Hell)
Robert Parrish (Benmar)
1975 Inside Out
Peter Duffell (Warner Brothers)
1975 The Diamond Mercenaries (Killer Force)
Val Guest (Michaelangelo Productions)
1977 Capricorn One
Peter Hyams (ITC)

MAXIMILIAN SCHELL

Maximilian Schell won the Academy Award for Best Actor in 1961 at the beginning of his international film career, but it was not enough to really make him into a major star. The trouble was that he won the Oscar for his superb performance as the passionate but cunning lawyer defending the Nazi officials on trial in **Judgment at Nuremberg,** and the persona created by this film was not a viable one for top stardom. In effect, Schell portrayed an ultra-smooth villain (ie, he skilfully defends the ultimate evildoers of our time) and this kind of slick persuasive villain has been his usual role in international films ever since. In the recent **Cross of Iron** he is a sophisticated, well-connected German Army officer determined to win an Iron Cross, who turns out to be cowardly as well as villainous. In **St Ives** he is a smooth-talking psychiatrist in league with Jacqueline Bisset ❯ to double-cross John Houseman. In **The Odessa**

Above: Maximilian Schell talks to James Coburn in Sam Peckinpah's 1977 **Cross of Iron,** *about obsessive heroism among German soldiers in Russia.*

File he is a highly-respected German industrialist but Jon Voigt ❯ discovers he is actually the former commander of a Nazi concentration camp. In **The Deadly Affair** he is an old wartime friend of security agent James Mason ❯, but secretly the enemy spymaster and the lover of Mason's wife.

Even as a villain Schell retains a likeable personality, and this allows him occasionally to play more sympathetic roles, notably as the honourable German General Bittrich in **A Bridge Too Far,** the master thief in **Topkapi** and the German emissary from Vanessa Redgrave ❯ to Jane Fonda ❯ in **Julia.**

In real life Schell was not a German at all and was a refugee from Nazism; he was born in Vienna, Austria, on December 8, 1930, and his family fled to Switzerland in 1938 after the Nazis took control of the country. His older sister Maria became a successful film actress before him and he was given his first film role in 1955 by director Laszlo Benzedek in **Kinder, Mütter und ein General.** He acted in several German films during the next two years, made his English-language début in the Broadway play *Interlock* in 1958 and then was cast as Marlon Brando's ❯ commanding officer in the film **The**

Young Lions. He starred on American television in Abby Mann's play *Judgment at Nuremberg* and was asked to repeat his role for the film version; it made him a big, if not a major, star. Since then he has continued to work regularly in both German and international cinema and has become a director and producer as well. He produced and starred in a version of Kafka's **The Castle**, directed and acted in **First Love** and directed the widely-acclaimed **The Pedestrian**. He has also directed and acted in many controversial stage productions. His 1978 films include **Avalanche Express** and **I Love You, I Love You Not** and his strength as a star seems to be increasing.

BEST FILMS:
1958 The Young Lions
Edward Dmytryk (20th Century Fox)
1961 Judgment at Nuremberg
Stanley Kramer (United Artists)
1964 Topkapi
Jules Dassin (United Artists)
1966 The Deadly Affair
Sidney Lumet (Columbia)
1968 The Castle
Rudolf Noelte (Schell)
1974 The Odessa File
Ronald Neame (Columbia)
1976 St Ives
J. Lee Thompson (Warner Brothers)
1977 A Bridge Too Far
Richard Attenborough (Joseph E. Levine/United Artists)
1977 Julia
Fred Zinnemann (20th Century Fox)
1977 Cross of Iron
Sam Peckinpah (Anglo-EMI)

ROMY SCHNEIDER

Romy Schneider is possibly the most truly international modern film star, having successively had major periods of stardom in the German, American and French cinema. During the '50s she was the Viennese cream cake of German schmaltz in the **Sissi** films and other such sweet confections; in the '60s she was the sexy European featured in English and American films like **The Victors, The Cardinal** and **What's New, Pussycat?;** in the '70s she became one of the leading stars of the French cinema, especially in the films of Claude Sautet.

She has now been a major star for over 25 years and looks more glamorous in her latest films than she did in her early ones. But then she started very young, aged 15; she was born on September 23, 1938, in Vienna, Austria, the daughter of movie star Magda Schneider and actor Wolf Albach-Retty. She made her film début in 1953 as her mother's daughter and her career took off immediately—by 1955 her mother was supporting her in films. The 1956 **Sissi** and its two sequels made Schneider famous all over Europe, probably the first German star to

get wide Continental acceptance since Lilian Harvey ». In these films she played the young Austrian Empress Elizabeth with Karl-Heinz Böhm as the Emperor Franz-Josef. The films were not well received in English-speaking countries, though Paramount edited all three into one picture and released it in 1962 as **Forever My Life.** Schneider herself hated her butter-wouldn't-melt-in-the-mouth image, refused to make any more **Sissi** pictures and tried to break into the French cinema with the help of intimate friend Alain Delon ». The real break-through came in an Italian film, Luchino Visconti's episode **Il Lavoro (The Job)** in the 1962

Above: Romy Schneider looking beautiful under pressure as the outsider who becomes the focus of attention in a small italian town in La Califfa.

picture **Boccaccio 70.** She played a wife making her husband pay to go to bed with her in that film and then played a seductive nympho-maniac in Orson Welles' » **The Trial.** The old image was shattered and she was free to become an international star in **The Victors** (a musician forced to become a whore), **The Cardinal** (trying to seduce a priest), **What's New, Pussycat?** (loved by Peter O'Toole ») and **Good Neighbour Sam** (pretending Jack Lemmon » is her husband).

Her international films were not her best, but they gave her a stature and strength that came to fruition in the third period of her career in France in the '70s. It began with Alain Delon in **La Piscine,** but it was Claude Sautet's critical and commercial hit **Les Choses de la Vie** in 1970 which really won her French acclaim. Since then she has starred in many other films for Sautet including **Max et les Ferrailleurs, César et Rosalie, Mado** and **Une Histoire Simple.** She has also given out-standing performances in other French films including **L'Important C'est D'aimer** (as a married actress involved in a painful love affair), **Le Trio Infernal** (as part of a murderous trio) and **Une Femme à sa Fenêtre** (as a French aristocrat involved with a Greek Communist

in the '30s). She was superb in Visconti's **Ludwig,** once again play-ing Elizabeth of Austria but this time giving, as one English critic said, "one of the major perform-ances of the past ten years". Schneider was excellent in another Italian film, **La Califfa** (an aggres-sive outsider in a small town), the German picture **Group Portrait with Lady** (based on the novel by Heinrich Böll), and the interna-tional Joseph Losey film **The Assassination of Trotsky** (as assassin Alain Delon's mistress).

BEST FILMS:
1962 Boccaccio 70 (Il Lavoro)
Luchino Visconti (Concordia/Cineriz)
1962 The Trial
Orson Welles (Paris Europa)
1970 Les Choses de la Vie
Claude Sautet (Lira)
1972 The Assassination of Trotsky
Joseph Losey (De Laurentiis/Shaftel)
1972 La Califfa
Alberto Bevilacqua (Fair Film)
1972 Ludwig
Luchino Visconti (Mega/Cinetel)
1974 Le Trio Infernal
François Girod (Lira/Belstar)
1976 L'Important C'est D'aimer
Andrzej Zulawski (Albina)
1976 Une Femme à sa Fenêtre
Pierre Granier-Deferre (Lira)
1977 Gruppenbild mit Dame (Group Portrait with Lady)
Aleksandar Petrovic (United Artists)

GEORGE C. SCOTT

George C. Scott should turn out to be one of the great actors of the American cinema. All the ability and some of the achievement is there, but his movie career is still remarkably thin after 20 years, considering his stature. He won the Academy Award for his magnificent performance in **Patton** (and then refused the Oscar, which is still in the Academy's vaults), and was nominated on three other occasions, for his superb performances in **Anatomy of a Murder** (his second film, as the prosecuting attorney), **The Hustler** (the steel-hard promoter who nearly destroys Paul Newman »), and **The Hospital** (as the doctor working too hard to have a personal life, opposite Diana Rigg). He is universally admired for his disciplined energy, con-trolled vitality and ability to dominate—in short, his power-house presence. George Campbell Scott was born in Wise, West Virginia, on October 18, 1927. He came to acting after a short career as a teacher and made his stage reputation working with Joseph Papp in New York from 1957, making his film début in **The Hanging Tree** in 1958.

He has always been as interested in the theatre as in the cinema, but surprisingly his stage experience has not kept him from appearing to be a "natural" actor, probably because his screen persona is based on the same suppressed

rage/energy that he utilises in the theatre. His lack of sustained achievement in the movies is surprising, considering his abilities; he has not made very many films, and many of the ones he has chosen to appear in are of little importance. Apart from the films mentioned above, his only '60s movies of reasonable merit were **The List of Adrian Messenger, Petulia** and (outstanding as a Pentagon general) **Dr Strange-love.** In the '70s he has mostly been better than his films, which include **Jane Eyre, The Last Run, The New Centurions, Bank Shot, The Hindenberg, The Prince and the Pauper** and **Islands in the Stream.** The two most interesting

Above: George C. Scott in his Oscar-winning role (he refused the award) as the egocentric but brilliant General Patton *who values glory more than life.*

were **They Might Be Giants** (as a man who thinks he's Sherlock Holmes) and **The Day of the Dol-phin,** neither of which was well received, plus **The Hospital.** One can only hope for greater achieve-ments to come.

BEST FILMS:
1959 Anatomy of a Murder
Otto Preminger (Columbia)
1961 The Hustler
Robert Rossen (20th Century Fox)
1963 The List of Adrian Messenger
John Huston (Universal International)
1963 Dr Strangelove
Stanley Kubrick (Columbia)
1968 Petulia
Richard Lester (Warner Brothers)
1969 Patton (Patton: Lust for Glory)
Franklin Schaffner (20th Century Fox)
1971 The Hospital
Arthur Hiller (United Artists)
1972 They Might Be Giants
Anthony Harvey (Universal)
1972 The New Centurions
Richard Fleischer (Columbia)
1973 The Day of the Dolphin
Mike Nichols (Avco-Embassy)

GEORGE SEGAL

George Segal has come to repre-sent, in a genial and slightly ironic way, the modern American urban man. He is cynical but worried,

easy-going but hard-working, able to use humour as a defence when nothing else will work, and essentially decent and likeable (despite sometimes having a possessive mother). This is the persona he exhibits as the detective in No Way to Treat a Lady, the husband with a mistress in A Touch of Class and Loving, the bachelor with a yen in Where's Poppa?, Tenderly and The Owl and the Pussycat, and the husband lamenting the loss of a wife because of a mistress in Blume in Love. The persona is essentially New York Jewish and its characteristics do not alter significantly even in different environments (Japanese prison camp in King Rat, German spy centre in The Quiller Memorandum) and contrasting professions (gambler in California Split and The Duchess and the Dirtwater Fox, gangster in The St Valentine's Day Massacre, safety inspector in Rollercoaster etc). Middle-class cinemagoers like him because they can identify with him. But unfortunately for his career as a major star, the mass audience of young and non-middle-class moviegoers find this characterisation harder to identify with, and thus none of his many outstanding films has been a big commercial success and some have been failures in financial terms.

Segal was born in New York on February 13, 1934, led a jazz band for a while in his youth, and began acting off-Broadway in the late '50s. He made his film début in The Young Doctors in 1961, had his first starring role in the 1965 King Rat, and got an Academy Award nomination for his superb performance as the new professor guest-who-gets-got in Who's Afraid of Virginia Woolf? His acting is memorable in even his weaker films (Sam Spade, Jr, in The Black Bird, the ex-Mountie in Russian Roulette, the crazed zombie in The Terminal Man). In

Above: George Segal, with Lee Remick, in the macabre thriller **No Way to Treat A Lady** *in which he plays a New York detective hunting a theatrical murderer.*

his best films he is one of the real pleasures of '70s movie-going, most notably having an affair with Glenda Jackson ≫ in A Touch of Class, winning a lot of money with Elliott Gould ≫ in California Split and looking marriage full in the face in Loving and Blume in Love. His satirical exposure of upper-middle-class values via his marriage to Jane Fonda ≫ in Fun with Dick and Jane has become his most commercially successful film to date. He was also featured in Ingmar Bergman's 1973 TV play The Lie.

BEST FILMS:
1965 King Rat
Bryan Forbes (Columbia)
1966 Who's Afraid of Virginia Woolf?
Mike Nichols (Warner Brothers)
1968 No Way to Treat a Lady
Jack Smight (Columbia)
1970 Loving
Irving Kershner (Columbia)
1970 The Owl and the Pussycat
Herbert Ross (Columbia)
1970 Where's Poppa?
Carl Reiner (Tokovsky/United Artists)
1972 A Touch of Class
Melvin Frank (Avco/Brut)
1973 Blume in Love
Paul Mazursky (Warner Brothers)
1974 California Split
Robert Altman (Columbia)
1976 Fun with Dick and Jane
Ted Kotcheff (Columbia)

PETER SELLERS

Peter Sellers has created a very successful screen career out of being a mimic, and was for a time in the late '50s and early '60s one of the most popular comedians in the world. Unfortunately, he neglected to create a screen

persona for himself and his chameleon-like movie appearances almost led to his stardom fading away. He was saved by the role of the most popular character he ever embodied on screen, the bumbling, ineffectual, idiotic French policeman, Inspector Clouseau. Following the huge success of Sellers in this role in the '60s films The Pink Panther and A Shot in the Dark, directed by Blake Edwards, the character was revived in the '70s when Sellers' reputation was at its lowest ebb; The Return of the Pink Panther, The Pink Panther Strikes Again and The Revenge of the Pink Panther, again made by Edwards, continued the success of the earlier films and Sellers' personal popularity returned.

He was born in Southsea, Hampshire, England, on December 8, 1925, into a family with a show-business tradition, and first made his name on BBC Radio with The Goon Show (along with Spike Milli-

Above: Peter Sellers, as the bumbling French detective Inspector Clouseau, examines the **Pink Panther** *diamond.*

gan and Harry Secombe). He made his film début in the 1950 short Let's Go Crazy and then appeared with his fellow Goons in the 1951 feature Penny Points to Paradise. The zany style of humour originated by Sellers and his colleagues had an invaluable and lasting effect on the development of British humour on radio and TV and in the cinema.

Sellers began his rise to solo stardom in 1955 as the spiv in The Ladykillers and the old projectionist in The Smallest Show on Earth. Tom Thumb and Carlton-Browne of the FO, both with Terry-Thomas, made him really popular in England, while The Mouse That Roared made him almost as popular in the US. He was good in I'm All Right, Jack, satirising the trade union movement, but sometimes his films seemed like exercises in mimicry (funny Indian doctor in The Millionairess, funny Scots accountant in The Battle of the Sexes). His international reputation soared in two films for Stanley

Kubrick, Lolita (as the detective chasing James Mason ≫ and his little girl) and Dr Strangelove (in the triple role of German-American scientist, American President and British Air Force officer). After the very funny Clouseau films, the highly enjoyable Only Two Can Play and the excellent The World of Henry Orient, Sellers suffered a series of heart attacks and his career began to falter. He was good as a nutty psychiatrist in the baroque What's New, Pussycat? adequate in I Love You, Alice B. Toklas, and amusing in There's a Girl in My Soup with Goldie Hawn, but most of his other films were poor and his career revived only with the return of the Pink Panther films in the mid-'70s.

BEST FILMS:
1955 The Ladykillers
Alexander Mackendrick (Ealing)
1959 The Mouse That Roared
Jack Arnold (Columbia)
1959 I'm All Right, Jack
John Boulting (British Lion)
1961 Only Two Can Play
Sidney Gilliat (British Lion)
1962 Lolita
Stanley Kubrick (MGM)
1963 The Pink Panther
Blake Edwards (United Artists)
1963 Dr Strangelove
Stanley Kubrick (Columbia)
1963 A Shot in the Dark
Blake Edwards (United Artists)
1964 The World of Henry Orient
George Roy Hill (United Artists)
1965 What's New, Pussycat?
Clive Donner (United Artists)
1976 The Pink Panther Strikes Again
Blake Edwards (United Artists)

DELPHINE SEYRIG

Delphine Seyrig is a film star for intellectuals, the entrancingly beautiful and mysterious heroine of important films by major directors which are unlikely ever to be widely shown. Her best known picture remains her first, the haunting Last Year at Marienbad in which Alain Resnais uses her beauty, grace of movement and mystery as the focus of the conflict between past and present. She was equally fine in her lesser-known second film for Resnais, Muriel, portraying an anguished 40-year-old woman in a provincial French town trying and failing to exorcise the ghosts of the past. She has been featured in two films by Luis Buñuel, as a prostitute in The Milky Way and as a woman with mysterious "scars" in The Discreet Charm of the Bourgeoisie. Marguerite Duras has utilised Seyrig's odd, distant persona superbly in four films: as the heroine involved in romantic intrigues in 1937 Calcutta in India Song, as the same heroine lending her voice to the same story in Son Nom de Venise dans Calcutta Desert, as the friend trying to probe beneath the surface in

Baxter, Vera Baxter and as the heroine in the earlier La Musica. She was superb as the Lilac Fairy godmother in the fantasy Donkey Skin, as Dirk Bogarde's ❯ old flame in Accident and as the seductive wife of the owner of the shop where Jean-Pierre Leaud works in Stolen Kisses. Her finest and probably least-seen performance in recent years however, was the extraordinary Jeanne Dielman in which she portrays with infinite detail the life of an ordinary housewife, who pursues her daily sideline as a prostitute as if it was just another household task.

Seyrig, as befits her mysterious persona, was born in Beirut, Lebanon, in 1932, where her father was the director of the Institute of Archaeology. She began working in provincial French theatre in the early '50s and then lived in New York from 1955 to 1960, working in off-Broadway theatre and studying at the Actors' Studio. She made her film début

Above: Delphine Seyrig, whose enigmatic beauty and grace has been superbly used by directors like Resnais, Buñuel and Losey.

in the 1958 underground short Pull My Daisy (with Ginsberg, Corso, Kerouac, etc) and then returned to Europe for Marienbad, probably the most famous "art film" of the '60s. She worked only occasionally in the cinema because of heavy theatre and TV commitments, but her other '60s films included William Klein's Who Are You, Polly Magoo? and Mr Freedom, and Marin Karmitz's Comedy. Other '70s films of note have been Harry Kumel's Daughters of Darkness (as a vampire), Joseph Losey's version of A Doll's House (as Kristine Linde) and Don Siegel's The Black Windmill. She starred in the semi-erotic German picture The Last Cry directed by Robert van Ackeren, the feminist-orientated Aloise directed by Liliane De Kermadec, and Le Jardin Qui Bascule.

BEST FILMS:
1961 L'Année Dernière à Marienbad (Last Year at Marienbad)
Alain Resnais (Courau)

1963 Muriel ou Le Temps d'un Retour
Alain Resnais (Argos)
1967 Accident
Joseph Losey (London Independent Producers)
1968 Baisers Volés (Stolen Kisses)
François Truffaut (United Artists)
1971 Peau D'âne (Donkey Skin)
Jacques Demy (Parc)
1972 Le Charme Discret de la Bourgeoisie (The Discreet Charm of the Bourgeoisie)
Luis Buñuel (Greenwich)
1974 India Song
Marguerite Duras (Sunchild)
1975 Jeanne Dielman, 23 Quai du Commerce, 1080 Bruxelles
Chantal Akerman (Paradise)
1976 Son Nom de Venise dans Calcutta Desert
Marguerite Duras (Cinema 9)
1976 Baxter, Vera Baxter
Marguerite Duras (Sunchild)

OMAR SHARIF

Omar Sharif became a movie star in 1954 in his first ever film, The Blazing Sun, but his reputation was limited to Arabic-speaking countries for the first ten years of his career. In 1962 he rode a camel into international stardom in David Lean's Lawrence of Arabia, won an Oscar nomination and began his career as an international heart-throb. Since then he has worked almost wholly in the American and European movie industry and starred in two of the biggest box office successes of all time, Doctor Zhivago with Julie Christie ❯ and Funny Girl with Barbra Streisand ❯. His film career reached its peak in the late '60s when he starred in a series of big-budget pictures; but the box office failure of expensive romantic films like Mayerling and The Appointment caused his career to tail off in the '70s.

He was born in Alexandria, Egypt, on April 10, 1932, as Michael Shalhoub, the son of a

Above: Omar Sharif gazes into the shimmering desert with Peter O'Toole in David Lean's Lawrence of Arabia, the film that made Sharif famous.

wealthy timber merchant. Youssef Shahin, one of Egypt's best directors and a close friend, offered him a starring role in The Blazing Sun in 1953 opposite Faten Hamama, then the top female star in Arabic cinema. The film was a hit, Shahin starred him in two more films and he married Hamama. He took the name Omar El-Sharif when he adopted the Moslem religion but dropped the El for his Western films. Of the 21 Egyptian films he made during the next ten years, the best were those for Shahin and for Salah Abu Saif, particularly the 1960 Beginning and End. He also starred in two French pictures in this period, as a wise fool in Jacques Baratier's Goha, and after his success in Lawrence of Arabia as a sheikh in The Fabulous Adventures of Marco Polo. Then he was a Spanish priest in Behold a Pale Horse, the Armenian husband of Sophia Loren ❯ in The Fall of the Roman Empire and the Yugoslav partisan lover of Ingrid Bergman ❯ in The Yellow Rolls-Royce. Although he was never typecast as an Arab, he was used normally as an exotic lover with flashing eyes, whether portraying an Austrian prince in Mayerling, a Russian doctor in Doctor Zhivago, a Neapolitan fairy tale prince in Cinderella Italian Style or an American Jewish gambler in Funny Girl. He played that last role for a second time in the weak 1975 sequel Funny Lady, but few of his '70s films have been more notable—among the reasonably interesting were The Horsemen (heroic in the desert as an Afghan horseman), Juggernaut (heroic as the captain of a ship with a bomb hidden on it) and The Tamarind

Seed (heroically in love with Julie Andrews ❯ despite international politics). His most recent film put him once more back in the desert, portraying the Prince in Richard Fleischer's Ashanti. In recent years, Sharif has become as well-known for his championship bridge-playing as for his movie-making.

BEST FILMS:
1954 The Blazing Sun (Sera'a Fil Wadi)
Youssef Shahin (Talhamy)
1959 Goha
Jacques Baratier (Baratier)
1962 Lawrence of Arabia
David Lean (Columbia)
1964 The Fall of the Roman Empire
Anthony Mann (Samuel Bronston)
1964 Behold a Pale Horse
Fred Zinnemann (Columbia)
1965 Doctor Zhivago
David Lean (MGM)
1967 Cinderella Italian Style (C'era una Volta)
Francesco Rosi (MGM)
1968 Funny Girl
William Wyler (Columbia)
1970 The Horsemen
John Frankenheimer (Columbia)
1974 Juggernaut
Richard Lester (United Artists)

ROBERT SHAW

Robert Shaw drove himself to stardom with the kind of steely determination and highly-trained skill that became a part of his screen personality. His death on August 28, 1978, just as he was beginning to achieve major star status, was saddening though oddly in keeping with the screen persona he had created: determined but almost invariably failing at the last moment just as he seemed to be win. In From Russia With Love, the 1963 film that made him a star, he portrayed a super-skilled, super-tough KGB agent whose attempt to kill James Bond ❯ (Sean Connery) failed at the final instant. In The Sting he is a super-clever, super-tough gangster, outwitted and swindled by Paul Newman ❯ and Robert Redford ❯ just at the moment he thinks he has won. In Jaws he is an experienced shark killer with his own boat, the most determined and able hunter, but it is he who is killed by the shark at the last moment while the others survive. In The Hireling he is a skilled and determined chauffeur who thinks he can rise up in society through the rich Sarah Miles, only to find out in the end he is totally wrong. In A Man for All Seasons he was King Henry VIII determined to make Sir Thomas More (Paul Scofield) bend to his will and approve of his break with Rome and, of course, failing. In Robin and Marian he was the tyrannical Sheriff of Nottingham defeated and killed by Robin Hood (Sean Connery ❯ again) despite all his skills and determination. In The Deep he was an underwater expert whose

Above: Robert Shaw as an Israeli agent in **Black Sunday,** *trying to prevent a Palestinian attack on a football stadium in Florida.*

vigour and skills fail to wrest a treasure from a sunken Spanish galleon.

Shaw was born in Westhoughton, Lancashire, in 1927, brought up in Cornwall and the Orkney Islands and studied at RADA. He began his stage career at Stratford in 1949 and made his film début in 1955 in **The Dam Busters.** His stage reputation grew in the late '50s and early '60s at the Royal Court and film stardom came with **From Russia With Love.** He was in the film version of Harold Pinter's **The Caretaker,** after his success in it on stage, and appeared in many more film versions of plays including **A Man for All Seasons, The Royal Hunt of the Sun** (as Pizarro) and another Pinter adaptation, **The Birthday Party.** He was excellent in the allegorical **Figures in a Landscape** and in **Young Winston** (as Randolph Churchill) but it was his appearances in the box office blockbusters **The Sting** and **Jaws** that made him into a really major star. Some of his more recent films were less successful (**Diamonds, Swashbuckler**) but both **The Deep** and **Black Sunday** (portraying a grimly determined Israeli guerrilla detective) were enormously popular. His last films before his death from a heart attack were **Force Ten from Navarone** and **Avalanche Express.**

In addition to acting, Shaw was an accomplished playwright and writer with five published novels and a high literary reputation. *The Man in the Glass Booth* and *The Hiding Place* were both made into films and he wrote several screenplays, including **Figures in a Landscape.**

BEST FILMS:

1963 From Russia With Love
Terence Young (United Artists)
1963 The Caretaker
Clive Donner (Caretaker Films)
1966 A Man for All Seasons
Fred Zinnemann (Columbia)
1970 Figures in a Landscape
Joseph Losey (Cinecrest)
1973 The Hireling
Alan Bridges (Columbia)

1973 The Sting
George Roy Hill (Universal)
1975 Jaws
Steven Spielberg (Universal)
1976 Robin and Marian
Richard Lester (Columbia)
1977 The Deep
Peter Yates (Columbia)
1977 Black Sunday
John Frankenheimer (Paramount)

Victor Sjöström

see Ingmar Bergman Stars

Alberto Sordi

Alberto Sordi's major importance as a star of the modern Italian cinema is not always recognised abroad. He is probably the most popular film actor of the past 30 years in Italy and his screen persona, representing the average Italian man, has been central to the development of the post-war Italian cinema. Although he works almost wholly in satirical comedy, it is comedy with a political and social edge and its targets have included the Mafia, the Italian legal system, corruption, heroism and masculinity. While Mastroianni ≫ and Gassman ≫ are probably better known internationally, Sordi is more of a key figure within Italy —though this has hardly been indicated in his American films, like **Those Magnificent Men in their Flying Machines** or **A Farewell to Arms.** He has worked with many of the finest Italian directors, including Fellini, Rosi, Petri, Lattuada, Comencini and Monicelli.

Born in Rome on June 15, 1919, Sordi entered the cinema at the age of 13, dubbing Oliver Hardy's voice, and had minor film

Above: Alberto Sordi, a popular star of the Italian cinema since the early '50s who specialises in socially conscious comedies.

roles from 1938. His first important film was Fellini's 1952 **The White Sheik,** where he was the embodiment of a photo-romance hero, and the following year Fellini used him as a central figure in his study of bored provincial young men, **I Vitelloni.** In the mid-'50s Sordi starred in a series of entertaining but revealing films about aspects of the Italian middle-class male and his ideas, including **The Seducer, The Bachelor, The Husband** and **The Widow.** His satirical, mass-appeal films then began to focus on tougher targets, such as black marketeers (**I Magliari**), official corruption (**Il Vigile**), the war (**La Grande Guerra**), the Mafia (**Il Mafioso**) and the economic boom (**Il Boom**). He began to direct himself in the mid-'60s, in **Fumo di Londra;** his popularity continued and serious critics began to recognise his importance.

In the '70s, Sordi's films have reflected the growing difficulties of Italian middle-class life, and the comedy is sometimes black and grim. In **While There's War There's Hope** he is an arms salesman in Africa, in **Detained While Waiting for Justice** he is wrongly arrested and his life virtually ruined and in **An Average Little Man** he turns against violent terrorist behaviour by becoming a vengeful killer himself. To really understand the Italian cinema, it is necessary to know the films of Alberto Sordi.

BEST FILMS:

1952 Lo Sceicco Bianco (The White Sheik)
Federico Fellini (PCDI-OFI)
1953 I Vitelloni
Federico Fellini (Peg-Cité)
1959 I Magliari (The Swindlers)
Francesco Rosi (Titanus-Vides)
1960 Tutti a Casa
Luigi Comencini (De Laurentiis)
1962 Il Mafioso
Alberto Lattuada (Cervi)
1963 Il Maestro di Vigevanao
Elio Petri (De Laurentiis)
1971 Detenuto in Attesa di Giudizio (Detained While Waiting for Justice)
Nanni Loy (Documento)
1972 Lo Scopone Scientifico (The Scientific Cardplayer)
Luigi Comencini (De Laurentiis)
1974 Finche C'e Guerra C'e Speranza (While There's War There's Hope)
Alberto Sordi (Rizzoli)
1977 Un Borghese Piccolo Piccolo (An Average Little Man)
Mario Monicelli (Auro)

Sylvester Stallone

Sylvester Stallone is the Cinderella of the modern cinema, the actor who came from nowhere to become a star with the Academy Award-winning **Rocky.** The sudden rise to fame of the prize-fighter in that film seems to have paralleled Stallone's own rise, while the street-boy-on-the-way-up screen persona he created in it

Above: Sylvester Stallone, whose manufactured image is classical Hollywood, as the prize-fighter **Rocky** *who goes the distance.*

has been identified with him and his roles in two further pictures, **F.I.S.T.** and **Paradise Alley.** He was, after all, the son of an Italian immigrant born in New York City's Hell's Kitchen area, and nobody had ever heard of him before **Rocky.** That's the myth, but it rings a little false; Stallone was born in Hell's Kitchen all right, but his family was by no means poor and he was brought up in suburban Maryland. After high school he was a teacher at the expensive American School in Switzerland (where he played Biff in a stage production of *Death of a Salesman*), then studied at the University of Maryland from 1967 to 1969. He moved to New York, made a living selling TV scripts and had bit parts in films like **The Out-of-Towners** and **Bananas.**

His real film career began with the 1974 **The Lords of Flatbush** portraying one of the three leads, Stanley Rosiello, the not-so-bright member of the gang who finally gets married (after getting the ring free). He says he was paid 25 tee-shirts for his excellent performance, but it made him well-known enough to move to Hollywood and try for other film parts. He was only a "Youth in Park" in **The Prisoner of Second Avenue,** but in **Capone** he was the gangster's lieutenant Frank Nitti, the man who eventually replaced Capone as the head of the mob. He was fifth billed, and moved up to third billing in Roger Corman's money-spinner **Death Race 2000** portraying Machine Gun Joe Viterbo, the loud-mouth chief rival of Frankenstein/David Carradine. He was thus hardly a total unknown without experience when he wrote **Rocky** and persuaded producers Irwin Winkler and Robert Chartoff to let him star in it. It cost $1 million, and it made $54 million in 1977 alone. Stallone was superb in his eloquent mumbling portrayal of a boxing bum who still has enough dignity to become a kind of hero. Critics and audiences loved it. His next film, **F.I.S.T.,** was an attempt to show how the gangster element crept into union organising with Stallone playing an idealistic union man corrupted during his rise to power and killed by the mob. Stallone then turned to directing for Paradise Alley, which he again wrote; his co-stars were virtual unknowns, and the Rocky-like story concerned three brothers who turned to wrestling as a means of breaking out of the poverty trap.

BEST FILMS:
1974 The Lords of Flatbush
Stephen Verona & Martin Davidson (Columbia)
1975 Capone
Steve Carver (20th Century Fox)
1975 Death Race 2000
Paul Bartel (New World Pictures)
1976 Rocky
John G. Avildsen (United Artists)
1978 F.I.S.T.
Norman Jewison (United Artists)
1978 Paradise Alley
Sylvester Stallone (Universal)

ROD STEIGER

Rod Steiger is a superb character star who alternates between being a great actor and being a very mannered one. He is never a natural performer (he had too much Actors' Studio stage training for that), but he has used his Method style to powerful effect and has established himself in a position similar to that of Charles Laughton ». Like Laughton, Steiger can be theatrical and mannered, tends to play heavies rather than romantic leads because of his looks and size, and is a brilliant technician of the acting craft; with his voice alone, Steiger created a sensation in the relatively minor role of the prosecuting attorney in The Court Martial of Billy Mitchell, and in No Way to Treat a Lady, emulating Alec Guinness », he flaunted his prowess with make-up and characterisation by playing in seven different disguises—theatrical, but a delight.

Steiger's early, villainous roles in On The Waterfront, The Big Knife and Jubal are powerful Method performances but, oddly, he is even better under Samuel Fuller's restraining hands in Run of the Arrow or when really allowing himself to go over the top in Al Capone. He may tend to be rather pretentiously artistic (The Pawnbroker, The Sergeant), but in the hands of a disciplined director like Francesco Rosi he can carry a truly serious film with great distinction (Hands Over the City, Lucky Luciano). It is not enough to be a brilliantly skilled actor to make good movies (W.C. Fields and Me, for example) even for character stars like Steiger and Laughton. His greatest success came from a more natural (although still studied and mannered) performance—the Southern, small-town police chief of In the Heat of the Night. He won an

Oscar and most of the other acting awards going for his superb, bigoted "naturalness".

Steiger was born in Westhampton, Long Island, New York, on April 14, 1925, and began acting on stage and TV in the late '40s. He made his cinema début for Fred Zinnemann in the 1951 film Teresa, but made his reputation with his second film, the 1954 On the Waterfront. That performance won him an Oscar nomination and made him the star of his next film, The Big Knife, playing the tough producer to Jack Palance's » declining movie star. He was good as Jud in Oklahoma!, but his Method style of acting jarred against the more appropriate musical-comedy style of the other actors. He was beautifully vicious in The Court Martial of Billy Mitchell, Jubal and The Harder They Fall, and then his solid string of good films ended.

Since 1956 he has made as many films that don't come off as he has made successful ones, and they are usually mixed with each other. These films are not necessarily bad, but for various reasons they don't jell and Steiger's acting style (despite good notices) is probably an important element in their failure—his performance

Above: Rod Steiger in his most famous role as the bigoted police chief in Norman Jewison's 1967 In the Heat of the Night.

as Pope John in Ermanno Olmi's And Came a Man helps to make the film unconvincing, the weakest movie ever made by that great Italian director. Steiger is often at his best in what he probably considers non-serious films, portraying the gangster boss in Al Capone, robbing a casino in Seven Thieves, and exploding as a brutal bandit in A Fistful of Dynamite. The "serious" ones, like The Illustrated Man and Happy Birthday Wanda June, get bogged down in their (and Steiger's) good intentions. One can expect Steiger to go on making good films for a long time (he's still young), but one can also expect him to go on making weak ones. The good ones, however, are worth waiting for.

BEST FILMS:
1954 On the Waterfront
Elia Kazan (Columbia)
1955 The Big Knife
Robert Aldrich (United Artists)
1956 Jubal
Delmer Daves (Columbia)
1957 Run of the Arrow
Samuel Fuller (Universal)
1959 Al Capone
Richard Wilson (Allied Artists)
1963 Le Mani sulla Città (Hands Over the City)
Francesco Rosi (Warner Brothers)
1965 The Pawnbroker
Sidney Lumet (Landau)
1967 In the Heat of the Night
Norman Jewison (United Artists)
1968 No Way to Treat a Lady
Jack Smight (Paramount)
1971 Giù la Testa (A Fistful of Dynamite)
Sergio Leone (United Artists)
1973 Lucky Luciano
Francesco Rosi (Vides)

BARBRA STREISAND

Barbra Streisand is the No 1 female movie star of the 1970s, with half-a-dozen blockbuster commercial successes including Funny Girl (for which she won an Oscar, portraying Jewish singer-comedienne Fanny Brice) and its sequel Funny Lady, What's Up, Doc?, The Way We Were and A Star Is Born. Financiers consider her to be the most bankable film actress now working (ie, the safest investment); she has been in the top ten box office list consistently since 1969. For all that, she is no glamour star. Her screen persona is one of mocking self-deprecation: she is the not-so-ordinary little Jewish girl from Brooklyn with a big nose and a small opinion of her beauty, but a grand line in Jewish humour and an unshake-

able faith in her talent. The persona burst full-blown on to the screen in Funny Girl, when Streisand sang I'm the Greatest Star, an opinion justified by her singing and acting talents in the film and one which apparently reflects her own off-screen beliefs.

Neither Hello Dolly! nor Funny Lady were as strong as Funny Girl, but A Star Is Born was a potent updating of the Hollywood film classic which had featured Judy Garland » and Janet Gaynor » in earlier versions. Streisand and co-star Kris Kristofferson » effectively transferred the drama to a rock setting; the songs included the Oscar-winning Evergreen, which Streisand co-wrote, and she was the executive producer of the movie as well as its driving force. There is no denying that Streisand has a large ego, but so far she has more than justi-

Above: Barbra Streisand with Kris Kristofferson in the 1976 version of A Star is Born, financially the most successful of all her films.

fied her high opinion of herself.

She was born as Barbara Joan Streisand in Brooklyn, New York, on April 24, 1942, and began to sing and dream about becoming a movie star while barely in her teens. As her subsequent screen persona shows, she was soon made aware of her apparent physical unloveliness and was dubbed "Big Beak" and "crazy Barbara". She began to work on stage with a summer stock company in 1957, while still a high school sophomore, and got her first break by winning an amateur singing contest. Despite pressures to make her become "normal"—ie, fix her nose, lose her Brooklyn accent and get rid of her kookie clothes and habits—she stayed pretty much herself except for dropping the "a" from Barbara. Her breakthrough came on Broadway in the musical *I Can Get It For You Wholesale*, stopping the show as Miss Marmelstein, but club singing also helped make her into a big name. *The Barbra Streisand Album* was an international success in 1963 and she was given the plum role of Fanny Brice in the 1964 Broadway production of *Funny Girl*.

By 1965 Streisand was one of the highest-paid entertainers in the world, a singing superstar, so it was not such a huge gamble as it might have appeared to feature an unknown in the lead of the big-budget film version of **Funny Girl**. In retrospect it seems impossible that anyone else could have taken the role. Her next film, **Hello, Dolly!**, was not, however, the most suitable vehicle; she had to "act" far away from her usual screen persona. She was back in form in a double role in **On a Clear Day You Can See Forever** as both a contemporary Brooklyn girl and a Regency woman who bewitches psychiatrist Yves Montand ➤, then very funny as a hooker with delusions of grandeur in **The Owl and the Pussycat**. She was equally enjoyable involved in screwball antics in **What's Up, Doc?**, very amusing giving comic monologues in **Up the Sandbox**, and was nominated for another Academy Award for her Jewish radical performance in **The Way We Were**. She tried screwball comedy again in **For Pete's Sake** (even getting involved with a stampede of rustled cattle in Brooklyn) before returning to musicals with **Funny Lady** and **A Star Is Born**.

COMPLETE FILMS:
1968 Funny Girl
William Wyler (Columbia)
1969 Hello, Dolly!
Gene Kelly (20th Century Fox)
1970 On a Clear Day You Can See Forever
Vincente Minnelli (Paramount)
1970 The Owl and the Pussycat
Herbert Ross (Columbia)
1972 What's Up, Doc?
Peter Bogdanovich (Warner Brothers)
1972 Up the Sandbox
Irving Kershner (First Artists)
1973 The Way We Were
Sydney Pollack (Columbia)
1974 For Pete's Sake
Peter Yates (Columbia)
1975 Funny Lady
Herbert Ross (Columbia)
1976 A Star Is Born
Frank Pierson (First Artists)

DONALD SUTHERLAND

Donald Sutherland is not so much a hero as a fanatic. His screen persona, based on his tall, gaunt figure, blank, impassive face and aloof attitude, is one of concealed and repressed turbulence, of obsessions that are not always allowed to show on the surface but which are the driving force of his actions. It is an ambiguous persona in that he can be villainous as well as heroic, and one is never sure that he is not a mixture of both. In **The Eagle Has Landed** he is the IRA fanatic helping to set up the kidnapping of Churchill. In **Casanova** he is the most famous sex fanatic of all time while in his other Italian film, **1900**, his obsession with fascism turns him into the cruel villain of the story. In **Klute** he is a detective so obsessed with finding a murderer, despite call girl Jane Fonda's ➤ reluctance to help, that he resigns from his police force to concentrate on the job. He was again a detective obsessed with his prey in **Lady Ice**. In **Steelyard Blues** he is a demolition derby fanatic attempting to destroy every possible make and year of car, while his obsession is with tanks in **Kelly's Heroes**. In **The Day of the Locust** his obsession with Karen Black and his repressed emotions eventually explode into the killing of a child actor and his own death at the hands of an outraged mob. In **Don't Look Now** his subconscious obsession with his daughter's death leads eventually to his own death at the hands of a

Above: Donald Sutherland as the gangling and insubordinate Hawkeye in Robert Altman's Army medical satire M*A*S*H.

midget wearing similar clothes. In **Little Murders** he is delightfully fanatic about not being fanatic, a non-involved minister who performs Elliot Gould's marriage ceremony without mentioning God. Sutherland's most popular film to date, however, remains **M*A*S*H**, which made him famous as the iconoclastic surgeon Hawkeye.

Sutherland was born in Canada (St John, New Brunswick) on July 17, 1934, worked as a radio announcer as a teenager and studied engineering at the University of Toronto. He went to England to study acting and made his film début in the 1964 horror film **The Castle of the Living Dead** after stage work. He was in other horror films, was one of the nastier members of **The Dirty Dozen** (a reprieved psychopath) and became a star in 1970 in **M*A*S*H** and **Start the Revolution Without Me** (as twins in the French Revolution). His ambiguous impassivity has made him an actor of interest to major directors, including Federico Fellini, Bertolucci, Robert Altman, Nicolas Roeg and John Schlesinger. His most recent films include **A Man, A Woman and A Bank, The First Great Train Robbery** and **Sherlock Holmes: Murder By Decree**.

BEST FILMS:
1970 M*A*S*H
Robert Altman (20th Century Fox)
1970 Kelly's Heroes
Brian G. Hutton (MGM)
1971 Klute
Alan J. Pakula (Warner Brothers)
1971 Little Murders
Alan Arkin (20th Century Fox)
1972 Steelyard Blues
Alan Myerson (Warner Brothers)
1973 Don't Look Now

1975 The Day of the Locust
John Schlesinger (Paramount)
1976 1900
Bernardo Bertolucci (PEA/20th Century Fox)
1976 Casanova
Federico Fellini (PEA/20th Century Fox)
1977 The Eagle Has Landed
John Sturges (ITC Entertainment)

JACQUES TATI

Jacques Tati is the greatest visual comedian of the modern cinema, the only rival in the sound era of the great comics of the silent film and the direct heir of Buster Keaton ➤. While there have been many great verbal comics in the sound film (Woody Allen ➤ is probably the greatest modern master), only Tati has continued the silent tradition. While his films utilise sound brilliantly, they have virtually no dialogue and the plot and humour depend almost

Above: Jacques Tati, as the romantic but hopelessly inadequate Monsieur Hulot, here on holiday and off to cause chaos.

entirely on what is seen. Like Keaton and Chaplin ➤, Tati directs his own films but he is such a perfectionist that he has produced only six during the past 30 years. He has created one of the great comic personas of the cinema, Monsieur Hulot, a gangling stork figure with pipe, hat and umbrella who can stand comparison with Keaton's "Stone Face" and Chaplin's "Tramp".

Hulot has become one of the myth figures of the cinema. He first appeared driving a battered old 1924 Hamikar in the 1953 film **Mr Hulot's Holiday** (where the only word he ever says is "Hulot") and his various mishaps included a disastrous encounter with a folding canoe, getting his spare tyre transmuted into a funeral wreath and igniting a hut full of fireworks. He returned in 1958 in **Mon Oncle** where his old-fashioned life style was contrasted with his brother-in-law's ultra-modern house and gadgets. In the 1967 **Playtime** Hulot's confrontation with the sterility and geometric horrors of modern life and architecture was carried to its pessimistic extreme. In the 1971 **Traffic** Hulot began to see that the mechanical aids of man could develop old-fashioned individuality, as the cars seemed to absorb and reflect the personality of their owners. In the forthcoming Hulot film, **Confusion**, Tati says he plans to show his alter ego baffled by the oddities of modern upside-down behaviour.

Hulot, according to Tati, is never really aware of what is going on around him. Where Chaplin and Keaton might try to overcome a difficulty, Hulot "never does anything intentionally" and invents, assumes and constructs nothing.

His impassivity, however, is like Keaton's in that it reflects a definite attitude to the world around him. He embodies old-fashioned middle-class virtues and remains imperturbable and unflappable in the most disastrous situations; he is the human element in the steel-and-glass "perfection" of the contemporary world and a hero for all his foibles and failings.

Tati was born in Le Pecq (Seine-et-Oise) on October 9, 1908, as Jacques Tatischeff; his family was originally Russian. He worked as a mime artist in music hall and appeared in his first film in 1932, the short **Oscar, Champion de Tennis,** but it was never finished. He appeared in other shorts in the '30s but his real career as a cinema actor/director began in 1947 with the short **L'École des Facteurs.** This was a trial run for his first feature, the 1948 **Jour de Fête,** in which he created the character of François the Postman. François is not Hulot; he is a characterisation in his own right, but like Hulot he is confronted with the modernisation of the world and is hopelessly in conflict with it. After being mocked for his old-fashioned delivery methods and seeing a film on new developments in America, François delightfully creates his own super-fast delivery system which includes using the tailboard of a speeding lorry as a sorting desk. The villagers are more than happy when he goes back to his old methods after one day. François was perfectly suited to his small village but could not be used as a developing character, so Tati created Hulot and his saga. Every trick of observation and mimicry that Tati learned in his years as a pantomime artist is embodied in this brilliant persona; Hulot has a personality which has made him as recognisable and as "real" as Tati himself and has become the perfect vehicle for conveying Tati's ideas: "Without seeking a message, I would like to express what is leading to the suppression of personality in an increasingly mechanised world". Tati's perfectionism over **Playtime** brought him to bankruptcy and all his films were taken over by a bank. They have recently been re-released to tremendous critical acclaim and box office success.

In addition to his other films, Tati has directed and starred in a video film for Swedish television, **Parade,** which features him re-creating some of his greatest mime routines including his agitated tennis player, disgruntled goalkeeper, punchdrunk prize fighter and incapable fisherman. Tati has won numerous awards and prizes for his films including the Best Foreign Film Oscar and New York Film Critics' Award for **Mon Oncle,** the Grand Prize at the Cannes Film Festival for **Mr Hulot's Holiday** and the Grand Prize at the Moscow Children's Film Festival for **Parade.**

BEST FILMS:
1947 L'École des Facteurs
Jacques Tati (Cady Films)
1949 Jour de Fête
Jacques Tati (Cady Films)
1953 Les Vacances de Monsieur Hulot
(Mr Hulot's Holiday)
Jacques Tati (Cady/Discina)
1958 Mon Oncle
Jacques Tati (Specta/Gray/Alter Film)
1967 Playtime
Jacques Tati (Specta Film)
1971 Trafic (Traffic)
Jacques Tati (Corona/Gibé Film)
1974 Parade
Jacques Tati (Gray Film)
1979 Confusion
Jacques Tati (in production)

Elizabeth Taylor

Many movie stars have contributed a part of themselves to the iconography of the cinema (Astaire's ➤ feet, Grable's ➤ legs, etc) but Elizabeth Taylor is probably the only star whose entire life both on and off the screen has become an icon. Movie audiences watched her grow up: she was a spirited child star (**Lassie Come Home, National Velvet**), a ravishingly beautiful young woman (**Father of the Bride, A Place in the Sun, Ivanhoe**), a developing screen personality (**Giant, Raintree County**) and then an acclaimed "actress" with an Academy Award (**Cat on a Hot Tin Roof, Suddenly Last Summer, Butterfield 8**).

She gained maturity with **Cleopatra** as the whole world followed her off-screen romance with Antony (Richard Burton ➤), and the two soon became the most famous cinema couple since Doug and Mary. If everything didn't always go smoothly for them, as audiences could see from their battling in **Who's Afraid of Virginia Woolf?** and **The Taming of the Shrew,** they kept on giving each other bigger and bigger presents just to prove it was all right. They married, divorced, re-married, re-divorced and generally led a very exciting life for the vicarious satisfaction of their attentive fans. In the '70s now permanently split with Burton, Taylor's life both off and on screen seemed dull and without sparkle, and films like **Ash Wednesday** and **The Blue Bird** were not successful. The icon was resting.

Born in Hampstead, London, on February 27, 1932, she moved to Hollywood at the beginning of the war, and was on screen by 1942 in **There's One Born Every Minute.** Her child stardom reached its zenith galloping to victory in **National Velvet,** she passed quickly through her awkward adolescent years in films like **Cynthia** and **A Date With Judy,** and she began to look very lovely indeed as Spencer Tracy's ➤ daughter in **Father of the Bride.**

She was certainly beautiful enough to give Montgomery Clift ➤ murderous ideas in **A Place in the Sun** and was ravishing and desirable as Rebecca in **Ivanhoe. Giant** with James Dean ➤ was the beginning of her acting phase; she got an Oscar nomination the following year for her Southern belle performance in **Raintree County** with Montgomery Clift again and unleashed her sexual frustrations on Paul Newman ➤ in **Cat on a Hot Tin Roof.** She cracked up under the strain of being so beautiful (and being used as boy bait) in **Suddenly Last Summer,** once more opposite Clift, and became a naughty call girl in **Butterfield 8;** illness helped her win a sympathy Oscar.

Taylor's films with new husband Burton in the '60s were generally of interest for biographical if not cinematic reasons (she had begun to put on a lot of matronly inches), but they had fun putting their private relationship on public show in **Virginia Woolf** (another

*Above: Elizabeth Taylor was the most famous movie star in the world in the early 1960s during the filming of the epic **Cleopatra** with Rex Harrison and Richard Burton. She earned over $2 million for the film, which cost nearly $40 million.*

Oscar for Taylor) and **Taming of the Shrew.** She also worked with some good directors in the '60s, including a fine film for John Huston (**Reflections in a Golden Eye**) and less successful ones for Joseph Losey (**Secret Ceremony, Boom**). Her '70s films have been mostly expensive failures, including the Soviet-US co-production **The Blue Bird** and the semi-musical **A Little Night Music.**

BEST FILMS:
1951 A Place in the Sun
George Stevens (Paramount)
1956 Giant
George Stevens (Warner Brothers)
1957 Raintree County
Edward Dmytryk (MGM)

INGRID THULIN

see Ingmar Bergman Stars

JOHN TRAVOLTA

John Travolta became the movie industry's hottest star in 1978 after a sensational and charismatic rise to fame on the strength of two films, **Saturday Night Fever** and **Grease.** Not since the sudden rocketing success of Valentino ❯ had a virtually unknown actor been boosted so far so fast. He set fashions for the way he dressed in **Saturday Night Fever** (white suits were sold out) and was acknowledged as the dance king who helped spark a disco boom around the world. In Britain 6000 fans went crazy with excitement at the première of **Grease** and nearly ripped off his clothes, and in America his two films and their companion LPs became enormous money-spinners. In addition to books and articles on the 24-year-old star, there was even a monthly magazine devoted to him. He was a combination of Fred Astaire and James Dean with a touch of Frank Sinatra—or so it seemed. How long his fame would endure was unclear, but there was no doubt that he was the major new star of the '70s, in fact, *the* '70s star.

He hadn't actually become a star overnight, though; he had spent eight tough years climbing to success. He was born in Englewood, New Jersey, on February 18, 1954, and both his parents had worked in the theatre. He quit school at 16 to turn professional actor and his first job was in a summer stock production of *Bye Bye Birdie.* After that he worked in TV commercials, off-Broadway theatre and finally bit parts in TV series like *The Rookies* and *Owen Marshall.* He went on tour with the stage musical *Grease* and stayed with the production for a year on Broadway. After that he returned to TV and finally won fame as Vinnie Barbarino, the brash, Italian wise guy in the series *Welcome Back Kotter* (based on the British series *Please Sir*). He became a teenage idol with some 10,000 fan letters a day and he also began to work in movies. He had

teenage supporting roles in **The Devil's Rain** and **Carrie,** and then was starred in the 1976 TV-movie **The Boy in the Plastic Bubble.** He portrayed a boy without immunity to disease forced to live in a germ-free plastic home that he realises is actually a prison. His mother in the film was actress Diana Hyland, 17 years his senior, with whom he fell in love and lived with until her sudden death in the spring of 1977. At the time Travolta had just signed a $1 million three-picture contract with the Robert Stigwood Organisation, and began filming **Saturday Night Fever.** Cross-promotion between the film and the record of the film's music, mostly by the Bee Gees, made it one of the major hits of all time; Travolta starred as a Brooklyn boy whose real life and glory is on the floor of the local disco on Saturday night. His next film, **Grease,** in which Olivia Newton-John co-starred, was based on the stage musical affectionately satirising the '50s, and was even more successful. This time Travolta sang as well as danced and reached the top of record charts around the world. He had been popular as a singer since 1976 when his first album, *John Travolta,* was released, but **Grease** made him a pop superstar. His third film

Above: John Travolta in the box-office bonanza **Grease** *which, along with the equally popular* **Saturday Night Fever,** *made him an overnight teenage idol.*

in late 1978 was the semi-autobiographical **Moment by Moment,** the story of a love affair between a young man and a much older woman, played by Lily Tomlin.

COMPLETE FILMS:
1975 The Devil's Rain
Robert Fuest (Sandy Howard)
1976 Carrie
Brian De Palma (United Artists)
1976 The Boy in the Plastic Bubble
Randal Kleiser (TV)
1977 Saturday Night Fever
John Badham (Paramount)
1978 Grease
Randal Kleiser (Paramount)
1978 Moment by Moment
Jane Wagner (Universal)

JEAN-LOUIS TRINTIGNANT

Jean-Louis Trintignant is best known to the international film public as the racing driver who gets Anouk Aimée ❯ in the roman-**A Man and a Woman** and as the

investigating magistrate resisting political pressure in the thriller **Z.** Although he has been a star since 1957 when he played Brigitte Bardot's ❯ husband in **And God Created Woman,** it is only in the past decade that he has come into his own as a major star. His cryptic, seemingly expressionless face hints at wide experience and repressed emotions and is equally effective whether those emotions are romantic, political or criminal. His greatest performances are based on this concept; in **My Night With Maud** he is a Catholic spending the night in bed with Françoise Fabian and talking about his feelings and his ideas,

Above: Jean-Louis Trintignant, shown here in **Le Train,** *has become one of the best-known French stars with his cryptic, experienced face.*

but unable to put principles into practice, and in **The Conformist** he is a repressed homosexual with a wife and mistress who becomes a Fascist in '30s Italy through his attempts to conform. to normality.

Trintignant was born in Point Saint-Esprit, Nîmes, in 1930, and made his feature film début in the 1956 **Si Tous les Gars du Monde.** The world-wide success of Bardot in **And God Created Woman** made him well known but major stardom eluded him for a long while. He was good as the jealous murderer of Gérard Philipe ❯ in **Les Liaisons Dangereuses,** outstanding as the serious young man Vittorio Gassman ❯ teaches to be less serious in **Il Sorpasso (The Easy Life)** and notable working for Georges Franju in the murder mystery **Plein Feux sur l'Assassin** and Jacques Doniol-Valcroze in the romantic comedy **Le Coeur Battant.** After a good performance as one of the suspects in Costa Gavras's **The Sleeping Car Murders,** he became internationally famous as the racing driver lover of **A Man and a Woman** (his father and four uncles had been professional racing drivers, so the role was a natural). He gave good performances for writer-turned-director Alain Robbe-Grillet in **Trans-Europ-Express** and **The Man Who Lied** and was exceptional as the man between Stephane Audran and Jacqueline Sassard in **Les Biches.** His position as a major star of the French cinema has been maintained in the '70s following his international fame in **Z** and **The Conformist** in such films as **Le Voyou, Sans Mobile Apparent** and **L'Attentat.** He co-starred with Alain Delon » in the tough detective thriller **Flic Story,** played opposite Catherine Deneuve » in **L'Agression** and turned director with **Une Journée Bien Remplie.** His recent films include **La Donna della Domenica (Sunday Woman), Les Passagers** and **L'Argent des Autres.**

BEST FILMS:
1957 Et Dieu Créa la Femme (And God Created Woman)
Roger Vadim (Iena/UCIL)
1961 Plein Feux sur l'Assassin
Georges Franju (Champs-Elysées Productions)
1962 Il Sorpasso (The Easy Life)
Dino Risi (Fair/Incie Films)
1966 Un Homme et une Femme (A Man and a Woman)
Claude Lelouch (Les Films 13)
1968 Les Biches
Claude Chabrol (Films La Boétie)
1968 Z
Costa-Gavras (Reggane Films)
1969 Ma Nuit Chez Maud (My Night With Maud)
Eric Rohmer (Losange/Carrosse)
1970 Il Conformista (The Conformist)
Bernardo Bertolucci (Mars/Marianne)
1975 L'Agression (Act of Aggression)
Gérard Pires (Gaumont/Jeudi)
1976 La Donna della Domenica (Sunday Woman)
Luigi Comencini (Fox Europa)

LIV ULLMANN

see **Ingmar Bergman Stars**

PETER USTINOV

Peter Ustinov has never quite become the major film star that one would expect, given his extraordinary personality and two Academy Award-winning performances. Part of the trouble, of course, is his amazing versatility at juggling careers in writing and directing as well as working in theatre and television, and never concentrating wholly on his screen acting career. His enormous personal success in 1978 as Hercule Poirot in the star-studded Agatha Christie movie **Death on the Nile** put him once again in the front rank of top character stars after a diminution in popularity. Ustinov has won two Academy Awards, for portraying a slave dealer in the 1960 epic **Spartacus**

and a sly conman in the 1964 heist film **Topkapi.** Slyness has been a prime ingredient of Ustinov's screen personality and it was his deft performance as Nero in the 1951 **Quo Vadis?** which started him on his path to international stardom.

He had already been acting for a long while. He was born in London in 1921 of White Russian parents, and made his stage début at the age of 17. He appeared in his first film in 1940, a short called **Hullo Fame,** and then began to climb to prominence as a multi-talented writer-director-actor. He began directing films in 1946 with **School for Secrets,** featuring Ralph Richardson, and starred himself in his own 1949 **Private Angelo.** After the role of

Nero made his name he began to get other Hollywood roles, and his playwriting career boomed. He was excellent as a lighthearted convict in **We're No Angels** with Humphrey Bogart » and then gave his greatest performance as the ringmaster to Martine Carol » in Max Ophuls' magnificent **Lola Montès.** The film was a financial failure, but many critics now consider it among the greatest movies of all time and Ustinov is central to it. His best directorial effort came in 1962 with **Billy Budd** in which he played the ship captain in an adaptation of Melville with Robert Ryan » as the evil Claggart.

In recent years Ustinov has given notable performances in Walt Disney films, first as the protagonist of **Blackbeard's Ghost** and then as a quack doctor in **The Treasure of Matecumbe.** His superb incarnation as the urbane Belgian detective Poirot in **Death on the Nile** (the fourth actor to play the role) has been hailed as one of the greatest screen detectives ever.

BEST FILMS:
1951 Quo Vadis?
Mervyn LeRoy (MGM)
1955 We're No Angels
Michael Curtiz (Paramount)
1955 Lola Montès
Max Ophuls (Gamma/Oska)
1960 Spartacus
Stanley Kubrick (Universal-International)
1962 Billy Budd
Peter Ustinov (Anglo-Allied)
1964 Topkapi
Jules Dassin (United Artists)
1967 Blackbeard's Ghost
Robert Stevenson (Buena Vista)
1968 Hot Millions
Eric Till (MGM)
1976 The Treasure of Matecumbe
Vincent McEveety (Buena Vista)
1978 Death on the Nile
John Guillermin (EMI/Paramount)

Above: Peter Ustinov and David Niven in Death on the Nile, *based on Agatha Christie's whodunnit. Ustinov was superb as super sleuth Hercule Poirot.*

MONICA VITTI

Monica Vitti has had two very different careers as a major film star, with entirely different screen personas. In the '60s she became internationally famous as the thinking man's sex star in pessimistic alienation fantasies by director Michelangelo Antonioni. In the '70s she became the leading female comedienne in Italy, the ordinary man's sex star, in a series of satirical social comedies with huge box office appeal. Her bubbling off-screen personality has always been closer to the second half of her career; the cool, bored and alienated persona of the early films **L'Avventura** and **The Eclipse** was invented by Antonioni.

Vitti was born in Rome on November 3, 1933, as Maria Luisa Ceciarelli. She began her acting career in the theatre, appearing in Machiavelli's *The Mandrake,* and made her film début in Eduardo Antan's comedy **Ridere Ridere Ridere (Laugh Laugh Laugh)** in 1954. Her collaboration with Antonioni began in 1957, when she started working with the Teatro Nuovo in Milan, which he directed, and when she

dubbed the voice of Dorian Gray in his **Il Grido.** They became inseparable friends; he starred her in two plays and then made her world famous in **L'Avventura, La Notte, The Eclipse** and **The Red Desert,** as the beautiful embodiment of his ideas. The persona was essentially the same in all these films. A modern woman, rich, bored and unable to love or discover what love is, seeking desperately for something to believe in; whether she leaves the man (**The Eclipse**), returns to him (**L'Avventura**), accepts him (**The Red Desert**), or consoles him (**La Notte**), she never achieves happiness. At the time Antonioni's ideas seemed terribly profound, now they seem merely romantic, their essential pessimism senti-

Above: Monica Vitti was at her beautiful best as the thinking man's neurotic sex star in her first film for Michelangelo Antonioni, L'Avventura *(1960).*

mental and glamourised, beautiful but self-indulgent.

Director Franco Zeffirelli broke the aloof, cool mould when he starred her in his 1964 stage production of Arthur Miller's *After the Fall* in the Marilyn Monroe » part. She also worked in other minor films and was featured by Joseph Losey in the title role of **Modesty Blaise.** In 1967 she turned completely to social satire comedy and had a huge hit **The Girl with the Pistol,** directed by Mario Monicelli. She had won many acting awards for **L'Avventura,** but she won just as many for this film, including Italy's equivalent to the Oscar. By 1970 she was the top female box office star in Italy, matched only by male comics like Alberto Sordi », with whom she co-starred in several films, including **Help Me My Love** and **The Couples.** She has worked primarily in comedy in the '70s, but starred for Miklós Jancsó in **The Pacifist** and had a small role in Luis Buñuel's **The Phantom of Liberty.** Recently she has co-starred with Claudia Cardinale » lightly promoting feminist ideas in **Lucky Girl** and **Midnight Pleasures.**

BEST FILMS:
1960 L'Avventura
Michelangelo Antonioni (Duca-Lyre)
1961 La Notte (The Night)
Michelangelo Antonioni (Nepi-Silva-Sofitedip)
1962 L'Eclisse (The Eclipse)
Michelangelo Antonioni (Hakim)
1964 Il Deserto Rosso (The Red Desert)
Michelangelo Antonioni (Federiz-Francoriz)
1966 Modesty Blaise
Joseph Losey (20th Century Fox)
1968 La Ragazza con la Pistola (The Girl with the Pistol)
Mario Monicelli (Documento)
1970 Nini Tirabuscio
Marcello Fondato (Clesi)
1971 La Pacifista (The Pacifist)
Miklós Jancsó (Lombarda-OCF)
1972 Teresa la Ladra (Teresa the Thief)
Carlo di Palma (Euro International)
1977 L'Altra Meta del Cielo (The Other Half of Heaven)
Franco Rossi (Plexus)

JON VOIGHT

Jon Voight, who became famous for playing a dumb Texas stud in **Midnight Cowboy,** is actually a university-educated, self-conscious New York intellectual who thinks of himself as a character actor rather than a screen personality. While it is true that he has not consciously created a screen persona, his extraordinary "healthy" presence has provided the basis for one all the same. His clean-cut All-American sportsman image has been used to reflect the modern American nightmare, the dream gone sour, with ideas of "success" turned upside down. In **Midnight Cowboy** his open and honest face contrasts remarkably with his occupation as a hustler; the sleaziness of the New York night scene a reflection of his own ambitions. In **Catch-22** he is Milo Minderbinder, the All-American-boy wheeler-dealer, everybody's friend, who will bomb his own base for business. In **Coming Home** the American nightmare is the Vietnam War which has embittered veteran Voight and caused the loss of his legs; he goes back to his old high school to tell the students about the reality of war. In **Deliverance** the imagined American joy of a back-to-nature trip turns nightmarish and deadly. In **The Odessa File** (set in Germany but the effect is the same) he is an investigator discovering a fascist nightmare concealed behind the facade of contemporary society. In **The Revolutionary** he is so disillusioned with the system that he drops out and becomes involved in every kind of revolutionary activity culminating in political assassination, while in **Conrack** he tries to change the system by

teaching black children. In **The All-American Boy** he is an alienated small town boxer desperate for success, and sure to be a failure.

Voight was born in Yonkers, New York, on December 29, 1938, the son of a professional golfer and the brother of singer-songwriter Chip Taylor. He studied at the Catholic University of New York and became a student of Sanford Meisner at the Neighborhood Playhouse in New York. He worked on stage and in TV (including Harold Pinter's *The Dwarfs*) and made his film début in 1967 in John Sturges **Hour of the Gun,** portraying one of Ike Clanton's gang. He also starred in two small-budget films which weren't released until 1969, **Fearless Frank** (in which he is killed and re-incarnated as a superhero) and **Out of It** (portraying a football star stud). His immense personal success in **Midnight Cowboy** was reflected in the New York Critics' best actor award and an Academy Award nomination. His latest film once again features him as a sports figure, a down-and-out boxer in a re-make of Wallace Beery's ≫ old '30s success **The Champ.**

BEST FILMS:
1969 Midnight Cowboy
John Schlesinger (United Artists)
1969 Out of It
Paul Williams (United Artists)
1970 Catch-22
Mike Nichols (Paramount)
1970 The Revolutionary
Paul Williams (United Artists)
1972 Deliverance
John Boorman (Warner Brothers)
1973 The All-American Boy
Charles Eastman (Warner Brothers)
1974 Conrack
Martin Ritt (20th Century Fox)
1974 The Odessa File
Ronald Neame (Columbia)
1976 End of the Game
Maximilian Schell (United Artists)
1977 Coming Home
Hal Ashby (United Artists)

MAX VON SYDOW
see **Ingmar Bergman Stars**

Below: Jon Voight became a star in **Midnight Cowboy** *(1969), portraying a Texas stud who befriends the sickly Dustin Hoffman and creating a persona that has kept him a top name.*

RAQUEL WELCH

Raquel Welch may have been a manufactured sex symbol, but then so was Brigitte Bardot ≫—and both ladies deftly abandoned their Svengali creators after achieving success. The man behind Welch's rise to fame was publicity genius (and second husband) Patrick Curtiz, who parlayed her remarkable physical attributes and rather ordinary acting ability into international stardom in only three years.

Welch was born in Chicago in 1940 as Racquel Tejada (her father was Bolivian). She got her surname from her first husband, a fisherman from whom she was divorced in 1964. That same year she was working as a model and cocktail waitress to support her two children and met Curtiz; they formed Curtwell Enterprises, she started entering and winning beauty contests (Miss La Jolla, Miss San Diego), and he got her a bit part in the 1964 Elvis Presley film **Roustabout.** Soon she was seen regularly on TV, had bits in other movies, and won a contract with 20th Century Fox, who hid

Above: Raquel Welch as Lilian Lust in Stanley Donen's 1967 re-working of the Faust legend, **Bedazzled,** *one of several movies which exploits her sex symbol image.*

most of her assets in a rubber suit for that blood-stream SF epic **Fantastic Voyage.** It was the 1966 British film **One Million Years BC** for Hammer that really made the world aware of her sex appeal and body, while Curtiz engineered one of the greatest star promotions of the modern cinema. Welch was featured on the covers of 192 European and 16 American magazines that year and became famous for being a movie star whose movies the public had never seen. Soon the publicity snowballed, so that she was famous just for being famous (and photogenic), and her marriage to Curtiz in Paris on St Valentine's Day, in a crocheted mini-dress, was a kind of frenzied publicity peak (they were even photographed in bed together).

Welch's films seemed rather pale in comparison to her real life, but there was a lot of her on display skin-and-sky-diving in the spy spoof **Fathom**, flirting with Frank Sinatra » in **Lady in Cement** and getting involved with Jim Brown in **100 Rifles**. She reached the zenith (or perhaps nadir) of her film career as the hero/heroine of **Myra Breckinridge**, set out to revenge her own rape in **Hannie Caulder**, and fought her way to roller-skating success in **Kansas City Bomber**. She was rather splendid in Richard Lester's sexy historical romp **The Three Musketeers** and its sequel **The Four Musketeers**, and gave an excellent performance as James Coco's mistress in **The Wild Party**, singing *Singapore Sally*. She was, not surprisingly, "Jugs" in the ambulance-driver, black comedy romp **Mother, Jugs and Speed**, and she looked pretty as Edith in **The Prince and the Pauper**. Since her divorce from Curtiz in 1971 she has cleverly managed her own career, and has not remarried. She has no illusions about her popularity and points out that "some people are meant to be the decorative things on the surface of the earth".

BEST FILMS:
1966 One Million Years BC
Don Chaffey (Hammer)
1966 Fantastic Voyage
Richard Fleischer (20th Century Fox)
1967 Fathom
Leslie Mortinson (20th Century Fox)
1968 Lady in Cement
Gordon Douglas (20th Century Fox)
1969 100 Rifles
Tom Gries (20th Century Fox)
1970 Myra Breckinridge
Mike Sarne (20th Century Fox)
1972 Kansas City Bomber
Jerrold Freedman (MGM)
1973 The Three Musketeers
Richard Lester (Film Trust)
1975 The Wild Party
James Ivory (AIP)
1976 Mother, Jugs and Speed
Peter Yates (20th Century Fox)

NATALIE WOOD

Natalie Wood began as a child actress, gained teenage renown opposite James Dean » in **Rebel Without A Cause**, and became a lovely if slightly clean-cut sex star in the '60s. Her films were certainly concerned with sex and there was no doubt that Wood was a very experienced veteran (by 1963 she had been making

Above: Natalie Wood sings the closing number "Somewhere" in **West Side Story** *in which she plays Maria, who falls in love with a non-Puerto Rican boy with tragic consequences.*

movies for 21 years), but it was all quite discreet. She began the decade by having an inter-racial affair in **West Side Story**, was warned off sex but discovered it anyway with Warren Beatty » in **Splendour in the Grass**, and then got down to the real nitty-gritty taking off her clothes as Gypsy Rose Lee in **Gypsy**. In **Love With The Proper Stranger** she went to bed with Steve McQueen », but when she got pregnant he didn't remember the experience and didn't want to marry her. In **Sex and the Single Girl** she was a sexologist and Tony Curtis » was a journalist investigating her sex life. She and Curtis were involved again in **The Great Race**, but in **Inside Daisy Clover** it was Robert Redford » who wed but couldn't bed her. Redford followed her into the Deep Tennessee Williams South for **This Property is Condemned**, and then she went a little nutty over Ian Bannen in **Penelope**. She ended the decade in a wife-swapping, husband-exchanging comedy called **Bob and Carol and Ted and Alice**. The sexy '60s exhausted her; she has hardly worked since except for the TV film, **The Affair**, and **Peeper**.

She was born as Natasha Gurdin in San Francisco, California, on July 20, 1938, and made her film début at the age of five in the 1943 **Happy Land**. She worked regularly as a child actor, without becoming a real name, and made the transition to teenage and adult roles without a pause. After her success in **Rebel Without A Cause**, she was excellent as the half-breed girl in John Ford's Western **The Searchers** and adequate in **Marjorie Morningstar** and **Kings Go Forth**. She has been married twice—both times to Robert Wagner.

BEST FILMS:
1955 Rebel Without A Cause
Nicholas Ray (Warner Brothers)
1956 The Searchers
John Ford (Warner Brothers)
1958 Marjorie Morningstar
Irving Rapper (Warner Brothers)
1961 West Side Story
Robert Wise & Jerome Robbins (United Artists)
1961 Splendour in the Grass
Elia Kazan (Warner Brothers)
1962 Gypsy
Mervyn Le Roy (Warner Brothers)
1963 Love With The Proper Stranger
Robert Mulligan (Paramount)
1965 Inside Daisy Clover
Robert Mulligan (Warner Brothers)
1965 The Great Race
Blake Edwards (Warner Brothers)
1969 Bob and Carol and Ted and Alice
Paul Mazursky (Columbia)

JOANNE WOODWARD

Joanne Woodward is an exceptionally gifted actress whose screen performances have won wide critical acclaim but who has not

Above: Joanne Woodward carries the groceries whilst real-life husband Paul Newman shoulders the luggage as they walk to their New Orleans apartment in the media thriller **WUSA**.

yet been able to break through to major stardom. She won an Oscar in 1957 for her tour de force triple performance as the divided personality of **The Three Faces of Eve**, received the New York Critics' Award in 1968 for her even better performance in **Rachel, Rachel** (directed by husband Paul Newman ») as a middle-aged schoolteacher finally experiencing love, and got another Oscar

nomination for her splendid job as the wife in **Summer Wishes, Winter Dreams**. For all these honours and her high reputation, she has never become a box office star, despite many appearances in films with husband Paul Newman. It is possible that the screen persona that she has developed is not one of wide appeal, as it consists basically of variations on helpless, fluttering, nervous, insecure and unhappy women, often floozies and slatterns, usually Southern. They are all victims in their various ways and mass audiences do not like to watch victims, even when beautifully and sensitively portrayed. Woodward has a fine sense of humour which helps make these women likeable, and it is possible that those warm comedy traits will yet make her a big star.

She was born in Thomasville, Georgia, on February 27, 1930, attended Louisiana State University, studied at the Actors' Studio, and worked on stage and in TV before going into films. She made her début in the 1955 **Count Three and Pray** opposite Van Heflin (he reforms her), starred opposite Robert Wagner in **A Kiss Before Dying** (she's pregnant and he kills her), and then made her major impact with **The Three Faces of Eve**. She married Newman in 1958 after appearing with him in **The Long Hot Summer** (she's the strong-willed daughter of Southern tyrant Orson Welles », he's the stranger in town). Their other films together include **Rally Round the Flag Boys, Paris Blues, A New Kind of Love, Winning** and **WUSA**, and Newman has also directed her in **The Effect of Gamma Rays on Man-in-the-Moon Marigolds**.

Other outstanding films have been with co-stars, most notably George C. Scott » in **They Might Be Giants**, Sean Connery » in **A Fine Madness** and Henry Fonda » in **A Big Hand for the Little Lady**. The Newmans' most recent film together was **The Drowning Pool**, in which she involves his private eye Harper in nefarious goings-on.

BEST FILMS:
1957 The Three Faces of Eve
Nunnally Johnson (20th Century Fox)
1958 The Long Hot Summer
Martin Ritt (20th Century Fox)
1959 The Fugitive Kind
Sidney Lumet (United Artists)
1960 From the Terrace
Mark Robson (20th Century Fox)
1966 A Fine Madness
Irvin Kershner (Warner Brothers)
1968 Rachel, Rachel
Paul Newman (Warner Brothers-Seven Arts)
1970 WUSA
Stuart Rosenberg (Paramount)
1971 They Might Be Giants
Anthony Harvey (Universal)
1972 The Effect of Gamma Rays on Man-in-the-Moon Marigolds
Paul Newman (Newman)
1973 Summer Wishes, Winter Dreams
Gilbert Cates (Columbia)

INDEX

This index supplements the cross-reference system (») used throughout the book, which indicates that a star has his or her own main entry.

The page numbers in **bold** denote a main entry; those in *italics* denote a caption.

Acknowledgements

The Publishers would to thank the following people and organisations for their help in obtaining illustrations for this book:

The John Kobal Collection
The Joel Finler Collection
The National Film Archive
MGM
Walt Disney Productions
Paramount
20th Century Fox
Embassy Pictures
Columbia Pictures
EMI
Warner Brothers
RKO
Rank/Two Cities

Hammer Films
First Artists
UniFrance
The Robert Stigwood Organisation
The Pickford Corporation
The Douglas Fairbanks Corporation
David Castell
Al Reuter
John Baxter
Tommy Keen